Handbook for Writers
CANADIAN EDITION

Celia Millward
BOSTON UNIVERSITY

Jane Flick
UNIVERSITY OF
BRITISH COLUMBIA

HOLT, RINEHART AND WINSTON OF CANADA, LIMITED

Toronto

D0743777

Canadian Cataloguing in Publication Data

Millward, Celia M.
  Handbook for writers

Includes index.
ISBN 0-03-921711-6

1. English language — Grammar — 1950–
2. English language — Rhetoric.   3. Report writing.
I. Flick, Jane, 1944–   II. Title.

PE1112.M49 1984   808'.042   C84-098408-1

Acquisitions Editor: Anthony Luengo
Developmental Editor: Brian Henderson
Managing Editor: Mary Lynn Mulroney
Copy Editor: Lenore d'Anjou
Cover Design: Public Good
Typesetting and Assembly: Compeer Typographic Services

Printed in Canada

  7   91

Contents

A Note of Introduction to the Canadian Edition

In preparing this edition of the *Handbook for Writers*, I have been acutely aware of the position in which we, as Canadians, find ourselves when we choose books, in particular, textbooks. We are accustomed to reading materials from within Canada and from without, notably from the United States and Britain. Our students, many of whom already enjoy a multicultural heritage, are encouraged to look beyond our boundaries, to develop a knowledge of the world, and to see Canada in the world context and its culture as it relates to others.

Our textbooks reflect these concerns. They suggest that we do not, by nature, look chiefly inward for our information as, for example, our American neighbors do. Yet we do not want our students so overwhelmed with "foreign information" that they lack familiarity with our own customs, our own writers, or our own culture. Thus, we find a growing and healthy tendency among university and college instructors to demand texts designed for the Canadian environment. Many American textbooks simply do not flourish when transplanted northward for the intellectual climate and the texture of life are different here, even though a cursory glance may not reveal the differences.

Yet two considerations lessen the desire for all-Canadian post-secondary texts. One is, pragmatically but importantly, the economics of producing books for a relatively small market. The other is the proven excellence of the structure and basic content of certain American textbooks.

Happily, some publishers have found a creative solution: bringing out Canadian editions of American texts, special editions that are Canadianized not merely in their place of publication and their cosmetics but in their examples, their references, their spelling, their content, and their emphasis. This Canadian edition of Celia Millward's *A Handbook for Writers* is such a book.

In tackling the Canadianization of *A Handbook for Writers*, I preserved the method, general organization, and much of the text of the original, for these have already proven successful. At the same time, I have taken care to consider the needs of students in Canadian universities and colleges; I have therefore incorporated materials—particularly in the rhetoric and research sections—that reflect current Canadian practices. These include a general guide to standard Canadian references, especially indexes and Statistics Canada publications, that will help students in preparing research papers; direction to Canadian dictionaries; and a discussion of and an appendix on the choices that exist in Canadian spelling. Given the strong feelings that the subject of spelling tends to raise among Canadians, I have given few prescriptions but have rather emphasized the differences between British-based and American-based practice and the need to select consistent patterns. In the text itself, I have followed the preferred spellings of the *Gage Canadian Dictionary* [Toronto: Macmillan of Canada, 1983], choosing such patterns as -or spellings over -*our*, *centre* over *center*, *defence* over *defense* and *levelling* over *leveling*.

Some of Millward's illustrative passages were primarily of interest to American readers, so I have replaced them with the work of Canadian writers or with passages of general interest. Similarly, in many examples I have substituted Canadian or international references for American place names, minor political figures, and so forth. Recognizing the reality of a bilingual country, I have added material on documenting French-language material and on the mechanics of handling French place names, organizational names, titles, and so on. I have also shifted to metric units and the Celsius scale where appropriate and ensured that style recommendations conform to SI practice.

Finally, I have made two kinds of changes that are more modernizing than Canadianizing. The first, in the grammar section, were responses to classroom experience. Readers familiar with Millward's second edition will note that I have re-ordered some of the information on adverbs and on pronouns and have re-classified isolates as interjections.

The second such group of changes were made after advance announcements of major shifts in the MLA's recommendations on documentation. The most important is its new preference for in-text references, rather than footnotes. (I have concurred in this recommendation but provided copious illustrations of notes for students whose instructors prefer the traditional pattern.) In addition, this edition follows the MLA's simplification of references—the omission of *p.* or *pp.*, *l.* or *ll.*, and the comma after a journal title, the use of a colon to separate volume and page number, and the use of Arabic, rather than Roman numerals for everything except titles and preliminary pages. I am indebted to the people at MLA and particularly to Joseph Gibaldi for his help in explicating details of the new recommendations.

In making the changes necessary fo this edition I have tried to keep the Canadian reader and writer in mind, and to hold Celia Millward's intention: to describe good written English.

Jane Flick

Grammar and Grammatical Problems

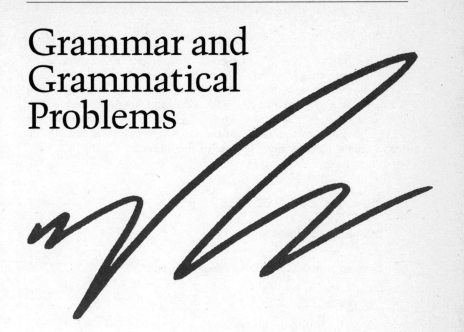

1 Sentence Patterns

The basic unit of the written language is the sentence. A **sentence** is a group of words that includes a subject (S) and a predicate (P) and that is not subordinated to—that is, dependent upon—any other group of words. In short, a sentence can stand alone as a single utterance. The **subject** of a sentence is what or who is talked about, and the **predicate** is what is said about or asked about the subject. In many but not all sentences, the subject is the first word in the sentence.

        S   P
<u>Elsa</u> <u>bought some green paint yesterday.</u>

              S
Last week <u>Peter</u> was sick.

                           S
Because of budget cuts, the <u>library</u> will close.

      S
Did <u>you</u> feed the dog?

The predicate of a sentence must contain a verb phrase (VP). A **verb phrase** is a word or words that express an action done by the subject or a state of existence of the subject. (Although the word *phrase* is commonly thought of as referring to two or more words, the term *verb phrase* can be used for single words as well.) As the fourth sentence below illustrates, the parts of a verb phrase are sometimes separated by other elements of the sentence (See the discussions of main verbs and auxiliary verbs in 4b.)

          VP
Elsa <u>bought</u> some green paint yesterday.

               VP
Last week Peter <u>was</u> sick.

                           VP
Because of budget cuts, the library <u>will close.</u>

VP   VP
<u>Did</u> you <u>feed</u> the dog?

All complete sentences contain a subject and a verb phrase. (Imperative sentences and some exclamations are apparent exceptions; see 16b.) In many sentences, the predicate also requires elements other than just a verb phrase. Depending on the nature of these other elements, sentences are classified into five basic patterns.

Subject + Verb Phrase (S + VP) A sentence may consist of only a subject and a verb phrase.

S   VP
Money talks.

S   VP
The rains came.

S   VP
Swallows are nesting.

Subject + Verb Phrase + Subject Complement (S + VP + SC) When the verb phrase of a sentence contains a special kind of verb called a linking verb (see 4b), the verb phrase is followed by a subject complement (SC). A **subject complement** is a word or words that define or describe the subject.

S VP SC
Time is money.

S VP SC
Time is valuable.

S   VP   SC
My sister became an archaeologist.

S   VP   SC
This milk has turned sour.

Note that the subject complement refers to the same thing as the subject. The verb phrase in such sentences is like an equal sign: saying "Time is money" is like saying "Time = money"; saying "This milk has turned sour" is like saying "This is sour milk."

Subject + Verb Phrase + Direct Object (S + VP + DO) In some sentences, the verb phrase is followed by a direct object (DO). The **direct object** of a verb is the person or thing that receives the action of the verb.

S   VP   DO
Familiarity breeds contempt.

S   VP   DO
Marilyn contradicted her mother.

S   VP DO
The children are eating clay.

Think of the direct object as answering the question *What?* or *Whom?* Thus, to the question *What does familiarity breed?* the answer is the direct object *contempt*. To the question *Whom did Marilyn contradict?* the answer is the direct object *her mother*.

A variant of the S + VP + DO sentence is the passive sentence. A

gr
1

passive sentence is one in which the direct object has been made into the subject and the form of the verb phrase has been changed. Sentences that are not passive sentences are called **active sentences.**

ACTIVE   The children are eating clay.

PASSIVE   Clay is being eaten (by the children).

Notice that the original direct object (*clay*) becomes the subject when the sentence is made passive. The original subject (*children*) is either omitted or becomes the object of the preposition *by.*

Subject + Verb Phrase + Indirect Object + Direct Object (S + VP + IO + DO) In some sentences, the verb phrase is followed by two objects, an indirect object (IO) and a direct object. The **indirect object** names the person or thing affected by the action of the verb or for whom or which the action of the verb was done.

> S   VP   IO   DO
> Paul sent his brother some money.

> S   VP   IO   DO
> Orson gave Eloise a camera.

> S   VP   IO   DO
> Hortense knit Andy a sweater.

Sentences of this type are sometimes made into passive sentences by substituting the indirect object for the original subject.

ACTIVE   Orson gave Eloise a camera.

PASSIVE   Eloise was given a camera (by Orson).

Subject + Verb Phrase + Direct Object + Object Complement (S + VP + DO + OC) In some sentences, the verb phrase is followed by both a direct object and an object complement (OC). An **object complement** is a word or words that refer to the same thing as the direct object.

> S   VP   DO   OC
> The team elected Tom captain.

> S   VP   DO   OC
> Judy likes ice cream soft.

> S   VP   DO   OC
> The Andersons named their baby Tricia.

Note that, just as a subject complement refers to the same thing as the subject, so the object complement refers to the same thing as the direct object.

Every English sentence is one of these five types. In the examples given here, only one or two words serve as subjects, objects, and complements. In many sentences, the basic elements of subject, verb, subject complement, direct object, indirect object, and object complement are accompanied by modifiers (M). **Modifiers** are words that describe, define, or limit other words (see also 20).

<pre>
  M   M   M   S   M   VP   M   M   DO
The large Persian cat contentedly licked its white paws.
</pre>

In this sentence, *the* and *Persian* modify the word *cat* by limiting it to a particular cat of a specific breed. *Large* describes the *cat*. *Contentedly* modifies the verb phrase *licked* by describing how the cat licked. The word *its* modifies *paws* by limiting the paws to the cat's own paws, and *white* modifies *paws* by describing the paws.

Exercises: Sentence Patterns

Write *S* above the subject and *VP* above the verb phrase in the following sentences. Then, using the letters corresponding to the five sentence patterns listed below, identify each sentence by type in the margin. If the group of words is not a sentence, write *NS*.

gr
2

    A. Subject + Verb phrase
    B. Subject + Verb phrase + Subject complement
    C. Subject + Verb phrase + Direct object
    D. Subject + Verb phrase + Indirect object + Direct object
    E. Subject + Verb phrase + Direct object + Object complement

1. The dachshund barked ferociously at the burglar.
2. Elena gave Juan a cold stare.
3. The vivid colors in the rainbow following yesterday's storm.
4. From his cage, the lizard greeted the restaurant's customers with an unblinking stare.
5. After the tragedy the silence seemed deafening.
6. The boys at the garage judged Leroy's old Chevy the best for the drag race.
7. The cathedral chimes broke the predawn stillness.
8. Before the race, the horse's owner gave the jockey an ultimatum.

---

2 Parts of Speech

We have thus far discussed the basic elements of sentences (subject, verb phrase, subject complement, direct object, indirect object, object complement, and modifiers). All of these elements are made up of words. But a moment's reflection will make it clear that not just any word can serve as a subject or as a verb phrase or as an indirect object. Words differ according to whether they name things or describe things or make assertions about things or connect things. Different words combine in different ways with other words. Different words appear in different positions in the sentence.

All Anglophones will understand what you mean if you say "Jimmy slept peacefully in his crib." But they will not know what you mean if you say *"The* slept peacefully in his crib" or *"Peacefully* slept in his crib" or *"In* slept in his crib." In other words, *Jimmy* can serve as the subject of a sentence, but *the, peacefully,* and *in* cannot.

Because different kinds of words have different kinds of meaning and serve different functions in a sentence, it is useful to classify words as **parts of speech** according to their meanings and functions. We usually identify seven parts of speech: nouns, verbs, adjectives, adverbs, pronouns, prepositions, and conjunctions. An eighth part of speech, the interjection, is unique in that it is not grammatically related to other words in the sentence.

At this point, we need a brief working definition and some examples of each part of speech to give us a vocabulary to use as we go along.

gr
2

PART OF SPEECH	FUNCTION	EXAMPLES
Noun	Serves as subject, object, or complement in a sentence	table, law, Marilyn
Verb	Serves as the main element in a predicate	take, distribute, suppose
Adjective	Modifies nouns and pronouns	hairy, impossible, large
Adverb	Modifies verbs, adjectives, and other adverbs	quietly, already, very
Pronoun	Substitutes for a noun	him, anyone, itself
Preposition	Is used before a noun or pronoun to form a modifier of some other part of the sentence	toward, upon, to
Conjunction	Connects words, groups of words, and sentences	and, until, although
Interjection	Is not grammatically connected with other elements in the sentence	hello, ouch, yes

2a ▪ Inflections

Of the eight parts of speech, five (nouns, verbs, adjectives, adverbs, and pronouns) have special endings that help to identify them. These endings are called **inflections.** They indicate such meanings as "more than one" (the plural inflection) or "action that took place in the past" (the past-tense inflection). For example, in the word *nations,* the *-s* is a plural inflection. In the word *showed,* the *-ed* is a past-tense inflection. Sometimes meanings are indicated by changes within a word; for example, *wrote* is the past tense of *write.* Such changes are also called inflections.

2b ▪ Phrases and Clauses

Two other terms needed in any discussion of the parts of speech are *phrases* and *clauses.* A **phrase** is a sequence of words arranged grammatically but not containing both a subject and a predicate (see also 11).

> over my dead body
> a dilapidated green Volkswagen van
> would like to have seen

Note that the definition states that a phrase is arranged grammatically. This is important. *Over my dead body* is a phrase because the words are arranged grammatically. *Body over dead my* is not a phrase. It is just a string of words because the words are not arranged grammatically.

A **clause** is a sequence of words arranged grammatically and containing both a subject and a predicate (see 12). Some clauses (**independent clauses**) can form complete sentences; some (**dependent clauses**) cannot.

INDEPENDENT CLAUSES	DEPENDENT CLAUSES
the traffic was light	although the traffic was light
you aren't home	if you aren't home
I hit my thumb	that I hit my thumb
this is what he wrote	which is what he wrote

A more complete discussion of kinds of phrases and clauses appears in 11 and 12.

gr
3

3 🦉 Nouns

The traditional definition of a **noun** is that it is the name of a person, place, thing, quality, or state. This definition by meaning is often helpful because most nouns do indeed name something or someone. Many nouns can also be identified by their forms, that is, by their inflections. And nouns can also be identified by their functions or by the positions they fill in sentences.

3a ▪ Characteristics

Nouns are characterized by their inflections for number and case and by their functions in a sentence as subjects, objects, and complements.

Inflections The **number** of a noun indicates whether it refers to a single thing (a singular noun) or more than one thing (a plural noun). Most English nouns have no inflectional ending in the singular and add -*s* or -*es* to form the plural. Some nouns have an irregular plural (see 45c for the spelling of irregular plural nouns).

SINGULAR   PLURAL

ribbon   ribbons
ditch   ditches
foot   feet (irregular plural)

The **case** of a noun shows its grammatical function in the sentence. English nouns have two cases, the **common** case and the **possessive** (sometimes called **genitive**) case. The possessive case is used to make the noun a modifier of another word; otherwise, the common case is used. (See 34a for the rules for forming possessive nouns.)

COMMON CASE   POSSESSIVE CASE

the burglar   the burglar's escape
a week   a week's vacation
sisters   my sisters' disappointment
men   men's clothing

Even when a noun is used as a modifier, it is often in the common case.

money market   college campus
coffee cup   city officials
weather forecast   nail clippers

Note English makes no change in the form of nouns to show case, except for the possessive (which is marked by the apostrophe). Case is otherwise evident from the grammatical position of the noun in the sentence.

Function and Position Nouns have characteristic functions and positions in a sentence.

FUNCTION   EXAMPLES

Subject   Misery loves company.
                      Sally Ride made history in 1983.

Subject complement   Honesty is the best policy.
                      America's first woman in space was
                         Sally Ride.

Object complement	Who appointed Irwin <u>boss</u>?
	The park named the amusement ride <u>Sally Ride</u>.
Direct object	We demand <u>justice</u>.
	Magazine articles profiled <u>Sally Ride</u>.
Indirect object	They wrote the <u>principal</u> a letter.
	The newscaster showed <u>Sally Ride</u> the telegrams of congratulation.
Object of a preposition	Jill climbed over the <u>fence</u>.
	The interest in <u>Sally Ride</u> was world-wide.
Appositive	William <u>the Conqueror</u> fought Harold in 1066.
	The astronaut, <u>Sally Ride</u>, attended Stanford.
Direct address	Don't be so sure, my <u>friend</u>.
	"Ride, <u>Sally</u>, ride!" cried spectators when the rocket was launched.
Nominative absolute	All <u>things</u> considered, I would rather be home.
	<u>Sally Ride</u> having proved herself, the question of putting women in space has not been raised again.

gr
3b

Note An **appositive** is a word, phrase, or clause that follows another word and that refers to the same thing or person (see 14). A **nominative absolute** (also called an **absolute phrase**) is a noun together with a particular form of a verb; the two together modify an entire clause or sentence (see 11c).

As the examples show, nouns can appear in almost any position in a sentence. Subjects are often near the beginning of sentences and before verb phrases. Subject complements normally follow linking verbs (see 4b). Object complements follow direct objects. Direct objects normally come after verb phrases. Indirect objects appear after verb phrases and before direct objects. Objects of prepositions typically follow prepositions. Appositives follow other nouns or pronouns. Nouns used in direct address most often come before or after the rest of their sentences, but sometimes appear in the middle. Nominative absolutes either precede or follow the rest of the sentence.

3b ▪ Classes

Nouns are traditionally divided into a number of different classes, depending on their formation, their meanings, and the kinds of modifiers that appear with them.

Simple and Compound Nouns   **Simple nouns** consist of a single word: *pan, miser, question, day*. **Compound nouns** consist of two—or sometimes more—parts of speech used as a single noun: *dustpan, tightwad, tossup, afternoon*. (See also Appendix B, "Glossary of Grammatical Terms," and 45c.)

Countable and Mass Nouns   **Countable nouns** have both singular and plural forms. The singular form may be modified by either *a* or *the*. **Mass** or **uncountable nouns** are a special kind of singular nouns that have no plural forms and cannot be modified by the words *a* or *one* but can be modified by *the*.

COUNTABLE NOUNS	MASS OR UNCOUNTABLE NOUNS
a chair, chairs	the furniture, furniture
a pebble, pebbles	the gravel, gravel
an enemy, enemies	the disgust, disgust

Proper and Common Nouns   **Proper nouns** designate or "name" specific entities such as one particular person, place, building, holiday, or the like. They may consist of more than one word. All important words in a proper noun begin with a capital letter. Proper nouns usually are not modified by such limiting modifiers as *the*, *a*, or regular adjectives. All nouns that are not proper nouns are **common nouns**.

PROPER NOUNS	COMMON NOUNS
Helen Keller	a woman
Charlottetown	the city
Westminster Abbey	that old building
Thanksgiving	an autumn holiday

Concrete and Abstract Nouns   **Concrete nouns** designate tangible, physical objects that we can see, hear, touch, smell, or taste (*child, carrot, dime, scream*). Concrete nouns may be either countable or mass nouns. **Abstract nouns** designate ideas, concepts, or anything that we cannot experience directly with our senses (*childhood, nutrition, wealth, loudness*). Most abstract nouns are mass nouns. Many nouns may be used either as concrete or abstract nouns. In such instances, the concrete noun is usually a countable noun, and the abstract noun is a mass noun. See also Appendix B, "Glossary of Grammatical Terms," and 46b.

ABSTRACT AND MASS	Beauty is in the eye of the beholder.
	The concept of honor has changed over the centuries.
CONCRETE AND COUNTABLE	Though plain as a child, Caroline grew up to be a beauty.
	Dr. Miles has received numerous honors.

Collective Nouns Collective nouns are used to designate an entire group of people or things (*audience, swarm, team, group*). Collective nouns are countable and may be made plural. See Appendix B, "Glossary of Grammatical Terms," and 18b.

SINGULAR COLLECTIVE The <u>team</u> is best known for its post-game celebrations.

PLURAL COLLECTIVE Four <u>teams</u> of workers are reseeding the oyster beds.

Exercises: Nouns

Underline every noun in the following sentences. Then write the appropriate letter from the list below over each noun to identify its function in the sentence.

A. Subject
B. Subject Complement
C. Object Complement
D. Direct Object
E. Indirect Object
F. Object of a Preposition
G. Appositive
H. Direct Address
I. Nominative Absolute

1. Dixie tells her dreams—in vivid, tedious detail—to the entire family.
2. Our cat, Beethoven, has an inordinate hatred of the piano.
3. But the driver did not stop for the light, officer.
4. Alfred considers bathing a waste of time.
5. The lawyer raised his eyes from his briefcase and surveyed the woman.
6. Their son Gene became a surgeon and moved to Regina with his wife.
7. The first orbit completed, the satellite beamed its signals to earth.
8. Jessica mailed her member of parliament the petition.

gr
4

---

4 Verbs

Verbs are traditionally defined as words that express an action, an occurrence, or a state of existence. This definition by meaning is not always satisfactory because other parts of speech, such as nouns, also express action or existence. But verbs can also be identified by their inflections and by their functions.

4a • Characteristics
Verbs are characterized by inflections for tense, person, voice, and mood, and by their function in a sentence as the main element of the predicate.

Inflections   Verbs have five forms, an infinitive and four inflected forms. The **infinitive** is either the base form of the verb (*carry*) or the base form preceded by *to* (*to carry*). The four inflected forms are (1) third-person singular present tense, (2) past tense, (3) present participle (also called progressive participle), and (4) past participle.

TYPE OF INFLECTION	FORM OF INFLECTION	EXAMPLES
Third-person singular present tense	-s	she talk<u>s</u>, it work<u>s</u>, he sing<u>s</u>
Past tense	-ed (or irregular)	she talk<u>ed</u>, it work<u>ed</u>, he sang
Present participle	-ing	she is talk<u>ing</u>, it has been work<u>ing</u>, he was sing<u>ing</u>
Past participle	-ed (or irregular)	she has talk<u>ed</u>, it has work<u>ed</u>, he had sung

gr
4a

The infinitive, the past tense, and the past participle of a verb are together called the **principal parts** of the verb.

PRINCIPAL PARTS	EXAMPLES
Infinitive	(to) talk, (to) grow, (to) work
Past tense	talked, grew, worked
Past participle	talked, grown, worked

Every form of a verb is either finite or nonfinite. **Finite verbs** are those that may stand alone as complete verb phrases or even as complete predicates. Infinitives, present participles, and past participles are **nonfinite verbs:** they cannot stand alone as complete verb phrases.

FINITE VERBS	NONFINITE VERBS
(The canary) sings.	(to) sing
(The canary) sang.	singing
	sung

In verb phrases containing more than one verb, only the first verb is finite, and the remaining verbs are nonfinite. Hence in the verb phrase *has been singing, has* is finite, but *been* (past participle) and *singing* (present participle) are nonfinite.

Function and Position   The verb forms the main element of the predicate; in simplest terms, it explains what is going on. Because the most common word order of English sentences is subject + predicate, the most common position of the verb phrase is after the subject. In many questions and in some other kinds of sentences, however, at least part of the verb phrase precedes the subject.

AFTER SUBJECT	The ambulance <u>was racing</u> across the square.
BEFORE SUBJECT	<u>Have</u> you any ideas for a costume?
BEFORE AND AFTER SUBJECT	<u>Will</u> Elmer <u>be eaten</u> by the lion?
	Rarely <u>do</u> we <u>encounter</u> exceptions.
	<u>Had</u> Orville <u>been born</u> with wings, he would not have <u>built</u> an airplane.

Tense, Mood, and Voice   Every verb phrase, whether it consists of a single verb or several verbs, contains three kinds of grammatical information—tense, mood, and voice.

1. **Tense** is the time or duration of the action or state named by the verb or verb phrase. The following table summarizes the five tenses of English.

TENSE	FORMATION	MEANING	EXAMPLES
Present	-*s* for 3d person singular; no ending for other forms	Universally true; not limited to a particular time	she talks; we talk
Past	-*ed* (or irregular)	Action completed at an earlier time	she talked; we talked
Progressive	A form of *be* plus the present participle of the verb	A continuing but limited action	she is talking; we are talking
Perfect	A form of *have* plus the past participle of the verb	Action begun earlier and still relevant at a later time	she has talked; we have talked
Future	*Will* or *shall* plus the infinitive	Future time; prediction	she will talk; we shall talk

The progressive and perfect tenses may combine with each other and with the present, past, or future tenses to form numerous compound tenses.

PAST PERFECT	she had talked
FUTURE PROGRESSIVE	she will be talking
PAST PERFECT PROGRESSIVE	she had been talking

A complete list of all possible tenses and their combinations is given in Appendix C, "Complete Conjugation of an English Verb."

2. The **mood** of a verb or verb phrase expresses the attitude of the speaker or writer toward the statement. The mood may express a fact or ask a question, it may express a command or request, or it may indicate that the statement is only a possibility or is contrary to fact. English has three moods: the indicative, the imperative, and the subjunctive. (See 17c for the uses of the different forms of the subjunctive.)

**gr
4a**

MOOD	FORMATION	MEANING	EXAMPLES
Indicative	(as in the preceding chart of the five tenses)	Ordinary statement or question	she is quiet; is she quiet?
Imperative	Infinitive with no subject, but "you" understood	Request or command	Be quiet.
Subjunctive	Infinitive or plural past tense of verb	Unreal, hypothetical, or doubtful statement	that she be quiet; if she were quiet

3. The **voice** of a verb indicates the relation of the action of the verb to the subject of the clause or sentence. The **active voice** means that the subject is the doer of the action. The **passive voice** means that the subject is the receiver of the action. The passive voice consists of a form of the verb *to be* and the past participle of a verb.

ACTIVE VOICE	Surgeons sometimes make mistakes.
	The surgeon has not taken a sponge count.
	Whom will the surgeon blame?
	The irate patient is filing a malpractice suit.
PASSIVE VOICE	Mistakes are sometimes made (by surgeons).
	No sponge count has been taken (by the surgeon).
	Who will be blamed (by the surgeon)?
	A malpractice suit is being filed (by the irate patient).

Exercises: Tense, Mood, and Voice of Verbs

Part A: Underline all the verb phrases in the following sentences, and identify the tense, voice, and mood of each.

1. Don stumbled into the classroom five minutes after the bell had rung.
2. Her mother does not know that she has been working at the club.
3. Karen will be furious when she learns that her roommate wrecked her car last night.
4. "See your lawyer first thing in the morning," Dmitri begged.
5. The wedding is being planned for the first week in October.
6. Mark insisted that Alice learn how to use a slingshot.

Part B: Complete the following sentences by writing in the specified tense and voice of the italicized infinitive.

1. The neighbors _____ on their vacation to-
                (*to leave*—future progressive)
  morrow.

2. The committee _____ already, long before we
              (*to decide*—future perfect)

  _____ a chance to present our argument.
  (*to have*—present perfect)

3. "She _____ here all evening," the landlady
       (*to be*—present perfect)

  _____ the police.
  (*to assure*—past)

4. You _____ everything that _____ to the
    (*to know*—past)   (*to know*—past passive)
  rest of us.

5. The theory _____ on a colony of ants.
        (*to test*—past progressive passive)

gr
4b

4b · Classes

Verbs can be classified in a number of different ways according to their forms and their functions in a clause or sentence. The most basic distinction is between main verbs and auxiliary verbs.

Main Verbs Main verbs (or **lexical verbs,** as they are sometimes called) are those that carry most of the meaning of the verb phrase in which they appear. Properly inflected, a main verb can stand alone as a complete verb phrase or even as a complete predicate.

Insurance rates have <u>increased</u> by 52 per cent.

You will have to <u>redraw</u> all the maps.

The lights <u>flickered</u>.

There are three major classifications of main verbs: (1) regular or irregular, (2) transitive, intransitive, or linking, and (3) finite or nonfinite.

1. Main verbs may be regular or irregular. For purposes of writing, a **regular verb** forms both its past tense and its past participle by adding -*d* or -*ed*. An **irregular verb** forms its past tense or past participle in a different way, such as by changing the vowel, by adding -*t* or -*en* instead of -*ed*, or by having no endings at all in the past tense or past participle. Out of thousands of verbs in English, fewer than two hundred are irregular, but the irregular ones are among those most frequently used. (See Appendix D for the past tenses and past participles of some common irregular verbs.)

REGULAR VERBS	IRREGULAR VERBS
talk, talked, talked	speak, spoke, spoken
drop, dropped, dropped	run, ran, run
amaze, amazed, amazed	cut, cut, cut

The verb *to be* is the most irregular verb in English. Unlike any other verb, it has a separate form for the first-person and third-person singular present and for the plural in both the present and past tenses.

PRESENT TENSE OF *TO BE*	PAST TENSE OF *TO BE*
I am	I was
you are	you were
he/she/it is	he/she/it was
we/you/they are	we/you/they were

2. Main verbs are also classified according to the kind of objects or complements that accompany them in a sentence.

Intransitive verbs are those with no direct object or subject complement.

The old man <u>slept</u>.
Time <u>passes</u> slowly here.
Snow <u>is falling</u>.

Transitive verbs have at least one direct object. Some transitive verbs are also accompanied by an indirect object or an object complement.

The old man <u>swept</u> the porch.
Time <u>changes</u> all things.
Snow <u>is covering</u> the shrubs.

Mother <u>handed</u> me a spoon. (direct and indirect object)
Schweitzer's work <u>made</u> him a hero. (direct object and object complement)

When the direct object of a transitive verb refers to the same thing or person as the subject, the verb is called **reflexive.** The direct object of a reflexive verb is always a pronoun ending in *-self.*

The old man <u>hurt</u> himself.

Linking verbs, sometimes called copula verbs, are followed by a subject complement.

The old man <u>is</u> tactless.
The old man <u>is</u> a coin-collector.
The snow <u>feels</u> wet.
The Ayatollah <u>turned</u> tyrant.

Some verbs are used only intransitively (*lie, rise, fall*), and some verbs are used only transitively (*have, need, want*). A few transitive verbs are used only reflexively (*pride, perjure, avail*). A very few verbs are used only as linking verbs (*seem*). Many verbs can be transitive or intransitive, reflexive or nonreflexive, linking or nonlinking.

TRANSITIVE	He <u>turned</u> the dial.
INTRANSITIVE	He <u>turned</u> slowly.
TRANSITIVE REFLEXIVE	He <u>turned</u> himself around.
LINKING	He <u>turned</u> green.

gr
4b

Finite Verbs Finite verbs are called finite ("limited") because they are inflected for person (*I am, he is*), number (*he is, they are*), and tense (*he is, he was*) and can serve as complete predicates in main clauses.

<u>Throw</u> me the towel.

Happiness <u>vanishes</u>.

He often <u>sends</u> them exciting presents.

The verb often has modifiers, as in the last example.

Nonfinite Verbs Nonfinite verbs cannot serve as complete predicates. Infinitives (*[to] walk*), present participles (*walking*), past paticiples (*walked*), and gerunds (*walking*) are nonfinite.

Auxiliary Verbs Auxiliary verbs, also called **helping verbs,** are used in forming verb phrases but cannot form a complete verb phrase by themselves. There are four major kinds of auxiliary verbs: (1) *be,* (2) *have,* (3) modal auxiliaries, and (4) *do. Be, have,* and *do* can also be main verbs: I *am* your captain; Oscar *has* athlete's foot; Can you *do* a split?

1. *Be* is used in forming the progressive tense and the passive voice.

PROGRESSIVE TENSE   she <u>is</u> helping, she <u>was</u> helping, she has <u>been</u> helping

PASSIVE VOICE   she <u>is</u> helped [by her friends], she <u>was</u> helped,
                       she has <u>been</u> helped

2. *Have* is used in forming the perfect tenses.

she <u>has</u> helped
she <u>had</u> helped
she <u>has</u> been helped

3. The **modal auxiliaries** are *will/would, shall/should, can/could, may/might, dare, need (to), ought (to),* and *must.* Unlike other verbs, the modal auxiliaries have only one form and are followed only by the infinitive form of the verb. (*Dare* and *need* can also be main verbs: Bert *dared* Cecily to jump off the slide; Mrs. Ryan *needs* a hearing aid.)

The modal auxiliaries *will* and *shall* are used in forming the future tenses. The other modal auxiliaries are used to express some degree of ability, necessity, obligation, uncertainty, or the like.

ABILITY   He <u>can</u> read.

NECESSITY   He <u>must</u> read.

OBLIGATION   He <u>ought to</u> read.

UNCERTAINTY   He <u>may</u> read.

**gr
4b**

4. *Do* is used when the grammar of the clause or sentence requires an auxiliary but no other auxiliary is appropriate. Thus, *do* is used primarily in asking questions and in negative sentences (those that deny an assertion). It is also used to avoid repetition of a verb used previously.

He reads, <u>doesn't</u> he?
<u>Does</u> he read?
He <u>does</u> not read.
<u>Does</u> he read French? He <u>does.</u>

Do is also the so-called **emphatic auxiliary**; it is used to contradict a previous assumption or statement or to emphasize the truth of the statement.

Despite what you say, he <u>does</u> read.
He truly <u>does</u> read French.

In addition to the four kinds of auxiliaries, a number of other verbs sometimes precede the main verb and act like auxiliaries. These **semiauxiliaries** are really idioms, that is, expressions whose meanings cannot be predicted from the meanings of their individual words.

He <u>kept on</u> reading.   She <u>is going to</u> read.
He <u>started to</u> read.   She <u>is to</u> read tomorrow.
He <u>has to</u> read.   She <u>is not about to</u> read.
He <u>used to</u> read.   She <u>is about to</u> read.
He <u>is supposed to</u> read.   She <u>happened to</u> read.

Exercises: Auxiliary Verbs

Underline all forms of the verbs *be, have,* and *do* in the following sentences. Indicate over each its function as either auxiliary verb (A) or main verb (M).

1. Have Alice and Don finally decided to get married?
2. The library is having some problems with its computer terminal.
3. Kirsten had taken the pictures without removing the lens cap from the camera.
4. The man did promise to return the coat.
5. The child has never had a very stable home.
6. "I am being good," the four-year-old assured his mother.
7. Kittens should be inoculated for distemper.

5 Adjectives

Adjectives are traditionally defined as words that modify nouns or pronouns by defining, describing, limiting, or qualifying those nouns or pronouns. Many adjectives also can be identified by their inflections or by their positions in sentences.

gr
5

5a ▪ Characteristics

Some adjectives have inflections showing comparative and superlative degrees. Adjectives are also identified by the positions they take as modifiers of nouns or noun substitutes.

Inflections   Many adjectives can be inflected to show comparison. The three degrees of comparison are **positive, comparative,** and **superlative.** The positive degree of an adjective has no ending, the comparative ending is *-er,* and the superlative ending is *-est.*

POSITIVE	COMPARATIVE	SUPERLATIVE
fine	finer	finest
poor	poorer	poorest

A few adjectives have irregular inflections.

POSITIVE	COMPARATIVE	SUPERLATIVE
good	better	best
bad	worse	worst
a little	less	least
many/much	more	most
far	farther/further	farthest/furthest
old	older/elder	oldest/eldest

Many English adjectives do not form their comparative and superlative degrees by inflection but with the separate words *more* (or *less*) and *most* (or *least*). As a general rule, adjectives of one syllable are inflected, and adjectives of more than one syllable form comparative and superlative degrees with *more* (*less*) and *most* (*least*). However, two-syllable adjectives ending in *-y, -ly, -le, -er,* and *-ow* are usually inflected.

accurate/more accurate/most accurate
brutal/more brutal/most brutal
curious/less curious/least curious

-y   heavy/heavier/heaviest
-ly   early/earlier/earliest
-le   little/littler/littlest
-er   clever/cleverer/cleverest
-ow   shallow/shallower/shallowest

Function and Position As modifiers of nouns and pronouns, adjectives appear near the words they modify. The following are four common positions:

(1) before nouns and the indefinite pronoun *one,*

The tiny nest was full of delicate eggs.
He'll take a pear if you have a ripe one.

(2) as subject complements following linking verbs,

Her explanation sounds fishy.
This fireplace is elegant but impractical.

(3) as object complements after direct objects,

I want that floor spotless.
You are driving us mad.

(4) after indefinite pronouns.

Anything small and furry delights Rupert.
None better could be found.

5b · Classes

Adjectives can be divided into a number of classes, depending on their formation, their relationship with other parts of speech, and their function in the sentence.

Descriptive The great majority of adjectives are **descriptive adjectives,** which specify a quality or state of the noun or pronoun they modify.

large, rare, old, strong, sweet
hasty, fatal, gracious, significant, merciless

A subclass of descriptive adjectives is **proper adjectives,** adjectives made from proper nouns.

> Italian, Turkish, Romanesque, Shakespearean

Others Another class of adjectives is the personal possessives used to modify nouns. When the demonstrative pronouns, interrogative pronouns, indefinite pronouns, relative pronouns, and cardinal and ordinal numbers are used to modify nouns, they are also classed as adjectives. Finally, the definite article and indefinite article are also kinds of adjectives. (See also Appendix B, "Glossary of Grammatical Terms.")

TYPE OF ADJECTIVE	FORMS	EXAMPLES OF USE
Possessive	my, your, his, her, its, our, their, one's	*my* hat; *its* completion
Demonstrative	this/these, that/those	*this* song; *those* stations
Interrogative	what, which, whose	*Which* path should we take?
Indefinite	another, each, both, many, any, some, no, etc.	*both* sides; *no* complaints
Numerical	two, five, third, eighth	*two* bricks; the *ninth* item
Relative	what(ever), which(ever), whose(ever)	He lost *what* little hair he had.
Definite article	the	*the* noise; *the* beachcombers
Indefinite article	a/an	*a* picture; *an* octopus

gr
5b

Exercises: Adjectives

Part A: Write sentences that include the specified form of the adjective given.

1. the comparative of *stubborn*
2. the superlative of *fragile*
3. the superlative of *bad*
4. the comparative of *much*
5. the superlative of *furry*
6. the comparative of *supple*

Part B: Underline *all* adjectives in the following sentences. Write above each one the letter from the list below that identifies the kind of adjective it is.

A. Descriptive   F. Indefinite
B. Proper   G. Numerical
C. Possessive   H. Relative
D. Demonstrative   I. Definite article
E. Interrogative   J. Indefinite article

1. That Irish dance is the most captivating part of their program.
2. Which mechanic worked on my car the last time?
3. Jon did not have enough money to pay for all of their lunches.
4. These prices are the lowest they have been in three years.
5. Millie loved to read German poetry aloud, but her bad pronunciation destroyed its subtle rhythms.
6. Kelly did not have any idea which tapes Randy had already bought.
7. Timid about making speeches of any kind, Dolores was especially upset when she had to welcome the new supervisor.

6 Adverbs

Adverbs are traditionally defined as words that modify verbs, adjectives, or other adverbs and that express such ideas as time, place, manner, cause, and degree. Many adverbs can also be identified by their inflections or by their position in the sentence.

6a ▪ Characteristics

Many adverbs are characterized by a distinctive *-ly* ending, and many by inflectional endings showing comparative and superlative degrees. Adverbs are also identified by their function and by their position near the words they modify.

Form   The adverbs characterized by an *-ly* ending are formed from adjectives by adding *-ly*. (These are sometimes called **adjectival adverbs**.)

odd	oddly	impressive	impressively
tight	tightly	egotistical	egotistically
final	finally	mistaken	mistakenly

Some adverbs are indistinguishable from adjectives. These adverbs are sometimes called **plain adverbs** (that is, they have no *-ly* endings to mark them as adverbs).

straight, hard, right, far, late, just, even

Function distinguishes these adverbs from adjectives.

ADVERB FUNCTION   The road runs <u>straight</u>.

ADJECTIVE FUNCTION   The <u>straight</u> road runs on to the horizon.

Many common adverbs are not derived from any other part of speech. They are recognized as adverbs by their unique form and by their function in the sentence.

also	maybe	quite	then
always	never	rather	there
anyhow	not	seldom	thus
anyway	now	so	too
ever	often	somehow	very
indeed	perhaps	somewhat	

Inflections Adverbs that are made from adjectives or that have the same form as adjectives may take comparative inflections (*-er, -est*). *Soon,* although it has no corresponding adjective, also takes *-er* and *-est*. The rules for forming and using the comparative inflection with adverbs are the same as the rules for adjectives (5a). A few adverbs have irregular inflections.

POSITIVE	COMPARATIVE	SUPERLATIVE
well	better	best
badly	worse	worst
far	farther/further	farthest/furthest

gr
6a

Function Adjectives modify nouns and pronouns; adverbs modify almost everything else, including verbs, adjectives, other adverbs, and entire clauses and sentences.

The policeman responded quickly. (*Quickly* modifies the verb *responded.*)

The very alert policeman responded quickly. (*Very* modifies the adjective *alert.*)

The policeman responded very quickly. (*Very* modifies the adverb *quickly.*)

Fortunately, the policeman responded quickly. (*Fortunately* modifies the entire sentence.)

Adverbs commonly "answer" the questions "how?" "when?" "where?" "why?" and "to what extent or degree?". They express many kinds of meaning, as the following examples illustrate.

MANNER   Examples: quickly, neatly, awkwardly, cheerfully
Mr. Potter speaks eloquently. (*Eloquently* modifies *speaks* and describes how Mr. Potter speaks.)

TIME   Examples: recently, tomorrow, nights, days
Mr. Potter spoke yesterday. (*Yesterday* modifies *spoke* and tells when Mr. Potter spoke.)

| FREQUENCY | Examples: twice, always, sometimes, never, occasionally |
| | Mr. Potter <u>often</u> makes speeches. (*Often* modifies *makes speeches* and tells when or how frequently Mr. Potter makes speeches.) |

| PLACE AND DIRECTION | Examples: here, there, East, left |
| | Mr. Potter spoke <u>here</u>. (*Here* modifies *spoke* and tells where Mr. Potter spoke.) |

| DEGREE AND EXTENT | Examples: very, quite, too, exceedingly, fairly |
| | Mr. Potter's speech was <u>rather</u> long. (*Rather* modifies *long* and tells the extent to which Mr. Potter's speech was long.) |

| AFFIRMATION | Examples: surely, definitely, undeniably, absolutely |
| | Mr. Potter <u>certainly</u> likes to talk. (*Certainly* modifies *likes to talk* and affirms or reinforces that phrase.) |

| NEGATION | Examples: not, never, no |
| | Mr. Potter <u>never</u> turns down a chance to speak. (*Never* modifies *turns down a chance to speak* and negates or denies that phrase.) |

| QUALIFICATION | Examples: perhaps, maybe, possibly, probably |
| | <u>Perhaps</u> Mr. Potter forgot his watch. (*Perhaps* modifies *forgot his watch* and expresses a qualification of the degree of certainty or probability.) |

Position Because adverbs modify so many different elements, they have greater flexibility of position in the sentence than any of the other parts of speech. In general, they appear near the words they modify. However, care must be taken in placing adverbs, for the meaning of the sentence may be affected by the psotion of the adverb, as the following sentences demonstrate. (See 20b and 20c for further discussion of adverbs and placement of modifiers.)

<u>Only</u> Mary passed the math test. (All others failed.)

Mary passed <u>only</u> the math test. (Mary failed all other tests.)

Mary <u>only</u> passed the math test. (Mary barely passed the test.)

6b ▪ Classes

Depending on their form and their function in the sentence, adverbs can be divided into several classes.

Simple **Simple adverbs** modify a single word or group of words.

He goes <u>tomorrow</u>.

She is <u>very</u> studious.

He eats <u>too</u> quickly.

We ran <u>almost</u> ten kilometres.

Sentence **Sentence adverbs** modify a sentence as a whole.

<u>Doubtless</u>, he will soon discover his error.
The telegram did not arrive in time, <u>unfortunately</u>.

Prepositional **Prepositional adverbs**, which are identical in form to pre-positions (see 8 for a list) generally express some kind of spatial relationship. They often stand at the end of a clause because the governing noun or pronoun is not expressed, though it is "understood."

He threw the stick over the fence, but he threw it too low and it went <u>under</u> (the fence).
We ran to the edge of the water and threw ourselves <u>in</u> (the water).

Interrogative *Where, when, why,* and *how* are **interrogative adverbs** when they are used to ask for information in indefinite situations.

<u>Where</u> did he go? <u>When</u> will she arrive?
<u>Why</u> did she do it? <u>How</u> did she do it?

gr
6b

Relative Some people call *where, when, why,* and *how* **relative adverbs** when they relate dependent clauses to independent clauses. In fact, in this use they function as subordinating conjunctions, and this text discusses them as such in 9b.

Bracken springs up <u>where</u> land has been overgrazed.
I left <u>when</u> the park closed.

Conjunctive A **conjunctive adverb** (sometimes called an **adverbial conjunction**) modifies some word in the clause in which it appears and also links that clause to the rest of the sentence:

We went to the library; <u>then</u> we went to class.

The adverb *then* modifies *went,* but it also joins two independent clauses (*We went to the library. We went to class.*)

A conjunctive adverb may be a single word or a phrase (for example, *therefore, accordingly, instead, otherwise, in other words*) that expresses the relationship between two main clauses. (See 9c for this use as a conjunction.) When a conjunctive adverb links main clauses, a semi-colon or a period must be used. (See 28c for punctuation with conjunctive adverbs.)

A conjunctive adverb may also be used within a clause; in this case it serves more as a parenthesis than a conjunction. (See 27d for punctuation of such parenthetical elements.)

JOINING MAIN CLAUSES	Candy is dandy; <u>however</u>, liquor is quicker.
	Candy is dandy. <u>However</u>, liquor is quicker.
WITHIN A MAIN CLAUSE	Cynthia, <u>for example</u>, prefers candy.
	Candy is dandy. Liquor, <u>however</u>, is quicker.
	Candy is dandy. Liquor is quicker, <u>however</u>.

Exercises: Adverbs

List all the adverbs in the following sentences. Beside each adverb write the letter from the list below that identifies what kind of adverb it is. If the adverb is a modifier, underline the word or words it modifies. If it is used as a conjunction, identify the clauses it joins.

A. Simple	C. Prepositional	E. Relative
B. Sentence	D. Interrogative	F. Conjunctive

1. Walter became very nervous when he saw the fireman furtively motion to the three policemen.
2. The police, unfortunately, had already been called in.
3. The minister never says publicly how he got the money so quickly or, indeed, precisely how much money is involved.
4. The wagon had just rolled to a stop when the girl jumped on.
5. The screams of "Who's there?" and "Where is my brother?" echoed in the lane.
6. Elinor's brother strongly encouraged her to apply to Dalhousie; in addition, he wrote to a friend in Halifax to ask about lodgings.
7. Robert stared harder at the spot where the needle had been inserted; however, his resolve did not grow stronger—he fainted.
8. Within minutes they arrived at the gates of the almost deserted park and went through.

**gr
7**

---

7 Pronouns

Pronouns are traditionally defined as words that substitute for nouns. Pronouns can also be defined by the positions they take in sentences.

7a ▪ Characteristics

Many pronouns have inflections for number, some for number and case, and some for number, case, person, and gender. Pronouns are also identified by their function as noun substitutes serving as subjects, objects, and complements.

Inflections The various inflections of English pronouns are best exemplified by examining the personal pronouns (*I, you, he,* etc.), which are inflected for person, number, gender, and case.

Inflection for the grammatical category called **person** distinguishes among the speaker (the first person, *I*), the person spoken to (the second person, *you*), and the person or thing spoken about (the third person, *he, she,* or *it*). Personal pronouns are inflected for **number** in the first and third persons (singular: *I, me; he, him; it;* plural: *we, us; they, them;* etc.). The third-person singular is also inflected for **gender** to indicate that a person is male or female and that a thing is neither. These genders are termed **masculine** (*he, him*), **feminine** (*she, her*), and **neuter** (*it*).

Like nouns, personal pronouns are inflected for **case** (see 3a), but, whereas nouns have just two cases (common and possessive), personal pronouns have three cases. The **nominative case** (also called the subjective case) is used for subjects and subject complements, the **objective case** is used for objects of all kinds, and the **possessive case** is used to substitute for a possessive adjective and a noun (see 7b).

All the possible inflections of the personal pronouns are summarized in the following table. The forms in parentheses are possessives used only as adjectives and not as pronouns.

PERSON	CASE	NUMBER	
		Singular	Plural
First	Nominative	I	we
	Objective	me	us
	Possessive	mine (my)	ours (our)
Second	Nominative	you	you
	Objective	you	you
	Possessive	yours (your)	yours (your)

		GENDER			
		Mas.	Fem.	Neut.	Plural
Third	Nominative	he	she	it	they
	Objective	him	her	it	them
	Possessive	his (his)	hers (her)	its (its)	theirs (their)

gr 7a

Note The possessive forms of the personal pronouns are not written with *'s*.

Inflections for other kinds of pronouns are indicated in the next section.

Function and Position Pronouns are used instead of nouns or noun phrases to avoid the noun or noun phrase.

        N   Pron
Let the dog in. He is scratching at the door. (*He* avoids repetition of the noun *dog*.)

               N   N   Pron

Ron wanted to take botany and geology, but neither was offered this semester. (*Neither* avoids repetition of *botany* and *geology*.)

Pronouns are also used when the appropriate noun is unknown or unspecified.

    Pron

<u>Someone</u> has taken Yvonne's tennis racket. (It is not known who took the racket.)

              Pron

I'm thinking of <u>something</u> old and brown. (You know what you are thinking of, but you do not care to specify it.)

Finally, pronouns are used when there is no appropriate noun but the sentence must have a subject.

   Pron

<u>It</u> will probably snow tonight. (There is no suitable subject for the verb *snow*, but the sentence must have a subject.)

**gr
7a**

    As substitutes for nouns, pronouns serve the same functions and take almost all the positions in a sentence that nouns do.

SUBJECT	<u>They</u> ate a whole watermelon.
	<u>Each</u> ate a slice.
SUBJECT COMPLEMENT	Determination is not <u>enough</u>.
	It was <u>he</u>.
OBJECT COMPLEMENT	We have to name the canary <u>something</u>.
	He tagged the girl "<u>it</u>" for the next game.
DIRECT OBJECT	Your country needs <u>you</u>.
	Don't eat <u>anything</u> after midnight.
INDIRECT OBJECT	Alice showed <u>me</u> her appendectomy scar.
	Tell <u>everyone</u> the news.
OBJECT OF PREPOSITION	Take the paper from <u>her</u>.
	Lift the awning over <u>everybody</u>.
APPOSITIVE	Mother wants a new vacuum cleaner, <u>one</u> with a headlight.
DIRECT ADDRESS	<u>You</u> in the striped shirt! Get out of the way.
NOMINATIVE ABSOLUTE	<u>Nothing</u> having been planned beforehand, disaster was the result.

7b ▪ Classes

There are nine classes of pronouns: (1) personal pronouns, (2) reflexive pronouns, (3) intensive pronouns, (4) interrogative pronouns, (5) relative pronouns, (6) demonstrative pronouns, (7) indefinite pronouns, (8) reciprocal pronouns, and (9) expletive pronouns.

Personal Pronouns Personal pronouns are so named because they are inflected for person. They are also inflected for case and number and in the third person for gender. The most common pronouns, personal pronouns function as nouns in almost all the grammatical positions usually taken by nouns. Note that the following illustrations use third-person pronouns.

SUBJECT	<u>Henry</u> took the children fishing. <u>He</u> took the children fishing.
SUBJECT COMPLEMENT	It was <u>Marian</u> who called. It was <u>she</u> who called.
DIRECT OBJECT	John does not recall the <u>number</u>. John does not recall <u>it</u>.
INDIRECT OBJECT	Betsy told the <u>child</u> the secret. Betsy told <u>him</u> the secret.
OBJECT OF PREPOSITION	Ellen arrived with <u>Mira</u>. Ellen arrived with <u>her</u>.
SUBSTITUTE FOR POSSESSIVE ADJECTIVE AND NOUN	<u>Henry's</u> bicycle is red and <u>Nan's</u> is yellow. <u>His</u> bicycle is red and hers is <u>yellow</u>.

gr
7b

Reflexive Pronouns Reflexive pronouns, which are compounds of certain personal pronouns and -*self*, refer to the same things as other nouns or pronouns in the same clauses, usually the subjects. When the subject and the object are identical in meaning, the reflexive must be used (for example, "the *fish* tore *itself* free," not "the *fish* tore the *fish* free"). Reflexive pronouns are inflected for number.

myself, yourself, himself, herself, itself, oneself (impersonal), ourselves, themselves	Joanne cut <u>herself</u> on the glass. Did you buy it for <u>yourself</u>?

Intensive Pronouns Intensive pronouns emphasize the nouns or pronouns they follow and usually stand right next to them. Intensive pronouns have the same forms as reflexive pronouns.

myself, yourself, etc.	He <u>himself</u> must answer the charge.

Interrogative Pronouns Interrogative pronouns introduce questions. The interrogative pronoun *who*, with its related *-ever* forms, is inflected for case: nominative ("*Who* spoke?"), objective ("To *whom* did you speak?"), and possessive ("*Whose* voice was that?").

what, which, who, whose, whom, and their forms ending in *-ever* (whoever, whichever, etc.)	<u>Who</u> invented the clothespin? <u>Whose</u> hat is on the table? <u>Whoever</u> could be calling at this hour? <u>Whatever</u> does he want?

Relative Pronouns Relative pronouns introduce subordinate clauses and serve as subjects or objects in those clauses. The relative pronouns are *that* and the various interrogative pronouns above.

that, what, which, who, whose, whom, whoever, etc.	Did you see the coyote <u>that</u> I shot? I do not know <u>what</u> you want. Gretchen is the one <u>who</u> dropped the tray. I don't know with <u>whom</u> he plays. The man has a daughter <u>whose</u> beauty he praises. <u>Whatever</u> he said was right. <u>Whoever</u> does it will do it well. She insists she will date <u>whomever</u> she likes. I won't carry it, <u>whosesoever</u> it is.

Demonstrative Pronouns Demonstrative pronouns point out or specify things as being nearer to or farther from the speaker. The demonstrative pronouns are *this* and *that*; both are inflected for number (*this/these*, *that/those*).

this/these that/those	<u>These</u> must go back tomorrow. I shall never believe <u>that</u>. Do you want <u>this</u> cup or <u>that</u> bowl? I shall buy <u>these</u> boots and <u>those</u> laces.

Indefinite Pronouns Indefinite pronouns refer to members or parts of a category without specifying which particular member or part. They are not inflected, but some have only a singular or a plural meaning (see 18d).

another, each, either, neither, many, few, more, enough, some, such, less, any, much, nothing, etc.	<u>Many</u> are called, but <u>few</u> are chosen. <u>Each</u> received a share. <u>Neither</u> was disappointed. <u>Any</u> of them will be adequate.

Reciprocal Pronouns   Reciprocal pronouns refer to interaction between two or more persons or things. They have a possessive case, which may be used freely.

each other, one another	Clio and I congratulated <u>each other</u>.
	The children all play well with <u>one another</u>.
	Elizabeth and Vera often use <u>each others'</u> books.

Expletive Pronouns   The general expletive pronouns serve as subjects of clauses and sentences when no other subject is appropriate or when the subject is a long clause.

it, there	<u>There</u> is no reason for despair.
	<u>It</u> seemed to me that nobody would ever come to answer the knocking at the door.

Exercises: Pronouns

List all pronouns in the following sentences. After each pronoun, write the letter from the list below that identifies its grammatical function and the number from the list that identifies the kind of pronoun it is.

gr
7b

A. Subject	1. Personal
B. Subject complement	2. Reflexive
C. Object complement	3. Intensive
D. Direct object	4. Demonstrative
E. Indirect object	5. Interrogative
F. Object of preposition	6. Relative
G. Appositive	7. Indefinite
H. Direct address	8. Reciprocal
I. Nominative absolute	9. Expletive

1. The parrot that the neighbors brought home from their vacation squawks day and night, and, even though everyone has complained, nothing has been done about it.
2. "That's it!" Nancy squealed. "That's the one I've wanted for so long!"
3. George offered to give me some of them, but I refused to take any.
4. There was a real absence of love in that house, felt by all who entered it.
5. "But she stood there herself and told me I could eat anything in the refrigerator," Keiren argued.
6. What did they give each other on their anniversary?
7. No one having remained behind to guard the camp, the hikers were worried about their food supplies.

8. It is important that you do it yourself rather than rely on others.
9. I thoroughly enjoyed myself at the concert last night.
10. This employer considered her someone with a very promising future.

8 Prepositions

Prepositions are words used before nouns or pronouns to form phrases that modify some part of the sentence. Prepositions have no inflections. The combination of a preposition, its noun or pronoun object, and any modifiers of that object is called a **prepositional phrase**.

PREPOSITIONAL
PHRASES
> The mice <u>in the attic</u> are driving me <u>out of my mind</u>. <u>Despite the traps</u> that I put <u>behind the chimney</u> and <u>by the door</u>, they seem to have multiplied <u>during the past two months</u>.

English has fewer than a hundred different prepositions, but they are used very frequently. Most prepositions have a basic meaning concerned with space (*above, beyond, from, through,* and so on) or time (*during, since, until,* and so on) or both space and time (*around, before, following, near,* and so on); most of these also have extended meanings that have little to do with actual time or space (for example, *beyond my comprehension, from my experience*). The remaining prepositions express many different kinds of relationships, including, for example, exclusion (*but, except*), cause (*because of, due to*), and focus (*concerning, with regard to*). Notice that the partial list of preopositions below contains a number of phrasal prepositions, that is, prepositions consisting of more than one word.

gr
8

about	below	for	prior to
above	beneath	from	regarding
according to	beside	in (into)	since
across	besides	in the	through
after	between	middle of	to
against	beyond	in spite of	toward(s)
ahead of	but	including	under
amid(st)	by	like	underneath
among	by means of	near	until (till)
around	concerning	next to	up
as	despite	of	versus
as for	down	off	via
at	due to	on (upon)	with
away from	during	out	with regard
because of	except	out of	(respect) to
before	except for	over	within
behind	following	past	without

Many of these words serve both as prepositions in the ways outlined above and as adverbs of a special type used in verb-preposition combinations. When the preposition is attached to a single-word verb, the meaning of the verb changes. For example, the verb *look* may become *look after* ("take care of"), *look over* ("review"), *look up* ("search for"), *look up to* ("admire"), and *look forward to* ("anticipate"). Some of these verb-preposition combinations may be separated by their subjects (I will *look* the *word up*; I will *look up* the word) and others may not (I *look after* a garden; I *look forward to* a party).

It is not always easy to tell whether a given word is serving as a preposition or as an adverb. One way to make the distinction is to think of prepositions as "transitive" and prepositional adverbs as "intransitive." That is, prepositions always have an object somewhere in the sentence, most often directly after the preposition. Prepositional adverbs have no object.

PREPOSITION · If you don't stop running <u>around</u> that pole, you'll get dizzy. (<u>That pole</u> answers the question "what?" and is the object of <u>around</u>.)

PREPOSITIONAL ADVERB · If you don't stop running <u>around</u>, you'll be exhausted. (<u>Around</u> has no object and thus is an adverb.)

PREPOSITION · <u>What</u> is the dog sleeping <u>on</u>? (<u>What</u> is the object of the preposition.)

PREPOSITIONAL ADVERB · The burglars even dropped the TV set, but the dog slept <u>on</u>. (<u>On</u> has no object.)

Exercises: Prepositions

In the following sentences, underline each preposition and circle the object of the preposition.

1. His cousin Gertrude had always been the subject of the most gossip among members of the family.
2. Looking around the room, Mrs. Badenoch found all but two of the kittens.
3. During the summer Banff is an artists' mecca, filled with the hordes of students who come to attend the Summer School of the Arts.
4. Prior to 1867, Alaska was owned by Russia, but in that year the United States purchased it for $7.2 million; it did not, however, become a state until almost a hundred years later.
5. Without her hat, the girl with the red hair reminded Mr. Pahlitzsch of an actress he had seen in a play in Toronto.
6. The stunt pilot flew his plane under the bridge and, with a burst of speed, made three loops over the crowd watching from the riverbank.
7. Whirling about like spinning tops, the Cossack dancers spellbound the audience, ending the performance only at midnight.

gr
8

9 Conjunctions

Conjunctions are words that link single words, phrases, and clauses. Like prepositions, they have no inflections. Many conjunctions are identical in form with prepositions (for example, *but*, *after*, *since*, *for*), and only their function identifies them as conjunctions. There are two major classes of conjunctions: co-ordinating conjunctions and subordinating conjunctions. In addition, conjunctive adverbs may act as conjunctions in certain ways.

9a ▪ Co-ordinating Conjunctions

Co-ordinating conjunctions connect elements that serve the same grammatical function. The primary co-ordinating conjunctions are *and*, *but*, *or*, and *nor*. The word *yet* is often used as an adverb but may also be used as a co-ordinating conjunction with almost the same meaning as *but*.

> Daffodils <u>and</u> violets bloom early. (*And* connects *daffodils* and *violets*, both of which are nouns and both of which are subjects of the sentence.)
>
> We planted crocus <u>but</u> not lily of the valley. (*But* connects two nouns, both of which are direct objects.)
>
> Would you prefer to weed <u>or</u> to transplant? (*Or* connects two infinitives.)
>
> I cannot find the rake, <u>nor</u> is the trowel on the shelf. (*Nor* connects two independent clauses.)
>
> She watered the hydrangea faithfully, <u>yet</u> it still died. (Note that "*but* it still died" would have the same meaning.)

Even though they connect not grammatically parallel elements but related or subordinate ones, *for* and *so* are punctuated as co-ordinating conjunctions (see 27a). *For* introduces a clause expressing cause, and *so* introduces a clause expressing result.

> We sprayed the birch, <u>for</u> Japanese beetles were eating its leaves. (*For* introduces the clause that explains why we sprayed the birch.)
>
> The garden hose had a leak, <u>so</u> we patched it with tape. (*So* introduces the clause the explains the result of the fact that the garden hose leaked.)

Note *Then* is not a co-ordinating conjunction, although it is used as one colloquially. It is better used as a conjunctive adverb, with or without a true co-ordinating conjunction.

> COLLOQUIAL   Drive two kilometres north, then turn left at the stop sign.

gr
9

REVISED   Drive two kilometres north, and then turn left at
                 the stop sign.

REVISED   Drive two kilometres north; then turn left at the
                 stop sign.

Correlative co-ordinating conjunctions are special types of co-ordinating conjunctions that are used in pairs. One part of the correlative conjunction appears in the first element being connected, and the second part appears before the second element.

CORRELATIVE CONJUNCTION	EXAMPLE OF USE
both . . . and	Hemophilia is <u>both</u> hereditary <u>and</u> incurable.
either . . . or	Can you <u>either</u> type <u>or</u> take shorthand?
neither . . . nor	I can <u>neither</u> type <u>nor</u> take shorthand.
not only . . . but (also)	Keys are made <u>not only</u> of steel <u>but also</u> of brass.
whether . . . or	Katie didn't know <u>whether</u> to laugh <u>or</u> to cry.
the . . . the	<u>The</u> more I look at it, <u>the</u> less I like it.
as . . . as	Marie is <u>as</u> messy <u>as</u> Ruth is neat.
(just) as . . . so	<u>Just as</u> adjectives modify nouns, <u>so</u> adverbs modify verbs.
such . . . as	<u>Such</u> unsanitary conditions <u>as</u> these produce epidemics.
no (or not) . . . or	Ellen did <u>not</u> phone <u>or</u> write for a year.
not so much (that) . . . as	He was <u>not so much</u> evil <u>as</u> ill-advised.

**gr
9b**

9b ▪ Subordinating Conjunctions

Subordinating conjunctions connect clauses that are not grammatically equal; one is dependent on the other. The relationship between the two clauses is indicated by the particular subordinating conjunction used. This relationship may be one of condition, cause, time, manner, or contrast.

CONDITION   Do not attempt this climb <u>unless</u> you are in top physical shape.

CAUSE   The Fords are inconsolable <u>because</u> their TV is broken.

TIME	<u>After</u> she had learned to drive, Bianca felt independent.
MANNER	Do <u>as</u> I say.
CONTRAST	<u>Although</u> seldom entered in shows, Maine coon cats are beautiful.

The most important single-word subordinating conjunctions are listed below:

after	lest	when
although (though)	once	whenever
as	since	where
because	that	wherever
before	unless	whereas
if	until (till)	while

Many subordinating conjunctions are phrases (a notable number end in *that*):

as if	in the event that
as far as	in the hope(s) that
as long as	in order that
as though	on condition (that)
assuming that	on the ground(s) that
but that	provided (providing) that
even though	save that
for fear that	seeing that
given (provided) that	so that
if only	the day (the month, year, moment, etc.) that
inasmuch as	
in case	so that
	to the end that

Some subordinating conjunctions are formed in phrases with the addition of *the fact that*:

because of the fact that   notwithstanding the fact that

Like co-ordinating conjunctions, subordinating conjunctions sometimes come in pairs. The most important of the **correlative subordinating conjunctions** are these:

if . . . then	If the ridgepole is removed, <u>then</u> the roof will collapse.
no sooner . . . than	<u>No sooner</u> had the rebellion been put down <u>than</u> a foreign invasion began.
scarcely . . . when	<u>Scarcely</u> had the rebellion been put down <u>when</u> a foreign invasion began.
so . . . that	The circuits were <u>so</u> overloaded <u>that</u> a fuse blew.
such . . . that	He is <u>such</u> a liar <u>that</u> no one trusts him.

gr
9b

9c ▪ Conjunctive Adverbs

When they are used to join two independent clauses **conjunctive adverbs** (sometimes called **adverbial conjunctions**) act as co-ordinating conjunctions rather than adverbs that modify (see 6b).

CO-ORDINATING CONJUNCTION	Cotton is cool, <u>but</u> it wrinkles.
	Cotton is cool, <u>and</u> it is easy to launder.
CONJUNCTIVE ADVERB	Cotton is cool; <u>however</u>, it needs ironing.
	Cotton is cool; <u>in addition</u>, it is easy to launder.

Note Conjunctive adverbs are not, however, full conjunctions. For example, they cannot be punctuated like co-ordinating conjunctions. A comma is not sufficient punctuation for a conjunctive adverb; a period or semicolon is needed. (See 28c on the punctuation of conjunctive adverbs.)

INCORRECT	Cotton is cool, <u>thus</u>, it is a popular fabric in summer.
REVISED	Cotton is cool; <u>thus</u>, it is a popular fabric in summer.
REVISED	Cotton is cool. <u>Thus</u>, it is a popular fabric in summer.

A further difference between conjunctive adverbs and co-ordinating conjunctions is that, whereas there are only five (or seven, if *for* and *so* are included) co-ordinating conjunctions, scores of words serve as adverbial conjunctions, and they express very diverse meanings.

ILLUSTRATION	for example, incidentally, namely, that is
ADDITION	after all, also, besides, further(more), likewise, moreover, second, similarly, what is more
CONTRAST	alternatively, however, in contrast, instead, nevertheless, on the other hand, otherwise, still
QUALIFICATION	certainly, indeed, in fact, perhaps, possibly, undoubtedly
RESULT	accordingly, as a result, consequently, hence, therefore, thus
ATTITUDE	frankly, happily, unfortunately, luckily
SUMMARY	in other words, in sum(mary), to conclude
TIME	at first, finally, meanwhile, now, then, thereafter

Exercises: Conjunctions

In the following sentences, list all conjunctions (including all elements of correlative conjunctions) and conjunctive adverbs. Next to each, write the letter from the list below that identifies it.

A. Co-ordinating conjunction

B. Correlative co-ordinating conjunction

    C. Subordinating conjunction

    D. Correlative subordinating conjunction

    E. Conjunctive adverb

1. Hal not only sloshed a pitcher of water in the waiter's face, but he also tore up the bill as the manager stood helplessly by.
2. After Sue won the marathon, the track and field association was so impressed that it gave her a lifetime membership; further, the association provided both financial and moral support for her next race.
3. The closer Mars gets to Earth, the brighter Mars appears to be.
4. I know that Bobby Nichols is either a golfer or an actor.
5. The old man had been generous to her, for she was his only living relative; indeed, she seemed to be the only person he loved.
6. No sooner had Su-ling stepped into the bathtub than the telephone began to ring; nevertheless, she decided to tune out not only the telephone but any other obstacles to a quiet bath.
7. When he began work on the newspaper's copy desk, John could neither change the ribbons on the Teletype machines nor put paper in the wirephoto transmitter; what is more, he considered these chores so menial that he did not want to learn how to do them.
8. Since the accident, Marty's father has forbidden her to ride the horse again; moreover, he is thinking of selling it if he can find someone who really likes horses as much as he and Marty do.

gr
10

10 🦉 Interjections

Interjections are grammatically isolated words or phrases. Many express sudden or strong responses (*ugh! whew! ah!*). Some are onomatopoeic; that is, they attempt to imitate sounds not used in normal speech (for example, *eek!* to represent a scream or *brrr!* to represent the rapid vibration of the lips by which people indicate that they are cold).

Traditionally, grammarians have designated interjections a part of speech, but not all interjections are one word (*good heavens!*) or fall neatly into one-word class; sometimes they belong to other parts of speech (*curses! ruined! hurry! there! by jove!*) Interjections are, however, recognizable by their independence from the grammar of the sentences in which or with which they appear. They may be found at the beginning or at the end of a sentence; they may be entirely separate.

Oh, that's how you do it.

The doctor arrived too late, alas!

He never answers his telephone. Really!

Good heavens! I thought he died years ago.

Punctuation is used to indicate the grammatical separation of inter-jections. Note that meaning determines what punctuation is used. An emphatic interjection (*Quick! Never! No, no, no!*) requires an exclamation mark. Mild interjections (*hello, okay*) need only a period or comma. Many interjections have several different meanings, depending on the way in which they are spoken. For example, the word *well* in a rising tone means the speaker is waiting for a response of some kind from the listener (*Well?*). *Well*, spoken with heavy emphasis and a falling tone, indicates indigna-tion (*Well!*), and a drawled *well* with a level tone indicates doubt or hesitation (*Well . . .*).

Most interjections take a set form or are highly conventional; that is, synonyms cannot be substituted for the words in interjections without changing the meaning completely. In general, interjections can be recog-nized by their set forms and by the situations in which they are used.

USE AND MEANING	EXAMPLES
Emotional reactions	Range from mild interjections such as *Wow!* and *Darn it!* to swear words (which usually involve religious terms) and taboo words (which usually refer to bodily func-tions)
Meeting and parting	Hello, Hi, Good-bye, So long, How are you?, How do you do?, Fine, and you?, Nice to see you
Agreement and disagreement	Yes, No, Okay, Right, Sure, No way!, Uh-uh, Maybe
Asking and receiving	Please, Thank you, Thanks, You're wel-come
Apology	Sorry, Excuse me, Whoops, Think nothing of it, That's all right
Direct address and name-calling	Dad, George, Good girl!, You idiot!
Alarm or attention-getting	Sssh!, Look out!, Help!, Boo!, Hey!, Psst!
Special occasions	Happy birthday! Merry Christmas! Good luck! Here's to you! Congratulations!
Hesitation	Uh, You know, I mean, Of course, Well, Why
Physical comfort or discomfort	Whew! Mmmm! Ugh! Eek! Yum! Brrr!

gr
10

11 🦉 Phrases

A **phrase** is a sequence of words arranged grammatically but not containing both a subject and a predicate. A phrase functions as a single component in a sentence. That is, a phrase may serve as a subject, the main part of a predicate, a complement, an object of some kind, or a modifier.

Phrases can be classified into several different types according to the nature of the most important word in the phrase and the function of the phrase in the sentence. These include (1) noun phrases, (2) verb phrases, (3) verbal phrases, and (4) prepositional phrases.

11a ▪ Noun Phrases

A **noun phrase** consists of a noun and all of its modifiers. Noun phrases are used in the same positions as single nouns, that is, as subjects, objects, or complements.

SUBJECT	The medium-sized vase with the starburst design was made in Czechoslovakia.
DIRECT OBJECT	Mrs. Prentice wore sunglasses too large for her face.
SUBJECT COMPLEMENT	The culprit was a seedy-looking, middle-aged man with a long, jagged scar over his right eyebrow.

As these sentences illustrate, a noun phrase may itself include other types of phrases. For example, in the last sentence, the noun phrase includes two prepositional phrases, *with a long, jagged scar* and *over his right eyebrow.*

11b ▪ Verb Phrases

Verb phrases consist of a main verb and all of its auxiliaries or semiauxiliaries, if any. Verb phrases serve as the essential elements of predicates.

You forgot the mustard.
Did you remember a bottle-opener?
I was supposed to bring potato salad.
The dog has eaten all the olives.

11c ▪ Verbal Phrases

Verbal phrases are those whose main component is a nonfinite verb. Types of verbal phrases include (1) infinitive phrases, (2) participle phrases, and (3) gerund phrases.

gr
11

Infinitive Phrases Infinitive phrases consist of the infinitive (*to* followed by the base form of the verb) and any objects or modifiers of the infinitive or its object. Infinitive phrases serve as modifiers, subjects, objects, or complements.

MODIFIER	Sheila has errands <u>to run</u>. (*To run* modifies *errands*.)
MODIFIER	Napoleon was happy <u>to leave Elba</u>. (*To leave Elba* modifies *happy*.)
SUBJECT	<u>To own a motorcycle</u> is Kurt's only ambition.
SUBJECT COMPLEMENT	My summer project is <u>to brush up on my tennis</u>.

Participle Phrases Participle phrases consist of the present participle or past participle of a verb along with any modifiers, objects, or complements of that participle. The phrase may contain a perfect participle (present participle plus past participle). Participle phrases modify subjects or objects.

PRESENT PARTICIPLE	<u>Smiling confidently</u>, the batter strode to the plate. (*Smiling confidently* modifies *batter*.)
PAST PARTICIPLE	<u>Alarmed by a wave of burglaries</u>, Mr. Leland put glasses of water on his windowsills. (*Alarmed by a wave of burglaries* modifies *Mr. Leland*.)
PERFECT PARTICIPLE	<u>Having refueled at Lisbon</u>, the plane flew on to Rabat. (*Having refueled at Lisbon* modifies *plane*.)

gr
11c

A special kind of participle phrase is the **nominative absolute,** or **absolute phrase,** which consists of a noun or pronoun plus a present or past participle phrase. Absolute phrases serve as modifiers; they modify, not just a single word or phrase, but an entire clause or sentence.

<u>All things considered</u>, I'd rather be rich than poor.

Clara and Henry separated, <u>she returning to Montreal</u> and <u>he staying in Chicago</u>.

Gerund Phrases Gerund phrases consist of a gerund and its modifiers and objects, if any. (A gerund is a noun made from a verb by adding *-ing*.) **Perfect gerunds** consist of a gerund plus a past participle. Gerund phrases are used as subjects, objects, or complements.

SUBJECT	<u>Building the pyramids</u> took many years and many lives.
OBJECT OF PREPOSITION	The boss was worried about <u>my not having worked before</u>. (*Having worked* is a perfect gerund.)
COMPLEMENT	Her hobby is <u>collecting stamps</u>, but her husband says it should be <u>designing them</u>.

11d ▪ Prepositional Phrases

A **prepositional phrase** consists of a preposition, its object, and any modifiers of that object. Prepositional phrases normally function as modifiers.

> I bought the camera <u>with the carrying case</u>. (*With the carrying case* modifies *camera*.)
> Students wrote papers <u>during the reading period</u>. (*During the reading period* modifies *wrote papers*.)

gr
11d

Exercises: Phrases

Identify each of the underlined phrases in the following sentences by writing above each a letter from column one below to indicate its type and a number from column two to indicate its function. If the underscored phrase includes other phrases, classify only the larger phrase.

A. Noun	1. Main verb (with or without modifiers)
B. Prepositional	2. Subject (with or without modifiers)
C. Verb	3. Direct object
D. Infinitive	4. Indirect object
E. Participle	5. Subject complement
F. Gerund	6. Object complement
G. Absolute	7. Object of preposition
	8. Adjective
	9. Adverb
	10. Sentence modifier

1. <u>Weeding the strawberry plants</u> was a tiresome chore to Gary, who loved <u>to eat strawberries</u> but not to tend them.
2. <u>Purring softly</u>, the kitten snuggled <u>into the cushions</u> on the sofa <u>to take its afternoon snooze</u>.
3. <u>The decision made at last</u>, the jurors <u>filed</u> back <u>into the courtroom</u> to give <u>their verdict</u>.
4. <u>The new sports car in the driveway</u> is a lavish graduation present <u>from Eileen's grandparents</u>.
5. <u>For getting a second F in French</u>, Doug <u>was put</u> <u>on academic probation</u>.
6. Francie checked <u>teaching swimming</u> as her first choice of the jobs offered <u>at the camp</u>.
7. Mr. Jonah is <u>the new supervisor</u> <u>of the quality control department</u>.
8. Most <u>of those</u> <u>questioned about personal values</u> ranked <u>being happy</u> much higher than they ranked <u>being rich</u> or being successful <u>in their professions</u>.

12  Clauses

A **clause** is a grammatical sequence of words that contains a subject and a predicate. The two most important types of clauses are independent clauses and dependent clauses.

12a ▪ Independent Clauses

An **independent clause** (or a **main clause**, as it is often called) is one that can stand alone as a complete sentence.

> When he pulled the shade, <u>it fell on his head</u>. (*It fell on his head* can stand as a complete sentence.)

> <u>Don't talk to Regina</u> until she has had a cup of coffee. (*Don't talk to Regina* can stand as a complete sentence.)

> <u>Jerry eats a pound of carrots a day; as a result, his skin has an orange tinge</u>. (*Jerry eats a pound of carrots a day* and *as a result, his skin has an orange tinge* are both independent clauses.)

gr
12

12b ▪ Dependent Clauses

A **dependent clause** is introduced by some kind of subordinating word and cannot stand alone as a complete sentence. In other words, a dependent clause requires an independent clause to complete it. Dependent clauses serve the same functions as nouns, adjectives, or adverbs.

Noun Clauses Dependent noun clauses fill the positions in a sentence that nouns may fill. They are typically introduced by *that, who, which, what, whom, whoever, whomever, whatever, whichever, whether, where, when, why,* and *how.*

> <u>Whoever painted this room</u> certainly likes purple and orange. (The noun clause is subject of the sentence.)

> I wonder <u>whether he is color-blind</u>. (The noun clause is the direct object.)

> The surprise is not <u>that there are stripes</u> but <u>that the stripes run sideways</u>. (The noun clauses are subject complements.)

Adjective Clauses Adjective clauses modify nouns, pronouns, or other groups of words serving as nouns. They follow the words they modify and are typically introduced by relative pronouns (*what, which, who, whom, that*) or relative adverbs (*where, when, why, how*).

The desk <u>that wouldn't fit through the door</u> was sawn in half. (The clause modifies the subject *desk*.)

That is an idea <u>whose hour will never come</u>. (The clause modifies the subject complement *idea*.)

Can you think of any good reason <u>why I should go to class today?</u> (The adjective clause modifies the direct object *reason*.)

Millie is still talking about the boy with <u>whom she played ping-pong last week</u>. (The clause modifies *boy*, the object of the preposition.)

Adverb Clauses   Adverb clauses modify verbs, verb phrases, adjectives, adverbs, or entire clauses or sentences. They are usually introduced by relative adverbs or subordinating conjunctions.

Laurie began to learn French <u>when she was eight years old</u>. (The adverb clause modifies the verb *began*.)

Laurie speaks French better <u>than her mother does</u>. (The clause modifies the adverb *better*.)

Within two months, Laurie's French was as fluent <u>as her mother's had been after two years' study</u>. (The clause modifies the adjective *fluent*.)

<u>Because she was so young</u>, Laurie was not embarrassed by her mistakes in grammar. (The clause modifies the independent clause *Laurie was not embarrassed by her mistakes in grammar*.)

12c ▪ Elliptical Clauses

Sometimes clauses are hard to identify because part or all of the subject or the predicate has been omitted and is understood only from the context. Such clauses are called **elliptical clauses;** they may be either independent or dependent clauses.

INDEPENDENT   I will drive the car and <u>Jane the van</u>. (The verb phrase *will drive* has been omitted.)

DEPENDENT   Amy does not work well <u>when under pressure</u>. (The subject *she* and the verb *is* have been omitted.)

DEPENDENT   You don't explain irregular verbs <u>as well as he</u>. (The verb *explains* and the direct object *irregular verbs* have been omitted.)

12d ▪ Conditional Clauses

Conditional sentences are made up of a dependent **conditional clause**— one that states a condition and usually begins with *if* —and an independent result clause. The mood of the verb in the conditional clause depends on whether the condition is **real** (possible) or **unreal** (contrary to fact, impossible, or unlikely). The form of the verb in the result clause follows from the mood of the conditional clause and thus reflects the likelihood of the result.

Real Conditions If the condition is possible, even barely possible, the mood of both clauses is indicative.

> If it is sunny tomorrow, we shall go to the park.
>
> If the child is hurt, he will cry.

The first condition is possible—it may be sunny, or it may not—so the result is also possible. The second condition is possible and the result is highly probably—the child usually cries when he is hurt. *Unless*, meaning "if you do not," is also common in clauses of real condition.

> Unless you do your homework, you may not go to the movies.

Unreal Conditions If the condition is impossible or unlikely, the mood in the *if* clause is subjunctive, and the verb in the result clause is marked by the modal auxiliary *would* (or *should*) and the past tense (see 17c).

> If I were you, I would not press him for an answer.
>
> If he had eaten his dinner, he would not have been hungry at bedtime.

The first condition is impossible—I am not you. The second condition is also impossible—he did not eat his dinner.

gr
12d

Exercises: Clauses

Identify each underlined clause in the following sentences by writing the appropriate letter code beside it.

I	independent clause	I-E	independent elliptical clause
D-NC	noun clause	D-E	dependent elliptical clause
D-ADJ	adjective clause	D-C-R	conditional clause (real)
D-ADV	adverb clause	D-C-U	conditional clause (unreal)
		NC	not a clause

1. Galloping across the meadow toward the stable, the huge black horse seemed the most majestic animal that Jeffrey had ever seen.
2. After the winter storm had subsided, thousands of families found that they were without electricity.
3. After following his career in the newspapers for many years, my aunt was thrilled to be able to meet the great boxer.

4. Sven and Ingrid <u>enjoyed refinishing old furniture</u> for their apartment, and <u>they had found several good pieces at local</u> secondhand stores.

5. <u>Because no one had been there to show the guests their quarters,</u> Kate had taken the blue room and <u>Will the downstairs bedroom.</u>

6. After dinner the men all settled down <u>to watch football on television,</u> and <u>their sons decided to go to a movie.</u>

7. <u>Whichever flight Lucie takes</u> is always the one <u>that is delayed for</u> one reason or another.

8. I told you not to do handstands <u>while you are in the shower.</u>

9. <u>If we leave the party on time,</u> we can catch the last bus.

10. <u>If you had used common sense,</u> you would not be stranded here at midnight.

---

13 🦉 Restrictive/Nonrestrictive Phrases/Clauses

Phrases and clauses used as modifiers are either restrictive or nonrestrictive. A **restrictive modifier** is essential to the meaning of the sentence or clause in which it appears. A **nonrestrictive modifier** provides additional information but is not essential to the basic meaning of the sentence or clause. Nonrestrictive modifiers are set off by commas in writing; restrictive modifiers are not. (See also 20d, 27e.)

RESTRICTIVE CLAUSE	The shells <u>that she sells by the seashore</u> are overpriced. (The restrictive clause limits the shells being discussed to those sold by the seashore.)
NONRESTRICTIVE CLAUSE	The shells, <u>which she sells by the seashore</u>, are overpriced. (All the shells being discussed are overpriced; the nonrestrictive clause simply gives additional information about the shells.)
RESTRICTIVE PHRASE	The car <u>parked in front of the bank</u> was ticketed. (The phrase *parked in front of the bank* identifies the specific car being discussed.)
NONRESTRICTIVE PHRASE	My car, <u>parked in front of the bank</u>, was ticketed. (The word *my* specifically identifies the car; the phrase *parked in front of the bank* simply gives additional information about it.)

Exercises: Restrictive and Nonrestrictive Phrases and Clauses

Write one sentence using each of the following phrases and clauses as a restrictive modifier and another sentence using it as a nonrestrictive modifier. Be sure that you punctuate correctly. Example:

RESTRICTIVE   The woman *wearing a green jumpsuit* is my physics instructor.

NONRESTRICTIVE   Ms. O'Leary, *wearing a green jumpsuit,* went out to milk her cow.

1. running through the crowd
2. with a mouthful of feathers
3. who had seen the entire incident
4. given two days extra vacation
5. which polluted the atmosphere
6. from a local department store

14 Appositives

Like a modifier, an **appositive** refers to the same thing as the word, phrase, or clause with which it is associated. However, unlike other modifiers, an appositive has the same grammatical function as the word or phrase with which it is associated. That is, an appositive to a subject could also serve as subject, an appositive to a subject complement could also serve as complement, and so on. Appositives are most often nouns or noun substitutes, but appositives may also serve as adjectives, adverbs, or even predicates.

NOUN PHRASE APPOSITIVE TO SUBJECT
The manatee, <u>an aquatic mammal native to Florida,</u> is in danger of extinction. (*An aquatic mammal native to Florida* refers to *the manatee.*)

NOUN PHRASE APPOSITIVE TO SUBJECT
A few people were invited, <u>all close friends.</u> (*All close friends* refers to *a few people.*)

ADJECTIVES APPOSITIVE TO SUBJECT COMPLEMENT
Ferdinand I was a true Hapsburg, <u>shrewd and stubborn.</u> (*Shrewd and stubborn* refers to *a true Hapsburg.*)

PREPOSITIONAL PHRASE APPOSITIVE TO PREPOSITIONAL PHRASE
The train left on time, <u>at exactly 09:37.</u> (*At exactly 09:37* refers to *on time.*)

PAST PARTICIPLE PHRASE APPOSITIVE TO PAST PARTICIPLE
Computer programs must be edited, that is, <u>checked for errors,</u> before being run. (*Checked for errors* refers to *edited.*)

Most appositives are nonrestrictive, but noun appositives are sometimes restrictive, particularly if the appositive is a proper noun.

RESTRICTIVE   My son <u>Warren</u> broke his wrist. (The appositive
                     Warren limits the meaning of *my son* to one
                     specific son.)

NONRESTRICTIVE   My son, a <u>soccer player</u>, broke his wrist. (The
                     appositive *a soccer player* merely gives fur-
                     ther information about *my son*.)

Exercises: Appositives

Underline all appositives in the following sentences, and punctuate the sentences correctly.

1. The new reporter was sent to the morgue that is the newspaper's library to find background information about the commission's public hearings.
2. For late spring the ice storm was a freakish happening a trick of nature.
3. During the nineteenth century the period of the Industrial Revolution perhaps nothing stirred up so much controversy as did one invention namely the steam locomotive.
4. The performer one of the greatest ballet dancers of the twentieth century refused to tour the United States.
5. In his painting the effect that Imre wanted to create the effect that his teacher encouraged him to create was an almost photographic rendering of the violence of modern society.
6. The colors lemon yellow, cantaloupe orange, and pagan purple turned the room into a garish nightmare.

gr
15

---

15 Nominals, Adjectivals, Adverbials

One outstanding characteristic of English is the ability of a single word to serve in various functions without changing its form. For example, the word *here* is normally considered an adverb, and adverbs are normally modifiers. However, in the sentence "Khartoum is a long way from *here*," *here* serves as the object of a preposition, although we usually think of the object of a preposition as being a noun or a pronoun. In instances like this, where the form of a word conflicts with its function in the sentence, it is convenient to have a separate label for the function. Because *here* in this sentence is serving as a noun, we can call it a nominal.

Distinguishing labels are particularly useful for describing the function of phrases and clauses in a sentence. For example, in the sentence

"Go to the dentist *before you get a toothache*," the dependent clause, "*before you get a toothache*," modifies the main clause. The entire clause is not an adverb, yet it is serving the same function as an adverb. We can call it an adverbial. Similarly, in the sentence "Pour the ink *in this bottle*," the prepositional phrase "*in this bottle*" functions as an adverb modifying the verb *pour*. But in the sentence "The ink *in this bottle* had dried up," the phrase "*in this bottle*" functions as an adjective because it modifies the noun *ink*; it is an adjectival.

15a ▪ Nominals

Any word or group of words that serves the function of a noun is a **nominal.**

KIND OF NOMINAL	FUNCTION	EXAMPLE
Noun	Subject	My <u>brother</u> loves Mexican food.
Infinitive phrase	Subject	<u>To eat spicy food</u> is his chief pleasure.
Infinitive phrase	Direct object	He likes <u>to cook Mexican food</u>.
Gerund phrase	Subject	<u>Cooking with hot peppers</u> is his favorite pastime.
Gerund phrase	Object	He likes <u>concocting hot sauces</u>.
Gerund phrase	Object of preposition	He surprised me by <u>winning a cooking competition</u>.
Adjective	Subject	<u>The hottest</u> is not hot enough.
Dependend clause	Subject	<u>How his stomach can stand it</u> is a mystery to me.
Adverb	Object of preposition	I've had enough tamales for <u>now</u>.

15b ▪ Adjectivals

A word or group of words that serves the function of an adjective is an **adjectival.**

KIND OF ADJECTIVAL	FUNCTION	EXAMPLE
Adjective	Modifies subject complement	There will be an <u>indefinite</u> delay.
Noun	Modifies subject	The <u>plane</u> ticket cost more than I had expected.

gr
15b

Infinitive	Modifies direct object	I have several complaints to make.
Participle	Modifies object of preposition	We had reservations on the postponed flight.
Adverb	Modifies subject	People here are suspicious of strangers.
Prepositional phrase	Modifies direct object	Will you cash an out-of-town cheque?
Dependent noun clause	Modifies object of preposition	When will I be paid for the luggage that you lost?

15c ▪ Adverbials

A word or group of words that serves the function of an adverb is an **adverbial**.

ADVERBIAL	FUNCTION	EXAMPLE
Adverb	Modifies past participle	The koala's body is thickly covered with fur.
Prepositional phrase	Modifies main clause	Without eucalyptus leaves, koalas will die.
Dependent clause	Modifies verb phrase	The infant koala remains in the mother's pouch until it is three months old.
Infinitive phrase	Modifies adjective	Koalas are difficult to breed in zoos.

Exercises: Interjections, Nominals, Adjectivals, and Adverbials

Write the identifying letter from the list below over each underlined word, phrase, or clause in the following sentences.

    A. Interjection C. Adjectival
    B. Nominal   D. Adverbial

1. "Yum! Smelling that baked ham is making me hungry," said Ralph.
2. To find out won't be a problem; we can just call up the reference desk.
3. Professor Craig is always at his worst on Mondays, but saying when he is at his best is difficult.
4. "I last saw your chemistry book on the front seat of the car," Natalie told Tom as he frantically scrambled through his books and notes, "and your calculus text is over there."

5. We live in two different worlds, yes, but we must learn to speak to each other if either world is to survive beyond the twentieth century.
6. The scowling customer clutched a newspaper advertisement in his left hand as he searched in vain for the floor manager.
7. Where Agatha was last week is a mystery that we will perhaps never solve.

---

16 ![owl] Classification of Sentences

In addition to describing sentences according to the elements of which they are composed (see 1), sentences can also be classified by the types of clauses they contain, by their function, and by whether they are affirmative or negative.

16a ▪ Classification by Types of Clauses

Sentences are made up of grammatically related phrases and clauses. One classification of sentences is based on the number and types of clauses they contain. The four basic types of sentences are (1) simple sentences, (2) compound sentences, (3) complex sentences, and (4) compound-complex sentences.

gr
16

Simple Sentences Simple sentences consist of one independent clause. This independent clause may, however, have a compound subject or a compound predicate.

SIMPLE SENTENCE	Fiona ran away from home.
SIMPLE SENTENCE WITH COMPOUND SUBJECT	Fiona and Nigel ran away from home.
SIMPLE SENTENCE WITH COMPOUND SUBJECT AND COMPOUND PREDICATE	Fiona and Nigel ran away from home and joined the circus.

Compound Sentences Compound sentences consist of two or more independent clauses and no dependent clauses.

Fiona joined the circus, and Nigel joined too.
Fiona ran away from home; she intended to join the circus.

Complex Sentences Complex sentences consist of one independent clause and one or more dependent clauses. The dependent clauses may either precede or follow the independent clause.

After Fiona ran away from home, Nigel ran away too.
Nigel joined the navy because Fiona had run away from home.

Compound-Complex Sentences Compound-complex sentences contain at least two independent clauses and at least one dependent clause.

> Fiona ran away from home, and, as soon as she had left, Nigel ran away too.
> Before Nigel could stop her, Fiona ran away from home; she intended to join the circus.

16b ▪ Classification by Syntax and Function

Sentences are also classified according to their function or purpose. The usual classifications are (1) declarative sentences, (2) interrogative sentences, (3) imperative sentences, and (4) exclamatory sentences. Each kind has a typical word order.

Declarative sentences make statements of fact or opinion. Normally, the word order is subject + verb phrase + object or complement, if the sentence contains an object or complement.

> Ms. Loomis borrowed a set of golf clubs.
> The mills of the gods grind slowly.

Occasionally, the word order of a declarative sentence is inverted for the sake of emphasis. The first sentence below has the order complement + subject + verb in both its independent clauses. The second sentence begins with an adverb, followed by the verb and then the subject.

> A pragmatist he is and a pragmatist he will always be.
> Down came the pile of boxes.

Interrogative sentences ask questions. There are two types of interrogative sentences, those with a WH-word (*who, what, which, when, where,* and *why*) and how and yes-no questions (questions to which an answer of *yes* or *no* is expected). WH and how questions normally begin with the WH-word or *how* followed by the verb. Yes-no questions usually begin with an auxiliary verb followed by the subject.

> WH/HOW   Why did he leave? How do you know? Where is Jean?
>
> YES-NO   Are you coming? Did they call? Have you heard yet?

Imperative sentences make a request or command. Typically, the implied subject is *you*, but the word is omitted, and the sentence begins with the verb. Ocassionally the subject is expressed.

> Turn left after two stop lights.
> Someone please tell me what is going on.

Exclamatory sentences usually express an attitude or strong emotion. They frequently begin with *what* or *how* and have inverted word order.

> How happy you must be!
> What a high price to pay for a ticket!

gr
16b

16c ▪ Affirmative and Negative Sentences

Sentences may be either affirmative or negative. An **affirmative sentence** makes an assertion; a **negative sentence** denies an assertion by means of a negating word such as *not, no,* or *never*. (For problems with double negatives, see 20b.)

AFFIRMATIVE   Seats are available.

NEGATIVE   Seats are not available. No seats are available.

Exercises: Classification of Sentences

Write the letter and number from the lists below in front of each of the following sentences to classify each sentence by the type of clauses it contains and by its function.

A. Simple sentence   1. Declarative sentence
B. Compound sentence   2. Interrogative sentence
C. Complex sentence   3. Imperative sentence
D. Compound-complex sentence   4. Exclamatory sentence

1. Never trust a man who speaks well of everybody.
2. When I play with my cat, who knows but that she regards me more as a plaything than I do her?
3. The great pleasure of a dog is that you may make a fool of yourself with him, and not only will he not scold you, but he will make a fool of himself too.
4. Generals cannot be entrusted with anything, not even with war.
5. When the cat's away, the mice will play.
6. Love your neighbor, but don't pull down the hedge.
7. How awful to reflect that what people say of us is true!
8. Take care to get what you like, or you will be forced to like what you get.

gr
17

---

17 Problems with Verbs and Verb Phrases

Using verbs correctly is sometimes difficult because verbs have more inflections than other parts of speech, because many common verbs are irregular, and because verbs and verb phrases must be changed to indicate changes in tense, mood, and voice.

17a ▪ Forms of Verbs *(vbf)*

Problems involving the forms of verbs include using a present form when
past meaning is intended, using an incorrect form of a past tense or past
participle, and using incorrect auxiliary verbs.

Regular Verbs All regular verbs form both their past tense and their past
participle by adding *-ed* or *-d* and form their third-person singular present
tense by adding *-s* or *-es*. In speech, these endings are often said so rapidly
as to be indistinct. In some dialects, they may be omitted entirely. In
writing, however, remember to include these *-s* and *-ed* endings.

> INCORRECT   Yesterday we <u>ask</u> her to meet us at the pool.
>
> CORRECT   Yesterday we <u>asked</u> her to meet us at the pool.
>
> INCORRECT   I have never <u>walk</u> so far in my life.
>
> CORRECT   I have never <u>walked</u> so far in my life.
>
> INCORRECT   Joe always <u>act</u> silly when he is around girls.
>
> CORRECT   Joe always <u>acts</u> silly when he is around girls.

The idioms *be supposed to* and *used to* are particularly troublesome
because they can be confused with the verbs *to suppose* and *to use*. Remember that *supposed* in *be supposed to* (meaning "required to, obli-
gated to") and *used* in *used to* (meaning "formerly accustomed to") always end in *-d*. In other words, in these idioms, *supposed* is always a past
participle and *used* is always a past tense. Both are always followed by
the infinitive form of the main verb.

> Do you suppose we are <u>supposed to</u> (not <u>suppose to</u>) call first?
> The twins <u>used to</u> (not <u>use to</u>) buy Ivory, but now they use another
> brand.

Irregular Verbs Irregular verbs are troublesome because their past tenses
and past participles have different and unpredictable forms. Some irregular verbs have the same form in all three principal parts (*cut, cut, cut*),
some have vowel changes but no inflectional endings (*sing, sang, sung*),
still others have vowel changes and an *-n* in the past participle (*drive,
drove, driven*), and some change the final *-d* of the infinitive to *-t* in the
past tense and past participle (*build, built, built*). The principal parts of
some common irregular verbs are listed in Appendix D. Your dictionary
can also guide you; most dictionaries list the principal parts of all irregular verbs.

If you are unsure which form of an irregular verb is required in a
given verb phrase, see 17b. In particular, avoid using a past tense form as
a past participle or a past participle form as a past tense.

> INCORRECT   The temperature this week has <u>broke</u> all records.
>
> CORRECT   The temperature this week has <u>broken</u> all records.

Especially confusing are pairs of verbs with similar forms and meanings. Of these, the chief offenders are *lie/lay*, *sit/set*, and *rise/raise*. In each case, the first member of the pair is an irregular verb that is intransitive (takes no direct object), and the second is a verb that is transitive (takes a direct object). You may find it helpful to remember that the intransitive verbs *lie, sit*, and *rise* always have a vowel change in the past tense and past participle, whereas the transitive verbs have no vowel change.

I lie here every day. Yesterday I lay here. I have just lain down.
I lay my books on my desk every day. Yesterday I laid my books on my desk. I have just laid my books on my desk.

I sit here every day. Yesterday I sat here. I have just sat down.
I set my mug on the shelf every day. Yesterday I set my mug on the shelf. I have just set my mug on the shelf.

I rise at seven every morning. Yesterday I rose at seven. I have just risen.

I raise the shade every morning. Yesterday I raised the shade. I have just raised the shade.

---

gr 17a

Exercises: Irregular Verbs

Fill in the blanks in the following sentences with the correct form of the verb that is given in parentheses.

1. During the three years when he had lived alone, Luke always _____ (awake) an hour later than usual on Sunday mornings and _____ (lie) in bed while he _____ (drink) a pot of mint tea and _____ (read) the newspaper.
2. Marjorie _____ (wring) out her towel and her T-shirt, but before she could get away her three brothers _____ (come) along and _____ (throw) her into the pool again.
3. Chuck laughed heartily as he _____ (sit) down to enumerate all the delicacies he had neither _____ (eat) nor _____ (drink) in this first terrible week of his latest diet.
4. No matter what the soprano _____ (sing), the critics were always so kind that other members of the opera company _____ (become) jealous and _____ (do) everything possible to jeopardize her performances.
5. The prisoner, whom the authorities had _____ (forbid) to see either his wife or his lawyer, _____ (hang) himself just before dawn.
6. Although Sergei had _____ (lie) in bed sick for more than a week, an invitation to accompany his aunt to New York for three weeks miraculously cured him: he _____ (fling) back the covers, _____ (lay) aside his heating pad and pills, and _____ (spring) from his bed.

7. When the man had _____ (set) the basket down, everyone _____ (sit) around him on the ground, watching as he _____ (take) out the snakes and _____ (lay) them across his bare shoulders.
8. The sailor _____ (dive) from the deck of the ship and _____ (swim) straight to the fisherman, who _____ (cling) to an overturned lifeboat.

Auxiliary Verbs The auxiliary verbs are *be, have, do,* and the modal auxiliaries. Most problems with auxiliary verbs occur in verb phrases that have one of the modal auxiliaries (*will/would, shall/should, can/could, may/might, dare, need, ought, must*).

1. ***Shall-will.*** The future tense is formed with *will* or *shall* plus the infinitive form of the main verb. Many Canadians feel that formal usage requires the use of *shall* with first-person subjects and *will* with second- and third-person subjects. Other Canadians follow American practice, using *will* for all persons even in formal writing. Almost all North Americans use *will* for all persons in informal writing and colloquial usage.

gr
17a

Shall is, however, generally used in asking first-person questions, especially questions that are requests for instructions.

Reversing *shall* and *will* changes meaning; for example, "He *shall* do it!", rather than "He will do it," expresses determination rather than a matter-of-fact statement.

INFORMAL	I <u>will</u> inform you of our decision.
	She <u>will</u> inform you of our decision.
FORMAL	I <u>shall</u> inform you of our decision.
	She <u>will</u> inform you of our decision.
EMPHATIC	I <u>will</u> inform you of the decision, whether he wants me to or not.
	She <u>shall</u> inform you of the decision, whether you want to hear it or not.

<u>Shall</u> we leave now?

<u>Shall</u> I take this package to the post office?

Should and *would* are the past-tense forms of *shall* and *will* respectively. They are also used as modal auxiliaries indicating desire, intent, or habitual action and in result clauses that follow unreal conditional clauses (see 12d). In all uses, *should* and *would* follow the distinctions of person for *shall* and *will.*

2. *Ought.* No verb phrase should contain more than one modal auxiliary. Hence it is incorrect to write *should ought to* or *shouldn't ought to.* Use either *should* or *ought to,* but not both in one verb phrase.

INCORRECT   They <u>shouldn't ought to</u> treat us like children.

CORRECT   They <u>shouldn't</u> treat us like children.

CORRECT   They <u>ought not</u> treat us like children.

It is also incorrect to write *had ought to* or *hadn't ought to;* omit the *had* or *hadn't.*

INCORRECT   You <u>had ought to</u> write to Action Line.

CORRECT   You <u>ought to</u> write to Action Line.

3. *Of* for *have.* In speech, *have* as an auxiliary verb is usually spoken so rapidly that it sounds like *of. Of* is not an auxiliary verb and should never be written as one.

INCORRECT   We <u>should of drained</u> the pipes last fall.

CORRECT   We <u>should have drained</u> the pipes last fall.

INCORRECT   He <u>wouldn't of sold</u> the textbook before the examination.

CORRECT   He <u>wouldn't have sold</u> the textbook before the examination.

**gr
17b**

17b ▪ Tense of Verbs *(t)*

Problems involving verb tenses include special and conventional uses of the present tense and the correct tense of verbs in subordinate clauses (the so-called sequence of tenses).

Special Uses of the Simple Present   The simple present is used (1) in expressing universal truths, (2) in indicating future time with an adverbial of time, and (3) in discussing the contents of literary works.

1. **Universal truths.** The present tense is used when there is no limitation on the time to which the statement applies.

Four plus three <u>equals</u> seven.
Milk of magnesia <u>tastes</u> awful.
All the stars visible from the earth <u>orbit</u> around the Milky Way.

2. **Future time.** The present tense is often used as an alternative to the future tense when there is an adverbial of time in the clause.

The barbershop <u>opens</u> an hour from now.
We <u>leave</u> for Toledo next week.

3. **Literary works.** The simple present is conventionally used in discussing the contents of literary works, even though these works were, of course, written in the past and even though the author may have used the past tense throughout his or her work.

> After betraying Miss Brodie, Sandy becomes a nun and writes a book on psychology.

An easy way to check for consistency in the sequence of tenses when you write about literature is to check that the *first* part of every main verb is in the present form (for example, Swift *says/ is* saying/ has *said/ has* been arguing/ *cannot* be understood, etc.). When discussing the facts of writing and publication of a book, use the past tense.

> Muriel Spark's first novel, *The Comforters*, <u>was published</u> in 1957, and *The Prime of Miss Jean Brodie* <u>appeared</u> four years later.

Sequence of Tenses   The term "sequence of tenses" refers to the relationship between the verb in the main clause of a sentence and the verb in a subordinate clause or phrase of the same sentence. (Some instructors also use the "sequence of tenses" to refer to what this textbook calls a shift in tense. See 23b.)

**gr
17b**

1. **Sentences with subordinate clauses.** If the verb in the main clause is in the present tense, there is normally no problem because the tense of the verb in the subordinate clause corresponds to the "actual" time meant. However, if the main verb is in any past or future tense, confusion can arise because the tense of the verb in the subordinate clause does not clearly correspond to "actual" time. For example, in the sentence *Guinevere will be shocked when she sees Merlin's beard*, the verb *sees* is in the present tense even though Guinevere's seeing of Merlin's beard is still in the future; at the time of speaking, Guinevere has not yet seen Merlin's beard.

The chart below summarizes the rules for sequence of tenses. For the first column, "present" refers to any verb phrase in which the first verb of the main clause is in the present tense (simple present, present progressive, present perfect, or present perfect progressive). "Past" refers to any verb phrase in which the first verb of the main clause is in the past tense (simple past, past perfect, past progressive, or past perfect progressive). "Future" refers to any verb phrase in which the first verb of the main clause is in the future tense (simple future, future progressive, future perfect, or future perfect progressive) and to cases in which the verb of the main clause implies a future tense, as with an imperative or the phrase *be going to.* Thus, to express simultaneous action in the past, the verb of the subordinate clause is always in a past tense, no matter what kind of past tense the verb of the main clause is in.

> The lecturer <u>frowned</u> when the bell <u>rang</u>.
> The lecturer <u>had begun</u> when the bell <u>rang</u>.

The lecturer <u>was</u> just <u>beginning</u> when the bell <u>rang</u>.
The lecturer <u>had been speaking</u> for five minutes when the bell <u>rang</u>.

These rules apply regardless of whether the subordinate clause precedes or follows the main clause:

When the bell <u>rang</u>, the lecturer <u>frowned</u>.
The lecturer <u>had been speaking</u> for five minutes when the bell <u>rang</u>.

TENSE OF MAIN CLAUSE	RELATIONSHIP OF ACTION IN SUBORDINATE CLAUSE TO ACTION IN MAIN CLAUSE	TENSE IN SUBORDINATE CLAUSE	EXAMPLES
Present	Simultaneous	Present	I know that I <u>am</u> late.
Present	Earlier	Past	I know that I <u>was</u> late.
Present	Later	Future	I know that I <u>shall be</u> late.
Past	Simultaneous	Past	I knew that I <u>was</u> late.
Past	Earlier	Past perfect	I knew that I <u>had been</u> late.
Past	Later	would + infinitive	I knew that I <u>would be</u> late.
Future	Simultaneous	Present	I shall call if I <u>am</u> delayed
Future	Earlier	Present perfect	I shall call if I <u>have been</u> delayed.
Future	Later	Future	I shall call if I <u>shall be</u> (<u>am going to be</u>) delayed. Call if you <u>will be</u> delayed.

gr
17b

2. **Participle phrases.** The tenses of participle phrases used as modifiers vary according to their relationship to the main verb. A present participle expresses action simultaneous with that of the main verb. A perfect participle expresses action earlier than the action of the main verb.

<u>Eating</u> a radish, he <u>left</u> the dining room. (He ate the radish and left the dining room at the same time.)

<u>Having eaten</u> a radish, he <u>left</u> the dining room. (He ate the radish before he left the dining room.)

3. **Infinitive phrases.** A present infinitive expresses the same time as or a time later than the action of the main verb. A perfect infinitive expresses time earlier than the action of the main verb.

> We want to see that movie. (At present, we want to see that movie in the future.)
>
> We wanted to see that movie. (In the past, we wanted to see that movie.)
>
> We had wanted to see that movie. (In the more distant past, we had wanted to see that movie in the less distant past.)
>
> We would like to have seen that movie. (At present, we wish that we had seen that movie in the past.)

4. **Direct and indirect discourse.** Direct discourse is the exact quotation of a speaker's or writer's words. The tense of the verbs should be whatever the speaker used. Indirect discourse is a paraphrase, a report of what someone said rather than the exact words used. The same sequence-of-tense rules apply to indirect discourse as to other subordinate clauses.

gr
17b

> DIRECT   She said, "It is raining here."
>
> INDIRECT   She says (that) it is raining there. (It is raining while she
>   is speaking.)
>
>   She said (that) it was raining there. (It was raining•
>   while she was speaking.)

Exercises: Sequence of Tenses

In the following paragraph, change the verb forms as necessary to make the sequence of tenses correct.

Because he was out of touch with the scientific community when he died in 1955, Albert Einstein, who saw many of his theories lauded and many others ridiculed in the course of his seventy-six years, did not realize fully the great contributions his discoveries will make to modern life. He had never been a disciplined student, and his lack of motivation to study subjects in which he had no interest caused him to fail the entrance exam at the prestigious Swiss Federal Institute of Technology. Later, after he has been admitted, he antagonized his teachers and relied on his friends' notes in order to have graduated in 1900. Beginning in 1905, Einstein, who by this time married Mileva Maric, begins to shake the foundations of Newtonian physics with several theories: an explanation of the photoelectric effect, an explanation of the movements of particles in liquid, and, of course, his theory of relativity. His famous theory, $E = mc^2$, fathers the atomic age, but Einstein himself is a pacifist and urged the end of all warfare. After the atomic bombs were dropped at Hiroshima and Nagasaki, he has claimed in great remorse that his motivation for working on the bomb was fear that Germany, his native country, will also develop it. Although he will die having seen the destructive force of his work, he did not realize the extent to which many of his theories opened up avenues to great discoveries that benefit our generation.

17c ▪ Mood of Verbs *(mood)*

Of the three moods of English verbs (indicative, imperative, and subjunctive), normally only the subjunctive creates problems for the writer. The subjunctive is troublesome because it occurs so infrequently that we simply lack practice in using it. In modern English, the subjunctive is used only in (1) certain kinds of clauses introduced by *that*, (2) subordinate clauses expressing unreal conditions, and (3) certain idioms.

That **Clauses** In subordinate clauses beginning with *that*, the present subjunctive is required after many verbs of requesting, ordering, and recommending, such as *ask, demand, command, suggest, recommend, order*, and *insist*. The present subjunctive is also required in subordinate clauses after adjectives expressing urgency, such as *necessary, important, imperative, crucial, essential*, and *urgent*, and after phrases such as *of great importance*. The present subjunctive has the same form as the infinitive of the verb.

> We asked only that she <u>be</u> careful.
>
> It is important that he <u>understand</u> how the timer works.

Unreal Conditions To express unreal (contrary to fact) conditions after the verb *wish* or in clauses beginning with *if*, the so-called past subjunctive is used. (See also 12d.) The past subjunctive has the same form as the plural past indicative of the verb (*were, had, saw*, and so on).

> I wish he <u>were</u> my father.
>
> I wish that I <u>had</u> more energy.
>
> If he <u>were</u> able, he would leave tomorrow.

In highly formal usage, *if* is omitted and the subjunctive verb precedes the subject.

> <u>Were</u> he able, he would leave tomorrow.

To express actual past time with the past subjunctive, use the past perfect form of the verb.

> I wish he <u>had been</u> my father. (not *I wish he would have been my father*)

gr
17c

If he <u>had been</u> able, he would have left yesterday. (not *If he would have been able*)

<u>Had</u> he <u>been</u> able, he would have left yesterday.

Idioms A few idioms take the present subjunctive in an independent clause.

God help us   far be it from me
suffice it to say   come what may
Heaven forbid   be that as it may
so be it   come rain or come shine

The past subjunctive is used in the idiom *as it were* and as an alternative to an infinitive phrase after *it's time.*

It's time we <u>went</u> home. (compare *It's time for us to go home*)

Food faddists have, <u>as it were</u>, redefined the word *natural.*

17d ▪ Voice of Verbs *(voice)*

gr
17e

Most writing problems involving the voice of verbs are really stylistic problems, not grammatical problems. That is, we may overuse the passive at the expense of the active voice, but we rarely have difficulty with the appropriate grammatical form of the passive. (See 4a.)

In speech or very informal writing, *get* is sometimes used instead of *be* as the auxiliary for the passive voice. As a general rule, avoid *get* as an auxiliary in formal writing.

ACTIVE   Someone <u>stole</u> Joshua's pacifier.

PASSIVE   Joshua's pacifier <u>was stolen</u>.

COLLOQUIAL   Joshua's pacifier <u>got stolen</u>.

17e ▪ Incomplete Verb Phrases

When a sentence has two or more verb phrases, we often need to write only one of them out in full. Every phrase must have an auxiliary, but other parts may be omitted if they are identical in form and grammar.

The second game <u>was taped</u>, but the first <u>was</u> not. (The second occurrence of *taped* can be omitted because it is identical to the first; both are past participles.)

The players <u>wanted to</u> but <u>could not leave</u> immediately after the game. (The first occurrence of *leave* can be omitted because it is identical to the second; both are infinitives.)

Do not, however, omit parts of a compound verb phrase that are not identical. The result will be an incomplete verb phrase. (See also 23f "Parallelism.")

INCORRECT   The players <u>have</u> not and <u>will</u> not <u>sign</u> the proposed contract. (The omitted verb *signed* is a past participle and not an infinitive.)

REVISED   The players <u>have</u> not <u>signed</u> and <u>will</u> not <u>sign</u> the proposed contract.

It is best not to omit the verb *to be* in a compound predicate unless the omitted verb has exactly the same form and the same grammatical function in the two verb phrases.

QUESTIONABLE   The players <u>were</u> defiant and the manager indignant. (The omitted verb *was* is singular and the first verb is plural.)

REVISED   The players <u>were</u> defiant and the manager <u>was</u> indignant.

CORRECT   The players <u>were</u> defiant and the coaches indignant. (The omitted verb *were* is plural, as is the first verb.)

**gr
17e**

Exercises: Summary of Verb Problems

Correct all errors in the underlined verb phrases of the paragraphs below. Not every underlined verb phrase is incorrect.

The flea market—a popular institution otherwise <u>known</u> as a garage sale, a bazaar, or a rummage sale—<u>are</u> a stage where the adage "one person's trash is another person's treasure" <u>be enacted</u> each week to standing-room-only audiences across the nation. Particularly in the spring, the urge <u>to have cleaned things out</u> fills the sellers' tables with varied goods—antique china dolls with <u>broke</u> heads, dusty books, and assorted bric-a-brac <u>laying</u> unused on shelves of its prior home. Just as bizarre as the variety of goods is the motley collection of buyers who <u>gather to dicker</u> over the mountains of goods haphazardly <u>lain</u> around. Usually, long before the hour when a sale is <u>suppose to begin</u>, a long line of hopeful buyers <u>agitates</u> for the sale doors <u>to have been opened</u>.

Once the sale officially begins, there is a stampede: two women argue over who <u>shall buy</u> a banged-up hassock, a mob <u>succeeds</u> in overturning a table and demolishing the merchandise that <u>might of</u> sold for ten dollars, and others remark that the sellers <u>shouldn't ought to of</u> let people run wild and <u>had ought to mark down</u> the prices if they really <u>wanted</u> to sell their goods. One woman picks up a broken toaster, <u>sits</u> it back on the table, and quickly <u>picks</u> it up once again. Then she <u>demands</u> that she should get a money-back guarantee if she will buy it. Having double-checked the price, two men are wanting to buy a set of golf clubs, although neither of the men has ever or will ever play golf. Meanwhile, the sellers are being relieved of numerous unwanted items, and their cash boxes have gotten fattened with money to be used by their club, to have been given to a charity, or to be enjoyed personally.

18 🦉 Problems with Subject-Verb Agreement *(agr)*

Agreement is the correspondence between grammatically related words whereby the use of one form of one word requires the use of a specific form of another word. For example, the use of *he* as a subject pronoun requires the use of *has* (as opposed to *have*). Except for the verb *to be*, the only kind of agreement required between subject and verb is number agreement for third-person singular subjects. Further, again except for the verb *to be*, number agreement appears only in the present tense. However, because all nouns and the majority of pronouns are third person and because so many verb phrases include a present-tense verb, subject-verb agreement is potentially a problem in almost all kinds of writing.

To be, the most irregular verb in English, has the following forms.

	PERSON	PRESENT	PAST
Singular	I	am	was
	you	are	were
	he, she, it	is	was
Plural	we, you, they	are	were
Subjunctive	(all persons and numbers)	be	were
Imperative		be	—
Participles		being	been
Infinitive		(to) be	—

18a ▪ Identifying the Real Subject

We sometimes get confused about the proper form of a verb because we forget or do not recognize the grammatical or "real" subject of the sentence.

Intervening Modifiers Between Subject and Verb Do not mistake a modifier for a subject. This error is most likely to occur when a modifier comes between the subject and the verb.

gr
18

A collection of amateur paintings <u>is</u> on display. (The real subject is *collection.*)

The members of the panel, one of whom is a student, <u>meet</u> every Thursday. (The real subject is *members.*)

Inverted Order of Subject and Verb When the verb precedes its subject, be sure the verb and subject agree.

After examination week <u>come</u> the winter holidays. (The real subject is *the winter holidays*, a plural subject requiring a plural verb.)

<u>Has</u> any one of you done as much? (The real subject is *one;* compare *Any one of you has done as much.*)

Subject and Complement with Different Numbers Singular subjects may have plural complements and vice versa. Regardless of whether the complement is singular or plural, the verb should agree with the subject.

Computers <u>are</u> a teller's best friend.

A teller's best friend <u>is</u> computers.

Our problem <u>was</u> too many critics and not enough writers.

18b · Special Kinds of Subjects

Sometimes we know what the real subject is but are uncertain whether it is singular or plural.

Collective Nouns Collective nouns (those that refer to groups, not individuals) normally take a singular verb. However, they take a plural verb if attention is being focused on the various individuals making up the group.

The family <u>is</u> at the movies. (focus on the family as a unit)

The family <u>are</u> all avid movie fans. (focus on the individuals making up the group)

Proper Nouns The proper names of books, works of art, places, and the like that are plural in form nonetheless take a singular verb because they are considered a single unit.

Niagara Falls <u>is</u> a popular tourist attraction.

Father and Sons <u>provides</u> a picture of Russia in the 1860s.

Nouns with Special Forms A few nouns look plural because they end in -*s* but nonetheless always take a singular verb. Examples include *news, measles, billiards,* and *molasses.*

Good news <u>is</u> always welcome.

Molasses <u>adds</u> flavor to pecan pie.

Nouns ending in *-ics* take a singular verb when they refer to a field of study but a plural verb when they refer to individual practice or application. Examples of such nouns are *ethics, athletics, physics, ceramics, politics,* and *mathematics.*

> Ethics is a branch of philosophy.
> His ethics are questionable.

Some nouns have the same form in both singular and plural; the meaning of the sentence determines the form of the verb. Among such nouns are *means, barracks, series, gallows, sheep,* and *deer.*

> Four series of lectures were offered.
> A series of lectures was offered.

A fairly large number of nouns have no singular form and always take a plural verb. Examples include *people, clergy, clothes, fireworks, tongs, cattle, bowels, manners, remains, soapsuds, wages,* and *thanks.*

> The cost of living has gone up, but my wages have not.
> The soapsuds were flowing all over the bathroom floor.

gr
18b

Words as Words   Words being cited as words take a singular verb, regardless of their form.

> *Indices* is one of the plural forms of *index.*

Expressions of Quantity   In expressions of addition and multiplication, either a singular or a plural verb is correct.

> Three and five is (or *are*) eight.
> Three times five equals (or *equal*) fifteen.

In expressions of subtraction and division, a singular verb is correct.

> Four minus two is two.
> Four divided by two equals two.
> Two into four is two.

As a subject, the phrase *the number of* takes a singular verb, but the phrase *a number of* takes a plural verb.

> The number of applicants was small.
> A number of applicants were disqualified.

Plural expressions of quantity take either a singular or a plural verb, depending on whether the expression is considered a single unit or not.

> Three days is too long to wait. (*Three days* is being treated as a single
>   unit of time.)
> Three days remain before the deadline. (Each day is considered as a
>   separate unit.)

18c ▪ Compound Subjects

Compound subjects (those connected by a conjunction) take either a singular or a plural verb, depending on the conjunction.

Connected by *and* Compound subjects connected by *and* always take a plural verb except in the rare instances when both subjects refer to the same (singular) individual or thing.

> My sister and best friend <u>are</u> visiting me. (My sister and my best friend are not the same person.)
> My sister and best friend <u>is</u> visiting me. (My sister is also my best friend.)

Some compound subjects are so closely associated that they are thought of as a single unit. In such instances, a singular verb is correct.

> Research and development <u>is</u> a key activity in many firms.
> Law and order <u>was</u> the theme of his campaign.

Connected by Correlative Conjunctions In sentences with a compound subject connected by the correlative conjunctions (*either*) . . . *or, neither . . . nor, not only . . . but, both . . . and,* or *not . . . but,* the verb agrees with the subject nearest the verb.

> <u>Are</u> the boys or their mother driving today?
> <u>Is</u> either the mother or her sons driving today?
> Neither the boys nor their mother <u>drives</u> to work.
> Neither the mother nor her sons <u>drive</u> to work.

Connected by *along with*, etc. When a compound subject is accompanied by a prepositional phrase beginning with (*along*) *with, as well as, rather than, more than,* or *as much as,* the verb agrees with the real subject, not the object of the preposition.

> Mr. Menotti, along with his neighbors, <u>opposes</u> rezoning.
> Insects, rather than drought, <u>are</u> responsible for the poor harvest.

18d ▪ Pronoun Subjects

When the subject of a clause or sentence is a pronoun, subject-verb agreement can be confusing, because pronouns do not have an *-s* ending that clearly marks the plural forms.

Indefinite Pronouns The indefinite pronouns *either, neither, each, another, one,* and all pronouns ending in *-one, -body,* or *-thing* take a singular verb.

> She went to both offices, but neither <u>was</u> open.
> Each of these organisms <u>is</u> microscopic.

The pronouns *all, any, most, more, none,* and *some* take a singular verb

gr 18d

if their antecedent is a mass noun (see 3b) but a plural verb if their antecedent is a plural noun.

> Sarah made a big pot of soup. Is any left? (The verb is singular because the antecedent of *any* is a mass noun, *soup*.)
>
> Sarah baked four dozen brownies. Are any left? (The verb is plural because the antecedent of *any* is a plural noun, *brownies*.)

Note *None* with a plural antecedent may also take a singular verb.

> Sarah baked four dozen brownies. None are left. (No brownies are left.)
>
> Sarah baked four dozen brownies. None is left (Not one brownie is left.)

Expletive Pronouns The expletive pronouns *it* and *there* differ from each other in their rules for subject-verb agreement. *It* always takes a singular verb, regardless of the following noun.

> It was Carmen who spilled the beans.
> Who is it? It is the Wristons and the Scotts.

The form of the verb after the expletive pronoun *there* is determined by the number of the following noun or pronoun.

> There is a letter to be typed. (*A letter* is singular, so the verb is singular.)
>
> There are letters to be typed. (*Letters* is plural, so the verb is plural.)

Relative Pronouns When a relative pronoun (*that, which, who*) is used as the subject of a clause, the verb agrees with the antecedent of the pronoun.

> She gave them a box of clothes that were too small for her. (*Clothes* is the antecedent of *that*.)
>
> She gave them the box of clothes that was in the back hall. (*Box* is the antecedent of *that*.)
>
> Gregory is one of the clerks who work late. (*Clerks* is the antecedent of *who*; the implication is that several clerks work late.)
>
> Gregory is the only one of the clerks who works late. (*One* is the antecedent of *who*; the meaning of the sentence would not be changed if *of the clerks* were omitted.)

18e ▪ Phrases and Clauses as Subjects

Phrases and clauses as subjects usually take a singular verb.

> Throwing coins in a fountain is a custom in many countries.
> Before lunch is too early for a martini.
> How I learned that is none of your business.
> That all of you disagree with me comes as a surprise.
> To avoid a scene was very important to him.

Clauses beginning with *what* are generally treated like collective nouns. That is, if the complement of the clause is thought of as a single unit, a singular verb is used; if the complement is thought of as separate units, a plural verb is used. As a rule of thumb, use a singular verb if you can substitute *the thing that* for *what*, but use a plural verb if you can substitute *the things that* for *what*.

What I want <u>is</u> three more chances.
What once were beautiful rivers <u>are</u> now open sewers.

Exercises: Subject-Verb Agreement

Correct all errors in subject-verb agreement in the following sentences.

1. Neither Abe nor his nephews is ever prompt in keeping appointments.
2. Dolores, along with Dave and Cecil, have taken up gliding this year.
3. *The Snows of Kilimanjaro* were shown on television last week.
4. Each of the boys are the pride of their family.
5. Mr. Hill is one of those fussy bosses who is never satisfied with anything that their employees do.
6. Six months are much too long for us to wait; none of us have enough money to remain here for that length of time.
7. On his bookshelf stands many rare editions bound in leather.
8. That the compromise annoyed both the men and the women were obvious.
9. Both the childen and the dog is afraid of thunderstorms, but everyone else in the house, including the grandparents, actually enjoy them.
10. There is bacon and a couple of oranges in the refrigerator.
11. The number of motorcycles on the road this morning were unbelievable.

gr
19

---

19 Problems with Pronouns *(pron)*

Pronouns are substitutes for nouns or nominals. The noun or nominal for which a pronoun substitutes is called its **antecedent,** and we say that a pronoun **refers** to its antecedent.

Little Miss Muffet was distressed when <u>she</u> saw a spider near <u>her</u>. (*She* and *her* are personal pronouns whose antecedent is *Little Miss Muffet*.)

Newfoundland, <u>which</u> joined Confederation in 1949, has a long and interesting history. (*Which* is a relative pronoun whose antecedent is *Newfoundland*.)

Pronouns should always agree with their antecedents in **gender** (masculine, feminine, or neuter), **number** (singular, mass, or plural), and **person** (first person, second person, or third person). However, the **case** of a pronoun (subject, object, or possessive) is determined by its function in its own clause, and a pronoun does not necessarily have the same case as its antecedent.

19a ▪ Pronoun Reference *(ref)*

Whenever a pronoun is used, its number and gender should be determined by its antecedent, and the antecedent should be clear.

Reference to Collective Nouns   To refer to a collective noun, use the singular pronoun *it* if attention is being focused on the group as a unit. Use the plural pronoun *they* if attention is on the individuals making up the group.

> The army congratulated <u>itself</u> on <u>its</u> performance in the war games. (Focus is on the army as a unified group.)

> The legislature voted <u>themselves</u> an increase in salary. <u>They</u> must now explain this inflationary move to their constituents. (Focus is on the individual members who received the raise.)

gr
19a

Be sure that the pronoun chosen is consistent with both the antecedent and the number of the verb. (See also 23b.)

> ORIGINAL   The team <u>has gone their</u> separate ways.

> REVISED   The team <u>have gone their</u> separate ways. (Logically, the focus is on the individual members; pronoun and verb should make this clear.)

Indefinite Reference: *he* and *she*.   Because English has no "sex-neutral" third-person singular pronoun, the plural pronoun *they* is often used in speech as a substitute for (1) indefinite pronouns such as *anyone* and *everybody*, (2) indefinite nouns such as *person* and *individual*, and (3) the many nouns that can refer to either a male or female such as *citizen*, *parent*, *bystander*, or *artist*. In writing, however, the use of a plural pronoun to refer to a singular antecedent is ordinarily not acceptable.

Traditionally, the masculine pronoun *he* has been used to refer to such indefinite human beings. Today, however, some people feel that the exclusive use of the masculine pronoun is sexist and therefore offensive. *He* is still grammatically correct but may be resented by some readers. Unfortunately, there is as yet no universally acceptable alternative. Many writers use *he or she* instead of simply *he*, and this strategy often solves the problem.

> Every parent discovers that <u>he or she</u> cannot always be patient and sweet-tempered.

However, if a pronoun is used several times within one sentence, this solution is likely to be cumbersome.

Everyone had to decide for <u>himself or herself</u> whether <u>he or she</u> was willing to spend several years of <u>his or her</u> life mastering this new skill.

Sometimes the writer can avoid the problem by using a plural noun or pronoun as an antecedent.

Participants had to decide for <u>themselves</u> whether <u>they</u> were willing to spend several years of <u>their</u> lives mastering this new skill.

Alternatively, it is often possible to rewrite the entire sentence avoiding pronouns with gender.

ORIGINAL   No one will be accepted until he or she has passed a physical examination.

REVISED   No one who has not passed a physical examination will be accepted.

Indefinite Reference: *you, they, we, it,* and *one*. In speech, we often use *you, they, we,* and even *it* when we wish to refer to people in general or when the referent is unknown or irrelevant. In writing, however, the acceptable use of these pronouns is highly limited.

gr
19a

1. *You* is always appropriate when the reader is clearly being addressed personally. Hence *you* is correct in imperative sentences or in writing instructions, even if the writer does not know the reader.

Before arranging a foreign trip, be sure <u>you</u> have a passport.

You is also appropriate as a kind of indefinite pronoun in quoting proverbs or fixed expressions.

<u>You</u> can always tell a Harvard man, but <u>you</u> cannot tell him much.

<u>You</u> shouldn't count <u>your</u> chickens before they are hatched.

In informal writing, *you* is acceptable as an indefinite pronoun for statements that apply to every human being. In formal writing, however, *one* is preferred.

INFORMAL   When <u>you</u> are born, <u>you</u> are toothless and hairless.
FORMAL   When <u>one</u> is born, <u>one</u> is toothless and hairless.

2. *They* is not appropriate as an indefinite pronoun in writing. Fortunately, it can be avoided by rewriting.

UNACCEPTABLE   They say it will be a hard winter.

REVISED   A hard winter has been predicted.
Forecasters predict a hard winter.

UNACCEPTABLE   In my high school, they made us take biology.

REVISED   Biology was a required subject in my high school.

3. *We* as an indefinite pronoun is somewhat less formal than *one*. It can be employed to avoid overuse of the passive or to include the writer in a general statement.

PASSIVE   Even greater delays can be expected in the future.

REVISED   We can expect even greater delays in the future.

WRITER   We all know at least one or two handicapped persons.
INCLUDED

4. The indefinite *it says* (with reference to printed matter) is not acceptable in formal writing. Further, it is usually wordy because the true subject is also mentioned. Avoid *it says* by making the book, newspaper, or magazine being quoted the subject of the clause.

UNACCEPTABLE   It says in the *Herald* that Robbins has been indicted.

REVISED   The *Herald* says that Robbins has been indicted.

5. *One* is always correct as an indefinite personal pronoun, but it may sometimes seem stilted. In North American usage, *he* or *she* can replace *one* after the first reference.

FORMAL   One often faces situations that one would rather
                   avoid.

ACCEPTABLE   One often faces situations that he or she would
                   rather avoid.

Ambiguous Reference   The antecedent of a pronoun should always be clear to the reader. Correct ambiguous reference by rewriting the sentence or by repeating one of the nouns.

AMBIGUOUS   When Jim attacked George in public, he was very
                   angry. (Who was angry, Jim or George?)

REVISED   George was very angry when Jim attacked him in
                   public.

REVISED   Jim was very angry when he attacked George in
                   public.

AMBIGUOUS   There's a fly in your salad; do you want to eat it? (the
                   salad or the fly?)

REVISED   There's a fly in your salad; do you want to ask for
                   another salad?

Remote Reference   When a pronoun is too far removed from its antecedent, the reader may be at least temporarily confused. Correct remote reference by repeating the noun or a synonym of that noun, or by rewriting the passage so that the pronoun is closer to its antecedent.

REMOTE   Yesterday I bought a new toaster. The first slice of
REFERENCE   bread that I toasted turned to carbon. When I put in

a second slice of bread, a fuse blew. I am beginning to suspect that <u>it</u> is defective. (What does *it* refer to?)

REVISED   Yesterday, I bought a new toaster. The first slice of bread that I toasted turned to carbon. When I put in a second slice of bread, a fuse blew. I am beginning to suspect that the toaster is defective.

Broad Reference In many sentences, the pronouns *this, that, it,* and *which* refer to an entire preceding clause or sentence. This practice is natural in speech and is acceptable in writing if the idea is completely clear to the reader.

It rained all day long, <u>which</u> prevented us from taking pictures.

Often, however, broad reference produces ambiguity, lack of clarity, or awkwardness. In such cases, rewrite the sentence to make the antecedent clear or to eliminate the pronoun completely.

UNCLEAR   He told me that he had been arrested for embezzlement, <u>which</u> surprised me. (What surprised you? That he had been arrested? Or that he told you?)

REVISED   I was surprised to learn that he had been arrested for embezzlement.

REVISED   I was surprised that he admitted to having been arrested for embezzlement.

UNCLEAR   Myron has proposed to Sue. <u>This</u> is not what she wants.

REVISED   Myron has proposed to Sue, but she doesn't want to get married.

REVISED   Myron has proposed to Sue, but she doesn't want to marry him.

Implied Reference The antecedents of pronouns should be either nominals or, occasionally, entire clauses or sentences. Avoid using pronouns that have no antecedents or that refer to words or structures that are not nominals.

INCORRECT   The house has oak floors. <u>This</u> is more expensive than pine. (The implied antecedent is *oak*, but *oak* is a modifier here, not a nominal.)

REVISED   The floors of the house are made of oak, which is more expensive than pine.

REVISED   The house has oak floors; oak is more expensive than pine.

INCORRECT   Tanya dog-paddled down the lane, <u>which</u> is not a recognized stroke in competition swimming. (The implied antecedent is *dog-paddled*, but *dog-paddled* is a verb, not a nominal.)

gr
19a

REVISED   Tanya dog-paddled down the lane; the dog-paddle is
                   not a recognized stroke in competition swimming.

Unnecessary Reference Personal pronouns substitute for nouns. Therefore, a pronoun subject should not be used when a noun subject is already
present. Use either the noun subject alone or the pronoun alone.

INCORRECT   Those dogs they ought to be on leashes.

REVISED   Those dogs ought to be on leashes.

REVISED   They ought to be on leashes.

Exercises: Pronoun Reference

Correct faulty pronoun references in the following sentences.

1. Despite the recession, our firm had retail sales of $5 million last year
   and is planning to open a new branch in Toronto, which causes much
   concern among our competitors.
2. All children should receive measles shots because it is a highly con-
   tagious and often dangerous disease.
3. Laura was extremely annoyed because her friends were all late, but
   this did not seem to faze anyone in the group.
4. Everybody must decide for themselves what color hair they want to
   have.
5. After Frances insisted that Cora go home, she was very tactless and
   said some things that she will likely regret.
6. The party has told its members that you should vote early and often.
7. Bill's father bought the drill and some lumber, but it wasn't the kind
   he had wanted.
8. One should look before one leaps, and we should also make sure that
   no one is under us when we jump.
9. It says in the *Examiner* that Roberta was disqualified from the race.
10. Three competitors were disqualified in yesterday's race. Roberta was
    the only female; the other two were male. They should have been
    more careful.
11. Those race officials they were certainly watching carefully.

**gr
19b**

19b · Pronoun Case (*case*)

The proper case of a pronoun depends on its use in its own clause. Normally, this causes no problem; no one would say or write, for example, "I
talked to she." Anglophones would automatically use the objective case
of the pronoun and say "I talked to her." Problems with pronoun case
usually arise only when other elements in the clause create confusion
about the actual role of the pronoun.

Ordinarily, problems with the appropriate case of pronouns occur in only a few types of constructions, including (1) compound constructions, (2) relative constructions, (3) appositive constructions, (4) constructions with *than*, *as*, and *but*, (5) after the verb *to be*, and (6) possessive constructions.

Compound Constructions   In compound constructions, use the form of the pronoun that would be correct if it were not part of a compound. When in doubt about the proper form of a pronoun after *and* or *or*, mentally omit the first part of the compound.

INCORRECT	Belle and <u>him</u> moved to Belgium in 1974. (You would not write "Him moved to Belgium.")
REVISED	Belle and he moved to Belgium in 1974.
INCORRECT	Loud music annoys Frank and <u>I</u>. (You would not write "Loud music annoys I.")
REVISED	Loud music annoys Frank and me.
INCORRECT	This rule applies to both you and <u>I</u>. (You would not write, "This rule applies to I.")
REVISED	This rule applies to both you and me.
INCORRECT	Pat embarrassed both of us, Ellen and <u>I</u>. (You would not write, "Pat embarrassed I.")
REVISED	Pat embarrassed both of us, Ellen and me.

**gr
19b**

Similarly, do not use the reflexive pronouns ending in *-self* as subjects or objects. Again, confusion most often arises in compound constructions.

INCORRECT	Edward and <u>myself</u> volunteered to work on Saturday. (You would not say, "Myself volunteered to work on Saturday.")
CORRECT	Edward and I volunteered to work on Saturday.
INCORRECT	This dispute is between Edward and <u>myself</u>.
CORRECT	This dispute is between Edward and me.

Relative and Interrogative Constructions   Of the relative and interrogative pronouns (*who*, *which*, *what*), only *who* is inflected for case (*who/whom/whose*).

1. **Who and whom.**   The relative and interrogative pronouns *who* and *whom* probably cause more problems to writers than all the other pronouns put together, chiefly because, in speech, *whom* is virtually ignored except when it immediately follows a preposition. Further, clauses with *who* or *whom* often have an inverted word order, causing the writer to lose track of whether the pronoun is functioning as a subject or as an object.

Although you can usually let *who* and *whom* fall where they may in speech, formal writing reserves *who* for subjects and *whom* for objects. As always, the function of the pronoun in its own clause determines the correct form. When in doubt, find the subject and the verb in the clause. If there is no other subject for the verb, then the pronoun must be the subject, and *who* is the correct form. If there is another subject, then the pronoun is an object, and *whom* is correct.

> <u>Who</u> put the Limburger cheese in my closet? (The only possible subject of *put* is *who*.)

> <u>Whom</u> did Washington appoint ambassador to France? (*Washington* is the subject, so *whom* is an object.)

> My curses on the scoundrel <u>who</u> put the Limburger cheese in my closet.

> Monroe, <u>whom</u> Washington had appointed ambassador to France, became governor of Virginia in 1799.

Especially confusing are clauses that contain parenthetical phrases such as *they said, I think, we feel*, and the like. Here the parenthetical phrase is often misinterpreted as the subject and verb of the clause, and the object form *whom* is incorrectly used.

gr
19b

> <u>Who</u> do you think I am? (That is, "Who am I?")

> <u>Whom</u> did they say Ginny would marry? (That is, "Ginny would marry whom?")

> Perry is the only person <u>who</u> we know is going to Hong Kong. (That is, "Perry is the only person we know <u>who</u> is going to Hong Kong.")

> Perry is the only person <u>whom</u> we know in Hong Kong. (That is, "We know whom in Hong Kong?")

Confusion can also arise when a noun clause beginning with *who* or *whom* is the object of a preposition. The grammar of the following clause (*not* the preposition) determines the correct form of the pronoun.

> We are worried about <u>who</u> might get hurt. (*Who* is the subject of the verb phrase *might get hurt;* the entire clause is the object of the preposition.)

> We are worried about <u>whom</u> the new rules might hurt. (*Whom* is the object of the verb phrase *might hurt*.)

> Send an invitation to <u>whoever</u> is in town. (*Whoever* is the subject of *is in town;* the entire clause is the object of the preposition.)

> Send an invitation to <u>whomever</u> you like. (*Whomever* is the object of the verb *like*.)

The only exception to these rules occurs when the pronoun is the subject of an infinitive. Any pronoun serving as a subject of an infinitive should *always* be in the objective case.

> I told <u>him</u> to find a new adviser. (*Him* is subject of *to find*.)

> They asked <u>whom</u> we wanted to go first. (*Whom* is subject of *to go*.)

2. **Whose.** *Whose* is a correct possessive form for both persons and things, although some people prefer to use *of which* for things and *whose* for persons. Use *of which* when it does not seem awkward, but use *whose* if *of which* seems stilted and artificial.

Taxes are a subject the mere mention <u>of which</u> upsets my uncle. (It would be awkward to write "whose mere mention.")

This town, <u>whose</u> taxes are the highest in the area, just approved new park buildings. (It would be awkward to write "This town, the taxes of which are the highest.")

If both *whose* and *of which* seem awkward to you, you can usually rewrite the sentence to avoid the possessive entirely.

The mere mention of the word *taxes* upsets my uncle.

The taxes in this town are the highest in the area, but the voters have just approved new park buildings.

Note Do not confuse the possessive *whose* with *who's*, the contraction for *who is*.

Appositive Constructions A noun in apposition to a pronoun does not affect the case of the pronoun. Use the form of the pronoun that would be correct if the noun were not present.

> gr
> 19b

INCORRECT	<u>Us</u> students are worried about the rising cost of books. (You would not write, "Us are worried.")
REVISED	<u>We</u> students are worried about the rising cost of books.
INCORRECT	The rising cost of books concerns <u>we</u> students. (You would not write, "The rising cost of books concerns we.")
CORRECT	The rising cost of books concerns <u>us</u> students.

After *than*, *as*, and *but* Writers are often confused about the proper form of pronouns after *than*, *as*, and *but* because they are unsure whether these words are conjunctions or prepositions. Conjunctions introduce clauses, and the proper form of a pronoun depends on its function in the clause. Prepositions, on the other hand, always take the objective form of the pronoun.

1. **Than.** *Than* is a conjunction and not a preposition, so the appropriate case of a pronoun after *than* depends on its function in the following clause. Confusion occurs when clauses introduced by *than* are elliptical, that is, when the verb and either the subject or the object of the clause are omitted. When in doubt, mentally supply the missing words to determine whether the pronoun should be in the nominative case or the objective case.

Mr. Gregg has more faith in her than <u>me</u>. (Meaning: "Mr. Gregg has more faith in her than Mr. Gregg has faith in me.")

Mr. Gregg has more faith in her than <u>I</u>. (Meaning: "Mr. Gregg has more faith in her than I have faith in her.")

2. **As.** In *as . . . as* constructions, the second *as* is a conjunction, and the following clause is often elliptical. Again, the case of the pronoun depends on its function in the elliptical clause.

Clara argues with Geri as much as <u>him</u>. (Meaning: "Clara argues with Geri as much as Clara argues with him.")

Clara argues with Geri as much as <u>he</u>. (Meaning: "Clara argues with Geri as much as he argues with Geri.")

3. **But.** In the meaning "except," the word *but* is usually considered a preposition and should therefore be followed by the object case of the pronoun.

I know everyone here but <u>him</u>.

After the Verb *to be*.   Theoretically, the nominative case of a pronoun should always be used as the complement of the verb *to be*. However, such sentences as *That was him* and *It's me* are universally used in speech, and many people find *It is I* uncomfortable even in writing. If the subject case seems stilted or awkward, rewrite the sentence to avoid the dilemma.

gr
19b

AWKWARD	Ms. Harvey thought that Ross was <u>I</u>.
REVISED	Ms. Harvey mistook Ross for me.
CORRECT	It was <u>I</u> who chopped down the cherry tree.

Exercises: Pronoun Case

Correct errors in pronoun case in the following sentences.

1. Fred wanted to know who we had asked to be publicity director.
2. The new neighbors never spoke to anyone, and they seemed to go out of their way to avoid Dave and I.
3. Billings is the student who, as you should remember, the administration tried to throw out of school because of his antinuclear demonstrations.
4. I can run longer than her, but she is as fast as me.
5. No one was willing to risk the president's wrath but she, although Marston and myself did abstain from voting.
6. This office will provide a letter of introduction for whomever may need one.
7. Angie was sure that the girl who waved to we three on the beach was her, that same girl who we had met at the disco two nights before.

8. Although he denies it, it was him who leaked the story to the newspapers.

9. Whom did he say is favored to win the tournament?

---

20 Problems with Modifiers *(mod)*

Modifiers, words that describe or limit other words, are either adjectivals or adverbials (see 15). Modifiers may be single words, such as the adjective *heavy* or the adverb *then*, or groups of words, such as the phrase *in the midafternoon* or the clause *until I find my umbrella*. Grammatical problems with modifiers can occur with the form of the modifiers or with the placement of the modifiers.

20a ▪ Single-Word Adjectivals *(adj)*

The two most important problems with single-word adjectivals are (1) incorrectly using an adverb instead of an adjective and (2) using an incorrect form of a possessive adjective.

Predicate Adjectives Linking verbs (see 4b) are properly followed by adjectives rather than adverbs. Linking verbs include verbs of sensation and verbs expressing a state of existence or a change in a state of existence. The adjectives that follow linking verbs are called **predicate adjectives**.

VERBS OF SENSATION	VERBS OF EXISTENCE	
feel	act	prove
look	appear	remain
smell	be	seem
sound	become	sit
taste	continue	stand
	grow	turn

Confusion occurs because many linking verbs can also be used as ordinary verbs. However, the grammar and meaning of linking verbs and their corresponding ordinary verbs differ. If the subject is being modified, the verb is a linking verb, and the modifier should be an adjective. If the verb is being modified, it is not a linking verb, and the modifier should be an adverb.

Stephanie looked <u>angry</u> about the referee's decision. (*Angry* describes Stephanie; *looked* is a linking verb.)

Stephanie looked <u>angrily</u> at the referee. (*Angrily* describes the way in which Stephanie looked at the referee.)

Bob grew <u>tall</u>. (*Tall* describes Bob; *grew* is a linking verb.)

Bob grew <u>rapidly</u>. (*Rapidly* describes how Bob grew, not Bob himself.)

gr 20

Possessives as Adjectivals All possessives are adjectivals and function as adjectives. Problems involving possessives include selecting the correct form of the possessive and knowing when to use possessive forms.

1. **Indefinite pronouns.** Some indefinite pronouns can be made into possessive adjectives by adding an apostrophe and *-s*.

another's	anyone's	anybody's	anybody else's
(the) other's	everyone's	everybody's	everybody else's
one's	no one's	nobody's	nobody else's
either's	someone's	somebody's	somebody else's
neither's			

Mrs. Rossoni questioned both Livia and Susannah, but <u>neither's</u> answer satisfied her.

One can never predict <u>someone else's</u> tastes.

All other indefinite pronouns (*any, each, both, few, many, several, all, much,* and so on) form their possessives with *of*.

Mrs. Rossoni questioned Livia and Susannah, and the answers <u>of both</u> satisfied her.

The interests <u>of some</u> are not the interests of all.

2. **The group possessive.** In spoken English, the *-'s* of the possessive does not always appear on the end of the noun that is the logical modifier. Instead, it often appears on the end of the last word of the entire noun phrase. It may even appear on a word that is not a noun or pronoun. Such possessive constructions are called **group possessives.** Except for possessives of a proper noun, such as *the Czar of Russia's death,* avoid the group possessive in writing. Instead, use a phrase with *of* or rewrite the sentence.

COLLOQUIAL	the man I talked to's opinion
FORMAL	the opinion of the man that I talked to
COLLOQUIAL	the girl in the corner apartment's dog
FORMAL	the dog owned by the girl in the corner apartment

3. **Possessives before gerunds.** Gerunds function as nouns. Like nouns, gerunds are modified by possessive forms of nouns and pronouns.

Dad objects to <u>Paul's</u> sleeping on the roof.

Were you surprised at <u>our</u> having won the lottery?

Because gerunds and participles both end in *-ing,* it is sometimes difficult to tell one from the other and to determine the proper form of a preceding noun or pronoun. If the *-ing* word is the subject or object, it is a gerund, and the preceding noun or pronoun should be possessive.

<u>Martin's</u> swimming amazed even the coach. (It was the swimming that amazed the coach.)

I watched <u>his</u> swimming with great envy. (You watched the *swimming: swimming* is a gerund and the possessive *his* is correct.)

gr
20a

Participles function as adjectives. If the noun or pronoun is the subject or object, the -*ing* word is a participle modifier, and the noun or pronoun should not be possessive.

> <u>Anyone</u> swimming after dark is endangering his or her life. (*Anyone*, not *swimming*, is the subject.)

> I watched <u>him</u> swimming in the surf. (You watched *him*: *swimming* is a participle modifying *him*.)

20b • Single-Word Adverbials *(adv)*

Problems with single-word adverbials include the improper use of adjectives as adverbs, double negatives, and the improper use of *so*, *such*, and *too*.

Adjectives as Adverbials   Although such adjectives as *real*, *sure*, *awful*, *pretty*, *bad*, and *good* are frequently used to modify verbs in the spoken language, this practice should be avoided in writing. If you are in doubt about whether a word is an adjective or an adverb, consult your dictionary.

INCORRECT	The new pencil sharpener works <u>good</u>.
CORRECT	The new pencil sharpener works <u>well</u>.

Frequently the best solution to an incorrect use of an adjective as an adverbial is to omit the intensifying modifier completely.

INCORRECT	The Night Owl is a <u>real</u> fast train.
QUESTIONABLE	The Night Owl is a <u>really</u> fast train.
REVISED	The Night Owl is a fast train.

Double Negatives   The unacceptable double negative occurs when additional negative words in a clause are used merely to intensify the negative meaning. To correct a double negative, rewrite the sentence to eliminate all but one of the negative words.

INCORRECT	There <u>wasn't nobody</u> under the bed.
REVISED	There wasn't anybody under the bed.
REVISED	There was nobody under the bed.
REVISED	Nobody was under the bed.
INCORRECT	The parrot <u>didn't hardly</u> talk at all.
REVISED	The parrot hardly talked at all.
INCORRECT	Christmas <u>doesn't only</u> come <u>but</u> once a year.
REVISED	Christmas comes but once a year.
REVISED	Christmas comes only once a year.

gr
20b

So, such, and too   In speech, the words *so, such,* and *too* are often used simply to intensify the statement being made. In writing, do not use *so, such,* or *too* without a following clause or phrase that completes the statement.

COLLOQUIAL	It was <u>so</u> cold in the house!
REVISED	It was <u>so</u> cold in the house <u>that the plumbing froze</u>.
REVISED	It was unbearably cold in the house.
COLLOQUIAL	Alex Workes is <u>such</u> a good magician!
REVISED	Alex Workes is <u>such</u> a good magician <u>that he fools even children</u>.
REVISED	Alex Workes is an exceptionally good magician.
COLLOQUIAL	Your offer is <u>too</u> insulting.
REVISED	Your offer is <u>too</u> insulting to <u>accept</u>.
REVISED	Your offer is intolerably insulting.

20c ▪ Placement of Modifiers (*mm*) (*dm*)

Except for a few fixed expressions like *court-martial* or *attorney general*, single-word adjectives usually precede the words they modify, and adjectival phrases usually follow the words they modify. Adverbials are more flexible in their placement but, in general, should be placed as close as is grammatically possible to the words they modify.

Misplaced Modifiers   A misplaced modifier is one that appears to modify the wrong word or words. Correct a misplaced modifier by rewriting to put the modifier closer to the word it is intended to modify.

MISPLACED	A fish was found in the Atlantic Ocean <u>that had been considered extinct</u>. (Had the Atlantic Ocean been considered extinct?)
REVISED	A fish that had been considered extinct was found in the Atlantic Ocean.
MISPLACED	He <u>almost</u> understood every word. (Did he almost, but not quite, understand?)
REVISED	He understood almost every word.
MISPLACED	Everyone was born in July <u>in this room</u>. (Were all the people born in this room?)
REVISED	Everyone in this room was born in July.

Dangling Modifiers   A dangling modifier is one that apparently has nothing to modify. The most common kinds of dangling modifiers are dangling participles, dangling infinitives, dangling gerund phrases, and dangling elliptical clauses. (An elliptical clause is one in which words have been omitted because they are understood from the context.) Correct a dangling modifier by rewriting the sentence.

gr
20c

DANGLING PRESENT PARTICIPLE	<u>Budgeting his money carefully</u>, his debts were finally paid. (Who did the budgeting?)
REVISED	Budgeting his money carefully, he finally paid his debts.
DANGLING PAST PARTICIPLE	<u>Confused by the complicated wording</u>, the contract made no sense. (Who was confused?)
REVISED	Confused by the complicated wording, I could make no sense of the contract.
DANGLING INFINITIVE	<u>To lose weight</u>, fatty foods should be avoided. (Who wants to lose weight?)
REVISED	To lose weight, one should avoid fatty foods.
DANGLING GERUND PHRASE	<u>By digging test wells</u>, new oil sources were located. (Who did the digging?)
REVISED	By digging test wells, the company located new oil sources.
DANGLING ELLIPTICAL CLAUSE	<u>A brilliant performer</u>, her concert was quickly sold out. (Who was a brilliant performer?)
REVISED	Because she was a brilliant performer, her concert was quickly sold out.

**gr
20c**

Squinting Modifiers A squinting modifier is one that is ambiguous because it could refer either to what precedes it or to what follows it. Correct squinting modifiers by moving them so that they clearly modify only the intended words.

SQUINTING	Dentists remind children <u>regularly</u> to brush their teeth.
REVISED	Dentists regularly remind children to brush their teeth.
REVISED	Dentists remind children to brush their teeth regularly.

Split Infinitives A split infinitive occurs when, and only when, a modifier comes between the word *to* and the infinitive form of a verb. Thus, *to carefully plan* is a split infinitive, but *to have carefully planned* is not. Strictly speaking, there is nothing ungrammatical about split infinitives, but they are often stylistically awkward, and many people disapprove of them. Try to avoid split infinitives in general, but do not hesitate to split an infinitive if avoiding it would lead to lack of clarity or awkwardness. In the following example, the adverb *really* cannot reasonably be placed anywhere except directly before *understand* because it modifies *understand* and only *understand*.

To <u>really</u> understand calculus, one must do the exercises.

In the following sentence, on the other hand, a split infinitive is not necessary because the sentence is clear and idiomatic when the modifier is placed outside the infinitive.

<blockquote>
SPLIT   You ought to <u>carefully</u> weigh the alternatives.

PREFERABLE   You ought to weigh the alternatives <u>carefully</u>.
</blockquote>

In any case, avoid splitting an infinitive with a modifier several words long.

<blockquote>
AWKWARD   The cat began to <u>slowly and with much hesitation</u> back down the tree.

REVISED   The cat began to back down the tree slowly and with much hesitation.

REVISED   Slowly and with much hesitation, the cat began to back down the tree.
</blockquote>

Unidiomatic Modifiers   Modifiers are unidiomatic when their placement and order of occurrence in the sentence is not natural to English. For example, adverbials of place normally precede adverbials of time, and both normally follow the rest of the predicate. Adverbials of manner most commonly appear either before the main verb or after the entire predicate. When these orders are violated, the resulting sentence is likely to be awkward and unidiomatic.

<blockquote>
UNIDIOMATIC   Mary <u>on Wedneday</u> met me in the library.

REVISED   Mary met me in the library on Wednesday.

UNIDIOMATIC   You hurt <u>deliberately</u> her feelings.

REVISED   You deliberately hurt her feelings.

REVISED   You hurt her feelings deliberately.
</blockquote>

Most people who are fluent in English have a natural feeling for what is idiomatic and what is not but sometimes become careless or forgetful in writing. Reading your sentences aloud may help you spot unidiomatic placement of modifiers.

gr
20d

20d ▪ Restrictive and Nonrestrictive Modifiers

When a modifier is essential to the identification of the word or group of words being modified, it is called a **restrictive modifier.** When a modifier merely provides additional information about what it modifies and is not essential in identifying it, it is called a **nonrestrictive modifier.** In writing, problems arise when restrictive and nonrestrictive modifiers follow the word or words they modify. Nonrestrictive modifiers should be set off by commas, but restrictive modifiers should not.

RESTRICTIVE   People <u>who are allergic to smoke</u> make poor firefighters. (The restrictive modifier restricts the specific people being discussed to those who are allergic to smoke.)

NONRESTRICTIVE   Human beings, <u>who are among the larger animals</u>, are bipeds. (The nonrestrictive modifier merely supplies more information about all human beings. It does not restrict the kinds of human beings being discussed. If the nonrestrictive modifier is omitted, the meaning of the sentence is not greatly changed.)

The writer usually knows whether he or she intends a modifying phrase or clause to be restrictive or nonrestrictive, but often the only clue the reader has is the presence or absence of commas. If commas are omitted from a sentence with a nonrestrictive clause, or if commas are incorrectly used with a restrictive clause, the reader gets a false clue and may misinterpret the sentence.

If you have difficulty in deciding whether a modifier is restrictive or nonrestrictive and hence cannot decide what the correct punctuation for the sentence is, check the modifier against the following list. (See also 27e.)

gr 20d

RESTRICTIVE MODIFIERS	NONRESTRICTIVE MODIFIERS
Restrictive modifiers are essential to the meaning.	Nonrestrictive modifiers are not essential to the meaning.
In speech, restrictive modifiers are not preceded by a pause.	In speech, nonrestrictive modifiers are preceded by a short pause.
Restrictive clauses can be introduced by *that: Irma needs a loan for the portion of her tuition that she must pay by April 15.*	Nonrestrictive clauses cannot be introduced by *that: Irma needs a loan for the entire amount of her tuition, which she must pay by April 15.*
In a restrictive relative clause, the relative pronoun can be omitted if it is not the subject of the clause: *Irma needs a loan for the portion of her tuition she must pay by April 15.*	In a nonrestrictive relative clause, the relative pronoun cannot be omitted: *Irma needs a loan for her tuition, which she must pay by April 15.*
Restrictive modifiers follow the words they modify: *The woman reading a comic book is Irma.* (One cannot write *Reading a comic book, the woman is Irma.*)	Nonrestrictive modifiers often may precede the words they modify: *Irma, smiling nervously, said she did not like my poem.* Or *Smiling nervously, Irma said she did not like my poem.*

Exercises: Modifiers

Correct all mistakes in modifiers in the following sentences.

1. Mr. Fitzgerald still looked badly when he returned to work after his operation.
2. Randy only wants to buy milk and bread.
3. Mrs. Allison's remarks at the convocation were really too irresponsible.
4. After doing calculus problems for six hours, John's foot went to sleep.
5. Both ACTH and cortisone are valuable drugs, but both's side effects can be dangerous.
6. The woman in the balcony's comments could not be heard from the podium.
7. We were amazed at the doctor being so understanding.
8. The piano teacher urges Donna often to practice.
9. Because my dog is old, he doesn't hear very good.
10. The war hadn't hardly begun when refugees started pouring into the capital.
11. People, who are mistreated as children, often become poor parents.
12. There was a wreck while the Davises were eating supper in the road in front of their house.
13. The bartender seemed to unfailingly and with deadly accuracy spot patrons under the legal drinking age.

**gr
21**

21 🦉 Problems with Comparisons *(comp)*

Comparisons are sometimes difficult for the writer because there are so many different rules for the different kinds of comparison. Further, what is acceptable comparison in speech is not always acceptable in writing. Among the problems that arise are those of (1) "double" comparison, (2) comparison of absolutes, (3) misuse of the superlative, (4) illogical comparisons, (5) ambiguous comparisons, (6) incomplete comparisons, and (7) the idiom of comparisons.

21a ▪ Double Comparisons

Do not use both *more* and *-er* to make a single adjective or adverb comparative. Do not use both *most* and *-est* to make a single adjective or adverb superlative.

INCORRECT	I am <u>more lonelier</u> here than I was in the Yukon.
REVISED	I am lonelier here than I was in the Yukon.
REVISED	I am more lonely here than I was in the Yukon.

| INCORRECT | Joel kicked the pumpkin the <u>most farthest</u> of all. |
| REVISED | Joel kicked the pumpkin the farthest of all. |

21b · Comparison of Absolutes

Adjectives or adverbs such as *main*, *daily*, *prior*, *entire*, and *only* are inherently comparative or superlative in meaning, and one is normally not tempted to add a comparative or superlative ending to them. Such words as *complete*, *dead*, and *round* present more of a problem. Logically, they are also absolute and cannot be compared. Practically, however, one often wishes to express a comparison between two things that have qualities of completeness or deadness or roundness but that could never be perfectly complete or dead or round. For example, the expression "a round face" means only that the face resembles a circle more than it resembles a square or a triangle. It would be silly to write, "Amy's face resembles a circle more than Janet's face does," rather than "Amy's face is rounder than Janet's."

Some people object to making absolute adjectives and adverbs comparative or superlative. To avoid offending them, one can use the formal *more nearly* instead of *more*, and *the most nearly* instead of *the most*.

INCORRECT	In order to form a <u>more perfect</u> confederation, we adopted a constitution.
FORMAL	In order to form a <u>more nearly perfect</u> confederation we adopted a constitution.
INFORMAL	Hall's summary is <u>the most complete</u> of the three.
FORMAL	Hall's summary is <u>the most nearly complete</u> of the three.

Note For the use of the word *unique*, see Appendix A, "Glossary of Usage."

**gr
21c**

21c · Misuse of the Superlative

A superlative should not be used where a comparative is appropriate, nor should a superlative be used as an intensifying adverb.

Superlative with Two Items Use the comparative when making a comparison between only two items; use the superlative when making a comparison among three or more items.

INCORRECT	Of the two wars, the Boer War was <u>the longest</u>.
CORRECT	Of the two wars, the Boer War was <u>the longer</u>.
CORRECT	Of the three wars, the Boer War was <u>the longest</u>.

Superlatives as Intensifying Adverbs In speech, a superlative is sometimes used as a kind of intensifier to emphasize the adjective without
really intending any kind of comparison. Avoid this use of the superlative in writing; substitute an adverb for the superlative if necessary.

COLLOQUIAL	We saw <u>the funniest movie</u> last night.
REVISED	We saw a <u>very funny movie</u> last night.

21d ▪ Illogical Comparisons

Illogical comparisons imply a comparison between two things that are
not actually being compared or that cannot be compared. Illogical comparisons should be corrected by rewriting to clarify what things are being
compared.

ILLOGICAL	She has a car smaller than her brother. (Is her brother really bigger than a car?)
REVISED	She has a car smaller than her brother's.
ILLOGICAL	Mario's grades are better than last year. (*Grades* cannot be compared with *years*.)
REVISED	Mario's grades are better than they were last year.
ILLOGICAL	Denmark's taxes are higher than Holland. (Is Holland high?)
REVISED	Denmark's taxes are higher than those of Holland.

gr
21e

21e ▪ Ambiguous Comparisons

In the second part of a comparison of equality (for example, *as big as*) or
a comparison of superiority (for example, *bigger than*), some words in the
second part are often omitted because they are understood from the context.

I dislike handball as much as squash. (That is, "I dislike handball as
much as I dislike squash.")

Fran ate more macaroni than Christie. (That is, "Fran ate more macaroni than Christie ate macaroni.")

Such elliptical comparisons usually cause no problem because only one
interpretation of the sentence is reasonable. In some instances, however,
it may be unclear whether the second part of the comparison is intended
as a subject or as an object. To avoid such ambiguity, fill in as many
words as are necessary for clarity.

AMBIGUOUS	He likes Laura better than Nancy.
REVISED	He likes Laura better than he likes Nancy.
REVISED	He likes Laura better than Nancy does.

21f · Incomplete Comparisons

In general, do not make a comparison unless you state explicitly what the basis of the comparison is, that is, what two things or categories you are comparing.

> Smiladent gives you <u>whiter</u> teeth. (Whiter than you used to have? Whiter than anyone else's teeth? Whiter teeth than other toothpastes do?)

> Michael has <u>the worst</u> cold. (The worst cold he has ever had? The worst cold he has had this year? The worst cold of anyone in his family?)

The basis of comparison may be omitted in common expressions or idioms.

> I haven't <u>the faintest idea</u> where Kuala Lumpur is.

> Mr. MacFuddy disapproves of <u>the younger generation</u>.

21g · The Idiom of Comparisons

One of the major difficulties in writing comparisons is keeping track, not only of the words being compared, but also of the prepositions, conjunctions, and articles that belong to each type of comparison.

Like and **as** Introduce a comparative clause with *as* or *as if* and a comparative word or phrase with *like*.

CLAUSE	Helen's desk looks <u>as if</u> Napoleon's retreating army had abandoned it.
WORD	Helen's desk looks <u>like</u> mine.
PHRASE	Helen's desk looks <u>like</u> a disaster area.

Other and **any** When comparing members of the same class, use *other* or *any other*. When comparing members of different classes, use *any*.

INCORRECT	A Honda has better fuel efficiency than <u>any</u> Japanese cars. (*A Honda* is a member of the class of Japanese cars.)
CORRECT	A Honda has better fuel efficiency than <u>other</u> Japanese cars.
CORRECT	A Honda has better fuel efficiency than <u>any other</u> Japanese car.
INCORRECT	A Honda has better fuel efficiency than <u>other</u> North American cars. (*A Honda* is not a member of the class of North American cars.)
CORRECT	A Honda has better fuel efficiency than <u>any</u> North American car.

More and rather than   If you use *more* (or *less*) in the first part of a comparison, do not use *rather than* to introduce the second part of the comparison.

INCORRECT	That symphony sounds <u>more</u> like Haydn <u>rather than</u> Mozart.
REVISED	That symphony sounds <u>more</u> like Haydn <u>than</u> Mozart.
REVISED	That symphony sounds like Haydn <u>rather than</u> Mozart.

Different from and different than   It is always correct to write *different from*, but *different than* is gaining in acceptance, particularly if the object of *than* is a clause. *Different to* is not acceptable.

INCORRECT	Why is your solution <u>different to</u> mine?
QUESTIONABLE	Why is your solution <u>different than</u> mine?
CORRECT	Why is your solution <u>different from</u> mine?
ACCEPTABLE	Hawaii was <u>different than</u> he had imagined it.
CORRECT	Hawaii was <u>different from</u> what he had imagined.

gr 21g

Fewer and less   Use *fewer* in comparing plural, countable nouns and *less* in comparing mass or uncountable nouns.

INCORRECT	India has <u>less</u> natural resources and land than China.
REVISED	India has <u>fewer</u> natural resources and <u>less</u> land than China.

Equality and Superiority   When using both a comparison of equality and a comparison of superiority (or inferiority) in the same clause, do not omit the *as* after the first adjective or adverb.

INCORRECT	Rubber cement holds <u>as well</u> or <u>better than</u> glue.
REVISED	Rubber cement holds <u>as well as</u> or <u>better than</u> glue.
INCORRECT	Hang-gliding is <u>as dangerous</u> or <u>more dangerous than</u> parachuting.
REVISED	Hang-gliding is <u>as dangerous as</u> or <u>more dangerous than</u> parachuting.

Exercises: Comparisons

Correct all faulty comparisons in the following sentences.

1. Camembert and Roquefort are both good, but we like Roquefort best.
2. Harvey has always loved fishing more than Amy.
3. People were much more friendlier than Mary had thought they would be.

4. When the twins had finished their baths, the bathroom looked like a tidal wave had struck it.
5. I will never be satisfied until I get a more perfect score.
6. The men both bought suits at the sale, but Joe's is different to Bill's in the way the jacket is cut.
7. Edinburgh, Scotland, has more stone buildings than any other North American city.
8. Although she always finds time to volunteer, Elizabeth has far less money and opportunities than most of her friends have.
9. Ammonia cleans most floors as well or better than many higher-priced floor cleaners.

---

22   Problems with Prepositions *(prep)*

Prepositions and the rules for their use are highly idiomatic, so much so that beginning students of English as a second language often feel that every expression involving a preposition is a separate idiom. Fortunately, fluent speakers of English normally use prepositions automatically, and questions concerning their use are limited to occasional doubts about where to put them, when to repeat them, and which one to use with a given word.

gr 22

22a ▪ Placement of Prepositions

Although one normally thinks of prepositions as preceding their objects, they often follow their objects and appear at the end of a clause or sentence.

> What are you complaining <u>about</u>?
>
> The streets are dangerous to walk <u>in</u>.
>
> The house that the car stopped <u>at</u> had a For Sale sign on the lawn.

This kind of construction is natural in speech, but some people disapprove of it in writing. If, for some reason, highly formal writing is desirable or necessary, the sentence can usually be rewritten so that the preposition precedes its object.

> <u>About</u> what are you complaining?
>
> It is dangerous to walk <u>in</u> the streets.
>
> The house <u>at</u> which the car stopped had a For Sale sign on the lawn.

However, if moving the preposition so that it precedes its object results in awkwardness, leave it where it was; it is not ungrammatical to end a sentence with a preposition.

AWKWARD	It was the worst accident <u>of</u> which I had ever heard.
NATURAL	It was the worst accident I had ever heard <u>of</u>.
AWKWARD	His answer will depend on that <u>for</u> which you ask.
NATURAL	His answer will depend on what you ask <u>for</u>.

In fact, in some situations, there is no alternative to putting a preposition at the end of a clause or sentence.

| EXCLAMATION | What awful weather to go out <u>in</u>! |
| INFINITIVE | He is hard to talk <u>to</u>. |

22b ▪ Repetition of Prepositions

Do not repeat a preposition that has already appeared with its object earlier in the sentence.

INCORRECT	Marty could not find the man <u>with</u> whom he had been assigned to work <u>with</u>.
REVISED	Marty could not find the man <u>with</u> whom he had been assigned to work.
REVISED	Marty could not find the man whom he had been assigned to work <u>with</u>.
INCORRECT	<u>To</u> what devices could Sherman resort <u>to</u> now?
REVISED	<u>To</u> what devices could Sherman resort now?
REVISED	What devices could Sherman resort <u>to</u> now?

For the repetition of prepositions in parallel constructions, see 23f.

22c ▪ Idiomatic Use of Prepositions

Many nouns, verbs, adjectives, and phrases are associated with specific prepositions, making the use of any other preposition incorrect. Further, the correct preposition may vary, depending on the verb or the object of the preposition. For example, if you decide to use a pen instead of a pencil, you *substitute* the pen *for* the pencil, but you *replace* the pencil *with* the pen. You are *answerable to* a person or authority, but you are *answerable for* your own actions. It is impossible to list all of these prepositional combinations; a few of the most troublesome are given in the following list.

according to	disapprove of
amazed at *or* by	eager for
annoyed at *or* by	familiar to (someone)
beware of	familiar with (something)
capable of	in accordance with
coincide with	in search of
conform to	inferior to

consist of	married to
consistent with	prior to
convince	refrain from
(someone) of	responsible to (someone) for (something)
(something)	result from (a cause)
critical of	result in (an effect)
differ with	speak to (someone) about (something)
(someone)	succeed in
about	surprised at
(something)	take charge of
differ from	
(something else)	

When in doubt about the appropriate preposition for a particular word or expression, consult your dictionary. If it was written for fluent speakers of English, it lists the correct prepositions for some but not all nouns, adjectives, and verbs. You can find many more correct idiomatic combinations in a good dictionary for speakers of English as a second language (such as *The Oxford Advanced Learner's Dictionary of Current English*).

Exercises: Prepositions

gr
23

Rewrite the following sentences to correct problems caused by incorrectly placed or misused prepositions.

1. The second edition of the book differed greatly to the first edition.
2. His refusal was one of the meanest gestures of which I have ever heard.
3. I cannot understand why my professor was so critical with my term paper.
4. Until she was nearly thirty, Louisa always had to tell her parents with whom she went out with and where she was going to.
5. A large sign near the entrance warns visitors to beware about bears.
6. The young teacher's aide was terrified when Miss Abjornson asked her to take charge over the class during the arithmetic lesson.
7. To what ends could Smitty's boss expect him to go to to meet the deadline?

---

23 Problems with Sentence Form *(sen fm)*

Among the most common problems of sentence form are (1) sentence fragments, (2) shifted constructions, (3) mixed constructions, (4) comma splices and fused sentences, (5) faulty predication, and (6) faulty and false parallelism.

23a ▪ Sentence Fragments *(frag)*

A complete sentence is one that (1) has a subject, (2) has a finite verb, and
(3) is not preceded by any word making it dependent on some other group
of words. That is, a complete sentence must have at least one independent clause. In writing, a complete sentence begins with a capital letter
and ends with a period, a question mark, or an exclamation point. A
sentence fragment or incomplete sentence begins with a capital letter
and ends with one of the marks of ending punctuation but is missing
at least one of the other requirements of a complete sentence. Here are
some typical errors.

NO SUBJECT	I bought a snow shovel last week. <u>And had to use it almost immediately.</u>
NO FINITE VERB	Snow fell all day. <u>The powdery kind with tiny, businesslike flakes.</u>
NO FINITE VERB	I shovelled for an hour. <u>The snow having drifted heavily.</u> (*Having drifted* is a perfect participle, not a finite verb.)
NO SUBJECT OR FINITE VERB	I ached all over. <u>Especially in my shoulders and arms.</u>
PRECEDED BY A SUBORDINATING WORD	Then the plow came by and pushed snow into the driveway. <u>Which I had just finished shovelling.</u>

Sentence fragments are common in speech, especially as answers to
questions or as afterthoughts to statements.

"When did you go to the market?" "<u>This morning.</u>"

"You're standing on my foot. <u>And blocking my view.</u>"

In writing, on the other hand, sentence fragments are less acceptable,
except in writing dialogue to imitate speech. Most sentence fragments
consist of (1) dependent clauses, (2) incomplete clauses, (3) detached predicates, (4) modifying phrases, or (5) explanatory phrases. Many, although
not all, sentence fragments properly belong with the preceding sentence
and can be corrected by changing only the punctuation and the capitalization.

Dependent Clauses   Correct sentence fragments consisting of dependent
clauses by joining the clause to the preceding sentence.

FRAGMENT	The Arabs contributed much to astronomy. <u>Which they considered a branch of mathematics.</u>
REVISED	The Arabs contributed much to astronomy, which they considered a branch of mathematics.
FRAGMENT	I didn't want Leslie to come home. <u>At least until I had had a chance to wash the dishes and make the beds.</u>

gr
23a

REVISED   I didn't want Leslie to come home—at least until I had had a chance to wash the dishes and make the beds.

Incomplete Clauses   Sentence fragments consisting of incomplete clauses often occur in sentences with lengthy modifiers. By the time all the modifiers have been put in, the writer has forgotten that the main clause has not been completed.

FRAGMENT   The term "laissez-faire," referring to letting people do as they please and applying specifically to the economic theory that the state should excercise as little control as possible in trade. (The subject, *The term "laissez-faire,"* has no main verb; it has only the participles *referring* and *applying*.)

REVISED   The term "laissez-faire," referring to letting people do as they please, applies specifically to the economic theory that the state should exercise as little control as possible in trade. (The subject, *The term "laissez faire,"* has the main verb *applies* in the predicate.)

FRAGMENT   Whenever Eddie had to answer the telephone, which was equipped with more buttons and red lights than the cockpit of a Boeing 727. (There are two dependent clauses but no independent clause.)

REVISED   Eddie panicked whenever he had to answer the telephone, which was equipped with more buttons and red lights than the cockpit of a Boeing 727.

gr
23a

Detached Compound Predicates   Sentence fragments result when two verbs with one subject are separated, and the second verb consequently lacks a subject. Such fragments can be corrected by reattaching the second part of the predicate to the sentence in which its subject appears.

FRAGMENT   He went to market to buy a sheep. <u>And came home fleeced</u>.

REVISED   He went to the market to buy a sheep and came home fleeced.

FRAGMENT   Esther has always loved entomology. <u>But hates centipedes</u>.

REVISED   Esther has always loved entomology but hates centipedes.

Modifying Phrases   Sentence fragments consisting of modifying phrases include prepositional phrases, appositives, participle phrases, and infinitive phrases. Reattach the phrases to the preceding sentence, or rewrite the phrase to make a complete sentence.

PREPOSITIONAL PHRASE	George attended school for thirteen years. <u>Without missing a single day.</u>
REVISED	George attended school for thirteen years without missing a single day.
APPOSITIVE	The capital of Java is Jakarta. <u>Formerly called Batavia.</u>
REVISED	The capital of Java is Jakarta, formerly called Batavia.
PARTICIPLE PHRASE	We began to row furiously. <u>Believing we could reach shore before dark.</u>
REVISED	Believing we could reach shore before dark, we began to row furiously.
INFINITIVE PHRASE	After dieting for three weeks, Henry was pleasantly surprised when he weighed himself. <u>To discover that he had lost three kilograms.</u>
REVISED	When he weighed himself after dieting for three weeks, Henry was pleasantly surprised to discover that he had three kilograms.

gr
23a

Explanatory Phrases Sentence fragments consisting of explanatory phrases beginning with *such as, for example, namely,* and so on can be corrected by incorporating the fragment into the preceding sentence.

FRAGMENT	The hijacking ring specializes in high-value merchandise. <u>Such as jewellery, furs, and Oriental rugs.</u>
REVISED	The hijacking ring specializes in high-value merchandise such as jewellery, furs, and Oriental rugs.
FRAGMENT	One legislative item was not voted on before the session ended. <u>Namely, the child-abuse bill.</u>
REVISED	One legislative item, the child-abuse bill, was not voted on before the session ended.

Deliberate Fragments Some authors occasionally write deliberate sentence fragments, especially in descriptive passages in which no action is taking place and the goal is simply to list detail to convey a picture to the reader.

It was a large square room. There was a double bed with a pink bedspread, a table with a green cloth, two wooden chairs and an armchair, a cupboard, two or three skimpy carpets. <u>Pale gray walls in need of painting, a photo of King Paul, an oleograph ikon over the bed.</u> Another door led into a bathroom.

John Fowles, *The Magus*

Fragments are also sometimes effective in answering rhetorical questions, in exclamations, in citing proverbs, and in reporting dialogue.

ANSWER	What does Professor Digger know about fossils? <u>Everything</u>.
EXCLAMATION	How depressing Vladivostock is on a raw November day!
PROVERB	Least said, soonest mended.
DIALOGUE	"Nice day," Jerry said. "Yeah, for ducks," replied Pamela.

Students sometimes deliberately write a sentence fragment, only to have their instructors mark it as an error. Instructors do this because they cannot be sure that their students know the difference between a fragment and a complete sentence or because the fragment, deliberate though it may be, simply is not effective. In general, unless a student has a demonstrably fine command of sentences and sentence variety, an instructor is likely to view a fragment as an error—not as an adventurous device used for stylistic effect.

Sentences Beginning with a Conjunction   Some people object to beginning a sentence with a co-ordinating conjunction, regarding such constructions as sentence fragments. They are not fragments if there is a subject and a finite verb. Nevertheless, do not overuse such sentences, or the result will be choppy prose.

gr
23a

CHOPPY	Father praised my good grades. And mother sent her love. But they didn't enclose a cheque.
REVISED	Father praised my good grades and mother sent her love, but they didn't enclose a cheque.

Exercises: Sentence Fragments

Rewrite the following sentence fragments to make them complete sentences.

1. Dieters can be seen everywhere, clutching their Bibles. Better known as their calorie-counters.
2. The fisherman, settling down for a long, peaceful afternoon of casting, interspersed with catnaps and reeling in the fish.
3. The party finally ended at 03:00. The band having left at 02:00, and the police having arrived at 02:45 to quiet things down.
4. While one part of the TV screen carried the football game and another part showed the scores of other games being played and a storm warning was being flashed across the bottom of the screen.
5. When all of the family had finally gathered in grandmother's parlor, where mother had insisted that we meet to discuss the sale of the farm.
6. Businesses quickly sprang up along the new highway. Including fast-food restaurants, bowling alleys, used car lots, and a 24-hour launderette.

23b ▪ Shifted Constructions *(shift)*

Shifted constructions are unnecessary changes in such grammatical features as tense, voice, person, number, and mood. Obviously, some shifts are necessary in writing; for example, contrasting past action with present action requires an appropriate shift of the verb tense. Errors occur when the shift is unnecessary or illogical.

Shifted Tense Do not shift the tense of the verb unless you intend to indicate a shift in the time of action.

SHIFTED TENSE	I <u>asked</u> the clerk where I <u>could appeal</u> the fine, and he <u>tells</u> me that I <u>will have to go</u> to court. (shift from past to present tense)
REVISED	I <u>asked</u> the clerk where I <u>could appeal</u> the fine, and he <u>told</u> me that I <u>would have to go</u> to court.

Shifted Voice Do not shift from active to passive voice or vice versa in the middle of a sentence.

SHIFTED VOICE	After she <u>pressed</u> the fabric and <u>laid</u> the pattern on it, the pattern <u>was pinned</u> to the fabric. (shift from active to passive voice)
REVISED	After she <u>pressed</u> the fabric and <u>laid</u> the pattern on it, she <u>pinned</u> the pattern to the fabric.

Shifted Person or Number Do not shift unnecessarily from one person to another or from singular to plural.

SHIFTED PERSON	When <u>one</u> wakes up with a terrible headache after a party, <u>you</u> shouldn't blame the pretzels. (shift from third person to second person)
REVISED	When <u>one</u> wakes up with a terrible headache after a party, <u>he</u> (or <u>he or she</u> or <u>one</u>) shouldn't blame the pretzels.
SHIFTED NUMBER	When <u>someone</u> wakes up with a terrible headache after a party, <u>they</u> shouldn't blame the pretzels. (shift from singular to plural)
REVISED	When <u>someone</u> wakes up with a terrible headache after a party, <u>he or she</u> shouldn't blame the pretzels.
REVISED	<u>People</u> who wake up with terrible headaches after a party shouldn't blame the pretzels.

Shifted Mood Do not shift from one mood to another in the middle of a sentence.

gr
23b

SHIFTED MOOD	The doctor suggested that he <u>get</u> more sleep and that he <u>should exercise</u> less strenuously. (shift from subjunctive to indicative mood)
REVISED	The doctor suggested that he <u>get</u> more sleep and that he <u>exercise</u> less strenuously.
REVISED	The doctor told him that he <u>should get</u> more sleep and <u>should exercise</u> less strenuously.
SHIFTED MOOD	First, <u>take</u> the receiver off the hook; then you <u>should listen</u> for a dial tone. (shift from imperative to indicative mood)
REVISED	First, <u>take</u> the receiver off the hook; then <u>listen</u> for a dial tone.

23c ▪ Comma Splices and Fused Sentences (*cs*)(*fs*)

Comma splices (or **comma faults**) result from using only a comma to connect two main clauses. **Fused sentences** result from joining two main clauses with neither proper punctuation nor a co-ordinating conjunction. Because proper use of punctuation is the most important way of avoiding or correcting comma splices and fused sentences, these errors are discussed in the section on punctuation, 27a.

gr 23d

23d ▪ Mixed Constructions (*mix*)

Mixed constructions result from beginning a phrase, clause, or sentence with one type of construction and then changing to another type without completing the first construction. The possible types of mixed constructions are almost unlimited, but a few kinds are especially common.

Direct and Indirect Quotations   Do not mix a direct and an indirect quotation.

MIXED	He assured the customer I know how to make change.
REVISED	He assured the customer that he knew how to make change.
REVISED	He assured the customer, "I know how to make change."

Direct and Indirect Questions   Do not mix a direct and an indirect question.

MIXED	I wonder do ladybugs eat mosquitoes?
REVISED	I wonder if ladybugs eat mosquitoes.

Adverbials and Subjects or Complements   Do not use an adverbial phrase or clause as a subject. Many such problems arise from improperly using *when, why, where,* or *how* to introduce a complement after the verb *to be.*

MIXED	By turning to look at the dog was when I fell off the bicycle.
REVISED	I fell off the bicycle when I turned to look at the dog.
REVISED	Turning to look at the dog, I fell off the bicycle.
MIXED	Just because you read it in a book doesn't make it true.
REVISED	Your having read it in a book doesn't make it true.
REVISED	It isn't necessarily true just because you read it in a book.

Subjects and Objects Do not make an object the apparent subject of a sentence. This error usually occurs when the object is the real topic and the focus of the writer's attention. The writer begins the sentence with this topic and then switches to a construction that turns the topic into an object.

MIXED	<u>People who have bad backs</u>, doctors advise <u>them</u> to sleep on hard mattresses.
REVISED	Doctors advise people who have bad backs to sleep on hard mattresses.
MIXED	<u>The baby skunk we found in the barn</u>, we took <u>it</u> to the veterinarian to be de-scented.
REVISED	We took the baby skunk we found in the barn to the veterinarian to be de-scented.

Independent Clauses and Subjects Do not use an independent clause as the subject of a sentence. To correct this error, you can (1) change the independent clause to a noun phrase, (2) make the independent clause into a dependent clause and the predicate into an independent clause, or (3) completely rewrite the sentence.

MIXED	<u>The salesman's face looked very honest</u> was what persuaded me to buy the set of encyclopedias.
REVISED	The salesman's honest face persuaded me to buy the set of encyclopedias.
REVISED	Because the salesman's face looked very honest, I decided to buy the set of encyclopedias.
REVISED	It was the salesman's honest face that persuaded me to buy the set of encyclopedias.

gr
23e

23e ▪ Faulty Predication

Faulty predication occurs when the predicate of a sentence fails, in one way or another, to "match" the subject. Probably the most common kind of faulty predication involves sentences with linking verbs in which the complement does not match the subject. Sentences with linking verbs, especially the verb *to be*, are really like equations; the subject is the left side of the equation, the verb is the equal sign, and the complement (that is, the rest of the predicate) is the right side of the equation. The sentence "Cats are mammals" is, in effect, saying "Cats = mammals." But not all nouns can logically be equated with each other; one would not, for instance, say "Cats are a devotion" or "Cats are difference." These last two sentences are examples of faulty complements. Faulty complementation usually occurs when writers are writing so rapidly that they concentrate only on the ideas they want to convey and not on the proper form for these ideas. A faulty complement can be corrected by rewriting the sentence to make the subject and the complement logically and grammatically equivalent.

FAULTY   In my philosophy class, the discussion is only a few students and the instructor. (*Students* or *instructor* is not *a discussion.*)

REVISED   In my philosophy class, the discussion is carried on by only a few students and the instructor.

FAULTY   One of the best antiseptics is by washing with soap and water. (*By washing* is not *an antiseptic.*)

REVISED   One of the best antiseptics is soap and water.

Faulty predication can also occur with other types of verbs, especially when modifiers come between the real subject and the verb.

**gr
23e**

FAULTY   The purpose of the expedition failed because Pooh never found the Heffalump. (The *purpose* did not fail, though perhaps the expedition did.)

REVISED   The expedition failed because Pooh never found the Heffalump.

REVISED   The purpose of the expedition was defeated since Pooh failed to find the Heffalump.

FAULTY   The decision about the disposal of waste products has delayed construction of new nuclear power plants. (The *decision* has not delayed construction.)

REVISED   Construction of new nuclear plants has been delayed because no decision has been made about the disposal of waste products.

REVISED   Lack of a decision about the disposal of waste products has delayed construction of new nuclear power plants.

Faulty appositives are a type of faulty complementation in which the verb *to be* has been omitted.

FAULTY   Competition is intense for places in the higher-paid professions, such as doctors. (*Doctors* are not *professions.*)

REVISED   Competition is intense for places in the higher-paid professions, such as medicine and law.

Exercises: Mixed and Illogical Constructions

Correct mixed and illogical constructions in the following sentences.

1. Couples seen holding hands or kissing are indicators of affection.
2. Midway through the examination, Peter found his mind wandering and that his vision had become blurred.
3. The coach asked Sam how much sleep did he get last night.
4. His father suggested that he look around for a good used car and that he should see some agents about auto insurance.
5. While the children were swimming, Pat and Howard made the salad and set the table, and then the steaks were grilled by them.
6. Everyone has good intentions about filing their income tax returns early, but somehow you always end up staying up all night on April 29.
7. In running to catch the bus was how I twisted my ankle.
8. Sarah's painting is a work of art that never fails to elicit comments from visitors to her studio and which is the result of more than a year's hard work.

gr
23f

23f ▪ Parallelism (‖)

Parallelism means using the same grammatical structure for all items that have the same function. It holds sentences together, adds emphasis, and provides a smooth, rhythmic flow to writing. Parallelism helps both writer and reader organize the thoughts being expressed. It usually is economical; that is, fewer words are needed to express ideas if they are grammatically parallel. Finally, parallelism seems to satisfy a basic human love for symmetry. We understand and remember sentences better if they are in parallel form. This is why so many proverbs and famous quotations use heavy parallelism.

> <u>I came</u>, <u>I saw</u>, <u>I conquered</u>.
>
> God send <u>you more wit</u> and <u>me more money</u>.
>
> <u>Whither thou goest</u>, <u>I will go</u>, and <u>where thou lodgest</u>, <u>I will lodge</u>.

Grammatical problems with parallelism can involve either faulty parallelism or false parallelism.

Faulty Parallelism   Faulty parallelism occurs when ideas serving the same grammatical purpose do not have the same grammatical form, that is, when the second or successive items do not fit the pattern established by the first. Correct this problem by putting all the related ideas into the same grammatical form. Faulty parallelism can occur in almost any kind of grammatical construction but is especially common in series.

| INCORRECT | Eating is time-consuming, expensive, and it makes you fat. (The first two items in the series are adjectives, and the last item is an independent clause.) |
| REVISED | Eating is time-consuming, expensive, and fattening. |

Faulty parallelism is also common in items connected by co-ordinating or correlative conjunctions.

| INCORRECT | Mexico is overpopulated, but there are not enough people in Australia. (The first clause has a subject complement, whereas the second clause begins with an expletive pronoun.) |
| REVISED | Mexico is overpopulated, but Australia is underpopulated. |

| INCORRECT | It is easier said than it is to do it. (The first part of this comparison ends in a past participle, whereas the second part has an infinitive and a direct object.) |
| REVISED | It is easier said than done. |

| INCORRECT | Vitamin A is found not only in vegetables, but eggs and butter also have it. (The first clause has a passive verb and a prepositional phrase, whereas the second clause has an active verb and a direct object.) |
| REVISED | Vitamin A is found not only in vegetables but also in eggs and butter. |

If all the related ideas in a series cannot be put into the same form, break the series up into two or more parallel series.

| INCORRECT | The foundations of the house are sinking, it must have a new roof, the paint is peeling, and it doesn't have storm windows. |
| REVISED | The foundations of the house are sinking and the paint is peeling; furthermore, it needs storm windows and a new roof. |

False Parallelism False parallelism occurs when ideas that are not parallel in grammatical function or meaning are put into parallel or seemingly parallel form. Correct false parallelism by rewriting.

A common error of false parallelism is making a subordinate clause falsely parallel to a main clause.

| INCORRECT | We spent hours doing crossword puzzles and playing word games, and which most people would find boring. (The co-ordinating conjunction *and* connects an independent clause and a subordinate clause introduced by *which*.) |

gr
23f

REVISED   We spent hours doing crossword puzzles and playing
                   word games, activities that most people would find
                   boring.

Another kind of false parallelism is using the same word in two or more
different ways.

INCORRECT   They will complete the repairs *by* the bridge *by*
                   Wednesday *by* hiring extra workers.

REVISED   They will hire extra workers in order to complete the
                   repairs near the bridge by Wednesday.

Missing words with different levels of generality or with clearly unrelated meanings is also false parallelism.

INCORRECT   This wheelbarrow is available in red, orange, and
                   bright colors. (*Bright colors* is a general term that
                   includes *red* and *orange*.)

REVISED   This wheelbarrow is available in red, orange, and
                   other bright colors.

INCORRECT   The judge was well-educated, liberal, and grey-eyed.
                   (*Well-educated* and *liberal* are mental characteris-
                   tics, but *grey-eyed* is a physical characteristic.)

REVISED   The judge was well-educated and liberal.

gr
23f

Parallelism and Repetition   Parallel structures are frequently identified
and clarified by the repetition of words common to all the parallel elements. Such repetition often is optional; you may either omit the common word or repeat it, but be consistent. For example, if you repeat a
preposition before one item in a series, repeat it before all items in the
series.

INCORRECT   He collected the information <u>from</u> letters, newspa-
                   pers, <u>from</u> diaries, and city records.

REVISED   He collected the information <u>from</u> letters, newspa-
                   pers, diaries, and city records.

REVISED   He collected the information <u>from</u> letters, <u>from</u>
                   newspapers, <u>from</u> diaries, and <u>from</u> city records.

INCORRECT   Janice brought home <u>her</u> guitar, bicycle, <u>her</u> geology
                   textbook, and <u>her</u> roommate.

REVISED   Janice brought home <u>her</u> guitar, <u>her</u> bicycle, <u>her</u> geol-
                   ogy textbook, and <u>her</u> roommate.

Exercises: Parallelism

Correct faulty or false parallelism in the following sentences.

1. Madeleine is a woman with true compassion for stray animals, who
   tries to find their owners or getting them adopted.

2. All of this compassion means that she usually has quite a menagerie to care for while she makes phone calls, places ads in the newspapers, and she solicits help from the radio stations.
3. The animals not only require a lot of attention, but Madeleine finds that caring for them is expensive and she gets very tired.
4. At six each morning, Madeleine serves breakfast to her clientele, opening cans of food for the dogs and cats, crumbling up bread for the birds and ducks, and fresh vegetables are chopped up for the rabbits and raccoon.
5. Caring for her menagerie is important to Madeleine for two reasons: she deeply loves animals and to teach animals to trust people.

gr
23f

Punctuation and Mechanics

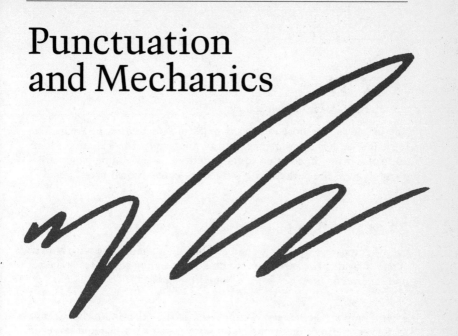

24  Periods (.)

Use a Period

- At the end of most sentences
- After abbreviations and initials
- In dramatic, poetic, and Biblical citations

The **period** is the most important mark of punctuation in English because it separates one sentence from another, and sentences are the basic units of writing. In addition to its structural use as ending punctuation for sentences, the period has a number of conventional uses.

24a ▪ As Ending Punctuation

Every sentence or deliberate sentence fragment should end with a mark of punctuation. The most common mark for ending sentences is the period (or *stop* or *full stop*, as it is sometimes called).

After Complete Sentences   Periods are used at the end of declarative sentences, indirect questions, and polite commands or requests, even though these commands may have the word order of a question.

DECLARATIVE SENTENCES	All cows eat grass.
	During the battle, General Wolfe was mortally wounded.
INDIRECT QUESTIONS	I asked how I could remove airplane glue from my clothes.
	People have often wondered whether there is life on other planets.
POLITE REQUESTS	Please turn down your radio.
	Would you kindly refund my money as guaranteed.

After Deliberate Sentence Fragments   Periods are also used after deliberate or conventionally acceptable sentence fragments. (See 23a for a discussion of sentence fragments.)

Yes.	Better late than never.
Good night.	So much for rose petals.

Exception   Titles at the tops of pages or otherwise set off from the text are not followed by periods, even when they are complete sentences.

Mountain Climbing Is an Uphill Job

The Failure of Western Medicine

24b · Conventional Uses

In addition to its use as a signal that a sentence has ended, the period has a number of conventional uses.

Abbreviations and Initials Periods are used after most abbreviations and initials. (See 42 for the appropriate use of abbreviations.)

Dr. Armitage is a Ph.D., not an M.D.

Ms. Paulsen lived in Georgetown, P.E.I., for more than three years.

Will A. J. Foyt win the Indianapolis 500 again?

1. Periods are used after the abbreviations for provinces, states, and the District of Columbia.

B.C.   Alta.   Nfld.   S.C.
N.B.   P.E.I.   Alta.   D.C.

These abbreviations are used chiefly in addresses, tables, and citations; their use is not recommended for formal writing. Note that the post office has developed two-letter abbreviations that are always in capital letters and have no periods: MB for Manitoba, PE for Prince Edward Island, and so on. These postal abbreviations should be used only for addressing mail.

2. Periods are not used after shortened word forms that have become accepted as independent words. Nor are periods used with nicknames.

She has an exam in the new gym this afternoon.

Ed and Flo send their love.

3. Many acronyms and initialisms do not use periods. However, because practice varies greatly, consult one dictionary and follow it consistently. Periods are never used with the call letters of radio and television stations and networks. See also 42d.

ACRONYMS	INITIALISMS	CALL LETTERS
UNESCO	YMCA	CKCW
laser	GNP	NBC
NASA	Q.E.D.	CBC
CIDA	RCMP	CBUFT

4. If a hyphen falls after an abbreviation in a French proper noun, the periods are omitted.

Ste-Anne-des-Monts   J-P Desbiens

Dramatic, Poetic, and Biblical Citations Periods separate act, scene, and

p
24b

line in citations from drama; chapter and verse in Biblical citations; and book and line in citations from long poetic works.

BIBLICAL CITATION	Psalm 23.3 (or Psalm xxiii.3)
	2 Kings 11.12 (or Kings II.xi.12)
DRAMATIC CITATION	*Othello* 2.3.24–27 (or *Othello* II.iii.24–27)
POETIC CITATION	*The Faerie Queene* 3.7.1. (or *The Faerie Queene* III.vii.1)

Some writers prefer colons to periods in such citations, especially in Biblical citations (see 29d).

Note Many modern authorities recommend using only arabic numerals in citations. For reasons of tradition, however, some authors and editors continue to use roman numerals as shown in parentheses in the examples. This practice is common within the text of an essay, in referring to plays and other literary works.

In *Othello* IV.ii we see that . . .

Othello says, "Be sure to prove my love a whore" (III.iii.359). . . .

25 Question Marks (?)

Use a Question Mark
- After direct questions
- After doubtful figures

Like a period, the **question mark** is used as a mark of ending punctuation. Unlike a period, it is used only after direct questions.

25a ▪ Direct Questions

A question mark is used after a direct question.

What is the difference between a duck and a goose?

Do you have a good book on bricklaying?

Even if the word order of a sentence is that of a statement, use a question mark if a direct question is being asked. In other words, if the voice would rise at the end when the sentence is spoken, a question mark should be used.

The newspaper was late again this morning?

You said you called the office and complained?

1. If a sentence contains a question within a question, use only one question mark.

Who was it that asked, "Of what use is a baby?"

2. When a sentence contains a series of words, all of which are being questioned, a single question mark may be placed at the end of the entire sentence.

What does he propose to do about rising taxes, crime in the cities, unemployment, the international situation, and inflation?

Less formally, you can place question marks after each separate question, even if the questions are not complete sentences.

What does he propose to do about rising taxes? crime in the cities? unemployment? the international situation? inflation?

To add greater emphasis, you can capitalize the first word of each item being questioned.

What does he propose to do about rising taxes? Crime in the cities? Unemployment? The international situation? Inflation?

25b • Conventional Use

A question mark is conventionally used to indicate a doubtful figure or date. In the sentence below, a question mark follows *1775* because the exact date of Chapman's birth is uncertain.

John Chapman (1775?–1845) is better known as Johnny Appleseed.

p
25c

25c • Superfluous Uses

Question marks should not be used after exclamations, indirect questions, or requests. Nor should they be used to indicate humor or sarcasm.

Exclamations Do not use a question mark after exclamations phrased as questions.

INCORRECT   Will you please leave immediately?
REVISED   Will you please leave immediately!

Indirect Questions and Requests Do not use a question mark after an indirect question or a polite request phrased as a question. (See also 23d.)

INCORRECT   George asked Harriet where she got her hat?
REVISED   George asked Harriet where she got her hat.

Humor and Sarcasm   Avoid the use of question marks to indicate humor or sarcasm.

INAPPROPRIATE   Our expert (?) guide led us directly into a swamp.

REVISED   Our supposedly expert guide led us directly into a
                      swamp.

26 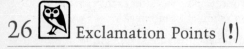 Exclamation Points (!)

Use an Exclamation Point
- After emphatic or emotional statements

The **exclamation point** is the most dramatic mark of ending punctuation. Because it does convey such a strong feeling of excitement, it should be used sparingly; otherwise, the writer is likely to appear somewhat hysterical.

26a ▪ Dramatic or Emotional Statements

The exclamation point is appropriate after interjections, exclamatory words and phrases, and exceptionally strong commands.

Help!   Ouch! You're standing on my fingers!

Look at him run!   There! That should do it.

Stop that!

The exclamation point is especially common after exclamations beginning with one of the question words *how*, *what*, and *who*.

Who would have thought it!

How generous of you!

What a job that will be!

In general, it is safest to reserve the exclamation point for reporting dialogue. But even in the reporting of dialogue, not every interjection requires an exclamation point.

Well! So this is what you do the minute my back is turned! (Genuine indignation is being expressed by the *Well!* and the following statement.)

Well, we'll just have to wait and see. (The *Well* is resigned and thoughtful, not excited.)

26b · Superfluous Uses

1. Do not use an exclamation point to indicate humor or sarcasm.

INAPPROPRIATE   Our expert (!!) guide led us directly into a swamp.

REVISED   Our supposedly expert guide led us directly into a swamp.

2. Never use more than one exclamation point after a word or phrase, and never combine exclamation points with question marks.

OVEREMOTIONAL   **You can't be serious?!!**

REVISED   **You can't be serious!**

Exercises: Periods, Question Marks, and Exclamation Points

Correctly punctuate the following sentences with periods, question marks, and exclamation points.

1. On the exam Ms Jones asked us to comment on *Othello* I iii 377–391
2. An automatic page turner What on earth will they think of next
3. Mr T P Perry, bureau chief for the CBC in Washington, DC, told his listeners, "This political problem has been with us a long time; think of Caesar in 44 BC"
4. Did you see the interview CBS arranged with the top directors of the CIA
5. "Oh my" she shrieked "Did you really get a job with the RCMP"
6. Mary wondered why Thomas Nast had chosen the elephant to represent the Republican Party in his famous 1872 cartoon that made the elephant the symbol of the GOP.
7. Volunteers who had done door-to-door campaigning poured into the local NDP headquarters to watch the election returns, and by 21:00 the hall was full.
8. The director bowed to the cast and exclaimed, "That was undoubtedly the most moving performance I have ever seen of *Who's Afraid of Virginia Woolf*"
9. Without looking up from his desk, Dr Morales said, "Miss, would you please sit down"

p
27

---

27 Commas (,)

Use a Comma

■ Between independent clauses
■ Between items in a series

- After introductory elements
- Around parenthetical elements
- Around nonrestrictive modifiers
- Before direct quotations
- Between geographic units
- Between parts of dates
- Between names and titles or degrees
- Between units of thousands
- After salutations and complimentary closings
- For clarity

The **comma** is by far the most important mark of internal punctuation. It serves as a separator—separating clauses and phrases from each other, separating items in a series, and separating nonessential elements from the rest of the sentence. The comma also has a number of other uses, both as a separator of words and numbers and simply as a mark that conventionally appears in certain places.

27a ▪ Independent Clauses

Independent clauses contain a subject and a finite verb and are not preceded by a subordinating word such as *that, until,* or *whenever*. (Finite verbs are those that can serve as complete verb phrases; see 4a.) When two or more independent clauses appear within one sentence, they must be separated by some mark of punctuation. If a co-ordinating conjunction connects these clauses, a comma is the appropriate mark of punctuation.

p
27a

With Co-ordinating Conjunctions   Use a comma before a co-ordinating conjunction connecting two independent clauses. The co-ordinating conjunctions are *and, but, or,* and *nor*.

> The land has been worked for centuries, <u>and</u> no effort has been made to maintain the fertility of the soil.

> Ballads appeared as early as the thirteenth century, <u>but</u> they did not become popular until much later.

> The architecture may have an English flavor, <u>or</u> it may display French influence.

> No photography courses are offered at the local high school, <u>nor</u> are any planned for the future.

Note   The comma is often omitted if the two clauses are short. However, it is not wrong to use a comma between them.

> The soil is poor and water is scarce.

> Her sins were scarlet but her books were read.

> I don't like rutabagas nor will I eat parsnips.

Note Then is often punctuated as a co-ordinating conjunction in in-formal writing. In formal writing, however, it should be treated as a con-junctive adverb.

INFORMAL   Fold your test paper in half, <u>then</u> hand it in.

FORMAL   Fold your test paper in half; <u>then</u> hand it in.

FORMAL   Fold your test paper in half, <u>and then</u> hand it in.

With *yet, for,* and *so* For purposes of punctuation, *yet* in the meaning of "but," *for* in the meaning of "because," and *so* in the meaning of "therefore" are often treated like co-ordinating conjunctions and are pre-ceded by commas to prevent misreading.

Diana, the Princess of Wales, often visits hospitals, <u>for</u> she takes her royal duties seriously.

He gets all A's, yet he never cracks a book.

There is no public transportation, so most people drive to work.

Comma Splices Using a comma to separate two main clauses that are *not* connected by a co-ordinating conjunction produces the very serious error called **comma splice** or **comma fault**.

COMMA
SPLICE   I knit an orange polyester scarf for my husband, he has never worn it.

Comma splices can be corrected in any of the following four ways:

1. By adding a co-ordinating conjunction.

   I knit an orange polyester scarf for my husband, but he has never worn it.

2. By using a semicolon instead of a comma.

   I knit an orange polyester scarf for my husband; he has never worn it.

3. By making two separate sentences.

   I knit an orange polyester scarf for my husband. He has never worn it.

4. By rewriting to make one of the clauses subordinate to the other.

   Although I knit an orange polyester scarf for my husband, he has never worn it.

There are, however, "allowable" comma splices. Commas alone are sometimes used to separate a series of short parallel independent clauses, even though the clauses are not connected by co-ordinating conjunctions. In such cases, semicolons may also be used.

Life is a toil, love is a trouble.

p
27a

I came, I saw, I conquered.

Church bells rang, sirens blew, people danced in the streets.

Church bells rang; sirens blew; people danced in the streets.

A conjunctive adverb such as *however, nevertheless, what is more,* or *incidentally* cannot substitute for a co-ordinating conjunction; a comma splice still results. (See 28c for punctuation with conjunctive adverbs.)

COMMA SPLICE	I knit an orange polyester scarf for my husband, however, he has never worn it.
CORRECT	I knit an orange polyester scarf for my husband. However, he has never worn it.
CORRECT	I knit an orange polyester scarf for my husband; however, he has never worn it.

Fused sentences   Failure to use either co-ordinating conjunctions or punctuation between independent clauses results in the error called **fused sentences**. (Fused sentences are also known as run-on sentences.)

FUSED SENTENCE	Housing is scarce in Japan apartments are hard to find and very expensive.

Fused sentences can be corrected in the same ways as comma splices:

1. By adding a comma and co-ordinating conjunction.

   Housing is scarce in Japan, and apartments are hard to find and very expensive.

2. By using a semicolon.

   Housing is scarce in Japan; apartments are hard to find and very expensive.

3. By making two separate sentences.

   Housing is scarce in Japan. Apartments are hard to find and very expensive.

4. By rewriting to make one of the clauses subordinate to the other.

   Because housing is scarce in Japan, apartments are hard to find and very expensive.

Note   A fused sentence cannot be corrected by simply putting a comma between the two clauses. The result will be a comma splice.

COMMA SPLICE	Housing is scarce in Japan, apartments are hard to find and very expensive.

p 27a

Exercises: Commas and Independent Clauses

Correctly punctuate the following sentences by inserting a comma wherever necessary between independent clauses. If the sentence is already correct, write C before the sentence. Write IC if the sentence lacks a comma before an independent clause. Write CS before sentences containing comma splices and FS before fused sentences.

1. For vacations Aubrey preferred the cool quiet of the mountains but Karen like hot, sunny days on the beach.
2. The play began at 20:30, however the theatre was only half full.
3. By applying an accounting trick, John saw that in copying the numbers he had transposed some figures for the difference in his total and that of the booklet was evenly divisible by nine.
4. The police car gave chase for two kilometres but then gave up on catching the speeder and returned to town.
5. Although it was past midnight, Dr. Williams was still out in his floodlit backyard practising his golf swing and hacking up the lawn.
6. Do you want to picnic on the lawn at Stratford or would you rather eat at the Terrace Restaurant?
7. The handsome man flashed a smile at the new teller and then he pushed the counterfeit bills toward her.
8. Allen said he would come to the party, nonetheless he did not show up.
9. Lisa and her fellow conspirator filled Joe's room with balloons they sprayed shaving cream all over both sides of the door.
10. In a bad mood for most of the day, Chuck would not answer the phone, nor did he go down to meals or attend class.
11. We should turn off a few lights wasting electricity is foolish.

p
27b

27b ▪ Items in a Series

When words belonging to the same part of speech or serving exactly the same function in a sentence appear consecutively, they form a **series**. Series may consist of single words, phrases, or even clauses.

Three or More Items   Use commas to separate three or more items in a series.

> Adam Smith, Jeremy Bentham, and J. S. Mill all contributed to classical economic theory.
> The nose of mammals is a structure of flesh, bone, and cartilage.
> St. John Chrysostom was born in Antioch, lived in Constantinople, and died in Armenia.
> Your arguments are vigorous, appealing, well phrased, but wholly impractical.
> I did all the driving, Ellen navigated by reading the road maps, and Will maintained a running commentary on the scenery.

Although some writers omit the comma before the conjunction and final item in a series, it is safest always to use a comma here because its omission often leads to ambiguity.

AMBIGUOUS   The audience consisted primarily of sick people, old men and women.

Here, the reader might think that the words *old men and women* are in apposition to *sick people*. A comma eliminates this ambiguity.

REVISED   The audience consisted primarily of sick people, old men, and women.

If there is no conjunction before the last item, a comma *must* be used.

Cockroaches were crawling in the sink, along the walls, over the floor.

A comma should never be used *after* the final item in a series.

INCORRECT   Lakes Superior, Michigan, and Huron, are all more than a hundred fifty kilometres wide.

CORRECT   Lakes Superior, Michigan, and Huron are all more than a hundred fifty kilometres wide.

No commas are used if all the items in the series are connected by co-ordinating conjunctions.

To keep in shape, Evan jogs and swims and lifts weights.

p 27b

Two Items   Except for independent clauses (see 27a for use of commas with independent clauses), do not use a comma when a series consists of only two items connected by a co-ordinating conjunction. In other words, the two parts of a compound subject, object, predicate, or modifier should not be separated by commas.

INCORRECT   Bluejays, and starlings are often very noisy.

CORRECT   Bluejays and starlings are often very noisy.

INCORRECT   Egypt borders on Libya, and the Sudan.

CORRECT   Egypt borders on Libya and the Sudan.

INCORRECT   He does not drink, or smoke.

CORRECT   He does not drink or smoke.

Series of Adjectives   Use a comma to separate a series of two or more adjectives not connected by a conjunction if the order of the adjectives can be reversed and still keep the same meaning.

Your son is a clever, sensitive child.
Your son is a sensitive, clever child.

If the order of the adjectives cannot be reversed, do not separate them by commas.

INCORRECT   Old, stone fences are a familiar sight in Vermont.

CORRECT   Old stone fences are a familiar sight in Vermont.

Exercises: Commas with Items in a Series

Correctly punctuate the following sentences by inserting a comma wherever necessary between items in a series.

1. Stamp collecting is an exciting educational hobby shared by young old rich and poor philatelists around the world.
2. From the very beginning, collectors have valued stamps that were printed in small quantities those that exhibited printing errors and those that had beautiful or peculiar designs.
3. Before they can think of specializing, however, serious beginners must first learn to view their tiny paper treasures with a magnifying glass to handle them with tweezers to store them carefully in pockets or paste them on with hinges in a moistureproof flat album and to revere them as amazingly detailed miniature works of art.
4. Some collectors accumulate only commemorative stamps of birds or reptiles or particular people some specialize in surcharged or semipostal stamps and some want stamps from only one or two countries or decades.
5. Although regular postage stamps in hundreds of shapes and sizes and designs provide a large resource for collectors, philatelists also buy trade and save airmail parcel-post special-delivery postal-savings newspaper and provisional stamps of all kinds.

p
27c

27c ▪ Introductory Elements

Introductory elements include modifying words, phrases, and subordinate clauses.

Introductory Words and Phrases   Use a comma to separate introductory phrases from the main part of the sentence.

Unfortunately, money does not grow on trees.

By the end of World War I, Europe was devastated.

Having checked the punctuation, the careful writer proofreads for spelling errors.

If the introductory phrase is short, the comma is sometimes omitted.

After lunch he took a nap.   In Ireland there are no snakes.

However, if the introductory phrase ends with a preposition, a comma is always used to avoid ambiguity.

> To sum up, the discussion was a waste of time.
> To begin with, the first page is missing.

Introductory Clauses If the order of two clauses in a sentence could be reversed, use a comma to separate them when the subordinate clause comes first.

> If the bowl is greasy, the egg whites will not stiffen.
> Because the lights were on, I assumed that he had paid his hydro bill.

27d ▪ Parenthetical Elements

Parenthetical elements are words or phrases that are not essential to the grammar of the sentence in which they appear, although they may be essential to its meaning.

Adverbs and Adverbial Phrases Use commas to separate parenthetical adverbs and adverbial phrases from the rest of the sentence.

> Used-car dealers were, on the whole, regarded with some suspicion.
> The Etruscans, on the other hand, were not Indo-Europeans.
> Warts, however, are generally found on the hands and fingers.

Contradictory Phrases Use commas to separate contradictory phrases from the rest of the sentence.

> It was Erica, not Eric, who dropped the typewriter.
> Wash this garment with a mild soap, never a harsh detergent.

Direct Address and Interjections Use commas to separate names used in direct address or interjections such as *yes, no,* and *thank you* from the rest of the sentence.

> Tell me, Miss Perkins, why you find grammar irrelevant.
> Yes, insurance is expensive, but a lawsuit is much more expensive.

Tag Questions Use commas to separate tag questions from the rest of the sentence. (Tag questions consist of an auxiliary verb and a pronoun added to a declarative sentence.)

> You aren't going to use fishing line as dental floss, are you?

> It is true, is it not, that Canada imports all of its coffee?

Illustrative Words Use commas to separate words and abbreviations that introduce an example or a list of examples or illustrations, including *namely, that is, to wit, i.e., e.g., for example,* and *for instance.* Because the examples themselves are nonrestrictive appositives, they too are separated from the rest of the sentence by commas.

> Many French impressionists, for example, Renoir, Monet, and Cezanne, painted still lifes.
>
> The double bridle, that is, a snaffle and a curb bit, is standard for well-trained riding horses.

Exception Do not use a comma immediately after *such as* or *such . . . as.* A comma is optional before *such as* when it introduces a nonrestrictive modifier.

> Left-handed people have trouble using such implements as can openers, scissors, and spatulas.
>
> Our local company performs only popular operas, such as *La Bohème, Madame Butterfly*, and *Carmen.*

27e ▪ Restrictive and Nonrestrictive Modifiers

Nonrestrictive modifiers are not essential to the meaning of the sentence. (In the statement "John, *who is clever*, went to France" the modifier is not essential to the main idea that John when to France; it simply provides additional information.) **Restrictive modifiers** are essential to the meaning of the sentence. (In the statement "The man *who is clever* will succeed" the modifier limits the meaning; success will be determined by whether a man is clever.) (For a detailed discussion of restrictive and nonrestrictive modifiers, see 20d.)

Nonrestrictive Modifiers Use commas to separate nonrestrictive clauses, phrases, and appositives from the rest of the sentence. (See 14 for a discussion of appositives.)

NONRESTRICTIVE CLAUSES	Tamerlane, who was a descendant of Genghis Khan, united the Mongols.
	The tarantula, which is a large and hairy spider, can inflict a painful bite.
	The topic of conversation all evening was cattle breeding, about which I know nothing.
	He doesn't play golf, unless you call chopping up the turf "playing golf."
NONRESTRICTIVE PHRASES	The dessert, soaked in brandy and served flambé, was the high point of the meal.
	Joel's mittens, dangling by a cord from his sleeves, seemed to fascinate our cat.
	The scout leader, overweight and out of shape, trudged painfully up the slope.

NONRESTRICTIVE
APPOSITIVES

Tamerlane, <u>a descendant of Genghis Khan</u>, united the Mongols.

The choir sang an old hymn, <u>"Bringing in the Sheaves."</u>

He comes from Huacho, <u>a small town in Peru</u>.

Restrictive Modifiers Do not use commas to separate restrictive clauses, phrases, or appositives from the rest of the sentence.

RESTRICTIVE
CLAUSES

It was Tamerlane <u>who finally succeeded in uniting the Mongols</u>.

A tarantula <u>that is fully grown</u> may have a leg spread of twenty to twenty-two centimetres.

The cattle <u>that Mr. MacDougall sells</u> are all Aberdeen Angus.

He won't play golf <u>unless he knows he is better than his partners</u>.

RESTRICTIVE
PHRASES

Not everything <u>soaked in brandy</u> is cherries jubilee.

The cat was fascinated by the mittens <u>dangling from a cord on Joel's sleeves</u>.

I hate to see scout leaders <u>overweight and out of shape</u>.

RESTRICTIVE
APPOSITIVES

The Oriental conqueror <u>Tamerlane</u> was a descendant of Genghis Khan.

Andrew went to New York with his roommate <u>Jacques</u>.

p
27e

Exercises: Commas with Introductory, Parenthetical, and Nonrestrictive Elements

Correctly punctuate the following sentences by inserting commas where necessary to separate introductory components; parenthetical words, phrases, and clauses; and nonrestrictive words, phrases, and clauses.

1. Her neck on the other hand was loaded down with ornate chains that sparkled and glistened in the candlelight.
2. Mrs. Petrovitch who had lived in Toronto all her life moved to Victoria when she retired.
3. After Gutenberg's invention of movable type in the fifteenth century printing was easier and more efficient.
4. Her brother Rob was the only one of six sons to finish college.
5. Isadora Duncan one of the founders of modern dance was a controversial woman who rebelled against classical ballet in favor of natural movement.

6. After the development of photography in 1839 and the discovery of the photoengraving process in 1852 newspapers were able to offer their readers pictures of news-making people and events.
7. As day dawned, the sunlight shimmering on the water was mirrored in the bow of the yacht that was moored at Mr. Kleindienst's dock.
8. His reluctance to accept the award really only a ploy on his part to get a larger grant irritated the members who had voted for him and made them determined to select someone who would seem more grateful than he.
9. We want to find the current address of the Mrs. Petrovitch who used to live in Toronto.
10. Begun in 1702 by Elizabeth Mallett the first English daily newspaper was the London *Daily Courant*.

27f ▪ Conventional Uses

The comma has a number of conventional uses that are determined more by accepted current practice than by grammatical logic.

Direct Quotations Use a comma to separate direct quotations from the phrase identifying the speaker.

> Samuel Butler said, " 'Tis better to have loved and lost than never to have lost at all."

> "You must fill out the application in quintuplicate," the person at the desk told me.

> "Well," she sighed, "I suppose I'll have to change the tire myself."

Do not use a comma if *that* precedes a direct quotation.

> Alexander Pope said that "an honest man's the noblest work of God," to which Samuel Butler replied, "An honest God's the noblest work of man."

Geographic Units Use commas to separate the names of smaller geographic units from the names of the larger units within which they are contained. Most writers prefer a comma after the name of the last geographic unit also, when this last unit appears in the middle of a sentence.

> My summer address will be 77A Colinton Road, Edinburgh, Scotland.

> The residents of Aberdeen, Hong Kong, would find life very different in Aberdeen, Scotland.

In French-language addresses, the rule of separating smaller geographic units from larger is carried to its logical extreme by using a comma between the street number and the street name.

> Send your reply to Denise DaJoie, 1234 est, rue Jean Talon, Montréal, Québec H2E 1S3

p
27f

Note No comma is used between the name of the province and the postal code, but an extra space is often left between the two in running text. If the code is typed on a separate line (as Canada Post prefers on envelopes), no punctuation is needed.

Oxford, England OX1 3B0   St. John's, Newfoundland A1B 3Z6

Missoula, Montana 59801   St. John's Newfoundland
                                              A1B 3Z6

Dates In dates, if the order is month–day–year, use commas to separate the day from the year. If the date appears in the middle of the sentence, use another comma after the year.

Harry was born on July 17, 1946, in a small town in upstate New York.

If the order is day–month–year, no commas are used.

The installation officially closed on 17 July 1946.

If only the month and year are given, the comma is optional.

We visited Lima in December 1972.

We visited Lima in December, 1972.

Titles and Degrees Use commas to separate names from titles or degrees that follow the name.

Elizabeth II, Queen of England

Cornelia P. Anderson, D.D.S.

Joe Clark, former leader of Canada's conservative party

Arthur Schlesinger, Jr.

Use no comma if the title precedes the name. Use no punctuation before a Roman numeral or an ordinal number used to differentiate persons or vehicles with the same name.

Her Majesty Queen Elizabeth II   Prime Minister Thatcher

Pope John XXIII   *Mariner III*

James Parker IV   Henry the Eighth

Numbers Use commas to separate digits by thousands when writing numbers over 999. Starting from the right, place a comma between every three-numeral group and the next numeral.

7,519,453   72,735

In strict metric usage, a space replaces the comma, and four-digit groups are kept closed unless they must align with five-digit groups. Some writers who are not using metric conventions also close four-digit numbers.

7 519 453   72 735   7146

Whichever convention you choose for large numbers must be used consistently throughout a given paper.

Note If you use French-language reference material, you will encounter a conventional use of periods and commas that is the reverse of English usage. Most Francophones use a comma to indicate a decimal point and periods to break large numbers into three-digit groups. This usage is so confusing to most Anglophone readers (is 7.343,245 slightly more than seven thousand or slightly more than seven?) that you should convert it to English or metric usage even in direct quotations.

Do not use commas to separate numbers in identification numbers, postal codes, telephone numbers, English-language street addresses, or years. Do not use commas to separate numerals after a decimal point.

Serial No. 863219677   19349 Crestwood Blvd.

Dorval, P.Q. H9P 2R2   2500 B.C.

Tel. 463–8750 π = 3.14159

Salutations and Complimentary Closings Use a comma after the salutation in informal writing and after the complimentary closing of a letter. (In formal letters, a colon is often used instead of a comma after the salutation; see 29d.)

Dear Ms. Peabody,   Sincerely,

Dear Alice,   Love,

Dear Mrs. Olsen:

p
27g

27g · Clarity

Use a comma to provide clarity and prevent misreading, even when none of the preceding rules applies.

To the young, blood pudding may not be appealing food. (Without the comma, the reader may at first interpret this as *To the young blood, pudding. . . .*)

We left him, assured that he would succeed. (*We* knew that he would succeed.)

We left him assured that he would succeed. (*He* knew that he would succeed.)

Omitted Words Commas are often used to mark allowable omissions of repeated words, especially verbs. Here the comma, like an apostrophe within a word, marks the point where the omission is made.

Your analysis is superb; your execution, appalling.

Marjorie was knitting a sweater; Paul, an afghan.

Consecutively Repeated Words   Commas are used to separate two or three consecutive occurrences of the same word within a sentence.

And still I cried, cried until my eyes were swollen and my nose was red.

What that is, is an anteater.

Rain, rain, rain—doesn't the sun ever shine around here?

Exercises: Other Uses of Commas

Correctly punctuate the following sentences by inserting commas as needed.

1. "It was Jonas not Sam who made the error" Mr. Quarles snapped.
2. "If she is really my friend" said Juanita "she won't hesitate to lend me the money."
3. Most leafy green vegetables for example turnip and collard greens, kale, and spinach, have few calories but supply large amounts of iron and vitamins.
4. "As of June 1 1978 your company's assets totaled $30 114 940.88," the auditor said.
5. When his girlfriend came by, Fred asked her in in spite of his mother's objections.
6. Luigi your three favorite dishes are chop suey ham and eggs and lasagna aren't they?
7. The cheque was sent to Loren Robertson M.D., whose office address is 2664 Dresden Avenue Winnipeg Manitoba R3C 3T1.
8. Some names of animals for instance *turkey*, *cat*, and *bull*, have enriched North American slang.

27h ▪ Superfluous Commas

The elements of a basic declarative sentence have the order adjective–subject–verb–complement (or direct object). This order represents the natural flow of an English sentence. The flow is interrupted if commas appear between any two of these elements.

Adjective and Noun or Pronoun   Do not use a comma to separate an adjective from the noun or pronoun it modifies.

INCORRECT   Solving differential equations can be a difficult and time-consuming, task.

CORRECT   Solving differential equations can be a difficult and time-consuming task.

Subject and Verb Do not use a comma to separate a subject (unless it is followed by a nonrestrictive element) from its verb.

INCORRECT	Delegates and newspaper reporters, crowded into the hall.
CORRECT	Delegates and newspaper reporters crowded into the hall.
CORRECT	Delegates and newspaper reporters, who had been waiting an hour for the doors to open, crowded into the hall.
INCORRECT	Using gasoline to light the logs in a fireplace, is inadvisable.
CORRECT	Using gasoline to light the logs in a fireplace is inadvisable.

Verb and Complement or Direct Object Do not use a comma to separate a verb from its complement or direct object.

INCORRECT	Brass is, an alloy made of copper and zinc.
CORRECT	Brass is an alloy made of copper and zinc.
INCORRECT	Charles Babbage set out to build, a calculating machine.
CORRECT	Charles Babbage set out to build a calculating machine.

Verb and Subordinate Clause Do not use a comma to separate the verb from the subordinate clause in indirect quotations or indirect questions. In such cases, the clause is actually the direct object of the verb. Thus, this rule is only a variation of the preceding rule.

INCORRECT	Marianne said, that she wanted to live in Copenhagen.
CORRECT	Marianne said that she wanted to live in Copenhagen.
INCORRECT	The landlord asked, if I had run out of cheques.
CORRECT	The landlord asked if I had run out of cheques.

Correlative Conjunctions Do not use a comma to separate sentence elements connected by the correlative conjunctions *so . . . that, as . . . as, more . . . than, both . . . and, either . . . or,* and *neither . . . nor.*

INCORRECT	Scott was so distracted, that he forgot to put on his hairpiece.
CORRECT	Scott was so distracted that he forgot to put on his hairpiece.

p
27h

| INCORRECT | Passengers receive neither gracious, nor competent service. |
| CORRECT | Passengers receive neither gracious nor competent service. |

Exercises: Comma Review

Correctly punctuate the following passage with commas.

Banking is not a modern innovation for records show that a crude form of banking existed by 2000 B.C. The Babylonians the Greeks of classical times the Egyptians and the Romans deposited valuables in temples and rudimentary banks. However it was only with the establishment of the Banco di Rialto in Venice in 1587 that modern banking really began. The term *bank* itself derives from the Italian *banco* a word meaning "bench" because the early bankers did their business at benches in the streets.

After 1500 something similar to the modern cheque appeared and in the seventeenth century English goldsmiths began to issue bank notes that came to be accepted almost universally as money. The cheque and the bank note having been developed the first clearinghouse was established in London in 1670 and the Bank of England in 1694. Branch banking another development associated with modern practices began in Scotland at this time too.

Banking in North America did not develop until a full century later. The Bank of North America the first bank in the United States was begun with the aid of the Continental Congress which needed a bank to help finance the American Revolution. Developing quickly after the founding of the Bank of Massachusetts in 1784 banks in the United States now number in the hundreds.

Canada which now has twelve chartered banks saw a slower growth. Although several attempts were made to establish banks the first permanent banking institution the Bank of Montreal was not formed until 1817. Canada's first bank of discount and deposit it was also the first to issue domestic currency. This bank and others founded soon after followed directly the charter of the Bank of the United States planned by Alexander Hamilton the first secretary of the treasury of the United States. In fact the Canadian banking system is a direct descendant—the only surviving one—of the first bank of the United States. (There are however tremendous differences between today's charters and the original.)

In the twentieth century banking changed in both countries. Bank crises in Canada in 1923 and in the United States in 1933 led to tightening of bank policies government inspection and insurance of banks; the Americans also put strict curbs on branch banking in many jurisdictions and sharply reduced the number of banks. Today's modern commercial banks provide security and service to all parts of the community.

**p
27h**

28 ![owl icon] Semicolons (;)

Use a Semicolon

- Between main clauses without a co-ordinating conjunction
- Between word groups already containing commas

The **semicolon** is a useful supplement to the comma and the period, intermediate in force between the weaker comma and the stronger period. The semicolon is used only between elements of equal rank.

Often the choice among comma and conjunction, semicolon, and period and new sentence is determined by the pace you want to establish. A comma and a conjunction provide the most rapid pace.

> Hopi women own the houses and fields, and Hopi men are the priests and leaders of the community.

A semicolon is slower.

> Hopi women own the houses and fields; Hopi men are the priests and leaders of the community.

A period together with a new sentence is slowest of all.

> Hopi women own the houses and fields. Hopi men are the priests and leaders of the community.

p
28

28a ▪ Main Clauses

Often two main clauses are so closely related that they should be included within one sentence. If no co-ordinating conjunction seems appropriate, or if the use of a co-ordinating conjunction would make the sentence ramble, the semicolon is the proper mark.

Note how the use of separate sentences produces a choppy, disjointed effect in the following two examples.

> The electrocardiograph records heartbeats and their variations. It can also be used to examine nerves and muscles.

> In his *Diary*, Samuel Pepys was extraordinarily frank about his personal and public affairs. John Evelyn's *Diary* is less intimate.

On the other hand, using simple co-ordination to connect the two parts of these sentences is also unsatisfactory. Because the two main clauses are not parallel, simple co-ordination produces a loose, rambling effect.

> The electrocardiograph records heartbeats and their variations, and it can also be used to examine nerves and muscles.

> In his *Diary*, Samuel Pepys was extraordinarily frank about his personal and public affairs, but John Evelyn's *Diary* is less intimate.

But a semicolon connects the two closely related clauses of each sentence without creating either a choppy or a rambling effect. This use of the semicolon is also one of the most effective ways of avoiding a comma splice (see 27a).

> The electrocardiograph records heartbeats and their variations; it can also be used to examine nerves and muscles.

> In his *Diary*, Samuel Pepys was extraordinarily frank about his personal and public affairs; John Evelyn's *Diary* is less intimate.

28b ▪ Co-ordinating Conjunctions

A semicolon is sometimes used before a co-ordinating conjunction if the first clause is very long and already contains commas as internal punctuation.

> After hitch-hiking for six hours in the blistering sunshine, we began to look for a hotel in the busy town of Aix in Provence; but there were no rooms available, and we had to go all the way to Marseilles to find a place to stay.

Short clauses connected by a co-ordinating conjunction should be separated by a comma, not a semicolon.

> INCORRECT   Ask me no questions; and I'll tell you no lies.

> REVISED   Ask me no questions, and I'll tell you no lies.

28c ▪ Conjunctive Adverbs

Just as a semicolon is used to join two main clauses without a co-ordinate conjunction, so it is used to join two main clauses with a conjunctive adverb. Conjunctive adverbs, such as *then, however, therefore, in addition, on the other hand, nevertheless,* and *fortunately,* often express the exact relationship between the two main clauses. (See the more extensive list in 9c.) A semicolon between the clauses emphasizes the relationship of the ideas.

When conjunctive adverbs are used with a semicolon, it follows the first main clause. If the conjunctive adverb is the first word or phrase of the second clause, it is followed by a comma.

> Father was cooking kidney stew; <u>therefore</u>, I decided to spend the day outdoors.

> Father was cooking kidney stew; <u>in addition</u>, the drain in the upstairs bath had backed up.

> Father was cooking kidney stew; <u>nevertheless</u>, I decided to hold a wine-tasting party that afternoon.

Punctuate carefully with these adverbs. Because they are not true conjunctions, they require a semicolon or period rather than a comma.

INCORRECT   Father was cooking kidney stew, <u>however</u>, no one was willing to eat it.

REVISED   Father was cooking kidney stew; <u>however</u>, no one was willing to eat it.

Note   When a conjunctive adverb is used within a clause, commas must set off the adverb from the rest of the clause. (See 27d for punctuation with parenthetical elements.)

Father, however, was determined to cook kidney stew again.

28d ▪ Separation of Word Groups

Use a semicolon to separate word groups when the elements of each are already separated by commas or other marks or punctuation.

The most common home knitting yarns are worsted, a heavy four-ply yarn used for outer garments; sport yarn, an intermediate-weight yarn; and fingering yarn, a light yarn often used for infants' clothing.

Participating in the Third Crusade were Philip Augustus, king of France; Richard I (Richard the Lion-hearted), king of England; and Frederick Barbarossa, Holy Roman emperor.

28e ▪ Superfluous Semicolons

p
28e

Once writers have discovered the semicolon, they may be tempted to overuse it or to misuse it. In general, avoid using the semicolon unless you are sure it is appropriate. Unlike the comma, the semicolon can be successfully avoided by the uncertain writer. The most common errors in the use of semicolons involve placing one where a comma or a colon would be appropriate.

With Elements of Unequal Rank   Do not use a semicolon between sentence elements of unequal rank (for example, between a dependent and an independent clause or between a modifier and the word or phrase it modifies).

INCORRECT   Although he was married to Hera; Zeus was not exactly a monogamist.

REVISED   Although he was married to Hera, Zeus was not exactly a monogamist.

INCORRECT   Vitamin C is unstable in solution; especially under alkaline conditions.

REVISED   Vitamin C is unstable in solution, especially under alkaline conditions.

With Direct Quotations Do not use a semicolon before a direct quotation. (See 27f for punctuation of direct quotations.)

INCORRECT	My mother said; "Close your mouth when you're eating."
REVISED	My mother said, "Close your mouth when you're eating."

With Listings or Summaries Do not use a semicolon before a listing or summary statement. (See 29b and 30b for punctuation of listings or summary statements.)

INCORRECT	Please bring the following; sleeping bag, tarpaulin, day pack, extra socks.
REVISED	Please bring the following: sleeping bag, tarpaulin, day pack, extra socks.
REVISED	Please bring a sleeping bag, tarpaulin, day pack, and extra socks.
INCORRECT	Aching muscles, sore feet, insect bites; these are the pleasures of hiking.
REVISED	Aching muscles, sore feet, insect bites—these are the pleasures of hiking.

p
28e

Exercises: Semicolons

Correctly punctuate the following sentences by replacing commas with semicolons wherever necessary.

1. George immediately introduced his crew of helpers: Caroline Serfis, a high school student, Dan Rossi, an unemployed painter, Sam DeKay, a fireman, and Muriel Brun, a former discotheque owner.
2. Charles has only one interest in life, consequently, I sometimes get tired of listening to tall tales about fishing expeditions.
3. Although French became the official language of England in 1066, Old English was still spoken by the common people, therefore, many words for basic goods and services remained English, while most legal, political, and artistic terms were replaced with French words.
4. The anaconda, a snake that entwines and strangles birds and small mammals with its body, grows to at least six and often to nine metres in length, in fact, it is the largest snake found in South America.
5. Golf developed in Scotland about 1100, nevertheless, it was banned in Scotland in the fifteenth century by James II because sportsmen were abandoning archery.

29 🦉 Colons (:)

Use a Colon

- Between general and specific main clauses
- Before listings and series
- Before long quotations
- In Biblical citations
- In time expressions
- With rhymes and grammatical forms

The **colon** is a strong mark of punctuation, as strong as the period. However, whereas the period tends to cut off one sentence from another, the colon points forward and indicates that the following material is closely related to the preceding material.

29a ▪ Main Clauses

A colon may be used to separate two main clauses if the second clause develops, details, or amplifies the first clause. The first clause is usually general; the second, specific. When a colon is used this way, it substitutes for such words as *namely*, *for example*, and *that is* or for the abbreviations *e.g.* or *i.e.* Hence a colon should not be used with these terms. Capitalization of the first word of a complete sentence after a colon is optional, though lower case is more common in Canadian usage.

> Marvin never forgot his manners: when his wife left him, he opened the door for her.
>
> There is only one solution: Drunken drivers must go to jail.

29b ▪ Listings and Series

A colon is often used to set off a listing or series of items, especially a listing introduced by the words *the following* or *as follows.*

> The poisonous species of the area are the following: scorpions, black widows, brown recluse spiders, tarantulas, conenose bugs, velvet ants, wasps, hornets, and bees.
>
> There are many kinds of needlework: knitting, crochet, embroidery, macramé, and so forth.

Note   A colon should be used only when the first clause is grammatically complete. Do not use a colon between a verb and its complement or its object, or between a preposition and its object.

p
29

INCORRECT	The most important monetary units of the world are: the dollar, pound, franc, mark, ruble, and yen.
CORRECT	The most important monetary units of the world are the dollar, pound, franc, mark, ruble, and yen.
INCORRECT	Jim is allergic to: feathers, dust, cat dander, and pollen.
CORRECT	Jim is allergic to feathers, dust, cat dander, and pollen.

29c ▪ Long Quotations

Although short quotations and dialogue are normally introduced by commas, a colon is often used before a long quotation if the clause preceding the quotation is grammatically complete.

> The preamble to Britain's Bill of Rights (1689) is written in lofty seventeenth-century prose: "Whereas the Lords Spiritual and Temporal, and Commons, assembled at Westminster, lawfully, fully, and freely representing all the Estates of the People of this Realm. . . ."

29d ▪ Conventional Uses

p
29d

In addition to its use as a grammatical signal indicating a close relationship between two elements of a sentence, the colon has a number of conventional uses.

Biblical Citations Use a colon between chapter and verse in citations from the Bible. (Periods may also be used for this purpose. See 24b.)

> John 3:16

Time Expressions Use a colon between hours and minutes in expressions of time.

> 05:43   17:06 (nonmetric: 5.43 A.M., 5:06 P.M.)

Salutations A colon is often used (instead of a comma) after the salutation in formal letters.

> Dear Dr. Ernst:

Rhymes and Grammatical Forms Use a colon between rhymes or to indicate a relationship between grammatical forms. (The slash is also appropriate in these uses.)

| RHYMES | moon : June |
| RELATED FORMS | go : went : gone |

Exercises: Colons

Correctly punctuate the following sentences with colons, replacing commas and semicolons wherever necessary.

1. A beginning carpenter needs six basic tools, a hammer, a handsaw, a screwdriver, pliers, a T square, and a vise.
2. Without consulting his son, Jim's father had completely planned the future, Jim would attend his former law school, marry a socialite, and become an influential and wealthy corporation lawyer.
3. The worst calamity in the town's history stuck at 10 28, a tornado ripped through the downtown area, killing 120 people and levelling 40 stores.
4. The answer to your problem is easy, get a better-paying job.

30  Dashes (—)

Use a Dash
- Around parenthetical statements
- Before summary statements
- In dialogue for interrupted speech

In most of its uses, the **dash** serves as an informal and usually more emphatic substitute for some other mark of punctuation—a comma, a colon, a semicolon, or parentheses. Properly used, the dash adds variety and lightness to writing; improperly used or overused, it gives the impression that the writer is flighty or disorganized. Use the dash, but sparingly, and not as a substitute for clear thinking and well-constructed sentences.

If the material to be set off by a dash occurs at the end of sentence, use one dash. But if the material occurs within the sentence, use a dash both before and after the inserted material. (See Appendix F for instructions on typing the dash.)

p
30

30a ▪ Parenthetical Statements

Use a dash to mark a sharp break in the thought or syntax of a sentence or to insert a parenthetical statement into a sentence. Sometimes the material set off by dashes is an appositive.

BREAK IN THOUGHT
    We were asked—well, actually we were told—to pick up our belongings and leave.

    The Dark Ages—though the term is really a misnomer—lasted from the fall of Rome until the eleventh century.

APPOSITIVE   *The Cyclops*—a drama first produced about 44
                B.C.—is a burlesque of Homer's story about Odys-
                seus and Polyphemus.

The dash should not be treated as a mark of desperation to be used
whenever the syntax of a sentence has gotten out of hand. In such cases,
rewrite the entire sentence to untangle the syntax.

TANGLED   It is interesting to speculate that human beings may
SYNTAX   start a new life on another celestial body, but certain
                things need to be given priority—such as the lives of
                humans on earth and the conditions in which they
                live—before governments allocate funds for plane-
                tary exploration and settlement.

IMPROVED   It is interesting to speculate that human beings may
                start a new life on another celestial body. However,
                in the allocation of funds, improvement of living
                conditions on earth should have priority over plane-
                tary exploration and settlement.

30b · Summary Statements

Before a summary statement and after an introductory list, the dash can
be used as an informal substitute for a colon.

"Penny-wise and pound-foolish," "Better late than never," "The
early bird gets the worm"—all of us have heard these proverbs.

Biology, chemistry, calculus—these courses are familiar to premedi-
cal students.

30c · Dialogue

In dialogue, use a dash to indicate hesitant or interrupted speech.

"To tell you the truth, I—we—aren't interested."

"He is a complete idi—uh—he's been acting rather foolishly."

31 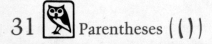 Parentheses (( ))

Use Parentheses
- Around nonessential information
- Around numbers or letters of enumeration

Parentheses (singular: parenthesis), commas, and dashes are all used
to enclose nonessential elements. However, parentheses are normally
used to set off material less essential than that set off by commas.
Whereas dashes emphasize the point and attract the attention of the

reader, parentheses de-emphasize and minimize the importance of the enclosed material. Parentheses are also more formal than dashes.

Parentheses, unlike commas and dashes, always occur in pairs. If the material enclosed within the parentheses forms a complete sentence and is not inserted within another sentence, the first word should be capitalized, and final punctuation (period, question mark, exclamation point) should be placed inside the closing parenthesis.

> Bake the chicken in a 180°C (350°F) oven for at least an hour. (Be sure to preheat the oven for fifteen minutes.)

Otherwise, the first word is not capitalized, and final punctuation, if any, follows the closing parenthesis, as in the following example:

> If the drumstick moves easily in your hand (you can test either drumstick), the chicken is done.

31a ▪ Nonessential Information

Use parentheses to enclose nonessential information, "asides," minor digressions, amplifications, or explanations. If the parenthetical information is lengthy, consider putting it into a footnote instead of including it in the main text.

> Definitions are given in Part 2 (pp. 75–154).
>
> Frédéric Chopin spent a winter (1838–39) on the island of Majorca.
>
> Dijon, France (pop. 156 787), is famous throughout the world for its mustard.
>
> Endive (the word is ultimately Egyptian in origin) is a variety of chicory.
>
> In preparing this survey, the author interviewed over two hundred individuals. (Their names are listed in Appendix 10.)

31b ▪ Numerals and Letters

Use parentheses to enclose the numerals or letters that number the items in a series.

> Some common taboos involve names of (1) deities, (2) wild animals, (3) parts of the body, (4) relatives, (5) bodily functions, and (6) death.

32 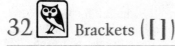 Brackets ([ ])

Use Brackets

- For editorial comments
- As parentheses within parentheses

The use of **brackets** is highly restricted, and brackets should be considered a supplement to parentheses, not a substitute for them.

p
32

32a ▪ Editorial Comments

Use brackets to enclose your own comments within a quotation from another writer. The two most common reasons for inserting your own editorial comments into a quotation are (1) to indicate that an error occurs in the original and (2) to fill in information when the quotation might otherwise be unclear or misleading. The conventional way of indicating an error in the original is to insert the bracketed Latin word [*sic*] (meaning "thus") into the quotation directly after the error.

> "In the months that followed, Napoleon's army continued the long siege of Moskow [*sic*], making the Russians very uneasy. In November, they were driven to foraging for potatoes in the frozen earth."

Here, the use of [*sic*] shows that the misspelling of *Moscow* appears in the original. Note that the word *sic* should be italicized (underlined).

To clarify a quotation for the reader, insert the necessary material in brackets at an appropriate place in the quotation. In the sentence below, the bracketed material indicates the referent of the pronoun *they*.

> "In November, they [Napoleon's forces] were driven to foraging for potatoes in the frozen earth."

32b ▪ Parentheses Within Parentheses

Brackets serve as parentheses within parentheses. However, be sparing in such piling up of parentheses because they tend to clutter up the sentence and distract the reader. The information in brackets can often be put into a footnote and the use of brackets avoided.

> Henri Bergson takes quite a different approach to the question (*Creative Evolution* [New York: Modern Library, 1944], chap. 4).

p
32b

Exercises: Dashes, Parentheses, and Brackets

Correctly punctuate the following sentences with dashes, parentheses, and brackets.

1. The new hospital administration has called for 1 the expansion of the central facility to 400 beds it now has 290, 2 the addition of an emergency room, 3 the hiring of an additional 35 nurses, and 4 the purchase of new equipment.
2. The satisfaction of printing her name all by herself for the very first time, her first acquaintance with the seashore, the arrival of her baby brother, her first trip on an airplane these scenes were indelibly pressed into Matilda's mind.
3. The fearsome Attila the Hun A.D. 406?–453 first invaded the Eastern Roman Empire and then pushed into France.
4. Douglas Greenwood's book *Who's Buried Where in England* New York: Academic Press, 1983 is a curiosity.

5. When he got home, Joe found Trip's toys six stuffed animals, a wagon, several cars, and what seemed like a million building blocks all over the living room.

6. A recent article in the local newspaper stated, "The town ranks first in the West in garft *sic* among municipal officials, and citizens who are aware of the corruption are too frightened to try to stop it."

7. Spiders, snakes, swinging bridges, and thunderstorms these have been objects of fear to Ivan since his childhood.

---

33 Quotation Marks (" ")

Use Quotation Marks
- Around direct quotations
- Around titles of shorter works
- Around words used in a special sense

Quotation marks are visual cues that isolate one group of words in a text from another group. The isolated groups may be the exact words of a speaker or writer, titles of various kinds, or words used in a special sense. Quotation marks always occur in pairs; do not forget to include the closing quotation marks when you quote directly.

p
33

33a ▪ Direct Quotations

Use quotation marks for direct quotation of the exact words of a speaker or writer. The name of the speaker or writer and the word *said* (or its equivalent) are for identification and are not enclosed within the quotation marks.

> Joel Chandler Harris said, "Licker talks mightly loud w'en it git loose fum de jug."

1. If the total quotation is split by the identification phrase, both parts are enclosed in quotation marks, and the first half of the quotation is followed by a comma.

> "I'm ready whenever you are," said Martha, "but don't let me rush you."

2. If each part of the quotation forms a complete sentence, the identification phrase is followed by a period, and the second part of the quotation begins with a capital letter.

> "Many hands make light work," declared Paul. "On the other hand, too many cooks spoil the broth."

3. In recording direct quotations, a question mark or an exclamation point appears directly after the question or exclamation to which it applies, even if the total sentence has not yet ended. No comma is used.

"Where have you hidden my sunglasses?" he asked irritably.
"The sky is falling!" cried Chicken Little.

4. In reporting the dialogue of more than one speaker, new quotation marks and a new paragraph are used every time the speaker changes.

"We'll reach Istanbul by tonight," Jim said.
"Istanbul!" exclaimed Sara. "We haven't even reached Belgrade."
"We'll make it if you don't insist on stopping every fifteen minutes."
"I'm not the one who wants to stop all the time."

5. If the words of a single speaker or writer involve more than one paragraph, opening quotation marks are placed at the beginning of each new paragraph, but closing quotation marks appear only at the end of the entire quotation.

"Simple. Here is your basic pantsuit. Take off the blouse, add a vest and you're ready for polo. Take off the slacks, put on the shorts and you're dressed for bicycling. Zip the lining into the shorts, add the halter and it's a bathing suit. Take the straps off the halter and it's a bra. Add a short skirt and you're ready for tennis.

"Now, turn the blouse inside out and it's a bathrobe. Turn down the cuffs on the slacks, take the belt off the overblouse and you're in your jammies."
Erma Bombeck, *If Life Is a Bowl of Cherries—What Am I Doing in the Pits?*

6. When it is necessary to have quotation marks within a quotation, single quotation marks are used. On the typewriter, the apostrophe serves as a single quotation mark.

Tylor reports, "The phrase 'raising the wind' now passes as humorous slang, but it once, in all seriousness, described one of the most dreaded of the sorcerer's arts."

33b ▪ Long Quotations

Relatively long quotations (more than four or five lines of prose or more than three lines of poetry) should be blocked, that is, separated from the main body of the text. Begin on a new line, indent the quoted material an extra paragraph indentation, and single-space the text of the quotation. (The *MLA Handbook* recommends double-spacing of indented quotations in manuscripts to be sent to publishers.) Do not enclose the quoted material in quotation marks; the material has been sufficiently set off by the indentation and single-spacing. Use a colon at the end of identifying phrases such as "The author says."

In his essay "The English Renaissance," L. M. Myers
says:

> It is a very curious fact that we seem to regard the
> roots and prefixes of Greek and Latin as the natural
> building blocks of new words, to be used with com-
> plete freedom, but are extremely conservative about
> making any combination with their English equiva-
> lents that are not already authorized by the dic-
> tionary. In this respect English is in strong con-
> trast with German, which still compounds native
> elements so freely that no dictionary pretends to
> list all of the legitimate combinations.

Not everyone would agree with Myers' conclusions, however. . . .

If the quotation is not preceded by such an identifying phrase, you can
simply end the preceding sentence with a period.

L. M. Myers believes that English no longer makes compounds out of native elements.

It is a very curious fact that . . .

33c · Titles

Use quotation marks to enclose the titles of shorter works of art or of
works that form part of a larger work. (A "shorter" poem is one that is
not divided into numbered parts, books, cantos, or the like.)

ARTICLES	"The Blossoms of Spring"
ESSAYS	"Philosophic Ants"
SHORT STORIES	"Polikushka"
CHAPTERS OF BOOKS	"White Dwarfs and the Dying Sun"
SHORT POEMS	"To a Waterfowl"
SHORT MUSICAL PIECES	"Drink to Me Only with Thine Eyes"

The titles of motion pictures, radio or television programs, paintings, and
sculptures are often enclosed in quotation marks. Some prefer, however,
to italicize (underline) these titles. Whichever you choose, be consistent
and *never* use both quotation marks and italics.

MOTION PICTURES	"How the West Was Won" (or *How the West Was Won*)
RADIO OR TELEVISION PROGRAMS	"Masterpiece Theatre" (or *Masterpiece Theatre*) "As It Happens" (or *As It Happens*)

PAINTINGS   "View of Delft" (or *View of Delft*)

STATUES   "Family Group" (or *Family Group*)

Titles of unpublished works, such as doctoral dissertations, are always enclosed in quotation marks, regardless of the length of the work.

33d ▪ Special Uses of Words

Use quotation marks with words being used in special ways, including:

1. An unconventional context or unusual meaning.

To Edgar, an "ancient" author is one who wrote before 1960.

2. Potentially confusing technical terms.

Proofreaders may have to "copyfit" their corrections.

3. Coined words.

The children spent their summer in an extended "hikeathon."

4. Words used to refer to themselves. (Some writers prefer to italicize words used as words.)

The word "very" is often overused.

Some writers use quotations marks to enclose slang or colloquial expressions that are included in a piece of more formal writing.

Several customers complained that they had been "ripped off."

Modern practice, however, tends to regard such use of quotation marks as overly apologetic, and hence they are often omitted. Effective slang is part of an author's style, and quotation marks should not single the slang out for special attention. In any case, slang expressions and colloquialisms, with or without quotation marks, should be used sparingly, or they will lose their effectiveness. It is usually best to rewrite the sentence, substituting another word or term that is less slangy.

Several customers complained that they had been cheated.

33e ▪ Superfluous Quotation Marks

By convention, quotation marks are not used with certain kinds of titles and quotations.

Titles Do not use quotation marks to surround the name of the Bible or parts or all of any sacred works. Do not use quotation marks to enclose mottoes or signs. Do not use quotation marks around the names of catalogues, directories, and political documents. (See also 36e, "Superfluous Italics.")

SACRED WORKS	Bible, Ecclesiastes, Talmud, Upanishads, Hail Mary, The Lord's Prayer, Nicene Creed
MOTTOES	In God We Trust, Remember the Alamo
SIGNS	No Smoking, Right Turn on Red
CATALOGUES AND DIRECTORIES	the Dominion Seed Catalogue, the Calgary Telephone Directory
POLITICAL DOCUMENTS	British North America Act, Magna Carta, Statute of Westminster, Gettysburg Address, Treaty of Utrecht, Commu-munist Manifesto

Do not use quotation marks around the title at the top of a paper or on the title page. But do use quotation marks if the exact title appears within the text.

He wrote a paper entitled "Extinct Animal Species."

Do not use quotation marks to enclose the titles of longer written works or works of art. (See 36 on italics.)

INCORRECT	She claims to have read "Paradise Lost" four times.
CORRECT	She claims to have read *Paradise Lost* four times.

Indirect Quotations Do not use quotation marks to enclose indirect quotations.

INCORRECT	Elinor said that "she hated to sew on name tapes."
CORRECT	Elinor said that she hated to sew on name tapes.
CORRECT	Elinor said, "I hate to sew on name tapes."

p
33e

Nicknames Do not use quotation marks to enclose familiar nicknames.

King Richard the Lion-hearted	my old friend Alex
Dief the Chief	the Lady with the Lamp

Exercises: Quotation Marks

Correctly punctuate the following sentences with quotation marks, adding periods, commas, question marks, and exclamation points where they are necessary. Adjust capitalization as necessary.

1. Don't you just love the songs from *Annie*, especially Tomorrow Joyce asked Louise
2. What you say isn't necessarily true argued Ernest if you will read Wednesday's editorial in the *Globe and Mail*, Strategy for the Middle East, I think you will see the errors in your reasoning

3. My teacher said we have to learn the new words for O Canada and know for tomorrow the chief points of the Bill of Rights passed in Parliament in 1960 Mark complained to his mother.
4. All night long I kept dreaming about being in a dark forest Celeste told her roommate at breakfast and that song Who's Afraid of the Big Bad Wolf? kept running through my head
5. Just wait here, Sir said the receptionist Mr. Jenkins is with a client.
6. Looking at these beautiful Greek vases always makes me think of Keats's poem Ode on a Grecian Urn Gene said and I always go home from the museum and reread that poem

34 Apostrophes (')

Use an Apostrophe
- With possessives
- With contractions
- For special grammatical endings

p 34

The primary uses of the **apostrophe** are (1) to indicate the possessive forms of nouns and some pronouns and (2) to indicate missing letters or numbers. The apostrophe is also sometimes used to prevent misreading of special symbols being used as words.

34a ▪ Possessives

The apostrophe is used to indicate the possessive (genitive) form of both singular and plural nouns and of some singular pronouns. Even though you may see the apostrophe omitted from possessive nouns (on signs, in newspapers, etc.), do not omit it in your writing unless it is omitted in the official form of a proper name, such as Periodical Writers Association of Canada or Smiths Falls, Ontario.

Singular Nouns and Pronouns Use the apostrophe, followed by -*s*, to form the possessive of singular nouns and some indefinite pronouns.

one cent's worth	Thailand's rice crop
Girl Guide's badge	someone's hat
Montreal's taxes	nobody's business
Marge's handwriting	a day's work

Though practice varies with nouns that end in an *s* or *z* sound, it is never wrong to add -'*s* to these nouns. Always add -'*s* if you pronounce the possessive as a separate syllable. If the possessive does not form a separate syllable in speech or if the following word begins with an *s* sound, you can use just an apostrophe without an -*s*.

> the class's performance
> Yeats's life *or* Yeats' life
> Tacitus's description *or* Tacitus' description
> for goodness' sake
> Myers' study *or* Myers's study

Plural Nouns   Add just an apostrophe to form the possessive of regular plural nouns.

> five cents' worth
> the students' complaints
> the Browns' dog (More than one person named Brown is implied.)
> the soldiers' uniforms
> a mayors' conference (The conference is for several mayors.)
> three weeks' vacation

With irregular plural nouns (that is, those that do not add -*s* or -*es* to form their plurals), add -'*s* to form the possessive.

> children's playground   women's rights
> men's clothing   alumni's reunions

Joint Possession   To indicate joint possession, add -'*s* only to the last item.

> Beaumont and Fletcher's comedies (They wrote them together.)
> Janice and Larry's children (They have the same children.)

But to indicate individual possession, add -'*s* to each item.

> Mozart's and Haydn's sonatas (Mozart and Haydn did not write the sonatas together.)
>
> the men's and women's rooms (The men and women do not share the same rooms.)

Compound Nouns and Pronouns   With compound nouns and pronouns, add -'*s* to the last element.

> attorney general's office
> sister-in-law's recipes (recipes from one sister-in-law)
> sisters-in-law's recipes (recipes from more than one sister-in-law)
> nobody else's business

**p
34a**

Gerunds   A gerund is a noun made from a verb by adding *-ing*. The possessive should be used before gerunds just as before other nouns. (See also 20a for a discussion of possessives with gerunds.)

> Brian's joining the soccer team surprised his father.
> They resented the girls' winning the wrestling meet.

Double Possessives   The so-called double possessive involves both an *of* phrase and an *-'s*. It is normally used only when the possession being indicated is one among several such possessions, and it is used only when the possessor is human.

> Sloppiness was a fault of Harry's. (Harry had more than one fault.)
> The sloppiness was Harry's fault. (Only one fault is being mentioned.)

If in doubt about the use of a double possessive, test to see if you could rewrite the phrase using *one of*; if you can, the double possessive is appropriate.

> She wore an old dress of her aunt's. (She wore one of her aunt's old dresses.)
> Sloppiness was a fault of Harry's. (Sloppiness was one of Harry's faults.)
> The sloppiness was Harry's fault. (This does not mean the same as "The sloppiness was one of Harry's faults." Thus the double possessive should not be used.)

If you omit the double possessive when it is appropriate, your reader may misinterpret the sentence. For example, if you want to say that you took a picture that belongs to your mother, you need to use the double possessive.

> AMBIGUOUS   I took my mother's picture.
> CORRECT   I took a picture of my mother's.

Personal and Relative Pronouns   Do not use an apostrophe in forming the possessive of personal pronouns or relative pronouns.

INCORRECT	CORRECT
their's	theirs
our's	ours
who's	whose
it's	its
a friend of her's	a friend of hers

Be especially careful to distinguish *its* (belonging to *it*) from *it's (it is)* and *whose* (belonging to *whom*) from *who's (who is)*.

> INCORRECT   The cinnamon had lost it's flavor.
> CORRECT   The cinnamon had lost its flavor.

p
34a

INCORRECT	Who's snoring is the loudest?
CORRECT	Whose snoring is the loudest?

Titles Do not form the possessive of the titles of books, plays, and so on, by adding -'s. Instead, use an *of* phrase.

AWKWARD	*Twelfth Night*'s language
PREFERABLE	the language of *Twelfth Night*

34b · Contractions

Apostrophes often replace missing letters in words and missing numbers in dates.

Missing Letters Use the apostrophe to replace the missing letters in accepted contractions. Be sure to place the apostrophe at the point where the missing letter or letters would have appeared. (See also 43 for a discussion of contractions.)

don't	let's	he'll
they've	o'clock	she's
ma'am	you'd	shouldn't
we're	I'm	jack-o'-lantern

Do not use the apostrophe before clipped or abbreviated words that have become accepted as complete words in their own right. If in doubt, consult your dictionary.

INCORRECT	CORRECT
'plane	plane
'flu	flu
'phone	phone
'cab	cab

Missing Numbers In highly informal writing, the apostrophe is used to indicate the missing century in dates. In more formal writing, express the date in full.

INFORMAL	FORMAL
the class of '68	the class of 1968
the '54 hurricane	the 1954 hurricane
a '75 Chevy	a 1975 Chevrolet

Do not use the apostrophe with the hyphen in expressions of inclusive numbers (dates and pages).

INCORRECT	CORRECT
pp. 275–'76	pp. 275–76
1921–'24	1921–24

p
34b

34c · Special Grammatical Endings

Use the apostrophe to avoid confusion or misreading of grammatical endings (plural, past tense, past participle) added to letters, figures, acronyms, or symbols being used as nouns or verbs.

CONFUSING   His *is* can be mistaken for *1*s.

CLEAR   His *i*'s can be mistaken for *1*'s.

Similarly,

Mind your *p*'s and *q*'s.

This table omits the 0's before a decimal point.

There are more +'s than −'s.

He k.o.'d his opponent in the third round.

If there is no possibility of confusion, the apostrophe may be omitted.

Your 3s look like 5s.

Do not use the apostrophe in forming the plurals of regular nouns, proper names, numbers that are spelled out, or decades or centuries expressed in arabic numbers.

INCORRECT PLURALS	CORRECT PLURALS
business's	businesses
Brown's	Browns
eleven's	elevens
the 1950's	the 1950s
the 1800's	the 1800s

p
34c

Exercises: Apostrophes

Correct all errors involving the use of apostrophes in the following sentences.

1. The coach's facial muscles tightened as he watched the teams' top player fumble the ball for the third time in the season's first game.
2. "When you've learned your ABC's," Kate told her kid brother, "youl'l be one of the teacher's favorite students."
3. Germany and Japan's citizens quickly rebuilt their nation's economies after World War II's devastations.
4. My brother's-in-law firm just gave each of its' employee's five hundred dollar's worth of company stock and promised all of them three weeks' vacation next year.
5. "Whose been eating my porridge?" growled Papa Bear.
6. Its' never too late to learn, I know, but, on the other hand, the leopard can't change it's spots.
7. Do'nt forget to review pages 182–'97 before you're quiz on Adam Smiths economic theory.

8. That mistake was your's and nobody's else, and you've got to accept the consequences.
9. Camilla and Marie found *War and Peace*'s plot too complicated to follow on they're first reading.
10. Im surprised at the Fosters' having built such a high fence between the Tremblay's property and their's.

---

35 Hyphens (-)

Use a Hyphen
- For word division
- With certain prefixes and suffixes
- For clarity
- With certain compounds
- For inclusive dates and pages
- For spelled-out words

The most common functions of **hyphens** are to unite words divided between two lines and to bring together the separate words that make up compounds.

35a ▪ Word Division

Use a hyphen after the first part of a word divided between the end of one line and the beginning of the next line. Hyphenated words should be divided only between syllables. The dictionary is your guide to syllabication; the raised dot between letters in the dictionary entry indicates a syllable division. Because different dictionaries do not always agree, choose one dictionary as your authority and stick with it.

Never divide words that have only one syllable when spoken, no matter how long the words may be. Do not isolate a single letter, even if it forms a separate syllable. If the word to be divided already has a hyphen in its spelling, break it only at that hyphen. Do not hyphenate the last word on a page or the last word of a paragraph.

Avoid hyphenating personal names. Do not use a hyphen to separate numerals, contractions, acronyms, or abbreviations used with numerals.

INCORRECT	CORRECT
Richard Bak- er	Richard Baker
have- n't	haven't
UNES- CO	UNESCO
200- B.C.	200 B.C.
$23 100- 000	$23 100 000

35b ▪ Prefixes and Suffixes

Use a hyphen after some prefixes, such as *ex-*, *self-*, *all-*, *quasi-*, *half-*, and *quarter-*. Use a hyphen before the suffixes *-elect* and *-odd*, and between any prefix and a proper name. Check a Canadian dictionary (see 45b) and be consistent in your usage.

ex-sailor	secretary-elect	pseudo-French
all-encompassing	sixty-odd	anti-American
half-drunk		trans-Siberian
self-propelling		

35c ▪ Clarity

Use a hyphen within a word to prevent ambiguity or misreading and to avoid a double *i* or the same consonant three times in a row.

two-bit players (insignificant players)

two bit-players (two players with small roles)

re-cover ("to cover again"; used to avoid confusion with *recover* "to regain")

semi-industrial (not *semiindustrial*)

hull-less (not *hullless*)

Many but not all Canadians also use a hyphen to avoid a double *o* or a double *e*.

co-ordinate (or coordinate)	co-operate (or cooperate)
re-enter (or reenter)	pre-empt (or preempt)

35d ▪ Compounds

Accepted usage for the hyphenation of compound words changes fairly rapidly; the trend is toward writing formerly hyphenated compounds as single words without a hyphen. Choose one dictionary as your guide, use it faithfully, and be consistent.

Letters or Numerals Normally, a hyphen is used between the elements of a compound in which one element is a letter or numeral. But practice varies, and some compounds of this type are often written without a hyphen. Check your dictionary for specific items.

A-line	4-ply	E sharp
U-boat	DC-10	U-turn *or* U turn

p
35d

Compounds of Equal Weight   Use a hyphen to connect compounds in which the elements are of equal grammatical weight.

city-state   yellow-green

Oilers-Islanders game   Monday-Wednesday-Friday classes

soldier-statesman   man-eater

Compound Modifiers   Use a hyphen to connect compound modifiers when these modifiers appear *before* nouns, but do not hyphenate them when they follow nouns or when they are used adverbially.

a nineteenth-century novel   *but*   The novel was written in the nineteenth century

icy-cold water   *but*   The water was icy cold.

spur-of-the-moment decision   *but*   He decided on the spur of the moment.

across-the-board increases   *but*   Increases were granted across the board.

Do not hyphenate a compound modifier if the first word is an adverb ending in *-ly*, even when the modifier precedes the noun.

sorely needed improvements   fully annotated edition
rapidly growing cities   heavily perfumed women

Long Compound   If the compound is very long, quotation marks can be substituted for hyphens.

p
35d

an I-told-you-so expression on his face
an "I told you so" expression on his face

Place Names   Most multiple-word place names in Quebec take hyphens. So do some in English Canada.

Cap-St-Jacques   Trois-Rivières
St-Jean-Port-Joli   Notre-Dame-de-Bon-Conseil
Stanstead-Est   Niagara-on-the-Lake

Be careful with French place names outside Quebec. They may follow some or all the conventions of English punctuation.

St. Boniface, Manitoba   St-Laurent-Grandin, Saskatchewan
Petite Rivière, Nova Scotia   Sault Ste. Marie, Ontario

Note   A reliable reference in which to check the spelling, capitalization, and hyphenation of Canadian place names is the *Canada Gazetteer Atlas*. Official provincial road maps are also generally accurate.

Other Compound Words Do not hyphenate compound words that are properly written as single words or as two separate words. Check your dictionary if you are not certain whether a hyphen should be used.

INCORRECT	CORRECT	INCORRECT	CORRECT
all-right	all right	in-so-far	insofar
out-side	outside	never-the-less	nevertheless
now-a-days	nowadays	where-as	whereas

Compound Numbers Use a hyphen to connect the two parts of a written-out compound number up to ninety-nine, even when the compound is part of a larger number.

thirty-three *but* five thousand and six
sixty-eight *but* two hundred sixty-eight

Some writers use hyphens to connect the parts of all written-out fractions unless either the numerator or the denominator already contains a hyphen.

one-half *but* a half   seven forty-fifths
seven-eighths   twenty-one twenty-seconds

Other writers prefer to hyphenate fractions used as modifiers but not to hyphenate fractions used as nouns.

Saunders has a two-thirds ownership in the company.
Saunders owns two thirds of the company.

Suspended Hyphen Use the so-called suspended hyphen when a series of compounds all have the same second element. Leave a space between the hyphen and the following word.

four- and five-year programs
pro- or anti-British

p
35e

35e ▪ Spelled-Out Words

Use a hyphen to express inclusive dates and pages.

pp. 276-381   A.D. 56-84   1899-1906

35f ▪ Inclusive Dates and Pages

Use hyphens to indicate the spelling-out of a word and to indicate stuttering.

t-h-e-i-r   "D-d-don't you know?"

Exercises: Hyphens

Correctly punctuate the following sentences by inserting hyphens to ensure correct spelling and clarity. Consult your dictionary if necessary.

1. "I d d dunno what you mean!" shouted the dirty faced eight year old boy as he scurried to his room.
2. Forty two people applied for the six new government funded jobs in Brandon.
3. The two anti American speakers asked the crowd to help them over-throw the government.
4. Gene doesn't remember if the car had an eighteen or twenty four month warranty.
5. Although the restaurant had had an A rating for years, the inspector was appalled at its grease covered walls, dirty floor, improperly washed dishes, and insect infested kitchen.
6. The Montreal-Boston game will be on television tonight.
7. Clive placed his new laminated T square on the glass topped drafting table.
8. For five years (1974 78), we lived in a rundown old house on Main Street.

36 Italics (*ital*)

Use Italics
- For titles of longer works
- For heavy emphasis
- For words used as words
- For foreign words

In printing, **italics** are special forms of letters that slant toward the right. (Regular, nonslanting letters are called roman letters.) Because italic letters are not available on standard typewriters, underlining is used instead. If your typewriter has only an italic typeface, underline to indicate italics just as if the typeface were roman.

36a ▪ Titles

Italicize the titles of books, newspapers, periodicals, plays, long poems, and long musical compositions. Italicize the names of individual ships, airplanes, and spacecraft. Many authorities prefer italics to quotation marks for the titles of paintings, sculptures, radio or television programs, and motion pictures. Do not italicize the word *the* when it appears as the first word in the titles of newspapers and periodicals unless it is regarded as part of the title by the newspaper or periodical itself.

p
36

BOOKS	*Wuthering Heights, The Tin Flute*
NEWSPAPERS	*The Globe and Mail,* the *Chicago Tribune*
PERIODICALS	*Saturday Night, Time, The New Yorker, Maclean's, Canadian Forum*
PLAYS	*Merchant of Venice, Oedipus Rex*
LONG MUSICAL COMPOSITIONS	*Madame Butterfly,* The *Messiah*
SHIPS AND AIRCRAFT	*Queen Elizabeth 2, Spirit of St. Louis, Apollo II, St. Roch*
PAINTINGS	*View of Delft, The Jack Pine*
SCULPTURES	*Family Group, Venus de Milo*
RADIO OR TELEVISION PROGRAMS	*Meet the Press, As It Happens*
MOTION PICTURES	*Chariots of Fire, The Grey Fox*

Note The names of types or makes of ships or aircraft should be capitalized but not italicized: Dash-7, DC-10, PT-boats. The abbreviations S.S., H.M.C.S., and U.S.S. should not be italicized, even when used with the name of an individual ship: H.M.C.S. *Athabaska.*

36b ▪ Emphasis

Italicize words or phrases to indicate particularly heavy emphasis.

> I can, I think, best explain by avoiding hackneyed words which *seem* to convey the correct meaning but in fact fail to do so.
>   Bertrand Russell, "Moral Standards and Social Well-Being"

Italicization for emphasis should be used sparingly in expository prose. When italics are overused, they lose their effectiveness and create the impression that the writer is immature and easily excited.

36c ▪ Words as Words

Italicize letters, words, or numerals being used to indicate the letters, words, or numerals themselves.

> *Technique* is spelled with a *q,* not a *g.*
> Your *3*s look like *5*s.

Alternatively, words used as words may be enclosed in quotation marks. Use either italics or quotation marks, but be consistent. In any case, never use both quotation marks and italics with the same word.

36d ▪ French and Foreign Words

Italicize French and foreign words or phrases that have not become fully Anglicized. If in doubt, consult a dictionary; dictionaries have special symbols or labels to indicate such words. (See 47c.)

> The judge issued a write of *capias* after Claxton failed to appear in court.

If the word is translated into English, put it in italics, and enclose its translation in quotation marks. Single quotation marks are normally used for the translation if it immediately follows the word in question.

> These latter subjects are still, for the most part, subsumed under what the Japanese called *kikenshiso* or "dangerous thoughts."
>
> Karl Mannheim, *Ideology and Utopia*

> The French word *orgue* 'organ' is masculine when singular and feminine when plural.

If the entire sentence is in French or a foreign language, do not italicize it. But do italicize non-English phrases that appear within an English sentence.

> "Pega, ladrão!" shouted the unfortunate peddler.

> "My *pièce de résistance* will be eel-and-octopus croquettes," announced the hostess.

Do not italicize French or foreign proper nouns. Italicize titles in another language only if you would italicize a similar title in English (see 36a). If a translation is desirable, follow the rule above, adding parentheses for clarity if necessary.

> Near the old Chemin du Roy ("King's Highway") in Batiscan stands the Manoir Presbytère des Jésuites, built of rugged fieldstone in 1640.

> Québec Amérique has published *L'enfant du cinquième nord* ("The boy on 5 north") and many other outstanding Québecois novels.

p
36e

36e ▪ Superfluous Italics

Do not italicize the names of sacred books, political documents, and certain other titles and names. (See 33c for the use of quotation marks with titles.) Do not italicize the title of your own paper when it appears at the top of the first page.

SACRED BOOKS	Ecclesiastes, the Talmud
POLITICAL DOCUMENTS	the Warsaw Pact
TITLES OF PAPERS	Belgium in the Hundred Years War
PROPER NAMES	François Mitterand, le Massif Central

37  Slashes (/)

Use Slashes
- For alternatives
- In quoting poetry
- For fractions and split years

The **slash** is also called the *slant, diagonal, virgule, solidus,* or *oblique;* it has more names than it has appropriate uses.

37a ▪ Alternatives

The slash is sometimes used to indicate alternatives; the terms *and/or* and *he/she* are the most familiar examples. However, it is generally preferable to rephrase the sentence and avoid the use of the slash.

QUESTIONABLE   The office provides outright grants and/or loans.

PREFERABLE   The office provides outright grants or loans or both.

A desirable use of a slash in some Canadian contexts is to indicate a bilingual name of an organization or journal.

See the interesting article in *Canadian Psychology/Psychologie canadienne.*

p
37

37b ▪ Quoting Poetry

Use the slash to separate lines in short quotations of poetry being quoted in running text.

"Thy root is ever in its grave, / And thou must die."

37c ▪ Fractions and Split Years

When fractions written with numerals are included within the body of a sentence (not set off on a separate line), use a slash to separate the numerator from the denominator.

A kilometre is 31/50 of a mile.

A slash is also useful for indicating a year that is not the same as a calendar year.

I attended Carlton University in 1983/4.

38 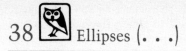 Ellipses (. . .)

Use Ellipses
- For omitted material

Ellipses are a series of three spaced dots used to indicate that material has been omitted from a quotation.

1. Use three spaced dots to indicate that material has been omitted from within a sentence.

ORIGINAL
: Wherever there are long, humid nights with crickets and fireflies, where lamps burn behind mosquito netting and whiskey is drunk from tin mugs, men on their own develop such a talent for recollection that every evening turns into a kind of ghostly party.[1]

ELLIPSIS
: Wherever there are long, humid nights with crickets and fireflies . . . men on their own develop such a talent for recollection that every evening turns into a kind of ghostly party.

2. Use a period followed by three spaced dots to indicate (a) that material has been omitted from the end of a sentence, (b) that material has been omitted from the beginning of a sentence, or (c) that an entire sentence, or more than one, has been omitted. In all of these cases, the material before and after the ellipsis should form complete sentences.

ORIGINAL
: It is the kind of road on which car crashes look like philanthropic gestures: they, at any rate, do something to provide a momentary relief in that monotony of sand and rusted oil drums. Skittering cola cans, blowing across the highway, make an ersatz wildlife; half-close your eyes, and you can imagine them as rabbits, surprised in a hedgerow on a country lane.

ELLIPSIS
: It is the kind of road on which car crashes look like philanthropic gestures. . . . Skittering cola cans, blowing across the highway, make an ersatz wildlife; half-close your eyes, and you can imagine them as rabbits, surprised in a hedgerow on a country lane.

ORIGINAL
: They had set up stalls in the walkways and constructed their own labyrinth in spaces which had been meant

P
38

[1]All quotations in this section are from Jonathan Raban, *Arabia: A Journey Through the Labyrinth* (New York: Simon & Schuster, 1979).

as routes of access. There were no straight lines to walk down: one had to zigzag through a maze of one-man businesses which were conducted from upturned packing cases under torn umbrellas.

ELLIPSIS   They had set up stalls in the walkways and constructed their own labyrinth in spaces which had been meant as routes of access. . . . one had to zigzag through a maze of one-man businesses which were conducted from upturned packing cases under torn umbrellas.

ORIGINAL   Toward evening, for the lucky ones, Abu Dhabi turns into a dizzy floating opera. When the fairy lights are switched on in the skeletons of the half-finished office buildings and hotels and the whole place begins to wink in the sea like the reflection of a giant, gaudy carousel, one can feel a tide of feverish elation rising in the city. The surrounding desert darkens and disappears.

ELLIPSIS   Toward evening, for the lucky ones, Abu Dhabi turns into a dizzy floating opera. . . . The surrounding desert darkens and disappears.

**p
38**

3. Use an entire row of spaced dots to indicate that a line of poetry, or more than one, has been omitted.

Good friends, sweet friends, let me not stir you up
To such a sudden flood mutiny.
. . . .
I come not, friends, to steal away your hearts:
I am no orator, as Brutus is;
                    William Shakespeare, *Julius Caesar*, 3.2.214–221

4. Do not use ellipses as a substitute for a dash or any other mark of punctuation.

INCORRECT   The air conditioner has two settings . . . high and low.

REVISED   The air conditioner has two settings: high and low.

REVISED   The air conditioner has two settings, high and low.

REVISED   The air conditioner has two settings—high and low.

39 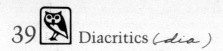 Diacritics (*dia*)

Use Diacritics

■ In spelling French and foreign words

Diacritical marks are special symbols that indicate the pronunciation of particular letters. English uses no diacritics as a regular part of its spelling system, but all diacritical marks in French and foreign words should be observed and copied. The most common diacritics are illustrated below.

ACUTE ACCENT	cliché, idée fixe	TILDE	cañon, señor
GRAVE ACCENT	à la carte, crèche	UMLAUT	Fräulein
CEDILLA	façade, aperçu	HAČEK	Kučera
CIRCUMFLEX	château, bête noire		

The **dieresis** is a diacritical mark formed like the umlaut and occasionally used over a vowel in English to indicate that the vowel is to be pronounced separately from the preceding vowel. This use of the dieresis is, however, nearly obsolete in English and is normally seen only in older printed books (for example, in such words as *coördinate* or *preëminent*).

Words that Have Entered English Words that are generally considered non-English words—those that are italicized in an English text (see 36d)—offer no choice as to diacritics. They must appear or the word is misspelled. Words that have entered the English vocabulary present more of a problem: some keep their accents (*résumé, corvée*); others shed them (*debacle, charabanc*); many others vary from one dictionary to another (*château/chateau, nöel/noel*). Writers are best advised to choose a good Canadian dictionary (see 47a) and follow its usage.

Proper Names The use of diacritics in French-Canadian proper nouns is highly individualistic. Some Francophones prefer to use the accents in their names; others drop them. In Canada outside Quebec, some French-language place names have diacritics where one would expect them; others do not. Writers must check a reliable reference (rarely the daily newspapers, most of which omit almost all diacritics to reduce production costs).

Montreal and *Quebec* present particular problems. Since both are well established in Anglicized forms, most Canadian authorities feel the accents can be dropped in English contexts but should be retained in French proper nouns and bibliographical references to French-Canadian books.

> I have lived in both <u>Montreal</u> and <u>Quebec</u> City.

> The <u>Musée du Québec</u> is located on the Plains of Abraham.

> Billon, Pierre. *L'enfant du cinquième nord*. <u>Montréal</u>: Québec Amérique, 1982.

**p
39**

Accents on Capital Letters in French Several conventions exist for using or dropping some or all French accent marks on some or all capital letters. When material comes from several sources, the conflict in style can be so confusing as to justify an exception to the rule of copying diacritics exactly. A writer who knows French well can choose which convention to follow in achieving a consistent style. A non-Francophone is best advised to drop the accents on all French capital letters, which is the simplest rule.

Exercises: Italics, Slashes, and Diacritics

Underline words that need to be italicized, and insert slashes and diacritical marks wherever necessary.

1. When the Titanic hit an iceberg in 1912, 1517 people lost their lives.
2. Toulouse-Lautrec reflected Parisian life in such paintings as The Laundress, At the Moulin Rouge, The Barmaid, M. Boileau in a Café, and The Ballet "Papa Chrysanthème."
3. In Book 1 of Paradise Lost, Milton explains that, through his poem, he intends to "assert Eternal Providence, And justify the ways of God to men."
4. The defendant, a stoop-shouldered, thin little man, entered a plea of nolo contendere.
5. Lunik II, launched by the Soviet Union in 1959, was the first spacecraft to make physical contact with the moon.
6. The author writes fire but must mean file.
7. Twelve large statues by Phillipe Hebert ornament the imposing facade of Quebec's Assemblee nationale.

---

p
40

40 Combining Marks of Punctuation

The marks of punctuation used to separate phrases, clauses, and sentences (commas, semicolons, colons, dashes, periods, question marks, and exclamation points) are mutually exclusive. A sentence, for example, should not end with both a period and a question mark, nor should a parenthetical statement be enclosed by both dashes and commas. Some marks of punctuation do occur together, but, by convention, they appear only in a given order.

1. Question marks and exclamation points always take precedence over other marks and replace them.

"But what will I tell my mother?" he asked. (Question mark replaces comma before identification of speaker.)

Don't you ever do that again! (Exclamation point replaces period.)

2. Within a sentence, the period as a mark of abbreviation can be used with other marks of punctuation.

Send it C.O.D.—I don't have enough money with me.

Several of these plants, e.g., azaleas, asters, and primroses, are perennials in warmer climates.

If, however, the last word in a declarative sentence is an abbreviation, use only one period at the end of the sentence.

In 1800, the capital of the United States was moved from Philadelphia to Washington, D.C.

3. Do not combine dashes with commas, semicolons, or parentheses.

INCORRECT	Before World War I,—but not afterwards,—Iceland was part of Denmark.
CORRECT	Before World War I—but not afterwards—Iceland was part of Denmark.
CORRECT	Before World War I, but not afterwards, Iceland was part of Denmark.
INCORRECT	Ariadne saves old pieces of string;—I can't imagine why.
CORRECT	Ariadne saves old pieces of string; I can't imagine why.
CORRECT	Ariadne saves old pieces of string—I can't imagine why.

p **40**

4. Commas, semicolons, and colons never precede parentheses within a sentence. They may follow parentheses if the logic of the sentence requires them to do so.

INCORRECT	After the processing of common salt, (sodium chloride) the salt must be recrystallized.
CORRECT	After the processing of common salt (sodium chloride), the salt must be recrystallized.

5. Commas and periods precede the ending quotation marks, regardless of the logic of the sentence.

Joan could recite all of "A Visit from St. Nicholas," but she did not know the words for "Jingle Bells." (Even though the comma applies to the entire first clause and not just the quoted material, it precedes the quotation marks.)

Note Some Canadian writers follow the British convention of placing commas and periods, like exclamation marks and question marks, inside or outside quotation marks according to the logic of the sentence.

6. Colons and semicolons *always* follow quotation marks.

Joan could recite all of "A Visit from St. Nicholas"; she did not, however, know "Jingle Bells."

Their apartment is furnished in "Graduate-Student Eclectic": Salvation Army antiques, garage sale finds, and family discards.

7. Exclamation points and question marks are combined with quotation marks according to the logic of the sentence.

What is meant by the term "exceptional children"? (The question mark follows the quotation marks because it refers to the entire sentence, not just to "exceptional children.")

We have just read Peter Taylor's "What You Hear from 'Em?" (The question mark is part of the title of the story and thus precedes the quotation marks. Note that no period is used at the end of the sentence.)

Exercises: Punctuation Review

Correctly punctuate the following sentences.

1. The barking of dogs the scraping of branches against the window the far-off echo of a train whistle all these sounds magnified Lucys uneasiness at being alone in the house
2. The leak was in a hard to get at pipe nevertheless the plumbers bill seemed exorbitant to Ms Schneider
3. Sir Edmund P. Hillary who with Tensing Norkay reached the 8848 m peak of Mount Everest on May 19 1953 recorded this pioneering climb in his book High Adventure
4. Grim faced Miss Taylor sternly asked the half frightened ninth graders Who said Conscription if necessary, but not necessarily conscription
5. Tom Thomson 1877 1917 born in Ontario is famous for his paintings of wilderness scenes e.g. The West Wind Spring Ice and The Jack Pine.
6. Edgar Allan Poe who wrote famous poems such as The Raven Annabel Lee and Ulalume and famous stories such as The Gold Bug and The Pit and the Pendulum was the inventor of the modern detective story
7. too many cooks spoil the broth A bird in the hand is worth two in the bush Dont count your chickens before they hatch these sayings were always Jessicas fathers advice for every problem
8. Its never Christmas for me Bob said until Ive heard Handels Hallelujah Chorus
9. After the meeting had ended Al told the president that he was dissatisfied because many members werent present because two of the committee chairmen gave half prepared hard to follow reports and because the members had spent too much time socializing
10. The word fortissimo a musical direction meaning very loudly is derived from the Latin adjective fortissimus the strongest

p
40

41 🦉 Capitalization *(cap)*

In general, the conventions of **capitalization** fall into two categories: capitalization of the first word only and capitalization of proper names. Capitalization of proper names includes the names of people, groups, religions, places, artistic works, official documents, and trade names. Many single letters used as words are also capitalized.

41a ▪ First Words

Capitalize the first words of sentences, lines of poetry, parts of letters, resolutions, and entries in outlines.

1. Capitalize the first word of every sentence or deliberate sentence fragment.

First, a cautionary note. You must use common sense.

Exception Do not capitalize a sentence inserted *within* another sentence by means of dashes or parentheses.

Yesterday—would you believe it?—he ordered a Cadillac.

Capitalization of the first word of a complete sentence after a colon is optional. If the material after the colon does not form a complete sentence, do not capitalize the first word.

There's just one problem: He doesn't know how to drive.

There's just one problem: he doesn't know how to drive.

Please buy the following: bread, milk, lettuce, and cat food.

Do not capitalize the first word of the second part of a direct quotation divided by the words *he said* (or their equivalent) unless the second part begins a new sentence.

"I'm lighting a candle to St. George," said Paula, "and another to the dragon."

"I'm lighting a candle to St. George," said Paula. "Perhaps I should light one to the dragon, too."

2. Capitalize the first word of every line of poetry provided that it was capitalized in the original.

There is a pleasure in the pathless woods,
There is a rapture on the lonely shore,
There is society, where none intrudes,
 By the deep sea, and music in its roar;

Byron, *Childe Harold* 4.177

p 41

41b ▪ Personal Names and Titles

Capitalize the proper names, nicknames, and official titles or degrees of persons, as well as most adjectives derived from proper nouns.

1. Capitalize the names, nicknames, and epithets of persons. Capitalize a person's name after a prefix, *unless* the compound is listed in your dictionary without a hyphen.

John A. Macdonald	anti-Roosevelt
Honest Abe	antichrist
Alexander the Great	pro-Trudeau

Capitalization of personal names with prefixes (e.g., *von, van, de, de la*) and of names beginning with *Mac* varies. Capitalize such names as your dictionary lists them or as the people themselves capitalize them. Names beginning with *Mc* usually capitalize the first letter after the *Mc*.

Arthur Vandenberg	*but*	Martine van Hamel
Ferdinand Delacroix	*but*	Walter de la Mare, Agnes de Mille
J.E.H. MacDonald	*but*	Sir John A. Macdonald
Cyrus McCormick, Nellie McClung, John McCrae		

2. Capitalize words derived from proper nouns unless your dictionary spells them without a capital letter.

McCarthyism	the Doppler effect	sherry
Bailey bridge	macadam	johnnycake
Melba toast	diesel engine	venetian blinds

3. Capitalize the titles of officials, nobility, and relatives when such a title precedes the person's name or when it is used as a substitute for the name of a specific individual. Do not capitalize a title used alone as a statement of the office or relationship. However, a reference to the reigning monarch is always capitalized in Canada.

General de Gaulle	*but*	the general
Lord Berners	*but*	a lord
Cardinal Richelieu	*but*	the cardinal
Aunt Helena	*but*	his aunt
Senator Ray Perrault	*but*	a senator
Queen Alexandra	*but*	the queen
Mama	*but*	my mother
Queen Elizabeth	*and*	the Queen

If the office or rank is a very high one, the title is sometimes capitalized even when used without a following name.

the Prime Minister (of Canada)	*but*	the club's president
The Duke (of Windsor)		the Attorney General

4. Capitalize the names or abbreviations of academic degrees or titles that appear after names.

Clarence V. Holmes, Ph.D.   Charlene Fraser, Attorney at Law
Frederic Larssen, M.D.   Douglas Fraser, F.R.S.C.

5. Do not capitalize occupational titles that appear after names.

Jean-Luc Pepin, former member of parliament for Ottawa-Carlton
General de Gaulle, commander in chief
Elton McNamme, president of the UNCO Corporation
Janet Rossi, our treasurer

6. Do not capitalize the generic (general) names of occupations or of social and academic classes.

She wants to become either a lawyer or an accountant.
Most North Americans belong to the middle class.
Special preference will be given to returning students.

41c ▪ Names of Groups

Capitalize the names of ethnic groups and the official names of organizations.

1. Capitalize the names of national, linguistic, ethnic, and racial groups and of adjectives formed from these names.

English	Mongol	Métis	Melanesian
Turkish	Asian	Algonquian	Ainu
Nordic	French	Semitic	Inuit

Canadian practice is mixed on the capitalization of two sets of words referring to linguistic and ethnic groups. Although *Francophone* and *Anglophone* are derived from proper nouns, many writers no longer capitalize them. (The term *francization*, which comes from the French, is always lower case, following the conventions of that language.) The words *black*, *white*, *oriental*, and *native people* may also be either capitalized or lower cased; treat them all consistently.

2. Capitalize all words except articles and prepositions in the names of officially organized groups of any kind but not the names of unofficial or loosely organized collections of people. Do not capitalize such general designations as *the army, the nation*.

Rotary International	University of Waterloo
Montreal Canadiens	United States Coast Guard
Canadian Historical Association	Hanseatic League
Vienna Philharmonic	Treasury Board
Del Monte Corporation	House of Commons
	Canadian Medical Association

p
41c

3. Francophone groups may follow one of several conventions for capitalizing organizational names. A simple one is to capitalize the first word and any proper nouns. (Notice that, in French, adjectives derived from proper nouns such as *québecois* and *français* are not capitalized.) This rule is generally acceptable and should be followed unless an authoritative source shows more capital letters in the name of a particular organization.

Parti québecois   Ministère de la santé

Théâtre Denise-Pelletier   Haut commissariat canadien

Note In French, an article (*Le, La,* or *L'*) appears before organizational names more often than an article would appear in English. Except in quoted material, such articles can be dropped or changed to English words (with appropriate adjustments to capitalization if necessary).

IN FRENCH TEXT   L'université de Montréal

IN ENGLISH TEXT   (the) Université de Montréal

41d ▪ Religious Terms

Capitalize the names or epithets of deities, organized religious groups, sacred texts and ceremonies, and adjectives derived from these names.

God, Christ, Allah, Jehovah, the Messiah, the Virgin, Buddha, the Prophet

Judaism, Roman Catholic, Shinto, Islam, Latter-Day Saints, the Church of England, Zen, Sufism, St. Paul's Cathedral, Protestant

the Scriptures, the Bible, the Vulgate, Genesis, Revelation, the Pentateuch, Koran, Talmud, Upanishads, Book of the Dead

Hail Mary, the Ten Commandments, the Litany, Hegira, the Crucifixion, Holy Communion

Christian churches, Moslem leaders, Gospel writers, Biblical exegesis

It is not necessary to capitalize pronouns referring to deities unless the pronoun could otherwise seem to refer to someone else.

41e ▪ Names of Places

Capitalize the names of political and geographical divisions and the names of individual structures or vehicles. Use lower case for any articles and prepositions.

1. Capitalize the English-language names of nations, provinces, states, counties, cities, towns, streets, highways, parks, mountains, rivers, lakes, and other recognized political and geographical divisions.

Thailand	the Grand Canyon
Quebec City	the Near East
Alberta	the Balkans
Dade County	the Black Forest
Schaffer Road	the Roman Empire
the Autobahn	the Gaspé Peninsula
Banff National Park	the Old World
Mount Everest	the Maritimes
the St. Lawrence River	the Bay Area
Lake Huron	the Lake District (England)
the Lascaux Caves	the Tropic of Capricorn
the Continental Divide	the Atlantic provinces

2. Do not capitalize the names of the points of the compass unless these names refer to specific geographic regions.

We walked east for about forty-five metres and then turned south.

The Western provinces often resent the large industrial tax bases of the East. (Here, *Western* and *East* refer to specific geographical —and hence political—areas of Canada.)

3. Capitalize the names of individual structures, buildings, monuments, ships, and aircraft.

Eiffel Tower	*Apollo II*
Lincoln Memorial	S.S. *France*
Houses of Parliament	Peace Tower

p 41e

4. French usage on place names varies considerably from English. Whenever possible, check a reliable source, such as the *Canada Gazetteer Atlas*; some government publications, including road maps published by the provinces, also give the correct forms. In general, town names are capitalized like English names. Words denoting roadways, parks, bridges, squares, and natural geographic features are lower cased, with the main modifying word capitalized.

rue St-Jacques	l'île de Montréal	Sept-Îles
place Royale	rivière Qui-Pleure	Trois-Rivières
mont Tremblant	baie des Anges	Baie des Roches

Buildings and other artificial objects are generally capitalized.

Théâtre du Nouveau Monde   Maison Maillou
Église de Saint-Joachim

Note The articles that appear in many French place names (*l'île d'Orléans*) may be dropped or changed to English articles except in direct quotations (see 41c).

41f ▪ Titles of Works

In the English titles of essays, articles, chapters, books, periodicals, newspapers, films, television programs, musical compositions, and works of art, capitalize all the words except articles, conjunctions, and prepositions. If the article, conjunction, or preposition is the first word of the title, it is capitalized.

"Moorish Influence on Medieval Art"	"The Tonight Show"
Encyclopedia of History	*Return of the Jedi*
Sports Illustrated	"The Marseillaise"
Winnipeg Free Press	*The Last Supper*
	Birth of a Nation

If a work is divided into parts, the names of these parts should also be capitalized.

Foreword	Book 3	Act 1	Index
Part 9	Chapter 17	Volume 2	Appendix B

Capitalization of a non-English title may be copied exactly. Or simply capitalize the first word and any proper nouns.

Les Cordes des bois or *Les cordes des bois*

Capitalize only the first word of and proper nouns in a parenthetical translation of a title.

Le médecin malgré lui ("The doctor in spite of himself")

41g ▪ Other Names

Conventions for the capitalization of other kinds of names are not always consistent; some are capitalized, some are not. The most important conventions are the following.

1. Capitalize the names of the days of the week, months of the year, and official holidays. Capitalize the names of geological time divisions but not the words *era, period, epoch,* and so on.

Thursday	Paleozoic era
February	Devonian period
Labour Day	Pleistocene epoch
May Day	Jurassic period

2. Capitalize the names of treaties, laws, historical documents, historical epochs or events, and legal cases.

Treaty of Versailles	Boston Tea Party
Habeas Corpus Act	War of Jenkins' Ear
Declaration of Independence	*Regina* v. *Drybones*
the Depression	*Anti-Inflation Reference* (to the Supreme Court of Canada)

3. Capitalize the names of flags, awards, and official brand names (but not the general name for a product).

Union Jack	the flag
Nobel Peace Prize	a grant from NRC
Sprite	bubble gum
a Yamaha guitar	

4. Capitalize the official name of an academic course, but do not capitalize the general name of the subject matter unless it is a proper name in its own right (such as the name of a language).

Physics 102 *but* My physics lab meets on Tuesday.
English 314 *and* My English seminar meets on Tuesday.

5. Do not capitalize the names of the seasons of the year. Do not capitalize the words *world, sun, moon, universe,* or *star.* Capitalize the names of planets, but do not capitalize the word *earth* unless it is being used as the name of a planet in contrast with other planets in the solar system.

Two-thirds of the earth's surface is covered with water.
The atmosphere of Mars is thinner than that of Earth.

6. Do not capitalize the names of centuries or the designations of most general historical periods. Check your dictionary to be certain: there is more tradition than logic in the capitalization rules for historical periods.

the eighteenth century	the Middle Ages
the space age	the Age of Reason
the colonial period	

p
41h

7. Do not capitalize the names for diseases, conditions, medical tests, and so on, unless the term contains a proper name.

tuberculosis	German measles
scratch test	Wassermann test
rubella	Hodgkin's disease
amblyopia	Pap smear

41h · Single Letters

Many—but not all—single letters used as words or as abbreviations for words are capitalized.

1. Capitalize the pronoun *I,* the interjection *O,* the letters used to designate grades in a course, letters used to describe or define a following noun, and letters used to designate musical notes. In designating musical

keys, capitalize letters indicating major keys, but do not capitalize letters indicating minor keys.

A-frame	G-string	T square
I-bar	vitamin C	A major
V-neck	B-girl	a minor

2. Capitalize letters of abbreviation if the words for which they stand would be capitalized when spelled out. Some abbreviations are always capitalized, even though the full words for which they stand are not capitalized. Always capitalize *A.D., B.C., R.S.V.P., M.P.* and abbreviations for time zones. Capitalize the first letter of abbreviations for chemical elements, whether the abbreviation stands for a single element (Na for sodium) or the elements within a compound (NaCl for sodium chloride). Capitalize the abbreviations for academic degrees, even if they do not follow names.

A.D. 24 (= anno Domini 24)
R.S.V.P. (= Répondez s'il vous plaît)
M.P. (= member of parliament)
EST (= Eastern Standard Time)
a Ph.D. in history (= a doctorate in history)
$AgNO_3$ (= silver nitrate)

3. Capitalization of the abbreviation for the word number (*No.* or *no.*) is optional.

No. 55   *or*   no. 55

4. Do not capitalize metric units when they are written out except the modifier in *degrees Celsius*. But do capitalize the metric abbreviations for units that are derived from proper names—*W, N, Pa,* and *C*—as well as the prefix symbols for large quantities, such as *M.*

three kilowatts, 3 kW   three newtons, 3 N
three megawatts, 3 MW   three milligrams, 3 mg

Exercises: Capitalization

Place capital letters wherever they are necessary in the following sentences.

1. "of all my courses," eric explained to jane, "I most enjoy art history and anthropology, but my german class, which is filled with obnoxious juniors, is the most unpleasant class I've taken since english 101."

2. july is an important month for national holidays in three nations: france, canada, and the united states. the french celebrate july 14, formerly called bastille day but now called simply "the fourteenth"; canadians celebrate july 1, formerly called dominion day but now called

canada day; and americans celebrate july 4, called independence day or the fourth of july.

3. neatly taped below the diploma of ernest schwartz, ph.d., issued in 1968 by the university of toronto, was the well-known quotation from robert browning's "andrea del sarto": "ah, but a man's reach should exceed his grasp,/or what's a heaven for?"

4. edvard grieg, the first norwegian composer to use scandinavian folk themes in his music written for ibsen's play *peer gynt.*

5. during the renaissance, copernicus challenged the ptolemaic philosophy of astronomy, which taught that the earth was a stationary body at the center of the universe.

6. in hamilton, provincial court judge william sharpe was to hear the case of the controller charged with larceny and embezzlement.

7. while vacationing on the baie des chaleurs last summer, i read several french novels, including georges duhamel's cécile parmi nous.

8. "have you got any asa or bufferin with you?" judge mcfadden asked his secretary. "believe it nor not, i have to spend the rest of the afternoon hearing testimony in the *towndes* v. *roper* case."

9. "should i write 60 w bulbs or sixty watt bulbs?" my father asked.

10. "if the premier does not quickly settle his differences with the back-benchers," the speaker continued, "he may very well be one of the least effective premiers the province has ever had."

11. seneca (5 b.c.–a.d. 65), an essayist and dramatist, was one of the leading proponents of stoicism.

p
42

42 Abbreviations *(ab)*

Abbreviations, or shortened forms of words, are both useful and widely used in informal writing, note taking, and many kinds of technical writing. Abbreviations, however, are much less acceptable in nontechnical writing. With the exception of the few almost universally used abbreviations explained in the following sections, a safe rule to follow is "When in doubt, spell it out."

In North American usage, most abbreviations are followed by a period. Do no space between periods *within* an abbreviation (Ph.D., A.D.) except when the abbreviation is the initials of a person's name (S. S. Stevens).

42a ▪ Abbreviations To Use

Certain titles of address, expressions of time and temperature, and certain Latin terms should always be abbreviated.

Personal Titles   Always abbreviate the following titles before personal names. French usage (and some English writers) will omit the period for *Mme* and *Mlle* but not for *M.*

| Mr. Francis | Ms. Francis | St. Francis | Mlle. Francis |
| Mrs. Francis | Dr. Francis | Mme. Francis | M. Francis |

Always abbreviate *Junior* and *Senior* and titles of degrees when they immediately follow the full personal name. Separate the name from the abbreviation with a comma.

| Peter Heath, Sr. | Peter Heath, Ph.D. | Peter Heath, F.R.S.C. |
| Peter Heath, Jr. | Peter Heath, S.T.B. | Peter Heath, LL.D. |

Time and Temperature   Always use the following abbreviations in expressions of time and temperature that are accompanied by a numeral.

10:30 a.m. (or 10:30 A.M.) (metric = 10:30)
8:16 p.m. (or 8:16 P.M.) (metric = 20:16)

7:30 PST (Pacific Standard Time; no periods are used in the abbreviation)
A.D. 734 (Note that A.D. precedes the year.)
in the eighth century A.D.
734 B.C.

20° C (Celsius or centigrade)
20° F (Fahrenheit)

When accompanied by a numeral, the word *number* may be abbreviated to either *No.* or *no.*

Train No. 504 will be leaving on track No. 7 (or track no. 7).

If the expression of time or temperature or the word *number* is not accompanied by a numeral, do not use the abbreviation in general writing.

INCORRECT	The hearing is scheduled for tomorrow a.m.
CORRECT	The hearing is scheduled for tomorrow morning.
CORRECT	The hearing is scheduled for 10:30 tomorrow.
INCORRECT	Many people have trouble converting temperatures from F to C.
CORRECT	Many people have trouble converting temperatures from Fahrenheit to Celsius.
CORRECT	A temperature of 22° C is approximately 72°F.

Latin Expressions   Always abbreviate common Latin expressions such as *e.g.*, *i.e.*, and *etc.* Many writers now prefer the English equivalents of the Latin words and avoid the Latin expressions entirely.

p
42a

42b ▪ Abbreviations To Avoid

Aside from the universally used abbreviations just discussed, avoid most other abbreviations.

Names Names of persons, names of geographical locations, and names of days, months, and holidays should not be abbreviated.

1. Do not abbreviate the first or last names of persons unless these persons are best known by their initials.

INCORRECT   Robt. Browning lived in Italy until his wife, Eliz. B. Browning, died in 1861.

CORRECT   Robert Browning lived in Italy until his wife, Elizabeth Barrett Browning, died in 1861.

CORRECT   O. J. Simpson has become a folk hero.

2. Do not abbreviate the names of countries, provinces, states, cities, towns, or streets.

INCORRECT   The Saint Patrick's Day parades held in Toronto cannot rival those on NYC's Bdway.

CORRECT   The Saint Patrick's Day parades held in Toronto cannot rival those on New York City's Broadway.

3. Do not abbreviate the names of the months of the year, the days of the week, or the names of holidays.

INCORRECT   Dec. 25 fell on Fri. in 1981, so we had a long Xmas weekend.

CORRECT   December 25 fell on Friday in 1981, so we had a long Christmas weekend.

p
42b

Parts of Books Within the text of an essay, do not abbreviate the names of the parts of a written work.

INCORRECT   The author discusses the effect of television on children in Pt. 1, Chap. 5.

CORRECT   The author discusses the effect of television on children in Part 1, Chapter 5.

Measurements Do not abbreviate terms for Imperial measurements and other quantities (*ft., yd., in., oz., lb., mi., yr., mon.,* and so on) in general writing; such abbreviations are, however, acceptable in some technical writing, recipes, and directions. In Canada, metric measures are preferable.

INCORRECT   By the time Sulak was three mo. old, she was sleeping 8 hrs. at night, but she still cried for 15 min. before falling asleep.

CORRECT   By the time Sulak was <u>three months</u> old, she was
               sleeping <u>eight hours</u> at night, but she still cried for
               <u>fifteen minutes</u> before falling asleep.

Metric terms are an exception. The rule is to use their abbreviations
whenever arabic numbers are used and to write them out whenever the
numerals are written out (see 44a and 44b).

INCORRECT   She had only enough money for <u>ten L</u> of gas, but she
               had to drive another <u>300 kilometres</u>.

CORRECT   She had only enough money for <u>10 L</u> of gas, but she
               had to drive another <u>300 km</u>.

CORRECT   She had only enough money for <u>ten litres</u> of gas, but
               she had to drive another <u>three hundred kilometres</u>.

Symbols Do not use ampersand (the symbol for *and*) or the symbols %,
¢, =, +, @, or # in general writing. However, these symbols may be used
in technical writing or in charts accompanying nontechnical writing.
Also use the ampersand when it is part of an official name or title (for
example, *Funk & Wagnall's Standard College Dictionary*).

INCORRECT   When Mr. *&* Mrs. Perry bought their Halloween
               candy, they found that prices had skyrocketed in
               the last year: a <u>20¢</u> candy bar was now <u>40¢</u>, an in-
               crease of <u>100%</u>.

CORRECT   When Mr. and Mrs. Perry bought their Halloween
               candy, they found that prices had skyrocketed in
               the last year: a <u>20-cent</u> candy bar was now <u>40
               cents</u>, an increase of <u>100 percent</u>.

Others Do not use such abbreviations as *gov't, cont., co.,* and *dept.* (But
see 42c for the names of particular companies.)

INCORRECT   The president of the <u>co.</u>, fearing bankruptcy, applied
               for a small-business loan from the <u>gov't</u>.

CORRECT   The president of the <u>company</u>, fearing bankruptcy,
               applied for a small-business loan from the <u>govern-
               ment</u>.

p
42c

42c ▪ Special Problems

Exceptions to the general rules for abbreviation in nontechnical writing
include many kinds of personal titles, company names, and a few special
cases.

Titles Preceding Names Titles that precede names (other than those listed earlier, which are always abbreviated) should not be abbreviated unless the *full* name of the person follows.

INCORRECT	Rev. Barrett; Prof. Lynde
CORRECT	Reverend Barrett; Rev. Thomas L. Barrett; Professor Lynde; Prof. Rachel Lynde

Company Names The official name of a company or other organization should be written exactly as the company itself writes it, including any abbreviations.

Algoma Steel Corp. Ltd.
IMB Corp.
McClelland and Stewart, Ltd.

Others Nicknames and short forms regularly used as full words are not treated as abbreviations. The abbreviations for certain geographical names follow special conventions.

1. Do not use a period after nicknames or after abbreviations that have become accepted words in their own right; check your dictionary when in doubt.

Chris, Al, Jo, Marge
gym, flu, taxi exam

2. The name *District of Columbia* is always abbreviated when it follows the city name *Washington* but is written in full when it occurs by itself.

Washington, D.C. *but* the District of Columbia

p
42d

42d ▪ Acronyms and Initialisms

An **acronym** is a special kind of abbreviation formed by the first letter or letters of each word of a multiword name or phrase, but pronounced as if it were an independent word. *Sonar* is an acronym for *so*und *na*vigation ranging, and *NATO* is an acronym for *N*orth *A*tlantic *T*reaty Organiza-tion. An **initialism** is formed just like an acronym, but the individual letters are pronounced. For example, the initialism *NAC* is pronounced N-A-C, not "nac."

Common Acronyms and Initialisms The use of acronyms and initialisms has increased greatly during the twentieth century, and many are now acceptable even in formal writing. In general, use the acronym or initialism in writing if it is universally used in speech. Because no one says "deoxyribonucleic acid" or "The Organization of Petroleum Export-ing Countries," it is acceptable to write *DNA* and *OPEC*. The most common acronyms and initialisms are usually spelled without periods, but consult your dictionary to be sure.

EEC	CARE	SEATO	Benelux	scuba
SPCA	SALT	UNICEF	Anzac	radar
CRTC	WASP	CUPE	Wrens	laser

Less Familiar Acronyms and Initialisms   Even if an acronym or initialism is not universally known, it can be used if the name is to be repeated many times within a paper. In such cases, spell the name in full the first time it is used. Place the acronym or initialism in parentheses immediately after the full name. All future references can then use the acronym or initialism.

> *The Dictionary of Old English (DOE)* Project is housed in Toronto's Robarts Libary; the making of the *DOE*, through the use of computer technology, is amazingly fast.

43 🦉 Contractions

A **contraction** is a special kind of abbreviation in which two words are spoken or written as one and in which one or more sounds or letters have been omitted. In written English, an apostrophe substitutes for the missing letter or letters.

We would not sound like English-speaking Canadians if our speech did not include the most familiar contractions. In writing, however, contractions are best reserved for informal papers. Avoid them in more formal writing such as research papers. When you do use contractions, be sure to spell them correctly and to put the apostrophe at the point where the letters have been omitted. Be especially careful to distinguish the contraction *it's* (= it is) from the possessive *its* (belonging to it), and remember that the form *its'* is *never* correct.

43a ▪ With *Not*

Among the most common English contractions are those consisting of a verb and a following *not*. The word *not* is abbreviated; the verb never is. The accepted contractions of verbs with *not* are the following.

aren't	wouldn't	doesn't	mightn't	needn't
isn't	shan't	didn't	haven't	oughtn't
wasn't	shouldn't	can't	hasn't	mustn't
won't	don't	couldn't	hadn't	

43b · With Pronouns

Another common type of contraction consists of a pronoun and a following auxiliary verb. In modern English, the verb is abbreviated, but the pronoun never is.

BE	HAVE	HAD	WILL	WOULD
I'm	I've	I'd	I'll	I'd
you're	you've	you'd	you'll	you'd
he's	he's	he'd	he'll	he'd
she's	she's	she'd	she'll	she'd
it's	it's	it'd	it'll	it'd
we're	we've	we'd	we'll	we'd
they're	they've	they'd	they'll	they'd
who's, who're	who's, who've	who'd	who'll	who'd
there's, there're	there's, there've	there'd	there'll	there'd

43c · *Is, Has, Had,* and *Would*

Other pronouns and noun subjects also form contractions with *is* and *has.* The rule is the same: The full form of the subject is followed by -'s.

Someone's eaten all the brownies.	=	Someone has eaten all the brownies.
Lionel's going to Australia.	=	Lionel is going to Australia.
My dog's just a mongrel.	=	My dog is just a mongrel.

When spelling out contractions of pronouns and verbs, be sure to use the correct full form. This can sometimes be confusing because both *is* and *has* are contracted as -'s, and both *had* had *would* are contracted as -'d.

He's a good friend of mine.	=	He is a good friend of mine.
He's caught a bad cold.	=	He has caught a bad cold.
I'd like to come.	=	I would like to come.
I'd better come.	=	I had better come.

**p
43c**

Exercises: Abbreviations and Contractions

In the following sentences, abbreviate words incorrectly spelled out, and spell in full the forms for which abbreviations and contractions would be incorrect in formal essay writing.

1. Forgetting the change from EST to EDT, the Hon. Frank Buscombe, a senator from the NWT, arrived red-faced almost an hour late for the stockholders meeting of Alpha Petroleum, Inc., at the corp. offices on Bay St.

2. Because the temperature had risen to a sweltering 33° C within the mechanism, scientists at the research ctr. estimated that they'd need at least two more weeks for tests in the U.S. and in Cold Lake, Alta.

3. P.M. Ghandi told the correspondents from India, Canada, and the U.K. (as well as those from the N.Y. and D.C. newspapers) that she hadn't expected the PLO to oppose her nation's policy.

4. Doctor Martin. M. Wong, a specialist in nutrition with the WHO, presented moving pleas for aid in Nicaragua when he spoke at meetings sponsored by UNICEF on Oct. 26 in L.A. and by Oxfam on Nov. 1 in Victoria.

5. Who'd have thought that the owner of sweepstakes ticket #4932 would've been Tracy Stevens, four yrs. old!

6. Who's going to support an increase in municipal taxes when the services the city provides (e.g., police protection, garbage pickup, fire protection, recreational facilities) aren't approaching the superior quality of two yrs. ago when the taxes were 12% less than they are now?

7. Nancy Cook, a prof. at Memorial Univ., told the rep. from Nfld. that unfortunately many women from her province's outports couldn't attend organizational meetings of the I.O.D.E.

44 🦉 Numbers (*num*)

The conventions for spelling out **numbers,** as opposed to using figures, vary from one kind of writing to another. In general, the more technical the writing, the greater the tendency to use figures rather than spelled-out forms. In any case, consistency of usage throughout a given paper is the most important rule.

Even in nontechnical writing, conventions for spelling out numbers vary. Some people prefer to spell out all numbers that can be expressed in one or two words. Others spell out numbers one through twelve and use figures for numbers over twelve. Still others spell out the numbers one through nine and use figures for numbers over nine. (See 35d for the hyphenation of spelled-out numbers.) If you will be expressing only a few numbers, you can spell them all out. But if you have many numbers to express, you will save time and space by using figures. Whichever rule you decide to follow, follow it consistently.

INCORRECT	Lucille has 152 pairs of shoes and eight hats.
CORRECT	Lucille has one hundred fifty-two pairs of shoes and eight hats.
CORRECT	Lucille has 152 pairs of shoes and 8 hats.

44a ▪ When To Spell Numbers

In addition to the general rule that small numbers should be spelled out, under certain conditions any number should be spelled out.

1. If a sentence begins with a number, the number should always be spelled out, regardless of its length or relationship to other numbers in the sentence. Often it is best to rephrase the sentence so that it does not begin with the number.

INCORRECT	125 years ago this area was virgin forest.
CORRECT	One hundred twenty-five years ago this area was virgin forest.
CORRECT	This area was virgin forest 125 years ago.

2. Approximate or indefinite expressions of number should always be spelled out.

There are roughly thirty-one centimetres in a foot.
Our house was built more than a hundred years ago.

3. Spell out a number used with a metric unit that is not abbreviated.

INCORRECT	The mass of the package is about 40 kilograms.
CORRECT	The mass of the package is about forty kilograms.

44b ▪ When To Use Figures

There are several exceptions to the general rules for spelling out numbers. Use figures in the following situations:

1. Except for extremely formal writing (such as wedding invitations), use figures to express street numbers, room or apartment numbers, telephone numbers, amounts of money, temperature, percentages, sports scores, Social Insurance and other identification numbers, air flight or train numbers, postal codes, and television channel numbers. Use figures for the pages of books or other written material and also for divisions such as chapters and volumes.

His address is Apartment 6, 68 Ava Road, Toronto, Ontario M6C 1W1.

Our mortgage is for $49,000 at 15 per cent interest.

I heard on Channel 6 that the Jays had won by a score of 3–1.

You will be responsible for all material in Chapters 1–6, pages 3–157.

She booked a seat on Flight 36 from Salzburg Airport and charged her ticket to VISA Card No. 5266-140-323-158.

If the name of the street itself is a low number, it is often spelled out to avoid confusion with the building number: *220 Fourth Avenue.*

2. Use figures to express numbers before an abbreviation or symbol of any kind.

27°3′N	60 km/h	3″ × 5″	16 cm × 90 cm
6 g	35 mm film	f/1.8	3 km/sec

p
44b

3. Use figures to express mixed whole numbers and fractions, or numbers with a decimal point.

The painters worked 6.5 h on Tuesday, 5 h on Wednesday, and 7.25 h on Thursday.

Plat No. 53 is 2½ times as large as Plat No. 52.

4. Use figures in charts (tables) and for numbering lists or series. In numbering a list, either place a period after the figure or enclose the figure in parentheses.

1. German	(1) German
2. Italian	(2) Italian
3. Russian	(3) Russian
4. Portuguese	(4) Portuguese

5. Use figures to distinguish one set of numbers from another set within the same sentence or group of sentences.

You will need two 3-inch nails and four 2-inch nails.

6. In expressions of time, use metric figures, but spell out the number before *o'clock*. Spell out numbers not using decimals, such as *half past, a quarter to, twenty of, in the morning*.

10:00 (*10 A.M.*)	ten o'clock	a quarter to eleven
22:00 (*10 P.M.*)	half past ten	ten in the morning

7. Dates may be expressed in a number of different ways.

May 6, 1945
6 May 1945 (no comma if the day precedes the month)
May 6
May 6th (but preferably not *May 6th, 1945* or *May sixth, 1945*)
the sixth of May (but preferably not *the 6th of May*)
45.05.06 (metric usage)

Use figures for specific years (e.g., 1800–1810) but ordinals, spelled out, for centuries (e.g., nineteenth century).

44c ▪ Inclusive Numbers

In writing inclusive numbers, that is, in indicating a series of continuous dates or pages, it is always correct to use the full figure for both the beginning and the ending numbers of the series:

the years 1917–1923   pages 554–558   numbers 503–509

If the number is over 110, those digits of the ending number that are identical to digits of the beginning number can be omitted when the inclusive numbers are connected by a hyphen. Always repeat the numbers in the units and tens positions, *except* when the number in the tens position is *0*. (The *MLA Handbook* recommends repeating a *0* in the tens position.)

the years 1917–23   pages 554–58   numbers 503–9

If the words *from* and *to* are used, the full figures should be written. Do not combine *from* with a hyphen.

INCORRECT	from 1923–1927
INCORRECT	from 1923–27
CORRECT	from 1923 to 1927

44d · Ordinal Numbers

Ordinal numbers indicate a specified position in a series of numbers:

I sat in the *fifth* row.

Cardinal numbers, on the other hand, indicate quantity but not order in a series:

The room had *five* rows of chairs.

Spelling   A suffix is added to the last element of a number to indicate that it is an ordinal number. The spelling of the ordinal numbers corresponding to *one*, *two*, and *three* is completely irregular, and the ordinals for *five*, *eight*, *nine*, and *twelve* have some irregularities. Other ordinal numbers simply add the suffix *-th*. When the cardinal number ends in *-y*, change the *-y* to *-i-* and add *-eth*.

CARDINAL	ORDINAL	CARDINAL	ORDINAL
one	first	ten	tenth
two	second	eleven	eleventh
three	third	twelve	twelfth
four	fourth	thirteen	thirteenth
five	fifth	twenty	twentieth
six	sixth	seventy	seventieth
seven	seventh	hundred	hundredth
eight	eighth	thousand	thousandth
nine	ninth	million	millionth

Abbreviating Ordinals   Most ordinal numbers are abbreviated by adding *-th* to the figures. The abbreviated forms of the ordinals for *one*, *two*, and *three* are irregular. No periods are used after the abbreviations for ordinals.

1 1st   3 3rd   12 12th
2 2nd   4 4th   29 29th

Ordinals as Parts of Speech   Ordinal numbers may be used as nouns,

p
44d

adjectives, or adverbs without any change in form, so there is no need to add *-ly* to ordinals when using them as adverbs.

| INCORRECT | We came early because, firstly, we wanted to get a good parking place and, secondly, we had to buy our tickets before the performance. |
| CORRECT | We came early because, first, we wanted to get a good parking place and, second, we had to buy our tickets before the performance. |

Spelling out Ordinals In general, the rules for using figures or spelled-out forms of ordinal numbers are the same as those for cardinal numbers. However, the spelled-out forms of ordinals are used, even for large numbers, when designating governmental units and religious organizations.

the eighty-ninth congress	Fifth French Republic
Fifteenth Concession	Third Reich
First Presbyterian Church	First Canadian Army

44e ▪ Roman Numerals

The ordinary figures we use to express numbers (1, 2, 3, 47, 9650) are called arabic numerals. Roman numerals are letters used as numbers. Although roman numerals are used relatively infrequently, everyone should be able to read them and to write at least small numbers in roman numerals.

Only seven letters are used in writing roman numerals. Depending upon the purpose, these numerals may be expressed in either capital or lower-case letters.

I (i) = 1		C (c) =	100
V (v) = 5		D (d) =	500
X (x) = 10		M (m) =	1000
L (l) = 50			

A line over any roman numeral indicates that its value should be multiplied by 1000.

$$D = 500 \quad \overline{D} = 500\ 000$$

Reading Roman Numerals The following are the rules for reading roman numerals.

1. When numerals are repeated, add them together.

$$III = 1 + 1 + 1 = 3$$
$$XX = 10 + 10 = 20$$

2. When a smaller number follows a larger number, add the two.

$$VI = 5 + 1 = 6$$
$$CLV = 100 + 50 + 5 = 155$$

3. Whenever any smaller number precedes a larger number, subtract the smaller number from the following larger number.

IV = 5 − 1 = 4
CM = 1000 − 100 = 900

Hence

DXLI   = 500 + 50 − 10 + 1 = 541
MCMXLIII   = 1000 + 1000 − 100 + 50 − 10 + 1 + 1 + 1 = 1943
MDCCXXIV = 1000 + 500 + 100 + 100 + 10 + 5 − 1 = 1724

Conventional Uses Although arabic numerals are now used on most occasions, roman numerals are still used for a few special purposes. Some writers also continue to use them in several conventional ways.

1. Capital roman numerals are used for main headings of outlines. Lower-case roman numerals are used for fifth-level headings in outlines. (See 52a for a sample outline.)

2. Ordinal numbers are used in speech to distinguish different persons or vehicles with the same name, but cardinal roman numerals are normally used for this purpose in writing.

George VI   *Mariner III*
Pope John XXIII   Queen Elizabeth II
Bronston Jacobs III *Bluenose II*

If the ordinal is used in writing, it is spelled out, not written in figures.

George the Third

3. Capital roman numerals are occasionally used to indicate dates. In particular, they are often carved on public buildings to indicate the date of construction. Older books often have the date of publication expressed in capital roman numerals.

MDCCCLIX = 1859

4. Traditionally, roman numerals have been much used in references to written texts and their parts. In this convention, capital roman numerals are used to indicate volume numbers, books, and other parts of a work, and lower-case roman numerals for the page numbers of a book's preliminary material (introduction, acknowledgements, table of contents, and the like), chapters, books of the Bible, and the cantos or major sections of a long poem. Current practice, however, favors arabic numerals in all these uses. Compare the following examples:

Volume IV of *Clarissa*   Volume 4 of *Clarissa*
in the *Iliad*, Book IX   in the *Iliad*, Book 9
Part VI, Chapter ii   Part 6, Chapter 2
on page ii of the Introduction on page 2 of the Preface
Luke xiv   Luke 14
Canto iv of *Don Juan*   Canton 4 of *Don Juan*

p
44e

5. Traditionally, acts of plays have been numbered with capital roman numerals and scenes with lower case. Current practice favors arabic numerals.

Twelfth Night IV.ii   *Twelfth Night* 4.2

Exercises: Numbers

Part A: Correct errors in the following sentences by changing figures to words or words to figures as necessary.

1. Flight three fifty seven was delayed for more than thirteen hours on March tenth, 1976, while 8 detectives questioned the two hundred and seven passengers and searched the plane.
2. Kim bought 2 four L cans of paint to cover the 2 6m × 4 m × 3 m walls.
3. Although twenty-four per cent of those interviewed said they favored city wards, only three per cent of them were registered to vote.
4. King Richard the 1st of England, known as Richard the Lion-hearted primarily for his exploits during the 3rd Crusade, was in England only for 2 brief periods during his reign of 10 years.
5. "I must have told at least 100 people today that the warehouse is located at 351 Heywood Road, not at twenty-seven Rutherford Street," snapped the irate secretary to what must have been the one hundred and first customer.
6. Mike was negotiating a 2nd mortgage on his twenty-year-old home in order to finance a 3rd car for the family—a 2nd-hand Ford to be driven by his 17-year-old daughter, Beth.
7. In the 9th inning, when Joey Mason hit the ball 93 m, the Giants scored 2 runs, tying the game 8 to 8.

Part B: Translate the following roman numerals into figures:

CXLVI, DCCVII, MDLXXI, MCMXXXIV, MCCXLIII.

 45 **Spelling** *(sp)*

Some people seem to be natural-born spellers, but many people have difficulty spelling at least some words or groups of words. **Spelling** is not necessarily related to intelligence or writing ability, yet it is one of the first things that readers notice. If there are a number of misspelled words, the writer will probably be classified as ignorant or careless. Furthermore, misspellings can confuse readers, diverting their attention from the subject matter.

Even if you are a terrible speller, your difficulties are not as insolvable as you may think. You already spell better than you realize. After all, you spell most words correctly. You never spell a word entirely wrong; you miss only a letter or two. A little attention to spelling can lead to a great improvement.

Keep a dictionary—one that shows Canadian usage (see 45f)—at hand while you are writing, and refer to it whenever you have doubts about the correct spelling of a word. When you find a misspelling in your writing or when one is pointed out to you, check the correct spelling. Spell the entire word aloud and write it down. Try to fix the correct spelling in your mind, making a mental image of the written word. Write the word on a file card and review your collection when you have a few minutes to spare.

Develop your own crutches for remembering the spelling of words that you misspell over and over again. It doesn't matter how silly the crutch is as long as it helps you. For example, many people have difficulty remembering whether a word ends in *-sede, -cede,* or *-ceed.* If you memorize the rather foolish sentence "The *proceeds succeeded* in *exceeding* estimates," you will have learned the only three words that end in *-ceed.* Then, if you remember that *supersede* is the only word that ends in *-sede,* you know that any other word with the same sound must end in *-cede (intercede, precede, recede, concede, accede, antecede, secede,* and all their derivatives, such as *procedure, antecedent,* and *conceded*).

Look for patterns in your spelling difficulties. For example, you may find it easier to remember that *pronounce* has an *o* that does not appear in *pronunciation* if you notice that other words have the same pattern: *denounce/denunciation; announce/annunciation; renounce/renunciation.* Some spelling problems, such as the confusion between *-ant* and *-ent (dominant, apparent),* are just historical accidents and cannot be resolved by memorizing a rule. Other problems, however, can be reduced greatly by applying a few basic rules. For example, the rule for adding the ending *-ly* is relatively simple (see 45e).

Be sure you have both the right spelling *and* the right word. In many so-called misspellings, the spelling is correct, but the wrong word has been chosen. This problem occurs most often when two words that are pronounced alike are confused. For example, in the sentence "Life is sometimes called a *veil* of tears," the word *veil* is spelled correctly, but the writer meant *vale* (valley) not *veil* (a piece of cloth worn over the face).

p
45a

45a ▪ Canadian Spelling Patterns

Canadian writers face an additional challenge—though not one that excuses misspelling—in their need to make consistent choices from the variants available for a number of words. Canadian spelling patterns clearly show the strong influence of both British and American practice. Some are characteristically American (*connection, curb, tire,* and *wagon*); others are characteristically British (*axe, cheque, racquet,* and *catalogue*). For words such as these, Canadian usage is so set that we are jarred by the American spelling in "squash or tennis *racket*" and by the British spelling in "car *tyre*." Yet Canadian usage is divided between the two traditions for other words (*plough/plow, programme/program, mould/mold, labour/labor, centre/center*).

Canadian spelling, then, follows neither the British nor the American pattern rigidly. In addition, spelling practices differ with the region, with the individual writer, and with the passage of time. Until recently, the British forms held the field, but today the American patterns seem to be establishing their dominance. (The growing preference for *-or* over *-our* in nouns and adjectives attests to this shift.) This development is not surprising in light of Canada's proximity to the United States and its constant exposure to the American media. Nevertheless, British-based spelling is entirely acceptable in Canada, and some readers, as well as writers, prefer it.

The important point to remember is consistency: whichever variant spellings you adopt, follow a regular pattern. Be consistent within each class of words; don't, for example, mix *favor* and *neighbour* or *centre* and *sombre*. Generally, if you tend to use British spellings, such as *pyjamas, ageing, jewellery,* and *sceptical,* then use British practice throughout (for example, double the final consonant of the root in words such as *marvellous* and *worshipped,* use one *l* in *enrol* and *skilful,* and distinguish between *licence* as a noun and *license* as a verb). Notice, however, that many Canadian writers whose spelling is British-based do use *-or* in words such as *honor* and *vigor.* (The *Gage Canadian Dictionary,* which this text follows, takes this approach.) Even more Canadians prefer *-ize* to *-ise* in verbs. (The *-ise* endings are not recommended by many British authorities, including the *Concise Oxford Dictionary.*)

Instructors at the university or college level are less likely than those in primary and secondary schools to insist on one pattern or the other. Make your decisions, get a good dictionary that shows Canadian usage (see 47a), and be consistent. Remember that the vast majority of English words do not change their spellings throughout the English-speaking world.

See Appendix E for a partial list of Canadian spelling variants.

p
45b

45b ▪ Spelling and Pronunciation

Everyone knows that, in many ways and for many words, there is a poor match between English spelling and English pronunciation. The reason for this poor match is historical: English spelling was fixed in all but minor details when printing was introduced in England at the end of the fifteenth century. But English pronunciation has been changing continually during the past five centuries. Hence today the same sound is often spelled several different ways (*go, grow, toe, though*), and different sounds are often spelled the same way (*good, food, blood*). But because we see the most common words in print nearly every day and because we

constantly write them ourselves, we seldom misspell them. Regardless
of how inconsistent the spellings are, the words are so familiar that we
usually spell them correctly. The words most often misspelled are normally somewhat less familiar ones. Many spelling errors caused by the
mismatch of pronunciation and spelling involve silent letters, omission
of letters, addition of letters, wrong letters, transposed letters, and homonyms.

Silent Letters   Silent letters occur in all positions of a word—at the
beginning, in the middle, at the end. Words beginning with silent letters
are especially frustrating because, if you do not know the first letter, you
cannot find the word in a dictionary. Words with silent letters must be
learned one by one. Try to form a mental picture of such words, concentrating on the position of the silent letter.

BEGINNING   gnaw, knapsack, psalm, pneumonia

MIDDLE   aisle, mortgage, handkerchief, silhouette

END   debris, depot, crumb, rendezvous

Omission of Letters   Letters are often incorrectly omitted because the
sounds they represent are dropped in rapid speech. Careful, even exaggerated, pronunciation will help you remember these neglected letters.

INCORRECT	CORRECT	INCORRECT	CORRECT
enviroment	environment	adultry	adultery
goverment	government	choclate	chocolate
Febuary	February	minature	miniature
libary	library	temprature	temperature
quanity	quantity	basicly	basically
suprise	surprise	accidently	accidentally

In words in which two letters stand for a single sound, try to concentrate on the two letters for the single sound.

INCORRECT	CORRECT	INCORRECT	CORRECT
aquaint	acquaint	disatisfied	dissatisfied
inteligent	intelligent	exagerate	exaggerate
embarass	embarrass	occured	occurred
tecnique	technique	accomodate	accommodate

Additional Letters   Letters are often incorrectly added because the words
are pronounced with an extra syllable or sound. Standard pronunciation
will assist in correct spelling.

INCORRECT	CORRECT	INCORRECT	CORRECT
drownded	drowned	atheletic	athletic
hundered	hundred	mischievious	mischievous

p
45b

In other instances, letters are incorrectly added by analogy with related words or similar words. Here you must concentrate on remembering the individual word.

INCORRECT	CORRECT	INCORRECT	CORRECT
explaination	explanation	arguement	argument
fullfil	fulfil	truely	truly
passtime	pastime	wonderous	wondrous
fourty	forty	hinderance	hindrance

Wrong Letters Probably the most common cause of wrong letters in
spelling is the fact that all unstressed vowels in English tend to become
one obscure vowel. Unfortunately, this sound is spelled in many different ways (compare *away, effect, imagine, occur, upon*). Again, focus your
attention on the correct spelling of the obscure vowel in the given word.
An exaggerated pronunciation is often helpful in remembering the spelling of obscure vowels. That is, as you write a word such as *separate*,
sound it out as *see-pay-rate*.

INCORRECT	CORRECT	INCORRECT	CORRECT
seperate	separate	hypicritical	hypocritical
catagory	category	prevelent	prevalent
analisis	analysis	speciman	specimen
contraversy	controversy	challange	challenge

Even the same consonant sound may have various spellings; the
sounds of *s* and *z* are especially troublesome. (Note, however, that such
spellings as *characterisation, realisation, apologise,* and *recognise* are
acceptable British spellings; check your dictionary.)

INCORRECT	CORRECT	INCORRECT	CORRECT
nesessary	necessary	consentrate	concentrate
fantacy	fantasy	conciderate	considerate
disguize	disguise	surprized	surprised
suffitient	sufficient	ficticious	fictitious

Transposed Letters Transposed (reversed) letters most often appear in
words that are slurred in pronunciation, especially in the vicinity of an *r*.
Careful pronunciation will aid correct spelling.

INCORRECT	CORRECT	INCORRECT	CORRECT
childern	children	preform	perform
prespire	perspire	prevert	pervert
revelant	relevant	perscribe	prescribe

**p
45b**

Words with silent letters also cause transposition problems when the writer knows there is a silent letter and knows what the letter is, but cannot remember exactly where it goes.

INCORRECT	CORRECT	INCORRECT	CORRECT
facsinate	fascinate	diahrrea	diarrhea
sutble	subtle	gehtto	ghetto
Britian	Britain	villian	villain

Homonyms Homonyms are two or more words pronounced in the same way, but differing in meaning and spelling. Most homonyms, such as *accept/except* and *fare/fair*, are more or less accidental and unpredictable, so we can only learn them item by item. However, one important group of frequently misspelled homonyms does form a kind of pattern. These are the words ending in *-nts* and *-nce*, words like *dependents/dependence* or *assistants/assistance*. In every case, the word ending in *-nts* is a plural noun, and the word ending in *-nce* is a singular noun. So, if you mean a plural, spell the word *-nts*; if you mean a singular, spell it *-nce*.

PLURAL	SINGULAR	PLURAL	SINGULAR
adherents	adherence	precedents	precedence
entrants	entrance	presents	presence
equivalents	equivalence	referents	reference
patients	patience	residents	residence

**p
45b**

Exercises: Spelling and Pronunciation

Part A: Use your dictionary to help you identify which of the following words are misspelled. List the misspelled words, and write the correct spelling next to them.

1. familiar
2. temperment
3. similiar
4. perrogative
5. knowledge
6. peculiar
7. alright
8. grammar
9. labratories
10. forrest
11. priviledge
12. bizare
13. lavatories
14. alltogether
15. willowy
16. mathematics
17. nusance
18. particular

Part B: Underline the misspelled words in the following sentences.

1. While dinning with his grandparents, the child spilled strawberry parfay and lasagnea down the front of his new kaki safarri suit.
2. Frederick, who had always thought he would remain a bachlor, found himself rehersing his proposal of marriage, ordering champaine, and ocassionally eyeing the two-carrat diamond with which he planned to suprise Marian.

3. Sitting in the dissorderly apartment and eating a sandwitch and vegtable soup, Beth began writting out a list of all the improvments necessary just to make her new quarters bearible.

4. Sam had always been stuborn, but as he grew older, he became so obstinate and tempermental that his friends' only cleu that anger was brewing and a firey arguement would ensue was his habit of twirling the ends of his moustashe when he was at the boiling point.

45c ▪ Four Standard Spelling Rules

Unpredictable as much of English spelling is, there are a few helpful rules. All of the rules have exceptions, but they are, nonetheless, applicable more often than not. The first rule uses pronunciation as a guide to spelling; the last three involve an automatic modification of the end of a word when a suffix is added.

ie* and *ei   If the sound is long *e* as in *me*, then *i* precedes *e* except after *c*. After *c*, the spelling is *ei*.

> LONG *e*   achieve, belief, field, grief, niece, siege, yield
>
> AFTER *c*   ceiling, conceit, deceive, perceive, receipt

Exceptions   caffeine, codeine, protein, seize, weird, financier. The words *either, leisure,* and *neither* will also be exceptions for speakers who use a long *e* in these words.

If the sound is something other than a long *e*, especially a long *a* as in *day*, then *e* precedes *i*.

> LONG *a*   eight, feign, freight, neighbor, weigh, rein, veil, vein
>
> LONG *i*   height, kaleidoscope, sleight, stein
>
> SHORT *i* or *u* counterfeit, forfeit, foreign, sovereign
>
> SHORT *e*   heifer, heir, their

Exceptions   friend, sieve, mischief.

If the *i* and the *e* are pronounced as two separate vowels, the rule does not apply: *atheist, fiery, science, variety.* If the *c* is pronounced like the *sh* in *she*, then *i* precedes *e*: *conscience, efficient, species, sufficient.*

Final -*y* before a Suffix   When a word ends in -*y* preceded by a consonant, change the -*y* to -*i* before adding a suffix, unless the suffix begins with *i*-. If the suffix begins with *i*-, keep the -*y* except before the suffix -*ize*.

BEFORE -*i*		BEFORE -*ize*
envy/envious, envies	copy/copyist	agony/agonize
forty/fortieth, forties	forty/fortyish	colony/colonize
likely/likelihood	study/studying	(also colonist)
plenty/plentiful	fry/frying	memory/memorize

If the -*y* is preceded by a vowel, -*y* does not change to -*i*.

joy/joyful   toy/toyed
journey/journeying valley/valleys

Exceptions

1. Proper names do not change -*y* to -*i* before a plural ending.

the Averys, the Stacys, the Harrys, the Martys

2. A few one-syllable words in which -*y* is preceded by a vowel change -*y* to -*i* before some endings.

pay/paid *but* payer, payment
say/said *but* says
lay/laid/lain/laity *but* layable, delayable
day/daily *but* days
gay/gaily *or* gayly; gaiety *or* gayety
slay/slain *but* slayer

3. Some one-syllable words in which -*y* is preceded by a consonant vary in their treatment before suffixes.

slyest *or* sliest
dryness *but* drier *or* dryer
wryness *not* wriness
shyly *not* shily

Final Silent -*e* If a word ends in a consonant followed by a silent -*e*, drop the -*e* before endings beginning with a vowel, but keep -*e* before endings beginning with a consonant.

	BEFORE A VOWEL	BEFORE A CONSONANT
excite	exciting	excitement
extreme	extremity	extremely
fate	fatal	fateful
shame	shaming	shameless

Exceptions

1. The following words are exceptions to the general rule.

acre/acreage   mile/mileage   whole/wholly
awe/awful   nine/ninth

Some exceptions are made to avoid confusion with another word.

dye/dyeing (to avoid confusion with *dying* from *die*)
line/lineage (to avoid confusion with *linage*)
singe/singeing (to avoid confusion with *singing*)

p
45c

2. The final -*e* is retained after *c* and *g* before suffixes beginning with *a*- and *o*- when the "soft" pronunciation of *c* and *g* remains.

notice/noticeable	courage/courageous
replace/replaceable	charge/chargeable
service/serviceable	disadvantage/disadvantageous
face/faceable	outrage/outrageous

3. In Canadian English, the final -*e* of words ending in -*dge* may be kept or dropped before -*ment*. The former practice is British, the latter American. Whichever you choose, be consistent.

abridgement *or* abridgment	acknowledgement *or* acknowledgment
judgement *or* judgment	dislodgement *or* dislodgment

4. If the word ends in -*ue*, the final silent -*e* is usually dropped even before a consonant. If the word ends in -*oe*, the -*e* is retained before -*ing*.

argue/argument	canoe/canoeing
due/duly	hoe/hoeing
pursue/pursual	shoe/shoeing
true/truly	

5. An increasing number of British writers retain the silent *e* in adding -*able* to many words that end in a stressed syllable. The American practice, which is common in Canada, is to drop the *e*.

livable *or* liveable   sizable *or* sizeable

6. The rule for dropping a silent -*e* holds for root words that Canadians end with an -*re*.

centre/centring   *but*   center/centering

Doubling of Consonants   If, after the suffix has been added, the stress is on the syllable before the suffix *and* if the last consonant is preceded by a single vowel, double the consonant before a suffix beginning with a vowel.

acquit	acquítted, acquítting, acquíttal
begin	begínning, begínner
occur	occúrred, occúrring, occúrrence
regret	regrétted, regrétting, regréttable
slip	slíppery, slípping, slípped, slíppage
refer	reférral, reférring (compare *réference* and *referée*, where the stress is not on the syllable before the suffix and where there is only one *r*)

Do not double the consonant before a suffix beginning with a consonant (*defer/deferment; sun/sunless*). Do not double the consonant if it is preceded by another consonant (*hurl/hurled; farm/farmer*). The letter *x* counts as two consonants and never doubles (*tax/taxable; fix/fixing*). Do not double the consonant if it is preceded by *two* vowels (*sour/soured; roam/roaming*).

Exceptions

1. There is some variation when the final consonant is *-l*. Final *-l* may be doubled even though the stress is not on the syllable before the suffix: *éxcellence*. Some words have alternative spellings, either with or without a doubled *-l*: *quarrelling/quarreling; enrolment/enrollment*. These words fall into two classes. One comprises verb roots in which the final syllable is unstressed and ends in a single *l* preceded by a single vowel: *travel; label*. Here, the British practice is to double the *l* before a suffix; the Americans leave a single *l*. The second group has root words that end in a double *l*. In some combined forms, the British drop the second *l*, but the Americans keep it.

BRITISH	AMERICAN	BRITISH	AMERICAN
traveller	traveler	skilful	skillful
labelled	labeled	fulfilment	fufillment

Canadian writers generally prefer the British usage in both cases, but the American is acceptable. Consult your dictionary, and be consistent in your usage.

Note   In British practice, an unstressed final *-p* is also doubled in some words. Compare *kidnapped* with the American *kidnaped*.

2. Except for *-ing* and *-ish*, suffixes beginning with *-i* normally do not double the preceding consonant even when the stress is on the syllable just before the suffix.

sit/sitting	rapid/rapidity	violin/violinist
top/topping	moral/morality	solid/solidify
sot/sottish	alcohol/alcoholic	Boston/Bostonian
snob/snobbish	atom/atomic	

p
45c

Exercises: Four Standard Spelling Rules

Part A: List the words below that are misspelled. Write the correct spelling beside each.

1. recipeint	7. shriek	13. concieve
2. counterfiet	8. soveriegn	14. theif
3. forfeit	9. freind	15. heist
4. resileince	10. wierd	16. beige
5. hygeine	11. preist	17. feind
6. releive	12. piety	18. sieze

Part B: Add the ending given in parentheses to each of the following:

1. carry (er)	7. defy (ance)	13. tidy (ing)
2. essay (ist)	8. manly (ness)	14. February (s)
3. purvey (or)	9. sympathy (ize)	15. fantasy (ize)
4. cry (ing)	10. betray (al)	16. wary (ly)
5. cry (er)	11. employ (ment)	17. wry (er)
6. annoy (ance)	12. glory (ous)	18. convey (ance)

Part C: Add the ending given in parentheses to each of the following:

1. note (able)	7. pressure (ize)	13. trace (ing)
2. tiptoe (ing)	8. blame (less)	14. guide (ance)
3. grace (less)	9. value (able)	15. appease (ing)
4. trace (able)	10. live (lihood)	16. appease (ment)
5. alternate (ly)	11. clue (ing)	17. confine (ing)
6. use (able)	12. salvage (able)	18. confine (ment)

Part D: Using prefixes and suffixes, make as many words as possible from each of the following roots. Many of the words on your list will have two acceptable Canadian spellings. List both, indicating which form is British and which American.

1. knowledge	4. jewel	7. shovel
2. parallel	5. worship	8. model
3. fill	6. wool	9. focus

45d ▪ Noun Plurals and Verbs

The rules for forming noun plurals and those for the third-person singular present of verbs are identical in most cases. Nouns or verbs ending in -*y* follow the rules for final -*y* (see 45c). Some nouns, of course, have irregular plurals; these are discussed separately below.

Adding -*s*   The majority of nouns form their plurals and the majority of verbs form their third-person singular present by adding -*s*. This rule includes words ending in -*a*, -*i*, and -*u*.

cup/cups	banana/bananas
take/takes	ski/skis
inspection/inspections	guru/gurus
implant/implants	Somali/Somalis

Adding -*es*   Words ending in -*ch*, -*s*, -*sh*, or -*x* add -*es* to form the plural or the third-person singular if the ending makes an extra syllable.

watch/watches	rush/rushes
miss/misses	tax/taxes

One-syllable words ending in a single -s or a single -z preceded by a vowel may double the final consonant before adding -es, but practice varies. Check your dictionary when in doubt. Words of more than one syllable do not double the final consonant.

MONOSYLLABIC WORDS	POLYSYLLABIC WORDS
bus/buses *or* busses	trellis/trellises
gas/gases *or* gasses	callous/callouses
fez/fezzes	rumpus/rumpuses
quiz/quizzes	

Words Ending in -f or -fe Words ending in -f or -fe vary in the way they form their plurals. All *verbs* ending in -f or -fe take a regular third-person singular ending in -s (*knife/knifes; dwarf/dwarfs*, and so on). Some of the most common *nouns* drop the -f or -fe and add -ves. Some simply add -s. A few form their plural either way. Since no hard-and-fast rule can be made, check your dictionary when in doubt.

NOUNS IN -ves	NOUNS IN -s OR -ves
half/halves	dwarf/dwarfs *or* dwarves
knife/knives	scarf/scarfs *or* scarves
leaf/leaves	
shelf/shelves	
thief/thieves	
wife/wives	

NOUNS IN -s

belief/beliefs
giraffe/giraffes
proof/proofs
roof/roofs
(and most other nouns)

Nouns ending in -ff form a regular plural in -s.

sheriffs, tariffs, stuffs, tiffs

Words Ending in -o Very few verbs end in -o; those that do form their endings like the corresponding nouns (*echo/echoes*, and so on). Nouns ending in -o preceded by a consonant vary in their formation of the plural. Some add -es, some add -s, and some may take either -s or -es. A few others are irregular in that the plural form may be the same as the singular (*buffalo*) or may have an added -s or -es (*buffalos, buffaloes*). Dictionaries do not agree on every noun ending in -o, so choose one dictionary and follow its listings consistently. Almost all dictionaries agree on the following spellings.

-es	-s or -es	-s	-s
echoes	haloes *or* halos	altos	oratorios
embargoes	mementoes *or*	bassos	photos
heroes	mementos	cantos	pianos

-es	*-s* or *-es*	*-s*	*-s*
Negroes	mosquitoes *or*	dynamos	quartos
potatoes	mosquitos	embryos	solos
tomatoes	mottoes *or* mottos	Filipinos	sopranos
torpedoes	volcanoes *or*		
vetoes	volcanos		
	zeroes *or* zeros		

Words ending in *-o* preceded by a vowel take a regular plural in *-s*: cameos, stereos, patios, studios, kangaroos, zoos.

Compound Words Compound words normally form their endings according to the rules for the last element of the compound.

NOUNS	VERBS
handfuls	freeze-dries
jack-in-the-pulpits	brainwashes
merry-go-rounds	water-skis
ceasefires	shadowboxes
court-martials	side-steps
madmen	bypasses
three-year-olds	outdoes
sit-ins	cold-shoulders

In a few compound nouns in which the first element is a noun and clearly the most important part of the compound, the first element takes the plural ending.

mothers-in-law	presidents-elect	commanders in chief
passers-by	cousins-german	sums total
men-of-war	poets laureate	battles royal
rules-of-thumb	attorneys general	knights-errant

In a very few combinations in which both elements are words for human beings, both elements take a plural.

menservants   women teachers   gentlemen farmers

Irregular English Plurals A very few words have totally irregular plurals.

child/children	foot/feet	tooth/teeth
ox/oxen	goose/geese	man/men
brother/brethren	louse/lice	woman/women
	mouse/mice	

Note The plural *brethren* is restricted to religious contexts; otherwise, the regular plural *brothers* is used.

Irregular Non-English Plurals Words borrowed from other languages, especially Latin and Greek, sometimes retain their non-English plurals. The tendency, however, is to regularize French and foreign words, and many have alternative English plurals. In general, if the singular of such a word ends in -*s*, the non-English plural is more likely to be used. A few common patterns are listed here. Check your dictionary when in doubt.

SINGULAR	PLURAL	MODEL	OTHER EXAMPLES
-us	-i	terminus/termini	alumnus, cactus, focus, fungus, locus, nucleus, radius, stimulus
-us	-era	genus/genera	corpus, opus
-is	-es	crisis/crises	analysis, axis, basis, diagnosis, hypothesis, neurosis, oasis, parenthesis, synthesis, thesis
-um	-a	memorandum/ memoranda	bacterium, curriculum, datum, medium, ovum, rostrum, stratum
-on	-a	criterion/criteria	automaton, ganglion, phenomenon
-eau	-eaux*	tableau/tableaux	beau, bureau, chateau, plateau, trousseau
-a	-ae	larva/larvae	alga, alumna, amoeba,* antenna,* formula,* nebula*
-ex, -ix	-ices*	index/indices	matrix, apex, appendix, vortex
-ma	-mata*	stigma/stigmata	enigma, stoma
No change in plural		species/species	apparatus, chamois, chassis, corps, hiatus, insignia, nexus, series, status

*These words may also take a regular English plural in -*s* or -*es*.

Note The singular *datum* is used to indicate a fact (*data* is the usual plural). But *data* is also used as a singular noun (with a singular verb) to indicate information for a computer.

No Separate Plural Forms   A few nouns have the same form in singular and plural. Many of these are the names of wild animals and fish. Tribal or national names from languages often have the same form in singular and plural, but usage varies. If the name ends in -*ese*, no plural ending is added.

ANIMAL NAMES	TRIBAL NAMES	NAMES IN *-ESE*	OTHERS
cod	Swahili	Chinese	barracks
bass	Bantu	Burmese	(air) craft
trout	Bedouin	Portuguese	means
salmon	Sioux	Sinhalese	gross
mackerel	Algonquian	Lebanese	bellows
pike	Kwakiutl	Japanese	
fish	Micmac	Vietnamese	
deer	Beothuk	Senegalese	
moose	Haida	Guyanese	
mink	Métis		
sheep			
swine			
wildfowl			

Note The plural form *fishes* is used for species.

Irregular Plurals of Titles The plurals of *Mr.* and *Mrs.* are irregular.

Mr. White	Messrs. White and Redd
Mrs. Tanner	Mmes. Tanner and Puce

Exercises: Noun Plurals and Verbs

Write the plural forms of the nouns and the third-person singular forms of the verbs in the following list. If the plural form or verb form is the same as the form given, write *correct*. If there are two correct forms, give both.

1. midwife
2. tablespoonful
3. bonus
4. menu
5. study
6. couch
7. blitz
8. leash
9. thief
10. wish
11. oasis
12. fiasco
13. hobo
14. pliers
15. curriculum
16. Javanese
17. stepchild
18. laundress
19. shrimp
20. cactus
21. member-at-large
22. taco
23. ghetto
24. plateau
25. lady-in-waiting
26. poncho
27. shelf
28. whiz
29. sheep
30. basis

---

p 45e

45e • Prefixes and Suffixes

Few people have trouble spelling the most common everyday words such as *eye*, *thought*, or *one*, regardless of how mismatched the spelling is to the pronunciation. A glance at any list of the words most frequently misspelled by students (see Appendix E) reveals that the majority of them are borrowed from other languages, especially Latin. Most of them consist of a prefix, a stem (or base, to which prefixes and suffixes are attached), and a suffix.

Spelling words with prefixes and suffixes is difficult for several reasons. First, many of them are words that are used relatively infrequently. Second, the various elements of the words are not recognized for what they often are—a prefix and stem; consequently, their spelling is not associated with the spelling of other words containing the same prefix or stem. Third, the same prefix, stem, or suffix may be spelled in different ways in different words.

You need not be a Latin scholar to analyse words into prefix–stem–suffix. You already know the meanings of many prefixes and suffixes, even if you have not consciously memorized them. For example, you know that *pre-* means "before, in advance" because you know the meaning of such words as *prejudge, preheat,* and *prepay.* You also know that it is almost a sure bet that any word ending in *-ion* is a noun. You may not recognize the stem *-dict-;* but if you think for a moment, you will recall several words with this stem, such as *dictate, diction,* or *dictionary,* and conclude that *-dict-* must mean something like "speak, pronounce, say." Thus, the word *prediction* consists of a prefix *pre-* meaning "before," a stem *-dict-* meaning "to speak," and a suffix *-ion* meaning "noun." So the word *prediction* means "something that is spoken in advance."

The habit of analysing words in prefix–stem–suffix not only helps you spell them correctly; it also helps you develop your vocabulary. Because you already knew the meaning of *prediction,* analysing it into its parts did not increase your vocabulary. But let us assume that you encounter the word *premonition* in your reading and do not know its meaning. You know the meaning of the prefix *pre-* and of the suffix *-ion,* so you removed these from the word, leaving a stem *-monit-.* You surely know the word *monitor* and probably also the word *admonish.* A *monitor* is someone or something that gives a warning, and the verb *admonish* means "to warn, to scold." hence the word *premonition* must mean something like "a warning in advance." This would probably be enough to understand the word in the context of a written passage. If you wanted to use the word *premonition* in your own writing, you should check the dictionary for a more precise definition. In any case, if you take the time to break the word down into its parts, you will probably not forget the meaning of that word, and you will also add a new word to your vocabulary. Further, if you associate the word *premonition* with the word *monitor,* you will be less likely to misspell it.

Although there are numerous pitfalls and inconsistencies in spelling words with prefixes and suffixes, a few rules always apply and a number of other rules apply in most instances.

Words with Prefixes The spelling of the root word or stem is *rarely* changed by the addition of a prefix. The exceptions, which do not exist in American-based spelling but are common in Canadian usage, are a few words that drop an *l.*

    mis + spell = misspell
    trans + plant = transplant

**p
45e**

un + necessary = unnecessary
counter + revolution = counter-revolution
a + rouse = arouse
de + fuse = defuse
inter + act = interact
uni + cycle = unicycle
but en + roll = enrol

Many prefixes also keep the same form, regardless of the stem to which they are attached.

PREFIX	MEANING	EXAMPLES
be-	all over, around	bedeck, befriend, belabor, belittle
counter-	against	counterintelligence, counterpart
dis-	reverse, not	disinherit, displace, distrust
for-	away, off	forbid, forsake, forswear
fore-	ahead, before	forearm, forecastle, foresaid
hyper-	over, beyond	hyperactive, hypercritical, hypersensitive
inter-	between, during	interchange, interlocking, interrelate
mis-	wrong	mislabel, misstate, misunderstand
out-	beyond	outcry, outpost, outthrust
over-	excessive, complete	overheat, overhaul, overstuffed
poly-	many	polychrome, polysyllabic, polytechnical
post-	after	postgraduate, postnatal, postwar
pre-	before	predate, prehistoric, premedical
semi-	half	semicircle, semidetached, semifinal
trans-	across	transaction, transform, transmigration
tri-	three	triangle, tricolor, tripod
ultra-	excessive	ultramodern, ultrared, ultrasonic
un-	not	unflattering, uninteresting, unreliable

p
45e

PREFIX	MEANING	EXAMPLES
under-	beneath, below	undercoating, underrate, underestimate
uni-	one, single	uniform, unilateral, unisex

Other prefixes assimilate to (become similar to) the first letter of the stem to which they are attached.

PREFIX	MEANING	EXAMPLES
ad-	to, toward	admit, adjunct, accept, affect, aggression, allocate, announce, apply, aspire
com-	together, with	compare, commit, co-operate, cohere, contain, collect, correct
en-	in, on	engrave, enlace, embrace, empower
in-	not	inorganic, indecision, illiterate, impossible, irregular, inexplicable
ob-	against	obtain, obligation, omit, occur, offer, oppose
sub-	under, beneath	submarine, subdivide, suspect, suffer, suggest, summon, support, sustain
syn-	together, with	synthesis, synchronize, symmetry, syllable, system

Among the most troublesome prefixes are those that are pronounced alike or nearly alike but are spelled differently. Sometimes the meaning of such prefixes is the same; sometimes it is different. A few of the most commonly confused groups are listed below.

p 45e

PREFIX	MEANING	EXAMPLES
ante-	before	antedate, antecedent, antechamber
anti-	against	anticlimax, antibody, antiwar
en-	make, put into	encase, enslave, enlarge, endanger
in-	(1) in, toward	inaugurate, influx, inscribe, incisive
	(2) not	inactive, incorrect, infinite, insane
un-	not, reverse	unborn, undo, unfold, unutterable
enter-	variant of *inter-*	entertain, enterprise
inter-	between, among	interpret, interrupt, intermural, intersperse
intra-	within, inside	intracity, intramural, intravenous
intro-	in, into	introduce, introspect, introvert
hyper-	over, excessive	hyperactive, hyperthyroid, hyperbola, hypercritical
hypo-	under, insufficient	hypodermic, hypotenuse, hypochondria, hypothesis

PREFIX	MEANING	EXAMPLES
for-	completely, off	forbid, forever, forgo, forget, forlorn, forsake
fore-	before	forebode, forecast, forego, forehead, foresee
per-	through, completely	percolate, perennial, perfect, persist, pertain
pre-	earlier, before	precede, predict, prefer, preclude, premature
pro-	forward; in favor of	proclaim, procreate, procure, profess, program
pur-	variant of *pro-*	purchase, pursuit, purloin, purport, purpose

Words beginning with *de-* and *di-* are particularly difficult to spell because the pronunciation is often of no assistance and because the prefixes themselves have so many different meanings. In a few instances, the *di-* is part of the stem and not a prefix at all. The proper spelling of *de-* and *di-* words must be learned for each individual word.

de-	*de-*	*di-*	*di-*
despair	degree	divide	dimension
destroy	deliver	divine	direct
describe	demand	dilemma	divulge
device	descend	divorce	diversion
decide	design	diverge	divisible

p
45e

Stems of Words   Stems that are independent words cause few spelling problems because the stem is easy to recognize, because the stem usually keeps the same form when prefixes or suffixes are added, and because the meaning of the stem remains fairly clear even when prefixes or suffixes are added. For example, the stem *class* keeps its form and meaning even with prefixes or suffixes, as in *subclass, classify, classifiable,* and *unclassified*.

Bound stems, those that do not occur as independent words, create more of a problem. You may not realize that the words in which they appear consist of a stem with prefixes or suffixes. Even if you recognize the stem, its meaning may be unclear, both because it is likely to be Latin or Greek in origin and because the meanings of many bound stems are rather vague. For example, the bound stem *-doc-* comes from a Latin verb meaning "to teach," yet this meaning is not at all obvious in such English words as *docile, document, doctor,* or even *indoctrinate*. Finally, bound stems often change their forms when different suffixes are added. For example, a Latin stem meaning "touch" takes the form *tang-* in the words *intangible* and *tangent,* but the form *tac-* in the words *contact* and *tactile*.

Although there are thousands of bound stems, only a few hundred of them appear over and over in common words. Furthermore, these common stems tend to appear with the most common prefixes and suffixes. Many words form patterns that can be grouped and learned together. In the verb *conceive*, for example, the stem has the form *-ceive*, but in the noun *conception* the stem has the form *-cept*. This variation, though it may seem unnecessary, does at least have the advantage of being consistent; that is, once you have recognized the relationship between *conceive* and *conception*, you have also learned *receive/reception* and *deceive/deception*.

We do not have space here to list the scores of such patterns that occur with bound stems. However, the examples below of the spelling patterns of verbs and related nouns with bound stems illustrate how identifying the variant forms of bound stems can help you spell not just one but several pairs of related words.

VERB	NOUN	VERB	NOUN
ad*m*it	ad*m*ission	pro*pel*	pro*pul*sion
com*m*it	com*m*ission	com*pel*	com*pul*sion
re*m*it	re*m*ission	ex*pel*	ex*pul*sion
sub*m*it	sub*m*ission	re*pel*	re*pul*sion

---

p
45e

Exercises: Prefixes and Stems

Circle the prefix of each word given below, and underline the stem. Referring to the list of prefixes in the preceding section, make a new word using one of those prefixes and the stem that you have underlined. Try to use a different prefix for each of your new words.

1. forbid	6. propose	11. inverse
2. submission	7. interject	12. postnatal
3. purport	8. subtract	13. commit
4. pertain	9. transform	14. enact
5. introduce	10. divert	

Words with Suffixes With the exception of inflectional suffixes (see 2a), suffixes usually change a word from one part of speech to another. The pattern is normally clear and consistent for such suffixes as *-ful*, which makes an adjective out of a noun: *masterful, beautiful, thoughtful*. Once you remember that the suffix is spelled *-ful* and not *-full*, you should have no problem with this suffix.

Unfortunately, not all suffixes are as straightforward as *-ful*. When a suffix is attached to a bound form, we may not recognize it as a suffix. For example, the adjective-making suffix *-ite* is not particularly obvious in such words as *opposite, infinite,* and *erudite.* In addition, English is notorious for **functional shift,** that is, for using what was originally one part of speech as another part of speech. The word *precipitate,* for example, with the suffix *-ate,* was first used in English as a verb but today may be a noun, an adjective, or a verb. Hence we often cannot associate a particular suffix with a particular part of speech. Finally, and most troublesome of all, the same suffix may have different spellings for no reason at all other than an accident of history. There is no logical pattern behind *independent* versus *pleasant* or *falsify* versus *liquefy.* In sum, the spelling of most words with suffixes must be learned individually. There are, however, reliable rules for a few of the most common suffixes.

Words Ending in -*ly* The last two letters are always *-ly, never -ley.* Add *-ly* to the word, unless the word ends in *-ll* or *-le* preceded by a consonant. If the word ends in *-ll,* add only *-y.* If the word ends in *-le* preceded by a consonant, drop the *-e,* and add *-y.*

actual/actually	WORDS IN *-ll*
adequate/adequately	full/fully
cool/coolly	dull/dully
home/homely	shrill/shrilly
sole/solely	WORDS IN CONSONANT + *-le*
love/lovely	capable/capably
	humble/humbly
	subtle/subtly

Exception   whole/wholly

If the word ends in *-y,* the regular rule for changing *-y* to *-i-* before an ending applies (see 45c).

hearty/heartily   ready/readily   coy/coyly

Exceptions sly/slyly; wry/wryly; day/daily; gay/gaily or gayly

Adjectives ending in *-ic* take the suffix *-ally.* Many such adjectives have an alternate form in *-ical,* and thus the *-al-* can actually be considered part of the adjective.

basic/basically	fanatic(al)/fanatically
classic(al)/classically	historic(al)/historically

Exception   public/publicly

Words Ending in -ble The suffix *-able* is used after common nouns and verbs and for newly coined adjectives. The suffix *-ible* is most often used with bound stems and with stems that have a corresponding noun ending in *-ion*.

COMMON NOUNS AND VERBS	NEWLY COINED ADJECTIVES
comfortable	patchable
fashionable	swallowable
reasonable	
sinkable	STEMS WITH NOUNS IN *-ion*
washable	
	corruption/corruptible
BOUND STEMS	digestion/digestible
	division/divisible
compatible	permission/permissible
edible	
incredible	
plausible	

If the stem ends in "hard" *c* or *g*, the suffix is always *-able*.

applicable	indefatigable
despicable	navigable

If the stem ends in "soft" *-ce* or *-ge*, *-e* is retained before *-able* but dropped before *-ible*.

-able	*-ible*
charge/chargeable	deduce/deducible (cf. deductible)
notice/noticeable	force/forcible
place/placeable	tangible

Words Ending in -ize, -ise, yse, or -yze If the word is a verb, the most common ending is *-ize*, although the British practice of using *-ise* in verbs such as *apologise* and *characterise* is sometimes seen in Canadian usage. Check your dictionary and be consistent. If the word is a noun or can be used as a noun, it always ends in *-ise*. (Note that, in many of the words ending in *-ise*, the *-ise* is actually not a suffix but part of the stem.)

VERBS	NOUNS
apologize	compromise
characterize	demise
dramatize	disguise
emphasize	enterprise
legalize	exercise
realize	franchise
recognize	paradise
stylize	surprise

p
45e

Exceptions   A few verbs always end in *-ise*. Two others—*paralyse* and *analyse*—are sometimes spelled *-yze*, although most Canadians prefer *-yse*. In all of these, the *-ise* or *-yse* is actually part of the stem of the word.

advise	apprise	exorcise	despise
devise	comprise	incise	surmise
improvise	reprise	advertise	
revise	rise	chastise	
supervise	arise		
	uprise		

The *z* in the endings *-ize* and *-yze* is replaced by *s* when a word ending in *-ist*, *-istic*, *-ism*, or *-is* is made from the verb.

apologize/apologist	criticize/criticism
dramatize/dramatist	emphasize/emphasis
characterize/characteristic	hypnotize/hypnosis
stylize/stylistic	baptize/baptism

Words Ending in an *l* Sound   Most adjectives ending in an *l* sound are spelled with *-al*. Nouns made from verbs usually end in *-al*. Verbs that imply repeated action usually end in *-le*.

ADJECTIVES	NOUNS	VERBS
beneficial	approval	babble
brutal	arrival	dazzle
dual	denial	mumble
final	dismissal	ogle
intellectual	refusal	ripple
moral	trial	sniffle
occasional	withdrawal	startle
personal	survival	tickle
principal	recital	wrestle

Words Ending in *-ous*   Many adjectives end in *-ous*, *-uous*, or *-ious*. The most common ending is *-ous*. If the ending is *-uous*, the *u* can be heard clearly in pronunciation. In words ending in *-ious*, either (1) an *e* sound can be heard in pronunciation, or (2) a preceding *c*, *t*, or *x* is pronounced as *sh*, or (3) there is a preceding "soft" *g*.

ADJECTIVES IN *-ous*		ADJECTIVES IN *-uous*	
anonymous	mischievous	ambiguous	sensuous
barbarous	ridiculous	arduous	strenuous
grievous	synonymous	deciduous	vacuous
jealous	unanimous	innocuous	virtuous

ADJECTIVES IN -*ious*

e-sound	preceding *sh*-sound	preceding "soft" *g*
copious	conscious	prestigious
ingenious	conscientious	religious
various	anxious	sacrilegious

When -*ous* is added to words ending in -*er* or -*re*, the *e* is sometimes lost. For a few words, either spelling is acceptable.

disaster/disastrous	dexterous *or* dextrous
leper/leprous	thunderous *or* thundrous
lustre/lustrous	
wonder/wondrous	
monster/monstrous	

Instead of -*ious*, a few adjectives are spelled with -*eous*.

advantageous	miscellaneous
courageous	nauseous
erroneous	outrageous

Words Ending in -*our* Words that are spelled in the British style, with a final -*our*, rather than -*or*, keep the *u* with -*able*, -*ite*, and -*ful* suffixes but drop it with -*ous* and -*ious*.

honour/honourable	honor/honorable
glamour/glamorous	glamor/glamorous
favour/favourite	favor/favorite
labour/laborious	labor/laborious

Words Ending in -*ic* and -*ac* Before a suffix beginning with -*i*, -*e*, or -*y*, add *k*.

panic/panicking/panicked/panicky

This rule applies also to *frolic, mimic, picnic, politic, shellac, traffic*. Some Canadians also adapt this rule for the word *Quebecker;* others use the more regular *Quebecer*. Either is acceptable.

Exercises: Words with Suffixes

Part A: Use the endings given in parentheses to transform these verbs into other parts of speech.

1. terrorize (-ist)
2. modernize (istic)
3. idealize (-ism)
4. parenthesize (-s)
5. revolutionize (-ist)
6. moralize (-istic)
7. mesmerize (-ism)
8. finalize (-ist)
9. formalize (-ism)
10. synthesize (-is)
11. realize (istic)
12. organize (-ism)
13. paralyse (is)
14. analyse (ist)
15. exorcise (-ism)

p 45e

Part B: Circle the misspelled words in the following list and write the correct spelling for each.

1. scandel	7. mammel	13. vivacous
2. mimicing	8. councel	14. avaricous
3. advantagous	9. mendacous	15. wonderous
4. strenuous	10. vigel	16. picniced
5. channal	11. gorgous	17. fossel
6. marvle	12. kennal	18. prestigous

45f ▪ Variant Spellings

As Canadians are well aware, many English words have two (or even more) acceptable spellings. This situation is not restricted to British-American differences. In fact, it is especially common for words borrowed from languages that do not use the Latin alphabet. For example, the *Funk & Wagnall's Standard College Dictionary* (Canadian Edition) lists as alternatives of the Arabic word *caliph* the spellings *kalif, kaliph,* and *khalif*. More familiar words usually have no more than two alternatives (*useable/usable; sulphur/sulfur; controller/comptroller; grey/gray; lustre/luster*).

A good dictionary is an invaluable aid for dealing with alternates. The first spelling listed in the dictionary is either more common or as common as subsequent spellings. Unless your instructor advises you differently, use the form given first.

Remember, however, that a dictionary's compilers have prepared it for a particular community of users—British, American, or Canadian. You will want to pay attention to this matter, for there are very few Canadian dictionaries (for example, the *Gage Canadian Dictionary; Funk & Wagnall's Standard College Dictionary,* Canadian edition); some dictionaries that are advertised as "Canadian" are very poor for postsecondary students. If you use a dictionary prepared for the British market (for example, the *Concise Oxford Dictionary*) or the American market (for example, *Webster's New World Dictionary*), you must not expect to find preferred Canadian spellings. (See 47a for more on dictionaries.)

Variants with Quotations and Proper Nouns   Variant spellings may also seem puzzling when you are quoting materials. The rule to observe here is fidelity to the original: no matter what your own pattern of spelling, if you are quoting directly from an American source (for example, a discussion of a map that has been "colored and labeled") or from a British source (for example, an account of a "programme of mediaeval studies"), use the spellings in the originals. Do this even if a Canadian (or other) text seems to be irregular in its usage.

Students sometimes also wonder what to do when their spelling patterns conflict with those of proper names. Here the rule is to spell the proper name in its exact form, even if doing so means a loss of consistency. Canadians celebrate *Labour* Day and have a Ministry of *Defence*, no matter how American the context in which they are discussed. Similarly, references to Lincoln *Center* and the *Travelers* Insurance Company must appear in texts that otherwise use very British spellings.

p
45f

Diction

46   Choosing the Right Words

Whether we are speaking or writing, we use words to convey our message. But choosing the right word is more crucial in writing than in speech. When we speak to a live audience, we can use gestures, facial expressions, tone of voice, and often the physical setting itself to clarify our meaning. If a friend and I were refinishing a piece of old furniture, I might say, with perfect clarity for that particular situation, "Hand me that curvy thing." On the other hand, if I were writing instructions on how to refinish wood, I could not say, "For finishing details, you will need a curvy thing." Instead, I would have to be much more precise and say something like "For finishing details, you will need a bent riffler." When our audience is present, sometimes no words at all are needed: a raised hand or a raised eyebrow can often communicate more effectively than a dozen words. But when we write, we have nothing to point to, so we must use words, and we must choose the words more carefully than we usually do in speech.

Which words? There are thousands of words to choose from. English has a huge vocabulary, the largest of any language in the world. Just to express the notion of "lack of size of physical objects relative to other physical objects of the same class," we have

> small, little, petite, runty, wee, diminutive, tiny, puny, elfin, minuscule, itsy-bitsy, stunted, minute, shrimpy, Lilliputian, microscopic, minikin, pigmy, infinitesimal.

All of these words mean "not big, not large," but they are not interchangeable. The choice you make should depend on the context. In describing a person, for example, you could say *tiny* but not *minute*. If you wanted to convey a favorable impression, you could say *diminutive*, *elfin*, or *petite* but not *stunted*, *runty*, *shrimpy*, or *puny*. You can apply the word *small* to almost any object, but you cannot use the word *elfin* to describe a potato, a pickup truck, or a prism. In a research paper on insects, you could describe some insects as *microscopic* but not as *itsy-bitsy*.

The right word at one time or place may not be the right word at another time or place. A *puny* nobleman in earlier centuries was inferior in rank, but a *puny* nobleman today is undersized. In Scotland today, you can call a young child a *wee* boy, but in North American, *wee* sounds affected or humorous. Indeed, the very decision to use any word meaning "not big" depends on what you are describing and the total context in which you are describing it. A small meal for a football player is not a small meal for a dieter; a small lake is a very large puddle.

The use of words, or **diction**, is more subtle than just "good" words and "bad" words. The same word may be good in one context and bad in another. For example, the words you use to describe your reaction to a low grade on an examination will differ depending on whether you are talking to your roommate or to your instructor. It is completely appropriate to tell your roommate that you are really *ticked off* about that grade and to tell your instructor that you are *distressed* about that grade. It is less appropriate to tell your roommate that you are *distressed* and your instructor that you are *ticked off*.

Thus, the definition of the "right" word is very complex. It depends on the medium (speech or writing), the topic, the level of formality, the audience, and even the time and the place. All of this may seem very confusing, and you may feel that it is impossible to keep track of so many different variables simultaneously. Don't despair. As an English-speaking Canadian, you already know intuitively a great deal about choosing the right words. If you do have occasional problems with diction, they probably involve appropriateness, exactness, economy, or freshness.

46a ▪ Using Appropriate Words *(app)*

Appropriate means "suitable for the occasion." There are various types of appropriateness, including geographic appropriateness, temporal appropriateness, and stylistic appropriateness.

Geographic Appropriateness Writing is geographically appropriate when the words used are suitable for, and familiar to, the audience. If you were writing in Britain for a British audience, for example, you would use the British term *lift* instead of the North American term *elevator*. In Canada and the United States, the term *lift* would be inappropriate.

Fortunately, geographic appropriateness rarely causes problems for writers in North America, because written English is highly homogeneous. Regional differences in pronunciation are hidden in the uniform spelling system. There are a few differences in acceptable grammar from one region to another; for example, *in hospital* (rather than *in the hospital*) is common in eastern Canada but not in the western provinces. Avoid such regionalisms if you are aware of them.

Differences in vocabulary are somewhat more extensive. For example, a large sandwich made with a small loaf of bread may be called a *submarine*, a *sub*, an *Italian sandwich*, a *hero*, a *grinder*, or a *hoagie*, depending on the region. Similarly, in some regions of Canada a *bluff* is a high, steep bank or cliff; in others it is a clump of trees standing on the flat prairie. What Canadians call *runnings shoes*, most Americans call *sneakers* or *tennis shoes*. Luckily, most regional differences in vocabulary involve homely, everyday items such as food products and farm implements, seldom mentioned in essays.

Student essays do, however, often include some of the few words that distinguish Canadian vocabulary from American. For example, Canadians travel by *railway*, Americans by *railroad*. Some of Canada's *native people* live on *reserves*; U.S. *Amerindians* live on *reservations*. In Canada, companies are owned by their *shareholders*, in the U.S. by their *stockholders*. Although the American media have made most of

d
46a

that country's vocabulary familiar north of the border, Canadian students should try to use Canadian terms unless they are directly quoting American sources.

Temporal Appropriateness   Temporal appropriateness means using words appropriate both to the time *at* which you are writing and to the time *about* which you are writing. To ensure that your writing is temporally appropriate, you should avoid archaisms, obsolete words, and anachronisms. A good dictionary will help you identify such words.

Archaisms are words or constructions no longer in general use and normally found only in old texts, religious works, and poetry. For example, *forsooth*, an adverb meaning "indeed," is an archaism. **Obsolete words** are words that have passed out of use entirely and are not used even in special contexts: *gnarl* as a synonym for "snarl, growl" is obsolete. Although some writers do employ them for humorous purposes, archaisms and obsolete words usually strike the reader as affected or even downright ridiculous. Avoid them.

Anachronisms place persons, events, objects, or customs out of their proper time. Thus, anachronisms are words that are inappropriate for the time about which one is writing. To say that Hamlet "had been dating Ophelia" is an anachronism because dating is a twentieth-century custom completely unknown in Shakespeare's—or Hamlet's—day. Similarly, although Queen Elizabeth II still has attendants, calling them *courtiers* is anachronistic because the former conventions of royal courts are not observed today. You may not always be certain whether a word or expression is anachronistic, but you can avoid such obvious anachronisms as calling a seventeenth-century person who cares for someone else's child a *baby-sitter*.

Stylistic Appropriateness   Stylistic appropriateness means writing in a manner that is suitable for both the subject matter and the audience. Stylistic appropriateness involves sentence structure as well as diction. Because sentence structure is discussed elsewhere (see 48), this section concentrates on the choice of words. There are many terms that refer to various aspects of stylistic appropriateness, some of them overlapping, some of them often misunderstood, some of them with more than one meaning. A few definitions may be helpful.

1. **Idiom** has several slightly different meanings. In one use, *idiom* means simply the normal language of a particular area or group of people. More often the term *idiom* refers to a phrase whose meaning cannot be predicted from the meanings of the separate words of which it is composed. For example, *give someone a hand* is an idiom because it does not mean that you remove your hand and give it away. *Stand a chance* is an idiom because *stand* normally means "be in an upright position" and does not take a direct object.

d
46a

The adjective *idiomatic* can have a slightly different meaning from the noun *idiom*. It refers simply to the usual and grammatical way of expressing things. For example, both *I bought my dog a collar* and *I bought a collar for my dog* are idiomatic. But *I bought for my dog a collar* is unidiomatic because English normally does not put the prepositional phrase that substitutes for an indirect object before the direct object. Good writing may or may not use many idioms, but it is always idiomatic.

2. **Slang** is the most casual type of vocabulary. It may consist of coined words (*twerp* for "silly person") or of extended meanings of existing words or phrases (*on the rocks* for "moving toward an unhappy ending"). Slang almost always expresses an irreverent or exaggerated attitude toward the subject matter. Most slang expressions have a short life: a few years ago, *heavy* was an all-purpose expression of approval, but today it is rarely used in this meaning. Effectively handled, slang adds vividness to your writing, but it should never be used only because you cannot immediately recall a more formal word. If you use slang in writing, use it deliberately, not carelessly or accidentally.

The word *slang* can sometimes refer to the specialized vocabularies of particular occupations or social groups. For example, in the terminology of computer scientists, a computer *crashes* when it ceases operating because of a malfunction, and a *loop* is a sequence of repeated steps. In the language of printers, a *widow* is a single syllable or very short line at the top of a page, and *to put to bed* is to lock printing plates into place and put them on a printing press. Such specialized vocabulary may also be called **technical terminology** (if one approves of it), **jargon** (if one feels neutral about it), or **cant** (if one disapproves of it). Occupational slang is longer-lived than more generally used slang.

3. **Formal English** is the language in its Sunday best. It is the language of much scholarly and technical writing, found in academic journals, textbooks, some essays, and many research papers. It is dignified, precise, and usually serious. It may use many polysyllabic words, but it does not have to; indeed, the best formal English avoids overuse of big words. It often gives the impression that the writer is impersonal and distanced from the reader, an impression that becomes stronger as the writing moves further away from normal speech patterns. The term *formal English* is a stylistic label, not a value judgement—there can be bad formal English as well as good formal English.

d
46a

Formal English

The great and simple appeal of fiction is that it enables us to share imaginatively in the fortunes of these created beings [fictional characters] without paying the price in time or defeat for their triumphs and frustrations. One moves with them in lands where one has never been, experiences loves one has never known. And this entrance into lives wider and more various than our own in turn enables us more nicely to appreciate and more intensely to live the lives we do know. It is impossible to say how much novelists teach us to look at our fellow beings, at "their tragic divining of life upon their ways."

Irwin Edman, *Arts and the Man*

This paragraph illustrates several characteristics typical of formal English:

a. Avoidance of the first-person singular (*I, me*) and the second person (*you*) and use of the more impersonal first-person plural (*we, us*) and one (*One moves with them* rather than *You move with them*)
b. Avoidance of contractions (*It is impossible* rather than *It's impossible*)
c. Avoidance of colloquial terms or slang
d. Precise and conservative use of words (The author uses *nicely* in its more formal meaning of "accurately, precisely," as opposed to its more common meaning of "pleasantly." He uses *various* in its less common meaning of "having different qualities" rather than the more familiar meaning of "several, many.")
e. Inclusion of learned quotations
f. Fairly long and carefully constructed sentences, often with parallelism.

The following passage illustrates the formal English of scientific writing.

Formal English

d
46a

Nutrient procurement by animals usually involves much more activity than it does in plants. Animals must often resort to elaborate methods of locating and trapping their food. Their incredibly varied feeding habits may be classified in any number of ways. We have already mentioned one possible classification, which distinguishes carnivores, herbivores, and omnivores, depending on whether the diet consists primarily of animals, plants, or both. Another possible criterion for classification is the size of the food. Thus we can recognize microphagous feeders, which strain microscopic organic materials from the surrounding water by an array of cilia, bristles, legs, nets, etc. And we can recognize macrophagous feeders, which subdivide larger masses of food by teeth, jaws, pincers, or gizzards, or solely by the action of enzymes.

William T. Keeton, *Biological Science*

Like Edman, Keeton avoids *I* and *you*, contractions, and colloquial expressions. He includes a number of technical words from Latin and Greek not because he is trying to parade his learning but because he wants to be as precise as possible. For example, the term *microphagous*, imposing as it may look, is actually more economical than *feeding on small particles. Nutrient* is more precise than *food.* Where scientific exactness is not essential, the author uses familiar words such as *trapping, size, dirt,* and *legs.*

4. **Informal English** is more casual and closer to normal speech than formal English is. It is typically the language of magazine articles, newspaper editorials, many essays, and well-written personal letters.

Informal English

In the primitive days of 1959, when I worked at a playground in Flushing, Queens, and carried Faulkner in my pocket, lived on *The Adventures of Augie March* and *The Viking Portable James Joyce,* I wouldn't have considered touching any women writers. Who were Doris Lessing and Muriel Spark? I was both an idiot and a snob. Then I discovered something in a barrel outside a Fourth Avenue book shop. It was an old reviewer's copy of *The Little Disturbances of Man.* I was witless for the next 24 hours.

> Jerome Charyn, review of *Mara* by Tova Reich,
> *The New York Times Book Review*

Like Edman's passage, this selection concerns literature, but it is more casual. The author uses the first-person singular (*I*) and contractions (*I wouldn't have considered*). Although none of the words or phrases are exclusively informal, a number of the words are used less precisely than they would be in formal English. In particular, the author tends to exaggerate: strictly speaking, he was not an *idiot* nor was he ever *witless.* In the first sentence, *primitive* is an exaggerated term for a period only a few years earlier. Sentences are shorter and looser in construction than in the corresponding passage of formal English.

Like Keeton's selection, the next passage is about food. But it is a highly subjective and personal discussion.

d
46a

Informal English

"A cold potato at midnight . . ." [about] the turn of our century, a Midwestern writer put this haunting phrase in one of her forgotten essays, although I can find no reference to it. I remember it clearly from when I first heard it in about 1940. She was lonely. She felt comforted, or perhaps merely revived, when she could sneak down to the silent family kitchen and pull out a boiled potato from a bowl of them in the icebox. As I see it now, she ate it standing up in the shadows, without salt, but voluptuously, like a cat taking one mouseling from a nest and leaving the rest to fatten for another night.

> M. F. K. Fisher, "The Midnight Egg and
> Other Revivers," *Bon Appétit*

Typical of informal English are the first-person singular and the colloquial expressions such as *sneak down* and *pull out*. The simile at the
end of the paragraph (*like a cat taking one mouseling . . .*) is intended to
create a mood, not to analyse or classify the experience in any objective
sense.

5. **Colloquial English** is natural conversational English, our everyday speech. It is not substandard or disreputable in any way. Indeed, it
would be highly inappropriate to use formal English in discussing, say,
your vacation plans with a friend. It is, however, the language of speech
and not of writing, and many words and phrases that are completely
acceptable in speech are not suitable in most types of writing. Examples
include such "fillers" as *you know* and *I mean* or vague classifiers such
as *kind of* and *sort of*. Other colloquialisms include *funny* in the meaning of "strange," *guy* in the meaning of "man or person," and *dumb* in
the meaning of "stupid."

Closely related to the term *colloquial* is the term **vernacular,** which
refers to the spoken as opposed to the written language. The term dates
from the time when all serious writing was done in Latin but people
usually spoke other languages such as English, French, or German. Since
people almost never write in Latin today, *vernacular* has come to mean a
common term for which there is a corresponding technical term. For
example, *buttercup* is the vernacular equivalent of *Ranunculus acris*,
and *leprosy* is the vernacular term for *Hansen's disease*.

The three levels of formal English, informal English, and colloquial
English form a continuum. No sharp lines divide formal and informal
English or informal and colloquial English. The vocabularies of all three
levels overlap to a large extent. Most of the words we know and use are
appropriate for all three levels.

6. **University and College Writing.** What is the appropriate stylistic
level for writing for university and college courses? Appropriateness
depends on what you are writing about and the audience for whom you
are writing. In general, most of your writing should range between high-
informal and low-formal. Use colloquialisms sparingly and only when a
more formal word is not available. Avoid slang except for special purposes such as dialogue and humor. Even in dialogue, be sure that the
slang is suitable for the person to whom it is attributed. Thus, do not put
phrases such as "Yeah, that really bugs me" into the mouth of a judge in
a courtroom.

INAPPROPRIATE	Dr. Wickens and two other members of the panel have submitted a report that is really a gasser.
IMPROVED	Dr. Wickens and two other members of the panel have submitted an extraordinary report.

In your writing, try to avoid careless inconsistency of diction, that
is, mixing words that clearly belong to extreme ends of the stylistic spec-
trum. For example, the word *sibling* is appropriate only for formal, technical English, but the words *brother* and *sister* are appropriate at all levels. In a term paper on the sociology of family life, it might be appropriate

d
46a

to write, "Disputes among siblings are not uncommon." But in a brief paper about an incident in your childhood, it would be inappropriate to write, "When I was little, I often fought with my female sibling."

The jarring effect of inconsistency of diction is well illustrated in the following passage.

> Last summer I landed a job as a grease monkey in Fredericton. That's where I met Sally. We got pretty serious. Her folks used to ask me weekends to their place at Lake Magaguadavic. They were really great to me. But somehow, things didn't work out. Even hashing over our problems didn't help much.
>
> First Sally became ambivalent about our relationship. Then, I told her she had better get to work on her interpersonal dynamics, and she became truculent in consequence. So I dropped her.

The author obviously intends to establish a very casual tone and uses such slang and colloquialisms as *landed a job, got pretty serious, hashing over*, and *get to work on*. But in the second paragraph, the author abruptly shifts to words used in a more formal context—*ambivalent, relationship, interpersonal dynamics*, and *truculent in consequence* (a highly formal phrase)—only to end with *So I dropped her*. Such sudden and apparently unjustified shifts in style can be as disturbing to a reader as the heavy use of slang.

Exercises: Using Appropriate Words

Part A: In the following sentences, underline the words and phrases that would be inappropriate in *formal* written English. For each underlined word or phrase, indicate by one of the letters below in what way it is inappropriate. Then substitute a more appropriate word or phrase for the inappropriate ones.

d

46a

    A. Archaic or anachronistic
    B. Too informal (too colloquial or slangy)

1. Albeit the women's suffrage movement had got off the ground in the 1860s, led by Dr. Emily Howard Stowe in Canada and Susan B. Anthony and Elizabeth Cody Stanton in the United States, women did not win the right to vote in Canada until 1917 and in the United States until 1920. It took the pressures of World War I to boot women into positions of public authority and to guarantee them a slice of the political pie.

2. At the close of World War I, India was on the brink of revolution against British rule. However, the movement for Indian independence did not get its act together until Gandhi came on the scene. In the decades following 1919, Gandhi achieved worldwide fame not only as India's number one man but also as the mouthpiece of subjected peoples. He drove his opponents around the bend with his techniques of non-violence and passive resistance as means of protest.

3. One of the most famous tapestries in the world is the Bayeux Tapestry, which is concocted of red, green, blue, and yellow wool on white canvas. The tapestry illustrates how William the Conqueror, in days of eld, hotfooted it over from France, defeated Harold's army, and grabbed the English throne for himself. William's wife, Matilda, may have had the tapestry made as a gift to Odo, the bishop of Bayeux, to spruce up the cathedral there.

Part B: Choose one of the following general topics and write two or three good sentences about it in (1) colloquial English, (2) informal English, and (3) formal English.

Example: One sentence in each style on the topic of eye and hair color.

Colloquial: You're stuck with the eye color your old man and your old lady gave you, but the blah color of your hair is something you don't have to put up with.

Informal: We can't do much about the color of our eyes, but we can change the color of our hair if we don't like it.

Formal: Heredity determines both the color of one's eyes and the color of one's hair. However, although it is difficult to change the color of one's eyes, it is relatively easy to alter the color of one's hair.

1. Embarrassment: How To Cope
2. The Computer: Friend or Foe?
3. Coincidence Shrinks the World
4. "You Cannot Judge a Book by Its Cover"
5. Spring: Herald of Hope

**d
46b**

46b ▪ Using Exact Words *(exact)*

Exact means "accurate, precise, correct, not approximate." Exactness in writing means selecting words with the proper denotations and connotations. It also implies the careful use of abstract and concrete words and of general and specific words.

Denotation and Connotation Words have both denotations and connotations. The **denotation** of a word is what it refers to, its direct, literal meaning, its dictionary meaning. The **connotation** of a word is its emotional meaning, the associations people make with it and the feelings they have about it.

Incorrect denotations can result either from confusion of similar referents (the things words refer to) or from confusion of similar words. If you write *bacteria* when you mean *viruses*, you have confused the referents of these words: bacteria are one-celled microorganisms, and viruses are submicroscopic protein molecules. On the other hand, if you call a *diary* a *dairy*, you have confused the two words; you know perfectly well the difference between the referents, that is, between a written record of events and a place where milk and milk products are kept.

A confusion of similar words that results in a ridiculous image is called a **malapropism.**

Tarbell discussed the business practices of Japanese typhoons.

This sentence contains a malapropism because *typhoons* means "tropical cyclones or hurricanes." The writer should have used the word *tycoons*, meaning "wealthy and powerful business people." You can usually avoid wrong denotations and malapropisms by checking your dictionary for the definitions of words with which you are not thoroughly comfortable and familiar.

The connotations of a word are its implications, the meanings that the word suggests beyond its literal, dictionary meaning. For example, the denotations of the words *authoritative* and *dictatorial* are similar; some dictionaries even list one as a synonym of the other. Their connotations, however, are not the same. People who are *authoritative* are often admired; people who are *dictatorial* are not.

The connotations of words may vary along a number of dimensions, for example, from "colorful" to "colorless," from "weak" to "strong," from "optimistic" to "pessimistic," or from "interesting" to "boring." Perhaps the most common dimension is from "favorable" to "unfavorable."

FAVORABLE	NEUTRAL	UNFAVORABLE
famous	well-known	notorious
nourishing	rich	fattening
summer home	cottage	shack
aroma	smell	stench

Connotations may be conveyed by all parts of speech. The sentence *Betsy is lively and strong-willed* uses adjectives to convey a favorable connotation, whereas the sentence *Betsy is a brat* uses a single noun to convey a correspondingly unfavorable connotation. In the sentence *Wolfe was supposedly a great general*, the adverb *supposedly* suggests that Wolfe was not, in fact, a great general. Unfavorable connotations are often created by using colloquial or slang expressions with reference to a serious subject: *Economists are always fooling around with figures* has unfavorable connotations because the colloquial verb phrase *fooling around with* suggests contempt for what economists do. Changing this to *Economists are always working with figures* neutralizes this impression.

Improper and unintended connotations in writing often result from carelessness. When writers cannot easily think of the exact word they want, they may use a word with similar denotations but different connotations. If you are uncertain about a word you want to use, check your dictionary. Sometimes words are specifically labelled as favorable or unfavorable. More often, you can get a general idea of the connotations of a word from the synonyms used to define it. (See also 47c.)

d
46b

Exercises: Denotation and Connotation

Part A: For each of the following relatively neutral words, list another word or phrase that has a similar denotation but an unfavorable connotation. Then list a word that has a similar denotation but a favorable connotation.

Example:
Neutral: legislator
Unfavorable: politician
Favorable: statesman

1. thin   4. thrifty   7. unusual
2. to talk   5. old   8. steadfast
3. simplicity   6. criticism   9. argument

Part B: Imagine a man who is 185 cm tall, weighs 115 kg, and is about fifty-five years old. He has relatively long hair and light-blue eyes and is wearing a tweed jacket that he has owned for the past fifteen years. Now write two brief descriptions of this man. In the first, give your reader a good impression of the man by choosing descriptive words and phrases that convey favorable connotations. In the second, give your reader a bad impression of him by using words and phrases that convey unfavorable connotations. You may add details not listed above, but be sure to include the same basic information in both descriptions.

Euphemism A euphemism is a word or phrase with pleasant or at least neutral connotations that is used to avoid a word with unpleasant connotations. Euphemisms often reflect a society's fears and feelings of guilt. For example, three current subjects about which many euphemisms have developed are death, bodily functions and malfunctions, and social problems. The following list includes only a few common euphemisms; you can easily add to the list. As a rule, euphemisms should be avoided in university and college writing.

d
46b

SUBJECT	EUPHEMISM	MEANING
death	pass away	die
	funeral director	undertaker
	remains	corpse
	memorial park	graveyard
bodily functions or malfunctions	dentures	false teeth
	bathroom tissue	toilet paper
	matter	pus
	irregularity	constipation
social problems	inner city	slum
	correctional officer	prison guard
	senior citizens	old people
	poorly motivated	lazy

Doublespeak Doublespeak is a kind of euphemism that is used to cover up one's own faults and to deceive others. A fairly recent example of doublespeak is the use of the term "income enhancement" to refer to a tax raise. Military and government officials use doublespeak when, for example, they call bombs designed to kill people "antipersonnel devices." Manufacturers who label used wool "reconstituted fibres" are doublespeaking. Euphemisms have at least the marginal justification that they are often used to avoid offending others: after all, some people really are embarrassed by the word *toilet* and prefer to hear *lavatory* or *bathroom.* But there is no excuse for doublespeak.

Exercises: Euphemism and Doublespeak

Underline all examples of euphemism and doublespeak in the following sentences. Rewrite each sentence to eliminate them.

1. Because his family was of a low socioeconomic profile, Sam qualified for substantial grants toward his education.
2. "It's your decision," the boss told her disgruntled employee. "Either you will accept the downward adjustment in your salary or the duration of your relationship with this company will be sharply curtailed."
3. When we went into the powder room, Addie said that dancing so vigorously had given her underarm wetness.
4. Many of the district's youthful offenders had grown up in broken homes, but most had lived in state-operated children's homes.
5. The general announced that prisoners who did not willingly participate in the re-education process would be terminated at once.

Slanting The conscious use throughout a piece of writing of words and phrases with particularly favorable or unfavorable connotations is called **slanting** or **slanted writing.**

d
46b

> Eventually, after her breakdown, Mrs. Trudeau left her husband with their three sons and went off to seek her fortune. Like many other rich young women who are newly single, she pretended for a time to be a photographer. She followed the Rolling Stones around and danced a lot in Studio 54. She attempted to become a movie star. The fact that the press reported her exploits as if she were a rational being no doubt contributed to her belief in her own importance.
>
> Nora Ephron, "First Ladies, Fourth Estates,
> Six Shooters," review of *Beyond Reason*
> by Margaret Trudeau, *Esquire,* 8 May 1979

One does not have to approve of Margaret Trudeau to see that Nora Ephron has attacked her in this review. For example, *to seek her fortune* places her in a fantasy, gold-digger's world. *Pretended for a time to be a photographer* and *attempted to become a movie star* suggest that real commitment and talent are lacking—surely not Margaret Trudeau's own view. The phrases *like many other rich young women, danced a lot,* and *followed the Rolling Stones around* dismiss her as frivolous; *left her husband with their three young sons* expresses a judgement of her action; *as if she were a rational human being* insults her directly. Perhaps the best way to demonstrate the slanting is to rewrite the review with essentially the same denotation, but with favorable instead of unfavorable slanting.

> Eventually, after her breakdown, Mrs. Trudeau and her husband separated; she left their three sons to his care and pursued a career. Entering enthusiastically into her new life, she worked first as a photographer and, in this capacity, followed the tour of the Rolling Stones. She was seen frequently, dancing, in Studio 54. After working as a photographer, she turned to acting in a film. The press followed her activities with interest, and this attention strengthened her belief in herself.

Absolute objectivity in writing is impossible—and not even necessarily desirable. But deliberate slanting is irresponsible. Further, it is often so annoying that the reader rejects completely the author's point of view. See also 46f, "Tone and Point of View."

Exercises: Slanting

Read the following selections carefully. Underline the words and phrases that seem to slant each selection. Then rewrite the passages, using words and phrases that give the opposite connotations. For example, you might change the first sentence below to "Foreigners can now freely visit about a dozen Chinese cities."

d
46b

1. China has hundreds of cities; only about a dozen are open to ordinary foreigners. In each one, the foreigners are always put in the same hotel—usually a huge palace, set like a fortress in the middle of a vast garden, far away in a distant suburb. In these hotels, the guests enjoy a restaurant that offers the best cooking available in the province, a barbershop and hairdresser, a bookstore that sells luxury editions and art reproductions unavailable in the city itself, an auditorium where films are shown and where artists sometimes come to give special performances for the foreign guests. Needless to say, the local public is not admitted: watchmen at the gate check the identity of all Chinese visitors. In this way, the only contact the travelers have with the towns they "visit" is as they speed past along the boulevards, driving to factories and hospitals in the routine way.

   Simon Leys, *Chinese Shadows*

2. The peculiar inertness of Axelrod's book stems from its refusal to face up to any of these questions. Lip service is paid, but in superficial ways, to Lowell's compositional powers. Imagery is doggedly pursued. Absurd ambiguities are "found" where none exist. The semblance of literary criticism is maintained while, to my mind, all that is essential goes unremarked.

Helen Vendler, review of *Pudding Stone*
by Steven Gould Axelrod, *The New York Review of Books*

Concrete, Abstract, General, and Specific Words   **Concrete** words refer to tangible, material things that can be experienced with the senses (*nectarine, nail polish*). **Abstract** words refer to qualities or conditions rather than to specific objects or examples (*sweetness, fulfilment*). **General** words refer to entire groups or classes (*people, fuel*). **Specific** words refer to explicit, particular examples of a group or class (*Boy Scouts, kerosene*). Unlike *abstract* and *concrete, general* and *specific* are relative terms. That is, there are degrees of generality. The words *house* and *swim suit* are more general than the words *log cabin* and *bikini* but more specific than *building* and *clothing*.

Abstract words are often general, but are not necessarily so. Similarly, concrete words may be either general or specific.

ABSTRACT AND GENERAL	old age	authority	amusement
ABSTRACT AND SPECIFIC	senility	dictatorship	the game of football
CONCRETE AND GENERAL	old people	rulers	football games
CONCRETE AND SPECIFIC	my grand- father	Czar Nicholas I	the Edmonton- Toronto game today

d
46b

One of the chief causes of vagueness in diction is the overuse of abstract and general words. It is a good practice, therefore, to select concrete words and examples whenever you can. This is not to say that you should never use abstract or general words: effective writing employs both abstract and concrete words and both general and specific words. Abstract and general words are often essential for introducing a topic and for summarizing.

Problems arise, not because abstract and general words have no meaning, but rather because they have too much meaning or too many meanings. Further, abstract and general words often mean different things to different people. Hence, when using abstract and general words, be sure you make your intended meaning clear to your reader by defining the words or by giving concrete and specific illustrations.

General words are needed in classification and definition. You could not classify a *zebra* without mentioning *animal* or define *mauve* without using the general word *color*. Even in description and narration, general words are occasionally as suitable as specific words. For example, if you were describing your experiences in obtaining a driver's licence, it would be appropriate to say, "After having my picture taken, I *went* upstairs to pay the fee." Whether you sauntered or walked briskly or stumbled up the stairs or took the elevator is irrelevant to the main point of your story. The general verb *go* is all that is required if your focus is not on your physical motions but on the process of getting a licence.

On the other hand, when you are discussing or describing something crucial to your central topic, be as specific as possible.

Overly General

The St. Elias Mountains, a very high and extensive range, are especially dangerous because the terrain is rugged and the weather is severe and unpredictable. For these reasons, only experienced mountaineers should venture to climb there.

More Specific

Canada's tallest peak, Mount Logan, pierces the glaciers of the St. Elias Mountains to a height of 6050 m. It does not tower alone; in this range, which extends from the British Columbia–Yukon border into Alaska, eight of the peaks are more than 4500 m high. These peaks lance up through a complex of glaciers as much as a kilometre thick in some places. With their awesome cliffs, sunless crevices, and unpredictable weather—even in July fierce blizzards are common—these montains are daunting to even the most experienced climbers. Canada's team making the assault on Everest would find these mountains good practice ground.

d
46b

Although the first paragraph is not inaccurate, it lacks interest and conveys little real information because it is too general. The second paragraph replaces the general *very high and extensive* with specific figures. The first paragraph's description of the weather as *severe and unpredictable* is so unspecific that it could apply just as well to the Mojave Desert as to the St. Elias Mountains; the second paragraph gives a specific example of the severity and unpredictability. Instead of the first paragraph's *the terrain is rugged*, the second paragraph describes particulars (*peaks, glaciers, cliffs, crevices*). The reader who might pass right over the final sentence of the first paragraph should be highly impressed by the final sentence of the second paragraph, which explicitly puts the St. Elias Mountains into the same category as Everest and the Himalayas.

Abstract words are essential to language, but writing about abstractions is full of pitfalls if you do not define the abstract words. For example, consider the question "Is faith in democracy justified?" This short question contains two dangerous abstract words, *faith* and *democracy*. What does *faith* mean? A dictionary will tell you that it means "unquestioning belief; belief that is not based on proof." Do you want to accept any form of government unquestioningly? Do you assume that democracy has no faults? Are you willing to accept democracy without any consideration of the alternatives? Will you demand no proof, no evidence of the superiority of democracy?

What does *democracy* mean? Again, a dictionary will inform you that it means "government by the people, either directly or through elected representatives." By this definition, the Soviet Union is a democracy because the governing officials are elected by the people. Indeed, a far higher percentage of the people vote for their representatives in the Soviet Union than in Canada, Great Britain, or the United States. Does the Soviet Union then have "more" democracy than these countries? Many of the restrictions and controls to which the citizens of the western democracies are subject are placed upon them by officials who are not elected—by regulatory agencies, by judges, by police. Do they then not have democracies after all? This brief example illustrates another problem with abstractions: dictionary definitions often do not capture the entire meaning of abstract words.

Good writing requires both abstract and concrete words and both general and specific words. But do not use abstract words to hide fuzzy ideas, and do not use general words as substitutes for specific information.

Exercises: Concrete, Abstract, General, and Specific Words

Each of the following sentences is dull because the language is too abstract and general. Rewrite each, substituting concrete, specific information for the generalities and abstractions.

1. The day was typical of early spring: the birds were singing, the grass was green, a breeze was blowing, and everything seemed fresh and new.
2. The restaurant was ugly on both the outside and the inside, and the food that we ordered was just like the surroundings—poor.
3. Very unattractive physically, Professor Adamson was equally unattractive as a lecturer because of his voice and mannerisms.
4. Seeing the Grand Canyon for the first time is really impressive because of its great size, lovely colors, and varied terrain.

d
46c

46c • Using Words Economically *(econ)*

Economical means "thrifty, sparing, frugal, avoiding waste or extravagance." Economical writing is concise and uses as few words as possible to convey its message clearly. Uneconomical writing is repetitious and wordy. To keep your writing economical, do not use more words than you need, and do not use complicated words when simple words can say the same thing.

Deadwood Unnecessary words are called deadwood. Deadwood is insidious; it can creep in and take over entire sentences and paragraphs without the writer's being aware of it. To combat deadwood, reread your first drafts, eliminating every word or phrase that does not contribute something essential.

> In my opinion, I think that clairvoyance, which is the perception of physical events that take place without the use of the five senses of sight, hearing, smell, taste, or touch, actually exists because it has been well demonstrated as a fact by scientific psychological research.

In this sentence, *I think that* is unnecessary because it merely repeats the meaning of *In my opinion*. The relative pronoun *which* and the verb *is* can be omitted because the word *perception* contains their meaning. Everyone knows what the five senses are, so they need not be specified. The words *actually exists because it* add nothing that is not implied by the following verb phrase. *As a fact* can be omitted because its meaning is implied by *demonstrated*. *Scientific* can be eliminated because psychological research is usually scientific. Some would argue that even the introductory phrase *In my opinion* should be deleted. Its inclusion is justified here because it tells the reader that the writer realizes that there are differences of opinion on the subject.

With the deadwood eliminated, the sentence is actually clearer than the original, yet contains fewer than half the words.

> In my opinion, clairvoyance, the perception of physical events without the use of the five senses, has been well demonstrated by psychological research.

d
46c

One common source of deadwood is the overuse of the expletive pronouns *there* and *it*. Examine all sentences and clauses beginning with these words to see if you can eliminate them without changing your intended meaning and emphasis.

DEADWOOD	It is lamentable that Hamlet is so indecisive.
IMPROVED	Hamlet's indecision is lamentable.
DEADWOOD	There are various uses of shale, such as in the manufacture of cement, bricks, and tile.
IMPROVED	Shale is used in the manufacture of cement, bricks, and tile.

Omnibus Words A relatively few words called omnibus words account for a great deal of deadwood. These words are sometimes both abstract and general, and they add little or no information to the sentence. Omni-

bus words may be nouns, adjectives, verbs, or adverbs. The following list
contains some of the most common ones.

aspect	factor	line	quality	state
case	feature	manner	situation	thing
character	field	matter	sort	type
fact	kind	problem		

Omnibus nouns usually detract from the effectiveness of a sentence.

WEAK   One of Clara's <u>problems</u> was her family <u>situation</u>.

IMPROVED   Clara was self-conscious because her husband was an
            alcoholic.

WEAK   A surprising <u>aspect</u> of the Easter Island sculptures is
            their solemn <u>quality</u>.

IMPROVED   The Easter Island sculptures are surprisingly solemn.

Common omnibus adjectives are *bad, crucial, fine, good, great, important, nice,* and *significant.* Sometimes the adjective can be eliminated
entirely.

WEAK   His falling asleep at the dinner table is a <u>good</u> indica-
            tion of how tired he is.

IMPROVED   His falling asleep at the dinner table is an indication of
            how tired he is.

Sometimes a more exact adjective is needed.

WEAK   She was saving her money to buy a <u>good</u> car.

IMPROVED   She was saving her money to buy a <u>reliable</u> car.

Among the omnibus verbs are *appear, be, do, exist, get, happen,
have, occur,* and *seem.*

WEAK   What <u>occurred</u> was that the wind blew the door shut.

IMPROVED   The wind blew the door shut.

WEAK   The noise level that presently <u>exists</u> is intolerable.

IMPROVED   The present noise level is intolerable.

**d
46c**

Omnibus adverbs include empty intensifiers and qualifiers such as
basically, completely, definitely, quite, rather, somewhat, and *very.*
These usually weaken rather than strengthen the sentences in which
they appear, yet sometimes two or three clutter up a single sentence.

WEAK   She was <u>basically quite</u> interested in politics.

IMPROVED   She was interested in politics.

WEAK   Summer was <u>definitely</u> over, but the weather re-
            mained <u>somewhat</u> warm.

IMPROVED   Summer was over, but the weather remained warm.

Circumlocution   Another variety of deadwood is circumlocution, the use of big words or long phrases instead of more common and shorter words and phrases. (See also 46b).

> WEAK   It came to my attention that the post office was not always to be relied upon.

> IMPROVED   I learned that the post office was not always reliable.

> WEAK   As far as the children were concerned, they considered that the purpose of the driveway was to enable them to rollerskate.

> IMPROVED   The children thought that the driveway was for rollerskating.

Tautology   Tautology, or the unnecessary repetition of a concept, is a particularly irritating source of deadwood. One of the most common forms of tautology is the modification of a noun by an adjective that means the same thing as the noun: *free gift, predicted forecast, necessary essentials, forthcoming future.* Tautologies also occur with other parts of speech. For example, in the tautology *repeat again*, the verb *repeat* contains all the meaning of the adverb *again. Consensus of opinion* is tautological because *consensus* means "collective opinion." Eliminate tautology by paying close attention to the denotations of words.

Exercises: Using Words Economically

Rewrite the following sentences to eliminate deadwood, circumlocution, and tautology. Eliminate omnibus words if possible, or replace them with specific expressions.

d
46c

1. It is a true fact that informed people who know a lot about Oriental rugs can usually identify the location where a rug was made simply by looking at the weave of it and the design of it.
2. With respect to the Far Eastern situation, India can be said to be a basically quite stable country, despite the fact that she has a significant overpopulation problem, which has led to the occurrence of food shortages and even famines in which people have actually starved to death.
3. Her own personal opinion about the matter of serious crime prevention seems to have changed somewhat as a result of her having experienced a robbery in which thieves broke into the apartment in which she was living while everyone was away and the apartment was unoccupied.
4. One important aspect of the current job market that should be kept in mind is that there are essentially quite a lot of openings for people in the field of highly skilled labor (like workers who make tool and die parts for machines and automobiles) and in the area of computer science.

5. Sharp types of implements, that is, cutting knives and scissors, should be stored away in safe places where small children who are not capable of handling these tools without incurring danger to themselves are unable to get access to them.

6. I often recall a memory from my young childhood in which I was in a state of anger of some sort and escaped from my mother by running away but soon found myself in a helpless condition due to having caught the back part of the sweater that I was wearing on a barbed-wire fence.

46d · Using Fresh Words *(fresh)*

The word **fresh** can mean "novel," "different," "original," but freshness of diction does not mean that you should try to invent new words. Instead, it means avoiding overfamiliar words and expressions. Very often it is not the individual words that have gone stale, but combinations of words. For example, both *lining* and *silver* are perfectly healthy English words, but their comination in the phrase *silver lining* has lost its freshness through overuse.

The greatest enemies of fresh diction are clichés, vogue words, nonce words, fine writing, and overuse of particular words and phrases.

Clichés   Clichés are trite, overworked, automatic phrases—the TV dinners of writing, and just as unappealing to the reader as TV dinners are to the eater. The person who first said or wrote *ice water in his veins* or *truth is stranger than fiction* was imaginative, but constant repetition over the years has worn such phrases out. Many clichés are overfamiliar metaphors, similes, and proverbial expressions.

avoid like the plague	bite the dust
sell like hot cakes	burn the midnight oil
spread like wildfire	face the music
stick out like a sore thumb	meet the eye
work like a dog	pave the way
down but not out	cool as a cucumber
gone but not forgotten	light as a feather
last but not least	neat as a pin
sadder but wiser	quick as a wink
slow but sure	sharp as a tack
dyed in the wool	better late than never
method in your madness	easier said than done
nip in the bud	hotter than hell
skeleton in the closet	more sinned against than sinning
soft place in my heart	no sooner said than done
all work and no play	bitter end
few and far between	broad daylight
hustle and bustle	fatal flaw

d
46d

pride and joy	happy couple
short and sweet	happy medium
crack of dawn	high noon
facts of life	proud father
sigh of relief	sorry sight
twinkling of an eye	sweet sixteen
walks of life	vicious circle

How can you be sure whether an expression is a cliché? If, when you think of one word, an entire phrase comes to mind, that phrase is probably a cliché. If you then ask a friend to complete the expression and he or she comes up with the same phrase that you did, it is certainly a cliché. For example, if you say *fresh as a . . .*, you automatically complete the phrase with *daisy*. *Fresh as a daisy* is anything but fresh. Try again for a comparison that is not so familiar.

The following passage is an example, admittedly exaggerated, of cliché-ridden prose.

When I first crossed the portals of learning, I was as innocent as a newborn babe, but I had a sneaking suspicion that I would have to toe the line or my education would come to a tragic end. I soon learned that I was not the centre of attention on campus, but just one of the rank and file of students. However, although it was easier said than done, I burned the midnight oil until the wee hours and walked the straight and narrow amidst all the hustle and bustle of life in the halls of academe. I stayed sober as a judge while my room-mates were out painting the town red. My untiring efforts allowed me to weather the storms of papers and examinations. After four years of honest toil, I left university as the proud possessor of a diploma and many fond memories.

Even the careful writer who shuns such clichés as *commune with nature* and *doomed to disappointment* often succumbs to expository clichés, especially as transitional devices.

d
46d

as a matter of fact	in the final analysis
believe it or not	it goes with saying
consensus of opinion	it is interesting to note
first and foremost	last but not least
in a nutshell	needless to say
in a very real sense	to all intents and purposes

It is almost impossible to avoid an occasional expository cliché, but weed out the most obvious of them. Such weeding also eliminates deadwood.

WEAK	It is interesting to note that the consensus of opinion in New England was to all intents and purposes against the War of 1812.
IMPROVED	Most New Englanders opposed the War of 1812.

Vogue Words Vogue words (sometimes called **buzzwords**) are words or terms that become very popular, are used and overused for a brief period of time, and then drop back into relative obscurity. For example, as we write this, the terms *syndrome, bottom line, optimize, interface, access* (as verb), and *supply-side* can be seen and heard everywhere. Three years from now, there will be a new set of vogue words, and such expressions as *bottom line* will seem out of date. In their overuse and normally brief life, vogue words resemble slang. Unlike most slang, vogue words often come from scholarly or professional vocabularies (for example, *syndrome* and *interface*). Further, vogue words are used by a wider range of people than slang and often appear in quite formal writing. Try to avoid vogue words because they give the impression that you are mindlessly repeating whatever you hear around you.

Nonce Words Nonce words, or **neologisms**, are words made up on the spur of the moment. There is nothing wrong with inventing a word if no other appropriate word exists. However, you should not invent a word such as *elasticness* when the word *elasticity* already exists. Most nonce words result from making one word or part of speech from another word by adding suffixes such as *-ize, -ish, -ment, -tion, -y,* and so on.

NONCE WORD	Despite all the <u>publicization</u>, few people voted in the last provincial election.
CORRECT	Despite all the <u>publicity</u>, few people voted in the the last provincial election.
NONCE WORD	His remarks showed his <u>prejudism</u>.
CORRECT	His remarks showed his <u>prejudice</u>.
NONCE WORD	Napoleon found himself in a <u>tightish</u> situation.
CORRECT	Napoleon found himself in a <u>rather tight</u> situation.

Check your dictionary if a word that you want to use does not seem completely familiar to you. If the word is not listed in a good college dictionary, it is probably a nonce word. Find the accepted form of the word in the dictionary and use it instead. If you cannot find an accepted form, try to rewrite the sentence to avoid the nonce word. For example, you might want to describe a piece of paper so old and fragile that it could not be picked up. Instead of using the awkward nonce word *unhandleable,* write *too fragile to be handled.*

d
46d

Exercises: Clichés, Vogue Words, and Nonce Words

Part A: Underline and identify by letter the clichés (C), vogue words (V), and nonce words (N) in the following sentences.

1. It is crystal clear that if we don't get a hedge against inflation, the unprofitability of continuing to fight for the program will be political suicide.

2. The government's threat of wage and price controls has brought forth a lot of constructive input from the private sector, especially with regard to the government's efforts to create a viable program for reducing unemployment.

3. I believe our survivability depends on our maintaining a low profile during the decision-making process, but once we see how the man on the street reacts to the policy, we can support the popular faction and milk the publicity for all it's worth.

4. "You are optimizing when you say that the power outages will be under control by early morning," the shop steward said, "but I suppose only time will tell."

Part B: Make a list of five or more different vogue words collected from radio, television, and magazine articles during a two-week period. How much overlap is there between your list and those of your classmates?

Fine Writing   Fine writing, or **flowery writing,** as it is sometimes called, is the unnecessary use of descriptive adjectives and adverbs, of polysyllabic and non-English words, of "poetic" expressions, and of artificial rhetorical devices. Fine writing, despite its label, is not good writing; it is affected writing. Although fine writing is usually motivated by the writer's desire to sound dignified and learned, the reader is usually more annoyed than impressed. Avoid the pretentiousness of fine writing.

WEAK	Undesirable waste material is removed on a semi-weekly basis by municipal employees specifically assigned to such activity.
IMPROVED	City collectors pick up garbage twice a week.
WEAK	*À propos* apprehensions, my *bête noire* has ever been altitude, albeit of late I have acquired a certain *sangfroid* with respect to the same.
IMPROVED	I have a fear of heights, but I'm conquering it.
WEAK	The heavy, dull, leaden *cumuli mammati* amassed menacingly and released upon the eager earth their life-sustaining burden, thereby effectively destroying our well-laid plans for a sylvan outing accompanied by comestibles.
IMPROVED	Clouds piled up, and it began to rain, spoiling our picnic in the woods.

d
46d

Exercises: Fine Writing

Part A: Translate the following examples of fine writing into good, plain English.

1. It is beyond the capacity of mortal mind to elucidate the tendency of domestic felines to express vocally their discontent with others of their species.

2. It was with decided alacrity that I hastened to respond to the reverberations of the signaling device at my portals.
3. He remains wedded to his books, still in the infancy of his cerebral *Wanderjahr*, clothing himself in the weeds of learning in preparation for launching himself on the great sea of life.
4. An imprudent man rarely, if ever, has the innate capacity and intellectual wherewithal to retain for a sustained period of time the profusion of currency that Fate has, in all of her bountiful generosity, heaped upon him.

Part B: Rewrite the following common English proverbs to make them into examples of fine writing.

1. You can't teach an old dog new tricks.
2. Sticks and stones may break my bones, but words can never hurt me.
3. Don't count your chickens before they are hatched.
4. One man's meat is another man's poison.

Overuse of Words or Phrases Perhaps you have recently learned the word *cogent* and enjoy using it as often as possible. Your reader, however, may not share your enthusiasm. If you have used *cogent* five times in a three-page paper, substitute a synonym such as *compelling, convincing,* or *forcible* for three or four of these uses.

A related problem is that of repeating one noun over and over again. It may be the correct noun, but excessive repetition is annoying to the reader. If there is no danger of ambiguity or improper connotations, substitute a pronoun or a synonym now and then to break the monotony.

d
46d

Repetitive

When I was in grade ten, I came down with chicken pox. Chicken pox is a childhood disease, and I was embarrassed to have to admit to my friends that I had chicken pox as an adult of fifteen. Although my younger sister had chicken pox at the same time, she didn't get as many spots as I did. Apparently, the older people are, the worse chicken pox affects them.

Improved

When I was in grade ten, I came down with chicken pox. This is a childhood disease, and I was embarrassed to have to admit to my friends that I had it as an adult of fifteen. Although my younger sister had chicken pox at the same time, she didn't get as many spots as I did. Apparently, the older people are, the worse the disease affects them.

However, do not feel that you must eliminate every repeated word. If a word has no good synonyms or if pronouns or synonyms would be ambiguous, repeat it as often as is necessary for clarity. Deliberate and parallel repetition can even be an effective way to create emphasis (see 48b).

Exercise: Overuse of Words or Phrases

The following paragraph suffers greatly from overuse of certain words. Rewrite it, retaining the sentence structure as much as possible but substituting synonyms or pronouns to break the monotony.

The man and the woman seated themselves on opposite ends of the park bench. They exchanged covert glances, and each moved from the opposite direction to a position a little nearer the middle of the bench. Each pretended to read—she a magazine, and he the newspaper—but all the while each peeked covertly at the other. Almost simultaneously each coughed and pretended to adjust his or her shoe, but each seized the opportunity to bend over as a covert opportunity for a second move closer to the centre of the bench. Now each was only centimetres from the other. The woman covertly blushed behind her magazine; the man smiled. Almost at once each moved almost into the lap of the other, a move that sent both jumping to their feet. "I arrest you," he shouted, waving a police ID covertly slipped from his pocket, but before he could finish his statement, she countered, "I hereby arrest you," displaying her police badge. Each looked at the other in amazement, both covertly pocketed their IDs, and both walked away in wonder that they could have been so wrong as all that.

---

d
46e

46e ▪ Figures of Speech

Figures of speech are expressions in which words are used not to convey a literal meaning but to add freshness and vividness to writing.

Metaphors and Similes The most familiar figures of speech are metaphors and similes. Both compare two things that are not of the same general class but that have something in common. The two figures of speech differ primarily in their grammar.

A simile makes an explicit comparison by means of such words as *like, as,* or *as if.*

The impatient tapping of her fingers on the table was <u>like</u> corn popping.

Myra's acceptance was <u>as</u> hesitant <u>as</u> one's first bite of squid.

A metaphor makes an implicit comparison by speaking of one thing as if it actually were the other. Metaphors often take the form *X is Y*.

> My hometown is a culinary desert; the traveler will find no oases, only the waterholes of Burger King and Church's Fried Chicken.

> His memoirs provide not so much a window on the past as a keyhole through which we may guiltily peep.

Both metaphors and similes are especially common in proverbs and proverbial expressions. *There's many a slip 'twixt the cup and the lip, Great oaks from little acorns grow,* and *The early bird gets the worm* are all metaphors. *As big as a barn, as welcome as water in your shoes,* and *like a bolt out of the blue* are all similes. Many of these expressions are so common that they have become "dead" metaphors or similes. We use them without being aware that they are actually figures of speech. In fact, it is almost impossible to write without using an occasional dead metaphor.

Rather than trying to rid your writing of all dead metaphors, concentrate on becoming more aware of their presence and on not letting them come back to life unexpectedly. For example, *to have a frog in one's throat* is a common dead metaphor for hoarseness, and, in most contexts, no one would take it literally. But in any context that includes animals, it is potentially dangerous.

> Professor Hawkins' lecture on amphibians was difficult to understand because he had a frog in his throat.

In the context of *amphibians,* the word *frog* suddenly takes on literal meaning and the resulting image is ludicrous. The skilful writer, however, may occasionally resurrect a dead metaphor to good effect.

> Unfortunately, Fred is an alarmist and cannot tell the difference between the handwriting on the wall and simple graffiti.

> I had finally found a man after my own heart; only later did I discover that he was also after my money.

In a **mixed metaphor,** several different and incompatible comparisons appear in one context. Mixed metaphors usually occur when the writer absentmindedly employs several dead metaphors.

> Deborah shot straight from the hip and didn't pull any punches.

> Although old MacAdoo had one foot in the grave, he kept his ear to the ground and always knew which end was up.

Strained similes and metaphors result from comparing two things that do not have enough in common or from making comparisons that suggest the wrong connotations.

STRAINED SIMILE	All my faith in technology has scattered like papers in a breeze.
STRAINED METAPHOR	Her mind was a veritable garbage truck; it picked up vast amounts of loose information, compressed it, and spewed it out again in compact form.

d 46e

In the first sentence, *faith* does not *scatter*, nor can one imagine how it possibly could scatter; the simile just does not work. In the second sentence, the writer apparently intends the comparison between a *mind* and a *garbage truck* to be complimentary, but the connotations of *garbage truck* are so unfavorable that the metaphor is not effective.

In sum, metaphors and similes are an important means of adding freshness and vividness to writing. Like most good things, they have some built-in traps and should not be misused or overused.

Irony is saying one thing and meaning something else—often just the opposite. Well-handled, irony is neither so obvious that it annoys the reader ("heavy" irony) nor so subtle that it escapes the reader.

> The apartment was adequate: six flights of stairs to keep me in shape, no closets to be cleaned or windows to be washed, and plenty of living creatures for company.

This sentence is ironic because the writer says *adequate* but means *inadequate*. The reader knows that a seventh-floor walk-up is *not* desirable, that good apartments have both closets and windows, and that the *living creatures* are vermin.

One danger in employing irony is its tendency to become sarcastic. Although sarcasm and irony are closely related, irony is relatively restrained and gentle, while sarcasm is more sneering, more vicious, and more personal; it is intended to hurt. Readers usually respond with pleasure to well-handled irony but are likely to turn against the author of sarcasm. The distinction between the two is fairly easy to maintain in speech, where facial expressions and tone of voice reveal intentions. In writing, there are only words, which are easily misinterpreted.

---

d
46e

Exercises: Figures of Speech

Part A: Use similes, metaphors, or irony to make the following sentences more specific and vivid. Avoid using mixed or strained metaphors or those that have become clichés.

1. When Inga got up and saw the cold rain outside, she felt really depressed—especially when she saw her unfinished homework on the desk and all of her dirty laundry scattered around the room.
2. At the school for handicapped children where Bob is a tutor, one of the children brought him a paper daisy she had made for him. He was very touched by this present. He felt like crying.
3. When the cop pulled us over and gave us a speeding ticket, we were really angry because he was so mean and nasty about it.
4. The owner of the store yelled a lot, but he didn't really mean it, and no one was scared of him.

Part B: Identify and label the strained and mixed metaphors and similes and the poorly used irony in the following sentences. Then rewrite the sentences, using more suitable figures of speech.

1. My first (and last) date with Jay was nothing short of heaven: he was fashionably late; his impeccable attire was punctuated with a brown shoe on one foot and a black one on the other; he took me to a lovely, intimate restaurant down in the boondocks; he delighted me to the brink of insanity with his elephant jokes; and then he allowed me to pay the bill!
2. The old man's agile body ticks along like a fine Swiss watch that never misses a beat and rarely needs rewinding.
3. "Hilda is," John remarked, "a woman with all the discretion of a full-blown sandstorm that knows no boundaries and respects no restraints."

46f ▪ Tone and Point of View

Tone is the attitude we express toward our subject, our reader, and even ourselves. Our tone determines to a large extent both the emotional and the intellectual effect of our writing on our reader. Tone may be formal or informal, tragic or comic, angry or cheerful, kindly or cruel, personal or impersonal. It can be bitter, hopeless, ironic, or sympathetic—in other words, tone reflects the entire range of human emotions. Choice of words is one of the most important components of tone, although choice of grammatical constructions and even content—what we include and what we omit—also contribute to our tone.

SYMPATHETIC TONE	Omar tends to be frustrated by mental tasks.
CRUEL TONE	Omar is too stupid to do anything calling for even a minimum of intelligence.
HUMOROUS TONE	Omar wasn't behind the door when they passed out the brains—he wasn't even in the house.

d
46f

Point of view is closely related to tone. It is the position from which we see our subject as we write. We may be emotionally moved, or we may be dispassionate observers. We reveal our point of view by the words we select and by what facts we include or exclude.

The following accounts of Louis Riel's activities illustrate how changing the tone and point of view also changes the message the reader receives.

In June 1884 Riel was invited by a group of settlers, half-breed and white, to return to Canada to lead a protest against the Canadian Goverment's indifference to Western grievances. He carried out a peaceful political agitation in the valley of the Saskatchewan, and sent a petition to Ottawa. During the spring of 1885 his actions became more and more irresponsible. He broke with the Roman Catholic Church, established a Métis provisional government and attempted to secure the support of the Indians.

Encyclopedia Canadiana

Riel and his family made the long journey northward over the trails from Montana to Batoche in the heart of the South Saskatchewan Métis country during the summer of 1884. The following winter, conferences were held and committees set up, not only among the Métis and English-speaking half-breeds but including white settlers as well, to discuss real or imaginary grievances against the Government of Ottawa. Caught up in the excitement, Riel began to lose his emotional balance. His mind became dominated by increasingly extreme and peculiar religious ideas. Moderates drew away from him but the simple, superstitious majority were stimulated by his very fervour and came to share it. On March 19, 1885, along with Gabriel Dumont, who would provide the real leadership, Riel proclaimed a provisional government.

D.G.G. Kerr and R.I.K. Davidson,
Canada: A Visual History

The tone of the first passage, taken from an encylopedia, is intended to be objective. Most of the words are neutral, although slanting appears in *irresponsible*. The author concentrates on relating facts, such as dates and events.

The tone of the second passage betrays an antagonistic point of view, revealed by such words and phrases as *imaginary, increasingly extreme, peculiar religious ideas, very fervour, lose his emotional balance,* and *the simple, superstitious majority were stimulated*. Note that the first passage states that Riel was invited by half-breeds *and* whites, whereas the second implies surprise that Riel worked "not only among the Métis and English-speaking half-breeds *but . . .* white settlers *as well*." Also, the authors of the second passage cast doubt on Riel's mental state, on his ability to attract any but the simple and superstitious, and on his ability to lead, by making the aside that Dumont (who is not mentioned in the encyclopedia entry) would provide *the real leadership* in the provisional government.

d
46f

Objectivity is not an automatic virtue, nor is subjectivity always a fault. Research papers should be as objective as possible; their purpose is to convey factual information. But a personal-experience paper may quite properly be highly subjective if its chief purpose is to convey impressions and emotions, not facts. The important things are that your readers understand your approach to your topic and that you not try to pass off opinions as facts.

Establish both tone and point of view in the opening sentences of a paper and maintain them consistently throughout the paper. Otherwise, the readers will not know how they are supposed to respond. Avoid excesses of tone. A pompous tone will bore the reader, a flippant tone applied to a serious subject will annoy the reader, and an overly sentimental tone will embarrass the reader. Tone should also be determined by the intended audience. For example, your description of a class that you are taking might have a humorous (or, for that matter, poisonous) tone in a letter to a friend but should be serious and objective in an official course evaluation.

Exercises: Tone and Point of View

The following problem requires several brief, well-written paragraphs of three to four sentences each. Write each paragraph from a different point of view and in a distinctly different tone. Use the same general information within each paragraph. Do not try to resolve the problem, but concentrate on point of view and tone.

Problem: Susan and Miriam were roommates during the previous term and therefore shared a telephone. When she left school, Susan did not pay her share of the telephone bill. The telephone company has disconnected the service, and Miriam cannot get service reinstated unless she pays the $112.82 that Susan owes.

1. Write the first paragraph of Miriam's letter to the telephone company.
2. Write the beginning of the telephone company's response to Miriam.
3. Write part of Miriam's letter to Susan.
4. Write part of Susan's response to Miriam.

47 The Dictionary (*dict*)

Your dictionary is the most valuable reference book you will ever own. What is more, dictionaries are real bargains; you get a well-bound, well-printed book with 1200 to 1800 pages for less than the price of most hard-cover textbooks. Because dictionaries are so valuable and because they are relatively inexpensive, every writer should own a good hard-cover edition. Paperback editions have only about half as many entries as hard-cover editions, and their bindings are not sturdy enough to withstand heavy use. A paperback is, however, convenient as a second dictionary to carry with you to class or to the library.

There are numerous misconceptions about dictionaries. The first and perhaps major misconception is that all dictionaries are alike. There are many differences among dictionaries. A second misconception is that dictionaries are infallible. Nothing is infallible, and if two dictionaries disagree on a point, obviously both cannot be "right." A third misconception is that, if a word is not in the dictionary, it is not a word. Even the largest unabridged dictionaries do not and could not include every new technical term, every ephemeral slang expression, every slight change in meaning of existing words.

Your dictionary should be up to date; if it is more than ten years old, keep it for cross-referencing and double-checking, but buy a new version of another dictionary. Every printing of good dictionaries includes many changes from the previous printing, so the edition number itself is not enough to ensure that you have the most recent version. Check the date of printing on the back of the title page.

d
47

47a • College Dictionaries

When buying a dictionary, be sure you have the exact title you want. The name *Webster* itself is not copyrighted, and many inadequate dictionaries include the word *Webster* in their titles. Some dictionaries are Canadian primarily in their titles. You may be required to buy a particular dictionary. If you are not, you can choose the one best suited to your own interests and tastes. All of the following are excellent college dictionaries:

Funk & Wagnalls Standard College Dictionary, Canadian Edition (Toronto: Fitzhenry and Whiteside)

The Random House College Dictionary (New York: Random House)

Webster's New Collegiate Dictionary (Springfield Mass: G. And C. Merriam Company; Toronto: Thomas Allen and Sons)

Funk & Wagnalls Standard College Dictionary, Canadian Edition, has an adequate type size and useful, though not numerous, illustrations. A good college dictionary for Canadian students, it has a large number of entries (about 155 000) and many notes on usage. The pronunciation guides are clear. Of the American-based college dictionaries that are widely used, the *Funk & Wagnalls* is the best for Canadian students because it contains more Canadian words than any other and clearly indicates preferred Canadian spellings as well as variants. (In addition, it provides such material as Canadian weights and measures, the prime ministers and governors general of Canada, and the Canadian Bill of Rights.)

The Random House College Dictionary has an exceptionally large number of entries (about 170 000). To achieve this while keeping the overall physical size of the dictionary relatively compact, the publishers used a small typeface. The number of illustrations is about average.

Webster's New Collegiate Dictionary has a clear and easily readable typeface but relatively few illustrations. It has many fewer notes on usage than the other dictionaries, but the brief contexts provided for a large number of words partially compensate for the absence of usage labels. The pronunciation guides may be slightly more difficult to interpret than those of the other dictionaries. The number of entries (about 150 000) is about average. It is the only one of the dictionaries listed here that includes an index.

Note Although it does not have as many entries as a college dictionary, the *Gage Canadian Dictionary* (Toronto: Macmillan Company of Canada) is useful for Canadian students because it has a wide range of Canadian words not found in standard college dictionaries. It gives Canadian spellings clearly, listing them first; its editors generally prefer British-based forms except for words such as *favor* and *labor*. (The spelling in this textbook is based on that of *Gage*.)

Another dictonary familiar to many students is the *Concise Oxford Dictionary*. Many Canadian writers who prefer British-based spelling regard it as indispensible for its clear and complete definitions and for the number of entries its editors have packed into a compact, easy-to-handle volume. It does not, however, indicate Canadian, as opposed to American, spellings; neither does it show syllable breaks.

47b ▪ Using the Dictionary

Unfortunately, many people use a dictionary only for information on spelling, definitions, and pronunciation. To get the most out of your dictionary, you should be familiar with the front and back matter, which includes explanatory notes on how the dictionary is organized, lists of abbreviations used, a statement of the editors' goals, and brief articles on the history of the language and on dialects and usage. Make a mental note of where the list of abbreviations is located so that you can refer to it easily when you encounter an unfamiliar abbreviation.

Unless you have no idea how to spell it, finding a word in the dictionary should not take longer than twenty to thirty seconds. Open the dictionary to the general location, and then use the guides at the tops of the pages; do not waste time scanning the page itself. If you are using the dictionary to check spelling, read the definition to be sure you have the right word: *discrete* and *discreet* are both English adjectives, but their meanings are different.

47c ▪ The Dictionary Entry

Within each dictionary entry, the information appears in a given order. This order varies slightly from dictionary to dictionary, but a typical order is (1) main entry, (2) pronunciation, (3) part of speech, (4) spelling of inflected forms, (5) definitions, (6) etymology. Following these may be additional information, such as synomyms and antonyms, information on usage, derived forms, alternative spellings, and idioms in which the word is used. A typical dictionary entry appears on page 244.

The Main Entry The main entry gives the spelling of the word; most dictionaries also list acceptable variant spellings at this point. If the word is a compound word, the main entry shows its treatment, which may vary considerably among dictionaries. For example, *Funk & Wagnalls* and *Random House* list the spelling *home-grown*, whereas *Webster's* lists *homegrown*. *Funk & Wagnalls* and *Random House* list *home-brew*, whereas *Webster's* lists *home brew*. All three agree on *home run*.

The main entry also gives the appropriate word division; the raised dot between letters corresponds to an end-of-the-line hyphen in writing or typing. All dictionaries agree on the division of the great majority of words, but occasionally they differ here too. For example, *Webster's New Collegiate* and *Random House* divide the word *flunky* as *flun·ky*, but *Funk & Wagnalls* divides it as flunk·y.

If the main entry is capitalized in the dictionary, the word should be capitalized in writing.

Pronunciation The pronunciation, including stress or accent, is indicated between parentheses (between diagonal slashes in *Webster's New Collegiate*). A pronunciation guide appears at the bottom of every right-hand page in *Webster's New Collegiate*, *Random House*, and *Funk & Wagnalls*. Acceptable alternative pronunciations follow the pronuncia-

d
47c

MAIN
ENTRY   PRONUNCIATION   PART OF
SPEECH LABEL   INFLECTED
FORMS

pret·ty (prit′ē) *adj.* **·ti·er, ·ti·est 1.** Characterized by delicacy, gracefulness, or proportion rather than by striking beauty: a *pretty* face. **2.** Pleasant; attractive: a *pretty* melody. **3.** Decent; good; sufficient: often used ironically: A *pretty* mess you've made of it! **4.** *Informal* Rather large in size or degree; considerable. **5.** Characterized by effeminacy; affected; foppish. **6.** *Archaic* Fine; elegant. **7.** *Archaic* or *Scot.* Bold; vigorous; strong. — **Syn.** See BEAUTIFUL. — *adv.* **1.** To a fair extent; moderately; somewhat; rather: He looked *pretty* well. **2.** *Dial.* Prettily; finely — **sitting pretty** *Informal* In good circumstances. — *n. pl.* **·ties** (-tēz) A pretty person or thing. [OE *prættig* sly, cunning < *præt* deceit] — **pret′ti·ly** *adv.* — **pret′ti·ness** *n.*

IDIOMS   SYNONYM   ETYMOLOGY   USAGE LABELS

DEFINITIONS

Funk & Wagnalls Standard College Dictionary, Canadian Edition. Copyright 1982 by Fitzhenry and Whiteside, Toronto. With permission.

tion that the editors judge to be most common. If no pronunciation is listed beside a word, it is pronounced like a preceding entry with the same root.

Part of Speech The part-of-speech category to which the word belongs is abbreviated in all dictionaries. If a single word can be more than one part of speech, most dictionaries include other parts under the main entry, with a new part-of-speech label preceding the definition.

Our sample entry indicates that *pretty* is used not only as an adjective but also as an adverb and a noun.

Inflected Forms If the spelling of inflected forms of words is irregular, the inflected forms are listed. In our example, the comparative and superlative forms of *pretty* are given because the final *-y* changes to *-i-* when these endings are added.

Etymology The etymology of a word is its history; the entry will note whether the word existed in Old English, was borrowed from another language, or has an unknown origin. In addition, the etymologies listed in dictionaries give, as far as possible, the original components of the word and earlier spellings and meanings. For obvious compounds such as *lampshade*, no etymology is listed because the etymology is that of the two parts of the compound.

Our sample shows us that the word *pretty* has been in the language since Anglo-Saxon (Old English) times but that its spelling and its meaning have changed a great deal over the years.

d
47c

Definitions Definitions typically consist of explanations or synonyms or both. Brief examples of words in context are sometimes provided. Even though dictionaries concentrate on the denotative and not the connotative meanings of words, the usage labels and synonyms give some information about connotations. For example, *Webster's* lists *frugal*, *thrifty*, and *economical* as synonyms of *sparing* but *close*, *niggardly*, *parsimonious*, and *miserly* as synonyms of *stingy*, thus clearly indicating that the connotations of *sparing* are more favorable than those of *stingy*.

Most dictionaries list what the editors feel is the most common or general meaning of a word first, followed by more restricted meanings. For example, regional or slang meanings appear late in the entry: an entry for *home-brew* would give the common meaning first, "any alcoholic beverage, especially beer, made at home." Variations of this definition appear in *Webster's Collegiate, Random House*, and *Funk & Wagnalls*, but only *Funk & Wagnalls* gives the slang use, "an athlete native to the country he plays in or place he represents" and notes it is Canadian.

Some dictionaries order definitions by historical occurrence, with the earliest meanings first. *The Oxford English Dictionary* (in thirteen volumes!) and the dictionaries based upon it follow this procedure. Of the collegiate dictionaries mentioned, only *Webster's Collegiate* uses historical order.

Dictionaries not intended primarily for use by postsecondary students are often helpful in presenting definitions that are simpler and clearer than those provided in the more advanced dictionaries. For example, *Webster's New World Dictionary* (Springfield, Mass.: G. & C. Merriam Company), which is intended primarily for use in homes and offices, makes a special effort to provide such definitions. Suppose, for example, you had encountered the word *plasmodium* in your reading and did not know its meaning. Compare the basic definitions you would find in *New World* and *Random House*. (The definitions in *Funk & Wagnalls* and *Webster's New Collegiate* resemble those of *Random House*.)

d
47c

NEW WORLD   a mass of protoplasm with many nuclei, formed by the fusion of one-celled organisms

RANDOM HOUSE   an amoeboid, multinucleate mass or sheet of protoplasm characteristic of some stages of organisms, as a myxomycete or slime mold

As a general dictionary, *New World* does not assume that you already know that *amoeboid* organisms have one cell or that *multinucleate* means "with many nuclei." On the other hand, *Random House* gives you more information and more detailed information about plasmodium.

Nearly every dictionary entry contains the basic information just discussed. Many entries also provide information about usage, idioms, and synonyms and antonyms.

Usage Information Information on usage takes two forms, brief labels before a definition and longer notes following a definition. If neither a label nor a note appears, the word is considered universally acceptable. Every dictionary has its own system for marking usage; this system is explained in the material at the beginning of the dictionary. In general, usage labels fall into four broad categories: occupational, geographic, currency, and status.

1. **Occupational labels** indicate that the word is limited in the given meaning to a specific occupational or intellectual field. Typical occupational labels include *Mathematics, Chemistry, Poetic,* and *Military.* For example, *Funk & Wagnalls* labels the word *mast* as a nautical term.

2. **Geographic labels** indicate that the word is limited in the given meaning to a specific geographical area of the English-speaking world. Typical geographic labels include *New England, British, Southern* (which in this context means the southern United States), and *Scottish.* For example, *Funk & Wagnalls* labels the noun *roundabout* as British in the meanings of "a merry-go-round" and "a traffic circle."

3. **Currency labels** refer to how commonly the word is used in modern English. **Rare** means that the word is uncommon. **Archaic** means that the word is still seen in books but seldom used; for example, *Webster's New Collegiate* labels *ouch* archaic in the meaning of a "clasp" or "brooch." **Obsolete** means that the word in the given meaning is never used today and that it is not familiar to the average educated person.

4. **Status labels** indicate the social acceptability of words or phrases. Dictionaries vary rather widely in the labels they use and in the extent to which they apply status labels. But in general, seven categories of status labels can be identified.

a. **No label.** The word or meaning is universally acceptable.

b. **Informal** or **colloquial.** The word is widely used in conversation but not in formal writing. For example, the noun *takeoff* is colloquial in the meaning "a burlesque imitation of someone."

c. **Slang.** The word is widely used but is extremely informal and usually expresses an irreverent or exaggerated attitude. For example, the use of the word *dog* to refer to an unattractive person is slang.

d. **Nonstandard.** The word is widely current, even among educated people, but is usually disapproved of. Examples of nonstandard usage would include *irregardless* (instead of *regardless*) or *like* as a conjunction.

e. **Substandard** or **illiterate.** The word or form is widely used but only by the least well educated people and not by prestige groups. It is considered incorrect, usually even by the people who regularly use it. An example of substandard usage would be *he ain't* (instead of *he isn't*).

f. **Dialectal** or **regional.** Dialectal or regional labels are similar to geographic labels but are normally restricted to small geographic areas. Forms labelled dialectal are acceptable within the particular region but are considered incorrect or at least old-fashioned outside of that region. An example of dialectal usage would be *het* as the past tense or past participle of *heat,* especially in the expression *all het up.*

d
47c

g. **Vulgar.** There is a social taboo attached to the word; many people consider it impolite or offensive. An example is the word *snot*. If the taboo is very strong, the word may be labelled **obscene** or **taboo**. Incuded in the general category of vulgar words are **derogatory** terms (such as *Polack*) and **profane** terms (such as *goddamn*).

Usage notes at the end of an entry discuss the usage of words in more details. Dictionaries differ rather widely in their employment of usage notes and in their "permissiveness." Of the college dictionaries discussed here, *Funk & Wagnalls* provides the most detailed discussions. For example, it carefully distinguishes *disinterested* and *uninterested*: "A person is *disinterested* if he does not stand to profit by the way he acts in a particular instance: *disinterested* advice; a *disinterested* bystander. A person is *uninterested* if he is simply without interest, as from boredom or indifference." *Random House* notes that *disinterested* and *uninterested* are not properly synonyms. *Webster's New Collegiate*, which has a policy of employing usage notes very sparingly, lists *uninterested* as a synonym for *disinterested*. Writers who feel somewhat shaky about their own usage will probably prefer one of the more prescriptive dictionaries.

Non-English Words   Dictionaries also specially indicate words that have not become fully assimilated into English. (French and foreign words should be underlined in writing.) *Random House* puts the main entry in italics; *Webster's New Collegiate* puts the language of origin and the meaning in that language in square brackets after the pronunciation. *Funk & Wagnalls* puts the language or origin in italics before the definition. For example, all the dictionaries treat *sine qua non*, meaning "something that is essential," as a foreign expression.

Idioms   All the dictionaries list some common idioms under main entries. *Random House* has probably the most complete coverage, followed by *Funk & Wagnalls*. *Webster's New Collegiate* lists the fewest idioms; many of these have separate main entries and are not listed under the key word. For example, *Random House* lists eighteen idioms with the word *play*, *Funk & Wagnalls* lists ten, and *Webster's New Collegiate* lists seven (including those under separate main entries). *The Oxford Advanced Learner's Dictionary of Current English*, which is intended for people whose mother tongue is not English and who, therefore, need special guidance in idioms, lists twenty-seven idiomatic uses of *play*.

d
47c

Synonyms and Antonyms   At the end of many main entries, dictionaries provide a list of synonyms and sometimes antonyms. Often a brief paragraph explains the differences in shades of meaning among the synonyms. For example, under the main entry for the noun *associate*, *Funk & Wagnalls* discusses the differences among the words *associate, companion, comrade, partner, mate, colleague,* and *ally* and also lists the antonyms *opponent* and *rival*. Dictionaries also cross-reference many entries, referring the reader to other entries for a list of synonyms and antonyms.

47d ▪ Special Features of Dictionaries

Besides their regular entries, dictionaries provide a great deal of other useful information. Nearly all dictionaries give, either in the main text or as separate sections at the end, biographical and geographical information, tables of weights and measures, signs and symbols, abbreviations, chemical elements, proofreaders' marks, and various alphabets. Some dictionaries have currency tables, forms of address, brief manuals of style, rhyming dictionaries, lists of common given names, and tables of Greek and Latin prefixes, suffixes, and roots used in English.

47e ▪ Unabridged Dictionaries

The college dictionaries discussed here are sufficient for most needs, but occasionally you may wish to refer to a larger, unabridged dictionary. These are usually located in the reference section of a library. There are four unabridged dictionaries in current use:

Funk & Wagnalls New Standard Dictionary of the English Language (the basis of *Funk & Wagnalls Standard College Dictionary*)

The Random House Dictionary of the English Language (the basis of *The Random House College Dictionary*)

Webster's Third New International Dictionary (the basis of *Webster's New Collegiate Dictionary*)

The Oxford English Dictionary (the basis of the *Concise Oxford Dictionary*; the unabridged *Oxford*'s 13 volumes plus supplements are unique in their extensive historical information about words).

47f ▪ Special Dictionaries

Special dictionaries provide information on a single class of words (slang, dialect words, economic terms, legal terms) or on a specific subject (book illustrators, battles, rubber, banking). Special dictionaries give readers in-depth information on a particular word or subject—more information than a general dictionary can.

Special-word dictionaries provide unusual information; as well, they give insights into the immense store of words in the language. The following dictionaries may be of particular interest to students of English:

Avis, Walter S. et al., eds., *Dictionary of Canadianisms on Historical Principles* (Toronto: W. J. Gage, 1967)

Follett, Wilson, *Modern American Usage*, ed. Jacques Barzun (New York: Hill and Wang, 1966)

Fowler, H.W., *Dictionary of Modern English Usage*, 2nd ed., rev. and ed. Sir Ernest Gowers (New York: Oxford University Press, 1965)

Lewis, Norman, *The New Roget's Thesaurus of the English Language in Dictionary Form* (New York: Putnam's, 1964)

Onions, Charles T., et al., eds., *The Oxford Dictionary of English Etymology* (New York: Oxford University Press, 1966)

Partridge, Eric, *Dictionary of Slang and Unconventional English*, 7th ed. (New York: Macmillan, 1970)

Partridge, Eric, *Origins: A Short Etymological Dictionary of Modern English* (New York: Macmillan, 1977)

Webster's New World Dictionary of Synonyms (Springfield Mass.: G.&C. Merriam, 1978)

Wentworth, Harold, and Stuart Berg Flexner, *Dictionary of American Slang*, 2nd supp. ed (New York: Crowell, 1975)

Exercises: The Dictionary

Part A. In the reference room of your library, locate the standard collegiate dictionaries discussed above. Read and take careful notes on each dictionary's treatment of the following words.

a. bigot   c. coarse   e. like (conj.)   g. silly   i. fiddlehead
b. bingo   d. gismo   f. promethium   h. yokel   j. bombardier

For each word, write a brief paragraph summarizing the differences in treatment among the dictionaries, taking into consideration such things as amount of information given in the definition, etymological statements, usage labels, pronunciation guides, mention of alternative spellings, and derived forms listed. Then write another paragraph explaining which dictionary you think is best for you and why you think so.

Part B. Find the unabridged edition of the *Oxford English Dictionary* in your library and look up the following four words. Write a brief paragraph summarizing how the meanings of each have changed over the years. Have the meanings become broader, narrower, or just different?

a. girl   b. kind   c. liquor   d. mere

Part C. Write your own brief dictionary (ten to twelve items) of slang expressions that you encounter among one particular group of people or in one place (for example, with members of an ethnic group or in the pool hall, the dorm, a disco, or the stables). Use terms peculiar to the chosen group or place as much as possible. Make as specific a definition of each as you can and guess at etymologies by looking up the words in a standard dictionary and comparing those meanings with definitions of the words found in slang dictionaries.

d
47f

Rhetoric

48 Words into Sentences

In many ways, a sentence is a miniature essay. Like a good essay, a good sentence has a definite and clear organization. It usually has a single purpose—to explain, to describe, to narrate, or to further an argument. It even has a thesis, a point that justifies its existence. The analogy, however, should not be carried too far: An essay has a purpose of its own, but the ultimate purpose of a sentence is to serve the essay as a whole. An occasional sentence may be so memorable that it is quoted independently of its context, but most good sentences are good only insofar as they contribute to the paragraph and to the entire paper in which they appear.

Good sentences must have clarity, emphasis, and variety. Clarity is the universal requirement—if the reader doesn't understand what you intend to say, the entire sentence is a failure. Emphasis and variety are relative matters. Everything you say should be clear, but you do not want to emphasize every single word that you use, nor is there much value in variety just for the sake of variety. In other words, proper emphasis and variety depend on the context in which you are writing. This context includes not only the sentences before and after the sentence you are writing, but also the subject matter, the audience, the type of writing, and the purpose of the paper.

As an illustration of how different contexts demand different arrangements, assume that you have the following ideas to express.

> Fumes kill things. Some fumes come from automobiles. These automobile fumes have killed maple trees. These maple trees are along the boulevard.

All these ideas can easily be combined into one simple, "neutral" sentence.

> Automobile fumes have killed the maple trees along the boulevard.

rh
48

If you had been discussing the different kinds of fumes that damage the environment, you might make fumes the subject of the sentence.

> Fumes from automobiles have killed the maple trees along the boulevard.

If you were stressing the different kinds of vegetation harmed by pollution, you could begin the sentence by naming a particular kind of vegetation.

> The maple trees along the boulevard have been killed by automobile fumes.

If your focus were on the various areas of the city where pollution damage has occurred, you might mention a particular area first.

> Along the boulevard, automobile fumes have killed the maple trees.

If you wished to correct an erroneous impression that it was old age or vandalism that killed the maple trees, you could write the sentence to stress that idea.

> It was automobile fumes that killed the maple trees along the boulevard.

All of these sentences are clear. The different orders provide different emphases suitable for different contexts.

These sentences also illustrate the importance of position in a sentence. In most English sentences, we expect the topic, or what we are focusing our attention on, to come early in the sentence, followed by the comment, or what we have to say about that topic. In the first of the rewritten sentences above, the topic is automobile fumes, whereas in the third sentence, the topic is maple trees.

Effective sentences fulfil the reader's expectations about topic and comment; weak sentences betray the reader's expectations. For example, if the third sentence appeared in a context focusing on types of harmful fumes, our expectations would be frustrated because the early position of the phrase *the maple trees* (and its use as subject of the sentence) makes us think that it is the focus of attention. A composition teacher would probably write "Weak Passive" beside that sentence, not because the passive is wrong as such, but because its use in such a context misleads the reader.

48a ▪ Clarity *(clar)*

The first essential of clarity is having something to say and then saying it in an organized fashion. However, many writers who do have something to say and who arrange what they have to say logically still have difficulty in making their sentences clear to their readers. To be clear, sentences must have proper grammar and punctuation, effective use of co-ordination and subordination, appropriate transitions, and careful placement of modifiers. They should not contain irrelevant detail or rely too heavily on speech patterns. Proper grammar and punctuation are discussed extensively in the first 44 sections of this book; see especially 23, "Problems with Sentence Form."

Co-ordination and Subordination   Proper co-ordination and subordination are essential for clarity. Co-ordination connects related ideas of equal importance. By far the most common way to co-ordinate ideas is with co-ordinating conjunctions and correlative co-ordinating conjunctions (see 9a).

> The word *skunk* comes from Algonquian, and *moose* is from Narragansett.
> Horatio Alger wrote over a hundred books, but he died penniless.
> Either I am seeing things, or that is a trooper behind us.

rh
48a

Less frequently, a semicolon replaces the co-ordinating conjunction.

> The word *skunk* comes from Algonquian; *moose* is from Narragan-
> sett.
> Horatio Alger wrote over a hundred books; he died penniless.

Faulty co-ordination occurs when the wrong co-ordinator is used or when items that should not be co-ordinated are connected by a co-ordinator. Overuse of *and* results in one of the most frequent kinds of faulty co-ordination. In the following sentence, the co-ordinator should be *but* because the idea in the second clause contradicts the expectation set up in the first clause.

FAULTY   Grey Owl, a handsome Indian in buckskins, created a
             sensation as he toured England to lecture, <u>and</u> he was
             really an Englishman named Archie Belaney.

REVISED   Grey Owl, a handsome Indian in buckskins, created a
             sensation as he toured England to lecture, <u>but</u> he was
             really an Englishman named Archie Belaney.

And is also misused if it connects ideas that are not really related or that are not of equal weight. Usually one of the ideas should be subordinated to, rather than co-ordinated with, the other.

FAULTY   The *Mona Lisa* was in the Louvre, <u>and</u> it was stolen from
             there in 1911.

REVISED   The *Mona Lisa* was stolen from the Louvre in 1911.

FAULTY   You misspell just one word, <u>and</u> she gives you an F.

REVISED   If you misspell just one word, she gives you an F.

Important as co-ordination is for connecting equal and related ideas, it should not be overused. Especially in narrative writing, one may be tempted to string one clause after another, all connected by *and* or *so*. Sometimes the relationship is completely clear without any co-ordinator at all; sometimes subordination makes the relationship clearer.

**rh
48a**

EXCESSIVE   We took the bus from Seattle to Vancouver, <u>and</u>
CO-ORDINATION   the bus driver was new to the route, <u>and</u> he got
                     lost, <u>and</u> he was supposed to come in on High-
                     way 1, <u>and</u> somehow he went all the way to
                     Horseshoe Bay, so even though it was sched-
                     uled to arrive at six o'clock, the bus arrived
                     at seven-thirty, <u>and</u> the man sitting next to
                     me said, "This must be the ten-cent tour of
                     Vancouver."

REVISED   When we took the bus from Seattle to Vancouver,
                     the bus driver, new to the route, got lost. He
                     was supposed to come in on Highway 1, but
                     somehow he went all the way to Horseshoe
                     Bay. Even though it was scheduled to arrive at

six o'clock, the bus arrived at seven-thirty. The man sitting next to me said, "This must be the ten-cent tour of Vancouver."

Like co-ordination, subordination connects related ideas. With subordination, however, the ideas should *not* be of equal importance. Instead, subordination should highlight the main idea by showing just how the less important idea relates to it. This is done by using the subordinating conjunction, correlative subordinating conjunction, or relative pronoun that best expresses the relationship. Many kinds of relationships are possible. A subordinate clause may identify something or state the reason for something in the main clause. Or it may limit the main clause by specifying a time, a condition, a purpose, or an exception. (See also 9.)

IDENTIFICATION The llama, <u>which</u> is a member of the camel family, is native to South America.

TIME <u>Until</u> the Spanish arrived, the most common beast of burden <u>in</u> Peru was the llama.

CONDITION A llama will refuse to budge <u>if</u> it is overloaded.

CAUSE The Quechua washed babies in llama urine <u>because</u> they thought it would keep evil spirits away.

Faulty subordination occurs when the wrong subordinator is used or when one idea is incorrectly subordinated to another.

FAULTY I hope I get into medical school <u>because</u> I've done well in all my science courses. (Doing well in my courses is not why I want to go to medical school.)

REVISED I hope I get into medical school; I've done well in all my science courses.

REVISED I think I have a good chance of getting into medical school because I've done well in all my science courses.

FAULTY We spent the entire day cleaning our room and didn't even go to classes, <u>in that</u> Eli's mother was coming to visit him.

REVISED We spent the entire day cleaning our room and even cut our classes because Eli's mother was coming to visit him.

Excessive subordination occurs when so many subordinated elements are piled into one sentence that, even though the sentence may be grammatically correct, the reader has a hard time wading through all the clauses and phrases.

EXCESSIVE
SUBORDINATION
I am writing this letter to you <u>because</u> the cassette tapes for "Beginning Hindustani," <u>which</u>

rh
48a

I ordered from you on December 13 and <u>which</u> were advertised on page 27 of your fall catalogue, still have not arrived, <u>even though</u> you promised delivery within four weeks, <u>provided</u> the tapes were to be mailed to an educational institution in North America, <u>although</u> I realize <u>that</u> mail deliveries are often delayed during the Christmas season, <u>so</u> I was not surprised <u>when</u> they did not arrive by February 1, but it has now been ten weeks <u>since</u> I ordered the tapes, <u>which</u> seems like an excessive delay under any circumstances.

REVISED I am writing this letter to you <u>because</u> an order I made on December 13 still <u>has</u> not arrived. I ordered the cassette tapes "Beginning Hindustani," advertised on page 27 of your fall catalogue. You promised delivery within four weeks, <u>provided</u> the tapes were to be mailed to an educational institution in North America. I realize <u>that</u> mail deliveries are often delayed during the Christmas season, <u>so</u> I was not surprised <u>when</u> the tapes did not arrive by February 1. However, it has now been ten weeks <u>since</u> I ordered the tapes; this seems like an excessive delay under any circumstances.

Even when it is completely grammatical and well balanced between coordination and subordination, a sentence may simply be too long. In the eighteenth and nineteenth centuries, good writers wrote sentences as long as sixty or seventy words. Today, readers are accustomed to shorter sentences and find long, involved sentences difficult to decipher. To avoid lack of clarity caused by extraordinarily long sentences (more than thirty or forty words), break them up into two or three shorter sentences.

rh 48a

TOO LONG It was not so much that I resented my father's advice—after all, I had often asked him for advice—as that I resented his giving it at that time, when I was having difficulty accepting authority from any source, whether it were that of a parent I knew loved me or an outsider who I felt was hostile to me, and therefore any advice offered was open to my suspicion, which I could not easily conceal.

IMPROVED I could not resent my father's advice because I had often asked him for it. However, at that time I was having difficulty accepting authority from any source, whether from a loving parent or from a hostile outsider. Therefore, I was suspicious of all advice, and I could not easily conceal this suspicion.

Transitions Transitional words do not necessarily co-ordinate two clauses grammatically or subordinate one clause to another. However, they do add clarity by relating what you have said previously to what you are going to say later. Readers, often unconsciously, rely heavily on transitional words to establish the logic of sentences and groups of sentences. For example, *the* often signals that its following noun is familiar or has already been mentioned. Personal pronouns serve the same purpose. An improper transitional word sends a false or ambiguous signal to the reader, resulting in loss of clarity.

Conjunctive adverbs are one of the most useful ways to achieve clear transitions. For example, each of the following sentences is well written, and each contains either co-ordination or subordination. But the relationship among the sentences would be clearer with a conjunctive adverb at or near the beginning of the second and the third sentence.

> Because Emily Carr did not paint in a popular style, her work was not well reviewed in 1911, and she gave up exhibiting. In the 1930s, she gained recognition, largely through the Group of Seven's support. Critics hailed her great originality, and she has since gained an international reputation.

The addition of *however* to the beginning of the second sentence lets readers know immediately that attitudes toward Carr's work changed. *Subsequently* placed at the beginning of the third sentence tells readers that what follows is a direct result of the change.

> Because Emily Carr did not paint in a popular style, her work was not well reviewed in 1911, and she gave up exhibiting. <u>However</u>, in the 1930s she gained recognition, largely through the Group of Seven's support. <u>Subsequently</u>, critics hailed her great originality, and she has since gained an international reputation.

Although properly used conjunctive adverbs add to clarity, it is better to omit one entirely than to use one improperly. An incorrect conjunctive adverb is less clear than no transitional word at all.

> I have always been a poor speller; <u>nevertheless</u>, I look up every word whose spelling I am uncertain of.

rh
48a

Here, *nevertheless* leads readers to expect that what follows will be a contradiction of or an exception to what has preceded. But the writer really wants to express a cause-effect idea and should have used *therefore* or *consequently* instead of *nevertheless*.

> I have always been a poor speller; <u>therefore</u>, I look up every word whose spelling I am uncertain of.

Conjunctive adverbs are not simply substitutes for co-ordination and subordination. A long series of short simple sentences each beginning with a conjunctive adverb is usually cluttered and jerky in rhythm.

AWKWARD   <u>Probably</u>, Billy Bishop is the most famous of Canada's
First World War heroes, as winner of the V.C., the
D.S.O. and bar, and the D.F.C. <u>Certainly</u>, his service
record as a "fighting airman" was remarkable. <u>That
is</u>, he shot down seventy-two enemy aircraft. <u>Fur-
thermore</u>, he was appointed in 1918 to the British
Air Ministry's staff. <u>Subsequently</u>, he had a hand in
forming the Royal Canadian Air Force as a separate
brigade. <u>Eventually</u>, he was promoted to honorary
air vice-marshal in the R.C.A.F. <u>Later</u>, during the
Second World War, he was promoted to honorary
air-marshal. <u>However</u>, he was almost forgotten by
one generation of Canadians until Allan Gray's play
Billy Bishop Goes to War revived his fame.

This passage is much smoother and at least as clear if some of the transitional adverbs are removed, others are tucked away inside their clauses,
and still others are replaced with co-ordination and subordination.

REVISED   Billy Bishop is <u>probably</u> the most famous of Canada's
First World War heroes, as winner of the V.C., the
D.S.O. and bar, and the D.F.C. His service record as a
"fighting airman" was <u>certainly</u> remarkable. He shot
down seventy-two enemy aircraft, and was appointed
in 1918 to the British Air Ministry's staff. <u>Subse-
quently</u>, he had a hand in forming the Royal Canadian Air Force as a separate brigade and <u>eventually</u>
was promoted to honorary air vice-marshal in the
R.C.A.F. During the Second World War, he was promoted to honorary air-marshal. He was almost forgotten by one generation of Canadians, however, until
Allan Gray's play *Billy Bishop Goes to War* revived
his fame.

Other Aids to Clarity Proper co-ordination and subordination and appropriate transitions are two important ways of making sentences clear.
Both primarily involve linking entire sentences or major parts of sentences. Other aids to clarity include careful placement of modifiers, appropriate use of detail, avoiding the overuse of nouns as modifiers, and
writing for the eye as well as for the ear.

1. **Careful Placement of Modifiers.** Modifiers should appear near the
words they modify, but they should not interrupt the natural flow of the
sentence. When a writer inserts modifiers as they come into his or her
mind and without concern for the most effective placement, the result is
lack of clarity. Probably the most distracting interruptions are long modifiers that split up a verb phrase or that separate a verb from its object or
complement. This fault can be corrected by moving the modifying

rh
48a

phrase to another position in the sentence; the beginning of the sentence is usually the best position (see also 20c)

AWKWARD A retail store may, through a special division established for the purpose, also conduct a mail-order business.

IMPROVED Through a special division established for the purpose, a retail store may also conduct a mail-order business.

AWKWARD Mendel was able to formulate, as a result of his long years of experimentation, three basic laws of heredity.

IMPROVED As a result of his long years of experimentation, Mendel was able to formulate three basic laws of heredity.

2. **Nouns as Modifiers.** Noun adjuncts, or nouns used to modify other nouns, are a familiar and convenient feature of English. Noun adjuncts can, however, easily become too much of a good thing. One noun adjunct per noun phrase is rarely a problem (*traffic control, oil refinery, shotgun pellet*). Lack of clarity begins when three or more nouns appear in succession. For example, the phrase *city hospital planning committee*, in addition to being ungraceful, is also unclear. Does it mean a committee to make plans for a city hospital? A planning committee established by the city hospital? A city committee for hospital planning? To avoid excessive use of nouns as modifiers, substitute prepositional phrases for some of the nouns. Sometimes you can rewrite the phrase, replacing one of the nouns with a verb.

UNCLEAR neighborhood traffic control regulations

PREPOSITIONAL PHRASE regulations for the control of neighborhood traffic

UNCLEAR There has been no citizen reassessment dispute participation.

VERB The citizens have not participated in the reassessment dispute.

3. **Use of Detail.** Carefully chosen detail ensures clarity and also adds interest to sentences. Irrelevant detail not only clutters sentences but may confuse readers by leading them to think that there is a relationship between the detail and the main statement that they do not understand.

In 1502, Leonardo da Vinci, <u>who was left-handed</u>, became Cesare Borgia's military engineer. (His left-handedness is irrelevant to his job as a military engineer.)

**rh
48a**

Context determines whether detail is relevant or not. In the following sentence, the clause *who was left-handed* is appropriate because left-handed people often smear their writing when they write from left to right and hence are more likely to want to do mirror writing.

Leonardo da Vinci, <u>who was left-handed</u>, left notebooks in mirror writing, writing that must be viewed in a mirror in order to be read.

4. **Writing for the Eye.** Because punctuation only imperfectly replaces the intonations and pauses of speech, sentences that are completely clear when spoken are sometimes confusing when written. In the following example, readers may at first interpret the comma after *epidemics* as separating items in a series and assume that the writer is saying that epidemics, heart disease, and cancer have all decreased.

UNCLEAR   With the decrease in epidemics, heart disease and cancer have become the leading causes of death.

If the first phrase is rewritten as a clause ending with the verb, the ambiguity disappears.

REVISED   Now that epidemics have decreased, heart disease and cancer have become the leading causes of death.

Exercises: Clarity

A. Rewrite the following sentences, correcting any problems with coordination, subordination, transitions, placement of modifiers, overuse of noun modifiers, irrelevant detail, or other flaws that detract from clarity.

1. We decided to cook a Chinese dinner, and it wasn't exactly a success, and the rice stuck to the pan. Besides, the vegetables were overdone, but the meat was almost raw.
2. Somebody has said that no one ever forgets where he buried the hatchet. Still, I will never forgive Isabelle for telling everyone that I wrote a letter to Ann Landers.
3. Lodge never, although he devotes thirty pages to the subject, succeeds in convincing the reader, perhaps because he himself is not convinced, that man is descended from dinosaurs.
4. The upright-model vacuum cleaner rug shampoo attachment instructions say that water should be added to the cleaning solution.
5. The Rogers Pass, where the Trans-Canada Highway was being repaired last summer, was the site of one of the outstanding feats of engineering in the opening of the West.
6. In lieu of the fact that they have been married for seventeen years, you might think that Ozzie would remember that his wife has blue eyes.

**rh
48a**

7. Thatcher is the most considerate and cheerful person I have ever known, but, when I asked him why, he said, "For I have promises to keep, and smiles to go before I weep."

8. Ebenezer, which is a Biblical name, is my favorite uncle because he tells such wonderful stories about his adventures when he was a young man working in the cod fisheries, whose annual catch has declined from 272 000 kg to 136 000 kg in the last decade, although the rest of the family claims that he never left St. John's because he was just a clerk and probably never even left shore, though his tales are so vivid that I can't believe that at least some of my favorites, which I never get tired of hearing, partly, of course, because Uncle Ebenezer is such a marvellous storyteller, are not true.

9. Surprisingly, private ownership of cars is forbidden. Nevertheless, there is a great deal of traffic on the streets. However, most of this consists of trucks. Moreover, bicycles are everywhere. Furthermore, pedestrians walk in the streets. In addition, there are many handcarts. Nonetheless, rickshaws are seen only in large cities. Also, they are not used by anyone except tourists.

B. Rewrite the following set of sentences according to the instructions.

Spring comes slowly and reluctantly to the mountains. Spring is delightful in the mountains. The observer may become impatient.

1. Using both co-ordination and subordination, rewrite the three sentences as one sentence, making it clear that the writer's focus is on the delightfulness of spring in the mountains.

2. Using both co-ordination and subordination, rewrite the three sentences as one sentence, making it clear that the writer's focus is on how slowly spring comes to the mountains.

3. Begin with the sentence "Spring is delightful in the mountains." Then rewrite the other two sentences as one sentence introduced by a conjunctive adverb and containing co-ordination.

4. Begin with the sentence "Spring is delightful in the mountains." Then rewrite the other two sentences as one sentence introduced by a conjunctive adverb and containing subordination.

rh
48a

48b • Emphasis *(emph)*

Emphasis is stress on or prominence of certain ideas. Appropriate emphasis adds to clarity by drawing the reader's attention to the most important points and keeping the less important ones in the background. Inappropriate emphasis confuses the reader. Appropriate emphasis is easy to achieve in speech by means of facial expressions, tone of voice, loudness of voice, pauses, and gestures. Writing does not offer these methods for creating emphasis, and the writer is limited to choice of words, arrangement of these words in the sentence, and, occasionally, punctuation and other graphic devices.

Do not feel that every sentence you write should be dramatically emphatic. Emphasis is effective only when it contributes to the whole paper, and the context determines what should be emphasized. If you try to emphasize every clause, every sentence, you will find—like the boy who cried "Wolf!"—that your audience no longer believes you.

By far the most important method of achieving emphasis in writing is careful placement of the elements. The end of a clause or sentence is normally the most emphatic position. The beginning of a clause or sentence is also a strong position because it is usually the place where the topic is introduced.

Rhetorical Types of Sentences   Sentences are traditionally classified as *cumulative* (or loose), *periodic*, or *mixed*, depending on the placement of the elements containing the most important ideas.

1. **Cumulative Sentences.** Cumulative sentences follow a natural, or "neutral," sentence order. Topic and comment appear first, followed by amplifying detail.

> He had large white hands like those in pictures of King David in the Bible.
>
> John Gardner, *The Sunlight Dialogues*

> But the story of Assyria lies outside the story of Greece, since the Greeks, except in one outlying corner, came into no immediate contact with the lords of Nineveh.
>
> J. B. Bury, *A History of Greece*

2. **Periodic Sentences.** In periodic sentences, the main idea is not completed until near the end, after amplifying detail has already been stated. Because the main idea is delayed, a certain amount of suspense builds up.

> But in the same rush of clear-headed detachment he had recognized, like Jacob of old when he found he'd got Leah, whose arms were like sticks and whose mouth was as flat as a salamander's, that he'd have to be a monster to tell her the truth.
>
> John Gardner, *The Sunlight Dialogues*

**rh
48b**

> While the Greeks were sailing their own seas, and working out in their city-states the institutions of law and freedom, untroubled by any catastrophe beyond the shores of the Mediterranean, great despotic kingdoms were waxing and waning in the east.
>
> J. B. Bury, *A History of Greece*

The independent clause of a periodic sentence usually carries the main statement. However, it may occur in a subordinate clause, as in the first sentence above. Occasionally, for special effect, the most important part is put into a modifying phrase.

> The place was crawling with cockroaches as big as your fist, like the one on your collar.

Virtually any cumulative sentence can be rewritten as a periodic sentence, and vice versa. The decision as to which sentence type to use depends on the amount of emphasis wanted. A periodic sentence is nearly always more emphatic than a cumulative sentence.

CUMULATIVE But the story of Assyria lies outside the story of Greece, since the Greeks, except in one outlying corner, came into no immediate contact with the lords of Nineveh.

J. B. Bury, *A History of Greece*

REWRITTEN AS PERIODIC Since the Greeks, except in one outlying corner, came into no immediate contact with the lords of Nineveh, the story of Assyria lies outside the story of Greece.

PERIODIC While the Greeks were sailing their own seas, and working out in their city-states the institutions of law and freedom, untroubled by any catastrophe beyond the shores of the Mediterranean, great despotic kingdoms were waxing and waning in the east.

J. B. Bury, *A History of Greece*

REWRITTEN AS CUMULATIVE Great despotic kingdoms were waxing and waning in the east while the Greeks were sailing their own seas and working out in their city-states the institutions of law and freedom, untroubled by any catastrophe beyond the shores of the Mediterranean.

3. **Mixed Sentences.** Although good writers use both purely cumulative and purely periodic sentences, a mixture of the two is probably more common than either. **Mixed sentences** begin with some amplifying detail, continue with the main statement, and end with more amplifying detail.

Even with their lights on, the houses looked abandoned, like habitations depopulated by plague.

John Gardner, *The Sunlight Dialogues*

In the seventh century, the mighty empire of Assyria was verging to its end; the power destined to overthrow it had arisen.

J. B. Bury, *A History of Greece*

Mixed sentences are especially useful when sentences contain several modifying phrases. Periodic structure would result in a long string of introductory material, leaving the reader wondering if the writer will ever get to the point. A cumulative structure would pile all the modifiers

rh
48b

at the end, weakening the end of the sentence. Notice how much weaker some mixed sentences become when they are rewritten either as periodic or cumulative sentences.

MIXED   Even with their lights on, <u>the houses looked aban-doned</u>, like habitations depopulated by plague.
                                John Gardner, *The Sunlight Dialogues*

PERIODIC Like habitations depopulated by plague, even with their lights on, <u>the houses looked abandoned</u>.

CUMULATIVE <u>The houses looked abandoned</u>, even with their lights on, like habitations depopulated by plague.

Exercises: Rhetorical Types of Sentences

Part A: Identify each of the following sentences as cumulative (C), periodic (P), or mixed (M). Underline the part of the sentence that contains the core meaning.

Example
When the car sputtered to a halt, <u>Karl put on the flashers and climbed out</u>, hoping that a passing motorist would stop to help.

1. Returning to their hotel room after spending the morning sight-see-ing, Jim and Marie found that they had been robbed of everything.
2. When the thunder and lightning became fierce and the air grew steamy, then the farmers knew the inevitable: a tornado would soon twist across the plains.
3. Ignoring the D that he had received on the chemistry midterm, Dave cut the next three classes after the test, finding out too late that those who had attended class that week had been allowed to retake the exam.
4. The old woman glowered at the children and they glowered back at her, pitiless and unyielding in their defiance.
5. Greg was fired after only one night's work in the supermarket because he stamped a whole case of cans with the wrong price, destroyed four cartons of eggs with the handle of a mop, and ran down a customer with a train of shopping carts he was returning to the front of the store.
6. To the delight of the cheering crowds lining the shore, the tall ships made their way into Sydney harbor—their sails flapping like great white sheets hung out to dry, their crews climbing like circus enter-tainers about the rigging.

Part B: Write one cumulative, one periodic, and one mixed sentence for *each* of the following groups of information. The main idea is given in the first sentence, and ideas to be subordinated are given in sentences within parentheses.

1. Our beach house had survived the storm. (It was protected by an enormous sand dune. All the neighboring houses lay in ruins. The contents of these houses were strewn about the beach like playthings.)
2. Socrates was sentenced to death in Athens in 399 B.C. (This act was the consequence of his public questioning of all state matters. Socrates was a renowned Greek philosopher.)

Emphasis by Position Achieving emphasis by position is a matter of taking advantage of the naturally strong positions at the beginning and especially at the end of a sentence.

1. **Periodic Structure.** Of the three rhetorical types of sentences we have seen, periodic sentences are the most emphatic. Most short sentences are periodic by nature.

Speed kills.
Many plants reproduce by means of spores.
The leadership of Europe fell into the hands of Prince Metternich.

In longer, complex sentences, you can achieve the more emphatic periodic sentence structure by placing subordinate clauses early in the sentence and leaving the end of the sentence for the main clause.

LESS EMPHATIC   It is disturbing to realize that we destroy several million brain cells whenever we sneeze.

MORE EMPHATIC   It is disturbing to realize that, whenever we sneeze, we destroy several million brain cells.

2. **Climactic Order.** When you have a series of parallel words, phrases, or clauses, you can achieve a periodic effect by listing them in an ascending order of importance, saving the strongest points for last.

UNEMPHATIC   For her birthday, Jeffrey bought his wife a cashmere sweater, a Jaguar, and a jigsaw puzzle.

EMPHATIC   For her birthday, Jeffrey bought his wife a jigsaw puzzle, a cashmere sweater, and a Jaguar.

rh
48b

Sometimes this climactic order is deliberately reversed for a humorous effect.

During her college years, Karen learned to think critically, question perceptively, write clearly, and play a mean game of gin rummy.

Careless anticlimax, however, simply destroys emphasis.

The Soviet Union is the largest nation in the world, the richest country in natural resources, and the world's leading exporter of caviar.

Context determines what is climactic and what is anticlimactic. Taken in isolation, the following sentence might appear anticlimactic, but in a narrative about a search for a missing hairbrush, it would be highly climactic and emphatic.

> I came down from the attic, carrying an antique doll's head, some love letters written by my grandfather, and my long-lost hairbrush.

3. **Adverbial Phrases at the Beginning.** You can often move adverbial phrases to the beginning of the sentence, leaving the subject or direct object in the emphatic position at the end of the sentence.

LESS EMPHATIC	A vicious-looking whip was in his hand.
MORE EMPHATIC	In his hand was a vicious-looking whip.
LESS EMPHATIC	The prospector struck gold after ten years of searching.
MORE EMPHATIC	After ten years of searching, the prospector struck gold.

4. **Conjunctive Adverbs at or near the Beginning.** Like subordinate clauses, clauses with conjunctive adverbs qualify a preceding clause or sentence. Sentences are more emphatic if conjunctive adverbs appear at or near the beginning of their clauses. Such placement also informs the reader at once about the relationship of the sentence or clause to the preceding material.

UNEMPHATIC	Smoking is bad for one's health; many people ignore this fact, however.
EMPHATIC	Smoking is bad for one's health; however, many people ignore this fact.

5. **Inversion.** The expected order of declarative clauses and sentences is subject + verb + object or complement. Violating this word order draws the reader's attention to the inverted words, and greater emphasis is the result. You are not free to make just any kind of inversion in English: obviously, inverting *John builds gliders* to *Builds John gliders* is not emphatic—it is simply ungrammatical. However, you can often place a direct object or complement before the subject and verb, thus lending emphasis to that object or complement.

LESS EMPHATIC	Steven has asked for trouble and he will get trouble.
MORE EMPHATIC	Trouble Steven has asked for and trouble he will get.
LESS EMPHATIC	Though Marie was poor, she was always generous.
MORE EMPHATIC	Poor though Marie was, she was always generous.

When you use position to achieve emphasis, be sure that the emphasis is appropriate to the context. False emphasis is a greater stylistic flaw than weak emphasis. For example, the sentence above (*Trouble Steven has asked for and trouble he will get*) would be appropriate if the focus were on Steven's behavior.

> Steven has always refused to co-operate, and now he has insulted everyone. Trouble he has asked for and trouble he will get.

However, if the context concerned a contrast between Steven and other people, the main focus would be on Steven, and the inverted word order would not be appropriate, as in the following example:

> Everyone else has been co-operative. Trouble Steven has asked for and trouble he will get.

Passive Voice   Some writers seem to feel that the passive voice adds authority and dignity to a sentence. This is rarely the case, and overuse of the passive makes for dull, wordy writing and detracts from proper emphasis.

WORDY PASSIVE   It is argued by the author that the cease-fire agreement was violated by the Egyptians.

IMPROVED   The author argues that the Egyptians violated the cease-fire agreement.

There are, however, four conditions under which the passive voice is normally preferable to the active voice and when its use adds to, rather than detracts from, proper emphasis.

1. **Focus on Receiver or Result of Action.** Use the passive to focus attention on the receiver of an action. Ordinarily, the sentence "A child was hit by a car this afternoon" would be preferable to "A car hit a child this afternoon" because one would normally be more concerned about the child than about the car. Context is the determining factor here. If the topic of discussion in the following example were provincial laws, the first sentence would provide the appropriate emphasis. But if the topic were employment standards, the second sentence, with the passive, would be more appropriate.

> All provinces have laws regulating the length of the work week.

> The length of the work week is regulated by law in all provinces.

If you want to create a picture of the *results* of action rather than to emphasize the action itself, the passive is appropriate. For example, if you were focusing on how hard a young man worked to make a good appearance, you might stress what he did by using only active verbs.

> Bruce got a haircut, cleaned his nails, shined his shoes, and pressed his best suit carefully.

**rh
48b**

On the other hand, if you wanted to emphasize how he appeared to someone else, you could create an effective static picture by using the passive voice.

> Bruce's hair was neatly trimmed, his nails clean, his shoes shined, and his suit carefully pressed.

2. **Doer of Action Unknown.** Use the passive when the doer of the action is unknown or irrelevant. The sentence "The meeting was adjourned at 3:30" is appropriate because it is unimportant—and probably unknown—who made the motion to adjourn and which people voted for adjournment.

3. **Long Clause as Subject.** Use the passive to avoid a lengthy clause or phrase as the subject of a sentence. Lengthy clauses make awkward and unemphatic subjects.

LESS EMPHATIC   To hear that the city plans to repair our street delighted me.

MORE EMPHATIC   I was delighted to hear that the city plans to repair our street.

4. **Avoidance of First Person.** Use the passive when convention demands it. In many kinds of technical writing, it is conventional to avoid the use of the first person, and frequently the only alternative is the passive voice.

INAPPROPRIATE   I placed four mice in the maze.

REVISED   Four mice were placed in the maze.

Balance and Parallelism   Parallelism, that is, using the same grammatical structure for all items that have the same function, is the chief component of balanced sentences (see also 23f). Balanced sentences are especially useful for emphasizing complementary or contradictory ideas.

> Do not let us speak of darker days; let us rather speak of sterner days.
> Winston Churchill, speech

> The race is not to the swift, nor the battle to the strong.

> A man of sense only trifles with them [women], plays with them, humours and flatters them, as he does with a sprightly and forward child; but he neither consults them about, nor trusts them with, serious matters.
> Lord Chesterfield, letter to his son

In these sentences, the clauses are parallel. For example, in the first sentence above, both clauses begin with an imperative and end in a prepositional phrase. The last sentence is a good example of how effective and emphatic even long sentences can be if they are balanced.

These sentences also illustrate that **repetition** reinforces parallelism and balance. The amount of repetition may vary according to the content. The Churchill quotation repeats the words *let, us, speak, of,* and *days.* But repetition alone does not create emphasis. The repetition must be parallel; careless, nonparallel repetition annoys the reader. For example, consider how ineffective Lincoln's famous lines "government of the people, by the people, and for the people" would have been if he had worded them differently.

> [we here highly resolve] that the government of the *people* shall not perish from this earth, that the *people* should control the government, and that the purpose of government is to serve the *people's* needs.

In Lincoln's original lines, *people* appears three times, each time as the object of a preposition. In the ineffective paraphrase, the repetition of *people* is not parallel; *people* is first an object of a preposition, then a subject, and finally a modifier of a noun.

Change in Sentence Length   A short sentence before or after a series of longer sentences is an effective way of adding emphasis by providing a change of pace.

> The fact is that Eichmann did not see much. It is true, he repeatedly visited Auschwitz, the largest and most famous of the death camps, but Auschwitz, covering an area of eighteen square miles, in Upper Silesia, was by no means only an extermination camp; it was a huge enterprise with up to a hundred thousand inmates, and all kinds of prisoners were held there, including non-Jews and slave laborers, who were not subject to gassing. It was easy to avoid the killing installations, and Höss, with whom he had a very friendly relationship, spared him the gruesome sights.
> Hannah Arendt, *Eichmann in Jerusalem*

> Brothers may separate and quarrel, especially when each is created with a separate, personal soul that he retains through all eternity. The lofty Hindu declares that "one should love his neighbor as himself because he *is* his neighbor." All selves are one.
> Herbert J. Muller, *The Uses of the Past*

rh
48b

In both these examples, the emphasis arises from the *contrast* between the short sentence and the long sentences, not from the short sentence in and of itself. Notice how much emphasis is lost from the first example if it is rewritten so that all the sentences are short.

UNEMPHATIC   The fact is that Eichmann did not see much. It is true, he repeatedly visited Auschwitz. It was the largest and most famous of the death camps. It covered an area of eighteen square miles. It was in Upper Silesia. Auschwitz was by no means only

an extermination camp. It was a huge enterprise.
It had up to a hundred thousand inmates. All kinds
of prisoners were held there. There were non-Jews
and slave laborers. They were not subject to gas-
sing. It was easy to avoid the killing installations.
He was very friendly with Höss who spared him
the gruesome sights.

Graphic Devices   The word *emphasis* may first suggest the practice of
underlining, capital letters, and exclamation points. And indeed, some
writers rely heavily on these graphic devices to achieve emphasis. Although such devices are occasionally justified, overreliance on them
makes the writer appear somewhat hysterical. The best writers achieve
emphasis through a judicious choice of words and careful sentence construction.

UNSUITABLE	There is *absolutely no* excuse for such behavior!
IMPROVED	Such behavior is inexcusable.
UNSUITABLE	In 1890, leg-of-mutton sleeves were THE THING in fashion.
IMPROVED	In 1890, leg-of-mutton sleeves were highly fashion-able.

Exercises: Emphasis

To get practice in achieving emphasis in a number of ways, write sentences according to the following specifications.

1. Using periodic structure to achieve emphasis, write a sentence about
   a moment when you were very frightened.
2. Using inversion to achieve emphasis, write two sentences about your
   least favorite teacher in elementary school.
3. Using climactic order to achieve emphasis, write a sentence about
   events during an industrial strike.
4. Use the passive voice to focus attention on the subject of a sentence
   about an experience in a department store.
5. Using balance and parallelism to achieve emphasis, write a sentence
   about the difference between selfishness and selflessness.

**rh
48c**

48c ▪ Variety *(var)*

The purpose of using a variety of sentence types in writing is to avoid
monotony, which bores and distracts the reader. Although too much of
anything results in lack of variety—too many short sentences, too many
long sentences, too much subordination, too many periodic sentences—
the most common problem of variety in student writing is an excess of
short, choppy sentences. Writing that consists only of a series of short

declarative sentences leads the reader to assume that the writer's thoughts are immature; that is, the constant use of short sentences suggests that the writer can think only in terms of simple statements and cannot see their interrelationships.

Variety is not a virtue in and of itself but only as it contributes to clarity and emphasis. Indeed, if you pay careful attention to clarity and especially to emphasis, you will probably find that variety results automatically. When revising for variety, always keep an eye on how your revisions affect clarity and emphasis.

Variety by Sentence-Combining One of the most basic and most obvious ways of achieving variety is to vary sentence length. This implies a variety of sentence types because simple declarative sentences tend to be short—there is a limit to the number of adjectives you can stick in front of nouns to stretch out the length of a sentence. So, to avoid an excess of short simple sentences, you can combine some of them into longer sentences. Sentence combination may take the form of (1) co-ordination, or making a single compound sentence out of two or more simple sentences; (2) subordination, or making a single complex sentence out of two simple sentences; or (3) embedding, or making one of the simple sentences into an adjectival or adverbial modifier or an absolute construction (see 11c) within the other simple sentence. The same set of simple sentences can frequently be combined in a number of different ways.

SIMPLE SENTENCES	Jeremiah prophesied the defeat of Judah. He was condemned as a traitor.
CO-ORDINATION	Jeremiah prophesied the defeat of Judah, and he was condemned as a traitor.
SUBORDINATION	After Jeremiah prophesied the defeat of Judah, he was condemned as a traitor.
	Jeremiah was condemned as a traitor because he prophesied the defeat of Judah.
EMBEDDING	Jeremiah, having prophesied the defeat of Judah, was condemned as a traitor.
	Jeremiah, who prophesied the defeat of Judah, was condemned as a traitor.
	Having prophesied the defeat of Judah, Jeremiah was condemned as a traitor.

**rh
48c**

Note When the subject (or the predicate) of the two sentences to be combined is the same, it can be omitted in the second clause. The result is technically a simple sentence with a compound subject (or predicate), but the principle is the same as that of a compound sentence.

Jeremiah prophesied the defeat of Judah and was condemned as a traitor.

To illustrate how sentence-combining adds variety to a series of sentences or paragraphs, let us assume that you are writing a paper on the *Titanic* disaster of 1912. As an introduction to the paper, you have decided to give some information about icebergs. You have consulted an encyclopedia, have discovered the following facts, and have written them all down in simple sentences.

Icebergs are frozen fresh water.[1] Ice floes are frozen salt water.[2] Pack ice is also frozen salt water.[3] Icebergs rise as much as 60 m above the waterline.[4] Icebergs reach below the waterline for seven to nine times their height.[5] The direction of drift of an iceberg depends on the wind.[6] Icebergs do not move into the wind.[7]

Most icebergs come from the glaciers of Greenland or from the shelf ice of Antarctica.[8] South Pacific icebergs come up almost to southern Australia.[9] North Pacific icebergs occur only in the Bering Strait.[10] There are many icebergs in the North Atlantic.[11] About 10 000 to 15 000 icebergs a year break off from western Greenland alone.[12] Other icebergs break off from eastern Greenland.[13] North Atlantic icebergs appear in shipping lanes.[14] Icebergs appear as far south as the Azores.[15]

The sentences are all short, and the result is clearly too choppy. Many of the sentences are related to each other and can be combined. By using co-ordination alone, you might produce the following.

Ice floes and pack ice are frozen salt water, but icebergs are frozen fresh water. (**1, 2** and **3** combined) Icebergs rise as much as 60 m above the waterline and reach below the waterline for seven to nine times their height. (**4** and **5** combined) The direction of drift of icebergs depends on the wind, and icebergs do not move into the wind. (**6** and **7** combined)

Most icebergs come from the glaciers of Greenland or from the shelf ice of Antarctica. South Pacific icebergs come up almost to southern Australia, but North Pacific icebergs occur only in the Bering Strait. (**9** and **10** combined) There are many icebergs in the North Atlantic. About 10 000 to 15 000 icebergs a year break off from western Greenland alone, and others break off from eastern Greenland. (**12** and **13** combined) North Atlantic icebergs appear in shipping lanes; they appear as far south as the Azores. (**14** and **15** combined)

By using subordination only, you could combine several of the original sentences, making complex sentences.

Although the ice floes and pack ice are frozen salt water, icebergs are frozen fresh water. (**1, 2,** and **3** combined) Icebergs rise as much as 60 m above the waterline. Icebergs reach below the waterline for seven to nine times their height. Because their direction of drift

rh
48c

depends on the wind, icebergs do not move into the wind. (**6** and **7** combined)

Most icebergs come from the glaciers of Greenland or from the shelf ice of Antarctica. Although South Pacific icebergs come up almost to southern Australia, North Pacific icebergs occur only in the Bering Strait. (**9** and **10** combined) There are many icebergs in the North Atlantic. About 10 000 to 15 000 icebergs a year break off from western Greenland alone. Other icebergs break off from eastern Greenland. North Atlantic icebergs appear in shipping lanes. Icebergs appear as far south as the Azores.

By changing some of the original sentences into adverbial modifiers or absolute constructions and embedding them in other sentences, you might produce the following:

Icebergs are frozen fresh water. Ice floes are frozen salt water. Pack ice is also frozen salt water. Rising as much as 60 m above the waterline, icebergs reach below the waterline for seven to nine times their height. (**4** and **5** combined) The direction of drift of an iceberg depends on the wind. Icebergs do not move into the wind.

Most icebergs come from the glaciers of Greenland or from the shelf ice of Antarctica. South Pacific icebergs come up almost to southern Australia. North Pacific icebergs occur only in the Bering Strait. Of the many icebergs in the North Atlantic, about 10 000 to 15 000 a year break off from western Greenland alone. (**11** and **12** combined) Other icebergs break off from eastern Greenland. North Atlantic icebergs appear in the shipping lanes as far south as the Azores. (**14** and **15** combined)

None of these revisions is completely satisfactory because a passage consisting primarily of co-ordination or subordination or embedded modifiers is almost as monotonous as a passage consisting solely of short, simple sentences. Therefore, you would want to select a mixture of various sentence types. The result might be the following:

Although ice floes and pack ice are frozen salt water, icebergs are frozen fresh water.[1] Rising as much as 60 m above the waterline, icebergs reach below the waterline for seven to nine times their height.[2] The direction of drift of icebergs depends on the wind, and they do not move into the wind.[3]

Most icebergs come from the glaciers of Greenland or from the shelf ice of Antarctica.[4] Although South Pacific icebergs come up almost to southern Australia, North Pacific icebergs occur only in the Bering Strait.[5] Of the many icebergs in the North Atlantic, about 10 000 to 15 000 a year break off from western Greenland alone; others break off from eastern Greenland.[6] North Atlantic icebergs appear in shipping lanes as far south as the Azores.[7]

rh
48c

In this final version, three simple sentences (**2, 4, 7**), two compound sentences (**3, 6**), and two complex sentences (**1, 5**) provide a good variety of sentence types. Sentence length varies from thirteen words (**7**) to twenty-six words (**6**), and there is a rough alternation of short and long sentences.

Using co-ordination to combine sentences usually does not greatly affect emphasis. Subordination, however, almost always results in at least a slight change of emphasis. When combining sentences by means of subordination, be sure that the resulting emphasis is appropriate. In the first sentence of the final version above—*Although ice floes and pack ice are frozen salt water, icebergs are frozen fresh water*—the emphasis is correct because ice floes and pack ice, which are introduced only to distinguish them from icebergs, are relegated to the subordinate clause. The real topic of the paragraph—icebergs—is placed in the stronger position, in the main clause and at the end of the sentence. If this position were reversed to read, "Although icebergs are frozen fresh water, ice floes and pack ice are frozen salt water," the reader would at first think that the topic of discussion was going to be ice floes and pack ice, not icebergs, and the emphasis would be inappropriate.

Combining sentences by means of embedding also affects emphasis. Making the sentence about the height of the icebergs into an absolute phrase—*Rising as much as 60 m above the waterline*—tends to de-emphasize it and to stress the importance of how far below the waterline icebergs reach. As always, the context determines where the emphasis should be.

Variety by Other Means   Sentence combination is by far the most important means of achieving a variety of sentence structures. However, for a bit of spice now and then, you might try a rhetorical question, inversion, or a short sentence fragment. Since these are all rather dramatic devices, however, they should be used very sparingly.

1. **Rhetorical Questions.** A rhetorical question is one used just for emphasis, one to which no answer is expected.

rh
48c

SIMPLE SENTENCES	Every student of modern poetry has heard of T. S. Eliot. Most do not know that he was a bank clerk.
RHETORICAL QUESTION	What student of modern poetry has not heard of T. S. Eliot? But few know that he was a bank clerk.

2. **Inversion.** Put an occasional complement or direct object before the subject and verb.

SIMPLE SENTENCES	The boy at the door was selling potato-peelers. I do not need potato-peelers.
INVERSION	The boy at the door was selling potato-peelers. Potato-peelers I do not need.

3. **Short Sentence Fragments.** Although sentence fragments are usually unacceptable (see 23a), short fragments can be an effective means of achieving emphasis, humorous anticlimax, or transition, provided you deliberately use them for these purposes and are fully aware of what you are doing.

EMPHASIS   My father told me I needed a haircut. A haircut!

ANTICLIMAX   At last, he had mastered the rules of cricket. Well, almost.

TRANSITION   We have enumerated the many advantages of organic gardening. Now for the disadvantages.

Exercises: Variety

Write the following paragraph according to the specifications listed. The result will, of course, be somewhat artificial, but the practice will help you to explore some techniques that you can use to improve your own style.

Write a description of your room. Avoid mentioning the obvious—bed(s), dresser(s), desk(s)—and concentrate on something unique—the giant spider web in your window, for instance. Do not begin any sentences with *there, it, this,* or *the.* Try to entertain your reader.

The eight sentences of your paragraph should be structured as follows:

1. Begins with a present participle, has at least one main clause and one subordinate clause, and has between fifteen and thirty words
2. Begins with the subject and has no more than ten words
3. Begins with a prepositional phrase, has at least two main clauses, and has from fifteen to twenty-five words
4. Begins with a subordinate clause, has at least one main clause, and has from twelve to seventeen words
5. Has no more than four words
6. Begins with the subject, has two main clauses, and has fifteen to twenty words
7. Begins with an adverb and has from ten to fifteen words
8. Begins with a subordinate clause and has fifteen to twenty words

**rh
49**

---

49 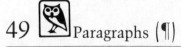 Paragraphs (¶)

Everyone understands, at least implicitly, what a sentence is because people speak in sentences. Regardless of how long and rambling or how short and incomplete the sentences may be, changes in the speaker's voice indicate when one sentence has ended and another has begun. Paragraph changes are not obvious; we may realize that a speaker has changed the subject but not hear the point at which he or she made the switch. We are not disturbed at not hearing these breaks because paragraphs are not essential to most kinds of speech.

Paragraphs are, however, conventional and essential in writing. Because we are accustomed to seeing paragraph divisions, we are uneasy when they do not appear or even when they appear only infrequently. Everyone is familiar with the sense of despair that comes from turning a page and discovering that the next page does not contain a single new paragraph. Paragraphs are both a physical and a mental convenience for readers. Physically, they provide a break and allow readers to keep the place on the page more easily. They also signal that one unit of thought has been completed and another is about to begin. Paragraphs are a convenience for writers too because they help them organize their ideas into manageable blocks.

A common definition of a **paragraph** is "a group of related sentences developing one idea." It often includes a topic sentence that summarizes that idea, followed by additional sentences that expand, qualify, analyse, or explain the idea. Ideas, however, are not like automobiles; they are not clearly distinct units with standardized parts that can be easily counted and classified. Ideas may be as simple as "I am eating a peanut butter and jelly sandwich" or a complex as "the role of technology in the universe." One idea may blend into another with no sharp division between the two. Yet if we are to deal with ideas at all, we must have ways of segmenting them—we cannot comprehend or express complex ideas all in one breath or all in one sentence. In writing, we use the paragraph to handle one segment at a time. Because ideas are so diverse in their content and complexity and because the possible ways of segmenting them vary greatly, there are no hard-and-fast rules for what constitutes a good paragraph. Rather, there are only "typical" paragraphs.

There is no absolute rule governing the length of a paragraph. Sometimes (though rarely) only a one-sentence paragraph is needed to make a transition between sections of a paper or to add dramatic emphasis. Sometimes a full typewritten page is appropriate if the paragraph treats an especially complex and closely knit argument. More typically, a paragraph has from one hundred to two hundred words or from three to ten sentences and fills from one-third to two-thirds of a double-spaced typewritten page. (Newspapers should not be taken as models because their conventions differ greatly from those of other kinds of writing.) If your paragraphs are very short, they probably lack completeness and need more development. If they are very long, they may lack unity or coherence or both.

**rh
49**

Despite great differences in content, organization, length, and function, all good paragraphs are unified, complete, and coherent. A paragraph is unified if it has a single focus. A paragraph is complete if the subject is adequately developed so that the reader is satisfied and not left with vague impressions and unanswered questions. A paragraph is coherent if all of the sentences are related to one another.

49a · Unity

Unity is oneness, the combination of all elements to form a single whole. A unified paragraph is internally consistent and has a single focus. In a unified paragraph, every sentence contributes to this focus by exemplifying it, explaining it, or expanding on it in some way. A unified paragraph may contain more than one simple idea, but all of the ideas expressed should be related to the same theme.

One of the greatest enemies of paragraph unity is the human thought process. We tend to think associatively rather than logically. One fact reminds us of another, even if the second is not logically related to the first.

Poorly Unified Paragraph

Most serious coin collectors carry special insurance on their collections. I became interested in coin-collecting when my aunt gave me sixteen old silver dollars on my sixteenth birthday. Insurance for coins can usually be added as a special rider on a homeowner's or apartment-dweller's policy. Although it is somewhat expensive, many coins in a good collection are irreplaceable, so insurance is well worth the cost.

Student paper

In the preceding paragraph, mentioning coin collections reminded the writer of how she began collecting coins. This may be an interesting fact, but it does not belong in a paragraph about insurance.

Poorly Unified Paragraph

It is a fact that capital punishment is not a deterrent to crime.[1] U.S. data show that in states with capital punishment, murder rates are the same or almost the same as in states without capital punishment.[2] It is also true that it is more expensive to put a person on death row than in life imprisonment because of the costs of maximum security.[3] Unfortunately, capital punishment has been used unjustly.[4] Statistics show that every execution is of a man and that nine out of ten are black.[5] So prejudice shows right through.[6]

Student paper

rh
49a

This paragraph has a promising beginning. Its first sentence makes a general statement, and its second sentence expands on the first by offering evidence to support it. But sentence 3 changes the subject from capital punishment as a deterrent to crime to the costs of capital punishment. Sentence 4 once again changes the subject—this time to the justice of capital punishment. Sentences 5 and 6 are related to sentence 4 if one agrees that executing men and blacks is evidence of injustice and prejudice, but the injustice of capital punishment is quite a different matter from the effectiveness of capital punishment as a deterrent to crime. The paragraph lacks unity because it contains not one but three main ideas: (a) capital punishment is not a deterrent, (b) capital punishment is expensive, and (c) capital punishment is unfair.

Unified Paragraph

> The punishment of criminals has always been a problem for society.[1] Citizens have had to decide whether offenders such as first-degree murders should be killed by being hanged, imprisoned for life, or rehabilitated and given a second chance in society.[2] Many citizens argue that serious criminals should be executed.[3] They believe that killing criminals will set an example for others and also rid society of a cumbersome burden.[4] Other citizens say that no one has the right to take a life and that capital punishment is not a deterrent to crime.[5] They believe that society as well as the criminal is responsible for the crimes and that killing the criminal does not solve the problems of either society or the criminal.[6]
>
> Student paper

Here the writer has stated the main idea in the first sentence. Sentence 2 then specifies the exact nature of the problem by listing the choices the society has. Sentence 3 breaks the topic down still further by stating the viewpoint of one group of citizens, and sentence 4 gives the reasons for this viewpoint. Sentence 5 states the opposing viewpoint. Sentence 6 lists the reasons for the opposing viewpoint. The paragraph as a whole has a unified and logical structure that follows a clear pattern of development.

To test whether a paragraph is unified, ask yourself first, "What is the main idea?" and then, "Does every sentence clearly relate to this main idea?"

Exercises: Paragraph Unity

Indicate which of the following paragraphs are good examples of unity and which are poor examples, and explain how the poor examples lack unity.

**rh
49a**

1. Dance is one of the oldest and most beautiful art forms. Figures of human dancers are recorded in paintings and on pottery made in northern Africa as early as 2500 B.C. Ballet, a very stylized dance form, flowered in Italy in the fifteenth century. In its early years it was a part of the opera, with dancers performing during the acts or intermissions. During the eighteenth century, Russian ballet gained world renown, but it was not until the twentieth century that North Americans showed any interest in supporting this art form. Learning to be a ballet dancer takes many years, and the student should begin training by at least age six. The training, as gruelling as that of any athlete, requires determination, constant self-discipline, and a special sensitivity toward this beautiful form of art.

2. The 1981 census revealed that rapid and dramatic changes in the Canadian labor force had occurred within just one decade. Statistics Canada reported that the labor force increased three times faster than the population as a whole and rose to 12 million. This figure represented almost 65 per cent of adult Canadians compared with 58 per cent in 1971. The highest rates of growth were observed in the Northwest Territories (76 per cent) and Alberta (75.2 per cent); the lowest were observed in Saskatchewan (22.7 per cent) and Manitoba (21.8 per cent). The statistics also show that Canada is increasingly a country of educated white-collar workers, for the number of workers with university degrees doubled during the decade, and the number of workers in managerial and administrative positions increased by 118 per cent. Women are becoming more prominent and have made considerable gains in some male-dominated occupations: in 1981 there were five times more female engineers, six times more female lawyers, three times more female accountants, and four times more female bus drivers than in 1971. Clearly, Canada's work force no longer fits the traditional picture of one comprised primarily of men working on the land's resources.

3. The twentieth century, with all its computer wizardry and electronic gadgetry, seems to be ringing the death knell for liberal arts education. A few students have always defied trends toward technical training so that they could "find themselves" by tracing their intellectual and spiritual insights back through the medieval teachings of the seven liberal arts to the roots of liberal education in ancient Greece and Rome. In Rome, the term *liberal education* meant education befitting a liberal, or free, person. The subjects taught were grammar, rhetoric, logic, arithmetic, geometry, astronomy, and music, subjects that continued to make up liberal arts curricula through the Middle Ages and Renaissance.

The Topic Sentence   In the unified paragraph about capital punishment, the first sentence is a **topic sentence,** one that summarizes the entire paragraph. Not every good paragraph has one particular sentence that sums up the point of the entire paragraph. In fact, most good writers probably aren't aware of whether their paragraphs have topic sentences. Certainly, if you have never had problems with paragraph unity, you need not worry about including a topic sentence in every paragraph. But if you do have difficulty in keeping paragraphs unified, topic sentences can be useful in helping you stick to the point as you write.

rh
49a

The most common position for a topic sentence is at the beginning of the paragraph.

Topic Sentence at Beginning of Paragraph

Never before have the English people been so vocal on so many issues at the same time.[1] Public participation has been encouraged to the point where the only contribution of which some are capable is a display of incoherence.[2] The fields of dissent are boundless.[3] Government measures, social injustices, financial policy, industrial relations, classical and modern literature, new trends in music, the causes of England's defeats in international sport—all these and a host of others are vigorously argued about.[4] Nothing is taken for granted.[5] No serious book can appear without at once stimulating a counterview.[6] Britain is indeed an isle full of noises.[7] The impression given abroad is of a bitterly divided, atrabilious, quarreling society.[8] What is actually happening is that a healthily skeptical English democracy is seeking to establish new foundations.[9]

> William Haley, "Will There Always Be an England?"
> *The American Scholar*

Here the author introduces the main idea—that the English are very vocal today—in the first sentence. Sentence 2 says that this speaking out has been encouraged. Sentences 3 through 6 list the many subjects of dispute. Sentence 7 restates the topic figuratively, and sentence 8 notes the foreign impressions of the British wrangling. Finally, sentence 9 says that all this vocal reaction is actually healthy. Note that every sentence after the topic sentence expands in some way on it.

A topic sentence sometimes appears in the middle of a paragraph following a transition from preceding paragraphs, as in the next example. The example below also shows that the topic sentence should be more than a bare statement of the topic. Particularly in a lengthy sentence, you should include material that develops the topic. Here the simple statement of the topic is "civilization takes the form of an authoritarian domination of nature." The rest of the sentence amplifies this assertion.

Topic Sentence in Middle of Paragraph

Why was there so little sense of participation? I think it was partly because of another unconscious assumption on the part of society, that Johnny should go to school because it was natural for him not to want to. That is, what he naturally wanted to do, according to this assumption, was play, and to be sent to school was enrolling him in a civilized operation. Civilization, then, was assumed to be antagonistic to nature. This assumption, that civilization takes the form of an authoritarian domination of nature, is exactly the same assumption which has produced, in other aspects of our society, the tedious grid pattern of our streets, our countrysides, and now even of our buildings. The same assumption is behind our pollution problems, behind the almost unimaginable hideousness of urban sprawl, behind the wanton destruction of trees and rivers and animals. There, if I had eyes to see it, was the central paradox of the contemporary world. It was all around me at school, and it was still around me after I went to college, enrolled in a course in philosophy, and settled down to grapple with some of its primary texts, including Aristotle's

Metaphysics, the first sentence of which reads, "All men by nature desire to know."

Northrop Frye, *Divisions on a Ground:*
Essays on Canadian Culture

Occasionally the topic sentence appears as the last sentence in the paragraph. This is one way to write an introductory paragraph because you build up a certain amount of suspense and tease the reader into continuing to the end to find out what the point is. You can also put the topic sentence at the end of a closing paragraph to summarize the entire argument. In the paragraph below, the author first states a generally held view (that taxonomy, the principles of classification, is considered dull), then explains his own view (that this view is unjustified because classification reflects human thinking), and finally summarizes with a topic sentence (that changes in taxonomy represent revolutionary changes in concepts).

Topic Sentence at End of Paragraph

Taxonomy is often regarded as the dullest of subjects, fit only for mindless ordering and sometimes denigrated within science as mere "stamp collecting" (a designation that this former philatelist deeply resents). If systems of classification were neutral hat racks for hanging the facts of the world, this disdain might be justified. But classifications both reflect and direct our thinking. The way we order represents the way we think. <u>Historical changes in classification are the fossilized indicators of conceptual revolutions.</u>

Stephen Jay Gould,
Hen's Teeth and Horse's Toes

When you have a paragraph with a fairly complicated argument, you may wish to state the topic sentence twice, once at the beginning to introduce the argument and again at the end to summarize it. (Obviously, you would not word the two topic sentences exactly the same.) In the next example, the author first states his topic in the negative— meteorites are not hot when they hit the ground. He then explains that they are initially cold, then are heated on the outside, then are cooled again. Finally, he summarizes by stating his point in the affirmative— meteorites are cold when they hit the ground.

rh
49a

Topic Sentence at Both Beginning and End of Paragraph

<u>It is a widely held but erroneous belief that meteorites arrive at ground level in a very hot condition.</u> In space meteorites are extremely cold and their temperature on entering the Earth's atmosphere is well below zero. During the brief few seconds of their blazing fireball flight the outer layers of a meteorite are melted and sprayed aside at a faster rate than heat penetrates inwards, so that

any heating effect is confined to just a few millimetres below the surface. After slowing to free fall at around 20 km height, the meteorite spends a minute and a half falling at about 200 km/hour through some of the coldest layers of the Earth's atmosphere and this cools the outer skin rapidly. <u>The meteorite arrives cold—usually very cold indeed.</u>

Keith Hindley, "Meteorite Photography,"
The Illustrated London News ·

Although the device should not be overused, writers occasionally make the last sentence of one paragraph the topic sentence for the next. In the following example, the writer first describes the qualities of an open fire. He then moves to observations about the transfer of energy from wood or coal and in his final sentence raises a question. This last sentence serves as a link between the two paragraphs and as a topic sentence for the second paragraph.

Topic Sentence at End of Preceding Paragraph

This is nothing quite so enjoyable on a winter's evening as an open fire. The warmth from the flames seems to have a special kind of charm that isn't shared by a central heating system, even though a physicist will tell you that the two kinds of heat are identical. If you think about it for a while, you will recall that heat generated from burning wood or coal can be harnessed by machinery to lift weights or move a vehicle. And yet, when you hold a piece of wood or coal in your hand it doesn't move, nor is it hot to the touch. <u>How can anything so inert produce all these effects?</u>

This is by no means a simple question. Some of the best minds in the history of science have stumbled over the relation between heat and motion, and it wasn't until the latter part of the nineteenth century that the issue was finally resolved. The difficulty is that there is no obvious connection between a quantity of fuel, a flame, and the work that can be performed by using that flame.

James Trefil, *The Unexpected Vista*

rh
49a

The purpose of a topic sentence is to let the reader know what the main point of the paragraph is, but it is usually not necessary to tell the reader overtly what you are going to do next. Try to avoid such sentences as "Now I am going to discuss . . ." or "In this section we explain. . . ." It is not exactly wrong to tell the reader openly what you plan to do before you do it, but it is wordy and inelegant. The topic sentence should be clear enough to let the reader know what is going on without your having to put up signposts.

As we mentioned earlier, many well-unified paragraphs have no single topic sentence or only an implied one. This is especially true of descriptive and narrative writing, where a topic sentence is normally unnecessary because, if there were to be one sentence that summarized the like" or "This is what happened." A good example of a paragraph without a topic sentence is the following description of the island of Ceylon by Michael Ondaatje.

No Topic Sentence in Paragraph

Ceylon falls on a map and its outline is the shape of a tear. After the spaces of India and Canada it is so small. A miniature. Drive ten miles an you are in a landscape so different that by rights it should belong to another country. From Galle in the south to Colombo a third of the way up the coast is only seventy miles. When houses were built along the coastal road it was said that a chicken could walk between the two cities without touching ground. The country is cross-hatched with maze-like routes whose only escape is the sea. From a ship or plane you can turn back or look down at the disorder. Villages spill onto streets, the jungle encroaches on village.

Michael Ondaatje, *Running in the Family*

Exercises: Topic Sentences

Underline the topic sentences in the following paragraphs.

1. Such neglected opportunities would hardly seem to recommend me as one to give advice on buying and selling antiques. But those were far from being my only mistakes. At the first show in which Betty and I sold antiques I took $10 for a $600 Steuben glass bowl. At an auction, much more recently than I can comfortably admit, I paid a ridiculously high price for a figural urn that, on delivery, I discovered to be marked "Deenie's Ceramics Studio." I once lost a $10,000 painting to a competitor who took it with a winning bid of $60. At a flea market I wasted half a day waiting for a dealer to show me a promised "art glass vase" that turned out to be worthless, while my neighbor casually strolled to the next table and picked up a fine Mettlach stein for $25.

Michael De Forrest, *Antiquing from A to Z: Buying and Selling Collectibles and Other Old Things*

2. All dogs came from two common ancestors millions of years ago. Even though they have changed in shape and size through the centuries, some breeds claim the wolf as their ancestor, while the rest claim the jackal. Collies, with their weather-resistant coats and their endurance and cleverness, were selected to be bred as herd dogs. The northern dogs, such as the husky, chowchow, and Samoyed, all with their heavy coats and curled tails to protect their noses while sleeping in the cold and their powerful build, were bred to be sled and draft animals. Terrier dogs, powerful little animals, were bred to catch rats and badgers, by farmers and hunters in the British Isles. The guard dogs, on the other hand, come from the Greek and Roman arenas, and the bull mastiffs are their ancestors. They were large and stouthearted and often had to fight lions in the arenas.

Louis L. Vine, *Your Dog: His Health and Happiness*

rh
49a

3. Rock. Hard rock. Live. That unmistakable driving, pulsating rock beat. Amplifiers way up. A kid in a leather jacket works the dials and periodically dashes half way up the aisle to check the decibels. Tall, lanky Valery Vernigor belts out *Evil Woman* and *Spinning Wheel*, hits made famous by the American group Blood, Sweat and Tears. He sings with feeling. In English. It could be the original except for sharp brassy riffs from trumpets and trombones. At the electronic organ, throbbing with rhythm, is a goateed dandy in a flaming red shirt. The drummer, lean and intense, is developing a handlebar mustache. A bank of electric guitarmen in neck-length hair give out with the vacant-eyed look and rolling body motion that go with rock. At center stage Lyosha Kozlov, with stringy beatnik hair and a full Solzhenitsyn beard, works over a wild, rippling alto sax. The room swims in sound. Then, sharp enthusiastic applause all around me. And Makhurdad Badi, a Moscow-born Persian lad with a high wavering tenor and kinky hair falling to his shoulders, joins in a medley from *Jesus Christ, Superstar*.

Hedrick Smith, *The Russians*

4. The writing of graffiti, perhaps because its practitioners are so elusive, is one human activity not given serious consideration or study by behavioral scientists—the historians, philosophers, sociologists, psychologists, psychiatrists, columnists. I consider this a grave oversight. Graffiti, too, are revelatory of developments, trends, and attitudes in man's history. Man is a natural communicator. A thought occurs to someone suddenly, or something is experienced during the day, and there is a compulsion to express it, if not to another person, then to whatever is close at hand: paper, wall, rock, tree, door. Graffiti, then, are little insights, little peepholes into the minds of individuals who are spokesmen not only for themselves but for others like them.

Robert Reisner, *Graffiti: Two Thousand Years of Wall Writing*

---

rh
49a

Other Kinds of Unity In addition to unity of ideas within the paragraph and the use of topic sentences as an aid to unity, grammatical unity and unity of diction are also important. Grammatical unity is achieved by correct agreement, consistency of tenses, proper placement of modifiers, and appropriate use of co-ordination and subordination. (See 17–23). Unity of diction means that the words are compatible with the subject matter and the purpose of the paragraph. Slang, for example, has no place in the description of a laboratory experiment. Fairytale diction ("Once upon a time") is not suitable for historical narration. See 46 for a discussion of choosing the right words.

Finally, what adds to unity in one context may detract from it in another. For example, extensive detail contributes to unity in descriptive writing but may detract from it in the summary of an argument.

Exercises: Review: Paragraph Unity

The following paragraphs lack unity. Explain what is wrong with each paragraph and rewrite *one* of the three, making it into a well-developed, unified paragraph.

1. Modern London, a swarming, sprawling city, is a city of great paradox. In every corner, ghosts of the past rise up to remind the visitor that this city is built on pageantry and splendor, suffering and deprivation, revolution and bloodshed, creativity and the unconquerable will of the human spirit. Samuel Johnson is almost afoot in Fleet Street; Admiral Nelson's ship is almost visible on the Thames; throngs of Londoners mass outside the Tower of London, eager for the next public execution of a nobleman; Queen Victoria's carriage seems to rumble through the narrow streets.

2. The modern consumer movement, which has brought about sweeping changes in the public's awareness of the political influence of its buying power, was largely spearheaded by the efforts of one man—Ralph Nader. Pressure by numerous buyers who have learned effective lobbying has forced stringent new safety standards on the automobile industry, more complete labelling of products in the food industry, new honesty in advertising, and new antipollution laws in industry.

3. People have always been fascinated by the world beneath the sea, but we know less about the surface of the ocean floor than about the surface of the moon. As early as the fourth century B.C., Alexander the Great had himself lowered into the sea in a large glass barrel. Basalt is the rock most commonly found on the sea floor. The most common forms of life on the ocean bottom are mollusks (octopuses, cuttlefish, as squid), brittle stars, worms, and strange fish. The deep-sea drilling projects for oil in the North Sea and the Beaufort Sea may incidentally provide additional knowledge about the earth's mantle.

49b ▪ Completeness

Completeness in a paragraph means that the topic is adequately developed by details, explanations, definitions, evidence, and the like, so that the reader is not left with only a fuzzy idea of what the writer means. How much development is "adequate"? Unfortunately, there is no simple answer. The amount of development necessary for any given paragraph will vary widely according to the topic, the audience, and the purpose of the paper of which the paragraph is a part. However, completeness does not mean simply that you should keep writing until you have 200 or 250 words and then start a new paragraph. Every sentence should be clearly related to the topic and to other sentences in the paragraph.

A paragraph may contain a fair amount of information but still be incomplete if this information is not developed.

rh
49b

Incomplete Paragraph

New filming techniques and new methods of creating special effects contribute to the influence a film will have on the industry. This influence is one aspect of whether or not a film is considered a classic. *King Kong* was one of the most important films in history and had a profound effect on the technical aspects of the film industry.

Student paper

This passage is really more an outline than a paragraph. The reader is left wondering about the nature of new filming techniques and special effects. What is the exact relationship between a film's influence on the industry and whether or not it is considered a classic? What were some of the new techniques of *King Kong?* What films did *King Kong* directly influence? This potentially good paragraph is ineffective because it is not complete.

Complete Paragraph

Railway travel in Spain is a nightmare which tourists should know about before embarking on a voyage.[1] Each compartment holds eight people, which usually results in a conglomeration of soldiers, tourists, farmers, and villagers.[2] Within minutes after the train pulls out of the station, the compartments become saturated with the mixed odor of wine, urine, and sweat.[3] Chickens and dogs casually stroll the narrow passageways.[4] Drunkards and perverts roam through the cars shouting obscenities and pinching the oversized rear-ends of standing or passing females.[5] Travellers suffer silently, passing the dreary hours by playing tic-tac-toe and poker.[6]

Student paper

rh
49b

This writer begins by stating the topic: Railway travel in Spain is a nightmare. A description of the size of the compartments and the different kinds of travellers follow. Sentence 3 states the results of the crowded conditions. Sentences 4 and 5 give details about the passageways of the cars. Finally, the writer describes how travellers respond to all these conditions. The reader is left with a vivid picture of why the writer called railway travel in Spain a nightmare. All this detail is justified because railway travel in Spain is the topic of the paragraph.

If, on the other hand, the topic of the paragraph were the broader one of the problems of vacationing in Spain, the details of railway travel might be limited:

Vacationing in Spain is not all bullfights and flamenco guitars. Potential tourists should know that they may find few people who speak English. Hotel accommodations often bear little resemblance to the pictures of rooms in travel brochures. The water is frequently unsafe to drink. Railway travel is a nightmare because of over-crowded cars and unsanitary conditions. An encounter with the Spanish police can be, at best, a traumatic experience.

Here, only two details about railway travel are provided because the topic is more general than in the first paragraph. In fact, if all those details were included here, the resulting paragraph would be badly out of proportion.

Types of Paragraph Development   One of the most serious and persistent problems in many student papers is underdeveloped paragraphs, paragraphs consisting of only one to three short sentences. What is more, underdeveloped paragraphs often lead to a lack of unity and coherence: The writer sees that a paragraph is too short, and so, rather than begin a new paragraph when taking up a new point, he or she simply adds that point to the preceding paragraph to bring it up to a respectable length.

Alternatively, a writer may try to fatten up an underdeveloped paragraph by sticking in miscellaneous facts not really related to the topic. Again, unity and coherence suffer: It takes two socks to make a pair, but not every two socks make a pair. Be sure that your development is appropriate to your material.

Most writers know enough about their subjects to write complete paragraphs. They simply do not know how to develop their information logically and interestingly. There are many ways to develop a paragraph. The **type of development** is the way in which the main idea is supported—by details, definitions, statements of cause and effect, and so on. The **sequence of development** is the order in which supporting sentences are presented—from the general to the particular, chronologically, by order of importance, and so on.

Among the most important types of paragraph development are development by (1) detail, (2) comparison and contrast, (3) analogy, (4) process, (5) classification and partition, (6) cause and effect, (7) definition, and (8) mixed development.

1.   **Development by Detail.** Development by detail is one of the most common and most useful types of development. Typically, the paragraph begins with a topic sentence or general statement that is then expanded by specific illustrations or examples.

**rh
49b**

Development by Detail

The Pueblos do not understand self-torture.[1] Every man's hand has its five fingers, and unless they have been tortured to secure a sorcery confession they are unscarred.[2] There are no cicatrices upon their backs, no marks where strips of skin have been taken off.[3] They have no rites in which they sacrifice their own blood, or use it for fertility.[4] They used to hurt themselves to a certain extent in a few initiations at the moments of greatest excitement, but in such cases the whole matter was almost an affair of collegiate exuberance.[5] In the Cactus Society, a warrior cult, they dashed about striking themselves and each other with cactus-blade whips; in the Fire

Society they tossed fire about like confetti.[6] Neither psychic danger nor abnormal experience is sought in either case.[7] Certainly in the observed fire tricks of the Pueblos—as also in the fire tricks of the Plains—it is not self-torture that is sought.[8] In the Fire Walk, whatever the means employed, feet are not burned, and when the fire is taken into the mouth the tongue is not blistered.[9]

Ruth Benedict, *Patterns of Culture*

This paragraph begins with a topic sentence and follows that sentence with details that support the assertion. Sentences 2, 3, and 4 support the argument by noting that the Pueblos do not maim themselves in any specific way. Sentence 5 cites situations in which Pueblo ceremonies may have led to accidental, but not deliberate, injury. Sentences 6 and 7 list ceremonies that are potentially dangerous but not intended to cause physical or mental damage. Details of fire ceremonies that do not involve self-torture are provided in sentences 8 and 9.

Development by Detail

I looked through the blindless windows of the Indian houses.[1] Half eaten meals littered the tables.[2] Because the tide had been right to go, bedding had been stripped from the springs, food left about, water left unemptied to rust the kettles.[3] Indians slip in and out of their place like animals.[4] Tides and seasons are the things that rule their lives: domestic arrangements are mere incidentals.[5]

Emily Carr, *Klee Wyck*

Unlike the paragraph by Benedict, this paragraph ends with a topic sentence that is prepared for by details. Here, however, the details are used to fill in a picture as well as support an assertion. The first sentence draws the reader into the scene within the Indian houses. Sentences 2 and 3 give physical details. Sentence 4 introduces one generalization about the Indians' way of life, likening its patterns to those of the natural world. Sentence 5 relates the human domestic details to the natural way of life to explain the significance of the scene described.

**rh
49b**

Exercises: Development by Detail

Use detail to develop a paragraph on one of the following subjects.

1. An event that impressed you at an early age (for example, a parade, circus, wedding, funeral)
2. The atmosphere of a particular place that you go to frequently (for example, a theatre, a disco, a library, a restaurant, or a shop)
3. The behavior of an eccentric person (real or imaginary)

2. **Development by Comparison and Contrast.** Strictly speaking, a comparison shows how two or more things are alike, and a contrast shows how they are different. In practice, comparison and contrast often appear together because two things that have everything in common and no differences are the same things, not two different things. Similarly, there is no point in grouping two things (say an eggshell and an earthmover) if they have nothing in common. Usually, the things being compared share a number of features and belong to a common and easily identifiable class—types of human behavior, diseases, warlike situations, kinds of games. If the similarities between the things being compared are so obvious that they need not be mentioned, the discussion may focus on the differences alone. In the following paragraph, the author does not mention that poets, dramatists, novelists, and historians are all human beings and are all writers because every reader knows this.

Development by Comparison and Contrast

The poet, the dramatist, the novelist are free to exercise their imagination as widely as they choose.[1] But the historian may not be allowed so long a tether.[2] He must fulfill his function as a creative artist only within very rigid limits.[3] He cannot invent what went on in the mind of St. Thomas of Canterbury.[4] The poet can.[5] He cannot suppress inconvenient minor characters and invent others who more significantly underline the significance of his theme.[6] The novelist can.[7] The dramatist can.[8] The historian, as Sir Philip Sidney has said, "is captive to the truth of a foolish world."[9] Not only is he captive to the truth of a foolish world, but he is captive to a truth he can never fully discover, and yet he is forbidden by his conscience and his training from inventing it.[10]

C. V. Wedgwood, *The Sense of the Past*

This paragraph is an example of almost pure contrast. Essentially, Wedgwood lists some of the many things that poets, dramatists, and novelists can do that historians cannot do. Note that sentences 9 and 10 do not overtly state a contrast, but, by their presence, they imply still another contrast: that poets, dramatists, and novelists are *not* "captive to the truth of a foolish world" as historians are.

rh
49b

Development by Comparison and Contrast

D. H. Lawrence and Katherine Mansfield had a good deal in common.[1] Both were outsiders in English society: Lawrence because of his working-class background, Katherine because of her colonial origins.[2] Though they left their birthplace, they were strongly influenced by it and frequently recreated it in their work.[3] They revolted against the conventional values of the time; and had considerable sexual experience in early life, though Lawrence had been strengthened and Katherine hurt by it.[4] They spent many impoverished years on the Continent and maintained a European rather than an insular outlook.[5] They had intuitive and volatile personalities, experienced life with a feverish intensity, were highly creative and passionately committed to their art, and achieved a posthumous fame far greater than their contemporary reputations.[6] Most important of all, they were seriously ill for a great part of their adult lives, and made their pilgrimage from country to country in search of a warm climate and good health.[7] They were subject to sudden fits of black rage, suffered the constant pain of disease and the fearful threat of death, and died of tuberculosis at an early age.[8]

> Jeffrey Meyers, "D. H. Lawrence: Katherine Mansfield
> and 'Women in Love,' " *London Magazine*

Meyers' paragraph illustrates almost pure comparison; only the last part of sentence 4 provides a contrast. Again, the author does not state the obvious contrasts—for example, that Lawrence was a man and Mansfield was a woman.

As these paragraphs show, comparisons and contrasts may be handled point by point. (For example, "X is big and Y is little. X is expensive and Y is cheap.") Alternatively, the features of one subject may be discussed first, followed by the features of the second subject. In this organization, a separate paragraph is often begun when the second subject is introduced.

Development by Comparison and Contrast

Choosing between the two [vinyl and aluminum], which are remarkably similar in panel sizes and shapes, mounting techniques and durability, is mostly a matter of taste and availability.[1] Vinyl is a bit easier to work, does not dent or show scratches and resists heat and cold better than aluminum.[2] But it can crack when struck in cold weather and cannot be repainted.[3]

Aluminum is usually less costly than vinyl, and comes in a brighter palette of factory-baked enamel finishes.[1] But it is easily dented and scratched, and some codes require electrical grounding.[2]

> Time-Life Books, *Roofs and Siding*

**rh
49b**

Here, sentence 1 of the first paragraph compares vinyl and aluminum siding. Sentences 2 and 3 contrast the two by stating the characteristics of vinyl that differ from the characteristics of aluminum. The second paragraph then states the distinguishing characteristics of aluminum.

Exercises: Development by Comparison and Contrast

Use comparison and contrast to develop a paragraph on one of the following topics.

1. The relative effectiveness of news presented in a newspaper or magazine as compared to that presented on the radio or television

2. The merits of two rock groups or two solo vocalists or instrumentalists
3. The characteristics of two elderly people of the same sex, people whom you know
4. Your tastes in clothes compared with those of an older person of the same sex as you

---

3. **Development by Analogy.** Development by analogy is similar to development by comparison and contrast in that both compare two different things. In analogy, however, one compares things that do not belong to the same class. In the next example, by Helen Keller, a ship is not a living creature as is a blind person; in the paragraph by James Michener, porridge is not related to lava.

Comparison and contrast and analogy are also used for different purposes. Comparison and contrast classify and differentiate similar things, and in the process both things are explained. Analogy explains the unfamiliar in terms of the familiar: most people have some notion of what it is like to be caught in a fog, but sighted people do not understand what it is like to be blind (Keller's paragraph). Similarly, porridge (oatmeal) is generally familiar, but the material beneath the earth's crust is not (Michener's paragraph). See 51d for a discussion of the proper uses of analogy.

Development by Analogy

Have you ever been at sea in a dense fog, when it seemed as if a tangible white darkness shut you in, and the great ship, tense and anxious, groped her way toward the shore with plummet and sounding-line, and you waited with beating heart for something to happen?[1] I was like that ship before my education began, only I was without compass or sounding-line, and had no way of knowing how near the harbour was.[2] "Light! give me light!" was the wordless cry of my soul, and the light of love shone on me in that very hour.[3]

Helen Keller, *The Story of My Life*

Here Keller states the familiar (a ship in a fog) in her first sentence. Sentence 2 then begins the analogy to the unfamiliar (the confusion of blindness) with the words "I was like that ship."

rh 49b

Development by Analogy

At the top of the mantle, only twenty-seven miles from the surface, rested the earth's crust, where life would develop.[1] What was it like?[2] It can be described as the hard scum that forms at the top of a pot of boiling porridge.[3] From the fire at the center of the pot, heat radiates not only upward, but in all directions.[4] The porridge bubbles freely at first when it is thin, and its motion seems to be always upward, but as it thickens, one can see that for every slow bubble that rises at the center of the pan, part of the porridge is drawn downward at the edges; it is this slow reciprocal rise and fall which constitutes cooking.[5] In time, when enough of this convection has taken place, the porridge exposed to air begins to thicken perceptibly, and the moment the internal heat stops or diminishes, it hardens into a crust.[6]

James A. Michener, *Centennial*

In this paragraph, Michener reverses the order used by Keller. Sentences 1 and 2 introduce the unfamiliar (the area beneath the earth), and sentence 3 begins the analogy with the familiar (porridge) with the words "It can be described as. . . ." Sentences 4, 5 and 6 continue the analogy by describing what happens to porridge as it cooks.

Exercises: Development by Analogy

Help your readers understand something unusual you know or do by making an analogy between it and something familiar to most people. For example, a computer programmer might make an analogy between the process of writing programs and the process of writing a composition. The following are some suggested topics for analogies.

1. Being in a tornado (or landslide, hurricane, earthquake, blizzard, or other violent natural phenomenon)
2. Coming out of the anesthetic after an operation
3. The appearance of a newly born animal
4. Preparing a meal for twenty or more people
5. Being in a country or area where you do not speak or understand the language
6. Being arrested for a crime you did not commit

---

4. **Development by Process.** Development by process is a step-by-step description of how something is done. Because the steps of a process must occur one after the other, this method of development usually follows a chronological sequence. If the purpose of the process statement is simply to give readers a general understanding of how something is done, as in the first paragraph below, you need fewer explicit details. If, as in the second paragraph below, you intend to teach the readers how to perform the task or activity themselves, you need more details. The exact order in which operations should take place is crucial, and supplementary comments about why an operation must be carried out may be necessary.

Development by Process

In the lost wax (*cire perdue*) technique of casting objects in metal, the object is first modelled in wax. The wax object is then coated in clay and baked, with vents being left through which the molten wax escapes. Then liquid metal is poured in through the vents to fill the cavity left by the wax. After the metal has cooled, the baked clay covering is broken. The resulting metal casting is an exact copy of the original wax object.

Because this paragraph is intended only as a general description for the reader's information, specific details such as the kind of metal used, the location of the vents, and the temperature at which the object is baked are not given. Nonetheless, the order of the steps is carefully indicated by the order of the sentences and by the use of such words as *then*, *after*, and *resulting*.

Development by Process

There are several ways of stopping, and it is wise to learn at least one (other than falling) early in your skating career.[1] If you are a skier, you are familiar with the *snowplow* move, which slows you down.[2] It works on ice as well as snow.[3] Skate in a glide, with your feet parallel but slightly apart; then push your heels apart farther, keeping your hands out at your sides for balance and your knees bent.[4] Your weight should be back.[5] The act of pushing your heels apart while your toes keep together makes you stop.[6] There also is a *one-foot snowplow* in which the heel and hip on one side are pushed forward strongly, causing the corresponding blade to skid.[7] With more pressure, this brings you to a stop.[8] This can be done with either foot acting as the brake.[9]

Tiny Noyes with Freda Alexander,
I Can Teach You to Figure-Skate

Here, the author intends the readers actually to carry out the process themselves, so she gives specific details (sentence 5, for example) and even provides helpful hints not directly related to stopping on ice (the comparison with skiing in sentence 2). Note how crucial the order of presentation is; for example, if you first pushed your heels apart and then tried to skate in a glide, the tips of your blades would cross and you would fall on your face.

**rh
49b**

Exercises: Development by Process

Use development by process to explain the techniques or steps involved in one of the following situations.

1. Learning an athletic skill or game (for example, how to punt a football, how to hold and swing a golf club, how to learn beginning chess)
2. Changing a tire on a car
3. Repotting houseplants
4. Avoiding obnoxious acquaintances: the art of self-defence
5. Giving a pill to a cat or dog

5. **Development by Classification and Partition.** Classification is the process of grouping individual items on the basis of their similarities and differences; classification collects individuals and fits them into a larger pattern. Partition, or analysis, is the reverse process: It divides larger wholes into smaller component parts. In other words, classification puts things together and partition takes them apart. In practice, classification and partition are often not easily distinguished—classification usually includes partitioning, and partitioning implies classification. In the following paragraph, the author first partitions the great apes into four groups. In the last two sentences, he then classifies all the great apes according to their common characteristics.

Development by Classification and Partition

The living great apes (Pongidae) fall into four groups: gibbons, orangutans, gorillas, and chimpanzees. All are fairly large animals that have no tail, a relatively large skull and brain, and very long arms. All have a tendency, when on the ground, to walk semi-erect.

                                    William Keeton, *Biological Science*

Both classification and partition are forms of definition, and both frequently appear in a single definition. Classification and partition are also similar to comparison and contrast in that the very acts of classifying and partitioning usually involve some comparison.

Development by Classification and Partition

The gibbons, of which several species are found in southeast Asia, represent a lineage that probably split from the others soon after the pongid line itself arose.[1] They are the smallest of the apes (about 3 feet tall when standing).[2] Their arms are exceedingly long, reaching the ground even when the animal is standing erect.[3] The gibbons are amazing arboreal acrobats and spend almost all their time in trees.[4]

                                    William Keeton, *Biological Science*

This paragraph uses primarily partition: Keeton distinguishes the gibbons from the other apes according to their habitat, lineage, size, proportions, and acrobatic ability. This very distinction implies a contrast with the other great apes, and Keeton uses an overt comparison ("the smallest of the apes") in sentence 2. Note also that the distinctions help define the gibbon.

In development by classification and partition, as in comparison and contrast, separate paragraphs are often used to develop each of the items being classified or partitioned.

Development by Classification and Partition

There are two kinds of late-snack invitations. One is the sort that a cheerful husband proffers the whole dance floor while the band plays

"Good Night Ladies." "Lesh all come over t'our housh for shcrambled eggsh!" (His wife is the feverish-looking lady by the door, with the armful of coats. She knows there are five eggs in the refrigerator, every one of them spoken for.) These occasions are seldom outstandingly successful.

The second kind is the invitation you issue yourself because these things are a community habit and it's your turn. If you can't move out of the community, you should make the first move—as part of your community endeavor—and suggest that everyone stop eating so much. But until you get around to this, the following late-snack ideas may be helpful. They are all easy and they take very little last-minute doing.

Peg Bracken, The I Hate to Cook Book

Here Bracken states the classification in the first sentence of the first paragraph and uses the rest of the paragraph to describe one kind of late-snack invitation. She devotes the next paragraph to describing the second kind of invitation.

Exercises: Development by Classification and Partition

Develop by classification and/or partition one or two paragraphs on one of the following subjects:

1. Varieties of secretaries or receptionists
2. Types of neighborhoods
3. Types of fashion magazines (or sports or news magazines)
4. Varieties of salesmanship
5. Breeds of university or college professors

---

6. **Development by Cause and Effect.** The basic purpose of a cause-and-effect paragraph is to explain why a condition or conditions exist or existed. Although some causes and effects are so complex that they require an entire paper to explain, simple cause-and-effect relationships can often be explained within a single paragraph. Normally, the effect is stated first and its cause follows.

rh
49b

Development by Cause and Effect

An enduring problem among the Scotch was that of personal nomenclature. As I have noted, a certain number of the clans transported themselves to Canada in bulk, or, in any case, reformed their ranks quickly on arrival. McCallums, Campbells, Grahams and McKillops were exceptionally numerous. That so many had the same surname would not have been serious had they not so often had the same Christian names as well. To call a son something other than John was to combine mild eccentricity with unusual imagination. And even an unusual imagination did not normally extend beyond Dan, Jim, Angus, Duncan or Malcolm. A fair proportion of the people we knew were called John McCallum. The John Grahams and the John Campbells were almost equally numerous.

John Kenneth Galbraith, *The Scotch*

In this paragraph, the effect (the problem of personal names) is stated first. Galbraith then explains in the following sentences what caused this problem (so many entire clans, all with the same surnames, came to Canada and all the people tended to name their sons John).

Development by Cause and Effect

There are three fundamental problems that have caused the current dilemma of environmentalism. First, there is the myth, which environmentalists have fashioned, of an ideal, preindustrial, prepesticide past, when crops were good, living was easy, and insects were few. This is a complete fantasy. Second, there is the false distinction between "natural" and "unnatural" chemicals, and the implicit assumption that chemicals like pesticides never occur in nature. Third, there is the myth that these "unnatural" chemicals are causing an equally mythical "epidemic" increase in cancer. Unfortunately, the genesis of all three of these ideas can be traced directly to *Silent Spring.*

William Tucker, "Of Mites and Men," *Harper's Magazine*

Like Galbraith, Tucker states the effect (the dilemma of environmentalism) in the first sentence. He then explicitly spells out three causes of this dilemma. Finally, the last sentence states that all three of these causes were brought about by the publication of Rachel Carson's *Silent Spring.* Later paragraphs in the article expand on each of these three causes. This device of summarizing all the causes or effects in one paragraph and then using following paragraphs to explain each cause or effect in detail is an especially clear and useful method for handling fairly complicated cause-and-effect relationships.

rh
49b

Exercises: Development by Cause and Effect

Use cause and effect to develop a paragraph. Make one of the following topics *either* the cause *or* the effect of something else.

1. The high cost of hospital care
2. Increased interest in Oriental philosophy
3. The trend toward "natural" fibres for clothing
4. An important change in your life, such as the loss of a friendship
5. The lost art of letter-writing

7. **Development by Definition.** In a broad sense, almost any kind of writing is definition—whatever we say about something helps to define it. In a narrower sense, a definition is an explicit statement of what a term means. Such definitions may be as simple as a synonym or a two- or three-word explanation or as elaborate as a full-length paper.

When a paragraph is developed by means of definition, the definition should be more than a simple sentence or list of synonyms. It may include examples or negative examples (what the term does *not* mean), analogies, and comparisons and contrasts. Extended definitions often include classification, partition, and statements of cause and effect.

Development by Definition

Hue, a term often used interchangeably with color, is the quality or characteristic by which we distinguish one color from another. The *primary* hues—red, yellow, and blue—are the basic building blocks of color from which all others are blended. The *secondary* hues, produced by mixing two primaries, are orange, green, and violet (purple). The *tertiary* hues (often called intermediates) stem from various combinations of the basic six; they are the "double-name" colors, such as yellow-green and blue-violet.

The Vogue Sewing Book

The simple, nontechnical definition of hue in this paragraph first gives a one-sentence general statement of what hue means. The next three sentences use partition to define different kinds of hues.

Definitions are particularly important for limiting the intended meaning of abstract or technical terms. If you use a familiar term in an unusual or technical sense, a definition explaining exactly what you mean by that term is essential. In the paragraph below, the writer must state exactly what he means by *literary dialect* because both *literary* and *dialect* mean different things to different people.

Development by Definition

**rh
49b**

One more type of standard dialect should be recognized at this point.[1] That is the *literary dialect.*[2] Any dialect may be a medium for literature, of course, as anyone knows who has read *Huckleberry Finn, Uncle Remus,* or the poems of Robert Burns.[3] But it often happens that a single dialect is considered the appropriate one for artistic and scholarly composition.[4] It may, of course, be the same as the standard spoken dialect, as is the case with most modern European languages.[5] This is likely to be true when literacy is widespread and many people engage in literature, whether it be reciting and listening to epic poems or writing and reading novels.[6] On the other hand, when literacy is restricted to a rather small and sometimes exclusive group—a scholar class—this group may use a special dialect for its writing.[7] Often this is an older form of the language, as it appears in literary classics which the scholar class is intimately familiar with.[8] Sanskrit is such an archaic literary dialect.[9] The extreme is reached when a literary dialect is actually another language, as was the case with classical Latin in Western Europe during the Renaissance.[10]

W. Nelson Francis, *The Structure of American English*

Exercises: Development by Definition

Use definition to develop a paragraph on one of the following subjects. You may check a dictionary first, but do not simply quote the dictionary's definition.

1. Ragtime
2. Eyeglasses
3. Boredom
4. Multiculturalism
5. Childhood disease
6. Inflation

---

8. **Development by a Mixture of Types.** As we have seen, a single paragraph often contains more than one type of development. In the *Vogue* paragraph, for instance, a brief analogy forms part of the definition. Almost any kind of paragraph may include examples or illustrations. The important thing is to avoid switching abruptly and apparently without reason from one kind of development to another in the middle of a paragraph. For example, you might be describing how to knit a sock and suddenly realize that the reader does not know what *stockinette* means. Rather than stop in the middle of your instructions and say, "Oh, by the way, stockinette means that you knit odd-numbered rows and purl even-numbered rows," you should include the definition in an earlier paragraph where you have defined such technical terms as *purl, yarn over,* and *fisherman's stitch.*

The following paragraph is a good mixture of definition and analogy. The first six sentences are devoted to straight definition. Sentences 7 and 8 switch to an analogy between the devotee of culture and a lover of games. Notice how much this analogy contributes to the definition.

**rh
49b**

Development by a Mixture of Types

The devotee of culture is, as a person, worth much more than the status seeker.[1] He reads as he also visits art galleries and concert rooms, not to make himself acceptable, but to improve himself, to develop his potentialities, to become a more complete man.[2] He is sincere and may be modest.[3] Far from trotting along obediently with the fashion, he is more likely to stick too exclusively to the 'established authors' of all periods and nations, 'the best that has been thought and said in the world'.[4] He makes few experiments and has few favourites.[5] Yet this worthy man may be, in the sense I am concerned with, no true lover of literature at all.[6] He may be as far from that as a man who does exercises with dumb-bells every morning may be from being a lover of games.[7] The playing of games will ordinarily contribute to a man's bodily perfection; but if that becomes the sole or chief reason for playing them they cease to be games and become 'exercise'.[8]

C. S. Lewis, *An Experiment in Criticism*

Exercises: Development by a Mixture of Types

Combine two or more of the methods of paragraph development to write a well-developed paragraph on one of the following topics.

1. Nonverbal communication
2. Shoplifting
3. Marriage in the 1980s
4. The most memorable place I have visited
5. Annoying habits of my friends

Sequences of Paragraph Development Sequences of development are not independent of types of development; that is, every type of development will follow some kind of sequence. Some sequences, such as general to particular, may be used with virtually any type of development. Other sequences are much more limited. For example, a spatial sequence would not appear in a cause-and-effect paragraph. The most important sequences of development are (1) general to particular, (2) particular to general, (3) climactic, (4) chronological, and (5) spatial.

1. **General-to-Particular Sequence.** A general-to-particular sequence is the most common type of sequence in nonfiction writing. A general statement, usually the topic sentence, introduces the paragraph and is followed by specific details that expand, explain, or illustrate the topic sentence. Readers can easily follow this sequence because they know the main point at once and so have it in mind as they read the rest of the paragraph.

The following selection illustrates a general-to-particular sequence in a paragraph with development by detail.

rh
49b

General-to-Particular Sequence

Most tropical animals are more sensitive to change—especially toward higher temperatures—than northern ones, and this is probably because the water in which they live normally varies by only a few degrees throughout the year.[1] Some tropical sea urchins, keyhole limpets, and brittle stars die when the shallow waters heat to about 99° F.[2] The arctic jellyfish Cyanea, on the other hand, is so hardy that it continues to pulsate when half its bell is imprisoned in ice, and may revive even after being solidly frozen for hours.[3] The horse-shoe crab is an example of an animal that is very tolerant of temperature change.[4] It has a wide range as a species, and its northern forms can survive being frozen into ice in New England, while its southern representatives thrive in tropical waters of Florida and southward to Yucatan.[5]

Rachel Carson, *The Edge of the Sea*

The first sentence states the general point—tropical animals are more sensitive to temperature change than northern animals. All the examples that follow list details: sentence 2 gives examples of tropical animals that die in overheated water, sentence 3 gives an example of a hardy northern animal, and sentences 4 and 5 modify slightly the general statement by mentioning a particular species that can survive in both cold and warm waters.

The following paragraph shows a general-to-particular sequence used for a slightly different purpose.

General-to-Particular Sequence

Natural history, to a large extent, is a tale of different adaptations to avoid predation.[1] Some individuals hide, others taste bad, others grow spines or thick shells, still others evolve to look consipicuously like a noxious relative; the list is nearly endless, a stunning tribute to nature's variety.[2] Bamboo seeds and cicadas follow an uncommon strategy: they are eminently and conspicuously available but so rarely and in such great numbers that predators cannot possibly consume the entire bounty.[3] Among evolutionary biologists, this defense goes by the name of "predator satiation."[4]

Stephen Jay Gould, *Ever Since Darwin*

In the first sentence here, the author also states the general point, namely adaptation to avoid predation. In sentence 2, Gould provides examples of common adaptations. In sentence 3, he narrows his focus to uncommon adaptation, particularly that of bamboos and cicadas. In sentence 4, he gives the name of this particular adaptation.

rh
49b

2. **Particular-to-General Sequence.** A particular-to-general sequence begins with a series of details and ends with a general statement (usually the topic sentence). This general statement is normally a conclusion reached by considering all the details. The particular-to-general sequence is less common than the general-to-particular sequence, in part because it places a greater burden on readers, who are not told the rationale for all the facts until they reach the end of the paragraph.

Particular-to-General Sequence

As I have noted, the revenues [from communications satellites] now exceed $140 million per year.[1] The total revenues received for all traffic routed by satellite, however, a figure no one tallies, is a much larger one, undoubtedly now exceeding \$1 billion per year.[2] Intelsat pays its member countries a 14 percent return on their investment.[3] This, plus the profits on earth-station operations, enables overseas telecommunications agencies in most countries to operate well in the black.[4] The global system seems profitable on all counts.[5]

> Burton I. Edelson, "Global Satellite Communications,"
> *Scientific American*

In the paragraph above, sentences 1 through 4 present details about revenues. Sentence 5 concludes that the global satellite system is profitable.

Particular-to-General Sequence

Birds breed almost everywhere.[1] Mammals of many species, ranging from squat, rotund lemmings to massive muskox occupy the lands.[2] The seas are home to whales, seals, obese walrus and sinuous white bears.[3] The seas are also rich in fishes as are the numberless inland lakes.[4] For those with eyes to see, the North is vitally and vividly alive.[5] Long, long ago, men of other races out of another time learned to call the northern regions "home."[6]

> Farley Mowat, *Canada North*

The author uses a paticular-to-general sequence here to refute the idea that the North is a lifeless wasteland. In sentences 1, 2, 3, and 4 he gives examples to show that the air, land, and waters are full of life. In sentence 5, the topic sentence, he states the general point directly. He ends, in sentence 6, by pointing out that human beings were long ago able to make their homes in this vital land.

3. **Climactic Sequence.** In a climactic sequence, the most intense or highest point of interest is saved for the final sentence, which may be, but is not necessarily, the topic sentence. For example, in the following paragraph, the first sentence is the topic sentence and the remaining sentences provide detail. The paragraph has a climactic sequence, however, because the final sentence both states the result of the narrative and provides a shock for the reader.

rh
49b

Climactic Sequence

The Horse, "Cobham's heroes" according to Enoch Bradshaw, did most of the murdering. They went hurrahing after every human being between Drummossie Moor and Inverness. Close by Barnhill, outside the town, some of them came up with "a very honest old gentlemen [*sic*] of the name of MacLeod" who had nothing to do with wars in general and the Rebels in particular. He had come to see the battle. He ran before the horsemen until he could run no further, and then he turned, going down on his knees with a cry for mercy. The dragoons swore at him and pistolled him through the head.

> John Prebble, *Culloden*

The next paragraph, which uses process (how Florida got its name) as its type of development, also has a climactic sequence of development. The author tells us that a land was to be named and describes in detail the process of making the decision. After a great deal of suspense has been built up, he finally tells us that the land was named Florida.

Climactic Sequence

Since he had not yet landed, he could not know what the Indians called that country, and in his impatience he wanted a name at once. Doubtless then he thought of many names, as a man does at such times. He might have called it for some place in Spain, perhaps New León after his own province; or he might have thought of honoring the King, or some saint. So, it would seem, as he hesitated in his own mind, or talked with his captains, he saw that one particular name was twice suitable. For, he remembered, the season was still that of Our Lord's Resurrection, only six days after the Easter of Flowers. At the same time, he thought that the green land toward which he now looked was at this season a flowered land. That there might be no doubt in the future, Herrera later wrote in plain words that Juan Ponce de León gave the name "for these two reasons." Thus they named it Florida.

George R. Stewart, *Names on the Land*

4. **Chronological Sequence.** A chronological sequence is one in which earlier things precede later things; items are listed in the order in which they occur in time. The most obvious use of a chronological sequence is in telling a story, as in the following paragraph, where the events of several years are narrated.

Chronological Sequence

Like the Eskimos the early Scandinavians were interested in the North for its own sake.[1] But at the beginning of the sixteenth century other Europeans began to look northward for a different reason.[2] Cut off by Spain and Portugal from voyaging to the Indies around Cape Horn and Cape of Good Hope, they dreamed of finding a usable northwest sea passage around the top of America.[3] As early as 1508 Sebastian Cabot sailed to the northwest on behalf of England searching for a strait leading to Asia.[4] He claimed to have got as high as 67 degrees north latitude on the Baffin Island coast and he reported the existence of a westward-trending strait (Hudson Strait), but nobody did much about it until 1576.[5] Then the buccaneering Martin Frobisher, who was to become one of the Armada men, took up the search and explored part of Frobisher Bay.[6] Frobisher initiated a gold rush to the northwest.[7] In three voyages between 1585 and 1587 John Davis examined most of the coast of the Davis Strait.[8] After 1600 a determined push to find a northwest passage via Hudson Strait was begun by George Weymouth.[9] He was followed in

rh
49b

1610 by Henry Hudson and later by a score of others who sailed their crank little vessels into Hudson Bay.[10] Not until two and a half centuries later did all hope of finding a usable passage to the west die out.[11]

Farley Mowat, Canada North

Notice that Mowat carefully keeps to a chronological sequence as he moves from the general, "the beginning of the sixteenth century," to the particular dates—1508, 1576, and 1587 in sentences 4, 5, and 8. He closes with a broad reference to "two and a half centuries later" in sentence 11. Notice, too, that Mowat amplifies the chronological sequence as he proceeds; in sentence 3 he provides historical context, in sentence 5 he gives details of Cabot's voyage, and in sentences 6 and 7 shows Frobisher's part in the exploration.

Chronological sequence is also frequently used for development by process. Woody Allen's humorous description of an imaginary dramatic production could justifiably be classified as either narration or process statement.

Chronological Sequence

A melodic prelude recounts man's relation to the earth and why he always seems to wind up buried in it. The curtain rises on a vast primitive wasteland, not unlike certain parts of New Jersey. Men and women sit in separate groups and then begin to dance, but they have no idea why and soon sit down again. Presently a young male in the prime of life enters and dances a hymn to fire. Suddenly it is discovered he is *on* fire, and after being put out he slinks off. Now the stage becomes dark, and Man challenges Nature—a stirring encounter during which Nature is bitten on the hip, with the result that for the next six months the temperature never rises above thirteen degrees.

Woody Allen, Without Feathers

5. **Spatial Sequence.** A spatial sequence is used in descriptions of various types. It starts the reader at a particular point and then moves logically in some direction.

rh 49b

Spatial Sequence

He followed her up the stairs, to find she had entered a room that faced north, over the large gardens below. It was an artist's studio. On a table near the door lay a litter of drawings; on an easel a barely begun oil, the mere groundlines, a hint of a young woman looking sadly down, foliage sketched faint behind her head; other turned canvases by the wall; by another wall, a row of hooks, from which hung a multi-colored array of female dresses, scarves, shawls; a large pottery jar; tables of impedimenta—tubes, brushes, color-pots. A *bas-relief,* small sculptures, an urn with bulrushes. There seemed hardly a square foot without its object.

John Fowles, The French Lieutenant's Woman

This sequence of details allows the reader to follow the character up the stairs and into the room and then see the room through his eyes.

Spatial Sequence

We went on, up a marvelously eroded road, like a deep trench in the red clay; on both sides of the road were deep canyons of erosion, in the clefts of which tall century plants bloomed like huge asparagus.[1] The banks of these canyons are full of burrows, and these are inhabited by small parrots; at our approach the parrots tumbled out and went squalling away down the canyon.[2] From the top of the road, one could look back on Orizona, nestled in the broad fronds of its banana trees, under its yellow spires.[3] Around it and beyond lay the green, rolling open range of Goiás.[4]

Peter Matthiessen, The Cloud Forest

Here Matthiessen uses a familiar and logical spatial sequence: The rider in the car first notices the road itself, then the sides of the road (sentence 1). Sentence 2 extends the vision to the banks beyond the sides of the road. In sentence 3, the rider looks back over the town he has just left, and in sentence 4, his gaze extends to the entire area behind him.

Exercises: Sequences of Development

Part A: Read the following paragraphs carefully. Then identify which sequence of development is used in each and explain why the sequence of development is appropriate for that paragraph.

**rh
49b**

A. General-to-particular sequence
B. Particular-to-general sequence
C. Climactic sequence
D. Chronological sequence
E. Spatial sequence

1. What I saw was a small man so short in the thighs that when he stood up he seemed smaller than when he was sitting down. He had a plum pudding of a body and a square head stuck on it with no intervening neck. His brown hair was parted exactly in the middle, and the two cowlicks touched his eyebrows. He had very light blue eyes small enough to show the whites above the irises, which gave him the earnestness of a gas jet when he talked, an air of resigned incredulity when he listened, and a merry acceptance of the human race and all its foibles when he grinned. He was dressed like the owner of a country hardware store. (On ceremonial occasions, I saw later, he dressed

like a plumber got up for church.) For all his seeming squatness, his movements were precise, and his hands in particular were small and sinewy.

Alistair Cooke, Six Men

2. Along with our overriding anxieties about the state of the world and our own country we are resentfully aware of shoddiness in cars, foods, services, in almost everything except the language we use. While an aroused public applauds the exposure of civic corruption and environmental pollution, neither the public at large nor officialdom has any concern with the corruption and pollution of language except to contribute to it. And this kind of corruption is quite as disastrous as any other, if not more so, partly because common violation of traditional usage is an ugly debasement of our great heritage, partly because sloppy English is a symptom and agent of sloppy thinking and feeling and of sloppy communication and confusion. To the famous question, "How do I know what I think till I hear what I say?" the answer might be "Do you and I know then?"

Douglas Bush, "Polluting Our Language," The American Scholar

3. A good watering schedule is to water plants once a week in early spring, twice a week in full spring, and three times a week in summer, which is when plants are in active growth. In fall, start tapering off water to twice a week, then once a week, to only occasional watering in winter—besides a rest from high temperatures, as we said, plants need a rest from watering. If you do water too much in the winter, your plants will bear abnormal growth, be susceptible to rot, and not bloom in summer. (Exceptions are Christmas and Easter cacti and hybrids, and Epiphyllums, which have leaflike stems and need winter watering.) Plants will give you hints as to when to resume your watering schedule: new growth and a perkier appearance. So adjust your watering schedule to the seasons; your plants will excel.

Jack Kramer, Cacti and Other Succulents

4. Everyone in Quebec recognized the artist, a slight little man who always wore a velvet suit and a round beaver hat. His eyes were bright and sharp, his wit was keen, and he told a story well. His friends were jolly, colourful roisterers, men about town, whose pranks reached every ear. Companions marvelled at his incredibly keen sight in the woods, for he could shoot game at a much greater distance than others. During evening celebrations at the neighbouring inn when the long and vigorous dancing had exhausted the musicians, the artist himself would jump on the platform and take over, playing on the violin, flute, guitar, or piano for his fun-loving set. Then in the morning, when the sun lit the eastern horizon, he would be among the last of the revellers to leave for home with throbbing temples and slightly tipsy gait. Such was Cornelius Kreighoff, patronized by Lord Elgin and many British officers, and by gentlemen in the English-speaking communities of Montreal and Quebec who were his friends, during the 1850s and 1860s.

J. Russell Harper, Painting in Canada

rh
49b

5. The next day we, the defendants, saw each other for the last time
   before the announcement of the individual sentences. We met in the
   basement of the Palace of Justice. One after the other we entered a
   small elevator and did not return. In the courtroom above the sentence was announced. Finally it was my turn. Accompanied by an
   American soldier, I rode up in the elevator. A door opened, and I stood
   alone on a small platform in the courtroom, facing the judges. Ear-
   phones were handed to me. In my ears the words reverberated: "Albert Speer, to twenty years imprisonment."

                                   Albert Speer, *Inside the Third Reich*

Part B: Choose two of the following subjects, and develop each into one
good paragraph. Use the specified sequence and type of paragraph development.

1. Movies as registers of society's needs (classification type, general-
   to-particular sequence)
2. Integrity (definition type, particular-to-general sequence)
3. The struggle between technology and humanism (comparison and
   contrast type, general-to-particular sequence)
4. A memorable childhood triumph (details type, climactic sequence)
5. The first day of your first job (details type, chronological sequence)

49c ▪ Coherence *(coh)*

Coherence is connection and consistency. A coherent paragraph is one in
which all the sentences are related logically and grammatically to make
a whole that allows the reader to follow the writer's train of thought step
by step. A paragraph may be unified (all the sentences related to one
topic) and complete (developed enough to cover the topic), but it will still
fail as a paragraph if it lacks coherence.

Incoherent Paragraph

In mountain-climbing, one must concentrate on each move he is to
make during the ascent.[1] A person must know his own limits and
learn that his moves will affect the entire group of climbers.[2] Therefore, when a climber endangers himself, he endangers his comrades
as well.[3] Many times during the climb you will find yourself being
supported by the tips of your fingers and toes, and you are aware that
one thin rope may at any time be called upon to save you from
death.[4] All the equipment from the smallest piton to the longest
stretch of rope must be meticulously inspected and packed, because
in this sport, mistakes may prove fatal.[5]

                                                            Student paper

rh
49c

Although this paragraph lacks an obvious topic sentence, it does not
totally lack unity because the reader can see that the writer's main point
is the great caution required in mountain-climbing. But the paragraph

does lack coherence. Sentences 1 and 2 stick together well enough, but the word *therefore* that begins sentence 3 leads the reader to expect a following statement of result. Instead, an amplification of sentence 2 follows; that is, endangering one's comrades is an *example* of how one person's moves affect the entire group. Instead of continuing the discussion of the entire group, sentence 4 shifts to the personal danger. Sentence 5 then switches abruptly from the personal danger to the importance of checking one's equipment. The change in voice from third person to second person in sentence 4 is jarring, as is that from future to present tense. Finally, sentence 5 is chronologically incoherent because one expects preparations for climbing to precede the climb.

Coherent Paragraph

The personal element is tremendously important in climbing.[1] It is one of the freest of sports in that it is entirely up to you and your colleagues on the rope to make your own decisions in the light of your judgment of the situation at the time.[2] To take responsibility in this way when the rewards and the penalties are both high is one of the most satisfying of the attractions of climbing.[3] At the same time the fact that things can so easily go badly wrong means that you must prepare yourself thoroughly in experience, in techniques, and physically, and that you must exercise a good deal of judgement and self-discipline when you are on the mountain, so that you always keep within your safety margin.[4]

Alan Blackshaw, *Mountaineering*

This paragraph achieves coherence by several means. The author announces his topic in the first sentence. Sentence 2 expands on sentence 1, explaining that the personal element of sentence 1 means that the climber must make his or her own decision and use his or her own judgment. Sentence 3 stresses the satisfaction of being responsible for one's own decisions. Sentence 4 then expands on the penalties mentioned in sentence 3 and states how one avoids them. Transitional devices that help relate one sentence to another include the pronoun *It* beginning sentence 2, which ties sentence 2 to sentence 1 by referring to the word *climbing* in sentence 1. In sentence 3, *in this way* refers to the decision-making discussed in sentence 2. The words *At the same time* link sentences 3 and 4 and show that the ideas expressed in sentence 4 restrict or contrast with the ideas of sentence 3.

rh
49c

Transition The most important components of coherence are logical order or sequence, adequate development, and appropriate transitions.

We have already discussed adequate development, but we might note here a special problem in paragraph development that relates to coherence. When you write about something you know very well, you make associations that may not always be clear to your readers. If they do not follow your jumps in logic, they will find your writing incoherent.

The more specialized the topic, the more likely this problem is to arise. If you know that your audience shares your knowledge and experience, you can omit many explanations and details. In fact, unnecessary explanations will annoy or even offend your audience. For example, you would insult almost any Canadian audience if you wrote:

> The university always had a public ceremony on Remembrance Day. In Canada, November 11 has been set aside to honor those men who died in the world wars.

On the other hand, many Canadians would be bewildered by the following apparent gap in logic:

> The day before had been Shrove Tuesday. Consequently, I couldn't bear the thought of eating pancakes for breakfast.

A Canadian audience might need to be told, at the very least, that Shrove Tuesday is popularly known as Pancake Tuesday in England and that it is an old custom to eat pancakes on this day in order to use up all the fat in the house before the beginning of Lent.

Appropriate transitions, the third component of coherence, are necessary between paragraphs, between sentences, and even within sentences. The best transitional device is a logical presentation; there is no substitute for getting ideas into their proper order in the first place, avoiding interruptions and irrelevant details. In addition to logical presentation, a number of specific devices aid transition. These include pronouns and pronominal adjectives, synonyms for or the repetition of important words and phrases, parallel sentence structure, consistent point of view, and transitional words, especially conjunctions and adverbs.

The following selection, containing two consecutive paragraphs and a third paragraph taken from a later section of the same essay, illustrates all of these transitional devices.

Transition Within and Among Paragraphs

rh 49c

Cell membranes are not, it turns out, just featureless, efficient, smooth sheets—a kind of smart cellophane.[1] They are studded with surface features that render the membrane as recognizable as a United States Marine in full-dress uniform.[2] Recognition, however, depends not on any visual process but rather on contact.[3] Another cell must bump up against the brass buttons, so to speak, to know that they are there.[4] And one kind of cell is usually capable of identifying only a limited number of other types.[5]

Nonetheless, the process of identifying one another by coming into contact is ubiquitous among cells and all-important to countless processes required to coordinate them into communities—as when they form large organisms.[6] Such recognition-by-contact serves a variety of purposes.[7] In some cases, one cell uses another to find its way to the proper location; as it brushes by, it reads a message that says, "Keep going."[8] Or two cells, as they touch each other, may be triggered to settle down and begin to specialize: "You be skin, I'll be muscle."[9]

....

What *is* this remarkable object on which life so critically depends?[10] Think for a moment what has to be achieved in designing a cell membrane.[11] It must accommodate the most extraordinary changes in size and shape of cells—and therefore must be both flexible and easily augmented or diminished as the occasion arises.[12] It must be reasonably tough (though not perfectly so; many cells utilize some kind of supplementary structural material to protect themselves from hard knocks).[13] It must be capable of performing an array of chemical tricks, and in higher organisms this repertoire changes during development.[14] It must carry distinctive features on its outer surface—and have a way to get them from the inside, where presumably they are made, to their final location on the exterior.[15] And it must always separate outside water from inside; passage of water and substances dissolved in water must be forever under strict control.[16]

William Bennett, "Brass Buttons, Fingertips, and the Fluid Mosaic,"
Harvard Magazine

1. Pronouns and pronominal adjectives. In sentence 2, Bennett uses the pronoun *they* to refer to the *cell membranes* in sentence 1. In sentence 6, *they* and *them* refer to *cells*, and in sentence 8, *its* and *it* refer to *cell*. In sentence 7, *Such* ties sentence 7 to sentence 6. In sentences 12 through 16, *it* refers to *cell membrane*.

2. Synonyms and repetition. Bennett repeats the key word *cell* several times throughout the paragraphs. In sentence 10, *this remarkable object* is used as a synonym for *cell membrane*.

3. Parallel sentence structure. Parallel structure is illustrated by the last five sentences of the third paragraph, all of which begin with *It must*.

4. Consistent point of view. Bennett uses the present tense and the third person consistently throughout the three paragraphs.

5. Transitional words. Specific transitional words include *however* in sentence 3, where it indicates that the analogy just made is not complete. In sentence 5, *And* indicates that Bennett is continuing the contrast. *Nonetheless* at the beginning of the second paragraph is also contrastive; in addition, it ties the second paragraph to the first paragraph.

rh
49c

Of the various ways of achieving clear transitions and hence coherence, transitional conjunctions and adverbs are both among the most important and among the most troublesome for insecure writers. Consider the following examples.

She owns three cats and a gerbil, although her apartment is already crowded.

She owns three cats and a gerbil. Consequently, her apartment is crowded.

She owns three cats and a gerbil. <u>In other words</u>, her apartment is crowded.

In the first example, the relationship between the two clauses is one of *concession;* that is, in light of the condition stated in the second clause, the fact stated in the first clause is surprising. In other words, one wouldn't expect her to own so many pets because her apartment is already crowded. In the second example, the relationship between the two sentences is one of *result;* that is, the fact stated in the second sentence is the result of the fact stated in the first sentence: Her crowded conditions result from her having so many pets. In the third example, the second sentence is a *summary* of the first. In effect, it implies *three cats and a gerbil = crowded apartment.*

These examples show how important it is that the transitional words you choose be appropriate for the kind of relationship you want to indicate. Be sure that you yourself know exactly what the relationship is before you pick a transitional word. Possible types of relationships and some of the transitional words that can be used to express them are listed below.

TIME	afterward, before, meanwhile, later, until, soon, during
PLACE	here, there, elsewhere, beyond, opposite, behind, in the background
RESULT	consequently, hence, therefore, accordingly, as a result, thus
COMPARISON	likewise, similarly, also, too, in like manner
CONTRAST	however, yet, nevertheless, on the other hand, but
EXAMPLE *or* ILLUSTRATION	for example, for instance, that is, such as, specifically, as an illustration
ADDITION	furthermore, and, next, besides, first, second, in addition, also, moreover
CONCLUSION	in conclusion, to conclude, finally
SUMMARY	to sum up, in other words, in brief, in short
CONCESSION	although, of course, admittedly, true, granted that
EMPHASIS	in particular, most important, indeed, chiefly, note that

Important as transitional conjunctions and adverbs are, they should not be used at the beginning of every sentence, or the result will be as painfully obvious as electrical wiring on the outside of walls. If you find that your paragraphs are cluttered with *therefores, howevers,* and *furthermores,* check to see whether your logic is clear without some of them. If it is, simply omit the transitional words, or bury a few of them within their sentences instead of having all of them at the beginnings of sentences. For instance, instead of writing "However, many people do object to lengthy paragraphs," try "Many people, however, object to lengthy paragraphs."

When writing transitions, try to avoid trite transitional clichés like *last but not least*, *strange as it may seem*, and *needless to say*. If you want to tell the reader that the next point is the final one, write *finally* instead of *last but not least*. Let the reader decide whether or not something is *strange as it may seem*. If something is really *needless to say*, don't say it.

Exercises: Coherence

Part A: Analyse the following coherent paragraph. List the logical, grammatical, and transitional devices that make it coherent.

> Analogy would lead me one step further, namely, to the belief that all animals and plants have descended from some one prototype. But analogy may be a deceitful guide. Nevertheless all living things have much in common, in their chemical composition, their germinal vesicles, their cellular structure, and their laws of growth and reproduction. We see this even in so trifling a circumstance as that the same poison often similarly affects plants and animals; or that the poison secreted by the gall-fly produces monstrous growths on the wild rose or oak-tree. Therefore I should infer from analogy that probably all the organic beings which have ever lived on this earth have descended from some one primordial form, into which life was first breathed by the Creator.
>
> Charles Darwin, *On the Origin of Species*

Part B: Rewrite the following paragraph to give it adequate subordination, co-ordination, and transition. Use grammatical and transitional devices to develop the simple sentences into a well-unified paragraph.

> All commercial airlines had grounded their planes. The winds were very strong. We had to be in Banff by 17:00. We had no car. There were no trains or buses. Someone told us about a pilot. He had a four-seater plane. He used to be a stunt pilot. He would fly in any weather. We found him. He agreed to fly us to Banff. We took off in the storm. He flew into the valleys between mountains. The wind tossed the plane violently. Sometimes the plane went six or seven metres up in the air. Then it plummeted down again. The plane rocked from side to side. We were terrified. We were very sick. We did not enjoy the scenery. Our eyes were closed. We reached Banff on time.

**rh
49d**

49d · Special-Purpose Paragraphs

On certain occasions, special-purpose paragraphs may be necessary. These include beginning and concluding paragraphs, transitional paragraphs, and dialogue. (Beginning and concluding paragraphs are discussed in 50h).

Transitional Paragraphs   Important as transition is for coherence, it is generally best to avoid devoting an entire paragraph to transition, especially in short papers. A very long paper, such as a research paper, may sometimes need a transitional paragraph between sections. If a transitional paragraph is used, it is normally brief—only a sentence or two. In the following example, Bergen Evans completes a series of sixteen paragraphs on popular misconceptions about animal behavior by describing the notion that animals can be buried for years and later revive when exposed to air. He then uses a short one-sentence paragraph as a transition between his discussion of land animals and the six following paragraphs on erroneous ideas about sea animals.

Transitional Paragraph

. . . In the classic version—one often sees it in the paper, date-lined from some place inaccessible to inquiry—the creature is at first seemingly lifeless. But he revives in the open air, and, to the astonishment of the excavator, hops away apparently none the worse for his strange experience. Unfortunately for the veracity of the anecdotes, a toad must have air to survive; and, even with all the air, food, and water that he can desire, he will not survive many years.

Of creatures that live in the sea, the whale, the shark, and the octopus appear most frequently in vulgar lore.

Although all that comes out of a whale's blowhole is his breath, he is commonly represented as spouting a jet of water into the air. If the artist is unusually naïve or unusually playful he sometimes puts a few small fish on top of the column. . . .

Bergen Evans, *The Natural History of Nonsense*

Although Evans uses a separate paragraph for the transition from land animals to sea animals, he could have made that transitional sentence the first sentence of the following paragraph.

Dialogue   In the paragraphing of dialogue (conversation), each direct quotation, along with the rest of the sentence of which it is part, requires a separate paragraph. Every time there is a change of speaker, there is a new paragraph indentation. If the conversation involves only two speakers, or if what is said makes it clear who is speaking, an identifying phrase like "she said" is not necessary for each change. However, an identifying phrase should be included every now and then to help the reader keep track of which character is speaking.

Dialogue

Honoria Waynflete flinched a little at the crudity of the language. She said, "I don't feel at all happy about her death. Not at all happy. The whole thing is profoundly unsatisfactory, in my opinion."[1]

rh
49d

> Luke said patiently, "But you don't think her death was a natu-
> ral one?"[2]
>
> "No."[3]
>
> "You don't believe it was an accident?"[4]
>
> "It seems to me most improbable. There are so many—"[5]
>
> Luke cut her short, "You don't think it was suicide?"[6]
>
> "Emphatically not."[7]
>
> "Then," said Luke gently, "you do think it was murder?"[8]
>
> Agatha Christie, *Easy to Kill*

Notice here that, whenever the speaker changes, a new paragraph is
made. Note also that, although paragraphs 3, 4, and 5 do not explicitly
identify the speaker, Christie adds "Luke cut her short" in paragraph 6
and "said Luke gently" in paragraph 8 to help the reader remember who
is speaking.

50 ▨ The Whole Paper

For most writing tasks, the whole paper is the whole point. All the details of grammar, punctuation, diction, and sentence and paragraph
structure are meaningful only as they contribute to this whole. In a composition course, the typical whole paper is nonfiction, relatively short
(less than ten pages), and relatively formal. It is also a source of unnecessary anguish for many students. This is not to say that writing is easy. It
isn't. It is hard work even for experienced writers. Alas, there are no
gimmicks to make good writing easy for everyone—or anyone. But there
are ways to make writing less agonizing and to ensure that the final
result is respectable.

50a ▪ Choosing a Topic

Students sometimes spend more time trying to decide on a topic than
they do on the actual writing. If the topic is assigned, there is, of course,
no problem. You may not care for it, but you have no choice, and you
may as well accept it gracefully. Even if you dislike the topic, do not
change it without permission. It was assigned for a reason. Most of the
writing you will do for the rest of your life will be on assigned topics.
When your boss tells you to do an analysis of the available labor force for
jewellery manufacturing in southwestern Ontario, you cannot say, "But
I just don't feel inspired by that topic." If your editor tells you to cover a
fund-raising lunch for an art gallery, you will not write up the local golf
tournament instead. Or, if you do, you will soon be looking for a new job.

Whatever the topic, your interest in it will increase as you learn
more about it and work with it. And even with assigned topics, you
normally have many options with respect to type of development, details
to be included, and conclusions to be reached.

Finding an Appropriate Topic   If the writing assignment is "open-ended," that is, if you must select your own topic, the problem is more serious. Your mind may be a total blank. But before giving in to despair, think of your resources. If your instructor has asked you to keep a journal, glance through it for ideas. Even brief notes about a strange impression, an overheard conversation, or a puzzling idea or incident can provide the nucleus for an entire theme. Your friends may offer suggestions that haven't occurred to you. And remember that you, like every other human being, have had unique experiences and have unique skills and interests.

1. **Personal Experiences.** Perhaps you grew up in a rural area and know a great deal about edible wild plants such as milkweed, dandelions, wintergreen, and wild blackberries and raspberries. You may not think that your expertise in this area is of much interest, but such information will fascinate many readers. You can write about the types of plants, how they are distinguished from nonedible plants, where they are found, or how they are prepared for eating.

But you need not have spent your childhood in the country—let alone in some exotic spot like Mozambique—to have had unique and interesting experiences. How did the residents of your neighborhood react to a crisis such as a major blizzard or a public-service strike? What are the problems of owning a pet in the city? How is the game of street hockey played? What did it feel like when you bumped into a glass door and swallowed the cap on your front tooth?

2. **Hobbies.** Hobbies are a rich source of topics for papers. Even if you are not an expert, you know more about the subject than most people do. What are the differences between a classical guitar and a bluegrass guitar? Should motorcyclists be required to wear helmets? Why do chess players read for hours about opening moves? What sorts of people enjoy solving crossword puzzles? Perhaps your hobby is an unusual one. I once read an excellent essay written by a popcorn buff. Maybe you spend your leisure hours in front of the television set: television programs and advertisements can provide a virtually unlimited number of topics. For example, you might discuss euphemism in advertisements for over-the-counter drugs, the portrayal of teen-agers in two different situation comedies, or the disadvantages of using former athletes as sports announcers.

3. **Reading.** Another source of topics is the reading that you have done for other courses or on your own. Perhaps you have read about conditioning in a psychology course and have suddenly realized that the kitten you had when you were eleven had conditioned you instead of your conditioning the kitten. You have here the nucleus of an entertaining narrative paper. Or, based on your own past experience, you may disagree with one of the principles set forth in your education textbook. Are you a science fiction fan? Compare the typical villains of Bradbury, Asimov, and Herbert.

If you have recently read a book that you found particularly interesting, you might consider a book review. A book review should provide a summary detailed enough to give the reader a clear idea of what the book is about but not so detailed that you spoil the book for the reader. However, a good review includes more than just a synopsis of the contents. You should discuss the type of book (for example, fiction, history, travel), the intended audience, and your opinion of the value of the book. A few details or a quotation or two will give the reader an idea of the flavor of the book. Be sure to state whether you think the book is good, bad, or mediocre, and give your reasons.

4. **Current Issues.** Current issues provide excellent paper topics: Should the Canadian distribution of American television programs be more restricted than it is now? Should the CBC be prohibited from purchasing U.S. shows? Pick a current issue about which you have thought carefully or with which you have had direct experience. If your only TV viewing is *Hockey Night in Canada*, this is not the topic for you. If you come from an ethnic neighborhood, you may have some ideas about the pros and cons of teaching heritage languages in the public elementary schools. If you live in a town where clothing or shoes are manufactured, you can probably say something about free trade versus protection.

5. **Likes and Dislikes.** Do you have likes or dislikes that run counter to popular tastes? Explain why you hate movies or enjoy going to the dentist. Or describe your own quirks and strange habits. Perhaps your total lack of a sense of direction has led to some embarrassing situations. Tell how you got lost coming back from your local supermarket. Maybe you find the letter *z* fascinating and will read anything that contains words like *guzzle, cozen, ooze, zephyr,* and *marzipan.*

6. **Character Sketches.** When you are gloomily pondering an assignment of "four pages on any topic at all," consider the character sketch or profile. Everyone knows interesting people because all people are interesting. If your family has an eccentric, as most families do, so much the better. But conventional people are interesting, too. Even those who seem to be perfect examples of "types" have many apparent contradictions in their behavior. For example, you may think of an aunt who appears to be the classic liberated woman. She works in the advertising department of a weekly magazine, discusses the stock market with authority, and hates to cook. But then you remember that she irons dish towels, puts down newspapers on freshly mopped floors, and does not know where the gas tank on her car is.

7. **Descriptions.** Instead of describing a person, you might describe a familiar place. What is your neighborhood like? What kind of architecture does it have? What kind of people live there? What do you see in the street? Has the neighborhood changed within your memory? Try to stand back and view it as a stranger seeing it for the first time. What impression does it make?

rh
50a

Or you might describe how to do something. Have you a favorite recipe for lasagna? How do you repair a faulty electrical plug? How do you determine your position at sea using dead reckoning? What is involved in using a wood-turning lathe? A good description of even a common activity such as operating a self-service gasoline pump can be entertaining and informative.

No topic is intrinsically boring—it is only made boring by a bored writer and dull writing. In this sense, writing is like speaking. You have surely known lecturers who managed to spoil the most exciting topics. And you have also known lecturers who delighted you with their presentation of material you had previously thought hopelessly dull. The most "common" or "boring" topics are entertaining if you capture for the reader the uniqueness of your own experience of them.

Topics To Avoid   As a general rule, avoid very broad or highly abstract topics. Even if you know quite a bit about the subject matter, you cannot handle it adequately within three to five pages. The following topics are far too broad for a short paper.

> The Lumbering Industry in North America
> The Development of Opera
> The Concept of Evil
> Changing Attitudes toward Child Rearing
> The Pros and Cons of City Planning
> The War of 1812
> The Novel and the Middle Class

You could use any of these topics for a short paper, but you would have to narrow it to one particular, small facet of the larger subject. Rather than trying to encompass all of the lumbering industry in five pages, you might write on the use of hemlock in the building trade (assuming you know something about hemlock). Instead of a paper on the concept of evil, you might describe your earliest memory of doing something wrong and your subsequent guilt feelings.

If you are given a choice, avoid such overused topics as "My High School Graduation," "Why I Came to College," "First Impressions of University Life," "The Values of a Liberal Arts Education," "A Trip to a Ball Game," and "Why I want To Be a Veterinarian." Either your experiences are likely to have been nearly identical to everyone else's ("My High School Graduation") or you really do not know why you came to college (nor should you feel guilty that you do not). That oldest of chestnuts, "My Summer Vacation," is not as bad a topic as it sounds, particularly if you did something unusual. Just don't entitle the paper "My Summer Vacation." Call it "Eight Weeks on a Coca-Cola Truck" or "House-Painting as an Art Form" or "Memoirs of a Tomato-Picker."

Finally, avoid topics about which you know little or nothing. If you cannot tell a prayer rug from a doormat, do not tackle "Buying an Oriental Rug." Do not write about the trials of motorcycle racing if you have never been on a bike. Steer clear of the problems of old age unless you have been surrounded by old people or have worked in a nursing home. If you are hopelessly ignorant about a subject but still fascinated by it, save the topic for a research paper, when you will have a chance to investigate the subject thoroughly.

Exercises: Choosing a Topic

Which of the following topics would *not* be suitable choices—as they are stated—for a three-to-five page essay? For each one that you consider too general or abstract, write a more specific topic that would be appropriate for a short essay.

1. Making Hand Puppets from Papier-Mâché
2. The Decline of the Movie Industry
3. The Benefits of Space Exploration
4. Ronald Reagan: His Rise to Political Power
5. Cooking with Wine
6. How To Build a Simple Wooden Plant Stand
7. The Riel Rebellion
8. The Development of Cubism
9. Wiring a House
10. Albert Einstein's Antiwar Stand

50b · Narrowing the Topic

Whether you have been assigned a topic or have selected the subject area yourself, you will always have to narrow it considerably before it is appropriate for a paper of only a few pages. This is true whether you know a good deal about the topic or very little. Indeed, the necessity of narrowing the topic is often greater in the latter case because, when you do not know very much about a subject area, you may be tempted to write vague generalizations about it.

Considering your audience helps in narrowing a topic. If you plan to write a short paper on hi-fi systems for a general adult audience, you should avoid a highly technical discussion that requires a great deal of background information. In writing about a particular book, consider whether your audience is likely to have read the book or to have a copy to refer to. A short essay on the problems of overpopulation probably needs one focus for an audience of retired civil servants and a very different focus for an audience of young married people.

How do you know when you have sufficiently narrowed your topic? The answer depends on the topic, the length of the final paper, and the level of generalization at which you discuss the topic. However, writing anything meaningful and interesting on a highly general level is very difficult, even for the expert writer, so you should plan to be as specific as possible.

rh
50b

First consider what you can tell your reader in, say, one thousand words (about four typed pages). You will probably need two hundred or so of these words to introduce and define your topic. For example, if you plan to write about purebred cats, you must introduce your subject and then tell the reader exactly what the term *purebred* means. You will have only eight hundred words left in which to say everything else you have in mind about purebred cats. You cannot cover all the different breeds, the problems of breeding, the most popular breeds, the advantages and disadvantages of each breed, and the conventions of cat shows in that space. Clearly, you must subdivide your topic before you can begin writing.

Narrowing a topic is not simply a mechanical process of chipping away at a subject until it fits predetermined limits. The very process of narrowing the topic forces you to focus your own thoughts about the topic and gives you specific ideas about what to say in the final paper.

Narrowing an Unfamiliar Topic   Perhaps you have read Thoreau's "Civil Disobedience" as a class assignment and your instructor has told you to write a paper about taxation. You realize, first, that you do not know very much about taxation and, second, that the topic is so broad that it must be cut down to size before you can say anything about it at all. Begin the narrowing process by jotting down things that come to mind when you think of taxes. Don't worry about the order of the items at this point; just put them down as you think of them. Your list might look like this:

1. Income tax
2. Purpose of taxation
3. Everybody hates taxes
4. Complicated system—nobody can figure it out
5. Many kinds of taxes—sales, property, income, hidden, on special products (cigarettes, gasoline), capital gains, import duties
6. Who decides on taxes?
7. What do taxes buy? Schools, fire and police, highways, defence, social programs
8. Alternatives to taxes—lotteries, legalized gambling, private funds
9. Fairness of taxes: progressive income tax
10. Should people vote on taxes?

rh
50b

When you cannot think of anything else to list, stop and look at what you have written down. As you scan the list, you see that No. 1, "Income tax," is really a subdivision of No. 5, "Many kinds of taxes." So you cross off No. 1. No. 2, "Purpose of taxation," looks like a subdivision of No. 7 "What do taxes buy?" Then you remember hearing that taxes are sometimes used to curb inflation, but you don't really understand that, so you decide to omit No. 2 also. No. 3 looks promising—you certainly have heard many different people complain about taxes. But you cannot think of anything else to say, and you decide you cannot expand "Everyone hates taxes" into a five-page paper. Cross out No. 3.

No. 4 looks discouraging at first because you do not understand the taxation system yourself. On the other hand, you remember several specific instances when you confronted the complexities of taxation. You decide to leave No. 4 on the list. No. 5 looks promising because you have already listed a number of different kinds of taxes. You leave No. 5 on the list, at least temporarily. You see that No. 6, "Who decides on taxes?" is related to No. 10, "Should people vote on taxes?" but you don't know enough about the making of tax laws, so you eliminate both No. 6 and No. 10 from the list.

No. 7, "What do taxes buy?" also has a number of entries after it, so perhaps you have a good start there. You leave No. 7 on the list. No. 8, "Alternatives to taxes," looks interesting, so you leave it too. You cross out No. 9 because you have already decided not to talk about income taxes in particular. Your list is now considerably shorter.

4. Complicated system—nobody can figure it out
5. Many kinds of taxes—sales, property, income, hidden, on special products (cigarettes, gasoline), capital gains, import duties
7. What do taxes buy? Schools, fire and police, highways, defence, social programs
8. Alternatives to taxes—lotteries, legalized gambling, private funds

As you look at your revised list, you decide that you are not especially interested in No. 7, so you eliminate it. You like the idea of writing on No. 8, "Alternatives to taxation," but you realize that you would have to do library research on the subject because you know little about lotteries, legalized gambling, or private funds. The assignment was not a research paper, so you cross out No. 8. You are now down to two items.

4. Complicated system—nobody can figure it out
5. Many kinds of taxes—sales, property, income, hidden, on special products (cigarettes, gasoline), capital gains, import duties

You see that you could add even more kinds of taxes to No. 5— excess profits taxes, one-time taxes, taxes marked for special purposes. Then you realize that explaining just one of these kinds of taxes would require an entire paper and involve research besides. You look at No. 4 again. You remember all the tax forms you had to fill out when you had a part-time job. You recall having had to pay customs duty on items you ordered by mail from the United.States. You know your parents hire an accountant to fill out their income-tax forms. You remember that your hometown newspaper published a series of articles on the complexities of the property assessment. You have seen the tax charts that retail clerks have to consult every time they ring up a sale. You make a brief note of each of these incidents.

rh
50b

Finally, you decide to write about the complexities of the tax system, arguing that it is too complicated for the average person. You can use the very fact that you do not understand it as part of the argument that the system is overly complex. The supporting evidence for your argument will be the confusing experiences you have had or have heard about. You can even salvage part of No. 5 from your earlier list ("Many kinds of taxes") by simply listing the various taxes and noting that the many different kinds of taxes add to the complexity of the system.

Narrowing a Familiar Topic   When you narrow a topic that you know little about, your first task is to find some aspect of it that you have enough information about to make an intelligent statement. When you know a good deal about the topic, your problem is that you have so much information that you cannot possibly include all of it in a brief paper. There are many broad subject areas about which you know a great deal (more than you realize).

the family	law	recreation	transportation
food	health	literature	history
education	television		

Suppose you wanted to write a paper on recreation. Clearly "Recreation" will not do as the title for a five-page paper. You can quickly subdivide the topic into kinds of recreation, purposes of recreation, attitudes toward recreation, and the history of recreation. You want to write about specific kinds of recreation. As you think about this, you see that there are a number of ways of subdividing kinds of recreation.

1. Team sports versus individual sports
2. Participatory sports versus spectator sports
3. Popular recreation versus unusual recreation
4. Strenuous recreation versus nonstrenuous recreation
5. Physical recreation versus mental recreation

You are not especially interested in the distinction between team sports and individual sports, and too much has already been written about participatory versus spectator sports. You decide that it would be too hard to draw the line between strenuous and nonstrenuous recreation. You do not want to talk about mental recreation, so you eliminate that. This leaves you with popular recreation versus unusual recreation. Unusual types of recreation sounds interesting, but you enjoy popular sports yourself. Further, you had originally had a hazy notion that you might write something about baseball. But, again, so much has been written about baseball that you are not sure you have anything new to say about it. Then you remember that your seventy-two-year-old grandmother is a dedicated Blue Jays fans who watches every televised game, knows the names and statistics of every player, and makes several excursions a season to Toronto's Exhibition Stadium to see the Jays play. At last you have a topic narrow enough to be handled in a short paper: "My Grandmother and the Blue Jays."

Any broad subject area can be similarly narrowed by the process of subdividing.

BROAD TOPIC	NARROWED TOPIC
The family	The perfect baby-sitter
Food	Baking bread in a reflector oven
Education	My two days as a teacher's aide
Law	Right turns on red should be outlawed

rh
50b

BROAD TOPIC	NARROWED TOPIC
Health	Hay fever isn't funny
Television	Local versus national news reporting
Literature	I love to read trash
Transportation	Taking Eurail across the Alps to Italy
History	Why the Mennonites settled in Alberta

Exercises: Narrowing the Topic

Assume that your instructor has assigned essays on the general subjects of hockey and birds. You have made the following lists of all your ideas on each subject. Now go over each list, striking off what you do not really know much about or what does not really interest you. Combine ideas that overlap. Most of what you have left will still be too broad and general. From these leftover general ideas, develop one good, specific theme topic for each subject.

A. Hockey
    1. Specatators at hockey games
    2. Differences between professional and amateur hockey
    3. The art of goal tending
    4. The history of hockey
    5. Officials at hockey games
    6. Basic hockey plays
    7. Play-off games
    8. Famous hockey players
    9. How hockey masks are made
    10. The development of hockey uniforms and equipment
    11. Recruitment of amateur players (even in boys' leagues)
    12. Recruitment of professional players
    13. How a hockey team trains
    14. Becoming a hockey coach
    15. Consistently good hockey teams
    16. Hockey outside Canada
    17. Violence in hockey
    18. Money and professional hockey
    19. My first hockey game
    20. The career of Wayne Gretzky

B. Birds
    1. Birds common in my region
    2. Birds that make good pets
    3. Exotic birds
    4. Birds of prey
    5. How to learn bird-watching
    6. Kinds of birds' nests

rh
50b

 7. Folklore about birds
 8. Extinct birds
 9. Bird songs and calls
10. Birds in literature
11. Birds and oil spills
12. Agencies that protect birds
13. The anatomy of birds
14. Birds in children's stories and nursery rhymes
15. Easy-to-build bird-feeders
16. Environmental problems and birds
17. Migration of birds
18. Birds in art
19. Kinds of beaks
20. Cooking fowl

50c ▪ Preparing to Write

Once you have selected a topic, you face the question "But exactly what am I going to say about it?" Actually, you probably have a number of good ideas already, or you would not have picked the topic in the first place. Begin by jotting these ideas down. Do not worry about order at this stage; just write ideas down as they come to you.

If you can wait several days before you have to begin writing, use the time to mull over the topic as you stand in line, wait for a bus, clean your room, or do other tasks that require no great mental effort. If you have the topic in the back of your mind, you will be surprised how often you will encounter something that relates to it and that gives you a new perspective on it. For example, you may be planning to write about the frustrations of city life. On your way to class you see a pigeon on the sidewalk walking rapidly around and around in tight circles. You do not understand why the pigeon is doing this, but it seems symbolic to you of the haste and aimlessness of the lives of many city-dwellers. You can incorporate this observation into your paper; such concrete examples add interest to an essay. Write it down as soon as possible so that you don't forget it—nothing is more annoying than to have forgotten an excellent idea.

Jot down quotations that you might use, anecdotes to make your point more forceful, and specific facts that should be included. Specific facts are very important because lack of detail in a paper makes it boring. If you need to check a fact, make a note to do the checking before you start writing. For example, you may be planning to write a paper on women as athletes and want to mention Gertrude Ederle. You think she was the first person to swim the English Channel. Or was she just the first woman to swim the Channel? Or did she just break a previous record? The correct answers to these questions may determine the turn your final arguments will take.

rh
50c

50d · Finding a Thesis

Perhaps the single most important component of a good paper is a clear thesis. The **thesis** of a paper is its main point, its central idea. It is the reason you are writing the paper (aside from the fact that your instructor told you to). A thesis statement sums up in one sentence the message you want to convey to your readers.

Formulate your thesis *before* you begin the actual writing. A good thesis statement helps you focus your thoughts about your topic before you start to write, and it helps you stick to your thesis as you write. It is much harder to revise an already written paper to provide a clear thesis than it is to begin writing with a thesis in mind.

Suppose you have been assigned a paper on interpersonal relationships, and you have narrowed that broad topic to "the generation gap." What precisely do you want to tell your readers about the generation gap? There are many possible thesis statements for this topic.

1. The generation gap is a fiction invented by sociologists and perpetuated by the media.
2. The generation gap has resulted from the breakup of family life.
3. There will always be a generation gap because parents will always be reluctant to allow children to make their own decisions.

If you had decided on the first thesis statement, you would probably develop your paper by suggesting that the very invention of the term "generation gap" had made people feel that one existed. Then, as the term was made popular by television and magazine articles, people came to believe that the generation gap *must* exist because everyone was talking about it. People might even have begun to feel that something was wrong with their own families if everyone got along well together. No one even tried to resolve any problems between generations because they thought that these problems were only natural.

Thesis statement No. 2 implies a very different development. You might use census data or other statistics to show that one generation has lost contact with the next because older people no longer live with their adult children. The high divorce rate has produced many households in which even young children are separated from at least one of their parents. The accelerated pace of modern life has meant that family members spend little time with one another.

If you chose thesis statement No. 3, you would suggest that the only thing new about the generation gap is the name. You might use historical examples of conflict between generations, and you could focus on the innate desire of parents to protect their children from what the parents feel are foolish decisions and behavior.

A good thesis statement is specific and unified but not self-evident. A **specific** statement not only indicates the main point of the paper exactly; it also avoids vague generalities.

rh
50d

OVERLY GENERAL	IMPROVED
Teaching is a noble profession.	The first-grade teacher is responsible for the most important skill we possess: reading.
Pollution is a serious problem in North America.	Acid rain is destroying fish stocks in the Great Lakes.
You don't have to be rich to be happy.	A vacation in a provincial park can be both delightful and inexpensive.

A **unified** statement includes only one idea or perhaps one main idea and one or two closely related subsidiary ideas. Consider the statement "The differences between moths and butterflies are often very subtle, but coloration, produced in only two ways, is not one of them, even though there are many, often contrary, explanations for color variation." This statement lacks unity because it contains at least three major ideas: (1) differences between moths and butterflies are often very subtle; (2) coloration in moths and butterflies is produced in only two ways; and (3) there are many, often contrary, explanations for color variation. Any one of these is a potential thesis statement, but you could not unify and develop all of them within the limits of a short paper.

NOT UNIFIED	IMPROVED
I like watching sports events on television, and I also like to participate in sports.	My love of spectator sports does not prevent me from participating in sports myself.
Many students do not like to read Chaucer, and they prefer Shakespeare, whose language is easier to understand.	Many students do not like to read Chaucer only because his language is hard to understand.
Even though we do not have much political terrorism in North America, it is an inexcusable way of trying to get one's demands.	Political terrorism is never excusable.

Self-evident statements are those that need not be made at all because everyone agrees with them; there is no point in writing a paper arguing that horses are bigger than rabbits.

SELF-EVIDENT	IMPROVED
Automobile accidents cause many injuries and deaths.	Playground equipment causes many injuries and deaths.

SELF-EVIDENT	IMPROVED
Poor people have less money to spend than rich people.	If doctors can opt out of Medicare, the rich may receive better medical care than the poor.

Although you should strive for a thesis statement that is specific, unified, and not self-evident, you need not try to make the thesis statement as dramatic or as shocking as possible. Do not claim more in your thesis statement than you can justify in the paper itself.

OVERLY DRAMATIC	IMPROVED
Overpermissive parents are the cause of juvenile crime.	Overpermissive parents are one cause of juvenile crime.
Napoleon was an incompetent general whose victories were due to luck alone.	Napoleon's victory at Wagram can be attributed more to his luck than to his military genius.

When you actually start writing the paper, include the statement of your thesis near the beginning. You may be able to use your original thesis statement in your paper, or you may have to reword it to make it fit in with your introductory material.

After you have started writing, you may find that your paper cannot be developed exactly along the lines of your thesis statement. If so, restate or revise your thesis rather than ignoring it or trying to justify an unworkable thesis. Even though you may have to revise your thesis as you go along, you should have some thesis in mind at every stage of your writing.

Exercises: Finding a Thesis

Label each of the following theses with the appropriate letter from the list below. Then, for each, write a specific, focused thesis statement that you could develop into an interesting paper.

rh
50d

A. Overly general   C. Self-evident
B. Not unified   D. Overly dramatic

1. Television breeds crime.
2. The rise in the number of working mothers has caused an increase in the number of day-care facilities, and it has contributed substantially to the phenomenal growth of the fast-food industry.
3. Sex education is necessary for adolescents.
4. Government deregulation of the airlines would lead to lower fares.
5. Dogs are great pets.
6. The electronic media are fostering illiteracy.
7. Baseball is one of the most popular Japanese sports.
8. Chess and crossword puzzles are stimulating.

50e ▪ Planning the Paper

Once you have a narrowed topic and a thesis statement, examine your thesis to see what approach it implies. Do you need to explain something, try to persuade your readers to accept your opinion, describe what something is like, or tell a story? When you have decided this, you must organize your material in the most suitable way. In other words, you must decide on the best rhetorical mode and on the order, or sequence, in which you will present your ideas.

Traditionally, there are four ways to approach a topic, or four **rhetorical types,** as they are called. These are *exposition, argument and persuasion, description,* and *narration.* The four rhetorical types are not completely independent of one another, and most papers contain elements of two or more. For example, you may need to relate a sequence of events (narration) in order to explain something (exposition). At least some exposition is required in argument and persuasion. Description is frequently part of narration. However, any one paper should have one of the four expository types as its primary approach.

Exposition   The purpose of exposition is to explain something. Exposition answers questions such as "What is it?" "What does it do?" "What does it resemble?" "How does it work?" "How did it come about?" "Why is it important?" An expository paper about the perfect baby-sitter, for example, might define "perfect" in the context of baby-sitters. It could explain that perfect baby-sitters are rare, that the very concept of a baby-sitter is a recent phenomenon, that many baby-sitters are teen-agers, and so on.

A clear thesis statement is especially important before writing an expository paper because the way in which you develop your paper depends on what you want to explain and how you want to explain it. Different thesis statements require different types of development. Most of the types of development discussed in 49, "Paragraphs," are also suitable for entire expository papers. You can centre your paper on a comparison and contrast, a cause-and-effect relationship, a process statement, a classification, or an extended definition. In a longer paper you may want to use several of these types within one paper, devoting a block of one or more paragraphs to a particular type of development. By the time you begin writing an expository paper, you should have decided which of these types best suits your narrowed topic and your thesis statement.

rh
50e

1. **Comparison and Contrast.** In comparison and contrast, you show your readers in what ways two things are similar and dissimilar, explaining both things as you do so. For a brief paper about skiing, you might have as your thesis statement "Although both downhill skiing and cross-country are termed skiing sports, there are distinct differences in the equipment used for each." You could develop your paper by comparing and contrasting the skis themselves, the ski boots, the poles, and the clothing usually worn. Your paragraph about ski boots might be the following:

In downhill skiing, the ski is a rigid extension of the leg and foot, and both the toe and the heel are fastened to the ski. This allows great control over the ski but also is potentially very dangerous because if the ski becomes twisted the skier is likely to end up with a broken ankle. To protect the ankle and lower leg, the downhill ski boot is made like a plaster cast: It is high, extremely heavy, and thickly padded inside to keep the ankle cushioned and locked securely in place. In cross-country skiing, on the other hand, only the tip of the toe is attached to the ski, and the heel rides freely up and down on the ski, greatly reducing the probability of broken bones in the case of an accident. A much lighter ski boot is used; in fact, the cross-country ski boot is little more than a leather sneaker. However, this arrangement gives the skier much less control over the ski.

The organization of this paragraph has the basic form of first A, then B; that is, downhill boots are first described and then cross-country boots are described. Other paragraphs comparing skis, poles, etc., would probably have a similar organization. The paper *as a whole* would have a point-by-point organization, with each item of equipment being taken up separately for comparison and contrast.

Another common way of organizing a comparison-and-contrast paper is to describe all the features of A first, followed by all the features of B. With this organization, your paper comparing downhill and cross-country skiing equipment would begin with several paragraphs describing downhill equipment and end with several paragraphs centring on cross-country equipment. The similarities and differences between the two would thus not be revealed until you began the second part, the description of cross-country equipment.

For some topics, still another kind of organization may be suitable. If you wanted to compare and contrast two things that most people believe are very different, you might begin by describing how they are indeed different but end by showing their many similarities. For instance, most people would not think that writing a computer program and writing an English composition have much in common: They are done for different purposes, use a different "language," and have very different conventions. You could begin your paper by explaining all this but continue by showing that they are similar in that both should have a thesis statement that defines their purpose, both have grammar rules to be observed, and both require careful attention to logic and organization.

2. **Cause and Effect.** In a cause-and-effect paper, you show the reader how something came about, what produced it. Sometimes an effect has a single cause; more often, effects have many and complex causes. And sometimes a single cause has several effects. In any case, your task is to show the relationship between the cause(s) and the effect(s).

Suppose you had decided to write about the rise in popularity of cross-country skiing. Your thesis statement is "Overspecialization in downhill skiing has brought about the boom in cross-country skiing." You could develop your paper by discussing the features of downhill skiing that have led many people to look for an alternative: the expense, the inconvenience, the lack of flexibility, the difficulty, and the dangers. In your section explaining how the overspecialization of downhill skiing equipment has caused people to turn to cross-country skiing, you might write the following:

> The very technology that has made downhill skiing an exciting Olympic sport has also caused some skiers either to abandon it or at least to look for an alternative. New surfaces eliminate the need for waxing but simultaneously limit the skier's mobility. Without wax, the skier cannot climb hills and must rely on tows to get to the top of a slope. Because building tows and preparing mountains for skiing is very expensive, the number of slopes is necessarily limited. Thus skiers cannot escape crowds or choose their own areas in which to ski.

This particular paragraph is almost pure cause; the effect will be stated elsewhere. Your other paragraphs describing the expense, lack of flexibility, difficulty, and dangers of downhill skiing could be developed in a similar way. You might choose to organize the paper *as a whole* on the principle of effect-to-cause, stating the effect (rise of cross-country skiing) in the opening paragraph and then listing the causes one by one. Or you could use a more dramatic cause-to-effect organization, first enumerating all the causes (the problems of downhill skiing) and saving the effect for the end of the paper.

3. **Process.** In a process paper, you tell the readers how something is done, so that they can either do it themselves or, at least, understand how the process works. The thesis statement for a paper on cross-country skiing might be simply "How to climb a hill on cross-country skis." Because the process is relatively easy to explain, you would describe several different hill-climbing techniques within one paper. Different sections of the paper would describe the different methods, such as running, sidestepping, and herringboning. One section might be the following:

> If the hill is extremely steep, the only way to climb it is by side-stepping. Align yourself at a right angle to the hill, skis parallel to each other and approximately 15 cm apart. You should be facing the side of the hill, not the top (or bottom!). Raise the ski on the upper side of the hill and bring it down, still parallel to your other ski, about 30 to 45 cm above its original position. Then bring the lower ski up so that you are again in your starting position but about 30 to 45 cm farther up the hill. Repeat—and repeat and repeat. It is a slow, tedious process, but also a safe and sure one for even the steepest slopes.

The most logical organization for a process paper is chronological: first things first and step by step. If, as in this paper on how to climb a hill, there are several different ways of achieving the same end, you would normally describe the easier ways (like sidestepping) first, followed by more difficult ways (like herringboning).

4. **Classification and Partition.** When you classify something, you show the readers how it fits into a larger category. When you partition something, you show how it can be broken down into smaller subdivisions on the basis of similarities and differences among its parts. For a classification-and-partition paper about different kinds of skis, your thesis statement might be "Different kinds of skis are designed for different purposes, different tastes, and different budgets." For a very short paper, you might classify and partition only by function—"Different kinds of skis are designed for different functions." For a longer paper, you would establish several kinds of groupings—by function, by design, by materials, by surface, by cost. When discussing function, you might write:

> Cross-country skis are of three basic groups, depending on their function: touring skis, mountaineering skis, and racing skis. Touring skis are all-purpose skis, of medium weight and length, designed for general use. They perform well in rolling countryside, are fast enough to make a downhill run exciting, yet can climb fairly steep slopes. Mountaineering skis are heavier and sometimes shorter; they have a steel edge for greater control. They are best suited for skiing on rugged terrain without a groomed trail. Racing skis are long and extremely light, designed for speed on a flat surface. Their additional length gives greater glide and speed, and their light weight lessens the strain on the skier.

This passage illustrates the easiest and clearest way to organize a classification-and-partition paper: from "big to small." The largest grouping here (cross-country skis) is mentioned first and then broken down into types of cross-country skis. The paper *as a whole* would show a similar organization, beginning, perhaps, by partitioning ways of moving on snow into snowshoes and skis, further partitioning skis into downhill and cross-country skis, and finally breaking cross-country skis down into types.

If your classification-and-partition paper relies more heavily on classification than partition, you can organize it according to the principle of "small-to-big." If your topic were defence mechanisms in insects, you could begin by discussing insects that bite or sting and then group these into a larger category of "aggressive defence." Insects that taste bad or that exude poisonous oils when touched might be grouped into a category called "passive defence." A third group of insects that look like twigs or have protective coloring could be classified as having "defence by appearance."

5. **Definition.** When we hear the word *definition*, we probably first think of a dictionary entry. Then we may think of definitions of specific abstract or technical terms like *impressionism, truth, microeconomics,* and *photosynthesis.* And, indeed, entire papers may be devoted to

rh
50e

defining a single term. They include a formal, or dictionary, definition, followed by an extensive discussion of different meanings of the term, a comparison and contrast with other related terms, and examples that illustrate the term.

But any writing that answers the question "What is it?" is also a definition. Whenever you explain something for your reader, you are defining it. For the general topic of skiing, one thesis statement for a paper devoted to development by definition could be simply "What cross-country skiing is." You could begin your paper by partition, explaining that both skis and snowshoes are designed to allow one to move over the surface of snow and that skis are faster but require open terrain. You might continue your definition by noting that cross-country skis and downhill skis are specialized descendants of a common ancestor. You would compare and contrast cross-country skiing with downhill skiing. One paragraph of such an extended definition might be the following:

> The outstanding feature of cross-country skiing is its versatility. Skiers can race down all but the steepest slopes and then climb back up again for a second run without having to rely on a tow. Or they can leave the trail entirely for a quiet excursion into the woods. As outdoor exercise, cross-country skiing can be gentle enough for people over sixty. But pursued more vigorously, it burns more calories per hour than any other sport, including running. It can be simple and safe enough to provide enjoyment for timid beginners on their first day out. It also can be developed into a skill of Olympic level.

The easiest organization for an extended definition is from the general to the particular. You first identify the broad area to which your definition applies, following this with specific details and examples. When defining something unfamiliar, it is best to proceed from the familiar to the unfamiliar. For instance, you might be writing an extended definition of painting and want to discuss the various media used. You would start with watercolors and oil paints because everyone is probably familiar with these. You would then discuss less familiar media such as egg white, gum, and wax, perhaps comparing the characteristics of these less familiar media with those of water and oil.

Argument and Persuasion The purpose of argument and persuasion is to bring the reader, by a logical reasoning process, to an acceptance of the writer's point of view. An argument-and-persuasion paper on the perfect baby-sitter might assert that there is no perfect baby-sitter because there is no substitute for a child's mother. Alternatively, it might argue that mothers are seldom the best baby-sitters. In either case, evidence would be provided to support the point of view and to persuade the reader to accept it. (See 51 for a detailed discussion of how to make a good argument.)

In an argument-and-persuasion paper, your thesis statement *is* your argument. When you are sure that you have a good statement of your argument, review the evidence you will need to support it and the

rh
50e

counterarguments you must refute. Think of who your audience is (even if it is a fictional audience). That is, if you were arguing that Canadians eat too much sugar, the main thrust of your argument would differ depending on whether your audience consisted of dentists, students, or parents of small children.

The most obvious organization for an argument-and-persuasion paper is general-to-particular. You state your argument first and then support it with detailed evidence. The evidence itself normally appears in the order of most important to least important.

Early in the paper, acknowledge opposing views by presenting and refuting counterarguments or, if you cannot refute them, by conceding the points. For instance, suppose you wish to persuade your readers that there is no place in Canadian academic institutions for intermural sports like those of the United States. You could begin by conceding that competitive athletics might attract badly needed financial contributions from alumni and provide enjoyment for many people within and without the academic community. You might then refute the argument that physical exercise is essential to health by noting that intermural teams provide exercise for only a few athletes.

Next you could cite the main evidence for your argument—that intermural sports are likely to draw attention away from the real purpose of a college or university, that the desire to get star athletes would eventually mean the admission of students on the basis of their athletic ability rather than their academic qualifications, and that intermural sports are potentially very expensive and would be likely to siphon away money, for equipment, facilities, and scholarships, that could better be used for academic purposes. You could cite examples from the United States. Less important evidence such as the erroneous public image of some American insitutions as athletic businesses, the normally heavy emphasis on contact sports, and the corruption that sometimes occurs would follow your main evidence.

Some arguments lend themselves to a particular-to-general organization. To persuade your readers that governments should protect citizens from business fraud, you could begin by citing a number of incidents in which consumers were cheated and end with the statement that more consumer-protection legislation is needed. In effect, you would present your evidence first and state your thesis afterward.

A third organization for an argument-and-persuasion paper is especially effective when you are trying to persuade your audience that one alternative is better than another. Here, you explain the advantages of A and the disadvantages of B point by point, normally using one paragraph for each point. In a paper arguing that cross-country skiing is preferable to downhill skiing, you could first note that cross-country equipment is much less expensive than downhill equipment. Then you note that cross-country skiing provides better exercise and gives the individual skier more freedom. You explain that cross-country skiing does not involve high tow fees or long hours of waiting in line. In the next paragraph, you argue that cross-country skiing is more flexible than downhill skiing and less dependent on weather conditions.

rh
50e

Strong winds will blow the powder from the surface of downhill slopes, making skiing treacherous or even impossible. When the wind-chill factor reaches −40°C or colder, downhill slopes often are closed because of the danger of exposure to skiers. Cross-country skiers, on the other hand, can simply plan a tour along more wooded trails where the trees provide protection from the wind. Furthermore, the strenuous exercise of cross-country skiing keeps skiers warm under virtually any weather conditions, and they rarely need worry about frostbite or hypothermia.

Description   The purpose of description is to convey a sensory impression, especially a visual impression. Exposition explains what it is; description tells the reader what it looks like, feels like, sounds like. A descriptive paper on the perfect baby-sitter might describe in detail the appearance of a baby-sitter that you once had. A description of an auction, on the other hand, might focus on sounds, while a description of a country scene could centre around odors.

Descriptive papers consist primarily of details. But if you are describing, for instance, your sister's appearance, do not restrict yourself to a head-to-toe description of the sort one might make from looking at a snapshot. Describe her gestures and mannerisms. What is her walk like? How does she look when she eats, falls asleep in front of the television set, gets caught looking in the mirror? If you are describing an object or a scene, what comparisons can you make? Don't limit your comparisons to vision alone—what does the object smell like, feel like, taste like, sound like? What does it remind you of? A good thesis sentence will provide a focus for your description. For example, the thesis sentence "I could tell that Clyde was a man who marched to a different drummer when I saw that he wore hiking boots with a three-piece suit" would allow you to focus your description on the contradictions in or eccentricities of Clyde's behavior.

Because the purpose of descriptive papers is to convey a physical impression, the most logical organization is according to the dominant impression that you wish to convey. If you were describing a policeman testifying before a royal commission, it would be impossible (and very boring for the reader) to itemize every single feature that could be observed. Instead, you might concentrate on a dominant impression of, say, nervousness. You might begin by describing his creased forehead, his habit of blinking, his way of continually licking his lips. You could then note that he constantly rubbed his forefingers and thumbs together, crossed and uncrossed his legs, and sat forward tensely in his chair. After this more or less general description, you could continue by noting exactly how he replied to particular questions, how he addressed his questioners, and so forth.

Organization by dominant impression can also be combined with an orderly spatial description. In a description of the interior of a Quaker meetinghouse, you might wish to give the reader an impression of starkness and simplicity. You could simultaneously give a spatially ordered description by beginning your description from a single seat within the meetinghouse and gradually moving outward from this seat. Thus, you might first describe the straight-backed cane-bottomed chairs, then the uncarpeted wooden floor, and then the plain ceiling with its single light fixture. From there you could move to the white walls without pictures and to the windows with small panes and no curtains, perhaps finally noting that even the tree branches visible through the windows are bare, without the ornamentation of leaves.

Assume that you want to describe the scene of a trip down a mountain on cross-country skis. You have selected a dominant impression of danger, and your thesis statement is "Downhill skiing on cross-country skis is only for the foolhardy." In order to emphasize this impression, you will leave out many other details not directly related to danger. You do not describe, for example, the weather or the clothing of the skiers. The basic organization is spatial, beginning with a glance behind the skiers and then moving to the appearance of the trail ahead of the skiers.

> Behind us were the weathered summit building, the roar of the machinery that controlled the gondola, and a few curious downhill skiers who openly stared at people crazy enough to ski down Wildcat Mountain on cross-country skis—and down the wrong side of Wildcat at that. Ahead of us was a terrifyingly steep, narrow, and sharply curving trail, little more than a path. Stunted though they were by the altitude and harsh climate, the twisted evergreen branches that hung over the trail were a menace to exposed faces or poorly controlled ski poles. A hundred metres straight down, a sign with a red arrow pointed right, but the trail beyond was invisible.

Narration   Narration tells a story, fictional or true. Narration is concerned with events and actions, usually in the past, and answers the question "What happened?" A narrative paper on the perfect baby-sitter might, for example, relate an incident in which a baby-sitter handled a crisis with great skill. The narration of a sports event describes the most exciting or crucial events of the game. A narrative paper about coming into a strange city would focus on the incidents that occurred during your arrival.

Usually you have a reason for telling a story. You may wish to entertain or amuse your reader, but you probably have another point to make: you want your reader to draw a conclusion or receive a particular impression. In a good narrative, the writer does not tell the reader in so many words what the message is. Instead, the writer selects details and presents them in such a way that the reader gets the point without being explicitly told what that point is. As with description, you should choose details carefully to convey a vivid impression and omit details that are not directly related to the point.

The most natural organization for a narrative paper is the chronological arrangement. The first events are narrated at the beginning and subsequent events later, following the natural order of time. You may

rh
50e

occasionally need to deviate briefly from a strictly chronological presentation in order to explain why a particular event is relevant or why it occurred, but in general the order is from earlier to later.

Alternatively, you might decide to state the outcome first and then narrate the events that led up to it. This method destroys suspense but has the advantage of letting the reader see beforehand just how all the events led inevitably to the outcome.

For many narratives, the end of the narrative will simply be the last event; when the last event happens, the story is over. This would be true if, for example, you were narrating a typical day in the life of a steelworker, a trip on a bus, or a riot in a federal prison. Other kinds of narrative are more effective if they have a climactic order, that is, an order that proceeds up to a dramatic occurrence and then stops, even if the entire story has not been completed. For example, in narrating an automobile accident, you might wish to end your paper with a sentence describing the moment of impact. To continue the story by relating the arrival of the police and tow trucks would be anticlimactic and would detract from the effectiveness of the story.

In a paper narrating a cross-country ski tour, you could begin with a brief mention of the skiers' inadequate equipment; this would be necessary to explain why the skiers found themselves in so much trouble. You would then give a chronological account of their experience. Note how such words and phrases as *at first, then, when,* and *as* help the reader follow the sequence of events.

> The extent of their foolishness was revealed when they began to descend. With no edges on their light touring skis, they had no control whatsoever on the thick icy crust. At first, they simply schussed until their speed became terrifying, and then they deliberately fell to brake themselves. When the trail became more winding, schussing was impossible, and Ginny and Bert both resorted to sitting down on their skis, trying to guide the tips with their hands. But when Bert tore his sleeve on a root, he decided to stand up again, regardless of the consequences. As he rocketed down the slope, he saw a large boulder directly in the middle of the trail. Attempting a quick step turn, he lost his balance, fell, and watched in dismay as his right ski continued down the mountain ahead of him.

rh
50e

Exercises: Planning the Paper

Choose one of the following general subjects. For it, write a narrowed topic and a thesis statement you could develop into an interesting paper. State the primary rhetorical approach you would use (exposition, argument and persuasion, narration, or description). Then list ideas, anecdotes, arguments, quotations, statistics, and details you could use in writing the paper.

1. Passive resistance
2. Soap operas
3. Early childhood development
4. Urban life
5. Advertising
6. Black holes in space
7. Solar energy
8. Postsecondary education

50f • Outlining the Paper

Suppose you have decided to write an expository paper about travel. You have narrowed the topic to a three-day stop you made in Iceland when you were en route to Belgium as a representative to an international youth conference. You have further restricted the topic to those things that impressed you most about Iceland. As you thought about the topic, you realized that you were actually more impressed by little things not mentioned in travel brochures than you were by the volcanoes and glaciers. You have formulated a thesis statement: "In a foreign country, it is the seemingly insignificant things, not the exotic things, that most impress me."

Your rough notes for the paper might include the following items.

Farming—sheep, hay, flax, cows in harnesses
Sheep get out of road
People—friendly, blond, good-looking
Newsboys wear rubber boots in summer
Glaciers, volcanoes, lava fields, hot springs, geysers
Arctic skuas, golden plovers, puffins
Hot springs heat—water always hot in rest rooms
Bananas growing in greenhouses
Whaling—meat looks like corned beef
Not much difficulty with language
Hotels and food very expensive
Plane crowded
Food—fish, carrots and peas, *skyr*
What travel brochures lead you to expect
Treeless or stunted trees
Corrugated tin roofs and siding
Cleanliness of Reykjavik—no dogs in city
Small bridges or no bridges at all
Near Arctic Circle, but mild climate

rh
50f

As you look at the list of ideas, you see that it has virtually no organization. Because your thesis statement makes a basic division between insignificant things and exotic things, you start organizing by dividing the list into "Exotic" and "Insignificant," with a third column for those items that do not seem to fit into either category.

EXOTIC	INSIGNIFICANT	OTHER
1. Glaciers, volcanoes, lava fields, hot springs, geysers	9. Flax fields in bloom	20. Farming—sheep, hay
2. Arctic skuas, golden plovers, puffins	10. Cows in harnesses	21. People—friendly, blond, good-looking
3. Hot springs heat	11. Sheep get out of road	22. Not much difficulty with language
4. Bananas growing in greenhouses	12. Newsboys wear rubber boots	23. Hotels and food very expensive
5. Whaling industry	13. Water always hot in rest rooms	24. Plane crowded
6. *Skyr* (like yogurt)	14. Whale meat looks like corned beef	25. What travel brochures lead you to expect
7. Treeless	15. Carrots and peas	26. Cleanliness of Reykjavik
8. Near Arctic Circle, but mild climate	16. Corrugated tin roofs	
	17. No dogs in Reykjavik	
	18. Small bridges or no bridges	
	19. Stunted trees	

When you examine your "Other" column, you decide that most of the items in it are not related to your thesis statement, so you cross items 20, 22, 23, and 24 off that list. You cannot decide about items 21 and 26, so you leave them on the list for the time being.

Your thesis statement implies a comparison and contrast, and your two columns "Exotic" and "Insignificant" are also contrasting lists. Clearly, you will need several comparison-and-contrast paragraphs in your final paper. (See 49b.) But how should the comparison and contrast be organized? One possibility is by categories.

Geography: (1) (7) (8) vs (19)   Everyday living: (3) vs (12) (13)
Animal life: (2) vs (10) (11) (17)   (16)
Plant life: (4) vs (9)   Industry and technology: (5)
Food: (6) vs (15)   vs (14) (18)

This division looks a little unbalanced—some categories have four entries, some only two. Probably some categories need to be combined or split up. However, you decide to leave the division as it is for the moment and consider the rest of the paper. How are you going to lead into the comparison? You decide to make a rough outline of the entire paper.

I. People often disappointed by great sights—Stonehenge, Grand Canyon

II. Travel brochures—I expected to be impressed with Iceland

III. Specific examples
    A. Geography
    B. Animal life
    C. Plant life
    D. Food
    E. Everyday living
    F. Industry and technology

IV. "Insignificant" things may actually be more important

When you examine this rough outline, you see that Items I, II, and IV will probably each take a single paragraph. Item III, however, is far too large to fit into one paragraph. On the other hand, some of the subdivisions, such as III.C., "Plant life," seem too small for a separate paragraph of their own. Perhaps you can combine some of these entries and end up with only four or five paragraphs under "Specific examples."

Item III.C., "Plant life," is rather skimpy. Further, as you think about it, the growing of bananas in greenhouses does not seem especially exotic. So you decide to eliminate the bananas and include the flax fields under III.A., "Geography." You can also put the present entries of III.D., "Food," in III.E., "Everyday living," eliminating another category. You see that most of what you have to say under III.F., "Industry and technology," really has to do with whales, and you have just recalled some more impressions of whaling. So you change the label of this subhead to "Whaling industry." But bridges are not related to the whaling industry, so you decide to move them to III.A., "Geography." Bridges are not really geography either, so you change the heading III.A. to "The countryside." Corrugated tin roofs are part of the countryside scene, so you move this entry from III.E., "Everyday living," to III.A., "The countryside." By this time, Item III in your outline is so marked up that you recopy it so that you can read it easily. As you recopy, you remember a few more details and include them in the outline.

rh
50f

III. Specific Examples
    A. The countryside

        1. Exotic
            a. Glaciers, volcanoes, lava fields, hot springs, geysers
            b. Treeless
            c. Near Arctic Circle, but mild climate

      2. Insignificant
        a. Stunted trees
        b. Small bridges or none at all
        c. Corrugated tin roofs and siding

  B. Animal life
    1. Exotic
      a. Arctic skuas, golden plovers, puffins
      b. Seals
    2. Insignificant
      a. Cows in harnesses
      b. Sheep stay out of road
      c. No dogs in Reykjavik

  C. Everyday living
    1. Exotic
      a. Hot springs heat
      b. Outdoor swimming all year round
      c. *Skyr*—national food
    2. Insignificant
      a. Newsboys wear rubber boots
      b. Water always hot in rest rooms
      c. Peas and carrots

  D. The whaling industry
    1. Exotic
      a. Small boats but big whales
      b. Processing stations
    2. Insignificant
      a. Whale meat looks like corned beef
      b. Strong odor of whale
      c. Sea birds all around dead whale

    You can see that there are still some inconsistencies in your outline, but since this is to be a fairly short paper, you decide not to make a formal outline at this stage. If required to do so, you will make a formal outline after you have written the paper itself.

rh
50f

Exercises: Making a Preliminary Outline

Take the topic you chose in the exercise "Planning the Paper." Consult the list of ideas you made in that exercise. Go over the list of ideas, eliminating those that do not fit anywhere, combining those that overlap, and subdividing those that are too general into specific facts and details. Now write a rough outline for an essay not to exceed 1000 words.

50g • Writing the First Draft

In reality, getting an idea, narrowing the topic, formulating a thesis, and deciding on the rhetorical type and organization of a paper are overlapping processes. By the time you have decided on a topic, you probably already have some notion of your thesis and the approach you will take. You may even become so interested in your paper that you start writing before you have completed all these other steps.

Some people, however, develop writer's paralysis when they reach the stage at which they must start composing sentences and paragraphs. If you have made an outline beforehand, paralysis is less likely to strike because you at least know what you are going to say and approximately where you are going to say it, even if you do not know exactly how you are going to say it. Knowing that your first attempt is only a rough draft can also help you overcome a block.

Try to begin writing when your mind is fresh. Whether you work better in the early morning, at midday, or late at night, do not wait for inspiration to strike: it will not. Reserve a fairly long, continuous period of time for writing the first draft; if possible, write the entire draft at one sitting. Such a procedure helps you maintain a uniform tone throughout the paper. Moreover, trying to write a draft in several sittings requires a warm-up period for each session. If you do write the rough draft in several sittings, refresh your memory by rereading what you have written previously.

If you are a fairly good typist, you may prefer to compose on the typewriter because typing is faster than handwriting. On the other hand, even good typists are often more comfortable writing rough drafts in longhand because crossing out and inserting are easier with a pen or pencil.

Refer to your preliminary outline as you write. You will probably find that your paragraph divisions generally correspond to the headings in your outline. But do not let your outline enslave you; if a heading requires two or more paragraphs, so be it. Conversely, you may find that two or more headings should be combined in one paragraph. If your outline is a good one, you will usually find that the order of points in your rough draft corresponds fairly closely to their order in the outline.

In general, try to avoid digressions that occur to you as you write. For example, as you are writing about your trip to Iceland, you may remember that your grandfather was stationed in Iceland during the Second World War. Or you may recall hearing a Japanese tourist in a cafeteria in Iceland ask for "a piece of Coca-Cola." These are interesting anecdotes, perhaps, but they are not related to your thesis statement and so should be omitted.

rh
50g

Exercises: Writing the First Draft

Write the first draft of an essay, using the preliminary outline you made in the exercise on "Making a Preliminary Outline." Your essay should be about 1000 words.

50h · Introductory and Concluding Paragraphs

The essential part of a paper is the middle, the body of the paper. But all papers have to begin and end in some way, although not every paper requires separate introductory and concluding sections. Whether or not you write a separate introduction or conclusion, the beginning and the end of a paper are important because these are emphatic positions. The beginning rouses—or fails to rouse—the reader's interest, and the ending strongly influences the reader's final impression of the paper.

Introductory Paragraphs At some time or another, you have probably had a good idea for a paper and a fairly detailed plan for developing the body of the paper. But when you sat down to write, you could get nothing down because you couldn't think of how to begin. When this happens, you may want to start in the middle; you will often find that after you have written a few paragraphs—or perhaps most of the paper—you will get a good idea for the beginning. Alternatively, you can put anything at all down just to get started and plan to revise it later. The problem with this second approach is that, by the time you have finished, you may be tired and tempted to leave the weak beginning as it is.

A beginning paragraph should set the tone for what follows and attract the reader's interest. Although you can begin a paper by plunging headlong into the topic, it is more effective to introduce the topic less directly, using the first paragraph to narrow the subject and to entice the reader to continue. There is no single way to begin a paper; almost any topic lends itself to several approaches.

Suppose you were writing a short paper on the Franco-Prussian War of 1870–1871. There are many possible ways of introducing this or almost any paper.

1. **Begin with a quotation.** It may be obviously related to the subject or it may be only indirectly related, requiring further explanation. Since it is often very difficult to find an appropriate quotation, don't insist on using one unless you have one in mind beforehand. Rather than force an unsuitable quotation into place, select another kind of beginning.

> "The great questions of the day will not be decided by speeches and resolution of majorities—that was the blunder of 1848 and 1849—but by blood and iron." So spoke Otto von Bismarck to the German parliament in 1862. Within a decade, the German states were to be involved in three European wars.

2. **Begin with a concessive statement.** Start with a statement recognizing an opinion or approach different from the one you plan to take in the paper.

> Many scholars attribute the Franco-Prussian War to the machinations of a single power-hungry man, Otto von Bismarck, and particularly to his editing and publication of the Ems Telegram. This may

have been the immediate cause, but wars do not have simple causes based on a single incident.

3. Begin with an interesting fact or statistic.

Today we call them guerrillas. In 1869 they were called *franc-tireurs,* "sharpshooters." They were not part of the French army, they had no uniforms, and when they were captured by the Prussians they were immediately shot.

4. Begin with a short anecdote or narrative. A short narrative is particularly effective for adding a touch of variety to an expository paper.

On July 30, 1898, the Iron Chancellor died in Friedrichsruh at the age of 83. The headstone on his grave has only one word: Bismarck.

5. Begin with a question or several questions.

How could France, seemingly at a peak of strength and prosperity, be so swiftly and so thoroughly defeated? How could the secret diplomacy of one man, a man who faced serious opposition in his own country, succeed in taunting France into war?

6. Begin with a paradox.

The Germans crushed the French army at Wörth and Gravelotte and Sedan—and the French Empire expanded in North Africa and Indochina. The Germans humiliated France in the Hall of Mirrors at Versailles—and all the world looked up to France for culture and beauty and spirit.

7. Begin with relevant background material. Background material should, however, be presented concisely and should be clearly related to your thesis. A rambling discussion of material only remotely related to your main point will bewilder and bore your reader.

Although the population was neither French nor German, Alsace had for centuries passed from French to German control and back again. But France had held it since the Treaty of Westphalia in 1648.

rh
50h

8. Begin by stating a long-term effect or effects without immediately stating the cause.

It brought about the Third Republic, one of the stormiest yet longest-lasting governments in France's history. Indirectly, it led to the Dreyfus affair. It was a test run for Germany's attack on France in 1914. Today it is called the Franco-Prussian War.

9. **Begin with an analogy.**

Before contractors begin constructing a new shopping centre, architects draw up plans and build mock-ups on a miniature scale. In this way, they can identify potential problems, test controversial innovations, predict traffic flow, and get an idea of the overall appearance of the completed center. The Franco-Prussian War was a mock-up for World War I, and Otto von Bismarck was the chief architect.

10. **Begin with a definition of a term that is important to your topic.**

This should not be a simple dictionary definition but an explanation of the term as it applies to your topic.

Nineteenth-century armies could no longer be persuaded that they would win because God was on their side. France had substituted a new mystique: *élan. Élan* was dash, fervor, impetuousness, ardor, and spirit, and, for the French, it was much more. It was a will to win that could triumph over antiquated matériel, poor leadership, and obsolete battle strategy and tactics. Or so they thought.

There are several ways of introducing a paper that are guaranteed *not* to attract the reader's interest.

1. Do not merely paraphrase your title. If your paper is entitled "The Franco-Prussian War," you will have made no real beginning if you start out by writing "In this paper, I will discuss the Franco-Prussian War of 1870–1871." But you will have bored the reader, who has already seen your title and knows what the topic is.

2. Do not begin with sweeping generalities or platitudes. "Wars cause much destruction and devastation" is so obvious a statement that it should not be made at all.

3. Do not apologize for your incompetence or lack of knowledge. A beginning sentence such as "Although I am no authority on wars or on the Franco-Prussian War . . ." will only convince the reader that it would be a waste of time to continue reading.

rh

50h

Concluding Paragraphs The purpose of a concluding paragraph is to strengthen the message conveyed by the whole paper and to leave the reader with a feeling of completion. Not every paper requires a separate concluding paragraph. This is especially true of short papers, where the reader can easily remember everything that you have said. Short narrative and descriptive papers in particular may require no concluding paragraph. Even a fairly lengthy process paper can end when the description of the process has been completed. If you have written all the rest of the paper and can think of nothing new that does not seem repetitious or otherwise unnecessary, you probably do not need a separate concluding paragraph.

Concluding paragraphs are more likely to be necessary in expository or argument-and-persuasion papers, but even here a strong final sentence can often replace a separate paragraph. If your entire paper is organized climactically, your most important points at the end will leave the reader with a sense of finality.

When you do write a concluding paragraph, avoid the following common problems.

1. Do not merely summarize what you have just finished saying. If a summary statement is needed because the paper is long or the argument rather complex, do not openly inform the reader that a summary is coming by such sentences as "Now I will summarize . . ." or "I have just shown that. . . ."

2. Do not apologize for your poor performance or lack of knowledge.

3. Do not throw your entire thesis into doubt by making a major concession to an opposing point of view. Concessions belong at the beginning of the paper, not at the end.

4. Do not trail off feebly with a row of dots after your final sentence.

5. Do not introduce a new idea that is really the subject of another paper.

6. Do not use the final paragraph as a catchall to include details or points that you forgot to include in the main body of your paper.

If you feel that a paper needs rounding off with a separate concluding paragraph, most of the devices suggested for introductory paragraphs are also suitable for concluding paragraphs. For example, a relevant quotation or anecdote might be used. If the argument has been complex, your thesis can be summarized, not step by step, but by restating only the key points and the conclusion. You may want to end by suggesting that, now that you have advanced the question one more step, it is up to the reader to take action on it.

A concluding paragraph may suggest implications or ramifications of your findings that go beyond the limits of your own paper. But don't confuse implications of your own presentation with the introduction of an entirely new idea. That is, if you have written a paper arguing that wind power is a feasible alternative to fossil fuels, your last paragraph might note that one implication of this conclusion is that industrial nations will have to switch from giant, centralized power plants to small, decentralized units. This is an acceptable concluding statement. What you should *not* do is conclude your paper on wind power by changing the subject and saying, "But, of course, we should also consider solar power and water power."

rh
50h

Exercises: Introductory and Concluding Paragraphs

Part A: Choose two of the following subjects, select a specific topic based on each, and write a thesis sentence for each topic. Then for each of the two topics write three different kinds of introductions.

1. Women artists   5. Nuclear energy
2. Country music   6. The Jazz Age
3. Jogging   7. Native land claims
4. Bilingualism in Canada 8. Imagination

Part B: For the two topics you selected in Part A, list the various types of conclusions you believe would be appropriate. For each type of conclusion, indicate the kinds of information you might conceivably use in it. If you do not believe that a concluding paragraph is necessary for your topics, explain why.

50i ▪ Titles

Every paper should have a title, which should specify or at least suggest the contents of the paper. A good title is more specific than simply a description of the general subject area of the paper. That is, if your instructor has assigned a paper on cheating in schools, your title should not be simply "Cheating in Schools." To avoid overly general titles, it is best to postpone deciding on a title until after you have formulated a thesis statement or, even better, until after you have written your first draft.

Titles should not be long; if your title takes up more than one line on the page, try to shorten it. For example, "A Description of the Old Open-Air Market in Kitchener" can easily be shortened to "Kitchener's Open-Air Market." Catchy titles are appealing to the reader but are more appropriate for informal or humorous topics than for serious topics. In any case, don't spend a great deal of time trying to think of a catchy title; a straightforward descriptive title is always acceptable.

UNACCEPTABLE	IMPROVED
Stamp-Collecting as a Hobby	Stamp-Collecting as a Hobby
Many people think of this as a hobby of fussy old men, but....	Many people think of stamp-collecting as a hobby of fussy old men, but....

rh
50i

Although a good title does not necessarily reveal the rhetorical type of a paper, it does provide an indication of it. Listed below are three broad subject areas. Possible titles are given for papers in each subject area and for each rhetorical type.

SUBJECT AREA	RHETORICAL TYPE	PAPER TITLE
tobacco	exposition	How To Roll Your Own Cigarettes
	argument	Why Snuff Should Replace Cigarettes
	description	The Paraphernalia of a Pipe-Smoker
	narration	My First Encounter with Chewing Tobacco

SUBJECT AREA	RHETORICAL TYPE	PAPER TITLE
automo-biles	exposition	Developing a Nonpolluting Engine
	argument	Teen-agers Make the Best Drivers
	description	My New Datsun 200 SX
	narration	Tragedy on the Trans-Canada
fires	exposition	Arson: The Fastest-Growing Crime
	argument	Smoke Detectors Are Worthless
	description	Our House After the Fire
	narration	The Great London Fire of 1666

50j ▪ Revising the Paper

Revising the First Draft   While you are writing the first draft, the most important thing is to get your ideas into words and the words onto paper. Once those words are on paper, you are probably proud of your act of creation and not a little relieved to have it completed. But unless you are a rare individual, the product is not yet ready for public viewing. You have been so wrapped up in the process of composing that you haven't seen the flaws. Although most writers do at least some revising as they write, this is not enough. No first draft is perfect; errors and inconsistencies are unavoidable. All writers must revise their work. The first draft of a paper is for the writer; the revisions are for the reader.

Plan to wait at least a few hours before starting to revise; a day or two is even better. This time lapse will give you a perspective on what you have written. In the meantime, ask a friend to read the paper and tell you what he or she thinks its strong and weak points are. Be sure your friend knows that you want an appraisal, not praise. You will probably be depressed or even annoyed if he or she makes serious criticisms—and the more valid they are, the more hurt you may feel. Nevertheless, consider them as objectively as possible.

If you simply do not have the time to wait even a few hours before beginning your revision, you can gain a little distance by rereading the paper aloud, rather than silently. As you reread, make brief notes about anything that strikes you as needing revision or correction. Then methodically check, point by point, all aspects of the paper, consulting the following checklist.

A. Content
  1. Does the paper as a whole develop your thesis statement?
  2. Have you unintentionally omitted something important from your outline?
  3. Is there irrelevant material that should be removed?
  4. Are all your statements accurate?
  5. Is your logic sound? Are there gaps in your logic? (See 51.)
  6. Are more details or more explanation necessary? Have you fully supported all your statements with facts?
  7. Have you anticipated counterarguments and responded to them?

rh
50j

B. Organization
   1. Is the organization logical and easy to follow? Or do you jump back and forth from one point to another?
   2. Are there clear transitions between sections? Are the transitions between paragraphs and between sentences easy to follow?
   3. Is the paper well-proportioned? Or is one section greatly underdeveloped or overdeveloped?
   4. Are the paragraph divisions logical? (See 49.)
   5. Is emphasis placed on the points you want to emphasize?
   6. Is the pace brisk enough to carry the reader along?
   7. Does the introductory paragraph lead logically and entertainingly into the main point of the paper?
   8. Does the concluding material leave the reader with the impression you intend?

C. Sentences (See 48.)
   1. Is there a variety of sentence types?
   2. Are sentences wordy and redundant?
   3. Are there completely unnecessary sentences?
   4. Is the syntax awkward or overinvolved?
   5. Are there failures in balance and parallelism?
   6. Are there unintentional sentence fragments or run-on sentences? (See 23.)

D. Use of Words (Diction) (See 46.)
   1. Is the language appropriate for the audience? Do you talk over the heads of your audience? Do you insult your audience by talking down to them?
   2. Do you use too many general or abstract words?
   3. Are words used precisely? Or are there incorrect denotations and improper connotations?
   4. Have you defined all necessary terms?
   5. Do you overuse the passive?
   6. Are there too many clichés?
   7. Are there mixed or inappropriate metaphors or similes?
   8. Is there "fine" writing?
   9. Will your reader believe what you say, or have you destroyed credibility by exaggeration or sarcasm?

rh
50j

E. Grammar (See 1–23.)
   1. Do you use standard grammar throughout?
   2. Are there unidiomatic phrases or expressions?

F. Mechanics (See 24–45.)
   1. Do punctuation, capitalization, hyphenation, and abbreviation all follow the conventions?
   2. Is your spelling correct? Have you checked in your dictionary any word about which you are uncertain?
   3. Have you made consistent choices among spelling variants for which Canadian preference is not firmly fixed?

G. Euphony

   Does the paper *sound* good? Read the entire paper aloud to check for awkward phrasing, clumps of indigestible consonants, excessive alliteration, and poor rhythm.

H. Acknowledgements (See 55.)

   1. Have you acknowledged any outside sources you may have used?
   2. Are your citations and bibliography in proper form?

I. Title

   Is the title accurate and appropriate?

J. Your Own Weaknesses

   Have you double-checked for particular weaknesses that have given you trouble in the past?

   If you have prepared the first draft carefully, you shouldn't have any huge flaws in logic or development. But you will likely have some unnecessary repetition, a poor transition here or there, an occasional word choice that is not quite right, and sentences that can be improved by combining or rearranging elements. You will almost certainly have a few mechanical errors such as misspellings and incorrect punctuation. As an example of how and why revisions are made, consider the following, which shows the first draft and the subsequent revisions of the second paragraph on page 345.

Plan to
~~If possible,~~ wait at least a few hours before

starting to revise; a day or two is even better.

This time lapse will give you a perspective on what

you have written~~.~~ ~~because you will not be so in~~

~~volved with the topic that you overlook many of the~~

In the meantime,   *tell*
~~problems.~~ a/Xsk a friend to read the paper and ~~to let~~

                      he or she thinks
you ~~know honestly~~ what, its strong and weak points

Be sure your
are. ~~Let you~~ friend know that you want an ~~honest~~

               will probably be depressed or even annoyed
appraisal, not ~~just~~ praise. You ~~may be hurt~~ if he

-- and the more valid they
or she makes serious criticisms, ~~but try to weigh~~
*   may*
are, the more hurt you~~feel~~. Nevertheless, consider
~~them objectively nevertheless.~~
them as objectively as possible.

In revising this paragraph, I first cut out the last half of the second sentence because I saw that it was unnecessary. I added "in the meantime" to the beginning of the third sentence to make a smoother transition. Because "to let you know honestly" was wordy, I changed it to "tell you." I added "he or she thinks" because the original implied that a friend would always be correct in his appraisal, and I didn't want to make such a strong assumption. All the changes in the fourth sentence were to make it sound smoother. When I reread the fifth sentence, I realized that I had not developed my point fully, so I noted that one's reaction to criticism may be either depression or annoyance and that people are often more offended by valid criticism than by foolish criticism. The fifth sentence was by now rather long, so I began a new sentence, moving "nevertheless" to a stronger position at the beginning of the clause. As I added "as possible" to the final sentence, I saw that I had begun the paragraph with "If possible." To avoid overusing "possible," I changed the opening words to "Plan to."

When you have made all your revisions, read the paper through once more to be sure that your revisions fit smoothly into the text. When you are satisfied with the revised draft, prepare the final draft according to the instructions for manuscript form given in Appendix F.

Exercises: Revising the Paper

Part A: Use the "Checklist for Revision" as a guide for revising the rough draft of the paper you have written in the exercise "Writing the First Draft." Be sure that your introduction and conclusion are effective.

Part B: Using the "Checklist for Revision" as your guide, revise the following first draft of a student essay.

Love is a rare phenomenon in our society. There are all kinds of relationships which are called love. There are the dominating themes that appear in the romantic songs and in the movies of sentimental impulses. No word is used with more meanings than this term, most of the meanings being dishonest in that they cover up the real motives in the relationship. But there are many other sound and honest relationships called love such as parental care for children, sexual passion, or the sharing of loneliness. The reality often discovered in when one looks underneath the surface of the individual in our lonely and conformist society, is how little love is actually involved in these relationships.

Our society is, as we have seen, thriving with competitive individualism, with power over others as a dominant motivation. Our particular generation is full of isolation and personal emptiness, which is not a good preparation for learning how to love. The capacity to love presupposes self-awareness, because love requires the ability to appreciate the potentialities of the other person. Love also presupposes freedom; because love which is not freely given is not love. To love someone because you are not free to love someone else is not love.

The error so common in our society is resorting to hypocrisy in trying to persuade himself that all of the emotions he feels are love. Learning to love will procede if we stop trying to persuade ourselves that to love is easy. And if we give up the disgiuses for love in a society which is always talking about love but has so little of it.

Preparing a Formal Outline Although a rough or informal outline is important in organizing a paper, you need not prepare a formal outline unless you are required to do so. If your instructor asks for an outline, prepare it from the completed paper, not from your rough outline because you probably did not follow your rough outline exactly as you wrote. An outline submitted with a paper should observe the conventions given in 52a.

Revising a Graded Paper Even if you have methodically checked your paper for all the problems in the checklist, you will probably find that your instructor has made a number of corrections and comments on the paper before returning it to you. It is, of course, depressing to see a paper on which you have worked hard marked up with red pencil. But that is what the instructor is for—to help you locate and correct writing problems that you yourself do not identify.

Whether or not you are required to submit a revised version of the paper to the instructor, read all the comments and corrections very carefully. Be sure you are familiar with the symbols used; if you are not, refer to the correction chart inside the front cover of this handbook. If there are comments that you do not understand, ask your instructor to explain them to you. Pay particular attention to general comments your instructor may make, such as "You seem to have difficulty with sentence structure" or "Paragraphs are underdeveloped." Refer to the appropriate sections of this handbook for guidance on these general problems.

**rh
51**

51 🦉 Making a Good Argument

Many papers assigned for university and college courses are argument-and-persuasion papers. Such familiar titles as "Why Bilingualism Is Essential," "The Basic Simplicity of Steinbeck's Style," "Home Computers Are Changing Our Lives," and "Evolution Proceeds by Jumps, Not Gradual Stages" all imply that an argument follows. But even narrative and descriptive papers usually include a certain amount of argument. This is not surprising, because, after all, there are few worthwhile subjects for which all the facts are available; most thinking about them involves a mixture of facts, opinions, and logical statements. If all the facts about a subject were available, there would be little point in writing—or reading—about it.

To be effective, an argument must be based on clear thinking. One cause of fuzzy thinking and poor arguments is the failure to distinguish among facts, opinions, and logical statements. A **fact** is something that is known to exist or to have happened; it is based on actual experience or observation. An **opinion** is a belief based on something less than absolute certainty or experience. In other words, an opinion is still open to dispute. A **logical statement** is a conclusion based on reasoning. Logical statements depend on inferences drawn from facts or assumptions, but the conclusions themselves are not necessarily facts. Further, if a conclusion is to be valid, the reasoning process used to reach the conclusion must follow certain universally accepted rules.

Whenever we draw conclusions, we normally follow one of two basic types of reasoning processes, **induction** or **deduction.** In induction, we examine particular facts or individual cases and draw a general conclusion from them. For example, if I eat strawberries and then break out in a rash, I might well suspect that the strawberries caused my rash. If I eat strawberries on four more occasions and break out in a rash each time, my suspicions will be even stronger, and I will probably conclude, by induction, that I am allergic to strawberries. One instance of a rash following the eating of strawberries would not be enough to justify this conclusion—some other food might have caused the rash, or I might have poison ivy, or I might be coming down with measles. Five instances is better evidence, although I might still be wrong—especially if I sometimes develop a rash even when I have not recently eaten strawberries.

Inductive reasoning leads to absolute proof if every possible instance or example is examined and supports the conclusion. If I notice that one of my keys opens several different doors in a building, I might hypothesize that I have a master key that opens all the doors. I then test my key with every door in the building and discover that it does indeed open every door. I have used an inductive process to prove absolutely that my key is a master key for the building. In most cases of inductive reasoning, however, every single instance cannot be tested. Energy specialists who conclude that natural oil is a more efficient fuel than wood do not reach this conclusion by burning every drop of oil and every stick of wood that ever existed or will exist in the future. Most inductive conclusions are based on a sample considered representative of the whole. Generally speaking, the larger the sample (that is, the more specific instances actually tested), the more confident we can be that our conclusions are correct.

Once we have drawn a conclusion based on inductive reasoning, we may use that conclusion to make further conclusions or predictions. After I have determined, by induction, that I am allergic to strawberries, I might reason as follows when I see a dish of strawberries before me:

rh
51

(1) Strawberries give me a rash; (2) These are strawberries; (3) If I eat these strawberries, I will brake out in a rash. This kind of reasoning from the general principle (Strawberries give me a rash) to the specific case (These particular strawberries will give me a rash) is called **deduction.** In deduction, general principles or **premises,** and not individual instances, lead to conclusions.

The basic formula for deductive reasoning is called the **syllogism.** It consists of three statements: two premises that have at least one term in common and a logical conclusion drawn from these premises. In the example below, (1) and (2) are the premises, and (3) is the conclusion.

1. All languages have consonants.
2. Navajo is a language.
3. Therefore, Navajo has consonants.

At this point, we must distinguish between **truth** and **validity.** Truth and validity are not the same. When we speak of facts, we are referring to truth. But when we speak of deductive reasoning, we must also talk about validity. The conclusion of a syllogism may be true but still not valid if the premises and conclusions are all facts but the reasoning process is not correct. An example of a true but invalid syllogism is

INVALID AND TRUE
1. All rodents are mammals.
2. A squirrel is a mammal.
3. Therefore, a squirrel is a rodent.

Here, the premises are true and the conclusion is true (squirrels *are* rodents), but the argument is invalid because many mammals are not rodents. The invalidity can be seen more clearly if we substitute *giraffe* for *squirrel.*

INVALID AND UNTRUE
1. All rodents are mammals.
2. A giraffe is a mammal.
3. Therefore, a giraffe is a rodent.

On the other hand, a syllogism may be valid but still untrue:

VALID AND UNTRUE
1. All mammals are rodents.
2. A giraffe is a mammal.
3. Therefore, a giraffe is a rodent.

rh
51

Here, the reasoning process is correct, so the conclusion is valid. But the conclusion is untrue because the first premise that all mammals are rodents is not true. A good argument requires both that the facts or premises be true and that the reasoning process be correct.

Most knowledge about the world and most beliefs are based on a combination of inductive and deductive reasoning. Human beings first use individual facts to form general conclusions (induction) and then use these general conclusions as premises to make particular statements or predictions (deduction). These deductions in turn may serve as examples to form new inductions, and thus the process begins again. When you were a very small child, you perhaps struck your steel high-chair tray with your spoon and discovered that noise resulted. When you banged two toy cars together, noise also resulted. By such induction, you soon formed the generalization that forcefully bringing two metal objects together produced noise. Later you perhaps saw two pot lids and deduced that they too would make a noise if you banged them together. You did not, of course, know the word *syllogism*, but you nevertheless had formulated one:

1. Banging metal objects together produces noise.
2. Pot lids are metal objects.
3. If I bang pot lids together, noise will result.

Now, at the same time, your mother may have told you to stop banging the pot lids together. On another occasion, your mother scolded you for screaming at the top of your lungs. On still another occasion, she was disturbed when you turned the television set up to full volume. From these examples, you could have induced that loud noises upset your mother. And, in turn, you could have used this generalization to predict that she would be annoyed if you burst a balloon near her ear.

The subject matter of reasoning changes as an individual grows up, but the basic reasoning processes remain the same. However, as the subject matter becomes more complex, the likelihood of drawing untrue or invalid conclusions increases. When you try to persuade others to accept your conclusions, you want to avoid logical fallacies—flaws in your reasoning—that weaken your argument. The following six rules are designed to make arguments as convincing as possible.

1. Define the argument clearly.
2. Define all terms used in the argument.
3. Limit the argument to the question at hand.
4. Present adequate evidence to support the argument.
5. Reason clearly and logically.
6. Anticipate contrary arguments and evidence.

rh
51

Exercises: Facts, Opinions, and Logical Statements

A. Identify each sentence below as a statement of fact (F), a statement of opinion (O), or a logical statement (L).

1. I know that Shelley ate the Hershey bar because she loves chocolate.
2. I know that Shelley ate the Hershey bar because it was there when I left, it is gone now, and she was the only one in the room afterwards.
3. I know that Shelley ate the Hershey bar because I saw her eating it.
4. Goldfish die if there is too much air in their water. Boris poured water straight from the tap into my fishbowl, so it was the air bubbles that killed my goldfish.

5. Blue whales will be extinct within fifty years.
6. Sabre-toothed tigers are extinct.

B. For each of the syllogisms below, indicate whether the conclusion is

> True and valid (TV)
> True and invalid (TI)
> Untrue and valid (UV)
> Untrue and invalid (UI)

1. Washington, D.C., has many famous buildings.
   The Lincoln Memorial is in Washington, D.C.
   Therefore, the Lincoln Memorial is a famous building.
2. Every moon is made of green cheese.
   Venus is a moon.
   Therefore, Venus is made of green cheese.
3. If you add one to any even number, the result is an odd number.
   Two is an even number.
   Therefore, two plus one equals an odd number.
4. Water contains hydrogen and oxygen.
   Sulfuric acid contains hydrogen and oxygen.
   Therefore, sulfuric acid is water.

51a ▪ Defining the Argument

The first step in defining an argument is to make sure that you really have an argument. An argument requires a statement about which there can be disagreement. Statements such as "Water is necessary for life" or "Most people resent being insulted" are not arguments because no one would disagree with them. Second, the statement must be one for which evidence for and against can be offered. "I have a bad headache" is not an argument because, even if you are lying, no one can refute it. Nor is "I dislike polka-dot ties" the statement of an argument because likes and dislikes are matters of taste, not of fact.

On the other hand, the sentence "Most people like mashed potatoes better than mashed turnips" could be the statement of an argument because you could present evidence for or against it—evidence in the form of the results of a poll, statistics on the sale of potatoes and turnips, the number of restaurant menus listing mashed potatoes and turnips, and so forth.

rh
51a

Stating the Argument When you have determined that you really have an argument, the next step is to state it clearly and fairly. In particular, avoid the fallacy of the **false dilemma,** which implies that there are only two alternatives when there may actually be several alternatives. The false dilemma frequently takes the form of an *if . . . then* statement or an *either . . . or* statement. The person who writes "If these malcontents don't like the way things are run in this country, they should go to Russia" has set up a false dilemma because he or she refuses to consider the alternative possibility of changing the society within this country. Similarly, the statement "Either we must agree that the pilgrimage of Chaucer's *Canterbury Tales* is an allegory of man's life on earth or we must assume that Chaucer had no overall theme in this work" is a false dilemma because it allows no alternative themes. A clearer and fairer statement of this argument would be "The pilgrimage of Chaucer's *Canterbury Tales* is an allegory of man's life on earth." (Of course, you would have to present evidence to support this statement.)

Exercises: Defining the Argument

Identify which of the following topics could be the basis for an argumentative paragraph or essay and which could not. For those that are arguable, explain what kinds of evidence and support you would use in making the argument. For those that are not arguable, explain why they are not.

1. Solar energy is superior to all other kinds of energy.
2. Integrity is one of the most admirable human qualities.
3. The freedom of the press should never be restricted.
4. In spite of its complexities, life in the twentieth century is not very different from the life in the Middle Ages or Renaissance.
5. A liberal arts education is the best foundation one can have as preparation for living in the modern world.

51b ▪ Defining All Terms

Words are slippery customers. They often have multiple meanings, and the same word may have very different meanings for different people. Many an apparent disagreement turns out to be no disagreement at all when people realize that they have been using the same word in different meanings. People may agree that they want "the good life," but individual definitions of "good life" vary greatly. The error of **undefined terms**, or failure to limit the definition of the words used in an argument, often leads to unacceptable conclusions. For example, before making the argument that parents should control their children, the word *control* should be defined. Does *control* include corporal punishment? Does it include selecting a husband or wife for the child? It is limited to physical behavior or does it include verbal behavior?

Using the same word in two different meanings is called **equivocation.** An absurd example will illustrate the point: "Chicken makes good soup, and John is chicken. Therefore, John must make good soup." Obviously, the words *chicken* and *make* are being used in two different meanings. Advertisements frequently employ equivocation to mislead the reader. If a pair of shoes is advertised as being made of *genuine vinyl*, the word *genuine* is equivocal because, in one sense, it means actual or real—and the advertiser could claim that "real vinyl" is all that is meant. On the other hand, *genuine* implies to many people "high quality." High-quality shoes are usually made of leather, so, by using the word *genuine*, the advertiser is trying to convey the impression that the shoes are made of high-quality material, that is, leather.

Most cases of equivocation are not so obvious; abstract words in particular tend to have several closely related meanings, and it is not always easy to see when the same word is being used in more than one meaning. For example, in the statement "She must not know French because she doesn't know the word *bêche-de-mer*," the word *know* is used equivocally. In the first phrase "know French" means "to have a practical understanding of"; in the phrase "know the word *bêche-de-mer*," it means "to be sure of the meaning of." One can of course have a practical understanding of a language without being familiar with every word in it.

51c ▪ Limiting the Argument

When an argument is somewhat shaky, a writer may try to divert attention from the argument itself by launching into a discussion of a side issue. He or she may **evade the issue**—ignore the real argument and attack something irrelevant to the main issue. One way in which writers make this error is by setting up a **straw man**. Here, you pretend that your opponent means something that he or she does not, or you take the weakest portion of your opponent's argument and attack that, evading the main point. For example, your opponent might argue that manufacturers should put lead in exterior house paints because lead makes the paint last much longer. You respond by saying that many small children have been poisoned by lead. But your opponent has not suggested that lead be used in interior house paints or on children's toys. You have set up a straw man.

Whereas setting up a straw man evades the issue by pretending your opponent's argument is something other than it is, **setting up a red herring** deliberately changes the subject of the argument by concentrating on an irrelevant issue: "You say it's too expensive, but just look at how well it fits." If, in response to the argument that Mussolini's government was very oppressive, you write, "Mussolini's government may have been a bit oppressive, but he finally got the Italian society organized and he made the trains run on time," you have introduced a red herring—the argument concerns oppression, not efficiency.

Another common way of evading the issue is by an **ad hominem** (Latin for "to the man") argument. Here, instead of attacking issues, you attack personalities. "How can you elect a person premier who couldn't even keep a clothing store from going bankrupt?" Or "I don't see how you can call anyone who's had six husbands a great actress." Of course, sometimes a person's character may be relevant to an argument; you

rh
51c

might quite reasonably hesitate to hire a person as cashier of a bank who had had four convictions for embezzlement. But the character flaw should be relevant to the issue under consideration.

Somewhat similar to the argument *ad hominem* is the **genetic fallacy,** which evaluates persons or things in terms of their origins: "How can anyone born and bred in Ungava understand the problems of the city?" Or "The money to set up that foundation was made through corrupt business practices, so you shouldn't accept a grant from it." Again, origins are not necessarily irrelevant, but they are not necessarily relevant either.

The **ad populum** (Latin for "to the people") argument evades the issue by playing on people's prejudices and emotions. Terms with strong connotations such as *radical, reactionary, democracy, traditional,* and *family* are used to make the audience respond emotionally rather than intellectually. An *ad populum* argument for film censorship might take a form such as "Do you decent, law-abiding citizens want to see inno-cent and helpless children exposed to this filthy vice and perversion?"

A variant of the *ad populum* argument is the **bandwagon** approach, which appeals to people's desire to be accepted as members of the group and their fear of being different or their mistrust of people who are differ-ent. The bandwagon approach is common in advertising: "Are you the only person on your block who still uses a hand mower?" But we can find the bandwagon approach even in serious writing: "Dr. Miller concen-trates primarily on classifying and describing the languages of Southeast Asia, despite the fact that most scholarly interest today focuses on the-ory and not on description."

The *tu quoque* error is still another way in which issues are evaded. **Tu quoque** (Latin for "you too") accuses your opponent of doing or being whatever he or she criticizes others of doing or being. We are all familiar with the less subtle forms of *tu quoque* as used by young children: "You can't tie your own shoes!" "Neither can you. So there!" But the adult who responds to a statement that he or she should get more exercise with the retort, "I don't see you out jogging at 06:00." is also using a *tu quoque* argument. If you respond to the argument that young people do not take their responsibilities as voters seriously enough by writing "Older people often fail to acquaint themselves with the candidates' rec-ords, and many do not even bother going to the polls," you are using *tu quoque* to evade the issue.

The best way to avoid the error of evading the issue is to define the question at hand clearly and carefully. Then ask yourself at each step in your argument if you are really addressing the issue or if you have al-lowed yourself to be sidetracked.

rh

51c

Exercises: Defining Terms and Limiting the Argument

Identify the logical fallacies in the following sentences by writing beside each sentence the name of the fallacy from the list below.

| Equivocation | Bandwagon | Genetic fallacy | *Ad populum* |
| Red herring | False dilemma | *Ad hominem* | *Tu quoque* |

1. How on earth can you bring yourself to vote for Jacobs? He divorced his wife of twenty-five years to marry a woman he had all but stolen from his best friend.
2. The prisoners who led the riot have received much tougher treatment. Just look at the way they treated the hostages!
3. Buy E-Z Mend Shoe Glue. More shoemakers use E-Z Mend than all other shoe glues put together.
4. I don't think you should hire Sam for that job. You know his father is a terrible alcoholic.
5. If you don't support me all the way, then I'll know you're my enemy.
6. Edward broke three ribs and an arm when he fell off the face of Stone Mountain. He's always trying to defy the law of gravity and now he's playing the penalty for being a law-breaker.

51d ▪ Presenting Adequate Evidence

In the long run, adequate evidence is the only way of proving an argument. Adequate evidence is reliable, sufficient, and verifiable. Evidence is reliable if it comes from trustworthy and informed sources. Evidence is sufficient if there is enough of it to represent all the points at issue. Evidence is verifiable if it is based on fact and not merely opinion. Facts can always, at least in theory, be tested; opinion cannot. For example, the argument that Unidentified Flying Objects from outer space have visited the earth cannot be proved—or disproved—because the evidence is inadequate. Since the trustworthiness (although not necessarily the honesty or good intentions) of the people who claim to have sighted UFOs is open to question, the evidence is not reliable. Since "sightings" are few, unpredictable, and often explainable as being due to other causes, the evidence is not sufficient. And since there are no UFOs to examine, the evidence is not verifiable.

Everyone relies heavily on informed opinion in making judgements. Many beliefs about the world are based, and properly so, on the opinions of others. Such **appeal to authority** (or **argumentum ad verecundiam**) can be a legitimate form of evidence. Faulty reasoning occurs when the authority cited is not really an authority on the subject. Although someone may be a famous athlete or TV star, he or she is not necessarily an expert on orange juice or political candidates. Further, yesterday's authorities are not necessarily today's authorities: Edward Gibbon was a great historian in his day, but many of his interpretations of history are unacceptable today.

Use authority to support an argument, but be sure that the authority really is reliable and that the appeal is based on the specialized knowledge of that authority and not on emotion—a cherubic child is very appealing but is no expert on the nutritional value of breakfast cereal. Finally, beware of using the authority cited as your sole evidence; authority should be one support of an argument, not the only support.

rh
51d

Improper evaluation of statistics is still another source of faulty arguments. For example, suppose a business firm's gross income was $1 million last year and is $2 million this year. Before jumping to the conclusion that the firm's profits increased by 100 per cent, you should take into account expenses such as labor and production costs, capital investment, and the effect of inflation during the year. Statistics is a highly sophisticated and technical subject whose methodology is not understood by the untrained reader. Be very cautious in citing statistics and particularly in drawing conclusions from unanalysed statistical data.

Biased evidence is another form of unreliable evidence. If you argued that the Canadian people are in favor of cutting timber in provincial parks on the basis of a poll taken among lumberjacks, your evidence would be biased.

One common way of deliberately biasing evidence is to take a statement out of context. Advertising blurbs for books and movies are notorious offenders here. Consider the following possible advertisement for a book:

> action . . . mystery . . . bright and bantering dialogue

The complete statement from which this excerpt was taken gives a very different picture.

> The action moves at a shuffle, the mystery is anything but mystifying, and the usually bright and bantering dialogue is exhausting.
>
> Review of Dick Francis, *In the Frame*, in *The New Yorker*

Such quotation out of context is deliberate and inexcusable. However, people sometimes unintentionally use biased evidence because they do not thoroughly understand the source of their information or the way in which it was collected. Insofar as possible, use information from sources that are generally considered highly respectable and disinterested.

Insufficient evidence weakens an argument. For example, we often hear or read such statements as "This book isn't any good—my brother read it and he didn't like it." Is your brother representative of all possible readers? Is whether a reader enjoys a book the only criterion of its value? To take a more obvious example, the conclusion that February is warmer than May because the temperature on February 1 was 15°C and the temperature on May 1 was 13°C is clearly based on insufficient evidence.

Inadequate evidence leads to **hasty generalization,** or the assumption that what is true in some situations is true in all similar situations. For example, the statement that health care in America is the most advanced in the world fails to take into account the fact that, in many parts of the United States, health care is very poor indeed. Or the hasty generalization that women are not as good scholars as men because so few women have won Rhodes Scholarships ignores the fact that, until recently, women were not even allowed to apply for Rhodes Scholarships. In other words, this generalization wrongly assumes that men and

rh
51d

women have always had equal opportunity to prove themselves as scholars.

To avoid errors in reasoning caused by hasty generalization, try to consider all possible aspects of the question. Ask yourself if you have ignored or forgotten conditions that may influence the situation.

The error of **post hoc, ergo propter hoc** (Latin for "after this, therefore, because of this") results from treating something as evidence that is not evidence at all. It ascribes a cause-and-effect relationship to two events when no such relationship exists, when their occurrence one after the other is simply a coincidence. A clearly absurd example of *post hoc* reasoning would be "Every year the trees lose their leaves before winter comes. Therefore, falling leaves cause winter."

A more typical example of *post hoc* reasoning was the belief, held for centuries, that night air is poisonous. People had observed that they developed fevers after they had been exposed to night air and concluded that the night air caused the fever. Not until the nineteenth century was it conclusively established that mosquitoes (which are especially prevalent at night) carried the organisms that produced the fevers. Canadian politicians would be guilty of the *post hoc* fallacy if they claimed that a Liberal prime minister would lead Canada into war because a Liberal prime minister was in office when Canada entered the Second World War.

Effects do, of course, have causes, but beware of assuming that events are causally related just because they are related in time.

Analogy involves a comparison of two different things that have some characteristics in common. Analogy can be useful in illustrating and clarifying unfamiliar objects or concepts, and a good analogy can be very persuasive. However, in analogies, there should be basic similarities between the things being compared. Important details should be shared, and the details that are not shared should be irrelevant to the point under discussion and should be included in the discussion. When a writer calls streets and roads *arteries*, he or she is making an analogy between a highway system and the circulatory system of a living organism. *Artery* is a good analogy to explain a highway *system* because both arteries and highways connect various points of a system and both are routes for carrying things from one point to another. However, in a discussion of the *costs of building and repairing* a highway, *artery* is not a good analogy because the creation and repair of organic circulatory systems in no way resembles the creation and repair of highways.

Analogies are in constant use in daily life, and this use is often justified. But even excellent analogies may break down. For example, by analogy with words like *schedule, scheme, scholar,* and *school,* one may assume that other words beginning with *sch-* are pronounced as if they were spelled with *sk-*. The analogy works with the word *scherzo,* but fails with the word *schist*. Analogies are dangerous because "like" does not mean "the same," and, therefore, we can never actually prove anything by analogy. Argument by analogy is really no argument at all, though analogy can help clarify what the argument is.

rh
51d

A **faulty analogy** assumes that, because two things are similar in one or two ways, they are also similar in other important ways. Faulty, or at least questionable, analogies are particularly common in arguments about history, when it is often assumed that because something happened in the past, it will happen in the future. For example, it is sometimes said that the United States is doomed to fall as the Roman Empire fell because, like the Roman Empire, the United States devotes a high percentage of its national income to military spending and public welfare. Among many other things, this analogy fails to take into account the fact that the United States has an extensive commercial and industrial base, whereas the Roman Empire had relatively little commerce or industry and relied heavily on booty or tribute from conquered nations for its national income.

Exercises: Presenting Adequate Evidence

Identify the logical fallacies in the following sentences by writing beside each sentence the name of the fallacy from the list below.

Appeal to unqualified authority   *Post hoc, ergo propter hoc*
Hasty generalization   Faulty analogy

1. It is ridiculous to say that private planes should be restricted or even banned because of the potential hazard to commercial jets. We don't make private motorists get off the roads just because they might get involved in an accident with a commercial bus, do we?

2. My priest said Sunday that a restructuring of the tax system in this country is imperative if its citizens are to prosper. Since Father Donahue is so well-educated, he must know what he's talking about.

3. We had an especially cold January and February this year, and the cold must have really hurt local business. All of the merchants complained that their sales for the two-month period were lower than they were at the same time last year.

4. Ninety-five per cent of all fatal accidents occur within 40 km of the victims' homes. Most fast-speed driving is done on long trips, farther from home. Fast driving must be safer than slow driving.

**rh
51e**

51e ▪ Reasoning Clearly and Logically

No matter how good your intentions, you will not be persuasive if the reader cannot follow the steps in your reasoning or if the reasoning is faulty. This is not to say that every single step in an argument must always be explicitly stated. For example, the sentence "If we don't get rain, the crops will die" does not state that crops need rain to survive, but you can safely assume that everyone accepts this fact and that it is unnecessary to state it explicitly. On the other hand, the sentence "The government of Canada should subsidize farm prices because the world's population is still increasing" has so many unstated assumptions that the reader may have difficulty in following the logic:

1. Farmers produce food.
2. People need food to live.
3. As the world's population increases, more people will need food.
4. It is desirable to produce enough food to feed all people.
5. Subsidies of farm prices will make farmers produce more food.
6. If Canada produces more food, there will be more food for all the world.

Of these unstated assumptions, numbers 1, 2, and 3 are common knowledge and need not be stated. However, assumptions 4, 5, and 6 are less obvious. Some people might actually argue that it is not especially desirable to produce enough food to feed all people. Not everyone will agree that subsidies of farm prices will automatically make farmers produce more food. And increased production of food in Canada will not lead to more food for all the world if distribution of this food is not adequate. The original statement can be expanded to include all the essential assumptions.

> The world's population is still increasing, and this population must be fed. Canada is capable of producing more food than it presently does and of distributing this additional food to the rest of the world. However, farmers need to be encouraged in some way to produce more food. One way of doing this is by having the Canadian government subsidize farm prices.

Although it is possible that not all readers will agree with all the assumptions, at least they know what the assumptions are and can see how you arrived at your final statement.

Conditional, qualifying, and concluding words are very important to a clear and logical argument. Overuse of *if, when,* and *unless* can lead to the fallacy of the false dilemma (see 51a). Qualifying words like *every, all, no, always, never,* and *probably* should be used with caution to avoid exaggerated claims. For example, the statement "Many politicians are corrupt" can be substantiated with evidence, but the statement "All politicians are corrupt" cannot be proved. Use concluding words like *thus, therefore, so, consequently,* and *as a result* only when the following statement is actually "a result" of what has previously been said.

Be sure the conclusions you state are justified by the evidence you have presented. When the evidence does not justify the conclusion, the argument is called a **non sequitur** (Latin for "it does not follow"). One common form of *non sequitur* argument is **guilt by association.** Suppose you argue that all Mafia members live in the East End of town, that John lives in the East End, and that John must, therefore, be a Mafia member.

rh
51e

Your conclusion does not follow from your premises because you have not considered the possibility that many people who live in the East End are not Mafia members. You have made John "guilty" of being a Mafia member by assuming that, just because he is like Mafia members in one way, he must be like them in other ways. The error of such conclusions can be more vividly illustrated by a ridiculous example: Someone could argue that all Mafia members like money, that John likes money, and that therefore John is a Mafia member. Clearly, this *non sequitur* argument is unacceptable.

The error of **begging the question** (or **circular argument**) lies in assuming that a point which is under dispute has already been proved. The statement "This essential legislation should be passed" begs the question because the word *essential* in this context means the same thing as *should be passed*. Similarly, "This harmless drug couldn't hurt anyone" begs the question because you have already assumed that it couldn't hurt anyone when you call it "harmless."

Sometimes it is hard to detect question-begging because it is hidden by the language of the argument itself. One of the most dangerous words is "because." Suppose the argument is that the federal government, not the provinces, should pay all the costs of education in English or French as a second language. A question-begging form of this argument might be: "The provincial governments should turn language education over to the federal government because the federal government should have responsibility for language education." Here the word *because* suggests that a reason will be given for turning this education over to Ottawa. But no reason follows. Instead, the original argument is just restated in slightly different words. Evidence could be produced for this argument. For example, one could use statistics to show that the provinces simply do not provide sufficient funds for this education or that the federal government, through its immigration policies, determines language-education needs. However, "they should do it because they should do it" provides no evidence at all. It simply begs the question.

Begging the question frequently takes the form of a **compound question,** or **double question,** as it is sometimes called. A compound question is one that really has two parts; it begs the question by assuming the answer to one of them. The classic example of the compound question is "When did you stop beating your wife?" Here the questioner assumes that the man being questioned has already beaten his wife at least once. The victim of this compound question cannot reply without agreeing to this assumption.

Advertisements and sales pitches frequently use or imply the compound question: "Will you have the pecan pie or the cheesecake for dessert?" (Perhaps you do not want any dessert at all.) Compound questions of the sort "Why did the mayor lie to us?" contain unstated assumptions (the unstated assumption here is "The mayor lied to us").

Although unstated assumptions are not necessarily wrong, the writer and the reader should be alert to their presence. For example, the statement "Don't bother reading that; it won't be on the exam" contains two questionable unstated assumptions: (1) "I know what will be on the exam" and (2) "Anything that won't be on the exam is not worth reading."

51f ▪ Anticipating Contrary Arguments

Any real argument involves opposing points of view and contrary evidence. To make a good argument, recognize these contrary points, and refute them as well as possible within the bounds of the evidence available to you. The most effective arguments usually follow the dictum of the good bridge player: "Take your losers first." In other words, anticipate and respond to your opponent's probable arguments early in the presentation of your own argument. If you cannot refute a point, concede it rather than ignore it.

For example, suppose you are arguing that deer hunting should be banned as a cruel and unnecessary sport. You know that your opponents may claim that (1) such hunting channels hostile instincts and that it is better for people to kill wild animals than to kill each other, (2) people have always killed wild animals for food, (3) some native people depend on deer hunting for part of their regular diet, (4) without controlled hunting, the population of deer would become too large for their habitats to support them, and (5) the fees for hunting licences help support the protection of all wildlife. You might answer these counterarguments as follows:

> Some may argue that deer hunting channels hostile instincts and that it is better that people kill wild animals than that they kill each other. However, there is no evidence that deer hunters are potential murderers or that murder rates are higher in areas where hunting is prohibited. Nor is the argument that men have always killed wild animals acceptable. Until the last century or so, men killed wild animals for food, for their own survival. Today we have ample food for everyone, and no one needs venison in order to survive. Indeed, many hunters do not even eat the deer they kill. Some native people regard the hunt as part of their tradition, and their regular diet does include a considerable amount of venison, but they now have other sources of food as well as other ways of maintaining their heritage.
>
> The contention that, without controlled hunting, the population of deer would become too large is also weak. We have much evidence that natural forces do an adequate job of controlling most wildlife populations without the intervention of man. Although the fees from hunting licences do help support the protection of all wildlife, this source of income is minuscule compared to the total costs of conservation and preservation, and other sources of income could easily be found.

rh
51f

You have openly and fairly recognized that there are contrary arguments to your point of view, but you have carefully and reasonably responded to each opposing point, refuting some of them and partially conceding others. You can now proceed with your own arguments in favor of banning deer hunting. By answering the opposition at the outset, you reserve the rest of your presentation for your own arguments and evidence, leaving the reader with an impression of the strength of your point of view. Further, when you acknowledge opposing points of view without being abusive to your opponents, your readers are more likely to be persuaded to accept your point of view because you appear to be fair and reasonable.

Exercises: Review of Making a Good Argument

Part A: Write one example for each of the following fallacies.

1. Faulty analogy
2. Hasty generalization
3. Evading the issue (use any of the kinds discussed in this section)
4. Guilt by association
5. False dilemma
6. Begging the question

Part B: Identify the fallacious arguments in the following passages—both are letters to the editor sent to a daily newspaper. Both passages contain several fallacies.

1. I am the father of three children. I try to do what I say I will do. This causes me to think about Japan. We signed a trade agreement with them over ten years ago. If our government does not keep to this agreement, what will our word mean to our allies? Is expediency morally right? How will the automobile industry be affected? How will other industries fare ten years from now? I am concerned about our good name! And I am concerned about our economy—in the long run!

2. Mrs. Simpson's interests concern us women. She is a member of many influential women's groups, and she supported the funding of a local shelter for battered wives and children.

   I am sure that if last week all the women in our riding had gone out to vote while their husbands were at work, Mrs. Simpson could have been elected. She has worked hard for us, and I believe that women have really let her down.

   When a woman as fine, as intelligent, and as well educated as Mrs. Simpson puts forth an effort, using her time and money to improve the lives and rights of women, the least we can do is to support her. Let's face it—women's salaries still do not equal those of men doing the same jobs!

52 Special Types of Writing

The principles of good writing apply to all kinds of writing, not just to essays assigned in English classes. Most of the rules and suggestions presented elsewhere in this handbook also apply to letter-writing, technical reports, essay examinations, and even to outlines. These other types of writing, however, have their own characteristics and their own special conventions.

52a • Outlines

Everyone uses outlines of one kind of another, even if they're not always thought of as outlines. The notes in a pocket calendar are an outline —however incomplete—of a day's activities. The list taken to the supermarket or stationery store is an outline of intended purchases. Before starting a letter to a friend, the writer has at least a mental outline of what he or she intends to say. All of these are informal outlines, used to help organize thoughts and activities.

For many kinds of writing, an informal outline, either mental or written in the form of sketchy notes, is adequate. However, for long papers or for papers with complex arguments or ideas, a more formal outline is usually necessary because it is difficult to keep a mental picture of all the important points and their relationships. A written outline helps provide coherence to the final paper and reveals imbalances, logical gaps, and inadequate development of the thesis before writing begins. A well-developed outline also helps a writer estimate the length of the final paper and provides a guide as he or she begins to write. Finally, an outline actually stimulates thought and ideas; seeing ideas written down makes the writer think of other ideas and of interrelationships among ideas.

In addition to their usefulness in writing papers, outlines are helpful in taking notes from material that has already been written. An outline reveals the structure of the author's argument more clearly and more quickly than several rereadings can. An outline of an unsatisfactory paper of your own can show what went wrong with it. An informal outline made before you answer an essay question on an examination helps you cover all important points in a logical order. Some classroom lectures lend themselves to note-taking in at least rough outline form. For other lectures, putting the notes into outline form after the class is over provides a more organized, coherent picture of what the instructor considers important.

A poor outline, however, is a hindrance, not a help, to the writing process. In particular, your outline should be logical, and its logic should reflect the type of development and sequence of development that you intend to follow in the paper. For example, if you were writing an argument-and-persuasion paper, the major headings of your outline should be the major points and conclusions of your argument, and the subheadings should be details that support your argument. On the other hand, if you were writing a paper on how to recondition an old bicycle, your major headings would probably be the most important systems of the bicycle (brakes, gear system, frame, and wheels), and your subheadings would be the component parts of each major system (cables, levers, and callipers as components of the brake system).

In preparing an outline for a paper that is yet to be written, don't try to make a formal outline the first time around. Begin by jotting down all the ideas you think might be included in the paper. Don't worry about their order at this stage; just write points down as they occur to you. When you have run out of ideas, look over your list and label with the same letter all items that seem to belong together.

Then examine all the items that are labelled with the same letter to get a rough idea of the level of importance of each item. For example, you might be outlining a paper on the pros and cons of buying your own house and put the letter *A* beside all the items dealing with financial matters, including "interest on the mortgage," "financial disadvantages," "taxes," "fee for title search," "maintenance," and "down payment." Clearly, the item "financial disadvantages" is at a higher or more general level than any of the others. Further, some of the expenses listed are paid only once, whereas others are paid over and over again. In the final outline, the above examples might appear in the following form.

A. Financial considerations
  1. Initial expenses
    a. Down payment
    b. Fee for title search
  2. Continuing expenses
    a. Interest on the mortgage
    b. Maintenance
    c. Taxes

As you put your rough notes into final form, you will probably discard some of your original items because they are not directly related to your topic. You will add new items that come to mind as you organize. Finally, you will probably continue to revise the outline as you write. Do not assume that once a formal outline has been prepared it must be followed slavishly and cannot be altered. If it doesn't work, revise it. If you are required to submit an outline along with a completed theme, it should be an outline of the actual paper submitted, not an earlier outline of what you had once thought the paper might be.

Informal Outlines   An informal outline consists of rough notes jotted down in no particular order but labelled either mentally or physically with letters (or some other such device) as a guide to the order of the final paper. Such an outline is suitable for a short paper or for the answer to an essay question on an examination.

Although informal outlines are personal and only for the use of the

rh
52a

writer, they are the basis of formal outlines. Because informal outlines are used more frequently than formal outlines, familiarity with their preparation is important. (For a discussion of the process of making an informal outline and an example of a rough outline, see 50f.)

Formal Outlines Formal outlines are suitable for long papers or for taking careful notes on written material. They are more carefully constructed than informal outlines and, unlike informal outlines, should be comprehensible to readers other than the author. Types of formal outlines include the paragraph outline, the topic outline, and the sentence outline.

1. **Paragraph Outlines.** Paragraph outlines summarize each paragraph with a single complete sentence. They are normally used for taking notes on written material. One disadvantage of a paragraph outline in taking notes is that not every paragraph is necessarily important enough to need a summary sentence. Further, a paragraph outline only lists topics in the order they have been discussed; it does not reveal their relative importance. A paragraph outline of the first four paragraphs of this section on outlines might take this form:

I. Everyone uses outlines of some kind.
II. Long papers require formal outlines.
III. Outlines are also helpful in taking notes and writing essay examinations.
IV. Outlines should reflect the logic of the material being outlined.

Paragraph outlines may also be used in preparing very short papers for which you know beforehand the number of paragraphs. Here, each entry is in effect a topic sentence for the paragraph it represents. For longer papers, you probably cannot—and should not try to—predict the exact number of paragraphs, and a topic or sentence outline is more suitable.

Exercise: Paragraph Outlines

rh
52a

Write a paragraph outline for two of the following subjects, giving the thesis sentences for a five-paragraph paper on each.

1. How to find a job.

2. Gifted elementary-school students should (should not) be sent to special public schools for bright children.

3. A person definitely should (should not) bother to vote.

4. The government should (should not) have some control over religious cults.

2. **Topic Outlines.** The most common type of formal outline is the topic outline. Points are listed in the form of words or phrases, and the outline is preceded by a thesis sentence that serves as a summary of the entire outline. The greatest advantage of the topic outline is that it reveals not only the subjects to be covered but also the logic (or illogic) of the organization of the entire paper.

Points are labelled with numbers and letters that indicate their order and relative importance. From most to least important, the order is large roman numerals, capital letters, arabic numerals, small letters, and, if necessary, arabic numerals in parentheses. Parallel headings are indented the same distance from the left margin. A period follows each number or letter, but there are no periods at the end of the entries themselves. The first word of every entry is capitalized.

Thesis sentence: The potential homeowner should be aware of both the disadvantages and advantages of owning a house.

I. Disadvantages
  A. Financial considerations
    1. Initial expenses
      a. Down payment
      b. Fee for title search
    2. Continuing expenses
      a. Interest on the mortgage
      b. Maintenance
        (1) Repairs
        (2) Improvements
      c. Taxes
      d. Capital all tied up in house
  B. Personal considerations
    1. Limited mobility of homeowner
    2. Responsibility of homeowner for upkeep
II. Advantages
  A. Financial considerations
    1. Profitable long-term investment, potentially tax-free on sale
    2. Long-term savings over renting
    3. Improved credit rating
  B. Personal considerations
    1. Satisfaction of owning property
    2. Freedom to remodel and redecorate
    3. No problem of living in house with strangers

rh
52a

To assure a logical, coherent structure for an outline—and for the paper based on the outline—you should observe the following conventions:

a. Put items of equal importance in parallel form. In the example above, both "Disadvantages" and "Advantages" are labelled with large Roman numerals, and the different types of continuing expenses are labelled with small letters. Grammatical structures within a given level should also be parallel. For example, prepositional phrases should not be mixed with noun phrases, nor should declarative statements be mixed with imperative statements. (Normally, complete sentences are not used at all in topic outlines.)

INCORRECT OUTLINE FORM

2. Continuing expenses
   a. Pay interest on the mortgage
   b. Maintenance
   c. Taxes
   d. Your capital is all tied up in your house

b. Make every subdivision a logical part of the topic under which it appears. In our example, "Down payment" and "Fee for title search" are part of the general category "Initial expenses."

c. Avoid single subdivisions under a heading. If you have only one point to make under a heading, incorporate it in the heading itself. For example, in the outline above, item IIA1, "Profitable long-term investment . . ." is a single entry, not an entry with a subdivision below it.

INCORRECT OUTLINE FORM

1. Profitable long-term investment
   a. No income tax on sale of principal residence
2. Long-term savings over renting

d. Insofar as possible, let each item in a topic outline deal with one concept and one concept only. Hence, it would have been improper to make "Maintenance and taxes" one entry.

e. Make each item as specific as possible. Avoid vague, overly general headings and subheadings such as "Conclusions," "Reasons," "Objections," and the like.

f. Avoid long series of parallel items under a single subdivision. Usually, lengthy subdivisions need further breaking down. For example, under II, "Advantages," the six points labelled with arabic numbers are properly subdivided into financial and personal considerations rather than strung together as six consecutive items.

g. Do not overlap headings and subheadings. For example, if "Disadvantages" had had two subpoints, "Expenses" and "Problems," the second subpoint, "Problems," would have overlapped with both "Disadvantages" and "Expenses."

h. Do not include in the outline introductory material that serves merely to lead into the topic. For example, if you plan to begin your paper with a relevant anecdote about life in the suburbs, you need not make a special heading for it. On the other hand, if the beginning material is an integral part of the paper, you should include it. If you plan to define an important term or state the problem in your first paragraph, include this term or statement in the outline. For example, an expository paper on various kinds of motorcycle racing might begin with an explanation of

rh
52a

how racing motorcycles are classified. The major point of the outline might take the following form.

Motorcycle Racing: Not for the Timid

Introduction: Motorcycles classed by engine size: 100cc, 125cc, 175cc, 250cc, open class

   I. Motocross
  II. Desert racing
 III. Cow-trailing
 IV. Café racing
  V. Speedway racing

Exercises: Topic Outlines

Rewrite the following topic outline, arranging the elements in a logical order, making the elements grammatically parallel, and punctuating, capitalizing, and spacing correctly. Add, delete, or combine elements as is necessary.

Thesis: Advertising on television and in magazines is a psychological game.

  I. Use of color.
    A. Suggests mood.
      1. conditioned responses awakened
 II. Catching the eye
    A. Combination of colors attracts attention.
    B. Importance of intensity of color
III. Language of ad
    A. Message's length
      1. Jingles can be effective.
      2. detailed, factual copy
IV. Targeting the language.
      1. How formal is the language?
        a. class appeal
        b. appeal to age.
        c. sex appeal.
    A. Using people in ads.
        a. Why celebrities are used.
      1. To transfer the appeal of celebrity to product.
      2. For transferring the glamor of the celebrity to the reader or viewer.
    B. The "beautiful" people
        a. appeal to vanity of reader or viewer
        b. sex appeal
        c. appeal to health

   C. Average people.
      1. Easy identification with the viewer or reader.
      2. Lends a sense of normalcy to product.
V. How the product is displayed
   A. setting
      1. Fantasy setting
      2. Setting is true to life.
   B. How prominently the product is displayed in the ad makes a psychological difference.
      a. Subtle treatment
      b. product is the central visual effect.

---

3. Sentence Outlines. The sentence outline is a variant of the topic outline. It has the same format and the same logic but uses complete sentences instead of single words or phrases. Making a sentence outline has the advantage of forcing writers to consider the specific things they want to say and not just the general topic they are going to discuss. Further, a sentence outline is easier for other readers to follow. One disadvantage of the sentence outline is that the writer may get carried away and make the outline almost as long as the paper itself, thus defeating the purpose of the outline.

The first part of the topic outline in the previous section is rewritten below as a sentence outline.

I. There are numerous disadvantages to owning one's own house.
   A. Home ownership is very expensive today.
      1. The initial expenses of buying a house are high.
         a. The down payment may be more than one-third of the cost of the house.
         b. The title-search can cost several hundred dollars.
      2. The continuing expenses of home ownership are also high.
         a. Today's interest rates are very high, so monthly mortgage payments are high and may go even higher when the mortgage is renegotiated.
         b. Maintenance costs, such as exterior painting, gutters, landscaping, roof repairs, plumbing, and the like, can cost several thousand dollars a year.
         c. Real-estate taxes will vary according to the neighborhood, the value of the house, and the city in which the house is located.
         d. The homeowner has thousands of dollars tied up in the property, money that is not available to be used in other ways.

rh
52a

When you have completed an outline of any type, check it carefully to be sure you have not omitted anything important. Before finishing your rough draft of a paper, check your outline to be sure you have included everything.

Exercises: Sentence Outlines

Make the outline in the exercise on topic outlines (pages 370–371) into a logical sentence outline that is correcly capitalized, spaced, and punctuated.

52b ▪ Letters

Even if you never write an essay after leaving university or college, you will write many letters in your lifetime. Their recipients will not put grades on them, but they will nonetheless judge you on the basis of your letters. Obviously, it is to your advantage to be able to write a good, clear letter that observes the conventions of letter writing.

Business Letters   A century ago, such phrases as "Yours of the 21st received" and "I remain, your faithful servant" were common in business letters. Fortunately, such artificial language is totally out of place today. The style of a business letter should be objective, direct, courteous, and relatively impersonal. The langauge should not be stilted or flowery. Include essential information such as order numbers, dates, and the like, but avoid wordiness and irrelevant information.

Type business letters on white, unruled paper 21.6 cm by 27.9 cm (8½ by 11 inches). Use only one side of the paper. The entire letter is single-spaced, with double-spacing only between sections and paragraphs. (The body of a very short letter of only two or three lines may be double-spaced.) If a second page is necessary, it should contain at least three or four lines of the text of the letter.

A business letter has six parts, as illustrated by the sample letter (page 373). These parts are (1) heading, (2) inside address, (3) salutation, (4) body, (5) complimentary close, and (6) signature.

1. **Heading.** Type the return address in the upper left or right corner of the page with the date below it. If you use a printed letterhead containing the return address, give only the date here. Such abbreviations as *St.* and *Ave.* are usually acceptable, but you will never be wrong if you spell these words out in an English address. The best place for the postal code is on a separate line; if it is not separate, no comma separates it from the name of the province, although there is at least one (often two) spaces between the two. There is no punctuation at the ends of the lines.

2. **Inside Address.** Type the inside address flush left and several spaces below the heading. You can adjust the space between the inside address and the heading in order to balance the letter on the page. The name and title of your addressee (if you have this information) comes first, followed by the name and address of the company or other organization. There is no punctuation at the ends of the lines.

```
          | 32 Luzon Street
HEADING   | Ottawa, Ontario
          | K1A OS5
          | October 17, 1985


          | Modern Age Book Club   INSIDE
          | 14 Abernathy Road      ADDRESS
          | Markham, Ontario
          | L3R 1B4


          | Ladies and Gentlemen: SALUTATION

          | As my October selection from your club, I ordered a copy
          | of Mavis Gallant's novel A Fairly Good Time.  When I received
          | my order three days ago, I discovered that you had sent
BODY      | three copies of this book and had billed me for all three.
          | I want only one copy and therefore wish to return the two
          | extra copies.

          | Please tell me the proper procedure for returning the books
          | to you.  Because the shipping error was not my fault, I
          | feel that I should receive credit not only for the extra
          | books but also for the postage costs of returning them.

          | Yours truly, COMPLIMENTARY CLOSE

          | Warren Jovin   SIGNATURE

          | Warren Jovin
          | Membership No. HS-515-2399
```

3. **Salutation.** Type the salutation flush left, two spaces below the inside address, and follow it with a colon. The salutation includes such titles as *Mr., Mrs., Ms., Miss,* and *Dr.* If you are on a first-name basis with the addressee, you may use his or her first name instead of last name (*Dear Martha*) and a comma instead of a colon at the end. When you know the title but not the name of the recipient, you can use just the title (*Dear Personnel Manager, Dear Admissions Officer*). If you know neither the name nor the title of the recipient, you can use *Dear Sir or Madam* for a letter addressed to an individual. Use *Gentlemen and Ladies* for a letter addressed to a company or other institution. Because business letters receive prompter attention if they are addressed to a specific person, always try to get the complete name of the person who will handle your letter.

4. **Body.** Single-space the body of the letter with double spaces between paragraphs. You may type the entire body flush left, or you may indent five spaces at the beginning of every paragraph. If the letter is more than one page long, put the addressee's name, the date, and the page number at the top of all pages after the first one. This information may all be on one line, separated by commas, or it may be typed flush left in three lines at the top left corner.

rh
52b

5. **Complimentary Close.** Type the complimentary close either flush left or in the centre of the page, and follow it with a comma. The conventional forms for a complimentary close are, in order of descending formality, *Very truly yours (Yours truly, Yours very truly), Sincerely yours (Sincerely, Yours sincerely),* and *Cordially yours (Cordially, Yours cordially).* For high-ranking church, government, or academic officials, the complimentary close *Respectfully yours* is appropriate.

6. **Signature.** Type the name of the sender four spaces below the complimentary close, and sign the letter by hand in the space between the complimentary close and the typed name. No title appears with the handwritten signature, but a title does precede the typed signature (however, the titles *Mr., Mrs.,* and *Ms.* are not used here except in parentheses for clarity). A woman may choose to indicate her marital status or preferred title in parentheses, as in the examples below.

Joyce Storey

Joyce Storey
(Mrs. Allan Storey)

Bridget Thébault

(Ms.) Bridget Thébault

If the letter includes an enclosure, such as a cheque, indicate this by typing *Enc.* flush left and two spaces below the typed signature.

Enc . : cheque

If copies of the letter are to be sent to persons other than the addressee, indicate this by typing *cc.* flush left and two spaces below the typed signature:

cc . : Walter French

If it is impossible to type a business letter, write it out neatly on unruled paper, following the same format as for typewritten letters and keeping the lines as straight as you can. A sheet of heavily ruled notebook paper placed under your stationery makes a convenient guide.

For a one-page letter, either a small—9.2 cm by 16.5 cm ($3^5/8$ by $6^1/2$ inches)—business envelope or a large one—10.5 cm by 24.2 cm ($4^1/8$ by $9^1/2$ inches)—is appropriate. For letters of more than one page or letters with enclosures, use the larger envelope. To fold a letter for the smaller envelope, fold the bottom up to within a centimetre or so from the top, and then fold it in thirds from left to right. For a large envelope, fold the letter in thirds from bottom to top.

The address on the envelope should be the same as the inside address. Addresses are single-spaced, except for two-line addresses, which are double-spaced. Type your return address in the upper left corner of the envelope. Special instructions such as "Attn: Credit Department" or "Personal" are typed in the lower left corner.

Exercises: Business Letters

Choose one of the following problems and write a suitable business letter to the addressee indicated. Type or write it in correct letter form.

1. You ordered three different leather-craft kits, one for making a belt, one for making a purse, and one for making a backgammon case. You sent payment in full with the order. The company has sent you three identical kits for making backgammon cases and has billed you for an additional $28.43. Write to Paul N. Saunders in the Customer Service Department of the N. F. Casbon Company at 1943 Micmac Trail in Dartmouth, Nova Scotia (the postal code is B2X 2H3).

2. You live alone in an apartment. Your water bill, which you have always paid on time, has increased by 50 per cent during the last three months. Your repeated calls to the water company have been ignored. You suspect that there is a leak or that someone else has tapped into your water line and is using the water that you are paying for. Write to Miss Anna M. Prentiss in the Consumer Complaint Department of the Water Accounts Office of the City of Vancouver at 453 West Twelfth Avenue in Vancouver, British Columbia (the postal code is V6R 2M5). Explain your predicament and what you expect to have done about it.

Letters of Application Perhaps the most important business letters you will ever write will be letters of application for jobs. Whether it is an application for a summer job or for a full-time position after you have left school, your letter and the reaction it elicits may determine your future; you obviously want to make the best possible impression.

Even if you are applying for several jobs at the same time, avoid using a form letter. Instead, rewrite and retype the letter for each prospective employer. (Of course, you may adapt the same general letter for each prospect. Access to a word processor is very helpful here.) Avoid gimmicks of any kind: this is not the place to be cute. Personnel managers have to read many letters of application every day, so be considerate of their time and keep your letter as concise as possible.

Begin your letter of application by telling how you heard of the position for which you are applying—through a newspaper advertisement, an agency, or a friend. If you are responding to an advertisement, the recipient will appreciate your mentioning the name of the newspaper and the date of the issue in which you saw the advertisement. Be as specific as possible about the position for which you are applying. If you are responding to no specific source but rather are "just checking," indicate why you are interested in working for that particular company or institution.

State your qualifications clearly, pointing out any special skills you may have gained from education or prior experience. Try to sell yourself without actually bragging. Keep your information positive. Do not talk

rh
52b

```
                                    Lister Hall
                                    University of Alberta
                                    Edmonton, Alberta
                                    T6G 2E9
                                    April 15, 1984


Andrea Osborn, Manager
The Everest Store
19 Summit Street
Banff, Alberta
T0L 2E0


Dear Ms. Osborn:

     One of your former employees, Stefan Moore, told me
that you often hire extra clerks during the summer months.
If you will be needing additional help for the coming summer,
I would like to apply for a job.

     I am at present a third-year student at the University
of Alberta and will be available for work from May 15 to
September 10.  I am an experienced climber and am familiar
with most kinds of climbing equipment.  In addition to
several years' experience climbing and backpacking in the
Rockies, I spent eight weeks during the summer of 1982 climbing
in the Olympic, Sierra, and Cascade Mountains.  During my
final year in high school, I taught mountaineering skills
in a special program and advised the school's purchasing
officer about the type of equipment to buy.  I am an avid
climber and would like very much to have the opportunity
to share my enthusiasm with others.

     I am free to come for an interview on any Thursday
or Saturday, but can arrange to come at some other time
if that is more convenient for you.

                                    Sincerely,

                                    Andrew MacIntyre

                                    Andrew MacIntyre
```

about your lack of experience. Do not say you need the job badly (even if you do). If you already have a job and want to leave it, do not say that you are unhappy in your present job because this may give the impression that you are a chronic complainer. Do not try to flatter prospective employers by stating that you think their firm is wonderful or better than any other company. Save questions about salary and benefits for the interview.

   If supplementary materials such as transcripts, samples of artwork, or letters of recommendation are pertinent to the job, offer to send these materials, but do not include them with the original letter of application. Be sure to ask permission from the people you want to use as references —and ask before you include their names.

If you have a great deal of information to convey in a letter of application, it should be summarized in a separate résumé or data sheet. (See 52c for information on preparing a résumé.) One advantage of a separate résumé is that it can be duplicated and enclosed in all letters of application, saving you the trouble and time of repeating the information in each letter.

You will probably want to end your letter of application with a request for an interview. State clearly any times or dates at which you will not be available for an interview. If at all possible, express a willingness to appear for an interview at any time convenient to the recipient of the letter. Enclosing a stamped, self-addressed envelope is a courtesy that will not pass unnoticed.

Letters of application follow all the conventions of regular business letters, as illustrated in the sample letter of application on page 376. Take particular care in proofreading a letter of application, and retype it rather than send it off with errors or messy corrections.

Exercises: Letters of Application

Write a letter of application for one of the following jobs. Because this letter will not include a résumé, include all the pertinent information in the letter itself.

1. A summer job as a guide at the Fortress of Louisbourg, the National Historic Park at Louisbourg, Nova Scotia. Write to Catherine B. Garneau, director of the park (the postal code is B0A 1M0).
2. A permanent job in the data-processing department of Fairbanks Chemical Corporation at 1661 Portage Avenue, Winnipeg, Manitoba (the postal code is R3G 0R9). Write to Kenneth M. Parson, personnel director.

52c · Résumés

The résumé is a fact sheet that summarizes one's education and experience for prospective employers. No single format is conventionally used for all résumés; the contents, the order of the contents, and the format vary according to the individual and the type of work being sought. The most important criteria are clarity and ease of reading. All résumés should include (1) an opening that gives your name, address, and telephone number, (2) a summary of your work experience, with the most recent experience first, (3) a summary of your education, in reverse chronological order, and (4) a list of at least three references who know you well enough to discuss your qualifications for the job you are interested in. For a university or college student, the references typically include at least one instructor and at least one former employer.

```
Resume of
Francine Milsom

9503 Peace River Road
Fort St. John, British Columbia
V1J 2S3
(604) 536-1678

EDUCATION            B.S.F. (Forestry), University of British Columbia,
                     1985: major in wood science and industry; minor in
                     forest management.  Area of concentration: tree
                     physiology

                     First-year program, College of New Caledonia
                     (Prince George, B.C.), 1980-81

                     Grade 12, Carson Graham Senior Secondary School
                     (North Vancouver, B.C.), 1980

WORK EXPERIENCE

    Summers          Forklift operator, Canadian Cellulose,
    1982 to 1984     Castlegar, B.C. Summers of 1983 and 1984

                     Fire spotter, British Columbia Forest Service
                     (Prince George District).  Summer of 1982

    1981 to 1982     Cashier, Oceanic Cost Plus Limited, Vancouver, B.C.
                     Part-time job, September 1981 to April 1982

AWARDS AND HONORS    WESCAN Tree Disease Control Technical Report Award,
                     1984
                     M.C. Bodden Fellowship, 1983
                     Northern Business and Professional Women's Bursary, 1982

PERSONAL             Birth date and place:  August 6, 1962, Cornerbrook, NFLD.
                     Marital status:  single
                     Languages:  English; conversational and technical French
                     Health:  excellent
                     Date of availability:  immediately

INTERESTS            Sky diving, sport fishing, playing the guitar, and
                     quilting

REFERENCES           Professor Donald Range
                     Faculty of Forestry
                     University of British Columbia
                     Vancouver, B.C., V6T 2W5

                     Mr. A.W. Wong, Director
                     Castlegar Division
                     Canadian Cellulose
                     305 Tamarack Street
                     Castlegar, B.C., V8N 8P2

                     Personal Reference:  Dr. Arlene Ochenko
                                          4620 West Tenth Avenue
                                          Vancouver, B.C., V6R 2J5

                     Academic references available from the Registrar, the
                     University of British Columbia, Vancouver, B.C. V6T 1W5
```

rh
52c

In addition to these four categories, you can add a personal-data section that includes such information as birthdate, health (if good), marital status, dependents, status under which you may work in Canada (citizen, landed immigrant, and so on), fluency in languages other than English, and date of availability for the job. Do *not* include race, religion, or sex: by law, employers are forbidden to use this information as a basis for hiring.

You may also want to include a separate section entitled "Career Objectives." This should be a brief but specific statement of what you eventually hope to do. One example might be "To teach English as a second language to adult immigrants and to prepare materials for TESL use." Or, for someone interested in marketing, the statement might be "To work as a marketing trainee and eventually to become a marketing specialist in children's clothing for a chain of department stores."

If you have received several high honors or awards or have other exceptional achievements, add a separate section listing these. Because some employers like to know about an employee's outside interests, you may want to add a category entitled "Other Interests." If you do, keep it brief and don't make up interests that you don't actually have. Alternatively, you can add information about outside interests to a personal data section.

Exercises: Résumés

Prepare a résumé that you could enclose with a letter of application for one of the following jobs. Use imaginary information if you like, but be sure the résumé is a believable one.

1. A position as an artist in the advertising department of a department store
2. A position as an editorial assistant
3. A position as a laboratory assistant for a drug company
4. A position as a truck driver for a logging company
5. A position as a proofreader for a daily newspaper

52d • Paraphrases and Summaries

rh 52d

Most students, at some point in their careers, have to write paraphrases and summaries, either of their own work or of the work of others. Both paraphrases and summaries are forms of rewriting, but they are quite different forms and serve quite different purposes.

Paraphrases   A paraphrase is a restatement of the original in words different from those used in the original. The purpose of a paraphrase is to help either the writer of the paraphrase or someone else understand difficult material. Paraphrases are especially useful for clarifying highly technical writing for the general reader. Here, the paraphrase often substitutes more familiar terms for specialized technical terms. Paraphrases of poetry restate the content of the poem in prose. Paraphrases of older texts "translate" these texts into modern English.

A paraphrase is not an evaluation, interpretation, or analysis of the original, simply a rephrasing. It adds no new material and should preserve the tone of the original insofar as possible. Paraphrases are normally about the same length as their originals but may be longer if the original is exceptionally difficult or concise.

In writing a paraphrase, first read the original carefully until you are sure that you thoroughly understand it. Then put the original aside and restate it in your own words. Avoid, whenever possible, using the original phrasing. If you do use the original wording, put it in quotation marks. After you have written the paraphrase, go back to the original to make sure that you have not left anything out or misstated anything. Note that even a complete paraphrase of someone else's writing must be footnoted if you include it in a paper of your own.

The following is a paraphrase of relatively technical writing, a paragraph discussing the organism that causes malaria. The paraphrase follows the original fairly closely but substitutes synonyms for some words and varies word order somewhat. It is approximately the same length as the original.

Original

The malarial plasmodium, for instance, is probably among the oldest of human (and pre-human) parasites; yet it continues to inflict severe and debilitating fevers upon its human hosts. At least four different forms of the plasmodium infect human beings, and one of these, *Plasmodium falciparum*, is far more virulent than the others. Conceivably, *Plasmodium falciparum* entered human bloodstreams more recently, and has not had time to adjust as well to human hosts as the other forms of malarial infection. In this case, however, evolutionary adjustment between host and parasite is complicated by the diversity of hosts to which the infectious organism must accommodate itself to complete its life cycle. Accommodation that would allow the malarial plasmodium to live indefinitely within the red blood corpuscles of a human being would make no provision for successful transmission from host to host.

                                   William H. McNeill, *Plagues and Peoples*

rh
52d

Paraphrase

Probably one of the oldest parasites to afflict human beings is the plasmodium, the organism that causes malaria. Despite its long association with human beings, it still produces serious fevers. There are at least four types of plasmodium that affect human beings, but *Plasmodium falciparum* is the most virulent by far. The explanation for its virulence may be that it has come to afflict human beings more recently. If so, it has perhaps had less time to adjust to life in the human bloodstream than have the other types of plasmodium. Further, because the plasmodium adapts itself to a number of different hosts in order to complete its life cycle, more time is required for its evolutionary adjustment. However, these different hosts are necessary; if the plasmodium lived indefinitely in one host, such as the human bloodstream, it could not reproduce or "spread" by going from host to host.

The following is the text of 1 Corinthians 13.1–3 from the King James version of the Bible, followed by a paraphrase of this text. The paraphrase modernizes the older language of the original and explains in simple words the meaning of the metaphors and similes in the original.

Original

1. Though I speak with the tongues of men and of angels, and have not charity, I am become as sounding brass, or a tinkling cymbal.
2. And though I have the gift of prophecy, and understand all mysteries, and all knowledge; and though I have all faith, so that I could remove mountains, and have not charity, I am nothing.
3. And though I bestow all my goods to feed the poor, and though I give my body to be burned, and have not charity, it profiteth me nothing.

Paraphrase

Even though I may speak very eloquently, everything I say is just noise if I do not have love. Even though I may be able to foretell the future and may know everything, and even though I may have enough faith to make mountains move, I am nothing without love. I can give everything I own to the poor and can even allow myself to be martyred by being burned, but it will do me no good if I do not have love.

Exercises: Paraphrases

Write a paraphrase of the following passage.

. . . the greatest single disservice to Johnson as a *mind*—as a guide to the human spirit to whom posterity could turn for courage and wisdom—was his own fame, after his death, as a talker. For it was the dramatic picture of Johnson as a supreme conversationalist that, more than anything else, swept attention away from his works to this one aspect of his life. The result, however engaging and picturesque, was to impoverish immensely his meaning and value as a fellow participator in human experience; and it is only within our own generation that we have at last begun to rediscover his real greatness.

W. Jackson Bate, *Samuel Johnson*

Summaries A summary, also called a **précis** or a **synopsis,** is an abridgment or condensation of its original. A summary is not an explanation of or a substitute for the original. Rather, its purpose is to refresh the writer's memory about what the original said or to give others enough information about the original to let them decide whether they want to read the original. Like a paraphrase, a summary adds no interpretation or evaluation and retains the approach and tone of the original. A summary normally follows the same organization as its original, omitting minor details, illustrations, quotations, anecdotes, and other material that is not absolutely essential. Unlike a paraphrase, a summary may include some of the same wording as the original, especially important terms and definitions. A summary is usually only about one-fourth to one-third the length of the original but preserves the general proportions of the original.

In writing a summary, read the original carefully two or three times, noting the author's main ideas and organization. Try to reduce entire paragraphs to topic sentences, either of your own composition or by the original author. Check the original carefully to be sure you have not omitted crucial points. Check your summary to see if it can be further condensed. A good summary will, of course, be abbreviated but should nevertheless be smooth and fluent and without confusing gaps in logic.

Here is a three-paragraph excerpt followed by a one-paragraph summary of the excerpt.

Original

We know today that the earliest forms of agriculture arose in Mesopotamia. Here, too, the first high cultures of humanity suddenly emerged from obscurity, after the long, historyless twilight existence of primitive peoples. These cultures sprang into being with a swiftness that is totally mysterious, in view of the hundreds of thousands of years that preceded them, and without explicable cause. First came the Sumerians, then the Babylonians and Assyrians along the Tigris and Euphrates, while about the same time the Egyptians were creating a culture in the valley of the Nile, the Indians in the valley of the Indus, and the Chinese along their great rivers.

These cultures achieved domestication of many plants and animals. They invented the wheel, lever, and plow, and soon devised writing.

Nothing of the sort is true for the cultures of North America, not even for the cultures of the Incas in the Andes, the Mayas in Central America, and the Aztecs in Mexico, which we also tend to regard as high cultures (so Spengler and Toynbee regard them). The American peoples invented neither the wagon wheel (in Central America the wheel does appear on *toy* animals) nor the plow and developed no alphabetic writing. And they failed to do something of equal importance in North America: they domesticated very few animals, or plants.

C. W. Ceram, *The First Americans*

rh
52d

Summary

The early cultures of the Middle East and Asia, including the Sumerians, Babylonians, Assyrians, Egyptians, Indians, and Chinese, made sudden, swift, and inexplicable advances in civilization. They domesticated many plants and animals, invented the wheel, lever, and plow, and devised writing. The early cultures of America, even the Incas, Mayas, and Aztecs, made none of these important inventions and domesticated few animals or plants.

Exercises: Summaries

Write a summary of the following passage.

Tying one's self-worth to performance standards leads to excessive concern about other people's opinions. It results in fearful, alert looking to the reactions of others for clues as to where one stands in life or how one measures up in their eyes. Such concern, of course, is a sure recipe for stress. Other people often do not know what they really value or believe. Their standards and preferences are often inconsistent and therefore unattainable. Pleasing others, by itself, even when possible, is always a hollow victory. One may escape censure or disapproval. But one achieves nothing in terms of increased self-esteem. That can come only from pleasing yourself, which has nothing to do with external standards of self-worth.
Robert L. Woolfolk and Frank C. Richardson, *Stress, Sanity, and Survival*

52e ▪ Essay Examinations

Essay examinations are an important part of nearly every college and university student's experience. In large classes, the instructor may be forced to judge ability and knowledge solely on the basis of your performance on one or two essay examinations. Obviously, the first requisite for good performance is knowledge of the subject matter, and no amount of strategy or verbal skill can substitute for study. On the other hand, many students who know the subject matter well receive lower grades than they otherwise might because they do not know how to take essay examinations.

Studying for the Examination When the examination is announced, listen carefully to what the instructor says about the examination and plan your studying accordingly. If the instructor says the examination will cover only four chapters, do not try to digest the entire book. If the instructor stresses the knowledge of factual material such as definitions, names, dates, or formulas, concentrate on learning this factual information.

If the instructor says that the examination will consist primarily of "thought" questions, consider the larger principles that have been emphasized in the class, try to formulate sample essay questions for yourself, and consider how you might answer them. Learn as many supporting details as possible, but focus on explanations, structure, and implications rather than on small details. For example, assume that in an anthropology class you have been studying the culture of the Inuit, and your instructor has told you that your examination will consist of "thought" questions. In lectures, the instructor has gone into detail about the building of houses; the making of tools, weapons, and boats; religious beliefs and ceremonies; child-rearing; and social organization. In an essay examination, the instructor will want you to make generalizations and draw conclusions from this detailed information. (You will, of course, be expected to support your generalizations with specific facts.) Typical "thought" questions might be something like the following examples.

How are the religious beliefs of the Inuit reflected in their social organizations?

How is the Inuit way of life influenced by the physical environment?

Discuss the roles of the sexes among the polar Inuit.

Compare child-rearing among the Inuit with that in Southern Canada.

Taking the Examination   Get to the examination early or at least on time. Take several pens with you to the examination. Bring a watch so that you will not have to rely on the instructor to tell you the time.

Before you start writing, scan the examination sheet to get a perspective on the entire examination. If percentages or expected times are indicated, mentally note these so that you can budget your time accordingly. Check carefully to see if a choice of questions is allowed. If so, plan to answer only the required number of questions. You will not receive credit for the extra answers, and you will waste time that would be better spent on improving the answers to required questions.

Start with the questions about which you know the most and feel most confident. They can serve as a warm-up and ensure that you are at your best when you get to the more difficult questions. Further, if you should find yourself running out of time at the end of the period, you will have answered those questions for which you expect to get full or nearly full credit. If possible, keep the order of your answers in the examination booklet the same as the order of the questions on the examination sheet. In any case, always number your answers according to the numbers of the questions on the examination sheet, not according to the order in which you answer the questions. Improbable as it may seem, instructors sometimes cannot tell from the answer alone which question is being answered.

Read each question very carefully; many students lose credit for not having read the question correctly. In particular, note whether a short

rh
52e

answer or a full-length essay is asked for. If it is a short answer, restrict your answer to a sentence or two. You will not receive extra credit for a lengthy answer; you will waste time needed for other questions; and you will probably annoy the instructor, who does not want to do all that unnecessary reading.

Note the language of each question. *Why* does not mean *what,* and if the instructor asks *why* a certain sequence of events occurred, do not give a description of *what* those events were. Similarly, pay particular attention to such instruction words as *discuss, evaluate, describe, compare, identify, explain, list, outline, summarize,* and *define.* For example, *evaluate* means that you are to make a value judgement, supporting this judgement with specific details, whereas *describe* asks only that you present the facts, not that you evaluate them. *Summarize* means that you should list the most important facts or conclusions, not that you should go into great detail about one or two aspects of the question. *Define* asks you to state the meaning of something, not merely to give one or two examples of it.

As an example, assume that one of the questions on a psychology examination is "Write a short paragraph defining classical conditioning." Possible poor, fair, and good answers to this question follow.

Poor

> Classical conditioning is when you make a dog salivate to a bell without any food. Pavlov discovered that this happens. He strapped his dogs into frames so that they couldn't move. Sometimes he used lights instead of bells. He thought that this was like telephone systems.

This answer is poor because, instead of defining classical conditioning, it gives a sketchy and disorganized description of the first experiments with classical conditioning. The information about strapping the dogs into frames is irrelevant. The writer does not say in what way Pavlov thought classical conditioning was like telephone systems. Even the sentence construction is weak.

Fair

> Pavlov showed his dogs food and then gave it to them. This made them salivate. Then he sounded a bell before he gave them the food. After a while, the dogs salivated when they heard the bell even though they didn't get any food. This salivation without the presence of food is an example of classical conditioning.

This answer is fair because, although it does not provide a general definition of classical conditioning, it does give a straightforward description of the process and then notes that this description is an example, not a general definition.

rh
52e

Good

> An unconditioned stimulus produces an inborn response (e.g., a dog automatically salivates when shown food). A neutral stimulus produces no such response (a dog does not salivate when it hears a bell). Classical conditioning occurs when a neutral stimulus (bell) is repeatedly paired with an unconditioned stimulus (food). The neutral stimulus eventually becomes a conditioned stimulus when it produces a response similar to that of the unconditioned stimulus, even when the unconditioned stimulus is not present.

This answer is good because, in addition to providing a general definition of classical conditioning, it also defines other terms (*unconditioned stimulus, neutral stimulus*) essential to a thorough understanding of the principle of classical conditioning.

When you are ready to answer a specific essay question, do not plunge right in, putting down all the points you can think of in whatever order they occur to you. Make a rough outline in the margin or on the back cover of the examination booklet. Examine these rough notes, and indicate the order in which points should appear by numbering them. Try to formulate a thesis sentence that will summarize your entire answer. If this thesis sentence rephrases the question as a statement, you can refer to it constantly as you write to be sure that you do not digress and that you direct the rest of your answer to this thesis sentence. In your answer, give as many specific illustrations, details, technical terms, names, and the like as you can think of, provided they are all related to the question and provided time allows. Avoid overgeneralizations that are not supported by details. Avoid digressions. Avoid repeating yourself and contradicting yourself. Do not try to put down everything you know about the subject; stick to what is asked for in the question. Be as economical as possible; the best answer is often not the longest answer. Above all, do not try to pad your answer or to bluff—your instructor will not be fooled.

Stop writing when you become uncertain of your answer. This is especially important with short-answer questions, where students frequently lose credit by not stopping when they run out of solid information.

If you are required to write on a question to which you have forgotten or simply do not know the answer, spend a few moments thinking of all that you do know about the area. The answer may come to you. Depending on the subject matter, you may be able to work out an answer by common sense and logic.

Instructors understand that students are under pressure when they take examinations and do not expect them to write elegant prose. On the other hand, the more polished your writing, the better off you are. Regardless of how hurried you feel, do not dash off disconnected words and phrases—if the instructor cannot understand what you are saying, you certainly will not get credit for it. Try to compose each sentence mentally before you write it.

Keep your handwriting as legible as possible. You will save very little time by scribbling, and you will lose a great deal of credit if the instructor cannot read what you have scribbled. Deletions and interlinear or marginal insertions are acceptable but should of course be clear.

Normally, you should use all the time allowed for an essay examination. When you have finished writing, read over both the questions and your answers. Make necessary corrections in grammar and spelling, and add or delete material as seems appropriate.

If you find that you consistently do poorly on essay examinations even though you feel that you know the subject matter well, consult your instructor about your problems. Make it clear to the instructor that you are not complaining about your grade but, instead, would like advice about how to improve your performance in the future. You might also ask a good student if you may compare his or her examination with your own in an effort to see exactly what constituted a good set of answers.

rh
52e

Research

53 The Research Paper

The research paper goes by many different names: term paper, source paper, library paper, reference paper, documented paper, investigative paper. Whatever the name, the use of sources outside the writer's own experience is implied. Of course, any paper, no matter how short or how long, may use outside sources, if only to verify a date or provide a quotation. Research papers, however, use at least several outside sources. Research papers are also normally much longer than other papers, typically ranging from 1500 to 5000 words in length. Because of their length, they require particular attention to organization. Some people may be able to write a 500-word paper without making an outline beforehand, but most need an outline for a paper that is to be 6 to 20 pages long.

The preparation of a research paper gives you practice in critical reading and in weighing evidence, practice that is valuable not only in your courses but in whatever you may do outside of and after college or university. It gives you a chance to learn how to use libraries and how to handle documentation. It gives you practice valuable for writing long papers in other courses, where the instructor usually assumes that you already know how to write a research paper. Finally, it gives you a chance to learn something new yourself. You learn more about a subject and learn it more thoroughly if you must sift evidence, organize various kinds of material, and then explain what you have learned to others in writing. It is always pleasant to discover that you have become somewhat expert on a subject about which you had previously known little.

53a ▪ Choosing a Topic

If, by chance, you are assigned a specific topic for a research paper, you may as well grin and bear it—at least, you have been spared the agony of trying to decide what to write about. More typically, instructors allow students a fair amount of freedom in their choice of topic. You may be given a list of topics from which to choose, or the assignment may be completely open-ended, allowing you to write on any topic you like. The following is a guide to the kinds of topics that are most appropriate for research papers.

    1. Pick a topic in which you are interested, potentially interested, or at least curious about. If you already know a little about the topic, so much the better. For example, if you are taking a religion course, you may be interested in investigating the history of Biblical translation, or Martin Luther's anti-Semitism, or the appeal of cult religions.

    2. Pick a topic that can be understood by a general audience. In other words, your topic should be one that can be made comprehensible and interesting to the average adult. For example, people do not have to be animal psychologists to understand and enjoy a paper about the language of dolphins and whales.

3. Pick a topic that can be treated objectively. Most topics can be so treated, but you should avoid topics about which final judgements must be primarily subjective. For example, a topic such as "Which was the greater composer, Mozart or Beethoven?" is unsuitable for a research paper because your conclusions will ultimately be subjective; there is no objective way of defining the greatness of outstanding composers. On the other hand, a musically knowledgeable student could treat objectively a topic such as the influence of literature on Beethoven's music.

4. Pick a topic within the range of your abilities. No matter how fascinated you may be by the concept of black holes in the universe, you will not be able to make intelligent conclusions about them if you lack the background in physics, mathematics, and astronomy necessary to evaluate the opinions expressed in your sources.

5. Although personal experience can sometimes be used as evidence, do not pick a topic that can be developed from your personal experience alone. The purpose of a research paper is to summarize and draw conclusions from a variety of sources outside your own experience and prior knowledge. Hence the topic "My impressions of Disneyland" is not appropriate for a research paper.

6. Do not pick a topic that can be developed from a single outside source. An example would be "Lenin's student days," the information about which could be drawn from any one biography of Lenin.

7. Do not pick a topic that is too controversial or about which you yourself have extremely strong prejudices. A topic such as "Which is the true Christian faith, Catholicism or Protestantism?" is not suitable for a research paper.

8. Do not pick a pseudoscientific topic such as pyramid power, astrology, the Bermuda triangle, or astronauts from outer space. Such topics are unsuitable for research papers because there is no respectable scientific evidence for—or against—the existence of these phenomena.

9. Do not pick a topic for which research materials are unlikely to be available. For example, libraries in Newfoundland will probably not have much material on the history of mining towns in Wyoming. For many topics, of course, you will not know whether sources are available until you actually start searching. However, you can be fairly certain in advance that topics that have just emerged in the past few weeks or months will have little or nothing about them in book form. Although your references should include periodicals, they normally should not be restricted to periodicals.

res
53b

53b · Getting Started

Once you have decided on a general topic for a research paper, the next step is a trip to the library to start collecting source material. If your topic is still rather broad and if you need more general background information, you may want to read an article or two on the subject in a good, up-to-date encyclopedia, such as the *Encyclopaedia Britannica*. Encyclopedias also provide brief bibliographies for many of their entries.

Other possible general sources include almanacs, yearbooks, who's whos, and handbooks. Browse for a while in the reference room; you will probably discover sources of information that you did not know existed. Consult periodical indexes for magazine and journal articles on your subject. (For a discussion of types of reference works, see 54d.) Finally, do not hesitate to ask your reference librarians for help—they are specially trained to help library users locate sources of information.

Even at this early stage in your research, you should have a thesis statement—or perhaps several alternative thesis statements—in mind. Even a tentative thesis will help you focus your search for additional information and will save you a great deal of unnecessary hunting and reading. (See 50d for a more extensive discussion of thesis statements.)

The Card Catalogue and the Stacks   The next step is the card catalogue. (See 54a for a detailed description of card catalogues.) If you already have the names of several authors or books on your topic, you can simply locate the cards for these books in the card catalogue. You will find other books in the subject index. If you get your books from the stacks yourself, browse along the shelves where your books are located. You will probably find other relevant books there for which you had no previous references.

The Preliminary Bibliography   As you locate potential sources of information, you will need to compile a preliminary bibliography. The simplest way is to use a separate 7.6 cm by 12.7 cm (3 by 5 inch) card for each reference. Put the call number of the reference at the top of the card, and include on the card all the information you will need for the final bibliography (author, title, place and date of publication, and so on). Use standard bibliographical form (see 55c) so that when you prepare your final bibliography, you can simply copy the necessary information directly from your preliminary bibliography without having to reorganize the material. Two sample bibliography cards, one for a book and one for an article, are reproduced on the next page.

Taking Notes   Everyone develops his or her own method for recording notes. The exact method used is not important; what is important is that the method be efficient, flexible, systematic, and relatively easy to use. Most people prefer to take notes on index cards that are relatively large —10.2 cm by 15.2 cm (4 by 6 inch) or 12.7 cm by 20.3 cm (5 by 8 inch). Cards can be rearranged easily and are sturdy enough to survive shuffling. Lined cards help keep the notes neat and easy to read.

On the top line of each note card, write down enough information to identify the source. Use a separate card for each reference. If you are making notes on more than one point from a single reference, use a separate card for each point. Do not write on the backs of the cards because you may forget to turn them over later. When you have more information than will fit on the front of a single card, use additional cards, identifying the source on each card and numbering the additional cards consecutively. Every card should include the specific page reference(s) for the information on it.

Bibliography Cards

> Periodicals
> Room
>
> Fowler, Mary Janet, Michael J.
> Sullivan, and Bruce K. Ekstrand.
> "Sleep and Memory." *Science*,
> 19 (Jan. 1973): 302-4.

> QP
> .D44
> 1974
>
> Dement, William C. *Some Must
> Watch While Some Must Sleep*.
> San Francisco: W. H. Freeman
> and Co., 1974.

Before actually writing down notes from a reference, skim the book or article. If the source is a book, glance at the table of contents, the preface, the introduction, and the index. Scan the various sections to get an idea of what the book contains and where the information you want is located. You may find that the book contains nothing useful to you. If so, make a note of this on the bibliography card for that book so that you will not needlessly come back to the book later. How closely you examine any particular source depends on the stage of your research. If you still lack a clear thesis statement, you will not reject many possible

Sample Note Card

> *Purpose of Sleep*
>
> Webb, 162-63
> Webb believes that the view that sleep
> is a state that restores our worn-out,
> diminished energies is less useful
> than the adaptive theory because "what
> is being diminished and, in turn,
> 'restored' has been so elusive that it
> has not been specifiable".

references. If you are at an advanced stage in your research, you will know exactly what kind of information you need and can ignore irrelevant references more easily.

As you read, try to evaluate the quality of your source. You can often judge from the tone and style of a reference whether the author is writing a scholarly or a popularized report. Does the author seem biased? Does he or she support the arguments with evidence? Is the book out of date? If you have doubts about the quality of a book, you may want to read reviews of it by experts in the field.

When you take notes, summarize the information in your own words. (Remember that even summaries must be documented in your paper.) Try to avoid lengthy direct quotations. When you do quote directly, use quotation marks so that you can properly credit the quotation and avoid plagiarism (see 53e). Double-check quotations for accuracy, including spelling and punctuation. If you omit material from a quotation, use an ellipsis to indicate the point of omission (see 38). Write down the numbers of *all* the pages from which you get information so that these page numbers will be available for your citations.

Put your own reactions to your reading in square brackets or, even better, in a different color ink so that you can easily distinguish your own ideas and opinions from those of your source. Distinguish opinion from fact in your sources by prefacing statements of opinion with "The author believes that . . ." or "The author concludes that. . . ." A sample note card is reproduced on the previous page.

If you find material that contains many facts, figures, important but lengthy quotations, charts, or helpful illustrations, you can have these pages photocopied to ensure accuracy and to save time in copying. Be sure to write the sources on the photocopied pages so that you can identify them later. Do not, however, photocopy everything you find that might conceivably be useful. Read the material carefully first, digest it, and then decide whether it is worth photocopying.

Review your notes occasionally as you read to see the direction in which your topic is developing and to determine what additional information you will need. As you read, you will probably get a clearer idea of how your topic can be narrowed and focused. Try to formulate a thesis or several alternative theses and a mental outline of your final paper while you are still reading your outside sources.

Organizing Notes By the time you have consulted several references, you should be able to put headings on your note cards to indicate subdivisions of your topic. For example, if you were planning a research paper on archaeology in Tunisia, headings on your note cards might include "History," "Methodology," "Specific Sites," "Findings," "Current Status." Additional reading will enable you to subdivide these headings further. The heading "Findings," for example, might be divided into "Pottery," "Architecture," "Tools," and so on. These headings and subheadings will serve as a guide for further research and for the final organization of your paper.

When you feel that you have a fairly clear idea about how to develop your topic and when you have either exhausted your references or find that all additional references merely repeat information that you already have, it is time to stop reading and start planning your paper. When you actually start writing, you may, of course, discover that you need to do additional reading.

53c ▪ Planning and Outlining the Paper

Before you have finished taking notes from sources, you should have a clear thesis statement and a rough notion of the structure of your final research paper. Read through all your notes to refresh your memory. Then, with your thesis statement in mind, sort your note cards into piles corresponding to the headings on the cards.

Next, make a rough written outline. You may find that you have some gaps in your sources; if so, plan to return to the library to do more reading. You will almost certainly find that you have some information that does not fit into a reasonable outline. Do not feel that you must force it into the paper; instead, make a discard pile of notes—far better to have taken a few unnecessary notes than to have a good research paper marred by irrelevant material. You will also probably discover that a number of your sources contain the same information. Select the best sources and discard the others. As you revise your rough outline, you will be able to narrow your topic further and focus it more sharply.

When your rough outline seems generally satisfactory, you are ready to make a detailed outline. You can use either a topic outline or a sentence outline, according to your own preference or the instructions of your teacher. (See 52a for the preparation of topic and sentence outlines.) The actual organization of the final outline will depend on the topic you have chosen and the approach you plan to take.

53d ▪ Writing the First Draft

Once you are ready to start the actual writing of your research paper, try to write as much as possible at one sitting to ensure continuity in your train of thought and consistency in your style. Most research papers are too long for the writer to complete the first draft in a single session, but you should plan to write each major section without interruption. Whether you compose the first draft in longhand or use a typewriter, leave ample space on each page for later corrections, insertions, and notes to yourself.

In general, the process of writing a research paper is similar to that of writing any other paper. There are, however, some differences in style, and there are greater problems in organization and transitions. Finally, there are conventional ways of handling citations and quotations.

Style The style of a research paper should be objective, impersonal, and more formal than that of short essays. Research papers are usually

res
53d

written in the third person, although the first person is sometimes acceptable to avoid excessive use of the passive. Even if you are accustomed to using contractions in your shorter, more informal papers, avoid them in a research paper. Slang is definitely out of place, as are emotionalism and extravagant language. Impersonality of style does not mean, however, that a research paper must be boring. The sample research paper on pages 404–420 is written in an impersonal, objective style, yet it is entertaining because the author has selected a topic of universal interest and captures the reader's attention at the very outset by relating three case histories.

Organization If you have a good outline to begin with, the overall organization of your research paper should not present a serious problem. Avoiding irrelevancies and repetition may cause greater difficulty because you may be tempted to include every bit of information from your notes. However, if you have previously discarded notes that contained repetitious or unnecessary material, you should have few problems with redundancy and irrelevancy.

As you write each section, be sure it is clearly related to the main idea and to preceding and following sections. Transition from one section to another is more difficult in research papers than in short papers because the greater length of a research paper makes it harder to keep all the parts in mind simultaneously. You will probably find that you need to write some transitional sentences or paragraphs. Notice how, in the sample paper (page 10), the author uses a question to make the transition from the chemistry of sleep to the effects of total deprivation of sleep. Most research papers need a separate concluding section or, at the very least, a concluding paragraph.

Presenting the Arguments Few research papers are so complete or so definitive that they leave no room for disagreement. Let the reader know what you are certain of and what you are uncertain of. When your sources disagree, note this and give both sides of the argument as well as your own opinion. Distinguish clearly between fact and opinion. You can usually indicate your own opinion without saying directly, "I think that . . ." or "I disagree with. . . ."

POOR   Peters attributes the interlace design to Celtic influence. I disagree. I think it can just as well be explained by native tradition.

REVISED   Although Peters attributes the interlace design to Celtic influence, native tradition is an equally plausible explanation.

**res
53d**

Handling Source Material Although one purpose of a research paper is to use outside references, the paper itself should not be simply a patchwork of unrelated facts and quotations strung together one after the other. Be sure that you have a good reason for every quotation—a reason other than proving that you consulted outside sources. Use quotations to fill in and support your own presentation, rather than using your own writing merely to tie the quotations together. When you quote or paraphrase several different sources on one point, do not feel that you must have a separate paragraph for each source. Each source used, however, must have a separate footnote.

Avoid large numbers of long quotations; most source material should be paraphrased or summarized instead of being quoted in full. If a particular sentence or phrase from one of your sources is especially appropriate or well stated, try to work the quotation into the grammar of your own sentence. (Quotation marks around what is directly quoted are still necessary, of course.) For example, if you were writing a paper on Mohammedanism, you might have read the following passage:

> Yet amongst the very earliest generations of Muslims, in all parts of the Islamic world, there were many men who brought the spirit of devotion into their daily activities, and to whom Islam was a discipline of the soul and not merely a collection of external rituals. Their creed was a stern ascetic creed, which bade every man go about his work with the fear of eternal punishment ever before his eyes, remembering that this world is but a temporary habitation, and that every gift it has to offer, power, riches, pleasure, learning, the joy of parenthood, is vanity and temptation—not indeed to be rejected or avoided, but to be used with a deep sense of the awful responsibilities which they entail.
>
> H. A. R. Gibb, *Mohammedanism*

Instead of quoting this entire passage verbatim, you could summarize most of it and include a small part of it as a direct quotation.

> For many early Muslims, Islam was a stern religion emphasizing the transitoriness and responsibility of life on earth, a creed "which bade every man go about his work with the fear of eternal punishment ever before his eyes."[6]

Copy out in full all the quotations you plan to use from your first draft on; this allows you to see if the quotations fit smoothly and logically into your text and also helps you keep down the number of overly long quotations. Put an abbreviated reference (author's name and a page number) in your text as you write to ensure that you do not forget to credit your source. Remember that summaries and paraphrases, as well as direct quotations, require documentation in your text, either in references with your text or in footnotes (see 55 "Documentation"). Your instructor will probably specify which form of documentation he or she prefers.

res
53d

Integrating Reference Material into the Text No matter which documentation system you use, you must pay attention, from the first draft on, to the way in which you handle the material for which you have references. Combining your own words with those of another writer to achieve a smooth "fit" is challenging; sometimes the contrast between your voice and that of a source is too jarring for a reader. You have to consider carefully whether to quote directly, paraphrase, or summarize. (The following section will help you with these points.)

If you are using in-text references for documentation, you face the additional challenge of weaving them into the text. Although this integration can be done at the revision stage (and you will certainly do some smoothing then), you can save yourself trouble if you begin to work at intergration from the beginning. Care on the first draft will also make it easier for you to prepare your bibliography later.

53e ▪ Avoiding Plagiarism

Plagiarism is taking the writings, ideas, or thoughts of others and passing them off as one's own original work. Plagiarism is not restricted to published material: if you submit an old paper written by your roommate, if you buy a paper from a "service," or even if you base a paper on a lecture you heard in a course without acknowledging that lecture, you are still guilty of plagiarism. Plagiarism is not restricted to long quotations; if you quote a sentence or even a memorable phrase without acknowledging it, you are plagiarizing. You can plagiarize without even using the exact words of the original author; if you paraphrase a passage without crediting it, you are plagiarizing.

Plagiarism is dishonest, stupid, and dangerous. It is dishonest because it involves both stealing (taking the work of someone else) and lying (pretending that it is your own work). It is stupid because people who plagiarize lose the opportunity to learn for themselves. It is dangerous because it is illegal; penalties for plagiarism range from an F on the individual paper, to an F for the entire course, to probation, to expulsion from college or university. Even if the immediate penalty is relatively light, the plagiarist has irretrievably lost the respect and trust of his or her instructor.

Although plagiarism is always an offence, not every plagiarist intends to cheat. Students sometimes do not know exactly what kind of information must be documented and what need not be. A student's high school may have allowed the use of outside sources without acknowledgement, so the student may not even understand that material clearly obtained from a specific outside source must be credited to that source. Sometimes writers unintentionally plagiarize through carelessness; they do not take notes properly and do not remember when they are quoting and when they are not. Or they may simply forget to document a passage or paraphrase that they had intended to acknowledge.

Deliberate plagiarism may result from fear; students may be so terrified of receiving a low grade or of not having enough time to complete an assignment satisfactorily that they deliberately plagiarize out of panic. But anyone who intentionally plagiarizes out of sheer dishonesty and an attempt to get a higher grade than he or she would otherwise receive deserves whatever penalties may result from the plagiarism.

To avoid plagiarism, follow the rule that *all outside information must be acknowledged.* The only exception to this rule is "common knowledge." That is, you need not footnote (1) information that everyone knows, (2) common proverbs and expressions, (3) information that is given in every source on the subject, and (4) general conclusions that anyone could reach. For example, you need not cite a source for the facts that Columbus discovered America, that "A penny saved is a penny earned," that John Diefenbaker died in 1979, or that watching television is a popular Canadian pastime.

What is sufficient acknowledgement and what are the proper uses of source materials? The following examples illustrate proper and improper acknowledgement.

> Trudeau's rise was meteoric. He did not join the Liberal Party until, in 1965, he and his friends Jean Marchand and Gerard Pelletier (former editor of *La Presse*) decided that it was the only party which could save the unity of Canada. He entered Parliament in 1966, and his advent, with that of his two associates, meant that, for the first time for a decade, the federal goverment included a group of French Canadians who were men of authentic intelligence, strong convictions, and forceful personalities, and who were in no way compromised by the errors of the past. Pearson accepted them with gratitude, and promoted them quickly. Trudeau became Minister of Justice in 1967, and set about immediately divising a bill to amend the Criminal Code in a number of radical directions, including the legalization of abortion under certain circumstances, of the dissemination of birth control, and of homosexual behaviour between consenting adults.
>
> George Woodcock, *Canada and the Canadians*

This quotation is too long to be included in most papers. But the material can easily be paraphrased or condensed because little about the language of the original is especially striking, nor is the original so well known that it would be an injustice to the author to change the wording. To include most of the information in a paper of your own, you could paraphrase the passage, using a footnote to acknowledge the source. The paraphrase should, however, be complete, not simply a slight rewording that merely substitutes a few synonyms and changes the order of a few phrases or clauses.

Plagiarism

res
53e

> Trudeau's rise was meteoric. He joined the Liberal Party in 1965. He and his friends Jean Marchand and Gerard Pelletier (who was formerly editor of *La Presse*) thought it was the only party capable of saving the unity of Canada. When Trudeau entered Parliament in 1966, his arrival and that of Marchand and Pelletier, meant that the federal government would have, for the first time in a decade, a group of French Canadians with authentic intelligence, strong convictions, forceful personalities and no fears about the errors of the

past. Pearson was grateful to have them, and he promoted them immediately. Trudeau was made minister of justice in 1967, and he quickly set about to plan a bill that would amend the Criminal Code radically, by legalizing abortion under certain circumstances, by legalizing the dissemination of birth control, and by legalizing homosexual behavior between consenting adults (see Woodcock 235).

Even with documentation included and even though the wording is not identical to the original, this rewriting would be plagiarism in a student paper because the implication is that most of the wording is that of the student author.

Acceptable Paraphrase

Trudeau rose brilliantly and suddenly into political prominence and power. In 1965 Trudeau, Jean Marchand, and Gerard Pelletier joined the Liberal Party because they felt it could preserve Canada's unity. Trudeau entered Parliament the following year. The arrival of Trudeau, Marchand, and Pelletier signalled a change; known for the strength of their intelligence, convictions, and personalities, and for their determination to ignore mistakes of the past, these three men brought the government a strong and new French-Canadian component. Pearson gladly advanced them in the government. Trudeau, made minister of justice in 1967, quickly undertook the amendment of the Criminal Code. He proposed radical changes: the legalization of homosexual behavior between consenting adults, the legalization of abortion, and greater access to and information about birth control. (See Woodcock 235.)

Documentation is still necessary here, but the passage has been so thoroughly rewritten that it would not be considered plagiarized.

If you do not need all the details from an original source, you can summarize it. Although the language of the summary below is almost completely different from the original, it still must be documented because the information it contains came from an outside source.

Acceptable Summary

Trudeau's political rise was swift and brilliant. He joined the Liberal Party in 1965 and entered Parliament in 1966 as a member of a group of French Canadians new to the government; in 1967, Pearson appointed him minister of justice. Immediately, he proposed radical changes in the Criminal Code through legalizing abortion, birth control, and homosexual relations between consenting adults. (See Woodcock 235.)

Often you may wish to use only a single fact or two from a source. Again, a citation is necessary.

Acceptable Use of Fact

The entry of Trudeau, Marchand, and Pelletier into Parliament in 1966 was important because French Canadians had not been part of a federal government for a decade (Woodcock 235).

If you borrow a metaphor, other figure of speech, or any kind of striking language from a source, place it in quotation marks and document it.

Acceptable Quotation

Trudeau, Marchand, and Pelletier were French Canadians "who were in no way compromised by the errors of the past" (Woodcock 235).

The best way to avoid plagiarism or charges of plagiarism is to take careful notes and to acknowledge all your sources. Whenever you have any doubt whatsoever about whether documentation is required, err on the generous side and provide it.

53f ▪ Revising the Paper

In planning a research paper, try to allow yourself at least two or three days between the completion of the first draft and the beginning of revision. If you begin revising immediately after completing the first draft, you will still be so close to that draft that you will lack perspective and may fail to see where revision is necessary.

Revision does not mean that every single sentence must be rewritten and the entire draft recopied. You can usually make the changes for a second draft on the copy of your first draft, although you may need to do some cutting and pasting if paragraphs or sections have to be rearranged. Recopy the entire paper only if the draft becomes so marked up with changes that it is difficult to read. (Of course, if you have access to a word processor, this is the point at which you will most appreciate it.)

When reading the first draft for possible revisions, always check the larger matters of organization, proportion, clarity, and emphasis first. When you are satisfied that these larger matters are in order, reread the paper sentence by sentence, following the "Checklist of Revision" in 50j.

After you have made your revisions, compare the new draft of the paper with your topic or sentence outline, making sure that you have not accidentally omitted any of the important points in the outline. If you have added material, changed focus, or reorganized the paper, make a new outline from the latest draft and check this new outline for logic, organization, and consistency. If you are required to turn in an outline along with your research paper, submit the revised outline, not the earlier version.

res
53f

53g ▪ The Final Draft

Prior to typing or writing the final draft, reread the entire paper carefully. If you are using in-text references, make sure each is a clear reference to the bibliography (see 55b). If you are using footnotes, check to be sure they are in numerical order; make sure that every reference has a corresponding footnote and every footnote a reference number in the text. (See 55b for proper footnote form.) Prepare your bibliography by listing in alphabetical order all the sources you have cited in your in-text references or footnotes. (See 55c for the proper form for bibliographies.) Check the title of your paper to be sure it is accurate but as brief as possible.

In its final form, the research paper has four parts: (1) title page, (2) outline (if required), (3) text (and footnotes if required), and (4) bibliography.

Title Page   Follow the directions of your instructor in preparing the title page. If you receive no directions, the format described here will be acceptable. Use a separate sheet of paper for the title page. Centre the title in the upper middle of the sheet of paper. Capitalize the first word and all subsequent words except articles and prepositions, but do not type the entire title in capital letters. The title page should also provide your name, the course, your instructor's name, and the date. (Some instructors appreciate having this information in the upper or lower right-hand corner of the paper to make sorting easy.) The title page is not numbered, nor is it counted in the page numbering of the paper. See page 404 for a sample title page.

Outline   Do not submit your outline with your paper unless you are told to do so. If the outline is included, it comes immediately after the title page. Type the word *OUTLINE* in all capitals, and centre it at the top of the page. Skip three spaces and type the thesis sentence. Skip three more spaces and type the outline, using the format described in 52a. The outline is not counted in the page numbering of the paper, but if the outline is more than one page long, you can number pages after the first page in small Roman numerals. See page 405 for a sample outline.

Text and Footnotes   Follow the instructions given in Appendix F for typing or handwriting the text of the research paper. If you are required to use footnotes rather than references integrated within the text, follow the instructions in 55b for footnote reference numbers and footnotes. If you put all your footnotes on separate pages at the end of the paper, continue numbering these pages as if they were part of the text.

Bibliography   Type the word *BIBLIOGRAPHY* (or *REFERENCES* or *LIST OF REFERENCES* or *REFERENCES CONSULTED*) at the top of a separate sheet of paper. Follow the instructions in 55c for the format of the bibliographical entries. Include the bibliography in the numbering of the text. See the sample bibliography on page 419.

res
53g

Finishing Touches   After the paper has been clearly typed or written, proofread it carefully from title page through bibliography for typographical errors or any other errors that you may have missed in previous readings. Make minor corrections and changes in black ink, using the conventions and symbols given in Appendix F.

Unless your teacher tells you to do so, do not staple the pages of your research paper. Instead, use a large paper clip so that the reader can easily separate the pages to compare sections or consult the bibliography. Unless you are instructed differently, there is no need to invest in fancy covers or binders for your research paper.

Before turning in your research paper, be sure you have a good copy of it for yourself, preferably a photocopy or carbon copy of the final version. Instructors have been known to mislay papers!

res
53g

*[Alternate place for
identifying information]*

*Title centred,
important words
capitalized*

Sleep: The Unconquered Realm   *Brief but vivid title*

Carol Andrews

*Complete information
for easy identification*

Fnglish 101
Section R2
Mr. Griffin
November 14, 1984

Heading centred, all caps
Triple-spacing

OUTLINE

Sleep, seemingly one of the simplest of human activities is actually a very complex and still poorly understood phenomenon.

Thesis statement

   I. Reasons for sleep

      A. Adaptive theory

      B. Restorative theory

  II. Quality of sleep

      A. Variations in sleep length

      B. Average amounts of sleep

 III. Components of sleep

      A. Non-REM states of sleep

      B. The REM stage of sleep

          1. Memory-consolidation theory

          2. Stress-assimilation theory

          3. Brain-development theory

      C. Chemistry of sleep

          1. The prior-sleep effect

          2. Neurochemicals and sedatives

  IV. Loss of sleep

      A. Physiological effects

      B. Emotional and mental effects

   V. The importance of continued research

Topic outline. Entries at the same level are parallel

Roman numerals aligned on final digit to allow for uniform spacing

*Three brief anecdotes attract the
reader's interest. No documentation
is needed because the author invented
the examples herself.*

*Identification of author on
every page after the title page*

Carol Andrews, 1

It is 4 a.m., and for the fourth consecutive night
Matthew Schneider, business executive, has been lying in
his bed counting sheep, trying frantically for five
hours to fall asleep. Matthew, who has become grouchy
and moody, has begun to fear that his loss of sleep will
drastically affect his on-the-job performance.

Mary Smith, a first-year elementary school teacher,
works hard all day with her thirty-two children, and in
the evening she plays tennis and swims. Mary, however,
never goes to bed until at least 2 a.m., always rising
at 6 a.m. sharp. She feels healthy and happy, but
lately friends have told her that her irreverence for a
proper night's sleep is shortening her life and dulling
her mind. No matter how hard she tries, though, after
four hours of sleep--even on the weekends--Mary simply
has to get out of bed.

Mr. and Mrs. Abe Kleitmann are the parents of a
lively three-year-old daughter, Jessica, who will not
sleep more than five hours at night. Repeatedly told
that children must have a lot of sleep, the Kleitmanns
are beginning to fear that Jessica is not normal.

Transition to the
specific topic These hypothetical cases, typical of those flowing
into sleep clinics springing up across North America,
are like experiences we all have had or like those we
have heard others describe. Sleep, in short, affects us
all. Most of us give up seven or eight hours a   *Well-known fact*
                                                      needs no
day--roughly a third of our lives--to sleep, and we *documentation.*
think very little about it unless it becomes a problem.

Carol Andrews, 2

Sleep is, however, a major problem for many. Wilse
Webb, one of the foremost sleep researchers, reports
that about 14 per cent of the population, or about one
person in seven, suffers sleep disorders (<u>Sleep</u> 114-15);
some estimates are higher (Lesley). A survey done in
the United States in 1977 showed sleep disorders to be
especially troublesome for "blacks, women, poor people,
the elderly, and those who were divorced, widowed, or
separated" (Gaylin 101). Clearly, large portions of the
population are troubled by sleep disorders, but available treatment is handicapped by the riddles of sleep
research, a study that has flourished only in the last
twenty years. Although the sheer abundance of current
information conveys the impression that science is
standing on the threshold of discoveries that would
affect millions of lives, sleep research is still a
giant maze of conflicting hypotheses and speculations.
Indeed, understanding sleep remains one of our most
challenging frontiers.

There are two central theories that attempt to
explain why human beings sleep: the adaptive theory and
the restorative theory. The adaptive theory claims that
our need for sleep results from evolution. Webb
theorizes that over millions of years each species
evolved the sleep pattern that best enabled it to
survive. His hypothesis is simply that "sleep . . .
evolved in each species as a form of 'non-behavior' when
<u>not</u> responding in the environment would increase

*Sources
indicated
in full
parentheses;
details in
bibliography*

Thesis

Part I of outline

*Part I.A
of outline*

*Use of ellipsis
for omitted material*

Carol Andrews, 3

survival chances" (Webb, _Sleep_ 158-59). The   *Title included*
                                                                   because
differences between the sleep patterns of various   *references*
                                                                   include more
species do not seem to depend on physiological   *than one work*
processes but reflect the species' needs for safety.   *by Webb*

A lion, which does not fear many other animals, may

sleep soundly sixteen hours a day, but a gazelle, prey

for many beasts, is a short, light sleeper (Scarf 86).

Prehistoric humans would have found it safer to sleep,

particularly in the dark nights not lighted up with

electric bulbs and neon signs, than to prowl in harm's

way.

Transition to Part   The adaptive theory is interesting and convincing
I.B of outline

in many ways, but it does not explain adequately why

people today with their twenty-four-hour lighting and

sophisticated methods of obtaining food and fighting off

predators have not evolved a sleep pattern of one or two

hours per night. If sleep is not restorative but is

simply an evolutionary result, why do modern human

beings need to sleep at all? Will our descendants,

continuing the evolutionary process, need less sleep

than we?

I.B   Ernest Hartmann, on the other hand, believes that

"sleep basically has a restorative function, in

accordance with our own commonsense notions" (145). He

believes that sleep consolidates disruptive, stressful

events of the days into a person's normal emotional and

learning systems, especially since it is clear that most

people do require more deep sleep and dream-sleep after

Notice that, throughout the paper, the author combines information from several sources within a single paragraph.

Carol Andrews, 4

stressful experiences or strenuous learning experiences

(147). Although tests with sleep deprivation bear out

some of Hartmann's theories, the hypothesis that sleep

Shortened book title underlined. Only the title needed in reference because Webb's name is given in the sentence

is basically restorative is problematic because, as Webb

states, "'what' is being diminished and, in turn,

'restored' has been so elusive that it has not been

specifiable" (<u>Sleep</u> 162-63). The only clear observation

is that the reasons we sleep are enormously complex.

A good deal of sleep research has been concerned

with pinpointing the amount of sleep a person needs.

Part II of outline

Although most young adults seem to need, or believe that

they need, six to eight hours of sleep per night,

II.A

scientists have found a great variation in the quantity

of sleep required by adults. For example, a husband

Development by use of examples

worried about his wife's habitual four-hour-per-night

sleeping pattern took her to a sleep clinic, where

doctors found her sleep "remarkably efficient" and

pronounced her very healthy. Doctors at the same clinic

examined a physics professor about fifty years old who

was concerned because he believed he needed to sleep at

least fourteen hours a night. They found that he was

absolutely correct in his assessment: he slept in nor-

mal patterns that stretched out over fourteen hours.

Cutting his sleep by even two hours left him tired

(Scarf 70). And, although older people generally do

not require as much sleep as young adults, some

astounding cases have been found of very old people who

hardly sleep at all, for example, a seventy-year-old

Carol Andrews, 5

physically sound woman who sleeps only one hour per
night (Webb, "On Sleep" 31).

Specific example   The story is also told--though it has not been
involving famous
person adds scientifically verified--of the artist Salvador Dali's
interest
famous method of sleep. Dali reportedly sits in a
chair, holding a spoon over a tin plate that he has
situated beside the chair. He relaxes. As he falls
asleep, the spoon drops from his hand, banging against
the tin plate and waking him. He says that the sleep he
gets in the very tiny interval that passes between the
time the spoon falls and the time it strikes the tin is
enough for him (Dement 5).

II.B. Note use of   How much sleep is normal? The amount of time a
question as
transition. human being needs to sleep may well be hereditary,
although such factors as prenatal care, illness,
nutrition, and environment play a role in determining
the necessary quantity of sleep (Webb, Sleep 66). Even
though most people seem to require about the same amount
of sleep (something close to the proverbial eight hours),
~~hours)~~ scientists agree that each person's requirement   *Correction*
of error
for sleep is individual. What they do not agree on is   *caught in*
proofreading
whether great variations in the quantity of sleep
reflect basic differences in personality and intelligence.

On the basis of two studies in his laboratories,   *Quotation*
blended into
Webb believes that sleep length shows "no more
the author's
difference in people than big or little ears," that it *own sentence*
shows no basic difference in intelligence or personality

Carol Andrews, 6

Article title in quotations or physical well-being (Webb, "On Sleep" 31). Dr. Hartmann maintains, however, that there are basic differences between short and long sleepers. Those who need more sleep tend to be more neurotic and depressed and under greater stress than the shorter sleepers, who seem more vivacious, self-confident, and aggressive. The longer sleepers, though worriers, tend to be more creative, less conventional thinkers than short

Because the author uses Hartmann's name, she does not need to repeat it in parentheses. sleepers. However, Hartmann admits that it is not clear whether the sleep pattern produces the personality or whether the personality requires the particular sleep pattern. He is convinced only that there is a correlation between the quantity of sleep and certain traits (65-68).

Part III of outline How we sleep--that is, the individual phases that make up a night's sleep--is one of the few noncontroversial areas of sleep research, but scientists do not know exactly why or how a person falls asleep. Even the electroencephalogram (EEG), which is used to chart the brain waves that reveal sleep patterns, cannot show the *III.A* precise instant when sleep begins (Dement 27). Once it has begun, however, normal sleep is made up of five distinct stages, which recur during the night in cycles of about ninety minutes. The normal sleeper passes fairly quickly through Stage-1 and Stage-2 sleep (light sleep phases differing in the kinds of brain waves) into the transitional Stage-3 sleep and into the intense, deep sleep of Stage 4. From Stage 4, or Deep Sleep as

This paragraph is rather long and could
easily have been made into two paragraphs.   Carol Andrews, 7

it is often called, the sleeper passes again through
Stage-1, Stage-2, and Stage-3 sleep into Stage-4, rarely
skipping a stage but changing stages about thirty-five   *No comma*
times (Webb, Sleep 26). After he or she has passed   *between page*
                                                                number
through the sleep stages once, however, this sequence is   *and source*
interrupted regularly--often at the end of Stage 2--by a
separate and very puzzling stage called Rapid Eye
Movement sleep, or REM sleep, so called because it is
characterized by bursts of eye movements along with
brain waves somewhat like those of Stage-1 sleep. Until
III.B this REM sleep was first observed in 1952 by Nathaniel
Kleitman and Eugene Aserinsky, sleep was thought to be a
process from waking to intense, deep sleep and back to
waking. Now, however, it is obvious that sleep is
cyclic (Hartmann 23). Most people follow this basic
sequence of stages, but no two people sleep in exactly
the same pattern.

Transition to The discovery of REM sleep revolutionized sleep
III.B.1 research. Studying the correlation of REM sleep and
dreaming has led to numerous hypotheses about the
significance and function of both REM sleep and
dreaming. Many of the theories that attempt to explain
the function of REM sleep claim that it is a necessary   *III.B.1*
tool for the consolidation of new material into long-
term memory. Dr. Peter Hauri, director of the Dartmouth
Sleep Laboratory at Hanover, New Hampshire, and Boston
researchers Chester Pearlman and Ramon Greenberg are   *III.B.2*
among the scientists who claim that REM sleep not only

One parenthesis contains two source references, separated by a semicolon.

aids memory but also allows the individual to absorb the stressful experiences suffered during the day (Scarf 81, 84; "Sleep for the Memory" 39).

On the other hand, Webb and William C. Dement, among others, find that REM sleep does not seem to aid memory at all. Webb finds that extreme deprivation of REM sleep has little effect on the individual (Sleep 154). Dement, whose first (and now largely disproved) theory about REM sleep was that it was a psychological stabilizer the loss of which caused emotional distur-

Reference in middle of sentence because final part of sentence is from a different source

bances (Scarf 81), has recently speculated that "perhaps REM sleep is necessary for the normal pre- and post-natal maturation of the brain" and its real function is served long before we become adults (Dement 31). In short, the precise function of REM--like so many other questions about sleep--continues to baffle researchers.

One particularly interesting recent discovery with regard to sleep and memory is the Prior-Sleep Effect, a phenomenon that suggests that certain sleep is detrimental to the memory. The Prior-Sleep Effect has shown that up to four hours of sleep just before learning has a detrimental effect on long-term memory. Even as little as one-half hour of sleep just before hitting the books is harmful to a student's memory. If the student sleeps as much as six hours before attempting to study, he or she will be more successful at remembering. Bruce Ekstrand and his co-workers, although convinced that "sleep facilitates memory"

III.B.3

III.C

III.C.1

Carol Andrews, 9

(419), have found that "four hours sleep prior to
learning resulted in more forgetting than no sleep prior
to learning" (431). The Prior-Sleep Effect does not,
however, affect short-term memory. Thus a student may
be able to learn enough information after three hours
sleep to pass a midterm test, but when final exams roll
around in a couple of months, he or she will have to
re-memorize the information.

III.C.2   Ekstrand and his team speculate that the Prior-
Sleep Effect is caused by the gradual buildup in the
brain of a chemical that blocks the integration of
information from the short-term memory into the
long-term memory. They believe that the chemical
subsides when a person wakes, gradually diminishing to *Correction*
allow the memory to function (435). This chemical, a *of error*
hormone called somatotrophin, has recently been found *caught in*
proofreading
to increase in the sleeper's body, beginning within a
half-hour after he or she falls asleep. Though the
hormone level diminishes toward the end of the night, it
is high during the first four hours of sleep (Hoddes
69).

Somatotrophin, which may account for the Prior-
Sleep Effect, is not the only body chemical that plays
an important role in sleep. The neurochemical seroronin
is now believed to be somewhat responsible both for the
onset of sleep and for Stage-4 sleep, and the chemical
norepinephrine may help to bring about REM sleep.
Sleeping pills of all kinds, though they do produce

Carol Andrews, 10

some phases of sleep, interfere with these chemicals and

other brain chemistry, upsetting regular sleep stages

(Scarf 77). There is, however, a natural sedative built

into certain foods, a sedative that is compatible with

these neurochemicals. This sedative, tryptaphane, is

found in milk, eggs, and meat. Its presence accounts

for the sleepiness we often feel after a big meal or

after the glass of warm milk that we may drink to help

us sleep (Scarf 69).

Part IV
of outline.   But what happens to a person who is deprived of all
Question sleep or deprived of all REM sleep or all Stage-4
is again
used for sleep? Experimenters have found some surprising data
transition about the effects of sleep deprivation. Though we

always feel terrible--and irritable--when we do not get

what we believe to be our proper amount of sleep, a lot

of our tired, grouchy attitude may result from our

expectations, for.   *Treatment of long quotation.*
                                            Note that it is typed to
                                            right-hand margin.

Indentation of   total wakefulness over a two- or three-day
ten spaces   period has no known harmful effects. . . .

Attention span, reaction time, and complex

decision making may be somewhat impaired, but
                                            Citation for indented
the major debilitating factor is related to *quotation follows the*

worry about not having slept. (Cohen 875) *final period.*

Triple-space between
quotation and Early sleep researchers doubtless believed that the   *IV.A*
text
loss of sleep was physically harmful because, in the

first sleep deprivation experiment conducted in 1894 by

Marie de Manaceine, puppies deprived of all sleep died

Carol Andrews, 11

after four to six days (Dement 5). Not only do human

beings not die when deprived of sleep, but the physio-   *Hyphenation of*
long words at
logical changes in a sleep-deprived person are few and   *ends of lines*

fairly insignificant, though after five days of sleep

IV.B   loss, emotional changes are noted (Webb, <u>Sleep</u> 123,

133). A sleep-deprived person can do well at almost any

brief laboratory test, although motivation is a crucial

problem, and performance on more complicated tasks may

be impaired.

Lengthy quotation   . . . the general conclusion about performance
begins with ellipsis
because first part   seems to be that highly motivated subjects can
of sentence has
been omitted   perform almost any task that requires a short-

term effort. On the other hand, sustained

periods of performance will typically show

deterioration, particularly if they are

Quotation marks   routine or "dull." Two major exceptions seem
within an indented
quotation   to be tasks that require rapid and complex

reaction time and short-term memory tasks.

These latter involve such things as listening

to a series of digits and immediately

recalling them. (Webb, <u>Sleep</u> 126-27)

If we are reasonably efficient when we do not sleep

and if our bodies do not suffer serious harm when

deprived of sleep, why then do we feel sleepy? Why do

we waste a third of our lives sleeping? Dement believes

that the time a person spends in sleep is "the depressed

phase of his circadian rhythm," that is, the cyclic,

rhythmic movement that permeates all things--the planets, the tides, the seasons, and all of life (18-19). This theory may account for the poorer performance of sleep-deprived persons who carry out tasks during periods when they normally would sleep. Webb observes that outside the laboratory, this decreased efficiency during the individual's normal sleeping time is evidenced in industry's need to provide more intensive quality control and more safety checks for those workers who rotate to the odd-hour shifts (<u>Sleep</u> 47, 134).

Part V of outline   Understanding how we sleep and why is obviously an enormously complex challenge that cuts across physiological, psychological, and biochemical research. Scientists are turning up more and more questions about *Conclusion raises unanswered questions about sleep* the extent to which sleep affects everyone. Can sleep deprivation be used to treat mental disorders? (Bhanji 540-41). To what degree are physical illnesses responsible for sleep disorders, and vice versa? Do sleep problems cause mental disorders? Sleep research has even entered the realm of the law. In 1961 after a British case in which an American soldier was acquitted of the murder of his girlfriend on the grounds that he was asleep when he killed her, the House of Lords debated whether the verdict in such cases should henceforth be "guilty, but asleep" (Casady 83).

To most of humanity, sleep seems a simple thing. In 335 B.C. Aristotle wrote, "When they are asleep you cannot tell a good man from a bad one, whence the saying

that for half their lives there is no difference between

the happy and the miserable" (quoted in "Sleep and

Citation of
secondary Dreams" 6). On the one hand, sleep is the great
source

equalizer of men, a common denominator in a world of

expanding diversity and complexity. On the other hand,

however, even though sleep universally demands our time

and respect, we are only beginning to understand--in a

way that Aristotle did not--that sleep exacts its due

with incredible variety and intricacy among people, a

variety and intricacy that make sleep one of the great

puzzles of science.

                                    Paper ends with restatement of thesis

Carol Andrews, 14

BIBLIOGRAPHY

Triple-space

Bhanji, S. "Treatment of Depression by Sleep
    Deprivation." <u>Nursing Times</u> 73 (1977): 540-41.

Hanging   Casady, Margie. "The Sleepy Murderers." <u>Psychology</u>
indentation   <u>Today</u> Jan. 1976: 79, 83.
of 5 spaces Cohen, Sidney. "Sleep and Insomnia." <u>Journal of the</u>
        <u>American Medical Association</u> 236 (1976): 875-6.

Dement, William C. <u>Some Must Watch While Some Must</u>
    <u>Sleep</u>. San Francisco: Freeman, 1974.

Ekstrand, Bruce R. et al. "The Effect of Sleep on Human
Accents put   Long-Term Memory." <u>Neurobiology of Sleep and</u>
in by hand   <u>Memory</u>. Ed. René R. Drucker-Colen and James L.
        McGaugh. New York: Academic Press, 1977.

Gaylin, Jody. "Sleep: Tracking the Elusive Sandman."
    <u>Social Science and Medicine</u> 10; rpt. <u>Psychology</u>
    <u>Today</u> Apr. 1977: 101.

Hartmann, Ernest L. <u>The Functions of Sleep</u>. New Haven:
    Yale Univ. Press, 1973.

Hoddes, Eric. "Does Sleep Help You Study?" <u>Psychology</u>
    <u>Today</u> June 1977: 69.

Lesley, Wanda. "Forty Winks Puts Psyche in Gear." <u>The</u>
    <u>Greenville</u> [S.C.] <u>News and Greenville Piedmont</u>, 22
    Jan. 1978: C1.
No author given.
Item entered "Nature's Sleeping Pill?" <u>Newsweek</u> 13 Oct. 1975: 69.
according to
first word of Scarf, Maggie. "Oh For a Decent Night's Sleep!" <u>The</u>
title (no a, an   <u>New York Times Magazine</u> 21 Oct. 1973: 36-37, 67,
or the)   70, 72, 77-78, 81, 84, 86.

"Sleep and Dreams: Where Are You When the Lights Go
    Out?" <u>Harper's</u> Dec. 1974: 5-12, 109-13.

"Sleep for the Memory." <u>Time</u> 23 Aug. 1976: 39.

Ten typed   Webb, Wilse B. "On Sleep: The Long and the Short of
hyphens used   It." <u>The New York Times</u> 22 Aug. 1975: 31.
when there ----------. <u>Sleep: The Gentle Tyrant</u>. Englewood
is more than   Cliffs, N.J.: Prentice-Hall, 1975.
one entry
by single   Webb, Wilse B., and H. W. Agnew, Jr. <u>Sleep and Dreams</u>.
author   Dubuque, Iowa: Wm. C. Brown, 1973.

Sample page with footnotes instead of in-text references

Carol Andrews, 5

physically sound woman who sleeps only one hour per
night.[1]

The story is also told--though it has not been
scientifically verified--of the artist Salvador Dali's
famous method of sleep. Dali reportedly sits in a
chair, holding a spoon over a tin plate that he has
situated beside the chair. He relaxes. As he falls
asleep, the spoon drops from his hand, banging against
the tin plate and waking him. He says that the sleep he
gets in the very tiny interval that passes between the

Raised time the spoon falls and the time it strikes the tin is
footnote
number enough for him.[2]

How much sleep is normal? The amount of time a
human being needs to sleep may well be hereditary,
although such factors as prenatal care, illness, nutrition, and environment play a role in determining the
necessary quantity of sleep.[3] Even though most people
seem to require about the same amount of sleep (something close to the proverbial eight hours), scientists
agree that each person's requirement for sleep is
individual. What they do not agree on is whether great
variations in the quantity of sleep reflect basic
differences in personality and intelligence.

First references to texts. For treatment of subsequent   *Quadruple-spacing between*
references, see 55a.   *text and first footnote*

5-space   [1] Wilse B. Webb, "On Sleep: The Long and the Short   *Single-spaced*
indentation   of It," The New York Times 22 Aug. 1975: 31.   *footnotes*

                  [2] William C. Dement, Some Must Watch While Some
                 Must Sleep (San Francisco: Freeman, 1974), 5.   *Double-spacing*
                                                                           between
                  [3] Wilse B. Webb, Sleep: The Gentle Tyrant   *footnotes*
                 (Englewood Cliffs, N.J.: Prentice-Hall, 1975), 66.

54 The Library

Because people have accumulated so much information of so many different types over the past few thousand years, libraries are necessarily complex. Further, no two libraries are exactly alike in their holdings, in their physical layout, or in their regulations and procedures. Consequently, the thought of using a library often frightens people. When they finally do venture inside, they sometimes waste their time wandering aimlessly around because they do not know how to get the information they want. This fear of the library is not unreasonable—after all, major libraries *are* intimidating places. But they are not as confusing as they seem at first glance. Standardized procedures for storing and retrieving information are common to almost all libraries, and once you have learned how to use one library, you will know how to use other libraries as well.

Familiarize yourself with the library system as soon as possible after you arrival at school; do not wait until you are forced to use its resources to write a paper. Many libraries offer guided tours to acquaint users with the library's layout and procedures. Free maps of and pamphlets about the library are often available. If you cannot go on an official tour, take your own informal tour and locate the card catalogue, the stacks, and the various reading rooms. Ask an attendant about the borrowing rules and the hours during which the circulation desk and the library as a whole are open (they may not be the same). Find out where the reference room and the reference librarian are located. Ask whether there are also branch libraries and, if there are, where they are located.

The library has much to offer you in addition to the books and periodicals you need to write a research paper for an English class. For example, most libraries have quiet reading rooms to which you can escape from a boisterous roommate. If you find your textbook for a course incomplete or confusing, the library will have books on the same subject to supplement your own texts. Many libraries contain such facilities as typing rooms, copying machines, listening rooms for records, and special displays.

Almost every library has a card catalogue, usually located on the main floor, and stacks, the area where most of the books are stored. The card catalogue consists of rows of filing drawers that contain index cards listing all the books owned by the library. Your library may also have a microcatalogue, with microfiches instead of cards. (Many libraries now use computers to produce catalogues on microfiche—small plastic sheets with information which has been photographed on a greatly reduced scale. Reading these sheets requires a special microfiche reader to enlarge the information, whose format is similar to that used on cards. The microcatalogue and microfiche readers are found in the same part of the library as the card catalogue.)

Some libraries have open stacks, in which users locate their own books. Other libraries have closed stacks, and users request books they

res
54

want by giving the necessary information to an attendant, who then finds the books and delivers them.

The stacks normally contain books that circulate, that is, that can be taken out of the library. Some of the library's other holdings have restricted circulation. For example, current periodicals, books placed on reserve by instructors, reference books, special collections, and rare books usually must be read in the library. Libraries normally have special rooms in which to use these materials.

Once you have a general idea of the layout of your library, return to the card catalogue. It is the "brain" of the library, and an understanding of it is essential.

54a ▪ The Card Catalogue

Cards in the **card catalogue** may be printed, typewritten, or, occasionally, handwritten. Every card has a call number, usually at the top left corner of the card. All cards for the same book have the same call number, and this call number also appears on the spine of the book.

In Canada, most college and university libraries use the U.S. Library of Congress cataloguing system, following publications from the National Library in Ottawa to adapt it to Canadian needs. Under the Library of Congress system, a unique combination of letters and numbers identifies each book. The twenty-one major categories and important Canadian subcategories are:

A   General (reference works, collections of essays, pamphlets, and so on)
B   Philosophy, religion, and psychology
C   Sciences related to history
D   History, eastern hemisphere
E   History, American
F   History, western hemisphere
FC History, Canadian
G   Geography, anthropology, sport and games
H   Social sciences
J   Political science
K   Law
L   Education
M   Music
N   Fine arts
P   Language and literature
PS Canadian literature
Q   Science
R   Medicine
S   Agriculture and forestry
T   Engineering and technology
U   Military science
V   Naval science
Z   Bibliography and library science

An additional letter and the numbers after the first letter indicate further subdivisions of the categories. The letters *I, O, W, X,* and *Y* are not used in the Library of Congress system, but some libraries employ these letters to designate books held in special collections.

Numbers may vary slightly from one library to another. Books are occasionally misclassified because they have misleading titles, so the call number of a book is not always a reliable indicator of its contents. Finally, the contents of many books include two or more categories. You should not assume, for example, that every single book with geographical information will have a Library of Congress number beginning with *G*; it may have been classified as being primarily a book on history and therefore be catalogued under *C, D, E,* or *F.*

Some libraries, including most public libraries, use the Dewey Decimal system, rather than the Library of Congress system, for classifying and cataloguing their books. The two systems differ somewhat in groupings and, of course, in the numbers given books, but both achieve the same goal: a logical system of classification that aids librarians and library users in locating holdings.

If you will be frequenting a library that uses the Dewey Decimal System (such as one of the large metropolitan reference libraries), ask an attendant to explain the system to you. Spend some time making yourself familiar with the way it works.

Author, Title, and Subject Cards   In almost all libraries, every book owned by the library has an **author card,** a **title card,** and one or more **subject cards.** If the book has more than one author or has been translated, edited, or compiled by someone other than the original author, there are also cards for these other authors, translators, editors, or compilers. The author card is the main card; the other cards are duplicates of it, with the additional information added at the top of the card.

Some libraries have a separate catalogue for subject cards, but many libraries put author, title, and subject cards together in one large file. Every card is filed alphabetically according to the first line of written information on the card. That is, an author card is filed by the last name of the author, a title card by the first words of the title of the book, and a subject card by the name of the subject.

Because card catalogues contain so many thousands of cards and because author, title, and subject cards are usually all filed together, locating a specific card can sometimes be a problem if you do not understand the principles of alphabetization used by the library. Libraries vary somewhat in the details of their alphabetization rules, but the following principles are the most common.

**res
54a**

1. At the beginning of a title, the articles *A, An,* and *The* and their equivalents in other languages (French *Le,* German *Der*) are ignored in alphabetizing. Thus, the title card for the book *A History of Greece* will be filed under *History.* The words *von* and *de* as parts of personal names are also ignored if they are written as separate words from the rest of the name but are included if the name is written as one word. Hence, you

would look for Karl von Clausewitz under *C*, but for Cornelius Vanderbilt under *V*.

2. *Mc* is treated as if it were spelled *Mac*. Hence, *McIntosh, Angus* would precede *MacIntosh, Charles*, and both would precede *Mack, Laurence*. Other abbreviations are filed as if they were spelled out. For example, *U.N.* and *Dr.* are treated as if they were *United Nations* and *Doctor*, respectively.

3. Identical words have the order of (a) person, (b) place, and (c) title. Thus *Paris, Matthew* would precede *Paris, France*, which in turn would precede the card for the play *Paris Bound*.

4. When one author has many works, the titles of collected works come before the titles of individual works. Several editions of the same work are filed in chronological order. Books about an author follow books by an author.

5. Within a main subject heading, cards are filed alphabetically by author. For example, under the subject heading *Mythology—Greek*, Thomas Bulfinch's *Mythology* would come before Robert Graves' *The Greek Myths*.

6. Within subject headings, historical subdivisions are arranged chronologically.

Great Britain—History—Anglo-Saxon Period, 449–1066
Great Britain—History—Medieval Period, 1066–1485
Great Britain—History—Tudors, 1485–1603
Great Britain—History—Early Stuarts, 1603–1649

7. In most libraries, all alphabetization is word by word or "short words before long words" and hyphenated words are treated as two (or more) separate words. For example, *Con Man* would come before *Concise*, and *Mouth-to-Mouth* would come before *Mouthpiece* but after *Mouth Organ*.

When using the card catalogue, read all the information printed on the card. The list of subject cards for the book may reveal that the book does not contain the kind of information you want. The date may tell you that the book is too old for your purposes. The title may reveal that the book is not in English. If the card indicates that the book has a bibliography, you may find it useful in locating other sources of information on the same subject. The author card shown on page 425 illustrates the different types of information that can be found on a card in the card catalogue. Unfortunately, library cards, and especially subject cards, are often incomplete and cannot substitute for an examination of the book itself.

The numbers in the following list correspond to those on the page that follows.

1. The call number of the book according to the Library of Congress system. In many libraries, special symbols or abbreviations below the call number indicate that the book is in a branch library or a special collection. Other symbols indicate an oversized book that is on special

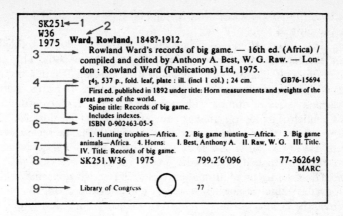

large shelves. If the library has more than one copy of the book, the number of copies owned may be indicated here.

2. The author's name, last name first. The author may be an organization or governmental agency. On many cards, the author's name is followed by the author's date of birth (and death if the author is not alive). On the sample card, the question mark after *1848* indicates that the date of Ward's birth is uncertain.

3. The title of the book and publication facts. The card tells us that the title is *Rowland Ward's Records of Big Game*, that it is the sixteenth edition of this book, that this edition was compiled and edited by Anthony A. Best and W. G. Raw, and that the book was published in London by Rowland Ward Publications Ltd. in 1975. The word *Publications* is in parentheses because, although it is part of the official name of the publisher, it does not appear on the book itself.

4. The collation or physical characteristics of the book. The collation includes such information as the number of pages, maps, illustrations, and the height of the book. If the book is one of a numbered series, the series name and number are listed here. On the sample card, [4] means that there are four preliminary pages; the brackets mean that these pages are not numbered. More typically, preliminary pages are numbered with small roman numerals. The words *fold, leaf, plate* mean that the book contains a folded page on which is an illustration of some kind. The entry *ill. (incl. 1 col.)* means that the book has illustrations, one of which is in color. *24 cm* indicates the height of the book.

The *GB76-15694* at the end of the line is the National Bibliography number of the book in Great Britain. It appears here because the description of the book is taken from the British card. Had the book been published in France, the letters *FR* would precede the numbers; had it been published in Germany, *GE* would precede, and so on.

5. Notes giving other information about the book. If the book is a reprint, a first edition, or a facsimile, this information is included. The notes also indicate whether the book has an index or a bibliography. The sample card tells us that the first edition had a different title from the

res
54a

current edition, that the title on the spine of the book is slightly different from the official title, and that the book has indexes.

6. The International Standard Book Number. Books published within the past few years have an ISBN printed in the book. This code number uniquely identifies the book and its publisher. The first number or set of numbers indicates the language of the text—0 means English. The second series of numbers identifies the publisher; for example all books published by Holt, Rinehart and Winston or its subsidiaries (such as Holt, Rinehart and Winston of Canada) have -03- as the second series of numbers in the ISBN. The sample book has a very long second series because it is published by a private press.

7. The tracings or additional entries under which the same book is catalogued. Arabic numbers list subject cards for the book, and roman numerals list second authors, sponsoring organizations, translators, the series name if the book is a member of a series, and so on. Roman numerals also indicate whether there is a title card for the book. The sample card lists two title cards, one for the official title and one for the title on the spine of the book.

8. Librarians' information. The first number is the Library of Congress number, the second the Dewey Decimal System number. The third number in this row is the order number for librarians to use when ordering additional cards from the Library of Congress.

9. Librarians' information. *Library of Congress* means that the book is in the Library of Congress. 77 means simply that the card was printed in 1977.

If your library has an open-stack system, it is a good idea to practise using the stacks by locating a book whose call number you have identified in the card catalogue. When you are looking for books on a specific subject for a research paper, you will of course use the card catalogue, but you should also go to the area of the stacks in which books on that subject are shelved. By browsing there, you will probably find several useful books on the subject that you previously had not known about.

Occasionally, you will need a book that your library does not own. If you are in a city with public libraries, check them for the book. Or you might ask the reference librarian to order the book for you from another library through an interlibrary loan service. Many university and college libraries in the same geographical area have microfiche copies of each others' catalogues. Many libraries have a copy of the *National Union Catalog*, which lists titles of books held in libraries across North America. Similarly, if you need to read an article in a periodical that is not listed in your library's card catalogue, the *Union Lists of Serials in Libraries of the United States and Canada* will tell you which libraries have this periodical. Periodicals normally cannot be borrowed through interlibrary loan, but you usually can obtain photocopies of particular articles through this service. If you plan to use interlibrary loan, be sure to make your request early; it will take a minimum of several days for the material to reach your library.

res
54a

54b • Periodical Indexes

If you are writing a paper on a current topic, you will want to consult recent magazine articles on the subject. Magazine articles cannot be located in the card catalogue because it lists only the title of periodicals and not the authors and titles of specific articles. Instead, you will need to consult a **periodical index**.

Periodical indexes are listings of articles published in newspapers, magazines, and journals. They appear on a regular schedule—monthly, bimonthly, or annually. Indexes often list articles within only a few weeks after publication. Most indexes are cumulated into larger quarterly, annual, or biennial volumes for easier use.

Periodical indexes are usually organized by subject areas and by authors. Within the subject areas, articles are listed alphabetically by title. Entries are heavily abbreviated to save space, so you will probably need to consult the material at the beginning of the index for an explanation of the abbreviations and of the method of organization. When you do not find a subject entry for the particular word you have in mind, try a synonym for that word. For instance, if you are looking for articles on roads and find no entry under "Roads," you should look under "Highways." If you cannot find an entry for a topic on which you are certain there have been recent articles, check other volumes of the periodical index; in fact, you will probably want to look at several volumes anyway to be sure you have located all the articles written over a period of several years.

After you have located the subject area in which you are interested, copy the information for the articles that seem promising. Then go to the card catalogue to see if your library has the periodicals. If it does, write down the call number of each periodical, including the number of the volume that you want. Current issues of periodicals are usually shelved by call numbers in a periodicals reading room. Older issues are bound into volumes and shelved in the stacks.

Most libraries restrict the circulation of periodicals. Current issues normally can be used only in the periodicals reading room. Back issues may have a limited circulation, such as one week, or they may have to be read in the library.

The best-known periodical index is the *Readers' Guide to Periodical Literature*, which indexes over 150 popular, nontechnical magazines like *Time, Fortune, Maclean's, The New Yorker,* and *Rolling Stone*. It appears once in February, July, and August, and twice in the other months. In addition, it is regularly cumulated into large volumes. *Readers' Guide* indexes only a few Canadian magazines, so you will have to consult the *Canadian Periodical Index* as well.

Suppose you are writing a paper on the Yukon's Mount Logan area and outdoor recreation, particularly skiing and climbing. You check *Readers' Guide* under "Logan" and find the following information:

res
54b

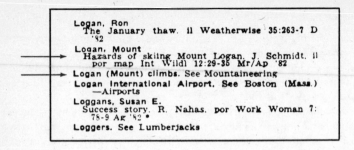

You would make a note of the article on ski hazards and then turn to "Mountaineering," where you find this information:

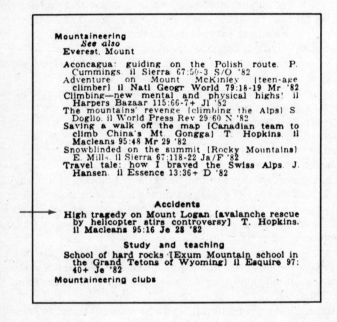

Because you are interested only in matters related to Mount Logan, you restrict your search to the article listed under "Accidents." The information in the square brackets indicates that this article may be less valuable for your purposes than the first one on ski hazards. When you consult the list of abbreviations at the beginning of this issue of *Readers' Guide*, you find that the Schmidt article, "Hazards of Skiing Mount Logan," appeared in *International Wildlife*, Volume 12, pages 29 to 35 of the March-April 1982 issue. It is illustrated, with pictures and maps.

If you had previously found a reference to an article by J. Schmidt on the subject of skiing, you could have looked in *Readers' Guide* under

"Schmidt" and have found the same information, but with the author's full name:

Schmidt, Helmut—*Continued*

about

Why spaceship Bonn crashed. T. Sommer. il por Newsweek 100:74 O 11 '82 •

Visit to France, 1982

A common front [meeting between H. Schmidt and F. Mitterrand] il pors Time 119:30 Mr 8 '82

Visit to the United States, 1982

Bitterness clouds a U.S.-German accord [Polish crisis] W. Lowther. il Macleans 95:28-9 Ja 18 '82

Secretary's news conference on Chancellor Schmidt's visit [press conference, January 6, 1982] A. M. Haig. por Dep State Bull 82:12-18 F '82

Visit of West German Chancellor Schmidt [joint statement, January 5, 1982] por Dep State Bull 82:12-13 F '82

Schmidt, Jeremy

Hazards of skiing Mount Logan. il por map Int Wildl 12:29-35 Mr/Ap '82

Schmidt, John

John Schmidt, founder of the first gay savings and loan, gives credit where credit is due. M. Wilhelm. il pors People Wkly 17:117-18 F 22 '82 •

Schmidt, Mike

An image in sharper focus. R. Fimrite. il pors Sports Illus 56:66-70+ My 31 '82 •

Schmidt, Peggy J.

Management-development courses. Work Woman 7:16+ Ag '82

At the beginning of the issue, *Readers' Guide* lists all the periodicals indexed, including cost of subscriptions and publishers' addresses. The entry for *International Wildlife* appears as follows:

The Humanist—$15. bi-m Humanist, 7 Harwood Dr, Amherst, NY 14226

International Wildlife—$10.50. bi-m National Wildlife Membership Services, 1412 16th St, NW, Washington, DC 20036

*Ladies' Home Journal—$17.97. m Ladies' Home Journal, P.O. Box 4565, Des Moines, IA 50340
Incorporating: Needle & Craft

Living for Young Homemakers. See House & Garden

The Living Wilderness—$20. q The Wilderness Society, 1901 Pennsylvania Ave, NW, Washington, DC 20006

**res
54b**

Readers' Guide also indexes current book reviews at the end of each issue, after the main author and subject index. This book review index is alphabetized by the last name of the author of the book being reviewed. The last item in the entry is the name of the reviewer.

```
Frye, N.  The great code
    America 147:96 Ag 21-28 '82. B. DePinto
    Christ Century 99:962-3 S 29 '82. J. P. Baum-
    gaertner
    Commentary 74:76-80 Ag '82. M. Fixler
    Commonweal 109:475-9 S 10 '82. J. D. Crossan
    Macleans 95:56 Ap 5 '82. J. Ayre
    N Y Rev Books 29:28-31 Ap 15 '82. J. M. Came-
    ron
    N Y Times Book Rev 87:10-11+ Ap 11 '82. H.
    Kenner
    New Repub 186:30-3 Je 9 '82. F. Kermode
    New Yorker 58:104-6 My 31 '82. N. Bliven
Fuentes, C.  Distant relations
    America 147:59 Jl 24-31 '82. R. Mahoney
    N Y Times Book Rev 87:3+ Mr 21 '82. G.
    Davenport
    Nation 234:57-8 Ja 16 '82. H. Koning
```

Useful as *Readers' Guide* is, it has some limitations, especially for Canadian students. It indexes only a few Canadian periodicals; as indicated previously, you should also consult *Canadian Periodical Index* for most topics. Also, *Readers' Guide* indexes only popular articles. Because these are usually not written by experts in the field, you will often want to consult more specialized indexes. The general format and the abbreviations used by most specialized indexes are similar to those of *Readers' Guide*. Suppose you were writing a paper on the decorated pottery of Corinth, Greece. You would find no entry for this in *Readers' Guide*, but if you consult *Art Index*, you might find the following article by I. McPhee about red-figured pottery excavated in Corinth:

```
CORINTH (Greece)
                    Antiquities
    Attribution  of  Corinthian  bronzes.  E.  G.
       Pemberton. bibl il Hesperia 50:101-11 Ap/Je
       '81
    City of Corinth and its domestic religion. C. K.
       Williams. bibl f il plans Hesperia 50:408-21
       O/D '81
    Classicizing  statue  in  ancient  Corinth.  M.  C.
       Sturgeon. bibl f il Am J Archaeol 86:219-26
       Ap '82
    Coins and amphoras—Chios, Samos and Thasos
       in the fifth century B.C.  H. B. Mattingly.
       bibl f il diags J Hell Stud 101:78-86 '81
    Corinthian developments in the study of trade in
       the fifth century. C. G. Loehler. bibl f il
       Hesperia 50:449-58 O/D '81
    Red-figured pottery from Corinth: Sacred Spring
       and elsewhere [with catalog] I. McPhee. bibl
       f il diag Hesperia 50:264-84 Jl/S '81
    Sculpture from Corinth. B. S. Ridgeay. bibl f il
       Hesperia 50:422-48 O/D '81
    Stoneworking in the Geometric period at Corinth.
       A. C. Brookes. bibl f il Hesperia 50:285-90
       Jl/S '81
CORINTH (Greece). Gymnasium
    Coin  hoards  from  the  Gymnasium  area  at
       Corinth [with catalog] J. A. Dengate. bibl
       il tabs Hesperia 50:147-88 Ap/Je '81
```

res
54b

This entry tells you that the title of the article is "Red-Figured Pottery from Corinth: The Sacred Spring and Elsewhere." It appeared on pages 449–58 of volume 50 of *Hesperia* in the July-September 1981 issue. The entry also tells you that the article has bibliographical footnotes (which will list other sources of information), illustrations, diagrams, and a catalogue.

54c ▪ Special Resources

Because they lack space for storing printed materials, today's libraries are relying more and more on microfilm and microfiche. Especially for older works, printed copies are often not available, so if the library is to contain these works at all, they must be on film. Each library has its own procedures for the use of materials stored on microfilm and microfiche. If you need to use these materials, ask an attendant to explain the procedure to you.

Most libraries also have special ways of classifying and storing government documents. Again, if you need access to government documents, check with a librarian.

An important source of Canadian data on an enormous variety of subjects is Statistics Canada. Your library has some of its publications and can obtain others. In addition, you can contact StatCan yourself; it maintains inquiry offices in ten Canadian cities and offers toll-free telephone service to all other areas of the country (check your telephone book). Staff members answer questions or direct you to appropriate publications.

Many other government offices, federal and provincial, will respond to student's inquiries (again, your telephone book can be an invaluable aid). So will many large companies and nonprofit organizations.

54d ▪ Reference Books

The reference room of the library is a good starting point for a research paper, particularly if you know relatively little about your subject when you begin your research. Most reference books do not circulate, so plan to use reference works in the reference room.

The names of the various types of reference works are not always self-explanatory, and sometimes terms used in library science have specialized meanings different from their everyday meanings. The following are among the most common terms for types of reference works.

Abstracts are brief summaries of articles or books in a particular field. By reading an abstract, you can often decide whether or not it is worth your while to find and read the full article or book. All major fields publish abstracts; examples include *Abstracts of English Studies*, *Astronomy and Astrophysics Abstracts*, and *Religious and Theological Abstracts*.

Almanacs are regularly published compilations of basic statistical information about politics, geography, education, sports, entertainment, and so on. They usually include useful tables of measures, world records, production figures, current events, and other miscellaneous subjects. Almanacs are particularly helpful for checking specific facts such as the date a treaty was signed, the names and titles of cabinet members in a given year, or the height of a particular mountain. Among the best-known almanacs are *The Canadian Almanac and Directory, Information Please Almanac, Facts on File,* and *World Almanac and Book of Facts.*

Atlases are books of maps or other illustrations. They usually include supplementary information on climate, population, natural resources, and the like. Atlases are not restricted to maps of geographical areas. There are, for instance, atlases of anatomy, historical events, and mineralogy. Examples include *Times Atlas of the World, Atlas of the Universe,* and *Oxford Regional Economic Atlas of the United States and Canada.*

Bibliographies are lists of sources of information. They normally include the names of authors, the titles of books or articles, and the publishers of the books or articles. Bibliographies may be very general or highly specialized. They may be mere listings, or they may be annotated (that is, they may include a description or evaluation of the contents). Most fields regularly publish bibliographies. Three of the many important ones are *MLA International Bibliography* (literature), *International Bibliography of Sociology,* and *Bibliography of North American Geology.*

Catalogues are complete lists of things, such as books on particular subjects or holdings in an art collection. They often contain brief notes explaining the listings. An example of a specialized catalogue is *Fiction Catalogue.* A more comprehensive one is *The National Union Catalog,* which lists all books known to exist in U.S. libraries.

Companions are small encyclopedias on a specific subject. Of particular interest are the Oxford Companions on many subjects in the humanities, social sciences, and fine arts. Examples are *Sandys' Companion to Latin Studies, Oxford Companion to Canadian History and Literature,* and *Oxford Companion to Film.*

Concordances list all the important words in a work or works of major authors. The words are cross-referenced to the passages in which they appear. For example, one important concordance is *The Harvard Concordance to Shakespeare.*

Dictionaries are alphabetically listed words or names with definitions or descriptions. Dictionaries may be general (for example, *Webster's Third New International Dictionary)* or specific to a foreign language or particular subject such as medicine, biology, electronics, art, or biography. A few examples are *Dictionary of Newfoundland English, McGraw-Hill Dictionary of Modern Economics, Aviation and Space Dictionary,* and *Dictionary of Canadian Biography.*

Directories are lists of names. These may be the names of persons, organizations, or publications. A directory usually includes not only the names but also addresses and other pertinent information. Some important directories are *Ulrich's International Periodicals Directory*, *American Art Directory*, and *Canadian Who's Who*.

Encyclopedias are summaries of knowledge. They may be general, including all subjects, or restricted to a particular field. Usually, they consist of alphabetically arranged articles varying in length from a few lines to several pages. Because they normally contain only general knowledge in a field, they are most useful to the nonspecialist. Examples include *New Encyclopaedia Britannica*, *Encyclopedia of Philosophy*, and *Encyclopedia of the Biological Sciences*.

Gazetteers are dictionaries of geographical names, giving information on the size, location, date of founding, and so on, of places and geographical phenomena. A gazetteer may or may not include maps. Two large gazetteers are *Webster's New Geographical Dictionary* and *Columbia Lippincott Gazetteer of the World*.

Glossaries are lists of technical terms in a particular field with brief definitions of these terms. An example is Abrams' *Glossary of Literary Terms*.

Handbooks are compact reference books for specific fields, providing information about important terms, formulas, persons, and the like in that field. They are similar to encyclopedias but are shorter and more specialized than most encyclopedias. Two examples are *Handbook of Chemistry and Physics* and *The Historian's Handbook: A Descriptive Guide to Reference Works*.

Indexes are descriptive lists of items in a collection of some type. The most common kind of index used by students is the periodicals index, which lists articles published in periodicals and newspapers. A few examples are *Canadian Periodical Index*, *Song Index*, *Applied Science and Technology Index*, *Social Sciences Index*, and *Education Index*.

Yearbooks are annual compilations of statistics from the preceding year. General yearbooks are often similar to almanacs (e.g. *Canada Year Book*), but specialized yearbooks concentrate on the occurrences in a particular field. Among the many yearbooks in various fields are *Current Biography Yearbook*, *International Yearbook of Education*, and *Yearbook of Comparative and General Literature*.

55 🦉 Documentation

Documentation is written acknowledgement of the sources of information used in the preparation of a paper. These are usually written sources but may also include oral sources such as recordings, interviews, or television programs. Careful, complete, and accurate documentation is essential to avoid taking the ideas and words of others and representing them as one's own. Documentation also shows that the writer has investigated the topic thoroughly, allows the reader to evaluate the sources of information, and, indirectly, reveals original contribution to the topic.

Over the years, writers in various disciplines have developed several systems for presenting documentation. The two that students are most likely to encounter are footnotes and in-text references.

Footnotes, which are used to provide the reader with several kinds of information additional to the text, are the traditional form of documentation. In the text, a number, raised above the line, signals the reader to look for a footnote pertaining to that part of the text. If the corresponding footnote is the first documentation of a work, it describes that work completely, giving the name of the author, the title of the work, and the full facts of publication, as well as any pertinent page numbers. Footnotes for subsequent references to the same work identify it more briefly; the reader looks for the details in the first note or in the **bibliography**, the complete list of references that is at the back of any research paper.

In-text references are a new form of documentation, but physical and social scientists have used them for decades, and they are becoming increasingly popular in other disciplines. In this system, the writer puts a brief citation (for example, the author's last name, a shortened title, and the relevant page numbers) parenthetically in the text; for full details, the reader refers to the bibliography. This practice reduces the number of footnotes and thus provides fewer distractions for the reader. It is also less work than footnotes for the typist or printer's compositor. For this reason, the most recent *MLA Handbook* recommends its use.

The sample research paper on pages 405 to 419 illustrates the in-text method of documentation. On page 420 is a representative page of the same paper with footnotes, rather than in-text references, so the two methods can be compared.

Students should be familiar with both systems of documentation because they will encounter both in their reading and because some instructors have a strong preference for one or the other. The two cannot be mixed (although in-text references are often combined with footnotes that are used for other purposes).

Both systems use bibliographies; in fact, the in-text system is, in effect, a system of cross-references to a bibliography. Because the mechanics of setting up bibliography entries are much like those of setting up documentation footnotes, the following sections describe the footnote system first and in somewhat more detail than the in-text system. However, we recommend in-text references to students whose instructors do not specify which system to follow.

res
55a

55a ▪ Footnotes

Footnotes are used for four purposes: (1) to cite sources of information, (2) to provide additional information or comments not suitable for inclusion in the text, (3) to direct the attention of the reader to other opinions, and (4) to refer the reader to other pages or sections of the text. Most students have occasion to use only the first two types of footnotes, source (or reference) notes, and, less often, comment (or substantive) notes.

When To Use Footnotes Comment or substantive notes are used when the writer wishes to add information not directly relevant to the text. This information may be further amplification, additional examples, or simply a digressive comment. Substantive notes should be used sparingly; if the information is important enough to be included at all, it probably should be incorporated into the text.

Reference notes should be used whenever information is borrowed from another source. All direct quotations must, of course, be acknowledged with a footnote, but indirect quotations, paraphrases, and summaries must also be footnoted. Even if you take only an isolated fact or a general idea from a source, that source must be documented. (See 53e, "Avoiding Plagiarism.") Whenever you quote directly from another source, even if it is only a few words, the quoted material must be enclosed in quotation marks. See 38 for the use of ellipses in omitting material from direct quotations; see 32 for the use of brackets to incorporate your own explanations into direct quotations.

Where To Put Footnotes All footnotes should be numbered consecutively throughout a paper, beginning with the number 1. Within the text of the paper, the footnote reference is a raised number placed at the *end* of the relevant words or sentence (or at the end of the quotation if you are quoting directly). Footnote reference numbers come after all punctuation except dashes.

The footnote itself should include the author's full name, the title of the publication, the facts of publication, and the page number or numbers on which the quotation or idea appears. Do not, however, repeat information already provided in the text of the paper. For example, if you give the author's full name in the text, it need not be repeated in the footnote.

Each footnote may be placed at the bottom of the page on which its reference number appears, or all notes may be put on one page at the end of the text. (Strictly speaking, notes that appear at the end are endnotes and not footnotes, but the term *footnote* is used to refer to both kinds of notes.) Either system has its advantages and disadvantages. Placing all the notes together at the end is easier for the typist but harder for readers, who must constantly shuffle pages if they want to consult the notes. Placing the notes at the bottom of the pages of text is easier for readers but presents spacing problems for the typist. Check with your instructor to find out which method of placement he or she prefers.

If you do place your footnotes at the bottom of the page, they should be separated from the text by a quadruple space (two double spaces). Each footnote should appear on the same page as its reference number, but the last footnote on a page may be continued on the following page, if

res

55a

necessary, by typing a solid line across the new page one full line below the last line of text, double-spacing twice, and continuing the note. Any footnote for the new page should follow immediately.

The first line of each footnote is indented five spaces. The footnote number is raised slightly (like the footnote reference number). Leave one space between the footnote number and the first word of the footnote. Footnotes should be single-spaced, with a double space between footnotes.

Form of Footnotes Different disciplines, publishing houses, and individuals follow slightly different conventions for the format of footnotes and bibliographies. The format presented here follows that of the previous edition of *MLA Handbook* (the most recent edition recommends in-text documentation). Follow the directions for documentation given by your instructor; if you receive no specific directions, the rules presented here will be acceptable. Completeness, clarity, and consistency are more important than specific details of format.

Books Always use the title page of a book as your source of documentation information because the information on the cover is often incomplete. If the date of publication is not on the title page, it can usually be found on the back of the title page. If the information on the title page is incomplete, you can often find it on the catalogue card for the book, where the missing information may appear in square brackets.

The basic information that every footnote reference to a book should include, in the following order, is:

1. **Author's Name.** The author's name is listed, first name first. The name is followed by a comma. If there are multiple authors, list their names in the order in which they appear on the title page, regardless of whether they are in alphabetical order. Degrees, titles, or affiliations that appear with the author's name on the title page are omitted in footnotes and bibliographies. Note that groups and organizations, as well as individuals, may be authors.

2. **Title of the Book.** The first word and all important words of the title are capitalized. The entire title is underlined. No punctuation follows the title if it is followed by information in parentheses. If the book has a subtitle, it is separated from the main title by a colon. Long subtitles may be omitted from footnotes but should be included in the bibliography. Short subtitles or subtitles that clarify the meaning of a vague main title should be included in both footnotes and bibliographies.

3. **Facts of Publication.** Facts of publication are put in parentheses. The city of publication is followed by a colon, then the name of the publisher, a comma, and the year of publication. If the publisher's name has been changed since the publication of the book, use the name as it appears in the book, not the current form of the name.

If the publisher's name is long, you may use an appropriately shortened form that eliminates unnecessary details such as "Publishing Co.,"

res
55a

"and Company Ltd.," and "Inc." (for example, *Scott, Foresman* instead of *Scott, Foresman and Company*). However, a university *press* must always be so designated, since a university may publish independently of the press (for example, many components of the University of Toronto publish studies, as does the University of Toronto Press). But it is not wrong to include the full name and, by doing so, you avoid having to decide what an appropriate shortened form would be. If the city of publication is not a familiar large city or if it could be confused with another city of the same name, add the name of the state or country of publication (for example, Don Mills, Ont. or Hillsdale, N.J.). The date of publication should be that of the *edition* used, not that of the latest *printing* of the book.

4. **Relevant Page Numbers.** Page numbers are followed by a period. For inclusive page numbers up through 99, write both numbers in full (for example, 27–29). For numbers over 99, only the last two digits need be given if the preceding digits are the same in the two numbers. For example, to indicate page 324 through page 359, write 324–59, but to indicate page 324 through page 417, write 324–417.

The footnotes reproduced here provide models for documenting many of the kinds of references you are likely to use in preparing a research paper. Section 55c gives the bibliographic listings for the same works and for various other kinds of references. Study the relationships between the two sets of examples. If you must footnote a type of reference not included in this section, you should be able to make appropriate adaptations to its bibliographic style. Above all, remember the need for clarity and completeness in all documentation.

Book with a Single Author

[1] Thomas Flanagan, <u>Riel and the Rebellion: 1885 Reconsidered</u> (Saskatoon: Western Producer Prairie, 1983), 94.

Book with Two or Three authors

[2] Wayne Barrett, Anne MacKay, and George MacBeath, <u>The St. John River Valley</u> (Toronto: Oxford University Press, 1981), 106–16.

Book with More Than Three Authors

[3] Richard G. Lipsey, et al., <u>Economics</u>, 4th ed. (New York: Harper and Row, 1982), 93.

Book with a Corporate Author

[4] Inter-Territorial Language Committee of the East African Dependencies, <u>A Standard Swahili-English Dictionary</u> (Oxford: Oxford University Press, 1939), 408.

res
55a

Book with a Translator

⁵ Shusako Endo, <u>The Samurai</u>, trans. Van C. Gessel (Toronto: Lester and Orpen Dennys, 1983), 73.

Article Collected in a Book

⁶ Dun Li, "The Taiping Rebellion," <u>China Yesterday and Today,</u> ed. Molly Joel Coye and Jon Livingston (New York: Bantam, 1975), 189.

Multivolume Book

⁷ Samuel Pepys, <u>The Diary of Samuel Pepys</u>, ed. Robert Latham and William Matthews, 11 vols. (Berkeley: University of California Press, 1970–83) 4: 154–55.

If a single book appears in several volumes, it is a courtesy to the reader to include the total number of volumes in the footnote, especially if all volumes are relevant. If the various volumes were printed in different years, the inclusive dates of publications are listed. The number of the volume actually being cited is then listed after the facts of publication with no intervening comma, followed by a colon and the page number or numbers from which the quotation is taken.

Book in a Series

⁸ C. L. Barber, et al., <u>Contributions to English Syntax and Philology</u>, Göteborg Studies in English No. 14 (Göteborg [Gothenburg]: University of Göteborg, 1962), 7.

Foreword, Preface, Introduction, and so on

⁹ Ira Dilworth, Foreword, <u>Klee Wyck</u>, by Emily Carr (Toronto: Clarke Irwin, 1971), [iv, ix].

Non-English Work

res
55a

¹⁰ Félix Leclerc, <u>Pieds nus dans l'aube</u> ("Barefoot in the dawn") (1946; rpt. Montréal: Fides, Bibliothèque canadienne-française, 1967), 103–4. My translation.

If you yourself have translated a direct quotation from a non-English work, your citation should say so. If the material is paraphrased or summarized, the language of the work's title shows the language you read it in. (Of course, if you read the work in translation, your documentation must be to the translated edition. See note 5 above.)

See 41f for the capitalization and translation of non-English titles.

Magazine Article

[11] Fred Bruning, "A Ticket to a Boring Sally Ride," Maclean's 25 July 1983:9.

Scholarly Journal Article

[12] Thomas R. Berger, "Conservation, Technology, and the Idea of Progress," Canadian Literature 96 (1983): 60–68.

Unsigned Newspaper Article

[13] "Tories Demand Ottawa Cease Tax on Artists," Edmonton Journal 12 Oct. 1983: A15.

Government Publication

[14] Statistics Canada, Business, Provincial and Municipal Relations Division, Index to Municipal Data 1982, cat. no. 11-515 (Ottawa: Supply and Services Canada, Apr. 1983), 129.

[15] Ontario Manpower Commission, Labour Market Research Group, Professional and Technical Manpower Requirements and Supplies in the Microelectronics Industry in Ontario: 1981–85 (Toronto: Ontario Ministry of Labour, 1981), table 9.

Publication with No Author or Editor Listed

[16] Discovering Britain (London: Drive, 1982), 43.

Publication without Page Numbers

[17] Richard Reece, Iona: Its History and Archeology (Glasgow: Iona Community Publishing Dept., n.d.), [4].

Secondary Source

Whenever possible, original sources should be used in preference to secondary sources. If the original publication is simply not available, give as much information about it as your secondary source lists, and also provide full information about your secondary source.

[17] Francis Bacon, Novum Organum, as quoted in Edward Burnett Taylor, The Origins of Culture (New York: Harper & Row, 1958), 136.

Subsequent References Subsequent footnote references to the same work are shortened by omitting at least the information on publication. Practice varies with respect to the amount of information given in shortened references. The easiest form of shortened reference includes only

res 55a

the author's last name and the appropriate page number or numbers. If the references include works by two authors with the same surname, use the full name of each author in subsequent references.

Full Form

[1] Thomas Flanagan, Riel and the Rebellion: 1885 Reconsidered (Saskatoon, Sask.: Western Producer Prairie, 1983), 94.

Shortened Form

[41] Flanagan 109.

If the work has more than one author, the last names of all authors listed in the first reference are included in subsequent references.

Full Form

[19] Kenneth Roberts and Philip Shackleton, The Canoe: A History of the Craft from Panama to the Arctic (Toronto: Macmillan, 1983), 246.

Shortened Form

[42] Roberts and Shackleton 197.

If a work has two authors (or editors) with the same surname or if you have references to two or more works by different authors with the same last names, use the full name of each author in subsequent references.

Full Form

[43] Margaret Howard Blom and Thomas E. Blom, ed. Canada Home: Juliana Horatia Ewing's Fredericton Letters 1867–1869. (Vancouver: University of British Columbia Press, 1983), 218.

Shortened Form

[44] Margaret Blom and Thomas Blom 126.

res
55a

An alternative form of shortened reference includes both the author's name and the title of the book or article. This form must be used if the references contain two or more works by the same author. If the title is more than five or six words long, it may be shortened, provided that the word order of the original is not changed.

Full form

[25] John Charles Marshall, "The Competitive Environment: Effects and Influences on the Young Athlete," diss. York Univ. 1980, 46.

Shortened Form

[45] Marshall, "The Competitive Environment," 49.

If the work has no author or editor, the shortened reference is to the title, which may be shortened as in the previous example.

Full Form

[8] "Trials and Tribulations of Victoria Synagogue Builders in 1863," Jewish Western Bulletin, 25 Sept. 1957: 6.

Shortened Form

[9] "Victoria Synagogue Builders" 80.

Subsequent References in Text If you quote one or two works extensively throughout a paper, the first footnote reference may note this fact, and subsequent references to page numbers may be made in the text itself, without footnotes. (Notice that this kind of documentation is similar to the in-text reference system described in 55b.)

First Reference

[46] Michel Tremblay, The Fat Women Next Door is Pregnant, trans. Sheila Fischman (Vancouver: Talonbooks, 1981), 86. All future references to this work appear in the text.

Subsequent Reference within Text

The fat woman wanted to "sit and look at the spring sunshine, instead of watching for its reflection in Madame Chagnon's window" (200).

Latin Abbreviations in Subsequent References The Latin abbreviations "ibid.," "op. cit.," and "loc. cit." were once popular for subsequent references. Though they are now considered superfluous, you will encounter them in your reading and should know their meanings.

res
55a

Ibid. (for *ibidem*, "in the same place") refers to an immediately preceding footnote. Neither the author's name nor the title of the work is given. The page number is given only if it differs from that of the preceding reference. (Ibid., p. 47.)

Op. cit. (for *opere citato*, "in the work cited") is used with the author's name and substitutes for the title of the work. (Tremblay, op. cit., p. 47.)

Loc. cit. (for *loco citato*, "in the place cited") is used only when referring to the same passage. It is also used with the author's name, but normally no page number is included. (Tremblay, loc. cit.)

Avoid these Latin abbreviations unless you are specifically asked to use them. Note that if used, they are no longer underlined or set italic.

55b ▪ In-Text References

An in-text reference system provides the reader with brief identification of sources within the text itself, leaving full documentation for the bibliography. Such a system has proved itself in the physical and social sciences because it is clear and uncluttered, involves no renumbering if the writer adds, deletes, or changes the order of material, and presents few difficulties for the typist. The *MLA Handbook* now recommends its use in the humanities.

When To Use References   In-text references are used whenever the writer has borrowed information from another source. Follow the rules about when to use documentation (see 53e, "Avoiding Plagiarism" and 55a "When To Use Footnotes").

The Form of In-Text References   The purpose of an in-text reference is to identify your source for readers, giving enough information for them to locate it in your bibliography. The basic form of an in-text reference is the same as that of the shortened footnote references illustrated on pages 440 to 441. You give the author's last name (or authors' last names) and any pertinent page numbers in parentheses at a logical point in the text.

The canoe's importance in early trade has been noted before (Roberts and Shackleton 116–25).

A whole book (Roberts and Shackleton) has been devoted to the history of the canoe.

If you use more than one book by the same author, you distinguish between them by adding shortened titles to the references. For example, if you are using Michel Tremblay's *The Fat Woman Next Door is Pregnant* and *Hosanna*, your in-text references might look like this:

(Tremblay Fat Woman 120)

(Tremblay Hosanna 86)

If a work has no author or editor listed, the in-text reference is to the title:

("Victoria Synagogue Builders" 80)

res
55b

Since one purpose of using in-text references is to avoid distractions for the reader, the information given in parentheses need not repeat any information already given in the text. For example, you might write:

```
Tremblay makes the point explicit (Fat Woman 120).
He repeats the theme in Hosanna (86).
```

The author's name appears in the first sentence here, so it need not be repeated in the parenthetical reference. In the context of the second example, *he* clearly refers to Tremblay as the author; the text also contains the name of the work. So you need give only the page reference in parentheses.

Sometimes you need no parenthetical reference at all:

```
Roberts and Shackleton have devoted an entire book
to the history of the canoe.
```

Assuming your references include no other work by these authors, the readers can find the bibliography entry with no additional information.

Occasionally you must add a word or two to your reference to make it clear.

```
(See Roberts and Shackleton 51)
(Tremblay Hosanna 85, my translation)
```

In general, the in-text parenthetical reference should contain only the information essential to identifying the work. If, however, you think the reader may miss the reference because it is very short (for example, a single page number in the middle of a paragraph), do not hesitate to repeat the author's name, the title, or both. Clarity is your primary consideration.

Integrating In-Text References Another important consideration with in-text references is introducing the documentation in such a way that it does not clutter your text and make your sentences hard to read. Some students find that learning how to integrate references into the text is as challenging as learning the technical points of writing footnotes. However, you can master the skill with practice.

The sample research paper on pages 404 to 419 provides some illustrations of integration. In your own work, keep the following points in mind:

1. Acknowledge your source briefly but clearly, letting the reader know exactly where you found the information.

2. Give the specific page number in parentheses as soon as possible after your use of the reference.

3. When you paraphrase or summarize, place the parenthetical reference so that it does not interrupt the syntax of your own sentences.

4. Just before preparing your final copy, check that your references make it absolutely clear what work each page number comes from. If it is not clear at any point, add the author's name, the title, or both. (For example, in the sample paper, see the references to the work by Hartmann and the two works by Webb.)

55c ▪ Bibliographies

The **bibliography** (or **list of references**) comes at the end of a work and lists, in alphabetical order, all the works cited in the footnotes or in the text. Some bibliographies also include other works consulted but not directly used in the preparation of the paper. (However, the MLA now urges that, in order to match the in-text method of documentation, the bibliography lists only those works cited.) Bibliographies are sometimes annotated: that is, they include after each entry a brief statement about the contents and the value of the work.

For very long research papers, the bibliography may be subdivided into primary and secondary sources. For example, the bibliography of a literary paper would include the works of the author under primary sources and criticism of those works under secondary sources. When a great many works have been consulted, the bibliogrpahy may be subdivided into separate lists for books and periodicals. For student research papers, one alphabetical list is usually sufficient.

Whether the documentation appears in in-text references or in footnotes, the format of the bibliography is the same. It is typed on a separate page or pages and placed at the end of the paper. If the footnotes also appear at the end of the paper, the bibliography follows them. The title "Bibliography" (or "List of References" or "Works Cited") is centred at the top of the page. Entries in the bibliography appear in alphabetical order by the last name of the author; the items are not numbered. If there is no known author, the entry is alphabetized by the first words of the title (excluding *A* and *The*). If the bibliography includes more than one work by the same author, the second and subsequent entries do not repeat the author's name. Instead, the name of the author is replaced by a long dash made by typing ten consecutive hyphens.

When a work is being prepared for publication, bibliographical entries are double-spaced, but for student papers, single-spacing with double spaces between entries is usually acceptable. Unlike footnotes, which have a paragraph indentation, bibliographical entries traditionally have a hanging indent; that is, the first line of the entry is at the left margin and subsequent lines of the same entry are indented five spaces.

A bibliographical entry includes the same information as a first footnote (see 55a). But the format differs slightly. The major differences are (1) the last name of the first author is listed before his or her given names, (2) periods separate the major parts of the entry, and (3) publication information is not enclosed in parentheses. Entries for entire shorter pieces (periodical articles or articles in a collection) include page numbers; entries for complete works (books, pamphlets) do not.

The examples provided earlier for footnotes are presented below in bibliographical form with some additions to illustrate other points. See page 419 for an illustration of a complete bibliography for a typed research paper.

Books The basic bibliographical information for a book is the author, the title, and the facts of publication—place, publisher, and date. Other information is added as necessary to identify the source or help the reader find it.

Book with a Single Author

Flanagan, Thomas. <u>Riel and the Rebellion: 1885 Reconsidered</u>. Saskatoon: Western Producer Prairie, 1983.

Book with Two Authors

Roberts, Kenneth, and Philip Shackleton. <u>The Canoe: A History of the Craft from Panama to the Arctic</u>. Toronto: Macmillan, 1983.

Book with Three Authors

Barrett, Wayne, Anne MacKay, and George MacBeath. <u>The St. John River Valley</u>. Toronto: Oxford University Press, 1981.

Book with More Than Three Authors

Lipsey, Richard G., et al. <u>Economics</u>. 4th ed. New York: Harper and Row, 1982.

Book with a Corporate Author

Inter-Territorial Language Committee of the East African Dependencies. <u>A Standard Swahili-English Dictionary.</u> Oxford: Oxford University Press, 1939.

Some works that have been written by a group, especially a government body, present a genuine choice of authors. For example, the government publication listed below by the Ontario Manpower Commission could equally well have been listed as written by Labour, Ontario Ministry of, or simply by Ontario. What is important is consistency, among citations and between citations and bibliography. Your readers will be confused if several publications from the Ontario Manpower Commission are listed in three different ways. And the point of in-text documentation is lost if your reference reads "Ontario" but your bibliography entry is alphabetized under L for "Labour."

res
55c

Books with a Translator

Endo, Shusako. <u>The Samurai</u>. trans. Van C. Gessel. Toronto: Lester and Orpen Dennys, 1983.

Book with an Editor

Hume, David. <u>Moral and Political Philosophy</u>. Ed.
    Henry D. Aiken. New York: Hafner, 1975.

Collection by One Author

Quirk, Randolph. ''Langland's Use of kind wit and
    inwit.'' <u>Essays on the English Language: Medieval
    and Modern</u>. Bloomington, Ind.: Indiana University
    Press, 1968. 20–26.

Collection by More than One Author

Li, Dun. ''The Taiping Rebellion.'' <u>China Yesterday and
    Today</u>. Ed. Molly Joel Coye and Jon Livingston.
    New York: Bantam, 1975. 189–93.

Multivolume Book

Pepys, Samuel. <u>The Diary of Samuel Pepys</u>. Ed. Robert
    Latham and William Matthews. 11 vols. Berkeley:
    University of California Press, 1970–83.

Multivolume Book, Separate Volume Title

Pelikan, Jaroslav. <u>The Growth of Medieval Theology
    (600–1300)</u>. Vol. 3 of <u>The Christian Tradition: A
    History of the Development of Doctrine</u>. Chicago:
    University of Chicago Press, 1980.

Non-English Work

Leclerc, Félix. <u>Pieds nus dans l'aube</u> (''Barefoot in the
    dawn''). 1946; rpt. Montréal: Fides, Bibliothèque
    canadienne-française, 1967.

Books in a Series

Barber, C. L., et al. <u>Contributions to English Syntax
    and Philosophy</u>. Göteborg Studies in English No. 14.
    Göteborg (Gothenburg): University of Göteborg, 1962.

If a book is published in a foreign city, use the spelling of the city's name
as it appears on the title or copyright page. In the example above, the
English spelling is given for readers who may be unfamiliar with the
Swedish spelling. If you do not know the spelling (e.g., Cologne/Koln;
Rome/Roma), look up the foreign spelling in a college dictionary; the
entry will list the English spelling.

Reprinted Book

Guillet, Edwin. <u>Pioneer Travel in Upper Canada</u>. 1933;
    rpt. Toronto: University of Toronto Press, 1972.

res

55c

Many paperback books are reprints of hardcover editions. The date of the hardcover edition is listed first, followed by a semicolon and the abbreviation *rpt*. Then the publication facts for the reprinted edition are given in regular form.

Subsequent Edition

Poucher, W. A.   The Scottish Peaks.   5th ed.   London:
Constable, 1979.

Foreword, Preface, Introduction, and so on

Dilworth, Ira.   Foreword.   Klee Wyck.   By Emily Carr.
Toronto: Clarke Irwin, 1971.

Articles in Reference Work

"Takuma School."   McGraw-Hill Dictionary of Art, 1969.

H[elmreich], E. C. "Imperialism."   Collier's Encyclopedia, 1957 ed.

If no author is listed, the first item in the citation is the title of the article. Do not use the abbreviation *anon*. If the article is signed by the author's initials, the full name of the author can usually be found at the beginning of the volume. The rest of the name is placed in square brackets in the citation, as in the example above.

Periodicals   The bibiographical format for periodicals differs from that for books in that (1) the title of the article as well as the title of the periodical is included, (2) no place of publication is listed, (3) month and even day of publication are given, and (4) for some types of periodicals, a volume number is included. The order of items and the punctuation of the entry are similar to that for books.

Weekly Magazine Article

Bruning, Fred.   "A Ticket to a Boring Sally Ride."
Maclean's 25 July 1983: 9.

Monthly Magazine Article

Jastrow, Robert.   "The Dinosaur Massacre: A Double-
Barreled Mystery."   Science Digest Sept. 1984:
50-53, 109.

Scholarly Journal Article

Berger, Thomas R.   "Conservation, Technology, and the
Idea of Progress."   Canadian Literature 96
(1983): 60-68.

res
55c

Scholarly journals usually have clearly displayed volume numbers, and pagination is continuous throughout all the issues of the one volume. Even though the volume number is sufficient to identify the year of publication, the year is placed in parentheses after the volume number as a convenience to the reader. The issue number may be shown separated from the volume number by a period.

```
Watson, William B. ''The Economics of Technology.''
    Policy Options / Options Politiques 4.2 (1983): 40-45.
```

Many Canadian journals have an English and a French title; giving both alerts the readers to the fact of bilingual publication. The language of the title of the article shows the language in which you read it.

Signed Newspaper Article

```
McDowell, Michael.  ''Jesuit from Salvador Describes
    Repression of Government Régime.''  The Globe and
    Mail, weekend ed. 15 Oct. 1983: 4, col. 1.
```

If the newspaper being quoted identifies the particular edition (for example, late edition, city edition, suburban edition), this information should be included in the entry because the contents of the various editions for one day's newspaper may vary. Inclusion of the column number for a short article will help the reader find the story more easily.

Unsigned Newspaper Article

```
''Tories Demand Ottawa Cease Tax on Artists.''  Edmon-
    ton Journal 12 Oct. 1983: A15.
```

Review

```
de Mott, Benjamin.  ''Domestic Stories.''  Rev. of The
    Moons of Jupiter, by Alice Munro.  The New York
    Times Book Review 20 Mar. 1983: 1, 26.
```

Unsigned reviews are treated exactly like signed reviews, except that the entry begins with the title of the review.

Editorial

```
Hutcheson, John.  ''To Love This Planet.'' Editorial.
    Canadian Forum 63.728 (1983): 4.
```

Letter to the Editor

```
Boivin, Pierre.  Letter.  Canadian Business Sept. 1983: 7.
```

Editorial

```
Hutcheson, John.  ''To Love This Planet.'' Editorial.
    Canadian Forum 63.728 (1983): 4-5.
```

res
55c

Other Sources of Information   Most of the information used in a research paper is normally taken from books or periodicals. You may, however, occasionally use other sources, including dissertations, pamphlets, government publications, conference proceedings, recordings, or legal references.

Unpublished Dissertation

Marshall, John Charles. "The Competitive Environment: Effects and Influences on the Young Athlete." Diss. York Univ. 1980.

A published dissertation is treated like any other book.

Interview or Other Personal Communication

MacDonald, Helen. Personal interview. 14 Feb. 1984.
Chari, Krisha. Letter to author. 15 Feb. 1984.

Pamphlet

Wells, Oliver Nelson. Salish Weaving: Primitive and Modern, as Practised by the Salish Indians of South West British Columbia. Rev. ed. Sardis, B.C.: Oliver Wells, 1969.

As this example shows, pamphlets are treated like books.

Government Publication

Statistics Canada. Business, Provincial and Municipal Relations Division. Index to Municipal Data 1982. Cat. no. 11-515. Ottawa: Supply and Services Canada, Apr. 1983.
Ontario Manpower Commission. Labour Market Research Group. Professional and Technical Manpower Requirements and Supplies in the Microelectronics Industry in Ontario: 1981-85. Toronto: Ontario Ministry of Labour, 1981.

The citation of government publications is complicated because so much information is involved. In listing the "author," put the name of the general division first, followed by subdivisions in descending order of size. The decision as to "who" to list as author is frequently arbitrary (for example, the examples above could have been listed as "Canada" and "Ontario" respectively). Try to treat similar bodies similarly (for example, in the same bibliography with the examples above, the author for another entry should be "Alberta Human Rights Commission," not simply "Alberta.")

Follow the title of a government publication with any other information that might help a reader to find it; including the catalogue number is particularly helpful for a Statistics Canada publication, which may be

res
55c

difficult to locate without it. Note that many federal government publications are printed by Supply and Services Canada (sometimes listed simply as Supply and Services), but the responsible ministries and departments do some themselves. Most U.S. federal government publications are printed by the Government Printing Office.

For more detailed information on documenting government publications, see *The Chicago Manual of Style* (University of Chicago Press, 1982), which is available in most libraries.

Conference and Symposium Proceedings

Paskievici, Vladimir. "Proposed General Principles and Safety Requirements for CANDU Nuclear Power Plants." CANDU Reactor Safety Design. Proc. of a Symposium, Canadian Nuclear Association, 28–29 Nov. 1978. Compiled by the Design and Development Division, Ontario Hydro. Toronto: Canadian Nuclear Association, [1979?].

Manley, Steve. "Forest Farming." Proceedings of the P.E.I. Conference on Ecological Agriculture. Ed. Martha Musgrove Pratt. Charlottetown: The Institute of Man/The Ark Project, 1979.

When a proceedings has no separate title, the name on the title page is treated as the title.

Recording

Thomas, Dylan. "Fern Hill." Dylan Thomas Reading "A Child's Christmas in Wales" and Five Poems. Caedmon, TC 1002, vol. 1, n.d.

Videorecordings and Computer Programs

The Chicago Manual of Style provides some useful guidelines for citing videorecordings, computer programs, and associated software. In general, entries should contain information on the nature of the materials (slides, films, texts from films, computer programs) and information that would help a user locate the material (date and place of production, producer or distributor, the owner of the rights to the materials).

res
55c

Legal References The conventions for legal references are very complex and differ greatly from those for citations of other published material. If you should need to use a Canadian legal reference, consult Douglass T. MacEllven, *Legal Reference Handbook* (Toronto: Butterworth, 1983) or Chin-Shih Pang, *Guide to Legal Citatation: A Canadian Perspective in Common-Law Provinces* (Toronto: Richard DeBoo, 1984). Information on U.S. legal references and some guidance for references from the entire British Commonwealth are in the latest edition of *A Uniform System of Citation* (Cambridge, Mass: Harvard Law Association).

Missing Information Especially if you consult older publications or special-purpose publications such as brochures and pamphlets, you may encounter sources that do not include all the standard information. Check the library card; it may have the missing information. If it does not, there are conventional ways of handling missing information.

1. **No Author.** If the author's name is not given, simply omit it and begin the entry with the title of the book or article. Do not use the abbreviation *anon.* Alphabetize under the first word of the title, skipping *A*, *An*, or *The*.

<u>Discovering Britain</u>.　London: Drive, 1982.

2. **No Date.** Use the abbreviation *n.d.* in the position where the date would normally appear.

Koch, Rudolf.　<u>The Book of Signs</u>.　New York: Dover, n.d.

3. **No Publisher or Place of Publication.** The abbreviation for both no publisher and no place of publication is *n.p.*

<u>American Youth Hostels Handbook</u>.　N.p.: n.p., 1977.

4. **No Pagination.** If the pages of a publication are not numbered, use the abbreviation *n. pag.* in the bibliography entry. If your in-text reference or footnote is to a specific page, count the pages (starting from the first page of text) and put the number in brackets.

Reece, Richard.　Iona: <u>Its History and Archeology</u>.　Glasgow: Iona Community Publishing Dept., n.d., n. pag.

Occasionally, you may wish to cite a publication that contains almost no publishing information. List all the information available, but indicate that the remaining information is missing so that the reader will not think that you are guilty of sloppy documentation.

<u>A History of Children's Book Illustration 1750-1940</u>. (N.p.: n.p., [1978]), n. pag. This book, a catalogue of an exhibition held at The Gallery, Stratford, Ont., contains 74 pages of text and illustrations.

Sometimes information missing from the publication itself is available on the catalogue card for that publication. The card will have the information in square brackets, and the bibliography entry should also list it in brackets.

Adrados, Francisco Rodrigues.　<u>Festival, Comedy, and Tragedy</u>.　[Trans. Christopher Holme.] Leiden: Brill, 1975

res
55c

Multiple Places of Publication of Multiple Publishers If the title page of a book lists several places of publication, only one need be listed in footnotes or bibliographies. In general, choose the Canadian city, if any, or the city listed first.

If a book is simultaneously published by two different publishers, the *MLA Handbook* rule is to list both. Other style guides say one is sufficient, generally the one in the writer's own country if that choice exists.

Zandvoort, R. W. A Handbook of English Grammar.
  3rd ed. London: Longmans; Englewood Cliffs, N.J.:
  Prentice-Hall, 1966.

Exercises: In-Text References, Footnotes, and Bibliographies

Part A: For each of the following quotations, assume that you are writing a research paper and wish to include some of the information contained in the quotation.

a. Compose a sentence or two incorporating the information that you want to use. If you use direct quotations, be sure to enclose them in quotation marks.

b. Incorporate an in-text reference in each of the brief passages you have written.

c. Write a correct bibliography entry for each passage.

d. If you feel that any quotation is "common knowledge" and could be used without a reference, state exactly why it need not be documented.

1. "The magic of the movies casts a spell, trying the tongues of Canada's storytellers and luring its film-makers to make American stories with American stars; even the streets were disguised as foreign avenues. Canada's struggle to break the spell has been protracted and at times humiliating. But . . . three new films—*The Tin Flute*, *Maria Chapdelaine*, and *The Wars*—will offer impressive evidence that the campaign has intensified dramatically." [p. 46, *Maclean's*, by Val Ross, "The New Screen Heroes," Volume 96, Number 39, September 26, 1983, total article pp. 46-54.]

2. "The Nile is the only river to flow northward across the Sahara, and only along its banks could an agricultural community survive the absence of rainfall. The Ancient Egyptians called their land 'Kemet,' the Black Land, because of the black silt which used to be deposited on the soil by the annual flood, caused by the rising waters of the Blue Nile when the river is swollen by the rainfall in Ethiopia. This silt is rich and fertile, and with careful irrigation enabled the Egyptians to produce two crops per year in some areas." [p. 11, Cornell University Press at Ithaca, N.Y., *The Egyptians: An Introduction to Egyptian Archaeology* by John Ruffle, 1977.]

3. "Today, logs cut in the group's forests (the Irvings own or lease 25% of New Brunswick's land area and are the biggest foreign landowners in Maine) travel on Irving-owned trucks burning Irving-refined fuel to Irving-owned lumber or newsprint mills, some of whose production ends up in an Irving-built prefab house or an an Irving-owned newspaper." [pp. 1, 20, *The Wall Street Journal*, by Allan Freeman and John

Urquhart, Tuesday, November 1, 1983, "All in the Family: Hardworking Irvings Maintain Tight Control in a Canadian Province," total article: pages 1 and 20.]

4. "Deacon did not spring out of the soil of the west by random chance or act of God. He had doggedly worked towards his ambition of becoming a Canadian man of letters since his articling days in Dauphin. Furthermore, in his years in the west, he had established and consolidated for himself a powerfully idealized view of Canada's destiny from which he never wavered." [p. 26, 1982, University of Toronto Press, Toronto, by Clara Thomas and John Lennox, *William Arthur Deacon: A Canadian Literary Life.*]

5. "In many respects, the imposition of a visa requirement is the most effective of all control mechanisms. It permits a screening of applicants abroad so that, at least, the most blatant cases of non-genuine visitors may be excluded." [p. 80, *Illegal Migrants in Canada,* a report to the Minister of Employment and Immigration from W.G. Robinson, special advisor, published in Ottawa in 1983 by Employment and Immigration Canada.]

6. "The French-speaking population unquestionably holds political power in Quebec, both provincial and municipal, which is essential in a decentralized federal system. But their troubles stem less from law or politics than from attitudes." [p. 116, *The Trouble with France,* by Alain Peyrefitte, published in 1981 in New York by Alfred A. Knopf, translated by William R. Byron.]

7. "Jamieson said one reason students from outside the Vancouver area might not do as well as local students is that they may have problems adjusting to living in Vancouver. Some may get too homesick to continue and withdraw to attend a local college closer to their homes, driving up their school's no-credit level." [p. A3, *The Sun,* "City Students Fare Better at UBC," by Carol Volkart, Tuesday, July 19, 1983, article on one page only.]

8. "St. Laurent's years were Canada's best, in terms of global prestige, economic progress, and general well-being. He even brought in balanced budgets and paid off a small part of the national debt. He put in place social programs that set Canada on the way to becoming the most highly socialized country in the developed world, not excluding the Scandinavian countries." [p. 127, *You Can't Print THAT! Memoirs of a Political Voyeur,* by Charles Lynch, published in 1983 by Hurtig Publishers in Edmonton.]

9. "With the arrival of the first steam railway lines in Ontario, in the early 1850s, channels through which urban centres could interact on a regular, indeed scheduled, basis appeared for the first time. Indeed, it could be argued that prior to that time it is questionable whether any transport 'network' actually existed." [p. 103, *Aspects of Growth in a Regional Urban System: Southern Ontario 1851–1951,* by W. Randy Smith, 1982, published by the Department of Geography, Atkinson College, York University; it is number 12 in the department's Geographical Monographs.]

res

55c

Part B: Correct all errors (spacing, punctuation, order, abbreviations, and so on) in the following footnotes and bibliography entries. Circle the number of any correct examples.

1. Footnote
   [13]Burnett, David, and Marilyn Schiff, Contemporary Canadian Art, Hurtig; Edmonton, 1983, pg.49.
2. Bibliography entry
   [2] Alderson, Brian, "Tracts, Rewards and Fairies: the Victorian Contributions to Children's Literature."In Essays in the History of Publishing: In Celebration of the 250th Anniversary of the House of Longman 1724–1974. Briggs, Asa, editor. New York: Longman, Incorporated, 1974, pgs. 245–282.
3. Bibliography entry
   Ericson, Richard V. *Making Crime: A Study of Detective Work.* Toronto: Butterworths, 1983.
4. Footnote
   [7]Eli Mandel, "The City in Canadian Poetry," in *An Anthology of Canadian Literature in English.* Vol. 2. Edited by Donna Bennett & Russell Brown, (Toronto, Oxford University Press, 1983) p. 133.
5. Footnote
   [14]Tanner, Adrian, "The End of Fur Trade History," *Queen's Quarterly* No. 90,(Spring 1983), p. 179.
6. Bibliography entry
   Tanner, Adrian. "The End of Fur Trade History." *Queen's Quarterly,* 90 (1983): 176–91.
7. Footnote
   [4]Martin Knelman, "Supporting Stratford's Role," *The Financial Post Magazine,* May 1, 1983, p. 30.

Part C: For each corrected footnote in Part B (ignore the bibliography entries), write an example of a subsequent reference to the source, making up a different page number for each. Do not use Latin abbreviations in this exercise.

Appendices

Appendix A
Glossary of Usage

Even in writing, accepted usage is often arbitrary. For example, there is no logical reason why *any more* should be written as two words but *anyhow* as one word, or why *different to* is seldom used while *dissimilar to* troubles no one. Further, usage is constantly changing; in the eighteenth century, many adjectives were acceptably used as adverbs (without an *-ly* ending), but today such usage is considered nonstandard. Finally, notions of usage are frequently vague and inconsistent—readers may object to slang as used by one writer and find it completely appropriate as used by another writer. The approach taken in this glossary is conservative, not as a protest against change and flexibility in language but on the principle that, if a word or construction is likely to offend even a few readers, it is best to avoid it.

This glossary lists only the most common problems of usage in student writing. For questions of usage not covered here, consult a good dictionary or other sections of this handbook.

The usage labels in the glossary entries below agree in general with those employed by most good dictionaries.

STANDARD	Acceptable at all levels of speech and writing
COLLOQUIAL AND SLANG	Acceptable in casual speech but not in writing
NONSTANDARD	Normally not approved of in either speech or writing
REGIONAL	Acceptable in speech in some geographical areas but best avoided in writing

A, AN. *A* is used before words beginning with a consonant sound, *an* before words beginning with a vowel sound: *a metaphor, a euphemism, an instant, an hour, a horse.*

A LOT, ALOT. The correct spelling is *always* as two separate words. The word *allot* is an entirely different word; it is a verb meaning "to assign, to distribute by shares." *A lot of* or *lots of* is colloquial for "a great deal, many" and is best avoided in writing.

ABOUT, AROUND. *Around* is used colloquially instead of *about* in expressions of time but should be avoided in writing.

COLLOQUIAL	The drought lasted <u>around</u> a year.
PREFERABLE	The drought lasted <u>about</u> a year.

It is not necessary to add *at* to *about; about* is sufficient.

WORDY	He came in <u>at about</u> midnight.
PREFERABLE	He came in <u>about</u> midnight.

app
A

ABOVE, BELOW. *Above* is an accepted way of referring to preceding written material; *below* refers to following written material:

the <u>above</u> illustration   the discussion <u>below</u>

Some people feel that this usage is stilted and overly formal and try to avoid it by alternative expressions:

the illustration on page 23   the following discussion

ACCEPT, EXCEPT. *Accept* is a verb meaning "to receive, to take." *Except* is either a verb meaning "to exclude" or a preposition meaning "with the exclusion of, other than."

ACTUALLY. Do not use *actually* as a simple intensifier *(He actually had the nerve to strike me!)*. Save it for expressing a contrast between fact and opinion *(George looks like an old man, but actually he is only 37)*.

AD. Although the shortened form *ad* is frequently used in speech, the full form should always be used in formal writing. Similarly for other shortened forms such as *auto, exam, gym, lab, math, phone, photo, prof,* and *Xmas.* Note that *add* is a verb and not an abbreviation for *advertisement.*

ADVICE, ADVISE. *Advice* is the noun, *advise* the verb. Similarly, *device* is the noun and *devise* the verb, and, in preferred Canadian spelling, *practice* is the noun and *practise* the verb. See also **LICENCE, LICENSE.**

AFFECT, EFFECT. *Affect* is normally only a verb; *effect* is most often a noun but is also used as a verb. The verb *affect* means either "to influence" *(This quiz will not affect your final grade)* or "to pretend, assume" *(He affected a British accent)*. The noun *effect* means "result" *(Painting the walls had a depressing effect)*. The verb *effect* means "to bring about, cause" *(The election effected a change of government)*. The noun *affect* is a rarely encountered technical term in psychology meaning "an emotion."

AGGRAVATE. *Aggravate* is widely used in informal speech to mean "to irritate, annoy." In writing, *aggravate* should be reserved for the meaning "to intensify, make worse."

AIN'T. Nonstandard and universally frowned upon except when used humorously.

ALL, ALL OF. Either is usually correct, but *of* can often be omitted to avoid wordiness. Only *all of* is correct before personal pronouns *(all of us, all of them)*. Only *all* is appropriate before abstract nouns *(All beauty is deceptive)*.

ALL READY, ALREADY. *All ready* is a pronoun plus an adjective; *already* is an adverb meaning "by a particular time." Similarly, *all together* is a pronoun plus an adjective, and *altogether* is an adverb meaning "entirely."

They were <u>all ready</u> by noon. It was <u>already</u> noon.

The ten of us were <u>all together</u>. There were <u>altogether</u> too many.

ALL RIGHT, ALRIGHT. The only acceptable spelling is *all right.*

ALL TOGETHER, ALTOGETHER. See **ALL READY, ALREADY.**

ALLUDE TO, REFER TO. *Allude to* means to mention indirectly, and *refer to* means to mention directly. You would allude to your neigh-

app
A

bor's loud radio by asking him if he was hard of hearing. You would refer to the loud radio by telling him that it was too loud. *Refer* with a direct object means to direct to a source for help: *She referred me to the almanac for information on temperatures.*

ALMOST, MOST. *Almost* is an adverb; *most* is a pronoun or adjective. Colloquially, *most* is often used as an adverb before a pronoun, but this should be avoided in writing.

COLLOQUIAL   <u>Most</u> everybody likes chocolate.

STANDARD   <u>Almost</u> everybody likes chocolate.

ALSO, LIKEWISE. *Also* and *likewise* are not co-ordinating conjunctions and should not be used as substitutes for *and.*

INCORRECT   He inherited a farm, <u>also</u> (<u>likewise</u>) a herd of cattle.

CORRECT   He inherited a farm <u>and</u> a herd of cattle.

ALTHOUGH, THOUGH. The words are interchangeable and both are correct. The abbreviated forms *altho* and *tho* should not be used in writing.

AMONG, BETWEEN. In general, *among* refers to more than two persons and things, and *between* refers to only two persons or things. *Between* is, however, often used with reference to more than two things if the things are being considered individually. Only *between* is correct if relationships are being considered two by two: *There were several marriages between members of the class.*

AMOUNT, NUMBER. *Amount* properly refers to mass or uncountable nouns, and *number* to countable nouns.

<u>amount</u> of water, rice, disagreement, furniture
<u>number</u> of cups, flowers, arguments, chairs

AND ETC. *And* is redundant because *etc.* is an abbreviation for Latin *et cetera*, which means "and the rest." Hence saying *and etc.* is like saying "and and so on."

AND/OR. Avoid if possible. See 37a.

ANY, SOME. The use of *any* and *some* as adverbs meaning "at all" and "a little" is colloquial and should be avoided in writing.

COLLOQUIAL   That didn't bother me <u>any</u>.

PREFERABLE   That didn't bother me <u>at all</u>.

COLLOQUIAL   He complained <u>some</u>, but did it anyway.

PREFERABLE   He complained <u>a little</u>, but did it anyway.

ANY MORE, ANYMORE. The correct spelling is as two separate words.

ANY ONE, ANYONE. *Anyone* means "anybody" or "any person at all." *Any one* means "a single person or thing and only one."

Choose <u>anyone</u> you like.

Choose <u>any one</u> of the three.

Exactly the same distinction applies to *everyone* and *every one;* *everyone* means "all persons" and *every one* means "each single individual." Similarly distinguish *someone* and *some one.*

ANY WAY, ANYWAY, ANYWAYS. *Any way* is an adjective plus a noun meaning "whatever way." *Anyway* is an adverb meaning "in any case." *Anyways* is a colloquial substitute for *anyway.*

Do it <u>any way</u> you like, but do it <u>anyway</u>.

APPROVE, APPROVE OF. *Approve* means to give official consent; *approve of* means to regard favorably.

The dean <u>approved</u> his petition even though he did not <u>approve of</u> it.

APT, LIABLE, LIKELY, PRONE. In careful usage, all four of these words are distinguished. *Apt* means "talented" *(apt at wood-working)* or "suitable for the occasion" *(an apt remark). Liable* means "susceptible to something unpleasant" *(liable to error)* or "legally responsible" *(liable for damages). Likely* means "probable" *(likely to snow). Prone* refers to a strong habit or predisposition *(prone to temper tantrums).*

AS. To be absolutely safe, reserve *as* to its functions as (1) a preposition meaning "in the role of" *(As a driver, he resented pedestrians),* and (2) a subordinating conjunction meaning "simultaneously" *(As the light turned green, a child stepped in front of his car).*

As is incorrect as a substitute for *that, which, who,* and *whether.*

INCORRECT   I'm not sure <u>as</u> I know Armand.

CORRECT   I'm not sure <u>that</u> I know Armand.

Do not use *as* after the verbs *nominate, name, elect, brand, vote, appoint,* or *consider.* Use *as* after the verbs *regard, pick, choose,* and *select.*

The class <u>named</u> him secretary.

The class <u>chose</u> him <u>as</u> secretary.

The class <u>considered</u> him qualified.

The class <u>regarded</u> him <u>as</u> a qualified candidate.

AS . . . AS, SO . . . AS. Positive comparisons take *as . . . as.* Negative comparisons may take either *as . . . as* or *so . . . as,* although some writers prefer *so . . . as.*

Today's news is <u>as</u> bad <u>as</u> yesterday's.

Today's news is not <u>as</u> bad <u>as</u> yesterday's.

Today's news is not <u>so</u> bad <u>as</u> yesterday's.

AS TO. Do not use *as to* to mean "about."

INCORRECT   The clerk inquired <u>as to</u> her credit rating.

CORRECT   The clerk inquired <u>about</u> her credit rating.

app
A

As to is redundant before the subordinators *who, what, when, which, whether, where, why,* and *how.*

WORDY   The clerk inquired <u>as to whether</u> she was healthy.

IMPROVED   The clerk inquired <u>whether</u> she was healthy.

AUTHOR, CRITIQUE, RESEARCH. Although these words are used colloquially as verbs *(He agreed to research the problem),* many people object to using them as verbs in writing. Substitute *write* for *author, do a critique* or *criticize* for *critique,* and *do research* or *investigate* for *research.*

AWFUL, AWFULLY. The adjective *awful* has lost its former meaning of "inspiring awe" and has come to have the colloquial meaning of "unpleasant, disagreeable." The adverb *awfully* has been so overused that today it means only "very." Both uses should be avoided in writing. The use of *awful* as an adverb *(I'm awful sick of his complaining)* is nonstandard.

AWHILE, A WHILE. *A while* may always be substituted for *awhile,* but only *a while* is correct after the preposition *for* or with *ago.*

Wait <u>awhile</u>. Rest <u>awhile</u> before you start again.

Wait <u>a while</u>. We waited for <u>a while</u>. He left <u>a while</u> ago.

BACK OF, IN BACK OF. Both mean simply "behind," but *in back of* is colloquial and best avoided in writing. When in doubt, use *behind.*

BAD, BADLY. *Bad* is an adjective and *badly* an adverb. Hence *bad* is the correct form after verbs of sensation (see 20a), and *badly* should be used with other verbs.

INCORRECT   I feel <u>badly</u> about the delay.

CORRECT   I feel <u>bad</u> about the delay.

INCORRECT   It doesn't hurt so <u>bad</u> now.

CORRECT   It doesn't hurt so <u>badly</u> now.

BARELY, HARDLY, SCARCELY. These are negative words and no other negative should be used in the same clause.

INCORRECT   hardly no trouble, barely didn't make, without hardly
               a word

CORRECT   hardly any trouble, barely made, with hardly a word

The same principle applies for the negative time adverbs *rarely* and *seldom.* Phrases with *barely, hardly,* and *scarcely* are followed by *when* or *before* and not *than.*

INCORRECT   She had scarcely left the garage <u>than</u> her brakes
               failed.

CORRECT   She had scarcely left the garage <u>when</u> her brakes
               failed.

BE SURE AND, COME AND, GO AND, TRY AND. The use of *and* in these expressions is colloquial. Substitute *to* in writing.

COLLOQUIAL   Be sure and leave a wide margin.

STANDARD   Be sure to leave a wide margin.

BECAUSE. Do not use *because* to introduce clauses after the verb *to be* and such words as *reason, excuse,* and *explanation.* The correct word is *that.*

INCORRECT   The reason he made a face is because he absentmind-
               edly licked the cat-food spoon.

CORRECT   The reason he made a face is that he absentmindedly
               licked the cat-food spoon.

INCORRECT   Her excuse for not coming is because two of her gup-
               pies died this morning.

CORRECT   Her excuse for not coming is that two of her guppies
               died this morning.

BEING AS (HOW), BEING THAT, SEEING AS (HOW). All are nonstand-ard for *because.*

BESIDE, BESIDES. *Beside* is a preposition meaning "at the side of." *Besides* is either a preposition meaning "in addition to" or an adverb meaning "in addition, moreover."

Beside the fishtank was a pump.

Besides the fishtank, there was a birdcage.

Besides, she had forty-two houseplants.

BETTER THAN. Colloquial for *more than* in such expressions as *Better than fifty people came to the barbecue.*

BETWEEN. See **AMONG.** The expression *between you and I,* though often heard in speech, is incorrect in writing because the objective form of the pronoun should always be used after prepositions: the correct usage is *between you and me.*

BROKE. Slang in the meaning of "having no money."

BUNCH. Colloquial when used to refer to a group of people or things, except for plants or fruit growing together, such as bananas or grapes.

BURST, BUST, BUSTED. The principal parts of the verb *burst* are *burst, burst, burst. Bust* is nonstandard; *busted* is slang for "arrested."

BUT THAT, BUT WHAT. Both are nonstandard for *that* or *whether.*

INCORRECT   I don't doubt but that he's a Martian.
CORRECT   I don't doubt that he's a Martian.

INCORRECT   Who knows but what he's a Martian?
CORRECT   Who knows whether he's a Martian?

CALCULATE, FIGURE, GUESS. All are colloquial in the meaning of "think, suppose, believe, expect."

app
A

CAN, MAY. In speech, *can* is widely used to indicate both "ability to do" and "permission to do." In writing, use *may* to express the idea of permission.

CAN BUT, CANNOT BUT, CANNOT HELP BUT. *Can but* is a somewhat stilted way of saying "have no alternative." *(We can but hope for the best)*. *Cannot but* is a rather illogical way of saying the same thing; use *can but* or *can only* instead. *Cannot help but* is often considered unacceptable; use simply *cannot help*.

QUESTIONABLE   I cannot help but feel that I have forgotten something.

PREFERABLE   I cannot help feeling that I have forgotten something.

CAN'T HARDLY. A double negative. Use *can hardly*. See also **BARELY, HARDLY, SCARCELY.**

CASE, INSTANCE, LINE. All three of these words tend to be overused and vague and are heavy contributors to deadwood. See 46c.

DEADWOOD   In the case of the manufacture of paper, air pollution is a serious problem.

IMPROVED   Air pollution is a serious problem in the manufacture of paper.

CHARACTER. Do not use *character* as a synonym for *person*.

COLLOQUIAL   He was a very methodical character.

PREFERABLE   He was a very methodical person.

COMMON, MUTUAL. Strictly speaking, *common* refers to something shared with others *(a common driveway, common interests)*. *Mutual* means "reciprocal, having the same relation to each other" *(mutal respect, mutual agreement)*. The distinction is often blurred in speech but should be preserved in writing.

COMPARE, CONTRAST. *Compare* focuses on similarities; *contrast* focuses on differences. In practice, *compare* is often used to include both similarities and differences.

COMPARE TO, COMPARE WITH. Although *to* and *with* are used interchangeably in speech, in more formal writing, *compare with* means "to examine in order to note similarities" and *compare to* means "to represent as similar, to liken." In other words, *compare with* is the act of comparing, and *compare to* is the statement of similarity.

CONSENSUS OF OPINION. Redundant because the word *consensus* means "agreement of opinion." *Consensus* alone is enough.

CONTACT. In the meaning of "get in touch with," the word is here to stay, despite the objections of some, because there is no suitable alternative when the means of communication is uncertain. However, if the means of communication is known, use a more precise word such as *speak, telephone, meet, call,* or *inform*.

CONVINCE, PERSUADE. You *convince* someone *that* something is right, but you *persuade* someone *to* do something. Hence, you might *convince* your instructor *that* your grade is too low but still not *persuade* him *to* change it.

COULD OF. *Could of* is a nonstandard spelling of the spoken contraction "could've." Always write *could have.* The rule is similar for *will of, would of, should of, may of, might of, ought of,* and *must of.*

CRITERIA. *Criteria* is a plural noun and should be used with a plural verb. The singular is *criterion.*

DATA. *Data* is the plural of *datum* and should be used with a plural verb. In formal writing the singular form is *datum.* However, *data* is today widely treated as a (singular) collective noun and is often used with a singular verb to indicate computer or processor information.

DEAL. Widely used colloquially to mean "business transaction, political bargain, arrangement, treatment, situation." It should be avoided in writing; choose a more precise word.

DEVICE, DEVISE. See **ADVICE, ADVISE.**

DIFFER FROM, DIFFER WITH. *Differ from* means "to be different from, to be unlike something." *Differ with* means "to disagree with someone."

DIFFERENT FROM (THAN, TO). *Different from* is always correct, but *different than* is widely used, even in writing, when followed by a clause. *Different to* is thought unacceptable by some writers. See also 21g.

DISINTERESTED, UNINTERESTED. Although both words are often used to mean "not interested," *disinterested* more properly is reserved for the meaning "impartial, unbiased, objective" and *uninterested* to mean "not interested, indifferent."

DIVED, DOVE. *Dived* is the preferred past tense of *dive,* but *dove* is also acceptable.

DOUBT. *Doubt* may be followed by *that, if,* or *whether.* It should not be followed by *but what* or *but that.*

DROWNDED. Nonstandard for *drowned.*

DUE TO, BECAUSE OF. *Due to* is widely used to mean *because of,* but this use is unacceptable in formal writing. *Due to* means "the result of" or "resulting from" whereas *because of* means "as a result of." *Due to* follows the verb "to be"; *because of* does not.

The speed skater's success was <u>due to</u> his self-discipline.

The speed skater succeeded <u>because of</u> his self-discipline.

DUE TO THE FACT THAT. This phrase is unnecessarily wordy and can always be replaced by *because.*

EACH AND EVERY. *Each and every* is unnecessarily wordy; either *each other* to refer to two persons or things and *one another* for more than two. For most people, the two phrases are interchangeable.

E.G., I.E. *E.g.* means "for example" and *i.e.* means "that is." Both are usually acceptable abbreviations in writing, and both should always be followed by a comma. If you tend to confuse the two, remember that *e.g.* moves from the general to the specific, but *i.e.* does not. *E.g.*

app
A

should be followed by one or more examples; *i.e.* should be followed by an explanation or rephrasing of what has just been said.

ENTHUSE, ENTHUSED. Although these words are widely used colloquially, many people object to seeing them in writing. Use *be enthusiastic* and *enthusiastic* instead.

EQUALLY AS. *Equally* should not be used in a comparison with *as*. If both elements of the comparison are expressed in the clause, use *as . . . as* or *just as . . . as*. If only one element of the comparison appears in the clause, use *equally*.

INCORRECT	Lentils are equally as nutritious as black beans.
CORRECT	Lentils are (just) as nutritious as black beans.
CORRECT	Black beans are an excellent food, but lentils are equally nutritious.

ETC. The abbreviation *etc.* is acceptable, even in formal writing, to avoid a long and tedious list that the reader can infer for himself. However, *etc.* should not be used just because the writer cannot think of any other examples. Rather than write *Vermin include rats, cockroaches, etc.,* try *Vermin include such pests as rats and cockroaches.* Do not misspell *etc.* as *ect.* Do not write *and etc.*

EXACT, EXACTLY. *Exact* is an adjective; do not use it to modify the adjective *same*. The correct form is *exactly the same*.

INCORRECT	He gave the exact same lecture last week.
CORRECT	He gave exactly the same lecture last week.

EXCEPT, UNLESS. *Except* is a preposition and should not be used to introduce a clause. To introduce a clause, use the conjunction *unless*.

INCORRECT	He never writes us except he wants money.
CORRECT	He never writes us unless he wants money.

EXPECT. Colloquial or regional in the meaning "suppose, suspect, think." *Expect* is standard in the meaning "anticipate."

COLLOQUIAL	I expect you already know who I am.
STANDARD	I expect you to respond immediately.
COLLOQUIAL	February 29 was an extra boring day.
STANDARD	February 29 is an extra day in the year.

FABULOUS. *Fabulous* has been so overused and misused to mean simply "pleasing" that it has almost no force left, and it should be avoided in writing. The same is true for *fantastic, grand, great, lovely, marvellous, sensational, terrific,* and *wonderful*.

FARTHER, FURTHER. In practice, the two words are almost interchangeable. However, some prefer to reserve *farther* to refer to

app
A

physical distance (*ten metres farther*) and *further* for other kinds of distance or degree (*a further observation*). Only *further* is correct in the meaning "in addition, moreover, furthermore."

FEATURE. *Feature* as a verb means "to make outstanding, to specialize in," and should not be used as a synonym for "offer, contain."

FEWER, LESS. In speech, *less* is often used before both plural and mass nouns. In writing, *less* should be reserved for mass or uncountable nouns (*less furniture, less control*); *fewer* should be used with plural or countable nouns (*fewer chairs, fewer controls*).

FIELD. The phrase *in the field of* is often nothing but deadwood and should be eliminated entirely.

DEADWOOD	He has been studying <u>in the field of</u> economics.
IMPROVED	He has been studying economics.

When a noun meaning "realm of knowledge or work" is necessary, try giving the overworked *field* a rest by substituting a synonym such as *subject, domain, region, theme,* or *sphere.*

FINALIZE. Although *finalize* is formed according to the same principles as the acceptable *popularize, legalize,* and *modernize,* some people still object to it. Try *complete, conclude,* or *put into final form* instead.

FIX. *Fix* is colloquial as a verb meaning "arrange, prepare" or "punish." It is also colloquial as a noun meaning "awkward situation." It is slightly colloquial in the meaning "repair." *Fix* is universally acceptable in the meaning "make secure or firm."

FOLKS. Colloquial in the meaning of "relatives, parents" or even "people." The formal plural of *folk* in the meaning of "tribe, nation, ethnic group" is *folk,* but the word is rarely used as a noun in this meaning today.

FORMALLY, FORMERLY. *Formally* means "in a formal way." *Formerly* means "earlier, in the past."

FORMER, LATTER. *Former* and *latter* should be used only when two—and only two—items have been mentioned. Otherwise use *first* and *last.* Even if you, as the writer, have only two things in mind, the reader may be confused if more than two things are mentioned in the same clause. Rewrite for clarity, avoiding *former* or *latter.*

CONFUSING	He often talked to my aunt about my cousin because the <u>latter</u> was his best friend. (Does *latter* refer to *aunt* or *cousin?*)
CLEAR	He often talked to my aunt about my cousin because my cousin was his best friend.

FUNNY. Colloquial in the meaning of "curious, odd, strange, queer." Standard English in the meaning of "amusing."

GENTLEMAN, LADY. *Gentleman* and *lady* should be reserved for reference to breeding and behavior and not used as synonyms for *man* and *woman.* Few men are gentlemen and few women are ladies.

app
A

GOOD AND. As an intensifier meaning "very," *good and* is colloquial; it should be avoided in writing.

COLLOQUIAL   Cleaning the cellar made him <u>good and</u> tired.

PREFERABLE   Cleaning the cellar made him <u>very</u> tired.

GOOD, WELL. *Good* is an adjective; its use as an adverb is colloquial or nonstandard. *Well* is either an adverb or an adjective meaning "in good health." Hence, *He plays good* is nonstandard, but both *I feel well* and *I feel good* are correct.

GRADUATE. Either *He graduated from McGill* or the more formal *He was graduated from McGill* is correct. *He graduated McGill* is nonstandard.

GUY. Colloquial for *man, boy*. The plural *guys* is colloquial for *people* (both male and female).

HAD BETTER. An acceptable idiom meaning "should, ought." However, don't omit the *had*.

UNACCEPTABLE   We <u>better</u> call the fire department.

ACCEPTABLE   We <u>had better</u> call the fire department.

HAD OF. Nonstandard for *had*.

NONSTANDARD   If you <u>had of</u> come earlier, you would have found me.

STANDARD   If you <u>had</u> come earlier, you would have found me.

HAD OUGHT, HADN'T OUGHT. Nonstandard for *ought, ought not (oughtn't)*.

NONSTANDARD   She <u>hadn't ought</u> to talk about sewers during dinner.

STANDARD   She <u>ought not</u> (to) talk about sewers during dinner.

In negative or interrogative sentences, *ought* may be used either with or without a following *to* before the infinitive.

HALF A, A HALF, A HALF A. Use either *half a (half a day)* or *a half (a half day)*, but not *a half a*.

HANGED, HUNG. *Hanged* is the past tense and past participle of *hang* used with reference to executions or suicides. Otherwise, the past tense and past participle are both *hung:* <u>The terrorist was hanged.</u> <u>The picture was hung.</u>

HAVE, HAVE GOT. Either *have* or *have got* is acceptable in many idioms, but why not save the extra word and simply say *have?*

ACCEPTABLE   She has got a bad cold.

PREFERABLE   She has a bad cold.

HEIGHT, HEIGHTH. *Height* is the correct form and *heighth* is nonstandard.

app
A

HOME, HOUSE. A *house* is a physical structure; *home* is an abstract noun meaning the place where one lives. Hence one buys a *house;* whether it is a *home* or not depends upon whether one lives there.

HOPEFULLY. *Hopefully* is always acceptable in the meaning of "in a hopeful manner" *(Minnie asked hopefully if there were any brownies left).* As a sentence modifier meaning "it is to be hoped," *hopefully* is attacked by many, who apparently have not noticed that *hopefully* is completely parallel to such acceptable sentence modifiers as *undoubtedly* and *preferably.* To be absolutely safe, you can reserve *hopefully* for the first meaning.

-IC, -ICAL. Many adjectives have alternative endings in either *-ic* or *-ical* with no difference in meaning (e.g., *problematic, problematical*). However, the meanings of a few adjectives differ, depending on whether they end in *-ic* or *-ical.*

classic "typical, outstanding" (a classic case of embezzlement, a classic performance)

classical "traditional, established" (classical music, a classical education)

comic "pertaining to comedy" (the comic tradition, comic opera)

comical "funny" (a comical face)

economic "pertaining to the economy" (economic indicators)

economical "thrifty, money-saving" (economical car)

electric "powered by electricity" (electric motor)

electrical "pertaining to electricity" (electrical engineering)

historic "having a history" (historic buildings)

historical "pertaining to history" (historical research)

politic "tactful" (politic response)

political "pertaining to politics" (political divisions)

-ICS. Nouns ending in *-ics* take a singular verb when reference is to a discipline or field of study but a plural verb when reference is to actual practice of the discipline.

Ethics is a branch of philosophy.

His ethics are questionable.

Other such words include *acoustics, athletics, economics, politics,* and *statistics.*

IF, WHETHER. *If* and *whether* are almost interchangeable after a verb and before a clause. *Whether* is preferred when an alternative is expressed *(Tell me whether you want to play Probe or Scrabble). If* is necessary in a statement of condition *(If you come, call me).*

IGNORANT, STUPID. *Ignorant* means "not having learned"; *stupid*

app **A**

means "not able to learn" or "characteristic of someone not able to learn." *Ignorant* people are not necessarily *stupid*.

IMPLY, INFER. *Imply* means "to hint or suggest indirectly, without stating directly." *Infer* means "to draw a conclusion based on evidence." You might *infer* that your roommate is angry because he *implied* it by throwing his track shoes at you.

IN, INTO. Strictly speaking, *in* refers to something inside an enclosure, and *into* refers to going from outside to inside. In practice, *in* is frequently used instead of *into*. However, *into* should not be substituted for *in*. That is, do not write *John is into trouble over his income tax*.

IN BACK OF, IN BEHIND, IN FRONT OF, BEFORE. The *in* is unnecessary in *in back of* and *in behind*. *Back of* is acceptable, though somewhat more colloquial than *behind*. *In front of* is always correct and often clearer and less awkward than the formal *before*.

IN LIEU OF. *In lieu of* means "instead of" or "in the place of." It does not mean "in view of." Even used correctly, the expression is somewhat affected and usually should be avoided.

IN REGARDS TO. Nonstandard for *in regard to* or *with regard to*. *As regards* is correct but sounds affected in Canadian English. All expressions with *regard* are wordy and often are better replaced with *about* or *concerning*.

INCLUDING, INCLUDE. The word *include* implies that only a partial listing is to be given. Hence the listing should not be followed by such expressions as *etc.* or *and others*.

INCORRECT   Hardwoods <u>include</u> oak, maple, ash, <u>and others</u>.

CORRECT   Hardwoods <u>include</u> oak, maple, and ash.

INDIVIDUAL, PARTY. The noun *individual* means a single thing or person as opposed to an entire group; it should not be used simply as a synonym for *person*.

INCORRECT   This job requires <u>an individual</u> with strong self-control.

CORRECT   This job requires <u>a person</u> with strong self-control.

Except to lawyers and the telephone company, a *party* is a group of people, not a single person.

INSIDE OF, OUTSIDE OF. In prepositional phrases referring to space, the *of* is redundant *(Don't wash the dog inside of the house)*. In time expressions, *inside of* is colloquial for *within (You'll hear inside of a week)*.

INSTEAD OF, RATHER THAN. Be sure to maintain parallelism when using these compound prepositions.

INCORRECT   We decided to buy two chairs instead of getting a sofa.

CORRECT   We decided to buy two chairs instead of a sofa.

app
A

| INCORRECT | Rather than skiing, Bill preferred to snowshoe. |
| CORRECT | Rather than ski, Bill preferred to snowshoe. |

INTO. The use of *into* to mean "involved in" or "greatly interested in" is slangy and should be avoided in writing. Instead of *I'm really into collecting 78 rpm records,* try *I enjoy collecting 78 rpm records.*

INVITE. As a noun, *invite* is nonstandard. Use *invitation* instead.

IRREGARDLESS, DISREGARDLESS. Both are nonstandard for *regardless.*

IS WHEN, IS WHERE. These phrases are often used incorrectly to introduce an adverb clause, particularly in definitions.

| INCORRECT | A marriage is when a man and woman are legally joined. |
| CORRECT | A marriage is the legal union of a man and woman as husband and wife. |

ITS, IT'S, ITS'. *Its* is a possessive adjective; *it's* is the contraction for *it is* or *it has (It's lost its flavor). Its'* is always incorrect.

JUST. *Just* is colloquial in the meaning of "completely, very, really" *(She's just delighted with her new can opener).*

KID. *Kid* is universally used in speech to mean "child, young person." In writing, use *child* instead.

KIND, SORT, TYPE. These words are singular and should be modified by *this* or *that,* not by *these* or *those.* In the phrase *this kind (sort, type) of a,* the *a* is redundant and should be omitted.

KIND OF, SORT OF. Colloquial for "somewhat, rather."

LAY, LIE. *Lay* is transitive; *lie* is intransitive. See 17a.

LEAD, LED. The correct past tense and past participle forms of the verb *lead* are *led,* not *lead.*

LEARN, TEACH. *Learn* means "to acquire knowledge." *Teach* means "to impart knowledge." Your teacher *taught* you arithmetic and you *learned* it.

LEAVE, LET. Before the word *alone,* the verbs *leave* and *let* are almost interchangeable *(leave him alone, let him alone).* Otherwise, *let* suggests a course of action and *leave* means "to allow to remain." *Leave* should not be used before an infinitive.

Let him speak for himself. Let the rope out slowly.

Leave him where he is. Leave the rope on the post.

LEND, LOAN. Traditionally, *lend* is the verb and *loan* is the noun. Today many people find *loan* acceptable as a verb, perhaps because they are uncertain about the past tense of *lend.* The principal parts of *lend* are *lend, lent, lent.*

LET'S US. Nonstandard for *let's.* Because *let's* is a contraction of *let us,* saying *let's us* is equivalent to saying *let us us.*

LICENCE, LICENSED. In preferred Canadian spelling, *licence* is the noun, *license* is the verb. The past participle of the verb is *licensed;* for example, a *licensed restaurant.*

app
A

LIKE, AS. Careful writers still use *like* as a preposition and *as* or *as if* as a conjunction to connect two complete clauses. However, if a verb has been omitted by ellipsis from the second clause, *like* is an acceptable connector.

COLLOQUIAL   He looked <u>like</u> he had just had a shock.

PREFERABLE   He looked <u>as if</u> he had just had a shock.

ACCEPTABLE   He looked <u>like</u> a man in shock.

LIKE FOR. Colloquial for simply *like* in such sentences as *I would like for him to help us.*

LINE, ALONG THE LINES OF. In the meaning of "glib way of speaking," *line* is slang *(He's handing you a line)*. As a catch-all term for "work, kind of activity," *line* is usually only deadwood. *Along the lines of* is a wordy way of saying *like* or *similar to.*

WORDY   Would your wife prefer something along the lines of a digital watch?

IMPROVED   Would your wife prefer something like a digital watch?

LITERALLY. *Literally* means "in a strict sense, exactly as spoken or written" and should not be used as an intensifier meaning "almost." *He literally crucified her* means that he actually nailed her to a cross. Similarly, *veritable* means "true, actual" and should not be used as a simple intensifier. *My nephew is a veritable monkey* makes you a monkey's uncle.

LOOSE, LOOSEN, LOSE. *Loose* is either an adjective meaning "free, unattached" or a verb meaning "set free, unfasten." The verb *loosen* means the same as the verb *loose*. *Lose* is a verb meaning "mislay, suffer loss."

You will <u>lose</u> an arm if that dog gets <u>loose</u>.

MAD (ABOUT). Colloquial in the meanings of "angry, annoyed" or "enthusiastic, fond of."

MAJORITY, PLURALITY. Save *majority* for use with exact counts, where a contrast between the majority and the minority is made or implied. *Majority* should never be used with mass nouns *(The baby ate the majority of his oatmeal)*. *Plurality* is a term used in elections; it means "the difference between the largest number of votes cast and the next largest."

MANY, MUCH. *Many* is used with countable nouns *(Many tears have been shed)*. *Much* is used with uncountable nouns *("Much madness is divinest sense," wrote Emily Dickinson.)*

MATERIALIZE, TRANSPIRE. Unnecessarily complicated ways of saying *occur, happen, appear,* or *take place.*

MAY BE, MAYBE. *May be* is a verb phrase indicating possibility. *Maybe* is an adverb meaning "perhaps." *Maybe* is somewhat colloquial; in formal writing, use *perhaps* instead.

MEDIA. *Media* is a plural noun and should be used with a plural verb. The singular is *medium.*

MEMORANDA. *Memoranda* is a plural noun and should be used with a plural verb. The singular is *memorandum.*

MIGHTY. Colloquial and regional as an adverb meaning "very, exceedingly." As an adjective meaning "strong, powerful," *mighty* is standard English.

MUCHLY. Nonstandard for *much* or *very much.*

MUST. Colloquial as a noun *(This asparagus peeler is a must for gourmet cooks).* Use *necessity* instead.

NICE. *Nice* has been so overworked as a general term to express mild approval that it is best avoided in writing. Choose a more precise word such as *amusing, polite, attractive,* or *entertaining.*

NO ONE. *No one* should always be written as two words.

NOHOW. Nonstandard for *in no way, not at all.*

NOR. *Nor* is correctly used as (1) the second member of the correlative conjunction *neither . . . nor,* or (2) to introduce a main clause after a preceding negative main clause. After a preceding *not, no, never,* etc., in the same clause, only *or* is correct.

INCORRECT	The refugees have <u>no</u> warm clothing <u>nor</u> shelter.
CORRECT	The refugees have <u>no</u> warm clothing <u>or</u> shelter.
CORRECT	The refugees have <u>no</u> warm clothing, <u>nor</u> do they have shelter.
CORRECT	He was <u>neither</u> a gentleman <u>nor</u> a farmer.

NUMBER, AMOUNT. See **AMOUNT.**

OFF OF. The *of* is unnecessary in sentences like *I took it off of the shelf.* The use of *off* or *off of* to designate source or origin is nonstandard *(I bought it off of a friend of mine).* Use *from* instead.

OFTENTIMES. An unnecessarily long way of saying *often.*

OK, O.K., OKAY. All are accepted spellings for the colloquialism. Except in the most informal writing, substitute more formal words such as *yes, all right, acceptable,* or *correct.*

OLD-FASHIONED. Spelled *old-fashioned,* not *old-fashion.*

ON ACCOUNT OF. Colloquial for *because of .* The use of *on account of* instead of *because* to introduce a noun clause is nonstandard.

NONSTANDARD	I stopped reading <u>on account of</u> the light was so bad.
STANDARD	I stopped reading <u>because</u> the light was so bad.

ONE. Highly formal usage still demands that the pronoun *one* be followed by *one (one's, oneself).* However, in all but the most formal contexts, it is acceptable to follow *one* with *he (his, him, himself).* If you prefer not to use the masculine pronoun, rewrite the sentence using a plural pronoun and avoiding *one.*

FORMAL	<u>One</u> cannot always solve <u>one's</u> problems by oneself.
ACCEPTABLE	<u>One</u> cannot always solve <u>his</u> problems by himself.

app
A

ONE OF THE, THE ONLY ONE OF THE. *One of the* is followed by a plural verb; *the only one of the* is followed by a singular verb.

Norman is one of the men who own their own boats.

Norman is the only one of the men who owns his own boat.

ONLY. In speech, *only* tends to appear toward the beginning of a clause, regardless of what part of the clause it modifies. In writing, it is best to place *only* just before the word or phrase it modifies. This is especially important if different placements could lead to different interpretations.

I only cooked the dinner. (I didn't wash the dishes.)

I cooked only the dinner. (Someone else cooked the lunch.)

OVER, UNDER. Careful writers avoid the colloquial substitution of *over* for *more than* and *under* for *less than*.

COLLOQUIAL	Over two hundred people died in the riot.
PREFERABLE	More than two hundred people died in the riot.

PASSED, PAST. *Passed* is the past tense and past participle of the verb *to pass*. *Past* is a noun, adjective, or preposition.

The time has passed rapidly.

in the past; past events; past our window

PER. Except in Latin phrases like *per capita*, *per* is best avoided in formal writing. In the meaning of "according to" *(per your instructions)*, *per* is outdated business jargon. In the meaning of "for each," *a(an)* is preferable to *per (twice a day, $2 a dozen)*.

PERSONAL. *Personal* is usually redundant and best omitted after possessive adjectives or nouns. For example, in the phrase *my personal feelings*, what else could your feelings be except *personal*? Reserve *personal* to contrast with *impersonal (highly personal remarks)*.

PHENOMENA. *Phenomena* is a plural noun and should be used only with a plural verb. The singular is *phenomenon*.

-PLACE. Adverbs ending in *-place (anyplace, everyplace, noplace, someplace)* are colloquial. In writing, use the forms in *-where* instead *(anywhere, everywhere, nowhere, somewhere)*.

PLAN ON, PLAN TO. *Plan on* is a colloquial substitute for *plan to*, perhaps by confusion with *count on*. In writing, use *plan to*.

PLENTY. As an adverb meaning "very," *plenty* is colloquial.

PLUS. *Plus* should be used only where addition and a specific sum are implied. *Plus* is not an acceptable substitute for *and* or *along with*.

UNACCEPTABLE	My brothers were there, plus my two cousins.
ACCEPTABLE	My brothers were there, along with my two cousins.
ACCEPTABLE	The total cost equals principal plus interest.

PRACTICE, PRACTISE. See **ADVICE, ADVISE.**

PRETTY. Colloquial as an adverb meaning "somewhat, rather" or "almost." Avoid it in writing.

PRINCIPAL, PRINCIPLE. *Principal* is an adjective meaning "chief, main" or a noun meaning (1) "the head of a school" or (2) "money used as capital, as opposed to interest." *Principle* is a noun meaning "rule, law, doctrine." It may help to remember that the adjective is always *principal.*

PROPOSITION. Always slang as a verb. Colloquial as a noun meaning "a situation or problem requiring special treatment." Reserve *proposition* for its more precise meanings of "a formal plan" or "a statement in logic."

PROVIDED, PROVIDED THAT, PROVIDING. All are acceptable in the meaning "on the condition that," but *provided* is preferred in more formal writing. The *that* can be omitted unless confusion would result. None of these need be used where *if* will express the same meaning.

QUOTE. In writing, use *quote* only as a verb. The corresponding noun is *quotation.* Similarly, use *in quotation marks,* not *in quotes.*

RAISE, REAR. In highly formal usage, one *raises* animals and *rears* children. But the use of *raise* with respect to children is widely established in North American English, and few people object to it today.

RARELY EVER, SELDOM EVER, SELDOM OR EVER. Instead of *rarely ever,* use *rarely* or *rarely if ever.* Instead of *seldom ever* or *seldom or ever,* use *seldom, hardly ever, seldom if ever,* or *seldom or never.*

REAL, REALLY. *Real* is colloquial as an adverb *(She was real pleased).* Use *really* or *very* instead. Or consider omitting the adverb entirely; *really* often sounds as if the writer is trying too hard to convince the reader *(You really must try this new shampoo).*

RIGHT ALONG (AWAY, OFF, NOW, OUT, etc.). As an intensifying adverb, *right* is colloquial. In writing, use more formal equivalents such as *directly, immediately,* or *at once.*

RUN. Colloquial as a transitive verb meaning "to operate, manage, maintain."

COLLOQUIAL	Leroy <u>runs</u> a supermarket.
STANDARD	Leroy <u>manages</u> a supermarket.

SAME, SAID. Except in legal or business writing, *same* or *said* should not be used as substitutes for *this, that, the foregoing.*

-SELF. The only correct forms of the pronouns are *myself, yourself, himself, herself, itself, oneself, ourselves, yourselves,* and *themselves.* Although *-self* forms are often used in speech when the subject of the sentence is not the same as the receiver of the action, this usage should be avoided in writing, and *-self* forms should be used only as intensive or reflexive pronouns.

COLLOQUIAL	He told a funny story to Paul and <u>myself</u>.
PREFERABLE	He told a funny story to Paul and <u>me</u>.

app
A

SHALL, WILL. In formal usage, most Canadians use *shall* for the first person *(we shall; he and I shall)* and *will* for the second and third persons *(you will, they will).* See also "Auxiliary Verbs" in 17a. *Will* is acceptable with all persons in informal writing.

SICK, ILL. In Britain, *sick* mean "nauseated" or "vomiting," and *ill* is the general term for being unwell. In North America, however, *sick* is completely acceptable for "unwell," and *ill* tends to sound affected.

SIMILAR TO. *Similar to* should introduce only adjectival phrases, not adverbial phrases. For adverbial phrases, use *like.*

INCORRECT	She talks <u>similar to</u> her mother.
CORRECT	She talks <u>like</u> her mother.
CORRECT	This knife is <u>similar to</u> that one.

SITUATION. Most sentences in which *situation* is used will be improved by its removal. It is often vague and should be replaced by more precise wording.

VAGUE	What about the shovel <u>situation</u>?
IMPROVED	Are there enough shovels for everyone?

Often, the word *situation* is completely unnecessary and simply makes the sentence wordy.

WORDY	The prairies were suffering from a drought <u>situation</u>.
IMPROVED	The prairies were suffering from a drought.

SIZE. *Size* in the meaning of "state of affairs" is colloquial *(That's about the size of it).* Also colloquial is the verb *size up* in the meaning "evaluate."

SLOW. *Slow* is acceptable both as an adjective and as an adverb. The adverb *slowly* is more formal and more common in writing. However, *slow* is more common before participial adjectives *(slow-moving, slow-speaking).*

SMART. Colloquial in the meanings of "intelligent" or "impertinent."

SO. (1) As an intensifier not followed by a qualifying phrase, *so* is colloquial and should be avoided in writing.

COLLOQUIAL	I was <u>so</u> excited!
STANDARD	I was <u>so</u> excited <u>that</u> I forgot to say goodbye.

(2) Before a result clause, *so* should be followed by *that.* No comma precedes the *so that* before result clauses.

He wore elevator shoes <u>so that</u> he would look taller.

(3) *So* or *and so* in the meaning of "therefore, consequently" is somewhat colloquial and should be used sparingly in writing.

COLLOQUIAL	He wears elevator shoes and <u>so</u> looks taller than he really is.
FORMAL	He wears elevator shoes and <u>consequently</u> looks taller than he really is.

app
A

SO, TOO, VERY. *So* and *too* are colloquial substitutes for *very* in negative clauses and should be avoided in writing. Either use *very* or omit the intensifier entirely. See also **SO . . . THAT.**

COLLOQUIAL	The eggplant quiche doesn't taste <u>so</u> good.
COLLOQUIAL	The eggplant quiche doesn't taste <u>too</u> good.
STANDARD	The eggplant quiche doesn't taste <u>very</u> good.

SOME. Colloquial as an adjective meaning "remarkable, extraordinary."

COLLOQUIAL	That was <u>some</u> speech that he gave.
PREFERABLE	He gave a <u>remarkable</u> speech.

See also **ANY, SOME.**

SOMETHING. Colloquial as an adverb.

COLLOQUIAL	The trapped badger fought <u>something</u> fierce.
PREFERABLE	The trapped badger fought fiercely.

SOME TIME, SOMETIME, SOMETIMES. *Some time* refers to a period or span of time *(I saw her some time ago)*. *Sometime* refers to a particular but indefinite time in the future *(Come to see me sometime)*. *Sometimes* means "now and then, at times" *(I see her sometimes, but not regularly)*. *Sometime* is also a slightly archaic adjective meaning "former" *(A sometime teacher, he is now a broker.)*.

SUCH (A). (1) As an intensifier not followed by a qualifying phrase, *such* is colloquial and should be avoided in writing.

COLLOQUIAL	We had <u>such</u> a good time in <u>St. John's</u>!
STANDARD	We had <u>such</u> a good time in St. John's <u>that</u> we plan to return.

(2) Before a result clause, *such* should be followed by *that*. Before an adjective clause, *such* should be followed by *as*.

His pain was <u>such that</u> he could not sleep.

I gave him <u>such</u> information <u>as</u> I was able to remember.

(3) *No such a* is nonstandard for *no such*.

NONSTANDARD	There is <u>no such a</u> word as "diversement."
STANDARD	There is <u>no such</u> word as "diversement."

SUPPOSED TO. Even though it is usually not heard in speech, the *-d* must be written. *Suppose to* is nonstandard in writing.

SURE (AND). *Sure* as an adverb is colloquial; use *certainly* instead.

COLLOQUIAL	Francis <u>sure</u> swims better than Gregson.
STANDARD	Francis <u>certainly</u> swims better than Gregson.

See also **BE SURE AND, COME AND, GO AND, TRY AND.**

THAN, THEN. *Than* is a subordinating conjunction used in making comparisons. *Then* is an adverb of time or a conjunctive adverb

app
A

meaning "consequently, therefore." Do not use the two interchangeably.

THAT (THERE). (1) *That* and *this* as adverbs are colloquial (*I can't believe it's all that bad*). (2) *That there, this here, those there,* and *these here* are nonstandard.

THAT, WHICH. *That* introduces only restrictive clauses. *Which* may introduce either restrictive or nonrestrictive clauses, although some writers prefer to use *which* only with nonrestrictive clauses.

THEIRSELF, THEIRSELVES. Nonstandard for *themselves.*

THEM. Nonstandard as a demonstrative adjective; use *those* instead.

NONSTANDARD   Try one of <u>them</u> epoxy glues advertised on television.

STANDARD   Try one of <u>those</u> epoxy glues advertised on television.

THERE, THEIR, THEY'RE. *There* is an adverb or an expletive pronoun; *their* is a possessive adjective; *they're* is the contraction of *they are.*

<u>They're</u> pitching <u>their</u> tent over <u>there</u>.

THESE KIND, THOSE KIND. See **KIND, SORT, TYPE.**

THING. Slang in the meaning of "enthusiasm for" or "dislike of" (*Maryann has a thing about macramé*). In other uses, *thing* is so vague that a more precise word should be substituted whenever possible.

THIS. Colloquial in the meaning "a, a certain" as in *I was standing at the bus stop, when this man came up and asked for a light.*

THROUGH. Colloquial in the meaning of "finished."

THUSLY. Nonstandard for *thus*. *Thus* is already an adverb and needs no additional *-ly.*

TILL, UNTIL. Either form is correct and the two words are interchangeable. The spelling *'til*, however, is incorrect.

TO, TOO, TWO. *To* is a preposition; *too* is an adverb; *two* is a cardinal number.

The <u>two</u> girls were <u>too</u> small <u>to</u> see over the fence.

TOWARD, TOWARDS. Either form is correct.

TRY AND, TRY TO. *Try to* is the acceptable idiom in formal English.

You should <u>try to</u> complete your work on time.

TYPE, -TYPE. *Type* instead of *type of* is colloquial.

COLLOQUIAL   I wouldn't buy that type bicycle for a child.

STANDARD   I wouldn't buy that type of bicycle for a child.

The addition of *-type* to a noun to make a modifier is awkward. Usually the *-type* can be omitted entirely.

AWKWARD   A tepee has a cone-type shape.

IMPROVED   A tepee is cone-shaped.

IMPROVED   A tepee has a conic shape.

UNDOUBTABLY. Nonstandard for *undoubtedly*.

UNIQUE. In careful usage, *unique* means "the only one, the sole example, having no equal." Hence you should not write *he was a very unique child* (or *more unique* or *most unique*) any more than you would write *he was a very only child*. If you mean simply "unusual," then write *unusual, rare, remarkable,* or *extraordinary*.

USED TO. Don't forget the final *-d* on *used*. Even though it is normally not heard in speech, its omission is nonstandard in writing.

UTILIZE, UTILIZATION. Unnecessarily long ways of saying *use*.

VERY, VERY MUCH. Strictly speaking, *very much* (or *greatly*) should be used to modify past participles and *very* to modify adjectives. The problem lies in deciding whether a past participle is also an adjective. If the participle has a different meaning from the verb, it is probably a true adjective (*determined, very determined*), but in many other instances, the line is not easy to draw. One way of resolving the difficulty is to omit *very* completely; *very* is overused as an intensifier and many a sentence is improved by its removal.

WANT IN (OUT/DOWN/UP/OFF, etc.). Regional and colloquial without an intervening infinitive such as *to go, to come,* or *to get*.

COLLOQUIAL   I got up because the cat <u>wanted out</u>.

STANDARD   I got up because the cat <u>wanted to go out</u>.

WANT THAT. The verb *want* should not be followed by a clause beginning with *that*. *Want* should be followed by an infinitive.

NONSTANDARD   Do you <u>want that</u> we should wait for you?

STANDARD   Do you <u>want</u> us <u>to</u> wait for you?

WAY, WAYS. (1) *Ways* for "distance, way" is colloquial.

COLLOQUIAL   That's a long <u>ways</u> to go by canoe.

STANDARD   That's a long <u>way</u> to go by canoe.

(2) *Way* for *away* is colloquial.

COLLOQUIAL   Don't go <u>way</u>—I need you.

STANDARD   Don't go <u>away</u>—I need you.

(3) The phrases *in a bad way* meaning "in poor condition" and *in the worst way* meaning "very much, greatly" are both colloquial.

WHERE (AT, TO). (1) *Where at* and *where to* are redundant colloquialisms. Omit the *at* or *to*.

COLLOQUIAL   Do you know where the fly swatter is <u>at</u>?

STANDARD   Do you know where the fly swatter is?

COLLOQUIAL   Do you know where the dog went <u>to</u>?

STANDARD   Do you know where the dog went?

(2) *Where* for *that* when no location is involved is colloquial.

COLLOQUIAL   I see <u>where</u> the mayor is on vacation again.

STANDARD   I see <u>that</u> the mayor is on vacation again.

app
A

WHICH, WHO, THAT. *Which* refers to nonhumans, *who* to persons, and *that* to either. See also **THAT, WHICH.**

WHILE. *While* is often vague or ambiguous in the meanings of "although," "but" or "and." Save *while* for expressions of time.

WHOSE, WHO'S. *Whose* is the possessive adjective or pronoun from *who* or *which*. *Who's* is the contraction of *who is* or *who has*. Note that *whose* is perfectly acceptable as a possessive for a nonhuman referent and often is far less awkward than *of which*.

AWKWARD   List all the planets the names of which you can remember.

IMPROVED   List all the planets whose names you can remember.

-WISE. The suffix *-wise* is completely acceptable in established words such as *clockwise*, *otherwise*, and *lengthwise*. However, its use to form new adverbs is abhorred by many. Even if *-wise* saves space, it is best to avoid it.

QUESTIONABLE   The house was satisfactory location-wise.

PREFERABLE   The location of the house was satisfactory.

COLLOQUIAL   I would like for you to wash your ears.

STANDARD   I want you to wash your ears.

YOU. In writing, *you* should be reserved for addressing the reader directly and should be avoided as an indefinite pronoun. Hence, *you* is correct in imperatives and in giving instructions or advice addressed specifically to the reader. As an indefinite pronoun, use *one*, *anyone*, *everyone*, *a person*, or the plural *people* or *those (who)*.

COLLOQUIAL   When you are deaf, you are cut off from the world.

PREFERABLE   A deaf person is cut off from the world.

Appendix B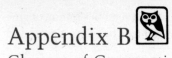
Glossary of Grammatical Terms

ABSOLUTE CONSTRUCTION. Also called *absolute phrase* or *nominative absolute*. A word group that modifies an entire clause or sentence but that is not linked to it by a conjunction, relative pronoun, or preposition. Absolute constructions most often consist of a noun or other nominal followed by a participle but may contain some other kind of verb. Sometimes the participle is only understood. See 11c.

The alarm jangling, Hubert jumped up with a start.

Henry II returned to France, his barons in rebellion. (*Being* is understood.)

Come the revolution, we'll all be riding bicycles.

ABSTRACT AND CONCRETE NOUNS. An *abstract noun* expresses an idea, characteristic, quality, or condition as opposed to a specific object or example: *lateness, fear, situation, insecurity, duty*. A *concrete noun* refers to something definite that can be perceived with the senses or to a specific example of a thing or action: *hair, earthworm, my house, that gorilla, his accident*. See 3b.

ACRONYM. A word formed from the first letter or first few letters of a group of words, *UNICEF* (from United Nations International Children's Emergency Fund) and *sonar* (from sound navigation ranging) are acronyms. See 42d.

ACTIVE VOICE. See **VOICE.**

ADJECTIVAL. A word, phrase, or clause that is used as an adjective, that is, to modify a noun, pronoun, or other nominal. See 15b.

I have lost the top to my pen.

We met a man who had been married nine times.

Giggling uncontrollably, they left the fun house.

ADJECTIVE. A word that modifies or limits a noun, pronoun, gerund, or other nominal. Types of adjectives include articles and descriptive, proper, demonstrative, indefinite, possessive, numerical, and interrogative adjectives. See 5.

   int. *num.*   *proper*   *art.*   *descrip.*
Which four Shakespearean plays will the slave-driving instructor
    poss. *indef.* *descrip.*   *dem.*
ask his many diligent students to read this week?

ADJECTIVE CLAUSE. A subordinate clause that modifies a noun or pronoun. Adjective clauses are usually introduced by relative pronouns or relative adverbs.

The man who ran into me had no insurance.

She returned to Repulse Bay, where all her relations lived.

ADVERB. A word that modifies a verb, adverb, adjective, or entire clause or sentence. Types of adverbs include simple, sentence, prepositional, interrogative, relative, and conjunctive adverbs. See 6.

   sent.   *rel.*
Unfortunately, when the exhausted runner reached the tape, he slid
prep. *conj.*   *simple*   *interrog.*
under; consequently, he was greeted noisily with cries of "How did you do it?"

ADVERB CLAUSE. A subordinate clause that functions as an adverb. Adverb clauses are usually introduced by subordinating conjunctions. In the sentence below, the subordinate clause modifies the verb *leave*. See 12b.

Leave the sauna before you faint.

ADVERBIAL. Any word, phrase, or clause that functions as an adverb. See 15c.

ADVERBIAL CONJUNCTION. See **CONJUNCTIVE ADVERB.**

AGREEMENT. The correspondence in form of words to reflect their relationship to each other. Subjects and predicates agree in number and person; pronouns and their antecedents agree in number, person, and gender; demonstrative adjectives and their nouns agree in number. See 18, 19.

ANTECEDENT. The words or words to which a pronoun or pronominal adjective refers. In the sentence below, *John* is the antecedent of *he*.

John thinks that he is Genghis Khan.

APPOSITIVE. A word or group of words that follows another word or group of words and that defines or supplements the words it follows. Appositives refer to the same thing and serve the same grammatical function as the words with which they are associated. See 14.

The hyphen, a mark of punctuation, is used to divide words.

ARTICLE. The *definite article (the)* indicates that the following noun is a particular individual; the *indefinite article (a/an)* indicates that the following noun is a member of a class.

The play that we liked best was a melodrama.

AUXILIARY. Also called *helping verb*. Auxiliaries precede main verbs and indicate the tense, mood, and voice of the main verb. The English auxiliaries are *be, have, do,* and the modal auxiliaries *will,* *would, shall, should, can, could, may, might, dare, need (to), ought (to),* and *must.* See 4b. See also **SEMIAUXILIARY**.

CARDINAL AND ORDINAL NUMBERS. A *cardinal number* refers to quantity (*one, two, seven, four thousand,* etc.). An *ordinal number* refers to position in a series (*first, second, third, twenty-seventh,* etc.). See 44d.

CASE. The inflectional forms of nouns and pronouns that show their relationship to other words in the sentence. English has three cases: (1) the *nominative* (or *subjective*), used for subjects and subject complements, (2) the *objective,* used for objects of verbs and prepositions, and (3) the *possessive* (or *genitive*), used to indicate possession and various other modifying relationships. Pronouns have all three cases (*I, me, mine*), but nouns have only one form for both nominative and objective cases (*girl*) and a form of possessive (*girl's*). The combined nominative-objective case is also called the *common case.* See 3a, 7b.

CLAUSE. A group of words containing a subject and a predicate. An *independent* clause (also called a *main* clause) can stand alone as a complete sentence. A *dependent* clause (also called a *subordinate* clause) cannot form a sentence by itself, but is dependent on some other element. Dependent clauses function as nominals, adjectivals, or adverbials. See 12.

COLLECTIVE NOUN. A noun that is singular in form but that refers to a group of persons or things. *Committee* and *herd* are collective nouns. See 3b.

COLLOQUIAL ENGLISH. The natural spoken English of ordinary conversation. If a dictionary entry labels a word or phrase "colloquial," that word is considered appropriate for conversation but not for formal written English. In the sentence below, the colloquialisms include the contractions *you're* and *don't,* the use of *going to* to express future tense, and the idioms *foul up* and *get down pat.* See 46a.

You're going to foul it up if you don't get the instructions down pat.

COMMA SPLICE. The joining of two independent clauses with only a comma and no conjunction between them. See 23c, 27a.

We knocked on the door, no one answered.

COMMON CASE. See **CASE.**

COMMON AND PROPER NOUNS. A *common noun* designates any member of a class of entities (*beer; a dog; the cities*). A *proper noun* names only one specific member of a class; proper nouns are usually capitalized and usually are not preceded by an article (*Carling; Rover; Ottawa* and *Hull*). See 3b.

COMPARISON. Changes in the form or syntax of adjectives and adverbs to indicate a greater or lesser degree of what is specified in the root word. The three degrees of comparison are *positive, comparative,* and *superlative.* See 21.

app
B

POSITIVE	hard	bad	ambitious	impressively
COMPARATIVE	harder	worse	less ambitious	more impressively
SUPERLATIVE	hardest	worst	least ambitious	most impressively

COMPLEMENT. *Subject complements* are nouns or adjectives that follow a linking verb and refer to the subject. Noun complements are also called *predicate nominatives* or *predicate nouns*, and adjective complements are called *predicate adjectives*.

PREDICATE ADJECTIVE	Harry is <u>inefficient</u>.
PREDICATE NOMINATIVE	Harry became a <u>politician</u>.

An *object complement* follows a direct object and refers to the same thing as the direct object.

OBJECT COMPLEMENTS	Ellen wears her hair <u>long</u>.
	They voted Joe <u>Man of the Year</u>.

Note: Some grammarians also treat direct objects and indirect objects as complements.

COMPLEX SENTENCE. See **SENTENCE.**

COMPOUND SENTENCE. See **SENTENCE.**

COMPOUND-COMPLEX SENTENCE. See **SENTENCE.**

COMPOUND WORD. A combination of two or more words used as a single word. Some compound words are written solid *(bloodhound)*, some are hyphenated *(bolt-action)*, and some are written as separate words *(boot camp)*.

CONCRETE NOUN. See **ABSTRACT AND CONCRETE NOUNS.**

CONJUGATION. The complete set of inflected forms or phrases in which a verb may appear to show number, person, tense, voice, and mood. See Appendix C for a complete verb conjugation.

CONJUNCTION. A word or group of words used to connect words, phrases, or clauses and to indicate the relationship between them. See **CO-ORDINATING CONJUNCTION, SUBORDINATING CONJUNCTION, CORRELATIVE CONJUNCTION,** and **CONJUNCTIVE ADVERB.**

CONJUNCTIVE ADVERB. Sometimes called an *adverbial conjunction*. An adverb that serves as a conjunction to relate two main clauses, either within one sentence or in two different sentences. Examples include *nevertheless, meanwhile, however, consequently, thus.* See 6b.

I dislike dogs; <u>moreover</u>, I dislike most pets.

CONNOTATION. The emotional meaning of a word; its implications, suggestions, or associations, as opposed to its explicit literal meaning. For example, although the literal meaning of both *tranquil* and *stagnant* is "still, inactive," *tranquil waters* seem much more pleasant than *stagnant waters* because *tranquil* has connotations of peacefulness, gentleness, and calmness, while *stagnant* has connotations of sluggishness, lifelessness, and even decay. See **DENOTATION** and 46b.

app
B

CONSTRUCTION. A somewhat vague term referring to a group of words arranged grammatically.

CONTRACTION. The shortening of a word or group of words by omission of one or more sounds or letters; an apostrophe usually replaces the missing letters in writing: *I've, won't, there's, nor'easter, bos'n.* See 43.

CO-ORDINATING CONJUNCTION. A conjunction that connects sentence elements that are grammatically parallel. The primary co-ordinating conjunctions are *and, but, or,* and *nor. Yet* is also used as a co-ordinating conjunction. See 9a.

CO-ORDINATION. The linking of parallel grammatical structures by means of specific words that express the relationship between the structures. See **CONJUNCTION, CO-ORDINATING CONJUNCTION.**

CORRELATIVE CONJUNCTIONS. Co-ordinating conjunctions used in pairs to join sentence elements that are grammatically parallel. Examples include *either . . . or, both . . . and, not only . . . but.* See 9a.

COUNTABLE AND MASS OR UNCOUNTABLE NOUNS. *Countable nouns* have both a singular and a plural form; the singular may be modified by the article *a* or the numeral *one; a bean/beans, one pen/pens, an idea/ideas. Mass or uncountable nouns* have only a singular form and cannot be modified by *a* or *one: granola, information, confidence.* See 3b.

DANGLING MODIFIER. A modifier that either appears to modify the wrong word or that apparently has nothing to modify. See 20c.

Having lived in Quebec for years, Seattle felt very warm.

DECLENSION. The change in form of nouns and pronouns to show number, gender, case, and person. English nouns decline for number and case; English personal pronouns for number, gender, case, and person. See **INFLECTION,** 3a, 7b.

DEMONSTRATIVE ADJECTIVES AND PRONOUNS. The demonstratives are *this* (plural *these*) for "near" reference and *that* (plural *those*) for "distant" reference. The demonstratives are pronouns when they serve as subjects, complements, or objects and are adjectives when they modify nouns or pronouns.

DEMONSTRATIVE PRON.   This is less expensive than any of those.

DEMONSTRATIVE ADJ.   That drug is a prescription item.

DENOTATION. The basic, specific, literal meaning of a word, as contrasted with its emotional meaning or the associations one makes with the word. The denotation of the word *cockroach* is "an orthopterous insect of nocturnal habits that frequents human dwellings." See also **CONNOTATION** and 46b.

DEPENDENT CLAUSE. See **CLAUSE.**

DESCRIPTIVE ADJECTIVE. An adjective that describes the quality,

app
B

kind, or condition of the noun it modifies. Only descriptive adjectives can be compared. See 5b.

happy warrior, *calmer* weather, *disreputable* business

DIRECT ADDRESS. A construction in which a name or other nominal is added parenthetically to a sentence to indicate the person or persons to whom the sentence is addressed:

I've told you, *Dick*, not to put teabags in the garbage disposal.

DIRECT OBJECT. See **OBJECT.**

DIRECT AND INDIRECT QUOTATION. Also called *direct* and *indirect discourse. Direct quotation* is the quotation of a speaker or writer using his or her exact words. *Indirect quotation* paraphrases a speaker's or writer's words without quoting them exactly. Indirect quotation usually takes the form of a subordinate clause.

DIRECT QUOTATION	Mme Roland said, "The more I see of men, the better I like dogs."
INDIRECT QUOTATION	Mme Roland said that the more she saw of men, the better she liked dogs.

DOUBLE NEGATIVE. Two negative words in the same clause. When the intended meaning is negative, double negatives are not acceptable in expository writing. A negated adjective can sometimes be correctly used with another negative word to express an affirmative meaning.

UNACCEPTABLE	She *wasn't never* willing to help. (= She wouldn't help.)
ACCEPTABLE	She was *not unwilling* to help. (= She would help.)

DOUBLE POSSESSIVE. A possessive form that uses both *of* before the noun and *-'s* on the noun. See 34a.

I went to England with a friend *of* my mother's.

ELLIPTICAL EXPRESSION. A phrase, clause, or sentence from which a word or words have been omitted but are understood and often can be supplied from a nearby phrase or clause. In the elliptical sentences below the words in parentheses are understood before the periods.

Nylon will last longer than rayon. (will last)

Does he read French? Yes, he does. (read French)

He is as tall as John. (is tall)

EXPLETIVE PRONOUNS. The pronouns *it* and *there* used as subjects of a sentence (1) when no other subject to appropriate, (2) when the logical subject is a long clause, or (3) when the writer wishes to emphasize a particular noun or pronoun in the sentence.

(1) *There* is no reason to fret.

(2) It is unpleasant to admit that I have been foolish.

(3) It was you who suggested taking this detour.

FINITE AND NONFINITE VERBS. *Finite verbs* are inflected for person, tense, and number and can serve as complete predicates in main clauses. *Nonfinite verbs* (infinitives, participles, and gerunds) cannot serve as complete predicates.

FORMAL ENGLISH. The variety of English used primarily for scholarly writing. It is characterized by relatively complex constructions, conservative usage, impersonality, objectivity, precision, seriousness, and conformity to accepted standards of written correctness. See 46a.

FRAGMENT. A part of a sentence punctuated as if it were a complete sentence. See 23a.

A part of a sentence. If it were a complete sentence.

FUSED SENTENCE. Also called *run-on sentence*. The joining of two independent clauses without any punctuation or conjunction between them. See 27a.

GENDER. The grammatical division of nouns and pronouns into masculine, feminine, and neuter. English overtly expresses gender only in the third-person singular pronouns *(he, she, it)* and in a few nouns *(actor/actress; widow/widower)*. See 7b.

GENITIVE CASE. See **CASE.**

GERUND. A nominal made from a verb by adding the ending *-ing*. In the sentence "Judy enjoys hiking," *hiking* is a gerund. See 20a.

HELPING VERB. See **AUXILIARY.**

IDIOM. An expression whose meaning is not predictable from the meaning of its individual words and which may even not fit the usual grammatical patterns of the language, but which is accepted and understood by the users of the language. See 46a.

In the long run, we'll make better time if we put off eating so early.

IMPERATIVE. See **MOOD.**

INDEFINITE ADJECTIVES AND PRONOUNS. Adjectives and pronouns that refer to unspecified persons or things. Examples include *another, each, much, any, some, such,* etc. and the compound indefinite pronouns like *anything, nobody,* and *someone.* See 5b, 7b.

INDEPENDENT CLAUSE. See **CLAUSE.**

INDICATIVE. See **MOOD.**

INDIRECT QUOTATION. See **DIRECT AND INDIRECT QUOTATION.**

INDIRECT OBJECT. See **OBJECT.**

INFINITIVE. The bare form of a verb with no ending (though it is often preceded by *to*). Infinitives are used in the formation of verb phrases and as nominals, adjectivals, or adverbials.

app
B

IN VERB PHRASE	Russ will <u>move</u> to Calgary if he can <u>find</u> a job there.
AS NOMINAL	Please try <u>to work</u> faster.
AS ADJECTIVAL	Sue wants a book <u>to read</u>.
AS ADVERBIAL	They went home <u>to eat</u> dinner.

INFLECTION. The change in the form of a word to indicate a change in meaning or in grammatical relationships with other elements in the sentence. Inflection of nouns and pronouns is called *declension;* inflection of adjectives is called *comparison;* inflection of verbs is called *conjugation.* See **DECLENSION, COMPARISON, CONJUGATION.**

INFORMAL ENGLISH. The variety of English used for lighter writing, such as magazine articles and newspaper columns. Compared to formal English, it tends to be characterized by shorter, less complex sentences, a more casual and personal tone, and occasional use of contractions and colloquialisms. See 46a.

INTENSIFIERS. Modifiers like *much, too, really, very,* and *so* that add emphasis (but not additional meaning) to the words they modify.

INTENSIVE PRONOUN. An intensive pronoun is used in apposition to a noun or pronoun to emphasize that noun or pronoun. The intensive pronouns are *myself, yourself, himself, herself, itself, oneself, ourselves, yourselves,* and *themselves.* See 7b.

The travel agent <u>himself</u> had never been outside Altoona.

INTERJECTION. A word, grammatically independent of the rest of its sentence, used to attract attention or express emotion. Examples include *ha! ouch! oh! hello, yes.* See 10.

INTERROGATIVE ADVERBS AND PRONOUNS. The words used in asking questions. The interrogative adverbs are *where, when, why, how,* and their compounds in *-ever (wherever,* etc.). The interrogative pronouns are *who, which, what,* and their compounds in *-ever (whoever,* etc.). See 6b, 7b.

INTRANSITIVE VERB. A verb that is not accompanied by a direct object. In the sentence "Puppies grow rapidly," *grow* is intransitive.

INVERSION. A change in the usual word order of a sentence, such as placing the subject after the verb or the direct object before the subject.

Down the alley ran the big rat.

Insolence I will not tolerate.

IRREGULAR VERB. Any verb that does not form both its past tense and past participle by the addition of *-d* or *-ed* to the infinitive form of the verb. See 4b and Appendix D.

LINKING VERB. Also called a *copula.* A verb that connects a subject with a subject complement (predicate adjective or predicate noun). The most common linking verbs are *be, become, seem, appear, remain,* and the verbs of sensation *see, smell, feel, sound,* and *taste.*

Other verbs, such as *turns, grow,* and *prove,* are also sometimes used as linking verbs, as in the sentence "The suggestion proved worthwhile." See 4b.

MAIN CLAUSE. See **CLAUSE.**

MAIN VERB. Also called *lexical verb.* The verb that carries most of the meaning of the verb phrase in which it appears. See 4b.

William <u>hiccoughed</u>.

Why have you been <u>stirring</u> the rubber cement?

I am <u>appalled</u> by his audacity.

MASS NOUN. See **COUNTABLE AND MASS NOUNS.**

MISPLACED MODIFIER. A modifier that appears to modify the wrong word or words, causing confusion or ludicrousness. See 20c.

Jody replanted the ivy for the secretary <u>in the hanging pot</u>.

MODAL AUXILIARY. See **AUXILIARY.**

MODIFIER. Any word or group of words functioning as an adjectival or adverbial. See also **ADJECTIVE, ADVERB.**

MOOD. A verb inflection that indicates the speaker's or writer's attitude toward what he or she says. English has three moods: *indicative, imperative,* and *subjunctive,* of which the indicative is by far the most frequently used. The indicative is used for ordinary statements and questions *(He takes; Does he take?).* The imperative is used for commands and requests *(Look!).* The subjunctive is used to express uncertainty, possibility, wish, or conditions contrary to fact *(If he were).* See 4a.

NOMINAL. A word, phrase, or clause that functions as a noun.

NOMINAL CLAUSE. See **NOUN CLAUSE.**

NOMINATIVE ABSOLUTE. See **ABSOLUTE CONSTRUCTION.**

NOMINATIVE CASE. See **CASE.**

NONFINITE VERB. See **FINITE AND NONFINITE VERBS.**

NONRESTRICTIVE MODIFIER. See **RESTRICTIVE AND NONRE-STRICTIVE MODIFIERS.**

NONSTANDARD ENGLISH. English usage that differs from what is generally considered to be correct. See 47c.

Between you and me, I ain't set to take trouble from nobody.

NOUN. A word that names a person, place, thing, or concept *(taxi-driver, New Orleans, jackknife, disruption).* Nouns are inflected for number *(sandwich/sandwiches)* and case *(toddler/toddler's)* and are used as subjects, complements, objects, and sometimes modifiers. See 3.

NOUN ADJUNCT. A noun used to modify another noun: *weather* prediction, *faculty policy* board, *discussion* section, *chain* reaction.

NOUN CLAUSE. A subordinate clause that can serve all the functions of a single noun.

SUBJECT	How you can read and knit at the same time amazes me.
DIRECT OBJECT	I know exactly what he will say.
INDIRECT OBJECT	Eva told whoever asked the entire story.

NOUN PHRASE. A phrase consisting of a noun or pronoun and all of its modifiers. See 11a.

She was carrying an orange umbrella with two broken ribs.

NUMBER. As a grammatical term, *number* refers to the inflections of nouns, pronouns, some kinds of adjectives, and verbs that indicate one (singular) or more than one (plural). In the sentences below, every word is marked for number.

SINGULAR NO.	This is a monkey-wrench.
PLURAL NO.	These are monkey-wrenches.

OBJECT. A noun, pronoun, or other nominal that is governed by, and usually follows, a verb or preposition. A *direct object* specifies what or who is affected by the action of the verb. An *indirect object* specifies who or what is the receiver of the direct object; indirect objects normally appear only in sentences with direct objects. An *object of a preposition* completes a prepositional phrase; its relationship to another part of the sentence is specified by the particular preposition used.

DIRECT OBJECT	Georgia carved the ham.
INDIRECT OBJECT	Georgia handed me a fork.
OBJECT OF PREPOSITION	Georgia ate her salad with her fingers.

OBJECTIVE CASE. See **CASE.**

ORDINAL NUMBER. See **CARDINAL AND ORDINAL NUMBERS.**

PARADIGM. A technical term for all the inflected forms of a word. The paradigm for *mouse* is

mouse   mice   mouse's   mice's

PARAGRAPH. A basic unit of written English, intermediate in size between the sentence and the total essay (or, for longer works, between the sentence and the chapter or section). Like a mark of punctuation, a paragraph sets off a portion of written material dealing with a particular idea, usually by means of indentation and a new line. Paragraphs may be as short as a sentence or two or as long as several hundred words. See 49.

PARALLELISM. Using the same kind of grammatical construction for all items that have the same function. *Faulty parallelism* occurs when ideas serving the same grammatical function do not have the same grammatical form. *False parallelism* occurs when ideas that are not parallel in grammatical function are put into parallel form. See 23f.

**app
B**

PARALLELISM	He is young, handsome, and rich.
FAULTY PARALLELISM	He is young, handsome, and a banker.
FALSE PARALLELISM	He is young and handsome, and which makes him attractive to many people.

PARTICIPLE. A nonfinite verb form used (1) in making verb phrases, (2) as an adjectival, or (3) in absolute constructions. The *present participle* ends in *-ing*. The *past participle* ends in *-ed, -d, -t, -en,* and *-n* or is formed by a vowel change *(stood, sung)*.

IN VERB PHRASE	Smoke was slowly <u>filling</u> the room.
	Stanley had deliberately <u>left</u> his hearing aid at home.
AS ADJECTIVAL	I was kept awake by that incessantly <u>barking</u> dog.
	Her teeth tightly <u>clenched</u>, Mrs. McNeill glared at Toby.
IN ABSOLUTE CONSTR.	The wind <u>rising</u>, they headed for shore.
	The stock market <u>having crashed</u>, many firms went out of business.

PARTS OF SPEECH. The classes of all words divided into groups according to their inflections, meanings and functions in the sentence. The exact classifications may vary according to different kinds of analysis, but nearly all analyses include nouns, verbs, adjectives, adverbs, pronouns, prepositions, and conjunctions. Most classifications also recognize interjections. See 2.

PASSIVE VOICE. See **VOICE.**

PERSON. The inflection of pronouns and verbs to distinguish the speaker or speakers (first person—*I, we*), those spoken to (second person—*you*), and those spoken about (third person—*he, she, it, they* and all other pronouns and nouns). Except for the verb *to be*, English verbs distinguish person only in the third person singular present indicative. See 7b.

PERSONAL PRONOUNS. Those pronouns that indicate grammatical person. English personal pronouns are inflected for three persons *(I, you, she)*, two numbers *(I, we)* and three cases *(I, me, mine)*. The third-person singular pronoun is also inflected for three genders *(he, she, it)*. See 7b for a complete chart of all personal pronoun forms.

PHRASE. A group of grammatically related words that does not contain both a subject and a predicate. Phrases function as a single part of speech within a clause or sentence. See 11.

<u>Inside the cave,</u> stalagmites had, <u>over the centuries,</u> created <u>an elfin city of calcium carbonate.</u>

PLAIN ADVERB. An adverb that has the same form as its corresponding adjective. Examples include *hard, fast, straight, far.* See 6b.

app
B

POSITIVE DEGREE. See **COMPARISON.**

POSSESSIVE CASE. See **CASE.**

PREDICATE. The part of a clause or sentence that expresses what is said about the subject. It consists of a verb or verb phrase and any objects, complements, or modifiers of the verb. See 1.

The quick brown fox jumped slyly over the lazy dog.

PREDICATE ADJECTIVE. See **COMPLEMENT.**

PREDICATE NOUN. See **COMPLEMENT.**

PREFIX. A bound form (one that is not an independent word) placed before another word or bound form to change its meaning. See also **SUFFIX.**

replay, uniform, unpleasant, declare, transplant

PREPOSITION. A part of speech used with a noun or other nominal (called the object of the preposition) to connect to the noun with another part of the sentence. The preposition together with its object forms a *prepositional phrase*. Prepositional phrases usually function as modifiers. See 8.

PREPOSITIONAL PHRASES   Give the money on the shelf to the paperboy.

PREPOSITIONAL ADVERB. An adverb that has the same form as a preposition. Examples include *up, across, outside, past.* See 6b.

PREPOSITIONAL PHRASE. See **PREPOSITION.**

PRINCIPAL PARTS. The forms of a verb from which all other forms can be derived. The principal parts of English verbs are the infinitive *(take)*, the past tense *(took)*, and the past participle *(taken)*.

PRONOUN. A member of a small class of words that serve the functions of nouns or replace nouns to avoid repetition of the nouns. See 7 and also **DEMONSTRATIVE** and **EXPLETIVE, INDEFINITE, INTENSIVE, INTERROGATIVE, PERSONAL, RECIPROCAL, REFLEXIVE,** and **RELATIVE PRONOUNS.**

PROPER ADJECTIVE. An adjective made from a proper noun. Examples include *Parisian, African, Swedish, Platonic.* See 5b.

PROPER NOUN. See **COMMON AND PROPER NOUNS.**

RECIPROCAL PRONOUN. A pronoun that refers to interaction between two or more persons or things. The English reciprocal pronouns are *each other* and *one another* and are used only as objects.

The room was so dark that we could hardly see each other.

REFLEXIVE PRONOUN. A pronoun that refers to the subject of a clause or phrase. Reflexive pronouns end in *-self* or *-selves* and are used only as objects. See 7b.

I can't envision myself as Marc Anthony.

REFLEXIVE VERB. A verb whose direct object refers to the same thing as its subject.

They <u>covered</u> themselves with suntan oil.

REGULAR VERB. A verb that forms both its past tense and past participle by the addition of -*d* or -*ed* to the infinitive form of the verb. See 4b.

RELATIVE ADJECTIVE. An adjective that introduces a relative clause. The relative adjectives are *what(ever), which(ever),* and *whose(soever).*

Seymour soon lost <u>what</u> little confidence he had had.

RELATIVE ADVERB. An adverb used to introduce a relative clause. The relative adverbs are *where, when, why,* and *how.*

The grandfather clock was in the corner <u>where</u> it had stood for forty years.

RELATIVE CLAUSE. A subordinate clause introduced by a relative pronoun or relative adverb. Relative clauses may be adjectival, nominal, or adverbial.

ADJECTIVAL	Use the scissors <u>that are in the drawer.</u>
NOMINAL	I will be grateful for <u>whatever you can tell me.</u>
ADVERBIAL	I'll sit <u>where I please.</u>

RELATIVE PRONOUN. A pronoun that introduces a subordinate clause and serves as subject or object in that clause. The relative pronouns are *what, which, who, whom, whose,* and their compounds in -*ever* (*whoever,* etc.). *That* is also usually regarded as a relative pronoun.

RESTRICTIVE AND NONRESTRICTIVE MODIFIERS. A *restrictive modifier* limits or uniquely identifies the word or words it modifies; if it is omitted, the meaning of the sentence will either be lost or be very different. Restrictive modifiers are not surrounded by commas. A *nonrestrictive modifier* describes the word it modifies or adds detail; if it is omitted, there is no essential change in the meaning of the sentence. Nonrestrictive modifiers are set off by commas. See 13 and 20d.

RUN-ON SENTENCE. See **FUSED SENTENCE.**

SEMIAUXILIARY. A verb, or a group of words including a verb, that precedes a main verb and functions like an auxiliary verb. Examples include *keep on, used to, be going to, have to.* See 4b.

SENTENCE. An independent utterance, usually containing a subject and a predicate. A sentence begins with a capital letter and ends with a mark of terminal punctuation. Sentences are often classified as being of four types: declarative, interrogative, imperative, or exclamatory.

DECLARATIVE	I want to see your master.
INTERROGATIVE	Where is your master?
IMPERATIVE	Take me to your master. (The subject *you* is understood.)
EXCLAMATORY	How fat your master is!

Sentences are also classified according to the number and type of clauses they contain. A *simple sentence* contains only one independent clause and no subordinate clause. A *compound sentence* contains at least two independent clauses. A *complex sentence* contains one independent clause and at least one subordinate clause. A *compound-complex* sentence contains at least two independent clauses and one subordinate clause.

SIMPLE	The cellar leaked.
COMPOUND	The windows rattled and the cellar leaked.
COMPLEX	Whenever it rained, the cellar leaked.
COMPOUND-COMPLEX	Whenever it rained, the windows rattled and the cellar leaked.

SENTENCE FRAGMENT. See **FRAGMENT.**

SEPARABLE VERB. A two-part verb consisting of a main verb and a preposition (or prepositional adverb) that function together as a single verb. Examples include *talk over, put on, mix up,* and *bring out.*

SEQUENCE OF TENSES. The grammatical requirement that the tense of verbs in subordinate clauses be determined by the tense of the verb in the main clause. See 17b. Some people also apply the term "sequence of tenses" to continuous prose (see 23b).

She <u>knows</u> that you <u>are</u> lying.

She <u>knew</u> that you <u>were</u> lying.

She <u>will know</u> that you <u>are</u> lying.

SIMPLE SENTENCE. See **SENTENCE.**

SLANG. Highly informal vocabulary typically consisting of newly coined words, extended meanings of old words, and exaggerated use of words. Slang is usually irreverent in tone, and most slang is short-lived. See 46a.

My <u>old man</u> <u>blew his stack</u> when he found out I had <u>gotten busted</u> by the <u>cops</u>.

SPLIT INFINITIVE. The insertion of one or more modifiers between the word *to* and the infinitive form of a verb: *to absolutely disagree.* See 20c.

SQUINTING MODIFIER. A modifier that is ambiguous because it could refer either to what precedes it or to what follows it. See 20c.

The man whom she addressed <u>eagerly</u> agreed with her.

SUBJECT. The noun or nominal in a clause or sentence about which something is said or asked. See 1. Sometimes a distinction is made between a *simple subject* and a *complete subject*. The *simple subject* of a sentence is a single noun or pronoun; the *complete subject* is the noun or pronoun along with all of its modifiers. In the following sentence, the simple subject is *firm*, and the complete subject is *The toy firm that made these blocks*.

The toy firm that made these blocks has gone out of business.

SUBJECTIVE CASE. See **CASE.**

SUBJUNCTIVE. See **MOOD.**

SUBORDINATE CLAUSE. See **CLAUSE.**

SUBORDINATING CONJUNCTION. A conjunction that introduces a subordinate (dependent) clause and connects it to a main (independent) clause. Examples of subordinating conjunctions include *because, if, although, whenever, until*. See 9c.

SUBORDINATION. Making one (or more) clauses of a sentence grammatically dependent upon another element in the sentence.

After he took his clothes out of the dryer, he folded them neatly.

SUBSTANTIVE. A noun or any word functioning as a noun in a sentence.

Charles has always wanted to help the poor.

SUFFIX. A bound form (one that is not an independent word) added to the end of a word or another bound form. *Inflectional suffixes* indicate such meanings as "plural" or "past tense" (e.g., the *-s* on *bands* changes the meaning from singular to plural). *Derivational suffixes* usually change the part-of-speech category of the words to which they are attached (e.g., the *-ful* on *joyful* changes the word from a noun to an adjective). See 45d.

SUPERLATIVE DEGREE. See **COMPARISON.**

SYNTAX. The way in which words are arranged to form phrases, clauses, and sentences; the word order or structure of sentences.

TAG QUESTION. A question consisting of a auxiliary verb and a pronoun and attached to the end of a statement.

The bolts aren't rusty, are they?

You play tennis, don't you?

TENSE. The time or duration of the action or state named by a verb or verb phrase. English has five categories of tense: present, progressive, past, perfect, and future. The progressive and perfect tenses may combine with each other and with the present, past, or future tense to form compound tenses, such as the present perfect progressive *(I have been trying)*. See 4a and Appendix C.

TRANSITIVE VERB. A verb that takes a direct object.

They burned their bridges.

app
B

VERB. A part of speech that serves as the main element in a predicate. Verbs typically express an action or state of being, are inflected for tense, voice, and mood, and show agreement with their subjects. See 4.

VERB PHRASE. The main verb of a predicate along with all its auxiliaries and semiauxiliaries, if any. See 1.

VERBAL. A word derived from a verb but used as some other part of speech, especially as a noun or adjective. The nonfinite verb forms (gerunds, participles, and infinitives) are often called verbals.

The <u>irritated</u> and <u>bickering</u> campers refused <u>to go</u> <u>swimming</u>.

VOICE. A characteristic of verbs that indicates the relation of the action of the verb to its subject. English has two voices, *active* and *passive*. When the verb is in the active voice, the subject is the doer of the action; that is, the subject acts or does something, or is, or is becoming something.

ACTIVE VOICE   People <u>eat</u> vegetables.

Susan and Charles <u>are making</u> bread.

James <u>is</u> an athlete.

Father <u>was becoming</u> anxious.

When the verb is in the passive voice, the subject is the receiver of the action; that is, the subject is acted upon.

PASSIVE VOICE   Vegetables <u>are eaten</u> by people.

The bread <u>is being made</u> by Susan and Charles.

The passive is formed with the verb *to be* and the past participle (e.g., *will be* + *carried*). Note that only transitive verbs can be made passive. See 4a.

Appendix C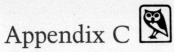

Complete Conjugation of an English Verb

Some of the following combinations occur only rarely, but all are grammatical and possible.

COMPLETE CONJUGATION OF THE VERB *TO TAKE*

INDICATIVE MOOD

ACTIVE VOICE		PRESENT	PAST	FUTURE
Simple	I/we	take	took	shall take
	you/they	take	took	will take
	he/she/it	takes	took	will take
Progressive	I	am taking	was taking	shall be taking
	we	are taking	were taking	shall be taking
	you/they	are taking	were taking	will be taking
	he/she/it	is taking	was taking	will be taking
Perfect	I/we	have taken	had taken	shall have taken
	you/they	have taken	had taken	will have taken
	he/she/it	has taken	had taken	will have taken
Perfect Progressive	I/we	have been taking	had been taking	shall have been taking
	you/they	have been taking	had been taking	will have been taking
	he/she/it	has been taking	had been taking	will have been taking

INDICATIVE MOOD

PASSIVE VOICE		PRESENT	PAST	FUTURE
Simple	I	am taken	was taken	shall be taken
	we	are taken	were taken	shall be taken
	you/they	are taken	were taken	will be taken
	he/she/it	is taken	was taken	will be taken
Progressive	I	am being taken	was being taken	shall be being taken
	we	are being taken	were being taken	shall be being taken
	you/they	are being taken	were being taken	will be being taken
	he/she/it	is being taken	was being taken	will be being taken
Perfect	I/we	have been taken	had been taken	shall have been taken
	you/they	have been taken	had been taken	will have been taken
	he/she/it	has been taken	had been taken	will have been taken
Perfect Progressive	I/we	have been being taken	had been being taken	shall have been being taken
	you/they	have been being taken	had been being taken	will have been being taken
	he/she/it	has been being taken	had been being taken	will have been being taken

SUBJUNCTIVE MOOD

ACTIVE VOICE		PRESENT	PAST
Simple	All persons	(that he) take	(if he) took
Progressive	All persons	(that he) be taking	(if he) were taking
Perfect	All persons	(that he) have taken	(if he) had taken
Perfect Progressive	All persons	(that he) have been taking	(if he) had been taking

PASSIVE VOICE		PRESENT	PAST
Simple	All persons	(that he) be taken	(if he) were taken
Progressive	All persons	(that he) be being taken	(if he) were being taken
Perfect	All persons	(that he) have been taken	(if he) had been taken
Perfect Progressive	All persons	(that he) have been taken	(if he) had been being taken

IMPERATIVE MOOD

Active Present	take
Passive Present	be taken
Infinitive	(to) take
Gerund	taking

Appendix D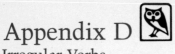
Irregular Verbs

The following list gives the principal parts of the very common irregular verbs; if a principal part has two forms, both are given. (If you are uncertain about a principal part of a verb not included here, look the verb up in a dictionary under its infinitive form. If the verb is irregular, the past tense and past participle will be given in the dictionary.)

INFINITIVE	PAST TENSE	PAST PARTICIPLE
arise	arose	arisen
awake	awoke	awaked, awoken, awakened
be	was	been
beat	beat	beaten
become	became	become
begin	began	begun
bend	bent	bent
bet	bet, betted	bet, betted
bid	bid, bade	bid, bidden
bite	bit	bitten
blow	blew	blown
break	broke	broken
bring	brought	brought
broadcast	broadcast, broadcasted	broadcast, broadcasted
burst	burst	burst
buy	bought	bought
catch	caught	caught
choose	chose	chosen
come	came	come
cut	cut	cut
dig	dug	dug
dive	dived, dove	dived
do	did	done
draw	drew	drawn
dream	dreamed, dreamt	dreamed, dreamt
drink	drank	drunk
drive	drove	driven
eat	ate	eaten
fall	fell	fallen
find	found	found
flee	fled	fled
fly	flew	flown
forget	forgot	forgotten, forgot
forgive	forgave	forgiven
freeze	froze	frozen
get	got	got, gotten

app
D

INFINITIVE	PAST TENSE	PAST PARTICIPLE
give	gave	given
go	went	gone
grow	grew	grown
hang	hung	hung
hang (execute)	hanged (executed)	hanged (executed)
have	had	had
hear	heard	heard
hide	hid	hidden
hit	hit	hit
hold	held	held
keep	kept	kept
know	knew	known
lay	laid	laid
lead	led	led
leave	left	left
let	let	let
lie	lay	lain
light	lit, lighted	lit, lighted
lose	lost	lost
mow	mowed	mown, mowed
pay	paid	paid
prove	proved	proved, proven
put	put	put
ride	rode	ridden
ring	rang	rung
rise	rose	risen
run	ran	run
say	said	said
see	saw	seen
seek	sought	sought
set	set	set
shake	shook	shaken
shine	shone	shone
shrink	shrank, shrunk	shrunk, shrunken
sing	sang	sung
sink	sank	sunk
sit	sat	sat
slide	slid	slid
speak	spoke	spoken
speed	sped, speeded	sped, speeded
spread	spread	spread
spring	sprang	sprung
stand	stood	stood
steal	stole	stolen
stick	stuck	stuck
swear	swore	sworn
swim	swam	swum

app
D

INFINITIVE	PAST TENSE	PAST PARTICIPLE
take	took	taken
tear	tore	torn
tell	told	told
throw	threw	thrown
wear	wore	worn
wind	wound	wound
write	wrote	written

Appendix E 🦉
Spelling Problems

Frequently Misspelled Words

Every word in the following list is in at least one list of words most frequently misspelled by students. For most words, only one form appears in the list. (For example, only *preferred* is listed here, although *prefer*, *preferring*, *preference*, and *preferable* are also frequently misspelled.) Alternate Canadian spellings are indicated.

absence	arctic	column
absorption	argument	coming
acceptance	around	committee
accidentally	arousing	comparative
accommodate	arrangement	completely
accompanies	article	conceive
accomplish	ascend	condemn
accustom	athletic	conscience
achievement	attack	conscious
acquaintance	attendance	considerably
acquire	attitude	consistent
across	author	continuous
actually	auxiliary	controlling
adolescence	basically	convenience
advice/advise	before	controversial
affect	beginning	council/counsel
against	believe	criticize
aggressive	benefited	curious
all right	boundary	curriculum
almost	breath/breathe	cylinder
already	brilliant	dealt
although	Britannica	decision
altogether	business	dependent
amateur	calendar	descendant
among	capital/capitol	description
amount	careful	desirability
analysis/analyse	carried	despair
angel/angle	category	destroy
annual	ceiling	development
answer	cemetery	difference
apparatus	certain	dining
apparent	challenge	disappearance
appearance	changeable	disappoint
appreciate	characteristic	disastrous
approach	chief	discipline
appropriate	choose/chose	disease
approximate	cloths/clothes	dissatisfied

app
E

distinction
divide
divine
dominant
during
easily
effect
efficient
eligible
embarrass
enemy
entertain
environment
equipped
escape
especially
exaggerate
excellence
except
excitable
exercise
existence
expense
experience
experiment
explanation
extremely
fallacy
familiar
fantasies
fascinate
favorite, or favourite
February
fictitious
field
finally
financially
foreigners
foresee
forty/fourth
forward
friendliness
fufil, or fulfill
fundamentally
further
generally
government
grammar

grateful
guarantee
guard
guidance
happiness
hear/here
height
heroes
hindrance
hoping
huge
humorous
hungry
hypocrisy
ignorance
imaginary
immediately
incidentally
independent
indispensable
influential
intellect
intelligence
interest
interference
interpretation
interrupt
involve
irrelevant
island
its/it's
jealous
jewellery, or jewelry
judgement, or judgment
kindergarten
knowledge
laborer, or labourer
laboratory
laid
larynx
later/latter
led/lead
leisurely
lengthening
library
license/license
likely
liveliest

loneliness
loose/lose
luxury
magazine
magnificence
maintenance
manoeuvre, or maneuver
marriage
mathematics
meant
mechanics
medicine
medieval, or mediaeval
mere
miniature
mischief
morally
muscle
narrative
naturally
necessary
Negroes
neighbor, or neighbour
neither
nickel
niece
ninety
ninth
noble
noticing
obstacle
occasionally
occurrence
official
omitted
operate
opinion
opportunity
optimism
origin
paid
parallel
parliament
particular
passed/past
pastime
peaceable
peculiar

perceive
permanent
permitted
persistent
personal/personnel
perspiration
persuading
pertain
phase/faze
philosophy
physical
piece
planned
playwright
pleasant
poison
political
possible
practical
precede
preferred
prejudice
preparation
prevalent
primitive
principal/principle
privilege
probably
proceed
professor
prominent
propaganda
prophecy/prophesy
proving
psychology
pursuing
quantity
quiet
really
receiving
recognize
recommend
referring
regard
relative
relieving
religious

reminiscent
repetition
representative
resistance
response
restaurant
rhythm
ridiculous
roommate
sacrifice
safety
satire/satyr
satisfied
scenery
schedule
science
seize
sense/since
sentence
separation
sergeant
several
shepherd
shining
shoulder
significance
similar
simile
simply
sophomore
source
specimen
speak/speech
sponsor
stopped
stories
straight/strait
strength
strenuous
stretch
strict
studying
substantial
subtle
succeed
summary
suppose

suppress
surprise
suspense
syllable
symbol
symmetrical
synonymous
temperament
temperature
technique
tendency
than/then
their/there
themselves
theories
therefore
thorough
those
though
thought
through
to/too/two
together
tragedies
transferred
tremendous
tried
truly
undoubtedly
until
unusually
using
vacuum
varies
vegetable
vengeance
view
villain
weather/whether
weird
were/where
wholly/holy
who's/whose
writing
yield
your/you're

Canadian Spelling Variants

Following is a partial list of the words for which two spellings are common in Canada. In each pair, the first spelling is British based, the second American. As in the previous section, the list shows only one form of each word *(for example, colour/color but not colourful/colorful)*.

-our/-or
colour/color
favour/favor
honour/honor
neighbour/neighbor
vigour/vigor

-ll- or -l-
cancelled/canceled
enrol/enroll
fuelling/fueling
fufil/fulfill
labelled/labeled
levelling/leveling
marvellous/marvelous
modelling/modeling
programmer/programer
quarrelled/quarreled
shovelling/shoveling
skilful/skillful
traveller/traveler

-pp/-p
kidnapped/kidnaped
worshipped/worshiped

re/-er
centre/center
fibre/fiber
metre, meter/meter
sceptre/scepter
sombre/somber
theatre/theater

-c/-s in nouns
licence/license
defence/defense

-c/-s/-z in verbs
analyse/analyze
paralyse/paralyze
practise/practice

silent -e retained/dropped
ageing/aging
abridgement/abridgment
acknowledgement/acknowledgment
judgement, judgment/judgment
liveable/livable
sizeable/sizable

diphthong kept/dropped
aesthetics/esthetics
archaeology/archeology
encyclopaedia/encyclopedia
manoeuvre/maneuver
mediaeval/medieval

open/closed/hyphenated
anti-inflation/antiinflation
co-operate/cooperate
co-ordinate/coordinate
co-worker/coworker
non-violent/nonviolent
per cent/percent
post-war/postwar

other
artefacts/artifacts
axe/ax
cheque/check
catalogue/catalog
cookie/cooky
doughnut/donut
grey/gray
jewellery/jewelry
mould/mold
plough/plow
programme/program
pyjamas/pajamas
sceptical/skeptical
veranda/verandah
whisky/whiskey

Appendix F 🦉
Manuscript Form

In preparing the final version of a paper, follow carefully any specifications that your instructor gives you. Make a carbon or photocopy of every paper that you submit in case you or your instructor should mislay the original. If possible, final copies should be typed (unless, of course, the paper has been written in class). Even if you find typing slow and painful, you still probably type nearly as fast as you write in longhand, and instructors always find typewritten papers easier to read and correct.

Unless you have received directions to the contrary, use the following conventions in preparing the final version of typewritten papers. (For the most part, the conventions given here agree with those recommended by the *MLA Handbook*; they differ somewhat in the instructions for single- and double-spacing.)

Preparation of Typewritten Papers

Typing or Writing Materials Use 21.6 cm by 27.9 cm (8½ by 11 inch) paper, white and unruled. The *MLA Handbook* recommends paper with a weight of 75 g/m^2 (20-pounds). Unless your instructor specifies otherwise, avoid A4 metric-sized paper; it does not fit into many file folders nor does it stack neatly with the more customary 21.6 cm by 27.9 cm sheets. Do not use colored paper or onionskin. Many readers object to the so-called erasable papers because they smudge very easily, are hard to make corrections on with a pen or pencil, and produce an unpleasant glare under most lighting conditions. (Erasable paper is also more expensive than other kinds of typing paper.) Type on one side of the paper only. Use a black typewriter ribbon, and be sure it is fresh enough to make a clear impression. Keep your typewriter keys clean to avoid blurred copy.

Margins For the main part of your paper, leave margins of 2.5 cm at the top, bottom, and both sides of the text. For the first page of any notes, the bibliography, or any page with a separate title (for example, an appendix in a long paper), leave a margin of 5 cm at the top.

Spacing Double-space the text of the paper, including quotations. (Your instructor may ask you to single-space quotations; this is a common convention in informal papers.) Do not use one-and-a-half line spacing because it does not leave enough room for comments and corrections. Quadruple-space between the title and the first paragraph. Triple-space between the text and a long quotation and between the end of the quotation and the beginning of your text.

Indentations Indent each new paragraph five spaces from the left margin. Indent all lines of long quotations ten spaces from the left margin.

Title Page   If your first page of text is also your title page, type your name, the name of the course, your instructor's name, and the date in the upper right corner. (Your instructor may direct you to type this information in the upper left corner and the page number in the upper right.) Double-space and then centre the title. Do not put the title in quotation marks, underline it, or capitalize it in full. You may follow the title with a question mark or an exclamation point if the grammar requires one (but consider carefully whether you really need an exclamation point).

If your title is too long to fit on one line, centre the second line below the first line. Break the title logically; a title such as *The Influence of Lester Pearson's Foreign Policy on International Relations in The Trudeau Years* might be divided after *Policy* or *Relations* but should not be broken after *Lester, International,* or *the.* Underline words in the title only if you would underline them in the text.

Triple-space between the title and the first line of your text.

Although a research paper does not ordinarily need a separate title page, your instructor may ask you to submit one. If you must provide a title page, place the paper's title, your name, the name of the course, your instructor's name, and the date in the centre of the page (approximately the middle 12 cm of the sheet of paper). Some instructors prefer another placement for your name and the course.

Outline   If your instructor requests an outline, you need a separate title page. The outline should follow the separate title page, if any, but precede the text. If it runs more than one page, number them with lower-case roman numerals.

Page numbers and labelling for identification   The first page of a paper may be left without a page number, or you may centre the page number just above the margin at the bottom of the page. Always count the first page of the text itself as page one. Number all subsequent pages in the top right corner. The page number should be from 2.5 cm from the right edge of the paper and 1.5 cm from the top. Use only arabic, not roman, numerals. It is a good idea to type your name just before each page number so if the pages become separated, your instructor can easily find and replace them.

Footnotes   Many instructors who require footnote documentation rather than in-text references allow students to group all notes on a separate page following the text (endnotes). Typing notes in this way is easier than typing them at the foot of the pages. If you do have notes at the bottom of the pages, remember to leave enough room for them as you type. Quadruple-space between your text and the first footnote on the page. Single-space all footnotes, but remember to double-space between them. (For detailed directions on the spacing and indenting of footnotes and for models, see 55a.)

Proofreading and corrections Proofread every page of your paper carefully before you remove it from the typewriter. Watch especially for
repeated or omitted words and for transposed (reversed) letters within
words. Make as many corrections as possible while the page is in the
typewriter. (Remember, it is easier to make corrections while the page is
still in place in the typewriter; once you remove the sheet of paper, you
may find it difficult to align the page exactly as you had it when you first
put it in the machine.) Use correction liquid or film, and type over mistakes, if space permits. Do not try to correct by striking over letters.

After you have finished typing, proofread the whole paper. You may
find this easiest to do by reading it aloud, including the marks of punctuation, and making light pencil marks in the margins to note errors. You
can then decide whether a page has so many errors as to require retyping,
or whether you can make neat corrections in black ink.

To correct a misspelled or otherwise incorrect word, draw a line
through it, and write the correct form neatly above the crossed-out word.
Do not put parentheses around words that are to be omitted.

> a ~~melancholly~~ *melancholy* state

To correct transposed letters, use an s-shaped line.

> ratin⌡al

To indicate that a word or words should be added, put a caret (^) at
the point where the word should appear, and write the word above the
line.

> put a caret at the ^*exact* point

To indicate that a word or words should be deleted, draw a single line
through the word or words.

> draw a single ~~solitary~~ line

To indicate that there should be no space where a space appears,
close up the space with curved lines.

> close up the space with cur⌒ved lines

To indicate that there should be a space between two words, draw a
vertical line between the words.

> between|the words

To indicate a paragraph division where one does not appear, use the
symbol ¶.

> within the year. ¶At last,

To indicate that there should be no paragraph division, connect the
two sentences with a line.

> before the sentence.⌐
> ⌐To indicate that

If a page is messy and contains many corrections, retype it. A neat paper makes a much better impression on the reader.

Use black ink to insert by hand any necessary symbols such as brackets, accent marks, or mathematical and scientific symbols that your typewriter keyboard does not have. Be sure to leave ample space for such symbols as you type. If you make a light checkmark in the margin with a pencil as you type the line, you can easily find the spot later where the insertion is to be made.

Fastening the Paper Fasten the pages with a paper clip before you hand the paper in. Do not staple it unless your instructor tells you to. There is no need to waste money on fancy plastic or paper binders for short papers. The reader usually has to remove the binder in order to grade the paper, and you may lose your binder in the process. Binders are appropriate for long papers that are too thick to secure with a paper clip.

Preparation of Handwritten Papers

Handwritten papers are prepared in the same way as typewritten ones, with a few exceptions.

Paper Use 21.6 cm by 27.9 cm *ruled* white paper. This may be either looseleaf notebook paper or essay paper designed specifically for handwritten essays. Write on one side only. Do not use paper torn from a spiral-bound notebook; the ragged edges tend to stick together and to shed scraps of paper.

Your instructor may ask you to write on every line or on every other line. If you use wide-ruled paper (lines 9 cm apart) and have reasonably small handwriting, writing on every line will probably be acceptable. If you use narrow-ruled paper (lines 6 cm apart) or have large handwriting, write on every other line.

Script Write in black, blue-black, or blue ink. Do not use other colors, such as red, violet, or green. Write as neatly and legibly as possible, avoiding ornate flourishes. Carefully distinguish capital letters from small letters, *a* from *o*, *n* from *u*, *v* from *r*, *g* from *q*. Cross all *t*'s and dot all *i*'s and *j*'s. Leave a definite space between individual words. If your handwriting is hard to decipher, print instead of using script. (And consider improving your handwriting—it can be done.)

Margins Margins should be the same as for typewritten papers. Do not write outside the line marking the left margin.

Typing Punctuation

There are a number of special conventions for typing punctuation, especially for the spacing of punctuation marks. The rules listed here also apply to handwritten papers, although spacing will, of course, be less exact than on typewitten copy.

Periods The spacing of periods varies according to whether the periods are used as ending punctuation or as marks of abbreviation.

Ending Punctuation Type the period directly after the last word of the sentence with no intervening space. Leave two spaces after the period.

```
no intervening space.  Leave two spaces
```

Mark of Abbreviation Type the period directly after the letter of abbreviation. Leave no space after a period within an abbreviation, *except* when the abbreviation is the initials of a person's name.

```
R.C.M.P.        R. C. Maples
```

Leave one space between the final period of an abbreviation and the next word.

```
R.C.M.P. Headquarters
```

If the abbreviation is the last word in a sentence, leave two spaces after the final period of abbreviation, as usual after any period ending a sentence.

```
in Victoria, B.C.  Many buildings have been
```

Question Marks and Exclamation Points Do not space before a question mark or exclamation point. Leave two spaces after these marks.

```
Is there a solution?  Few would care to
What nonsense!  Even a child
```

Colons Do not space before a colon. Leave one space after a colon.

```
They sent reports on three computers: an Apple, an
    IBM, and a Fujitsu.
Frye, Northrop.  Anatomy of Criticism: Four Essays.
    Princeton: Princeton University Press, 1957.
```

Commas and Semicolons Do not space before a comma or semicolon. Leave one space after both.

```
In sum, the function
citation; nevertheless, the council
```

Quotation Marks Do not space between quotation marks and the words or marks of punctuation that they enclose. See 33a for the handling of quotations within quotations.

```
The word "elbow" is sometimes
"Oh, no," she said, "I was seasick."
```

**app
F**

Hyphens and Dashes A hyphen is a single horizontal stroke. A dash is two consecutive hyphens with no space between them. Do not space before or after either a hyphen or a dash. Never begin a line of typing with a hyphen or a dash.

```
red-eyed        was red--not blue--and the
```

Try to avoid more than two consecutive hyphenated words at the ends of lines. By leaving a relatively wide margin on the right-hand side, you can type many words in full and not have to divide them.

Parentheses and Brackets Do not space *after* opening parentheses and brackets or *before* closing parentheses and brackets. Leave one space before opening parentheses and brackets and one space after closing parentheses and brackets. But if an entire sentence is contained within these marks, leave two spaces after the closing parentheses or brackets.

```
a winter (1838-1839) on the island

individuals.  (Their names are below.)  Some
```

If your typewriter has no brackets, leave an extra space for them when you type and insert them later by hand in black ink.

Apostrophes Do not space before or after an apostrophe unless the apostrophe appears at the end of the word.

```
hasn't       a day's work      Mr. Jones' family
```

Italics Use the underline key to indicate italics. When several consecutive words are underlined, some people prefer to underline the spaces between the words. Others prefer to underline each word separately. You can follow either rule; just be consistent in your practice throughout a single piece of writing.

<u>be consistent in your practice</u>

<u>be</u> <u>consistent</u> <u>in</u> <u>your</u> <u>practice</u>

Ellipses Leave one space before, between, and after each period that forms part of an ellipsis. If your ellipsis occurs at the end of a sentence, you need a period for end punctuation and three spaced ellipsis points. That period, like any period at the end of a sentence, has no space before it. See 38.

```
No Canadian shall be deprived of "the right to be
presumed innocent until proved guilty . . . in a public
hearing" or deprived of "the right to the assistance of
an interpreter in any proceedings in which he is
involved. . . ."
```

Slashes   When a slash is used to separate lines of poetry, leave one space before and one space after the slash. Otherwise, do not space before or after a slash.

```
What our contempts do often hurl from us / We wish
8/15    L/kg
```

Diacritical Marks   Many typewriters do not have keys for diacritical marks (accent marks). Insert them by hand in black ink. If you make a light pencil mark in the margin as you type, you can easily locate the spot where the diacritics are to be added.

```
       René Descartes       résumé
```

Some symbols can easily be created on a standard keyboard. Use a capital L with a dash through it for a British pound sign, two dashes with varied horizontal spacing for an equal sign, a capital (not a lower-case) L for a litre sign.

Be aware, however, that it is possible to obtain sets of four to eight special keys for many makes of typewriters (and word-processor printers). If you have frequent need of, say, French accent marks or mathematical symbols, they may be worth the small expense.

app
F

Index

Numbers in **boldface** refer to sections of the handbook, boldface capital letters to appendices.

Acknowledgements

Excerpt from *Without Feathers* by Woody Allen. Copyright © 1972 by Woody Allen. Reprinted by permission of Woody Allen and Random House, Inc.

From *Eichmann in Jerusalem* by Hannah Arendt. Copyright © 1963, 1964 by Hannah Arendt. Reprinted by permission of Viking Penguin Inc.

Excerpt from *Patterns of Culture* by Ruth Benedict. Copyright © 1934, and © renewed 1962 by Ruth Benedict Valentine. Used by permission of Houghton Mifflin Company.

Excerpt from "Brass Buttons, Fingertips, and the Fluid Mosaic" by William Bennett. Copyright © *Harvard Magazine*, 1977. Reprinted by permission.

Excerpt from *Mountaineering* by Alan Blackshaw, pp. 139–140. Copyright © Alan Blackshaw, 1965, 1968, 1970, 1973, 1975. Reprinted by permission of Penguin Books, Ltd.

Excerpt from *If Life is a Bowl of Cherries — What am I Doing in the Pits?* by Erma Bombeck. Copyright © 1978 by Erma Bombeck. Used with permission of McGraw-Hill Book Company.

Excerpt from *The I Hate to Cook Book* by Peg Bracken. Copyright © 1960 by Peg Bracken. Reprinted by permission of Harcourt Brace Jovanovich, Inc.

Excerpt from *History of Greece* by J. B. Bury and R. Meiggs. Reprinted by permission of St. Martin's Press, Inc.

Excerpt from "Polluting Our Language," by Douglas Bush. Reprinted from *The American Scholar*, Volume 41, Number 2, Spring 1972. Copyright © 1972 by the United Chapters of Phi Beta Kappa. By permission of the publishers.

From *Klee Wyck* by Emily Carr. Copyright © 1941 Clarke, Irwin & Company Limited. Used by permission of Clarke Irwin (1983) Inc.

Excerpt from *The Edge of the Sea* by Rachel Carson. Copyright © 1955. Reprinted by permission of Houghton Mifflin Company.

Excerpt from *The First Americans* by C. W. Ceram. Copyright © 1972 by C. W. Ceram. Reprinted by permission of Harcourt, Brace, Jovanovich, Inc.

Excerpt from *Riview of Mara* by Jerome Charyn. Copyright © 1978 by The New York Times Company. Reprinted by permission.

Excerpt from *Easy to Kill* by Agatha Christie. Copyright © 1945. Reprinted by permission of Dodd, Mead & Company.

Excerpt from *Six Men* by Alistair Cooke. Copyright © 1977. Reprinted by permission of Random House, Inc.

Excerpt from *Antiquing from A to Z* by Michael De Forrest. Copyright © 1972 by Michael De Forrest. Reprinted by permission of Simon & Schuster.

Excerpt from "Global Satellite Communications," *Scientific American*. February 1977, by Burton I. Edelson. Reprinted by permission of W. H. Freeman and Company Publishers.

Excerpt from *Arts and the Man* by Irwin Edman. Copyright © 1928, 1939 by W. W. Norton & Company, Inc. Copyright renewed 1956, 1967 by Meta Markel. Used by permission of W. W. Norton & Company, Inc.

Excerpt from Nora Ephron, "First Ladies, Fourth Estates, Six Shooters". Copyright May 8, 1979 from Esquire.

Excerpt from *The Natural History of Nonsense* by Bergen Evans. Copyright © 1960. Reprinted by permission of Random House, Inc.

Excerpt from "Midnight Egg and Other Revivers," *Bon Appétit*, May 1978, by M. F. K. Fisher. Copyright © 1978 Bon Appetit Publishing Corp. Reprinted by permission.

With permission from *Funk and Wagnalls Standard College Dictionary*, Canadian Edition. Copyright © 1982 by Fitzhenry and Whiteside Limited.

Excerpt from *The French Lieutenant's Woman* by John Fowles, by permission of Little, Brown and Co.

Excerpt from *The Structure of American English* by W. Nelson Francis. Copyright © 1958. Reprinted by permission of John Wiley & Sons, Inc.

Excerpt from Allan Freeman and John Urquhart, "All in the Family", November 1, 1983. Reprinted by permission of The Wall Street Journal.

Excerpt from Northrop Frye, *Divisions on a Ground: Essays on Canadian Culture*. Copyright © 1982 by House of Anansi Press Ltd.

Excerpt from *The Scotch* by John Kenneth Galbraith. Copyright © 1966. Reprinted by permission of Houghton Mifflin Company.

Excerpt from *The Sunlight Dialogues* by John Gardner. Copyright © 1973. Reprinted by permission of Random House, Inc.

Excerpt from *Ever Since Darwin* by Stephen Jay Gould. Reprinted by permission of W. W. Norton.

Excerpt from *Hen's Teeth and Horse's Toes* by Stephen Jay Gould. Reprinted by permission of W. W. Norton.

The "Riel" entry from *Encyclopedia Canadiana*. Reprinted by permission of Grolier Ltd.

Excerpt from "Will There Always Be an England?" *The American Scholar*, by William Haley. Reprinted from *The American Scholar*, Volume 47, Number 3, Summer 1978. Copyright © 1978 by the United Chapters of Phi Beta Kappa. By permission of the publishers.

Excerpt from *Painting in Canada* by J. Russell Harper. Reprinted with permission of University of Toronto press.

Excerpt from "Meteorite Photography," *The Illustrated London News*, April 1978 by Keith Hindley.

Excerpt from *Biological Science* by William T. Keeton, W. W. Norton & Company, Inc., New York, N. Y. Copyright © 1967 by W. W. Norton and Company, Inc.

Excerpt from *Canada: A Visual History* by D. G. G. Kerr and R. I. K. Davidson. Reprinted by permission of Nelson Canada, Ltd.

Excerpt from *Cacti and Other Succulents* by Jack Kramer. Reprinted with permission of the publishers, Harry N. Abrams, Inc., 1979.

Excerpt from *An Experiment in Criticism* by C. S. Lewis. Cambridge University Press, 1961.

Excerpt from *You Can't Print That* by Charles Lynch. Reprinted by permission of Hurtig Publishers Ltd.

Excerpt from *The Cloud Forest* by Peter Matthiessen. Copyright © 1961 by Peter Matthiessen. Reprinted by permission of Viking Penguin, Inc.

Excerpt from "D. H. Lawrence: Katherine Mansfield and 'Women in Love,' " *London Magazine*, May 1978, by Jeffrey Meyers. Reprinted by permission of *London Magazine*.

Excerpt from *Centennial* by James M. Michener. Copyright © 1975. Reprinted by permission of Random House, Inc.

Excerpts from *Canada North* by Farley Mowat. Reprinted by permission of The Canadian Publishers, McClelland and Stewart Limited, Toronto.

Excerpt from *The Uses of the Past* by Herbert J. Muller. Copyright © 1952 by Oxford University Press, Inc. Reprinted by permission.

Excerpt from *I Can Teach You to Figure Skate* by Tina Noyes with Freda Alexander. Reprinted by permission of Hawthorn Books from *Figure Skating* by Tina Noyes with Freda Alexander. Copyright © 1973 Associated Features Inc. All rights reserved.

Excerpt from *Running in the Family* by Michael Ondaatje, Copyright by McClelland and Stewart Ltd., 1982.

Excerpt from *The Trouble with France* by Alain Peyrefitte, published in 1981 in New York by Alfred A. Knopf, translated by William R. Byron.

Excerpt from *Culloden* by John Prebble. Copyright © 1963. Reprinted by permission of Martin Secker & Warburg Limited and Curtis Brown Ltd.

Excerpt from *Arabia: A Journey through the Labyrinth* by Jonathan Raban. Copyright © 1979 by Johathan Raban. Reprinted by permission of Simon & Schuster.

Excerpt from *Graffiti: Two Thousand Years of Wall Writing* by Robert George Reisner. Copyright © 1971 with the permission of Contemporary Books, Inc., Chicago.

Excerpt from "The New Screen Heroes," by Val Ross, Sept. 26, 1983. Reprinted by permission of Maclean's magazine.

Excerpt from *Senator Joe McCarthy* by Richard H. Rovere. Reprinted by permission of Harcourt Brace Jovanovich, Inc.

Excerpt from *The Egyptians* by John Ruffle. Copyright © 1977 by Phaidon Press Ltd., Oxford.

Excerpt from *The Russians* by Hedrick Smith. Copyright © 1976 by Hedrick Smith. Reprinted by permission of Times Books, a division of Quadrangle/The New York Times Book Co.

Excerpt from *Inside the Third Reich* by Albert Speer. Copyright © 1970 by Macmillan Publishers Co., Inc.

Excerpt from p. 16. *Household Facilities by Income and Other Characteristics 1982*, a publication of Statistics Canada, published in Ottawa, in 1983 by the Minister of Supply and Services.

Excerpt from *Names on the Land* by George R. Stewart. Copyright © renewed 1972 by George R. Stewart. Reprinted by permission of Houghton Mifflin Company.

Excerpt from *Williams Arthur Deacon: A Canadian Life* by Clara Thomas and John Lennox. Reprinted with permission of University of Toronto Press.

Excerpt from *Roofs and Siding: Home Repair and Improvement* published by Time-Life Books, Inc. Reprinted by permission of Time-Life Books, Inc.

Excerpt from *The Unexpected Vista: A Physicist's View of Nature* by James S. Trefil. Copyright © 1983 James S. Trefil. Reprinted with the permission of Charles Scribner's Sons.

Excerpt from *Of Mites and Men* by William Tucker. Copyright © 1978 by *Harper's Magazine*. All rights reserved. Reprinted from the August 1978 issue by special permission.